SAINT JOHN OF DAMASCUS

On the Orthodox Faith

ST VLADIMIR'S SEMINARY PRESS
Popular Patristics Series
Number 62

The Popular Patristics Series published by St Vladimir's Seminary Press provides readable and accurate translations of a wide range of early Christian literature to a wide audience—students of Christian history to lay Christians reading for spiritual benefit. Recognized scholars in their fields provide short but comprehensive and clear introductions to the material. The texts include classics of Christian literature, thematic volumes, collections of homilies, letters on spiritual counsel, and poetical works from a variety of geographical contexts and historical backgrounds. The mission of the series is to mine the riches of the early Church and to make these treasures available to all.

Series Editor
BOGDAN BUCUR

Associate Editor
IGNATIUS GREEN

* * *

Series Editor
1999–2020
JOHN BEHR

SAINT JOHN OF DAMASCUS

On the Orthodox Faith

A New Translation of
An Exact Exposition of the Orthodox Faith

Introduction, Translation, and Notes by
NORMAN RUSSELL

ST VLADIMIR'S SEMINARY PRESS

YONKERS, NEW YORK

2022

Library of Congress Cataloging-in-Publication Data

Names: John, of Damascus, Saint, author. | Russell, Norman, 1934- editor, translator.

Title: On the Orthodox faith : a new translation of An exact exposition of the Orthodox faith / Saint John Damascene ; introduction, translation, and notes by Norman Russell.

Other titles: Exposition of the Orthodox faith. English

Description: Yonkers, New York : St Vladimir's Seminary Press, 2022. | Series: St. Vladimir's Seminary Press popular patristics series ; number 62 | Includes bibliographical references and index. | Summary: "St John of Damascus is often regarded as 'the last of the fathers,' and his On the Orthodox Faith (or An Exact Exposition of the Orthodox Faith) is a summary and creative synthesis of all preceding patristic thought, touching upon every major aspect of the Christian faith. Norman Russell's new translation is based upon Kotter's critical Greek text, which is included on the facing page"—Provided by publisher.

Identifiers: LCCN 2021060613 (print) | LCCN 2021060614 (ebook) | ISBN 9780881416947 (paperback) | ISBN 9780881416954 (kindle edition)

Subjects: LCSH: Theology, Doctrinal—Early works to 1800.

Classification: LCC BR65.J63 E9713 2022 (print) | LCC BR65.J63 (ebook) | DDC 230.09—dc23/eng/20220207

LC record available at https://lccn.loc.gov/2021060613

LC ebook record available at https://lccn.loc.gov/2021060614

COPYRIGHT © 2022 BY
ST VLADIMIR'S SEMINARY PRESS
575 Scarsdale Road, Yonkers, NY 10707
1-800-204-2665
www.svspress.com

ISBN 978–088141–694–7 (paper)
ISBN 978–088141–695–4 (electronic)
ISSN 1555–5755

For

Fr Andrew Louth

Contents

Preface

John Damascene does not fit neatly into the Greek constellation of "the Fathers of the Church." He was an outsider, a Greek-speaking Syrian who was a presbyter of the Church of the Anastasis in Jerusalem in the first half of the eighth century and whose concerns were different from those of the great age of the fathers of the fourth and fifth centuries. He lived under the Umayyad caliphate, when Orthodox Christianity was no longer supported by the privileges it had enjoyed under the Christian Roman emperors and had to fight its own battles. He antagonized the imperial authorities in Constantinople at the time of the Iconoclast Controversy by his spirited defense of the icons—Mansur the traitor, they called him, using his Arabic name and alluding to the role played by his grandfather in surrendering Damascus to the Arabs in 635. It was only in the eleventh century that he was brought in from the cold as a result of the ecclesiastical policy of the emperor Alexios I Komnenos, who found John's compendious presentation of Orthodox doctrine well suited to his need, in a time of acute political crisis, to strengthen the Church's doctrinal discipline. By the fourteenth century he was being hailed as "the last of the fathers," his pronouncements now regarded as normative for Orthodoxy.

Through his rehabilitation in Byzantium, John came to the attention of Western theologians. In the early twelfth century he was translated into Latin by Burgundio of Pisa, thus becoming accessible to the teachers of the University of Paris. He soon became an authority appealed to by luminaries such as Alexander of Hales and Thomas Aquinas. The first printed edition of the Greek text was published in Verona by Bernardino Donato in 1531. The first critical edition, using

a restricted number of manuscripts, was published in Paris in 1712 by the great Dominican scholar, Michel Lequien, and reprinted in 1860 by Jacques-Paul Migne. A modern critical edition on the basis of a comparison of all the surviving manuscripts was published in Berlin in 1973 by the German Benedictine, Dom Bonifaz Kotter. It is this edition on which the present translation is based.

The two previous English translations, by S. D. F. Salmond and Frederick H. Chase, belong to the late-nineteenth and mid-twentieth centuries respectively. A translator of the twenty-first century has the great advantage of benefiting not only from the labors of the textual scholar Bonifaz Kotter but also from the work of the theologian Andrew Louth and the Byzantinist Vassa Kontouma. Louth has deepened our appreciation of St John's theological achievement. Kontouma has revolutionized our understanding of the context in which St John lived and wrote and of how he came to be regarded as a Church Father.

Since Michel Lequien, the *Exact Exposition of the Orthodox Faith* has been seen as the third part of a trilogy called *The Fount of Knowledge*. Kotter and Louth, however, have argued that the idea of a trilogy, bringing together three of John's compositions that had been written as independent works, came to the Damascene towards the end of his life and was not fully achieved, leaving its trace in only one manuscript. The *Exact Exposition of the Orthodox Faith* stands on its own, and in the present translation is treated as an independent work.

The division of the work into a hundred chapters and subsequently, in the Latin translation, into four books raises problems. Modern scholars tend to refer to the *Exact Exposition* by book number and the independent sequence of chapter numbers within each book. This is still the practice despite the protests of successive editors of the Greek text since the sixteenth century: Donato ignores the Latin division; Lequien includes it reluctantly; Kotter gives it in brackets in the table of contents and in the chapter headings and also in a concordance at the end. More recently, the Greek chapter

numbers themselves have been challenged by Vassa Kontouma. She sees them as a Byzantine "straightjacket" imposed on the text by John's first editor in the ninth century. Her proposal to remove them is attractive. Many of the chapters can be grouped together as larger units that are divided quite artificially by the chapter numbers. I have resisted the temptation, however, to follow Kontouma all the way. It is a bit like restoring an old painting. It is easy to strip off the modern varnish of the book divisions, but to go down as far as the chapter numbers might be to remove additions intended, even as an afterthought, by the author himself. I therefore keep the Greek chapter numbers but also give a concordance of Latin and Greek numbers for ease of reference.

I should like to thank Fr Ignatius Green for inviting me to contribute this volume to the Popular Patristics Series, and to express my gratitude to him and the book's sponsors for their patience during my long delay in submitting the translation. Moreover, Fr Ignatius not only carefully checked my translation against the Greek but also generously shared his patristic expertise with me, especially with regard to St Gregory of Nyssa, enriching the commentary at a number of places (as acknowledged in the notes by the initials IG). I am deeply grateful to him. Several other scholars have also helped me by answering queries and sending me papers: David Bradshaw, Sebastian Brock, Dirk Krausmüller, Chryssa Maltezou, and Petros Toulis. I thank them warmly and also Fleur Lynas, who skillfully typed my handwritten text. Lastly, it gives me great pleasure to dedicate the volume to Fr Andrew Louth in recognition of all that I have learned from him in the course of several decades of friendship.

Norman Russell
May 2021

Abbreviations and Sigla

ACO	Acta Conciliorum Oecumenicorum, ed. E. Schwartz
CCSG	Corpus Christianorum, Series Graeca
Constas	*Maximos the Confessor: On Difficulties in the Church Fathers, The* Ambigua, ed. and trans. N. Constas
CWS	Classics of Western Spirituality
FOC	The Fathers of the Church (The Catholic University of America Press)
Green	*Saint Gregory of Nyssa, Catechetical Discourse,* ed. and trans. I. Green
Heil	*Pseudo-Dionysius Areopagita De Coelesti Hierarchia,* ed. G. Heil
IG	Ignatius Green
Kotter 1	*Die Schiften des Johannes von Damaskos,* vol. 1, ed. B. Kotter
Kotter 2	*Die Schiften des Johannes von Damaskos,* vol. 2, ed. B. Kotter
Kotter 3	*Die Schiften des Johannes von Damaskos,* vol. 3, ed. B. Kotter
Kotter 4	*Die Schiften des Johannes von Damaskos,* vol. 4, ed. B. Kotter
Kotter 5	*Die Schiften des Johannes von Damaskos,* vol. 5, ed. B. Kotter
Lampe	*A Patristic Greek Lexicon,* ed. G. W. H. Lampe
Louth	*St John of Damascus, Three Treatises on the Divine Images,* trans. A. Louth
LXX	Septuagint
Morani	*Nemesii Emeseni de natura hominis,* ed. M. Morani
Moreschini	*Gregorio di Nazianzo, Tutte le Orazioni,* ed. C. Moreschini
MT	Masoretic Text
Naldini	*Basilio di Cesarea sulla Genesi,* ed. and trans. M. Naldini

NPNF   A Select Library of Nicene and Post-Nicene Fathers of the
           Christian Church
ODB   *The Oxford Dictionary of Byzantium*,
           ed. A. P. Kazhdan, *et al.*
PG   Patrologia Graeca, ed. J.-P. Migne
PL   Patrologia Latina, ed. J.-P. Migne
PPS   Popular Patristics Series
SC   Sources Chrétiennes
Suchla   *Pseudo-Dionysius Areopagita, De Divinis Nominibus*,
           ed. B. R. Suchla
TTH   Translated Texts for Historians
Wickham   *Cyril of Alexandria: Select Letters*, ed. and trans.
           L. R. Wickham

A   Munich, Staatsbibl., Codex Mon. gr. 310, 9th cent.
B   Messina, Bibl. Univ., Codex Messan. gr. 116 (olim S. Salvatoris,
       πε΄), 10th cent.
C   Grottaferrata, Bibl. della Badia, Codex Cryptoferr. II (Patr.) 11
       (B a 11), 10th cent.
D   Paris, Bibl. nat., Codex Paris. Suppl. gr. 8 (S. Hilar.), 12th cent.
E   Moscow, Historical Museum, Codex Mosqu. Synod. gr. 201,
       9th cent.
F   Athos, Monastery of Dionysiou, Codex Athous Dionys.
       175 (3709), 13th cent.
G   Rome, Bibl. Apost., Codex Vat. Chis. gr. 18 (R IV; 38),
       dated 1029/30
H   Sinai, Monastery of St Catherine, Codex Sinait. 383,
       9th–10th cent.
I   Moscow, Historical Museum, Codex Mosqu. Synod. gr. 202,
       11th cent.
K   Munich, Staatsbibl., Codex Mon. gr. 317, 13th or 14th cent.
L   Rome, Bibl. Apost. Vat., Codex Vat. gr. 490 (332), 12th–13th cent.
M   Oxford, Bodl. Libr., Codex Cromwell. gr. 13 (298), beginning of
       11th cent.
N   London, Brit. Mus., Codex Addit. 27862, 11th cent.

Introduction

The Greek *Life* and its Sources

The few reliable facts of John's life may be set out very briefly. He was born in Damascus early in the second half of the seventh century to a Melkite[1] Christian family, the Manṣūr, prominent in the fiscal administration of the city under successive Roman (Byzantine), Persian, and Arab regimes. The capture of Damascus in September 635 by Muslim forces led by Khālid ibn al-Walīd proved to be permanent, and in 661 the city was chosen to be the capital of the Umayyad caliphate (661–750). In the early eighth century, for reasons that are unclear but may be connected with the cultural changes brought about by the caliph ʿAbd al-Malik (685–705) when Greek was replaced by Arabic as the caliphate's administrative language, John resigned his post in the administration and became a monk and priest at a monastery in or near Jerusalem, where he remained until the last years of his life. A mention of him as apparently recently deceased in the acts of the iconoclast Council of Hiereia (754) has been taken to indicate that he died at an advanced age shortly before that date.[2]

[1]On the term "Melkite" (from the Syriac *mălkāyā*, "imperial"), indicating Christians who belonged to the church of the Roman Empire, i.e., to the Chalcedonian as opposed to the Monophysite community, see Sidney H. Griffith, "John of Damascus and the Church in Syria in the Umayyad Era: The Intellectual and Cultural Milieu of Orthodox Christians in the World of Islam," *Hugoye: Journal of Syriac Studies* 11/2 (2011): 207–37, esp. 218, note 42. Griffith says that the term did not come into currency until the end of the seventh century. It should not be confused with the way it is used today to refer to the members of the patriarchate of Antioch who seceded from Orthodoxy in the eighteenth century to become Catholics of the Eastern rite (today the Melkite Greek Catholics).

[2]With regard to the iconophiles George the Cypriot, the patriarch Germanos, and "Mansur," the Council of Hiereia said: "The Trinity has condemned [καθεῖλεν,

The difficulty in filling out this bare outline lies in the lateness and confusion of the biographical sources.[3] The standard Greek *Life*, by a patriarch called John, was long thought to have been written by either John VII (964–66) or John VIII (1106–56) of Jerusalem.[4] It has now been shown convincingly by Vassa Kontouma that the author of the *Life* was in fact John III Polites of Antioch (996–1021), who wrote it in about the year 1000.[5] In 969 the Byzantines had recovered Antioch and had set about restoring imperial rule in northern Syria.[6] John III at the time was the chartophylax of the Great Church of Constantinople.[7] In 996 he was chosen by the emperor Basil II (976–1025) to succeed Agapios II of Antioch, an independent-minded Arabic-speaking Melkite, who had been installed in Antioch after its recapture but had proved unsatisfactory from the imperial point of view and was forced to resign. John III (who no doubt acquired the sobriquet Polites because he was a Constantinopolitan) turned out, again from the imperial vantage-point, to be an excellent choice.[8] During

---

katheilen] all three." *The Acts of the Second Council of Nicaea (787)*, trans. Richard Price, TTH 68 (Liverpool: Liverpool University Press, 2020), 540. The verb καθεῖλεν (*katheilen*, literally "put a stop to") is understood as indicating their death. John himself refers to his advanced age in *Homily 2.1 on the Dormition of the Mother of God*, where "with an aging tongue" he offers the Virgin the flower of his oratory "in our wintertime of words [ἐν χειμῶνι τῶν ἐπῶν, *en cheimōni tōn epōn*]" (Kotter 5:517.30); *On the Dormition of Mary: Early Patristic Homilies,* trans. Brian E. Daley, SJ, PPS 18 (Crestwood, NY: St Vladimir's Seminary Press, 1998), 204.

[3]For a critical discussion of the documents relating to John's life that supersedes all previous work, see Vassa Kontouma, *John of Damascus: New Studies on his Life and Works*, Variorum Collected Studies Series CS1053 (Farnham, UK: Ashgate Publishing, 2015), Studies I and II. Kontouma gives John's dates as *c.* 655 to *c.* 745.

[4]The text is in PG 94:429–90.

[5]Vassa Kontouma, "John III of Antioch (996–1021) and the *Life of John of Damascus* (BHG 884)," in Vassa Kontouma, *John of Damascus: New Studies*, Study II. One of the manuscript traditions actually names John of Antioch as the author.

[6]Antioch remained in imperial hands, or at least after 1078 under imperial suzerainty, until it was surrendered to the Seljuk Turks by its Armenian governor, Philaretos Brachamios, in 1084.

[7]The chartophylax, head of the patriarchal chancery and keeper of the archives, was a very senior figure at the patriarchate.

[8]On John Polites' forceful character, see Kontouma, "John III of Antioch (996–1021)," 7–13.

his twenty-five years as patriarch (although he took possession of his see only in 999, when he accompanied the newly appointed military governor, the *doux* Nikephoros Ouranos, to Antioch), he did much to further the re-Hellenization of the Arabic-speaking Christians of his city and bring them firmly into the orbit of Constantinople.[9]

One of the instruments of Hellenization under Basil II was hagiography. This was the period when Symeon Metaphrastes was working at the imperial chancery reshaping and editing saints' *Lives* for the *Menologion*.[10] The aim of the project was to produce saints' *Lives* in correct but uncomplicated Greek suitable for liturgical reading, which would disseminate the social and cultural values that were important to Basil and his successors of the Macedonian dynasty. At Antioch both John Polites and Nikephoros Ouranos engaged in work on similar lines, the patriarch writing the *Life of John Damascene*, and the governor the *Life of Symeon Stylites the Younger*, "valorising two illustrious Greek-speaking Syrians," as Kontouma puts it, "especially John of Damascus, the great Chalcedonian author in Greek and offspring of the important Melkite family of the Manṣūr."[11] At about the same time, the task of translating the Damascene into Arabic was undertaken by Antony, *hēgoumenos* of the monastery of St Symeon the Younger on the Wondrous Mountain not far from Antioch, who translated a number of texts including the *Dialectica* and the *Exposition of the Orthodox Faith*.[12] It was thus only at the beginning of the eleventh century that work began on establishing John Damascene as a Father of the Church.[13]

[9]John drew up an official document which laid down that henceforth the patriarch of Antioch would be ordained by the patriarch of Constantinople.

[10]Symeon, who died *c.* 1000, was not an ecclesiastic but the Grand Logothete of the Drome, a high-ranking imperial official with a large staff whose duties were equivalent to those of a modern foreign minister. His sobriquet Metaphrastes ("Paraphraser") came from the technique he used to produce the saints' *Lives*.

[11]Kontouma, "John III of Antioch (996–1021)," 25.

[12]One of the texts he translated, the *Exposition and Declaration of the Faith*, has come down to us only in his Arabic translation (Latin version in PG 95:417–38).

[13]Kontouma draws attention to the fact that before the end of the tenth century "John of Damascus was not really venerated nor often cited, even in iconophile circles" ("At the Origins of Byzantine Systematic Dogmatics: the *Exposition of the*

For his "official" *Life* of the Damascene, John Polites did not start
with a *tabula rasa*. He had to hand at least two documents that he
corrected and reshaped in the metaphrastic manner. The chief of
these was a Greek text known as the *Life of the Melodists Cosmas
and John Damascene*.[14] Kontouma dates it to 842–43 and attributes
it to Michael Synkellos.[15] The *Life of the Melodists* is an extraordinary
mishmash—the Cosmas of the title is a conflation of at least three
different people of that name—but it does contain a few genuine
nuggets, such as the information that John was a monk and priest
in Jerusalem. Polites recognized the prosopographical and historical
confusion in the text (which he cites several times) and attempts in
his own *Life* to reduce the confusion to some order. The other source
mentioned by him is an Arabic *Life*, no longer extant, which seems
also to have been a source for the earliest surviving Arabic *Life*, written by a monk called Michael of the Monastery of St Symeon the
Younger towards the end of the eleventh century.[16]

Orthodox Faith of St John of Damascus," in Kontouma, *John of Damascus: New
Studies on His Life and Works*, Study VI, 3–4. The same point is made very emphati-
cally by Sidney Griffith, who laments the failure of Byzantinists to recognize that in
Byzantium St John was despised during his lifetime and only appreciated long after
his death. Such a failure, he says, "co-opts John of Damascus out of his own milieu
and into a Byzantine frame of reference that was never his own" ("John of Damascus
and the Church in Syria in the Umayyad Era," 229).

[14]Text in Athanasios Papadopoulos-Kerameus, Ἀνάλεκτα Ἱεροσολυμιτικῆς
σταχυολογίας, vol. 4 (St Petersburg: V. Kirsbaoum, 1897), 271–302; analysis in Vassa
Kontouma, "John of Damascus (*c.* 655–*c.* 745)," in Kontouma, *John of Damascus: New
Studies*, Study I, 11–15. Kontouma argues that the historical context of the text is "the
Restoration of Orthodoxy" after the ninth-century revival of iconoclasm under the
emperors of the Amorian dynasty and that the motivation for its composition was
"to establish spiritual paternity between three great hagiopolite composers—Andrew
'bishop of Crete', Cosmas the Melodist, and [John of Damascus]" and "to bring the
Melodist into the iconophile camp" (15).

[15]Kontouma, "John of Damascus (*c.* 655–*c.* 745)," 12. On Michael Synkellos, who
was born in Jerusalem *c.* 761 and died in Constantinople in 846, see Robert Browning
and Alexander Kazhdan, *ODB* 2:1369–70.

[16]Edited by Constantin Bacha, *Sīrat al-qiddīs Yūṣannā al-Dimashqī al-aṣlīya /
Biographie de Jean Damascène* (Harissa, 1912). Robert Hoyland notes that three manuscripts are extant, one of which states in the prologue that it was written by the monk
Michael in 1084; Robert G. Hoyland, *Seeing Islam as Others Saw It: A Survey and Evaluation of Christian, Jewish and Zoroastrian Writings on Early Islam*. Studies in Late

Besides these two sources, which were certainly known to Polites, there were others of which he might have been aware. One was the *Brief Life* of John Damascene, dating from the end of the ninth century.[17] In this *Life*, which is dependent on the *Life of the Melodists*, Cosmas is identified as John's adopted brother and the historical context for John's early life (the reign of Leo III) is more accurately drawn than in the *Life of the Melodists* (where it is set in the reign of Constantine V), but there are many fanciful details. John's father, for example, becomes an emir called Manṣūr, and John is represented as traveling around the world in the company of Cosmas and finally dying in Damascus. Other documents available in Polites' time include the record of the Council of Hiereia of 754, with its famous fourfold anathematization of John Damascene (preserved in the Acts of the Seventh Ecumenical Council of 787),[18] the brief notices concerning John in Theophanes' *Chronographia* (between 813 and 817),[19] and the entries in the *Synaxarion* of Constantinople and the *Souda* (latter half of the tenth century).[20] Even if he was aware of these documents, however, Polites make no direct use of them.

Antiquity and Early Islam 13 (Princeton, NJ: The Darwin Press, 1997), 483, n.100. On Michael's *Life*, and its near-contemporary translation via Greek into Georgian by the monk Ephrem Mtsire, see Bernard Flusin, "From Arabic to Greek, then to Georgian: A Life of Saint John of Damascus," in *Languages and Cultures of Eastern Christianity: Greek*, ed. Scott Fitzgerald Johnson, The Worlds of Eastern Christianity, 300–1500, vol. 6 (Farnham, UK and Burlington, VT: Ashgate Variorum, 2015), 482–93.

[17]Critical text by R. Gkenakou-Mporobilou in Βυζαντινά 22 (2001): 67–73; brief notice in Kontouma, "John of Damascus (*c.* 655–*c.* 745)," 16.

[18]"To Mansur, the ill-named and Saracen-minded, anathema! To Mansur, the worshipper of images and writer of falsities, anathema! To Mansur, the insulter of Christ and plotter against the kingdom, anathema! To Mansur, the teacher of impiety and false interpreter of divine scripture, anathema!" Acts of the Sixth Session, from the end of the *Horos* of 754 (TTH 68:540, lightly modified).

[19]The entry for the year AD 729 (AM 6221) reads: "In Damascus of Syria there shone forth in his life and discourse John the Golden Stream (Χρυσορρόας, *Chrysorroas*), son of Manṣūr, a presbyter and a monk, a most excellent teacher" (Theophanes, *Chronographia* 408 (trans. Mango, 565).

[20]Kontouma notes that the *Brief Life* is probably the source of the *Synaxarion* entry, whereas the *Souda* notice draws on the *Life of the Melodists*. Kontouma, "John of Damascus (*c.* 655–*c.* 745)," 16–17.

Polites' *Life* of John of Damascus owes many of its details to the *Life of the Melodists*. These are adjusted to fit a more credible historical framework and are augmented with new information. Polites, for example, distinguishes between the Cosmas who was John's tutor (whom he identifies as a Calabrian Greek monk redeemed from the slave-market by John's father, Sergios/Sarjūn) and the Cosmas who was his adopted brother. He moves the story of the severed hand (John's right hand was said to have been amputated on the orders of the caliph after he was falsely charged with being in treasonable communication with the Byzantine emperor, and then to have been miraculously restored by the Virgin) from the time of Constantine V (741–75) to that of Leo III (717–41), making it the reason for John's leaving Damascus. Polites is also the first writer to locate John as a monk at the Great Lavra of St Sabas, a monastery that still lies in the Kidron valley to the south of Jerusalem. The author of the *Life of the Melodists* had simply placed him in Jerusalem. Polites does not reveal his reason for transferring John to the Great Lavra, but it seems possible that it did not suit the purpose of the *Life* to embed John too firmly at the heart of the Jerusalem patriarchate. There may also have been a tradition that it was at the Great Lavra that John spent his last days after the death of his patron and spiritual father, the patriarch John V (705–35), and his leaving Jerusalem.[21] According to the *Life of the Melodists*, Cosmas was buried at St Sabas, but not John, who was buried "in the depths of Persia."[22] It was only at the time of the Crusades that John's relics are first mentioned as possessed by the Great Lavra.[23]

[21]This is the tradition at St Sabas today, where pilgrims are shown the cave-cell once occupied by St John.

[22]Kontouma, "John of Damascus (*c.* 655–*c.* 745)," 19, citing Papadopoulos-Kerameus, Ἀνάλεκτα Ἱεροσολυμιτικῆς σταχυολογίας, 4:299.

[23]Kontouma, "John of Damascus (*c.* 655–*c.* 745)," 21–22. Louth notes that when Abbot Daniel, a Russian pilgrim, visited the Great Lavra during his pilgrimage to the Holy Land in 1106–8, he was able to venerate the body of St John Damascene in the chapel above the tomb of St Sabas. Kontouma, *St John Damascene*, 22, citing John Wilkinson, with Joyce Hill and W. F. Ryan, *Jerusalem Pilgrimage 1099–1185* (London: Hakluyt Society, 1988), 140. Lequien notes that the twelfth-century Greek pilgrim,

John's own writings leave us in no doubt that he was a monk and priest in the city of Jerusalem. His references to himself are rare.[24] The most important of them is in a letter to an archimandrite called Iordanes on whether the Trisagion is addressed to the Trinity (as the Orthodox held), or to the Son alone (as the Monophysites, following Peter the Fuller, claimed).[25] John had heard that a Chalcedonian *hēgoumenos*, Anastasios of the monastery of Euthymios,

John Phokas, also saw the Damascene's relics at the Great Lavra (PG 94:485D–486A), and in the same footnote he draws attention to the claim in George Pachymeres' *De Michaele et Andronico Palaeologis* 1.13 that Andronikos II (reigned 1282–1328) gave the body of St John Damascene to the Arsenites (strict Orthodox who were strongly opposed to the Palaiologoi and their policy of union with Rome) in an attempt to appease them. This has led to the confident assertion—e.g., by Joseph Nasrallah, *Saint Jean de Damas* (Harissa: Imprimerie Saint Paul, 1950), 128–29—that St John's relics were transferred to Constantinople in the early fourteenth century, but it is very difficult to see how this could have been the case. The tradition at the Great Lavra today, as recounted by a modern pilgrim, is that the body was taken to Venice by the Crusaders. William Dalrymple, *From the Holy Mountain* (London: Harper Collins, 1997), 301. The Crusaders certainly did take the body of St Sabas to Venice (it was returned to the Great Lavra by Pope Paul VI in 1965) and it is not unlikely that the relics of St John, by then in the possession of the Lavra, were removed at the same time. An inventory of the relics in the *scrinium* of the Orthodox church of San Giorgio dei Greci in Venice, dated April 23, 1647, records a crystal reliquary containing the head of St John Damascene. Chryssa Maltezou, "*Nazione greca* καὶ *cose sacre*: Λείψανα ἁγίων στὸν ναὸ τοῦ Ἁγίου Γεωργίου τῆς Βενετίας," *Thesaurismata: Bolletino dell'Istituto Ellenico di Studi Bizantini e Postbizantini* 29 (1999): 9–31, at 23. Chryssa Maltezou, in a private communication, tells me that the church of San Giorgio today possesses a great number of relics housed in a *scrinium* (a chamber-like "screen") in the upper part of the "Oraia Pyli." "Unfortunately," she says, "no relic bears any sign of identification. It is not excluded that one of them belongs to St John Damaskinos but it is impossible to confirm it." The Kazan church of the Novodevichy monastery in St Petersburg possesses the right hand of St John in a silver reliquary. There are also relics of St John at the Monastery of St John the Evangelist on Patmos (founded in 1088 under the patronage of the emperor Alexios I Komnenos, who promoted the cult of St John Damascene in Constantinople), and at the Monastery of St George Alamanou in Cyprus.

[24]They are assembled and discussed by Kontouma in "John of Damascus (*c.* 655–*c.* 745)," 24–27.

[25]On the Trisagion (the "thrice holy [hymn]": "Holy God, Holy Mighty, Holy Immortal, have mercy on us"), see Robert F. Taft, SJ, "Trisagion," in *ODB* 3:2121. Peter the Fuller (Monophysite patriarch of Antioch three times in the late fifth century) added the invocation "who was crucified for us" after the third clause to make it clear that (in his view) the Trisagion was addressed to Christ.

was claiming that the patriarch of Jerusalem, John V, and John Damascene himself were both in agreement with the Monophysite interpretation. He rejects this indignantly, emphasizing the identity of his own teaching with that of the patriarch: "For who knows the mind of the most blessed John better than I do? Nobody. To tell the truth, he never breathed a dogmatic word without communicating it to me as his disciple."[26] John's insistence on his closeness to the patriarch is interesting, strongly implying that he was on the staff of the Anastasis church in Jerusalem. The superscriptions of some of his homilies appear to confirm this, particularly that of the *Homily on the Withered Fig Tree*, which describes John precisely as "presbyter of the Holy Anastasis of Christ our God."[27] It may be added that the homilies are clearly intended for a general, not a monastic, audience and would have been very appropriately delivered in the Anastasis church. Moreover, John's extensive hymnography appears to have been created specifically for the Jerusalem liturgy.

John Damascene's Career in its Historical Context

With the help of these and some later historical sources, we are now in a position to fill out our opening sketch of John's life with some degree of confidence. His full name in Arabic was Manṣūr ibn Sarjūn ibn Manṣūr.[28] The precise date of his birth is not known, but there is no doubt that he was a Melkite Syrian who grew up at the Umayyad court in Damascus, where his father, Sarjūn, and grandfather, Manṣūr, had served the caliphs faithfully as senior treasury officials in the *dīwān* (the state bureaucracy). Although by the tenth century it was thought necessary to account for John's mastery of Greek by importing a teacher from abroad, there is no difficulty in accepting that he received his education in Damascus from native teachers.

---

[26]*Epistula de hymno trisagio* 26.13–14 (Kotter 4:329) (my translation). Evidently the patriarch, referred to as "thrice blessed" (τρισμάκαρ, *trismakar*) and "most blessed" (μακαριώτατος, *makariōtatos*)—had recently died.

[27]*Oratio in ficum arefactam* (Kotter 5:121).

[28]He may have taken the name Yuhannā (John) only when he became a monk.

Sophronios of Jerusalem (*c.* 560–638) and John's contemporary, Andrew of Crete (*c.* 660–740), were both raised and educated there, and both of them were excellent Hellenists. There were others, too, such as the Palestinian monk, Amba Marianos, who is described by Stephen the Sabaite's biographer, Leontios of Damascus, writing in about 807, as a distinguished Christian of Damascene origin "who possessed a great knowledge of science and was also well acquainted with philosophy."[29] In the late seventh century Damascus was still an important center of Greek culture.

On completing his education, John followed in the family tradition of government service. According to the Arabic *Life*, he was secretary (*kātib*) to the fifth Umayyad caliph, 'Abd al-Malik.[30] The rule of 'Abd al-Malik (caliph from 685 to 705) was a time of change in which the visible symbols of Islam became increasingly more prominent. In 688 'Abd al-Malik began the construction in Jerusalem of the earliest Islamic monumental building, the Dome of the Rock, intending it, perhaps, as a shrine for Muslim pilgrims to rival the Church of the Anastasis. Completed in 692, the Dome of the Rock, resplendent with its gilded cupola, looked down on Jerusalem and the Anastasis church from Temple Mount, visibly proclaiming the superiority of Islam.[31] 'Abd al-Malik also took several decisive steps to Islamize the apparatus of government. One was to create the caliphate's own currency (previously the Byzantine and Sasanian

[29]Michele Piccirillo, OFM, "The Christians in Palestine during a Time of Transition: 7th–9th Centuries," in *The Christian Heritage in the Holy Land*, ed. Anthony O'Mahony with Göran Gunner and Kevork Hintlian (London: Scorpion Cavendish, 1995), 49. The quotation is from the *Life of Stephen the Sabaite* by his disciple Leontius, which survives in an Arabic translation made in 902.

[30]Arabic *Life* 15; Hoyland, *Seeing Islam as Others Saw It*, 481; Sidney H. Griffith, "The Manṣūr Family and Saint John of Damascus: Christians and Muslims in Umayyad Times," in *Christians and Others in the Umayyad State*, ed. Antoine Borrut and Fred M. Donner (Chicago: The Oriental Institute of the University of Chicago, 2016), 29–51, at 32. The Greek hagiographies magnify this, making John the caliph's vizier (πρωτοσύμβουλος, *prōtosymboulos*).

[31]Such symbolic matters were of great importance. See Oleg Grabar, *The Dome of the Rock* (Cambridge, MA: The Belknap Press of Harvard University Press, 2006), 118–19.

coinage had been used); another was to replace Greek with Arabic as the language of the *dīwān*. Officials who were fluent in Arabic could remain in their posts, but John may have seen this as the appropriate time to leave Damascus, especially in view of another factor: the restoration in 705 of the patriarchate of Jerusalem, which had been in abeyance, or at least dysfunctional, for nearly seventy years.

The history of the patriarchate of Jerusalem in this period is obscure. After the death of Sophronios in 638 the Muslims did not permit the election of a successor. For a time the patriarchate was administered by a patriarchal vicar, Stephen of Dora, assisted by John of Philadelphia (modern Amman). At the Sixth Ecumenical Council, held in Constantinople in 680–81, Jerusalem was represented by a presbyter and monk called George, who is described as the *apokrisiarios* (delegated representative) of Theodore, *topotērētēs* (locum tenens) of the see of Jerusalem. Then, eleven years later, the acts of the Quinisext Ecumenical Council (the Council "in Trullo" of 692), include among the signatories Anastasios, patriarch of Jerusalem. Since the eighteenth century, when Michel Lequien published the first critical edition of St John Damascene's works, it has been assumed that Anastasios was a nominee of Justinian II, the emperor at the time of the Council in Trullo, and that he lived at Constantinople. This has been challenged more recently,[32] but whether or not Anastasios was a resident patriarch, he left no trace in Jerusalem.

At about the same time as the re-establishment of the patriarchate of Jerusalem, the cathedral of St John the Baptist at Damascus was appropriated from the Melkites by ʿAbd al-Malik's son and successor, al-Walīd I (705–15), and turned into the city's Great Mosque. The coincidence of these events—the Melkites' loss of their cathedral at Damascus, the re-establishment of the patriarchate of Jerusalem, John's resigning his post to embark on a new career as a monk in Jerusalem—has led some scholars to see a causal connection

---

[32]F. R. Trombley, "A Note on the See of Jerusalem and the Synodal List of the Sixth Ecumenical Council (680–681)," *Byzantion* 53/2 (1983): 632–38.

between them.[33] Such a connection is not at all unlikely. Indeed, it is difficult to account for John's move to Jerusalem unless it was to support the newly revived patriarchate. The details, however, remain speculative.

In Palestine, unlike in Syria, Chalcedonian Orthodox Christians were in a majority. Under the new patriarch, John V (705–35), Jerusalem rapidly became not only their ecclesiastical but also their cultural and spiritual center. For more than a century after John V's enthronement, in contrast to Byzantium, which was facing strong if intermittent military pressure from the Arabs and struggling with a succession of internal crises, including Iconoclasm, Palestine remained a beacon of Greek learning and a center of literary production.[34] Things, however, were not as they had been when Palestine was a province of the Eastern Roman Empire. Then the Chalcedonians had the backing of imperial authority. Now they were competing on a level playing-field with other Christian communities (both miaphysite West Syrians and "Nestorian" East Syrians) and, moreover, with Muslims, Manichaeans, and Jews.[35] John Damascene's apologetic works are to be interpreted against this background. The need to defend Chalcedonian Christianity against its opponents on rational grounds, and strengthen the allegiance of Chalcedonians to their faith and their patriarch, sharpened the dialectical skills of Palestinians of John Damascene's generation.

[33]Most recently (and very plausibly) by Scott Ables, "Was the Reestablishment of the Jerusalem Patriarchate a 'Proto-Melkite' Gambit Orchestrated by John of Damascus—*Quid pro Quo*: Cathedral for Patriarchate?" *ARAM Periodical* (forthcoming); available at: http://oregonstate.academia.edu/ScottAbles.

[34]See Cyril Mango, "Greek Culture in Palestine after the Arab Conquest," in *Languages and Cultures of Eastern Christianity*, 375–86. For the paucity of literary production in Constantinople compared with Jerusalem in this period, see also Ihor Ševčenko, "Hagiography of the Iconoclast Period," in *Iconoclasm: Papers Given at the Ninth Spring Symposium of Byzantine Studies, University of Birmingham, March 1975*, edited by Anthony Bryer and Judith Herrin (Birmingham: Centre for Byzantine Studies, University of Birmingham, 1977), 113–31.

[35]"Miaphysite" is a modern term used as a neutral alternative to "monophysite," to which the non-Chalcedonians have always objected.

John's apologetic works comprise the most important portion of his oeuvre. *On Heresies* with its list of one hundred sectarian movements, summarizing Epiphanius' *Panarion* and concluding with a chapter on Monotheletism and a supernumerary chapter on Islam, was intended to inoculate his readers against the attraction of competitors' creeds. The compilation of fifty philosophical terms in the *Philosophical Chapters* (known in the West since the sixteenth century as the *Dialectica*) defined precisely the way in which such terms as "essence," "nature," and "hypostasis" were to be used in debate with Christian rivals, particularly Monophysites. The three treatises *On the Divine Images*, while occasioned by the Iconoclast movement in the Byzantine Empire, served to defend Christians against accusations of idolatry by Jews and Muslims. The *Exact Exposition of the Orthodox Faith* itself clearly demarcated the boundaries of the Chalcedonian community.

It was the same apologetic need to defend Chalcedonian Orthodoxy that drew John so passionately into the Iconoclast Controversy. The issue of the legitimacy of sacred images was a sensitive one in the Palestinian context, because it was a point on which the Chalcedonians were particularly vulnerable to attack from Muslims and Jews. When the Byzantines adopted Iconoclasm under Leo III (717–41) and especially under Constantine V (741–75), it undermined the position of the Chalcedonians in Palestine. Nor could the Chalcedonians count on support on this matter from the Monophysites.[36] Feelings were bitter on both sides of the iconoclast/iconophile divide. Hence the personal invective against John at the Council of Hiereia (754), where he was anathematized as "Saracen-minded" and "an enemy of the kingdom."[37]

[36]See Sebastian Brock, "Iconoclasm and the Monophysites," in *Iconoclasm: Papers given at the Ninth Spring Symposium of Byzantine Studies, University of Birmingham, March 1975*, ed. Anthony Bryer and Judith Herrin (Birmingham: Centre for Byzantine Studies, University of Birmingham, 1977), 53–57. Brock argues, however (55), that the Monophysite Michael the Syrian's approbation of Constantine V had more to do with hostility to St Maximus the Confessor's Christology than with opposition to images.

[37]See the end of the *Horos* of 754 in the Acts of the Sixth Session of the Seventh

After the death of the patriarch John V in 735, John Damascene left Jerusalem to spend the last years of his life in monastic seclusion.[38] Two letters, the one on the *Trisagion* already mentioned,[39] and the other addressed to a monk called Cometas that prefaces his treatise *On the Holy Fast*,[40] indicate that he was under stress from what Kontouma aptly calls the "climate of instability and infighting among the Chalcedonians of Palestine" that marked the end of his service at the patriarchate.[41] Although John Polites' *Life* claims that he spent his final days in editing his works,[42] Kontouma thinks it more likely that his works were edited by someone else after his death.[43]

An Exact Exposition of the Orthodox Faith

Literary Form

Since the beginning of the eighteenth century, when Michel Lequien first published his edition of the works of St John Damascene,[44] it

Ecumenical Council, translated by Richard Price, in *The Acts of the Second Council of Nicaea (787)* (Liverpool: Liverpool University Press, 2020), 540. Behind the insult "Saracen-minded" (σαρακηνόφρων, *sarakēnophrōn*) must lie the reputation of the Manṣūr family as traitors to the empire (which is why John is also characterized as "enemy of the kingdom"—ἐπίβουλος τῆς βασιλείας [*epiboulos tēs basileias*]—i.e., of the Byzantine Empire). A tradition recorded in the Arabic *Annals* of Eutychios of Alexandria (Melkite patriarch 935–40) held that Damascus had been betrayed to the Muslims by John's grandfather Manṣūr ibn Sarjūn, on which see Griffith, "The Manṣūr Family and Saint John of Damascus." Griffith translates the relevant section of the *Annals* on pp. 29–30.

[38] According to a tenth-century manuscript (Vaticanus gr. 2081) he went to St Chariton's monastery, the Old Lavra, near Bethlehem (Kotter 5:483–84). John Polites' *Life* says that he returned to the Great Lavra of St Sabas (PG 94:451). The *Life of Stephen the Sabaite* simply mentions a hermitage "in the desert." Kontouma in "John of Damascus (*c.* 655–*c.* 745)," 30.

[39] See p. 21 above.

[40] PG 95:64–68A. The relevant passages are translated by Kontouma in "John of Damascus (*c.* 655–*c.* 745)," 25.

[41] Kontouma, "John of Damascus (*c.* 655–*c.* 745)," 25.

[42] PG 94:454B.

[43] Kontouma, "John of Damascus (*c.* 655–*c.* 745)," 30.

[44] *S.P.N. Joannis Damasceni monachi et presbyteri Hierosolymitani opera omnia*

has been assumed that the *Exact Exposition of the Orthodox Faith* is
the third part of a trilogy called the *Fount of Knowledge*—the first
two parts being the *Philosophical Chapters* (in two versions of either
fifty or sixty-eight chapters, known since 1548 as the *Dialectica*) and
On Heresies (in 100 or 103 chapters).[45] There is no manuscript tradition, however, to support this arrangement. Lequien constructed the
trilogy on the basis of information contained in the preface to the
Philosophical Chapters, in the form of a letter addressed to Cosmas
of Maiuma, which Lequien unites with some further remarks which
John makes in the first two chapters of the same work. The *Letter to
Cosmas* announces a threefold program. First, John says, he will set
forth what may be learned from the Greek philosophers, then he will
describe the heresies as a guide to what is false, and finally he will
set forth the truth as taught by the prophets and apostles. But does
this statement refer to the three works that are thought to constitute
the *Fount of Knowledge*? In the *Philosophical Chapters* itself John
does no more than suggest that these chapters could be entitled
"Fount of Knowledge."[46] As Vassa Kontouma has pointed out, the
three works (the *Philosophical Chapters*, *On Heresies*, and the *Exact*

quae extant, cura et studio Michaelis Lequien (Paris, 1712), reprinted by Migne in PG
94–96 (Paris, 1857–64).

[45]In what follows I depend on on Vassa Kontouma, "The *Fount of Knowledge*
between Conservation and Creation," in Vassa Kontouma, *John of Damascus: New
Studies*, Study V.

[46]"Our purpose, then, is to make a beginning of philosophy and to set down
concisely in the present book, so far as is possible, every sort of knowledge. For this
reason let it be called a Fount of Knowledge" (Διὸ Πηγὴ γνώσεως ὀνομάζεσθω, *Dio
Pēgē gnōseōs onomazesthō*) (Kotter 1, *Dialectica* 2.6–9; trans. Chase, modified). Kotter
edited the texts separately in two different volumes (I and II) without using the title
Fount of Knowledge. Kontouma notes a shift in John's work from argumentation based
on patristic texts to argumentation based on philosophical speculation. Kontouma,
"John of Damascus (*c.* 655–*c.* 745)," 39. Scott Ables, building on Kontouma's observation, sees the *Dialectica* as a watershed in John's theological development. Fully aware
that much sectarian Christian debate was fuelled by a confusion over the meaning
of terms, John moves his discussions onto more philosophical ground. Scott Ables,
"Development in Theological Method and Argument in John of Damascus," *Journal
of Early Christian Studies*, forthcoming; available at: http://oregonstate.academia.
edu/ScottAbles.

Exposition of the Orthodox Faith) are reproduced in that order under the title "Fount of Knowledge" in only a single manuscript (out of the twenty-two that contain all three texts) and this manuscript was not among those used by Lequien.[47] Indeed, the usual way the *Exposition* is presented in the manuscript tradition is either as a book standing on its own (156 manuscripts), or as united with the *Philosophical Chapters*, in which case it is given the title *One Hundred and Fifty Chapters* (150 manuscripts).

This fact alone suggests that the text as we have it is the result of an editorial process that continued after John's death.[48] Andrew Louth believes that the original form of the *Fount of Knowledge* was probably a work consisting of 150 chapters, fifty philosophical chapters explaining the logical terms that John will use, followed by one hundred chapters on the content of the Orthodox faith. Louth agrees with Kotter that the prefatory letter to Cosmas was written later to introduce the longer version of the *Philosophical Chapters* (with its additional eighteen chapters), and that it was only then that John conceived of the threefold structure: "philosophical foundation : exploration of heresy : exposition of Orthodoxy." But John died, Louth thinks, before he was able to carry out his plan, which is why it has left almost no trace in the manuscript tradition, with only one copyist guessing John's final intention.[49]

[47]Kontouma, "The *Fount of knowledge* between conservation and creation," 2. The single manuscript with the title *Fount of Knowledge*, Codex Venet. Marcian. gr. app. II.196 (coll. 1403), however, is an early one, dating from the eleventh century.

[48]It may be added that within the manuscript tradition there are also two different ways in which the chapters are ordered. There is the order in which they are given in Kotter's critical edition and reproduced in the present translation (the *expositio ordinata*) and there is also, in a minority of manuscripts, the so-called "inverse order" (*expositio inversa*) in which the order of the chapters is 1–18, 82–100, and 19–81. The *expositio ordinata* is clearly the original order, since the opening words of Chapter 87 refer back to the discussion of the Virgin as Theotokos in Chapter 56.

[49]Andrew Louth, *St John Damascene: Tradition and Originality in Byzantine Theology* (Oxford: Oxford University Press, 2002), 33–34; idem, "The Πηγὴ Γνώσεως of St John Damascene: Its Date and Development," in *Porphyrogenita: Essays on the History and Literature of Byzantium and the Latin East in Honour of Julian Chrysostomides*, ed. Charalambos Dendrinos, et al. (Aldershot, UK and Burlington, VT: Ashgate, 2003), 335–40.

Vassa Kontouma's suggestions are more radical. Basing herself on John's feeling of discouragement at the time he left the patriarchate (as expressed in his own letters), and on her own analysis of the *Exact Exposition of the Orthodox Faith*, she does not believe that John did the work of editing himself. She argues that the text as we have it today is the work of two people, John himself and an unnamed editor who produced the text that circulated in his name. Two of her arguments are particularly telling. The first concerns the title itself of the *Exact Exposition of the Orthodox Faith*. "Exposition" (in Greek, ἔκθεσις, *ekthesis*) is not a strict translation of the corresponding word in the Greek title, which is actually ἔκδοσις (*ekdosis*), or "edition." The title of the work may be translated literally as *An Accurate Edition of the Orthodox Faith of the Holy Abba the Presbyter John Damascene*, which implies, as Kontouma suggests, that somebody else shaped the text for distribution.[50] The second argument concerns the table of contents (the *pinax*), which gives the chapter headings. The *pinax* in Byzantine texts was usually prepared by an editor, who also supplied the headings.[51] Kontouma believes that the editor in this case not only supplied the headings but also divided up the text into a hundred chapters. Freed from these divisions, the text flows more freely, revealing, in Kontouma's words, "its own structure, a looser structure, but one that follows a precise and coherent order of ideas."[52]

Kontouma characterizes the *Exposition of the Orthodox Faith* as "a great theological fresco," adding, "it is not a handbook, nor a dogmatic century."[53] Louth, too, regards the text as not set tightly within the "centuries" convention, describing it as a "dogmatic treatise prefaced by philosophical chapters."[54] The division of a text into self-contained sections ("chapters"), often arranged as a set of a hundred (a "century"), is a literary form that had been devised by

---

[50]Kontouma, "The *Fount of Knowledge* between Conservation and Creation," 8.
[51]See ibid., n. 29, for the evidence concerning this.
[52]Ibid., 8.
[53]Ibid., 14.
[54]Louth, *St John Damascene*, 32.

Evagrius Ponticus (346–99) for slow meditative reading and had quickly become popular in monastic circles.[55] Evagrius intended his brief chapters to be suitable for memorizing; they are terse and quite short, a feature that we still find in Maximus the Confessor (580–662), who in the preface to his *Four Centuries on Love* addressed to Elpidius says that he has condensed his material into short paragraphs so that it should be easy to commit to memory and assimilate. John's chapters are quite different. The ascetical context has gone and memorizing is no longer a consideration. The paragraphs are now generally quite long and are carefully interconnected, the flow of thought often moving seamlessly from one chapter to the next. Whereas the *Philosophical Chapters* may perhaps have been written as a set of distinct chapters defining philosophical terms, the *Exposition* is very likely to have been originally a continuous treatise with the chapter numbers imposed later, either by John himself, or, as Kontouma holds, by a subsequent editor.

Originality

The seventh century, an age of intense Christological debate, was also the great age of dogmatic florilegia. These were compilations of passages from the fathers that were intended to give authoritative support to contested points of mainly Christological doctrine. Their origin lies in the selection of patristic texts compiled by Cyril of Alexandria and read out at the Council of Ephesus (431) by Peter, the *primicerius* of the notaries in charge of procedure.[56] This florilegium

[55]On the origins of the "century" (in Greek ἑκατοντάς, *hekatontas*) and its development by Byzantine writers, see Joel Kalvesmaki, "Evagrius in the Byzantine Genre of Chapters," in *Evagrius and His Legacy*, ed. Joel Kalvesmaki and Robin Darling Young (Notre Dame, IN: University of Notre Dame Press, 2016), 257–87.

[56]Norman Russell, *Cyril of Alexandria* (London and New York: Routledge, 2000), 50. Elizabeth Jeffreys and Alexander Kazhdan (*ODB* 2:793) draw attention to the precedent set by Basil of Caesarea and Gregory of Nazianzus in the fourth century by their selection of texts from Origen for their *Philokalia*, but the conciliar example seems to me much more important. It should be noted that the provenance of the *Philokalia* is disputed, e.g., by Susanna Elm, *Sons of Hellenism, Fathers of the Church: Emperor Julian, Gregory of Nazianzus, and the Vision of Rome* (Berkeley and

was read out again at the first session of the Council of Chalcedon, accompanied by another florilegium, also from the Council of Ephesus, of passages selected from the works of Nestorius to prove his heterodoxy.[57] At the end of the Council of Chalcedon an address in defence of Leo's Tome was sent to the emperor Marcian, accompanied by a crudely dyophysite florilegium drawing on the Antiochene tradition.[58] Such florilegia set a precedent for the doctrinal disputes that followed the council, when each side had a need for handbooks that set out their respective authorities in a compendious form. The most important of these, and the most useful to the Chalcedonians, was the *Doctrine of the Ancient Fathers on the Incarnation of the Word*, known as the *Doctrina Patrum*, to which John Damascene has frequent recourse.[59] He also compiled three small florilegia of his own to accompany his three treatises *On the Divine Images*. There is another vast florilegium entitled *Hiera parallela* ["Sacred texts side by side"], traditionally, but probably wrongly, attributed to John, which gives the exegesis of the fathers on a selection of biblical passages arranged in a thematic rather than a scriptural order.[60]

Los Angeles: University of California Press, 2012), 22. It seems likely that Gregory of Nazianzus acquired a ready-made collection of excerpts in Caesarea, perhaps from the scriptorium of its bishop, Eusebius. On the current state of the question, see Elm, *Sons of Hellenism*, 22 n. 23. (I owe this reference to IG.)

[57]Richard Price and Michael Gaddis, *The Acts of the Council of Chalcedon*, TTH 45 (Liverpool: Liverpool University Press, 2005), vol.1, 301–10, 323–33.

[58]Price and Gaddis, *The Acts of the Council of Chalcedon*, vol. 3, 117–20. See also Price's commentary on this document, 105–7.

[59]Edited by F. Diekamp as *Doctrina Patrum de Incarnatione Verbi: Ein griechische Florilegium aus der Wende des 7. und 8. Jahrhunderts*, and revised by B. Phanourgakis and E. Chrysos (Münster: Aschendorff Verlag, 1981). The *Doctrina Patrum* contains 977 citations, of which 751 are from the fathers. According to Kotter, John has 80 citations from the *Doctrina Patrum*, of which 44 are exact (Kotter 2:252–3).

[60]The *Hiera parallela* exist in two versions (not edited by Kotter), the *Parallela Vaticana* (PG 95:1040–1588; PG 96:9–441) edited by Lequien from cod. Vat. gr. 1236, and the *Parallela Rupefucaldina* (PG 96:441–544), a small part of which was edited by him from cod. Berol. B. N. gr. 46. (The strange name of the latter version derives from the fact that the manuscript once belonged to Cardinal de la Rochefoucauld.) Lequien regarded the *Hiera Parallela* as a spurious work. At the end of the nineteenth century Karl Holl made a strong case for authenticity—*Die Sacra Parallela des Johannes Damascenus*,

It has long been taken for granted that the *Exact Exposition of the Orthodox Faith* is itself an elaborate work of compilation, in effect a disguised florilegium. After all, John had said in the *Letter to Cosmas*, with reference to the third part of his projected trilogy, "I shall say nothing of my own, as I have said, but shall gather together into one what has been elaborated by the most eminent teachers and, to the best of my ability, make their discourse succinct."[61] This is not to be taken as a merely conventional expression of modesty. After six ecumenical councils and nearly three centuries of Christological wrangling between Chalcedonians and their opponents, the need, in John's view, was not for another personal exposition of Christian doctrine, but for a reliable summary securely based on the best authorities. By John's time, the expression "the fathers of the Church" had already come into use.[62] Besides the large number of quotations from the fathers—usually attributed—from Athanasius of Alexandria, Basil the Great, Gregory the Theologian, Gregory of Nyssa, Cyril of Alexandria, and Dionysius the Areopagite,[63] there are also many unattributed passages from authors not recognized

---

Texte und Untersuchungen zur Geschichte der altchristlichen Literatur 16/1 (Leipzig: J.C. Hinrichs'sche Buchhandlung, 1897)—but opinion is now moving back to Lequien's view. See José Declerck, "Les Sacra Parallela nettement antérieurs à Jean Damascène: Retour à la datation de Michel Le Quien," *Byzantion* 85 (2015): 27–65.

[61]John Damascene, *Prooimion*, 60–62, ed. Kotter 1:54.

[62]The Thesaurus Linguae Graece attributes the earliest use of this precise expression (Πατέρες τῆς Ἐκκλησίας) to Leontius of Byzantium (d. *c.* 543), who declares in the second of his *Three Books against Nestorians and Eutychians* that what he has to say is not his own but that of the fathers who have received the charism of teaching from the Holy Spirit (*Leontius of Byzantium: Complete Works*, ed. and trans. Brian E. Daley, SJ [Oxford: Oxford University Press, 2017], 386). The "fathers" are not, as in modern usage, all the orthodox writers of the Early Church but those who by common consent are the Church's most distinguished teachers.

[63]Kontouma lists these—including Maximus the Confessor, although he is never mentioned by name—as "Gregory of Nazianzus (194 citations, 186 of which are exact), Athanasius of Alexandria, Cyril of Alexandria (73 citations, 58 of which are exact), Maximus the Confessor (70 citations, 66 of which are exact), Basil of Caesarea (69 citations), Gregory of Nyssa (49 citations, of which 42 are exact), and ps.-Dionysius the Areopagite (41 citations)" ("The *Fount of knowledge* between conservation and creation," 7). According to Kotter 2:249–50, Athanasius of Alexandria should be listed as 83 citations, of which 4 are exact.

at the time as patristic authorities, such as Nemesius of Emesa (late 4th cent.), Leontius of Byzantium (early 6th cent.), Maximus the Confessor (early 7th cent.), and John's older contemporary, Anastasius of Sinai. Until recently, it was also thought that a very large proportion of the early chapters on the Trinity was the work of an author conventionally named "Pseudo-Cyril" whom John Damascene had plagiarized without acknowledgement.[64] This was still the scholarly consensus when Kotter published his critical edition of the *Exposition of the Orthodox Faith* in 1973, with the result that his apparatus contains many references to Pseudo-Cyril's *On the Most Holy Trinity* as a major source. Now, thanks to the researches of the Spanish codicologist, Gregorio de Andrés Martinez (1919–2005), and the French Augustinian of the Assumption, Daniel Stiernon (1923–2015), brilliantly confirmed in 1995 by Vassa Kontouma, it has been established that the supposed work of Pseudo-Cyril is in fact a compilation drawn from John Damascene himself in the early fourteenth century by the Byzantine scholar, Joseph the Philosopher (also known as Joseph Rhakendytes).[65] It is no longer possible to dismiss the *Exposition of the Orthodox Faith*, as many scholars still do, merely as "a mosaic of quotations." John Damascene may have stayed close to the text of his sources, but he is nevertheless an important theologian in his own right.[66]

[64]This is the *De SS. Trinitate*, which Migne (following Jean Aubert's seventeenth-century edition of Cyril) prints in PG 77:1120–73 among Cyril's doubtful and spurious works. Lequien, however, believed that the *De SS. Trinitate* was a genuine work of John Damascene which he had excerpted himself from his *De fide orthodoxa* (see his *admonitio*, PG 95:9–10).

[65]Kontouma, "Pseudo-Cyril's ‹De SS. Trinitate›: A Compilation of Joseph the Philosopher," 119–29.

[66]For a strongly dissenting view, see John A. Demetracopoulos, "In Search of the Pagan and Christian Sources of John of Damascus' Theodicy," in *Byzantine Theology and its Philosophical Background*, ed. Antonio Rigo, in collaboration with Pavel Ermilov and Michele Trizio, Byzantios: Studies in Byzantine History and Civilization 4 (Turnhout: Brepols, 2011), 50–86. Demetracopoulos' learned and characteristically combative study takes issue with several scholars, notably Michael Frede and Vassa Kontouma, dismissing Kontouma's work on Pseudo-Cyril as restoring "some lines to John's pen" without affecting "the compilatory nature of the whole work" (p. 54, n.13). (The "some lines" are actually twenty-eight columns of Greek in Migne's edition of

No Byzantine theologian, of course, especially after the first four ecumenical councils, was going to claim originality. To produce theological writings meant to express the mind of the fathers. Personal innovation was bound to be unorthodox, especially if it was unsupported by the patristic tradition. With John freed from dependence on "Pseudo-Cyril," however, if not from dependence on Nemesius of Emesa, and the other "moderns" he quotes anonymously, we are now in a position to appreciate more fully the extent of his theological creativity. He is the first, for example, to introduce the concept of *perichōrēsis* (mutual coinherence), previously used only in Christological contexts, into a consideration of the Trinity; he deepens the doctrine of the Holy Spirit, emphasizing the Spirit's hypostatic character and clarifying its relations with the Father and the Son (the Spirit proceeds from the Father and rests in the Son); in the chapters on the economy of the incarnation he develops an "asymmetrical" Christology in which all the initiatives lie with the divine Word;[67] and in his analysis of how the human will operates, "in spite of all the internal tensions and unclarities which arise from John's use of disparate sources, the account which emerges is in some respects novel."[68] The *Exact Exposition of the Orthodox Faith* is more

Pseudo-Cyril.) Demetracopoulos has a very demanding (if somewhat anachronistic) standard of originality, even classifying as plagiarism anything he detects to be "latent paraphrasing" (p. 63). He is right, however, not to let us forget that John does often stay very close to his sources, especially on topics where he feels he has nothing new to say. The unacknowledged anthropological material from Nemesius of Emesa, for example, amounting to about ten columns in Migne's text quoted verbatim with another five columns paraphrased, is incorporated by John with scarcely any comment at all apart from cutting out references to pagan authors. Demetracopoulos' final judgement of John is that he was not a Father of the Church but a Byzantine author who produced "compilatory yet 'correct' theological pieces" (p. 85). This ignores the innovative aspects of John's work, yet would, I think, have been regarded as a compliment by John himself.

[67]See Louth, *St John Damascene*, 157. The phrase "asymmetrical Christology" is Florovsky's.

[68]Michael Frede, "John of Damascus on Human Action, the Will, and Human Freedom," in *Byzantine Philosophy and its Ancient Sources*, ed. Katerina Ierodiakonou (Oxford: Clarendon Press, 2002), 63–95, at 93. What is novel, says Frede, arises through John's integration of his sources into a new context.

than just a work of synthesis: it repositions Chalcedonian Christian doctrine so as to face the challenges of a world in which, without its former privileged status, it can only commend itself by rigorous argument, and it offers a potential way out of the impasses of the Chalcedonian/miaphysite debate.[69]

Purpose

After the Arab conquest, it was no longer possible for Chalcedonian orthodoxy to be imposed on the Monophysites by force. The Christian faith itself, whether Chalcedonian or not, no longer enjoyed a privileged position with regard to Judaism or Manichaeism. The dominant religion was now Islam. Although initially professed by a relatively small number of believers, Islam exerted a strong attraction simply because it was the religion of the victors. A new style of apologetic writing was needed that would strengthen the identity of Chalcedonian Christians and define their boundaries with regard to their opponents, both within the Christian family and outside it, without unduly provoking the Muslim authorities.

John was writing, probably in the 730s, principally for a monastic audience, the main readership in Palestine for theological texts in Greek. Palestinian monks had played a prominent role in the defense of Chalcedonian orthodoxy in the previous two centuries. Despite John's "perichoretic" Trinitarian theology and "asymmetrical"

---

[69]For a very helpful discussion of the innovative aspects of John's theological work see Ables, "Development in Theological Method and Argument in John of Damascus." Following Kontouma, Ables believes that the *Dialectica* was a watershed for John, after which his theological method became more philosophical and less reliant on the scriptural and patristic argument that in the previous two centuries had led to the impasse with the Monophysites. Ables, too, rejects the idea that John was no more than a compiler: "We find a creative theologian, who played a key role in the survival of Chalcedonian Christianity under the Umayyad Arabs by adapting his theological polemic to his local context with creative insight." He argues convincingly that in an effort to find common ground with his miaphysite West Syrian and "Nestorian" East Syrian interlocutors, John goes back to the Nicene Trinitarian settlement, recasting it with the help of the notion of perichoresis borrowed from Maximus the Confessor.

Christology, there was no longer much hope of reconciling the Monophysites (as they were now known by their opponents) to the imperial church by theological debate. There was still a pressing need, however, to continue the struggle, especially in view of the fact that in Syria Jacob Baradaeus (c. 500–78) had set up a parallel hierarchy that by John's time was well established as a separate church. Hence the very large number of chapters (45–81)—nearly half the text of the *Exposition*—devoted to Christology.

The Palestinian Orthodox themselves, after sixty-seven years without a patriarch, were a divided community. There were conflicts on liturgical matters. Even the cult of icons does not seem to have had much of a popular following.[70] The *Exposition of the Orthodox Faith*, while not being a dogmatic handbook, served to present the essentials of the Chalcedonian Orthodox faith as a coherent body of doctrine with a view not only to winning over the Monophysites but also to promoting the unity of the Chalcedonian community itself.[71]

With regard to Islam, pressure on Christians was not as intense in the early Umayyad era as it was to become later. There was no general demand that Christians should become Muslims so long as they respected Islam's dominant position. The accounts of martyrdom that we have from the seventh and eighth centuries concern individuals in particular circumstances rather than whole communities. After Gaza had been surrendered by its citizens in 636/7, the soldiers of the garrison were offered the choice of conversion to

---

[70]See the discussion in Marie-France Auzépy, "From Palestine to Constantinople (Eighth–Ninth Centuries): Stephen the Sabaite and John of Damascus," in *Languages and Cultures of Eastern Christianity*, 399–442, esp. 422–24.

[71]From Ananastasius of Sinai's *Questions and Answers*, a text written a few decades earlier than John's *Exposition*, "the daily observances of belief and Christian ritual [in the Muslim world] can be shown to be much less rigorously and uniformly observed within the neo-Chalcedonian community than the 'official line' represented by the canons of the Quinisext, for example, would suggest." John Haldon, "The Works of Anastasius of Sinai: A Key Source for the History of Seventh-Century East Mediterranean Society and Belief," in *Languages and Cultures of Eastern Christianity*, 323–63, at 346.

Islam or death. Sixty of them chose to die in their Christian faith.[72] In the 650s, George the Black, who had been taken prisoner as a child and had become a Muslim, returned to the Christian faith and was martyred as a Muslim apostate in Damascus.[73] In 715, again in Damascus, Peter of Capitolias was put to death for insulting Muhammad and Islam.[74] These were isolated cases. Chalcedonian Christians in Palestine were in a majority and relatively secure. They nevertheless needed to be equipped with rational arguments with which they could defend their faith.

A literary genre that had been found useful for giving guidance on disputed matters in the past was that of "Questions and Answers" (*Erōtapokriseis*). John's older contemporary, the Palestinian monk Anastasius of Sinai (died shortly after 700), wrote a work in that form for laypeople.[75] He was also the author of a general guide, the *Hodēgos*, which is not unlike John's *Exposition* in its polemic against Monophysitism and—more discreetly—Islam.[76] John did not write an *erōtapokrisis* but many of the last nineteen chapters of the *Exposition* deal with various topics of Christian practice in a similar manner.

The Islamic challenge also seems to have made itself felt on the level of theological debate. It may not be a coincidence that three of the *Exposition*'s chapters (92–94) discuss to what extent God is responsible for everything that happens, evil as well as good. This was precisely the chief theological issue that was debated among Muslim scholars at the time when John was employed as 'Abd al-Malik's secretary. The advocates of free will, the *Qadarīs*, posed a potential political threat to the caliph, who from a predestinarian perspective could claim that everything he did, even what was unjust, was decreed by God. A prominent *Qadari*, Ma'bad al-Juhani,

---

[72]Hoyland, *Seeing Islam as Others Saw It*, 347–51.
[73]Ibid., 351–52.
[74]Ibid., 354–60.
[75]On the *Erōtapokriseis*, see John Haldon, "The Works of Anastasius of Sinai," passim.
[76]John cites it several times (in Chapters 13, 35, 37, 42, 58, and 72).

was put to death by 'Abd al-Malik, a fact of which John could not have been ignorant.[77] John does not engage directly with Islamic thought, but the issues that concerned Muslim religious scholars were in the air around him.

Structure

The structure of the *Exposition of the Orthodox Faith* has puzzled scholars ever since Lequien published his edition of the text in 1712. The most commonly held view is that expressed by Martin Jugie nearly a hundred years ago. The general plan, he says, reproduces the sequence of the Creed of Nicaea-Constantinople. Although the manuscript tradition witnesses to only a hundred chapters, the four-book division of the medieval Latin translation, in Jugie's view, makes good sense. The fourth book, however, contains a rag-bag of topics without much order, so that the work tails off unsatisfactorily. There are also a number of lacunae. Particularly regrettable, says Jugie, is the lack of a chapter on the Church.[78]

Bonfaz Kotter, although rejecting the Latin division into four books in his edition of the text, nevertheless respects its grouping of chapters in his summary of the contents, with the difference that he detaches Chapter 100, *On resurrection*, regarding it as as a separate major topic.[79]

In his 2002 monograph on John Damascene, Andrew Louth is prepared to see more unity in the last group of chapters: "If there is a common theme linking the last nineteen chapters, it would seem to be the *practices* of Christians, and the way these distinguish them from Jews and Muslims, leading to a clarification of issues at stake

[77]On the theological culture of the Umayyad court, see Majid Fakhry, *A History of Islamic Philosophy*, third edition (New York: Columbia University Press, 2004), 39–49. Interestingly, Fakhry also mentions "reports of a conversation between Ma'bad, who initiated this whole current of discussion on free will, and a Christian from Iraq called Sausan" (p. 45).

[78]Martin Jugie, "Jean Damascène (Saint)," *Dictionnaire de théologie catholique* 8/2 (Paris: Letouzey et Ané, 1925), cols 693–751, at 697–98 and 715.

[79]Kotter 2:xxvii.

between Christians and their religious opponents in Umayyad Palestine."[80] Although cautious about making John's thought too systematic,[81] he too finds merit in the Latin fourfold division.

Writing in 2006, Vassa Kontouma breaks away not only from the division into four books but also from what she regards as the division into a hundred chapters imposed by the Byzantine editor: "Once released from these constraints, the text can reveal its own structure, a looser structure, but one that follows a precise and coherent order of ideas."[82] The structure of the *Exposition* as conceived by Kotter, Louth, and Kontouma may be presented synoptically as follows:

Kotter[83]	Louth[84]	Kontouma[85]
Ch. 1–14	Ch. 1–14	Ch. 1–3.44
1. *God and Trinity*	1. *God and Trinity*	1. *Knowledge of God*
	- Human knowledge of God	Ch. 3.45–7.44
	- The doctrine of the the Holy Trinity	2. *Natural knowledge of the divine*
		- Natural knowledge of divine properties
		- Natural knowledge of the hypostatic processions
		Ch. 8
		3. *Knowledge from tradition*
		- Traditional knowledge of divine properties
		- Traditional knowledge of the hypostatic processions

[80]Louth, *St John Damascene*, 85.

[81]"John is concerned about clarity, but he is not in any way systematic." Louth, *St John Damascene*, 86.

[82]Kontouma, "The *Fount of Knowledge* between Conservation and Creation," 8.

[83]Kotter 2:27.

[84]Louth, *St John Damascene*, 89–189.

[85]Kontouma, "The *Fount of Knowledge* between Conservation and Creation," 8–14.

- Union and distinction of the
hypostases of the Trinity

Ch. 9–12
*4. The divine activities,
principle of the divine names*
- Essence and "that which is
around the essence"
- Names known through
activities

Ch. 13–14
5. God the place of creation
- God uncircumscribed
- God unchanging

Ch. 15–44
*2. Invisible and
visible creation*
- angels, demons
- World, paradise,
human beings
with their
creative powers,
providence

Ch. 15–44
*2. Creation and
human kind*
- Creation
- The invisible
creation: angels
and demons
- The visible
creation: heaven
to paradise
- Human kind
- Human psychology
- Providence

Ch. 15–25
6. The creation of the world
- The invisible world
- The visible world
- The world made up of
the visible and the invisible

Ch. 26–45
7. The creation of man
- Man made up of the visible
and invisible
- "In the likeness": the soul in
the exercise of virtue
- "In the image": the soul in
the exercise of free will
-Providence and government
of creation
- The fall of man

Ch. 45–81

3. *Christ and his work of redemption*

Ch. 45–81

3. *The incarnate Oikonomia*

Ch. 46–81

8. *The economy of the Word*
- The hypostatic union
- Subsidiary problems related to the doctrine of the hypostatic union
- The two wills and activities of Christ: "each form wills and acts in communion with the other"
- Problems related to the doctrine of the two activities and two wills
- The restoration of like by like
- The life-giving death of the Lord
- Subsidiary questions and definitions

Ch. 82–99

4. *Individual questions*
- Baptism, veneration of the cross, relics and images, prayer towards the east, Eucharist, Theotokos, Scripture and its statements on Christ

Ch. 82–100

4. *Christian practices*
- Baptism
- Faith and the cross
- Prayer facing east
- The Eucharistic mystery
- Relics and icons of the saints
- Scripture
- Dualism
- Against the Jews
- Eschatology

Ch. 82–92

9. *Means of salvation bequeathed by the Lord*
- The life of the Savior, model of salvation
- The model of living images of the Lord
- The means of transmission of the preaching of the faith

- Against the
Manichees and Jews
-Virginity,
circumcision,
Antichrist

Ch. 100	Ch. 93–100
5. *Resurrection*	10. *Sin and liberation of man*
	- Evil, *para physin*, and the law of sin
	- The restoration *kata physin*
	- Spiritual law and the practice of virtue
	- The end times and the Second Coming

The most striking difference in these outlines is an increasing will-ingness by scholars to see a coherent structure and logic in the work, particularly in the last nineteen chapters. John was not a proto-scholastic, which is how his medieval Latin interpreters saw him. His chief concern was to show his readers how God may be known and salvation attained in a religious and political environment in which Chalcedonian orthodoxy enjoyed few privileges (apart from the restoration of the Jerusalem patriarchate) and needed to make its case as persuasively as possible.

John Damascene in the Byzantine and Western traditions

John Damascene was one of the most widely read Greek authors in the later Byzantine period. For his critical edition of the *Exact Exposition of the Orthodox Faith* Bonifaz Kotter collated no fewer than 752 manuscripts, of which 252 contain the complete text. It was only centuries after his death, however, that John attained the authoritative status he came to enjoy. Of the complete manuscripts of the *Exposition*, only three date from the ninth century and five from the tenth.

The number rises to forty-six from the thirteenth century, sixty-three from the fourteenth century and forty-nine from the fifteenth century.[86] The reason for the greatly increased interest in John's text in late Byzantium has been attributed by Vassa Kontouma to the work of the theologian Euthymios Zigabenos (*c.* 1050–*c.* 1120), who made extensive use of the *Exposition* in his systematic refutation of heresies, the *Dogmatic Panoply*.[87] This work had been commissioned from Euthymios by Alexios I Komnenos (1081–1118), an emperor who came to the throne after the decade of disorder that followed the catastrophic defeat of Roman arms at Mantzikert (1071) and who made it his responsibility to tighten up ecclesiastical and doctrinal discipline. Until the twelfth century, John Damascene was not considered part of the Byzantine world and was more or less ignored. But he attracted the attention of Alexios, to whom he was useful for the comprehensive way in which he presented Orthodoxy. As Euthymios explains in the Prologue to his *Dogmatic Panoply*, it was Alexios himself who drew up the list of passages from the fathers, including John Damascene, which were to be included in the treatise.[88] "As emperor, he therefore accomplished what the most fervent iconophiles did not: installing the traitor Manṣūr as an authority."[89]

After Zigabenos, John Damascene enters the canon of patristic authorities invoked in polemical or apologetic works, where he is sometimes cited as "the last of the fathers."[90] The precision of John's language was found to be extremely useful, especially during

[86]See the table in Kotter 2:xliii.

[87]Kontouma, "At the origins of Byzantine systematic dogmatics," 4–9.

[88]PG 130:24AB; trans. Kontouma, "At the origins of Byzantine Systematic Dogmatics," 8. This is all the more remarkable in view of John's blunt protest against imperial interference in church affairs: "It is not for emperors to legislate for the Church" (*Three Treatises on the Divine Images* 2.12; trans. Louth). Euthymios makes a point of meeting this reproof head on by emphasizing that Alexios was "not usurping the work of hierarchs, but encouraging them by his own example, making a pact of alliance with them" (PG 130:21D; trans. Kontouma).

[89]Kontouma, "At the origins of Byzantine Systematic Dogmatics," 9.

[90]Gregory Akindynos, for example, calls him "the last of the leading and most divine theologians" (Letter 62.79; trans. Hero). He shares December 4 with St Barbara as his feast day.

the fourteenth-century Hesychast Controversy. Both sides in this controversy frequently appeal to "the celebrated John, glory of the city of Damascus."[91] Gregory Palamas, as might be expected, found much to cite from the *Exposition*, especially from Chapters 8 (On the Holy Trinity) and 59 (On the energies).[92] These citations support his contention that distinctions can be made in the Godhead apart from those that exist between the three hypostases, for the "Damascene theologian" distinguishes between begetting, which belongs to the divine nature, and creating, which belongs to the divine will.[93] But Palamas' opponent, Gregory Akindynos, is also able to cite John by picking out balancing statements in the *Exposition* that emphasize the unity of the Godhead.[94] John does not lend himself to easy sloganizing.

It was John's rehabilitation under Alexios I Komnenos that also led to his being adopted as a Church Father by the Latin West. This came about through the Latin translation of the *Exact Exposition of the Orthodox Faith* made in 1153/4 by the jurist and Greek scholar, Burgundio of Pisa (1110–93), at the request of Pope Eugenius III (1145–53). Eugenius, a fellow-Pisan and the first Cistercian to occupy the papal throne, was keen to inform himself about how the theology of the Greeks differed from that of the Latins. In 1149 or 1150 he had heard from the German statesman and diplomat, Anselm of Havelberg (*c.* 1100–58), about a disputation on the theological points separating the two traditions that had been held in Constantinople in 1136 between Anselm and a leading Greek theologian, Niketas of Nikomedia, and had asked Anselm to write up an account of it for

[91]The expression is again that of Akindynos in *Refutation of the Dialogue between an Orthodox and a Baarlamite* 3.5 (ed. Cañellas, CCSG 31, 174).

[92]From Chapter 8, Palamas derives 33 citations, and from Chapter 59, 30 citations, out of a total of 113.

[93]See, for example, *Against Akindynos* 2.45, 2.49, and 2.56 ("the Damascene theologian" is from 2.56); *Against Gregoras* 1.29 and 2.54, and *Letter to John Gabras* 32, all from the same paragraph of John Damascene, *Exposition* 8, lines 63–88 (Kotter 2.21–2; trans. below, pp. 73–74).

[94]For example Akindynos, *Refutation* 1.12, citing John Damascene, *Exposition* 1.8, lines 268–74 (Kotter 2:29–30).

him.[95] It was in the context of wishing to learn more about Orthodox theology that he also asked Burgundio to translate the *Exposition of the Orthodox Faith* for him. Burgundio had himself attended the disputation of 1136 in the role of Pisa's ambassador to Alexios I's son and successor, John II (1118–43). An excellent Hellenist, he produced a good Latin translation.[96]

Burgundio's translation of the *Exposition* followed the 100-chapter form that its Byzantine editors had given to it. The division into four books (on analogy with the format of Peter Lombard's *Sentences*, the main theological textbook at the University of Paris) seems to have been made by Philip the Chancellor (*c.* 1160–1236). Philip, who was chancellor of the cathedral of Notre Dame in Paris and in that capacity also the rector of the university, is one of the first Latin theologians to make use of John Damascene in his own work. He borrows from John his account of the process by which we deliberate an action and come to a decision to put it into effect (Chapters 36–39) but modifies John's account by reducing the element of freedom simply to the final choice of action.[97]

The most important use of Burgundio's translation, however, was made by the Dominican Thomas Aquinas (*c.* 1225–74).[98] Despite not

[95]Anselm explains this in the introduction to Book II of his *Dialogues* (PL 188:1139–1248). For a fuller discussion, see Norman Russell, "Anselm of Havelberg and the Union of the Churches," *Sobornost incorporating Eastern Churches Review* 1:2 (1979): 19–41. Cf. Jay T. Lees, *Anselm of Havelberg: Deeds into Words in the Twelfth Century* (Leiden: Brill, 1998), 224–81. (Note that Lees critiques an earlier version of my article, published in *Kleronomia*, which through an unfortunate oversight on my part bears the same title as the more developed version that appeared in *Sobornost*.)

[96]*De fide orthodoxa: Versions of Burgundio and Cerbanus*, edited by Eligius M. Buytaert (St Bonaventure, NY: Franciscan Institute, 1955). Buytaert dates the translation (previously thought to have been made in 1150) to 1153/4.

[97]On Philip's work, see Colleen McLuskey, "Philip the Chancellor," The Stanford Encyclopedia of Philosophy (Summer 2019 edition), ed. Edward N. Zalta, <https://plato.stanford.edu/archives/sum2019/entries/philip-chancellor/>.

[98]John also became important in the Franciscan tradition. On his use by Alexander of Hales (c. 1186–1245) and his Franciscan successors at the University of Paris, see the chapters by Richard Cross ("The Reception of John of Damascus in the *Summa Halensis*") and Johannes Zachhuber ("John of Damascus in the *Summa Halensis*") in *The Summa Halensis: Sources and Content*, ed. Lydia Schumacher, Veröffentlichungen

knowing Greek well enough to read them in the original, Thomas was a keen student of the Greek fathers.[99] In his Orvietan period, when he was constructing his great compendium of Greek patristic commentenary on the verses of the Gospels, the *Catena Aurea*, he brought together very many Greek authors, including Theophylact of Ohrid (*c.* 1050–after 1126), the translation of whose work he had commissioned himself. Burgundio's translation of John Damascene left its mark on the *Summa theologiae*. Thomas relies on John, for example, for his knowledge of the Greek teaching on icons,[100] and also for his understanding of the role of the Holy Spirit (at the *epiclesis*) in the Eucharist.[101] Besides the *De fide orthodoxa* (as the *Exposition* was known in Latin), Thomas was also familiar with John's two homilies on the Transfiguration and uses them as a testimony.[102] John Damascene thus entered the Western canon of church fathers only a century after his elevation to similar status in the East.[103]

Editions and Translations

Other Latin translations (or revisions of Burgundio) were made in the Middle Ages but none supplanted Burgundio's work.[104] The first

des Grabmann-Institutes zur Erforschung der mittelalterlichen Theologie und Philosophie 66 (Berlin and Boston: Walter de Gruyter, 2020), 71–90, 91–116.

[99]Thomas's interest in the Greek patristic tradition has recently been explored in an important work, *Thomas Aquinas and the Greek Fathers*, ed. Michael Dauphinais, Andrew Hofer, and Roger Nutt (Ave Maria, FL: Sapientia Press, 2019).

[100]See John Sehorn, "Worshiping the Incarnate God: Thomas Aquinas on *Latria* and the Icon of Christ," in Dauphinais, Hofer, and Nutt, *Thomas Aquinas and the Greek Fathers*, 221–43. Sehorn points out that John Damascene's chapter on icons (*Exposition* 89) was Thomas's sole Greek source on the topic.

[101]See Joseph Wawrykow, "The Greek Fathers in the Eucharistic Theology of Thomas Aquinas," in Dauphinais, Hofer, and Nutt, *Thomas Aquinas and the Greek Fathers*, 274–302, especially 291–95.

[102]See Marcus Plested, "Thomas Aquinas and John of Damascus on the Light of the Transfiguration: Can we speak of a Greek patristic turn in Thomas?" in Dauphinais, Hofer, and Nutt, *Thomas Aquinas and the Greek Fathers*, 206–20.

[103]His feast day in the Western Church is also December 4 (formerly, before the reform of the calendar in 1969, March 27). In 1890 Pope Leo XIII proclaimed him a Doctor of the Universal Church.

[104]Burgundio's translation survives in 117 manuscripts (Buytaert based his

printed Greek edition of the *Exact Exposition of the Orthodox Faith*,
the *editio princeps*, was edited by Bernardino Donato (1483–1543) and
published in Verona in 1531.[105] Donato faithfully reproduces the 100
chapters of the Greek manuscript tradition. When Michel Lequien
(1661–1733) came to publish his great edition of John Damascene's
complete works in 1712, he decided, somewhat reluctantly, to keep
the four-book division of the *De fide orthodoxa* only because it was
so familiar to prospective readers. He was fully aware that no Greek
manuscript divides the text in this way, so he he gives the Greek
chapter numbers as well. This is the Greek text, accompanied by
Lequien's revision of a sixteenth-century Latin translation by Jacques
Billy, that was reprinted by Migne in 1860.[106]

A new era in the history of the text begins with Dom Bonifaz
Kotter (1912–87), a monk of the Bavarian Abbey of Scheyern. The
Byzantine Institute of Scheyern Abbey was founded in 1939, and
from the beginning adopted as its chief work the production of
a critical edition of the prose works of John of Damascus.[107] The
members of the Institute were originally just three of the monks,
Fathers Hildebrand (Hans-Georg) Beck (1910–99), Johannes Hoeck
(1902–95), and Bonifaz Kotter. When Hoeck was elected abbot of
Ettal in 1951 and left Scheyern, Kotter was sent to Munich to study for
a doctorate under Hoeck's former teacher, Franz Dölger (1891–1968).

critical edition on eleven of them). On the different Latin translations up to the
beginning of the sixteenth century, see Irena Backus, "John of Damascus, *De Fide
Orthodoxa*: Translations by Burgundio (1153/54), Grosseteste (1235/40) and Lefèvre
d'Etaples (1507)," *Journal of the Warburg and Courtauld Institutes* 49 (1986): 211–17.
Jacques Lefèvre d'Etaples' translation was the first to be printed (in Paris in 1507, by
Henri Estienne the elder).

[105]Bernardinus Donatus, Ἰωάννου τοῦ Δαμασκηνοῦ ἔκδοσις τῆς ὀρθοδόξου
πίστεως. Περὶ τῶν ἐν πίστει κεκοιμημένων. *Joannis Damasceni editio orthodoxae fidei.
Eiusdem de iis qui in fide dormierunt* (Verona: Apud Stephanum et Fratres Sabios, 1531).
Note that Donato translates the ἔκδοσις of the title as *editio*, following Grosseteste (*Editio diligens de fide orthodoxa*) rather than Burgundio (*Traditio certa orthodoxae fidei*).
Kontouma, too, holds that the title (no doubt supplied by the original Byzantine editor)
should be rendered "an exact edition" rather than "an exact exposition."

[106]PG 94:789–1228, preceded by the Greek *pinax* in columns 783–88.

[107]This had been suggested to to the Institute by Professor Albert Ehrhard
(1862–1940) of the University of Bonn.

In 1956 he defended his thesis on the manuscript tradition of the *Fount of Knowledge*. Then for thirty years he worked, mostly single handedly, on producing the first five volumes of the *Schriften des Johannes von Damaskos*, a series that stands as a model of textual scholarship. Kotter came to reject the idea that the tripartite *Fount of Knowledge* was put together as such by John Damascene himself, and he does not reproduce it in his edition of the texts. The *Exact Exposition of the Orthodox Faith*, occupying the second volume of the series, was published in 1973.

Translations into some of the non-Greek languages of the Orthodox world began very early, with Old Bulgarian and Arabic versions in the ninth/tenth centuries.[108] The first Church Slavonic version was made in the sixteenth century by A. Kurbiskii, followed in the eighteenth and nineteenth centuries by printed editions of further Church Slavonic versions and new translations into Russian and Georgian.[109] The first English translation was made in 1899 by S. D. F. Salmond (1838–1905) and published in volume 9 of the second series of A Select Library of Nicene and Post-Nicene Fathers of the Christian Church.[110] Another, by Frederick H. Chase, Jr, followed in 1958 in the Fathers of the Church series.[111] Both these translations were based on the text in Migne now superseded by Kotter.

The present translation is the first English version based on Kotter's critical text.[112] Its aim is to give as literal a rendering as possible

[108]The Arabic version remains unedited. For details of the two versions, see Kontouma, "At the origins of Byzanine systematic dogmatics," 3.

[109]For details, see Kotter 2:xliv–xlv. The Russian translation, *Tochnoe izlozhenie pravoslavnoi very* [Exact exposition of the orthodox faith], by Aleksandr Bronzov, was published in St Petersburg in 1894.

[110]*John of Damascus, Exposition of the Orthodox Faith*, trans. S. D. F. Salmond in NPNF, Second Series, ed. Philip Schaff and Henry Wace, vol. 9, part 2 (New York: Christian Literature Co., 1899; reprinted by T&T Clark and W. B. Eerdmans, 1997.)

[111]*Saint John of Damascus, Writings. The Fount of Knowledge: The Philosophical Chapters, On Heresies, and On the Orthodox Faith*, trans. Frederic H. Chase, Jr. Fathers of the Church 37 (Washington: The Catholic University of America Press, 1958; reprinted by Ex Fontibus Co., 2012.)

[112]The first modern translation in any language on the basis of Kotter's text was

of the Greek as is consistent with a readable English style. I consider this important because John Damascene pays close attention to the exact signification of his many technical terms, often discussing them in relation to their etymology. So far as possible, I translate any given term by the same English word. In the case of a handful of terms, however, following this method rigidly would have led to offense, infelicity, or even unintelligibility.[113]

Kotter still gives both the Latin and Greek numbering of the chapters in the main body of his text. The present translation, following the counsels of both Louth and Kontouma, abandons the Latin numbering altogether. A concordance of the Latin and Greek numbering is given for convenience, however, because the Latin numbering is still, regrettably, the usual way of referring to the *Exact Exposition of the Orthodox Faith* in the secondary literature.

John Damascene was almost certainly trilingual (in Syriac—perhaps the language spoken in his family—Greek, and Arabic), but so far as we know he wrote only in Greek, of which he had a perfect command. The power and beauty of his sermons, delivered in Greek, probably in the Church of the Anastasis in Jerusalem, earned him the title "flowing with gold" (χρυσορρόας).[114] His technical treatises may lack the poetry of his sermons and liturgical compositions, but

that of the Sources Chrétiennes edition, published in two volumes (SC 535 and 540) in 2010.

[113]The chief terms in this category are: ἄνθρωπος (*anthrōpos*)—"the human being," "the human person," "humanity," "humans," "humankind," or "man;" ἐνέργεια (*energeia*)—"energy," "activity," or "operation;" λόγος (*logos*)—"principle," "reason," "reasoning," or "word/Word;" οὐσία (*ousia*)—"substance," "essence," "being," or "reality;" and πνεῦμα (*pneuma*)—"breath," or "spirit/Spirit," or "gas."

[114]For excellent English translations of John's trilogy of homilies on the Dormition of the Theotokos and his homily on the Transfiguration of the Lord, see *On the Dormition of Mary: Early Patristic Homilies*, ed. and trans. Brian E. Daley, SJ, PPS 18 (Crestwood, NY: St Vladimir's Seminary Press, 1998), 183–239, and *Light on the Mountain: Greek Patristic and Byzantine Homilies on the Transfiguration of the Lord*, ed. and trans. Brian E. Daley, SJ, PPS 48 (Crestwood, NY: St Vladimir's Seminary Press, 2013), 205–31. In the first volume Daley also offers a translation of the Canon for the Dormition composed by John (241–46). The translations are based on the critical texts published in Kotter 5.

they are more than just exercises in logic and rhetoric.[115] They make strong demands on the translator, which I hope have not exceeded my abilities.

I owe most of my references to Kotter, who was indefatigable in tracing John's biblical and patristic sources.[116] In my explanatory notes I have tried not to forget the original purpose of the Popular Patristics Series as an aid to students. All the Greek text that is reproduced is furnished with an English translation. All the less familiar theological terms are explained. These are not as numerous as one might expect. By the eighth century the Christological debates had become highly technical with a specialized vocabulary, yet John sets out his discussions with exceptional clarity. His aim is not to engage in further debates with fellow-intellectuals but in an age of handbooks and compilations such as the *Doctrina Patrum* and the *Hodēgos* to give a reliable summary of the Orthodox faith for educated readers who needed to defend that faith in a hostile environment. In this respect our situation today is not all that different.

---

[115]Andrew Louth rightly points to "a kind of abstract and exhilarating poetry" even in these, "for instance, the first paragraph of *Exposition* 8, on the Trinity." Louth, *St John Damascene*, 223.

[116]A new area of research concerns the extent of John's reading among late antique commentators on Plato and Aristotle such as the pagans, Alexander of Aphrodisias, Porphyry, Ammonius, and Simplicius, and the Christian, John Philoponus. On this fascinating topic, see Demetracopoulos, "In Search of the Pagan and Christian Sources of John of Damascus' Theodicy;" Krausmüller, "Responding to John Philoponus."

An Exact
Exposition
of the
Orthodox Faith

Τάδε ἔνεστιν ἐν τῇδε τῇ βίβλῳ.

Contents

Τοῦ ὁσίου ἀββᾶ Ἰωάννου πρεσβυτέρου Δαμασκηνοῦ ἔκδοσις ἀκριβὴς τῆς ὀρθοδόξου πίστεως

1   Ὅτι ἀκατάληπτον τὸ θεῖον καὶ ὅτι οὐ δεῖ ζητεῖν καὶ
περιεργάζεσθαι τὰ μὴ παραδεδομένα ἡμῖν ὑπὸ τῶν
ἁγίων προφητῶν καὶ ἀποστόλων καὶ εὐαγγελιστῶν

«Θεὸν οὐδεὶς ἑώρακε πώποτε. Ὁ μονογενὴς υἱὸς ὁ ὢν ἐν τοῖς
κόλποις τοῦ πατρός, αὐτὸς ἐξηγήσατο». Ἄρρητον οὖν τὸ θεῖον
καὶ ἀκατάληπτον. «Οὐδεὶς γὰρ ἐπιγινώσκει τὸν πατέρα εἰ μὴ ὁ
υἱός, οὐδὲ τὸν υἱὸν εἰ μὴ ὁ πατήρ». Καὶ τὸ πνεῦμα δὲ τὸ ἅγιον
οὕτως οἶδε τὰ τοῦ θεοῦ, ὡς τὸ πνεῦμα τοῦ ἀνθρώπου οἶδε τὰ ἐν
αὐτῷ. Μετὰ δὲ τὴν πρώτην καὶ μακαρίαν φύσιν οὐδεὶς ἔγνω ποτὲ
τὸν θεόν, εἰ μὴ ᾧ αὐτὸς ἀπεκάλυψεν οὐκ ἀνθρώπων μόνον ἀλλ᾽
οὐδὲ τῶν ὑπερκοσμίων δυνάμεων καὶ αὐτῶν φημι τῶν Χερουβὶμ
καὶ Σεραφίμ.

Οὐκ ἀφῆκε μέντοι ἡμᾶς ὁ θεὸς ἐν παντελεῖ ἀγνωσίᾳ· πᾶσι
γὰρ ἡ γνῶσις τοῦ εἶναι θεὸν ὑπ᾽ αὐτοῦ φυσικῶς ἐγκατέσπαρται.
Καὶ αὐτὴ δὲ ἡ κτίσις καὶ ἡ ταύτης συνοχή τε καὶ κυβέρνησις τὸ
μεγαλεῖον τῆς θείας ἀνακηρύττει φύσεως. Καὶ διὰ νόμου δὲ καὶ
προφητῶν πρότερον, ἔπειτα δὲ καὶ διὰ τοῦ μονογενοῦς αὐτοῦ
υἱοῦ, κυρίου δὲ καὶ θεοῦ καὶ σωτῆρος ἡμῶν Ἰησοῦ Χριστοῦ,

---

[1] For a theological commentary on the first eight chapters, see Louth, *St John Damascene*, 89–116.
[2] Jn 1.18.
[3] Mt 11.27.
[4] Cf. 1 Cor 2.11.

An Exact Exposition of the Orthodox Faith by the Holy Abba the Presbyter John Damascene

1   *That the divine is incomprehensible and that it is not permitted for us to investigate that which has not been transmitted to us by the holy prophets, apostles, and evangelists and to inquire into it out of curiosity*[1]

"No one has ever seen God. It is the only-begotten Son, who is in the bosom of the Father, who has made him known."[2] The divine is therefore ineffable and incomprehensible. "For no one knows the Father except the Son, nor the Son except the Father."[3] And the Holy Spirit knows the things of God in the way that the spirit of human beings knows the things that are within them.[4] After the first and blessed nature no one has ever known God, unless he himself has revealed himself to them, not only no human being, but also not even any of the supramundane powers themselves, by which I mean the cherubim and seraphim.

Nevertheless, God has not left us in utter ignorance. For the knowledge that God exists is implanted naturally by him in all of us.[5] And creation itself in the way that it is maintained and governed proclaims the grandeur of the divine nature.[6] Moreover, first through the law and the prophets, then also through his only-begotten Son, our Lord and God and Savior Jesus Christ, he revealed knowledge

[5]Cf. Gregory of Nazianzus, *Oration* 28.6 (PG 36:33A; Moreschini, 660); Dionysius the Areopagite, *Divine Names* 7.3 (PG 3:869CD; Suchla, 197.17–23).

[6]Cf. Wis 13.5; Rom 1.20; Gregory of Nazianzus, *Oration* 28.3 (PG 36:29AB; Moreschini, 658).

κατὰ τὸ ἐφικτὸν ἡμῖν τὴν ἑαυτοῦ ἐφανέρωσε γνῶσιν. Πάντα τοίνυν τὰ παραδεδομένα ἡμῖν διά τε νόμου καὶ προφητῶν καὶ ἀποστόλων καὶ εὐαγγελιστῶν δεχόμεθα καὶ γινώσκομεν καὶ σέβομεν οὐδὲν περαιτέρω τούτων ἐπιζητοῦντες· ἀγαθὸς γὰρ ὢν ὁ θεὸς παντὸς ἀγαθοῦ παρεκτικός ἐστιν οὐ φθόνῳ οὐδὲ πάθει τινὶ ὑποκείμενος· «μακρὰν γὰρ τῆς θείας φύσεως φθόνος τῆς γε ἀπαθοῦς καὶ μόνης ἀγαθῆς». Ὡς οὖν πάντα εἰδὼς καὶ τὸ συμφέρον ἑκάστῳ προμηθούμενος, ὅπερ συνέφερεν ἡμῖν γνῶναι ἀπεκάλυψεν, ὅπερ δὲ οὐκ ἐδυνάμεθα φέρειν, ἀπεσιώπησε. Ταῦτα ἡμεῖς στέρξωμεν καὶ ἐν αὐτοῖς μείνωμεν μὴ μεταίροντες ὅρια αἰώνια μηδὲ ὑπερβαίνοντες τὴν θείαν παράδοσιν.

2   Περὶ ῥητῶν καὶ ἀρρήτων καὶ γνωστῶν καὶ ἀγνώστων

Χρὴ οὖν τὸν περὶ θεοῦ λέγειν ἢ ἀκούειν βουλόμενον σαφῶς εἰδέναι, ὡς οὐδὲ πάντα ἄρρητα οὐδὲ πάντα ῥητά, τά τε τῆς θεολογίας τά τε τῆς οἰκονομίας, οὔτε μὴν πάντα ἄγνωστα οὔτε πάντα γνωστά· ἕτερον δέ ἐστι τὸ γνωστὸν καὶ ἕτερον τὸ ῥητόν, ὥσπερ ἄλλο τὸ λαλεῖν καὶ ἄλλο τὸ γινώσκειν. Πολλὰ τοίνυν τῶν περὶ θεοῦ ἀμυδρῶς νοουμένων οὐ καιρίως ἐκφρασθῆναι δύναται, ἀλλὰ τὰ καθ' ἡμᾶς ἀναγκαζόμεθα ἐπὶ τῶν ὑπὲρ ἡμᾶς λέγειν, ὥσπερ ἐπὶ θεοῦ λέγομεν ὕπνον καὶ ὀργὴν καὶ ἀμέλειαν χεῖράς τε καὶ πόδας καὶ τὰ τοιαῦτα.

---

[7]Cf. Dionysius the Areopagite, *Divine Names* 1.4 (PG 3:589D; Suchla, 112.7–10).

[8]Gregory of Nazianzus, *Oration* 28.11 (PG 36:40B; Moreschini, 666).

[9]Prov 22.28. This verse, frequently quoted by the fathers since the time of Origen, was taken as a warning not to modify ancient doctrines.

[1]The phrase "it is necessary to know" or "one needs to know" (χρὴ εἰδέναι or χρὴ γινώσκειν, *chrē eidenai* or *chrē ginōskein*) is used many times in the text (the former 14 times and the latter 23 times) to introduce an axiomatic principle. A weaker form of the expression (ἰστέον, *isteon*) seems to be used (27 times) to introduce what it is

of himself in accordance with our capacity to receive it. Therefore we accept, know, and respect everything that has been handed down to us by the law, the prophets, the apostles, and the evangelists, and we do not seek out anything beyond that.[7] For since God is good, he supplies every good thing, not being subject to any envy or passion, "for envy is far from the divine nature, which is dispassionate and alone is good."[8] Therefore since he knows all things and provides each person with what is advantageous for them, he revealed to us what it is profitable for us to know and remained silent about what we are unable to bear. We shall be satisfied with these things and confine ourselves to them, not "moving ancient boundaries"[9] or going beyond divine tradition.

2   *On what is expressible and what is inexpressible, and on what is knowable and what is unknowable*

It is therefore necessary[1] for anyone who wishes to speak or hear about God to know clearly that with regard to what belongs to theology and what to the economy not everything is inexpressible nor is everything expressible, nor indeed is everything unknowable or everything knowable.[2] For what is knowable is one thing and what is expressible is another, just as speaking is one thing and knowing is another. Indeed, many of the things about God that are perceived obscurely by the mind cannot be expressed with precision. On the contrary, we are obliged to speak about what transcends us in terms of our own experience, as when we attribute to God sleep, anger, indifference, hands and feet, and so on.

useful or advantageous to know. I generally translate ἰστέον (*isteon*) as "one should know."

[2]"Theology" is the discussion of God as he is in himself; "the economy" is what belongs to the divine dispensation of the incarnation. John's sources for this first paragraph are *Doctrina Patrum*, Diekamp, 7.16–8.1; Dionysius the Areopagite, *Divine Names* 1.1 (PG 3:588AC; Suchla, 108.1–110.10) and 1.5 (PG 3:593AD; Suchla 115.19–118.1), and Gregory of Nazianzus, *Oration* 28.4–5 (PG 36:29C–32C; Moreschini, 658–60).

Ὅτι μὲν οὖν ἐστι θεὸς ἄναρχος, ἀτελεύτητος, αἰώνιός τε καὶ ἀίδιος, ἄκτιστος, ἄτρεπτος, ἀναλλοίωτος, ἁπλοῦς, ἀσύνθετος, ἀσώματος, ἀόρατος, ἀναφής, ἀπερίγραπτος, ἄπειρος, ἀπερίληπτος, ἀκατάληπτος, ἀπερινόητος, ἀγαθός, δίκαιος, παντοδύναμος, πάντων κτισμάτων δημιουργός, παντοκράτωρ, παντεπόπτης, πάντων προνοητής, ἐξουσιαστής, κριτής, καὶ γινώσκομεν καὶ ὁμολογοῦμεν. Καὶ ὅτι εἷς ἐστι θεὸς ἤγουν μία οὐσία, καὶ ὅτι ἐν τρισὶν ὑποστάσεσι γνωρίζεταί τε καὶ ἔστιν, πατρί φημι καὶ υἱῷ καὶ ἁγίῳ πνεύματι, καὶ ὅτι ὁ πατὴρ καὶ ὁ υἱὸς καὶ τὸ πνεῦμα τὸ ἅγιον κατὰ πάντα ἕν εἰσι πλὴν τῆς ἀγεννησίας καὶ τῆς γεννήσεως καὶ τῆς ἐκπορεύσεως, καὶ ὅτι ὁ μονογενὴς υἱὸς καὶ λόγος τοῦ θεοῦ καὶ θεὸς διὰ σπλάγχνα ἐλέους αὐτοῦ, διὰ τὴν ἡμετέραν σωτηρίαν, εὐδοκίᾳ τοῦ πατρὸς καὶ συνεργίᾳ τοῦ ἁγίου πνεύματος ἀσπόρως συλληφθεὶς ἀφθόρως ἐκ τῆς ἁγίας παρθένου καὶ θεοτόκου Μαρίας γεγέννηται διὰ πνεύματος ἁγίου καὶ ἄνθρωπος τέλειος ἐξ αὐτῆς γέγονε, καὶ ὅτι ὁ αὐτὸς θεὸς τέλειός ἐστιν ὁμοῦ καὶ ἄνθρωπος τέλειος, ἐκ δύο φύσεων, θεότητός τε καὶ ἀνθρωπότητος, καὶ ἐν δύο φύσεσι νοεραῖς θελητικαῖς τε καὶ ἐνεργητικαῖς καὶ αὐτεξουσίοις καὶ ἁπλῶς εἰπεῖν τελείως ἐχούσαις κατὰ τὸν ἑκάστῃ πρέποντα ὅρον τε καὶ λόγον,

---

[3]John's list of divine names begins with fifteen negative attributes (all beginning in Greek with the privative alpha), which are the province of apophatic theology, and then passes to the positive attributes, which belong to kataphatic theology. The latter are known because they have been revealed through the divine economy.

[4]The word John uses is οὐσία (*ousia*), a noun derived from the present participle of the verb "to be" (εἶναι, *einai*). Rendered in the translation variously as "being," "essence," or "substance," it must not be understood in any material sense. For the classic discussion of the various meanings of οὐσία (*ousia*), see Christopher Stead, *Divine Substance* (Oxford: Clarendon Press, 1977).

[5]The terms "hypostasis" (ὑπόστασις, *hypostasis*) and "person" (πρόσωπον, *prosōpon*) had been declared by the Second Ecumenical Council (Constantinople I) to be equivalent to each other (in the Synodal Letter preserved by Theodoret in *Ecclesiastical History* 5.9) and John himself declares that, along with "individual" (ἄτομον, *atomon*), they have the same referent (*Philosophical Chapters* 43). John, however, is always sensitive to the etymologies of words and in practice distinguishes between the two terms. In *Philosophical Chapters* 43 he says that πρόσωπον (*prosōpon*) denotes

So then, we both know and confess that God is without beginning, without end, eternal and everlasting, uncreated, immutable, unchangeable, simple, non-composite, incorporeal, invisible, impalpable, uncircumscribed, limitless, ungraspable, incognizable, unfathomable, good, just, almighty, the creator of all created things, sovereign over all, overseeing all, exercising foresight over all, having supreme power over all, and judge of all.[3] We also know and confess that God is one, that is to say, one substance,[4] and that he is acknowledged in three hypostases and exists as such,[5] by which I mean as Father and Son and Holy Spirit, and that the Father and the Son and the Holy Spirit are one in every respect except with regard to unbegottenness, begotteness, and procession, and that for our salvation the only-begotten Son and Word of God and God out of his deep compassion, at the good pleasure of the Father and with the cooperation of the Holy Spirit, was conceived without seed in an incorrupt manner and was born of Mary, the holy Virgin and Theotokos,[6] through the Holy Spirit, and became from her a perfect human being, and that the same is perfect God as well as a perfect human being, from two natures, divinity and humanity, and in two natures endowed with intellect and volition and with activity and free will, and, to put it simply, each severally possessing in a perfect manner its appropriate definition and principle, that is to say,

a distinct appearance, whereas ὑπόστασις (*hypostasis*) is derived from ὑφεστάναι (*hyphestanai*), "to subsist." When he first uses πρόσωπον (*prosōpon*) in *Exposition* 11, it is in the sense of a distinct appearance, i.e., "face." In my translation ὑπόστασις (*hypostasis*) is rendered consistently as "hypostasis," which means an entity that subsists in reality and not merely notionally.

[6]The title "Theotokos" (literally "God-birther") is of Alexandrian origin and received conciliar approval at the Third Ecumenical Council (Ephesus I) in 431. It is left transliterated because the usual translations, "God-bearing" or "Mother of God" are imprecise. ("God-bearing" is more strictly θεοφόρος [*theophoros*], which can be applied to any saint; "Mother of God" is rarely used by John—in the *Exposition* twice in Chapters 56 and 89 in the form θεομήτωρ [*theomētōr*], and once in Chapter 88 in the form θεοῦ μήτηρ [*theou mētēr*].) The accentuation is important. John Philoponus, in a work on the different meanings that words may have depending on the accent, says that theótokos, stressed on the first "o," is an adjective meaning "born of God," whereas theotókos, stressed on the second "o," is a noun meaning "she who gives birth to God."

θεότητί τε καὶ ἀνθρωπότητί φημι, μιᾷ δὲ συνθέτῳ ὑποστάσει, ὅτι
τε ἐπείνησε καὶ ἐδίψησε καὶ ἐκοπίασε καὶ ἐσταυρώθη καὶ θανάτου
καὶ ταφῆς πεῖραν ἐδέξατο καὶ ἀνέστη τριήμερος καὶ εἰς οὐρανοὺς
ἀνεφοίτησεν, ὅθεν πρὸς ἡμᾶς παραγέγονε καὶ παραγενήσεται
πάλιν εἰς ὕστερον, καὶ ἡ θεία γραφὴ μάρτυς καὶ πᾶς ὁ τῶν ἁγίων
χορός.

Τί δέ ἐστι θεοῦ οὐσία ἢ πῶς ἐστιν ἐν πᾶσιν ἢ πῶς ἐκ θεοῦ θεὸς
γεγέννηται ἢ ἐκπεπόρευται ἢ πῶς ἑαυτὸν κενώσας ὁ μονογενὴς
υἱὸς καὶ θεὸς ἄνθρωπος γέγονεν ἐκ παρθενικῶν αἱμάτων ἑτέρῳ
παρὰ τὴν φύσιν θεσμῷ πλαστουργηθεὶς ἢ πῶς ἀβρόχοις ποσὶ τοῖς
ὕδασιν ἐπεπόρευτο, καὶ ἀγνοοῦμεν καὶ λέγειν οὐ δυνάμεθα. Οὐ
δυνατὸν οὖν τι παρὰ τὰ θειωδῶς ὑπὸ τῶν θείων λογίων τῆς τε
παλαιᾶς καὶ καινῆς διαθήκης ἡμῖν ἐκπεφασμένα ἤτοι εἰρημένα
καὶ πεφανερωμένα εἰπεῖν τι περὶ θεοῦ ἢ ὅλως ἐννοῆσαι.

3   Ἀπόδειξις, ὅτι ἔστι θεός

Ὅτι μὲν οὖν ἔστι θεός, τοῖς μὲν τὰς ἁγίας γραφὰς δεχομένοις,
τήν τε παλαιὰν καὶ καινὴν διαθήκην φημί, οὐκ ἀμφιβάλλεται,
οὔτε δὲ τοῖς τῶν Ἑλλήνων πλείστοις· ὡς γὰρ ἔφημεν, ἡ γνῶσις
τοῦ εἶναι θεὸν φυσικῶς ἡμῖν ἐγκατέσπαρται. Ἐπειδὴ δὲ τοσοῦτον
ἴσχυσεν ἡ τοῦ πονηροῦ κακία τῆς τῶν ἀνθρώπων φύσεως,
ὥστε καί τινας εἰς τὸ ἀλογώτατον καὶ πάντων κακῶν κάκιστον
καταγαγεῖν τῆς ἀπωλείας βάραθρον, τὸ λέγειν μὴ εἶναι θεόν,
ὧν τὴν ἀφροσύνην ἐμφαίνων ὁ ἱεροφάντης ἔφη Δαυίδ· «Εἶπεν
ἄφρων ἐν καρδίᾳ αὐτοῦ· Οὐκ ἔστιν θεός», οἱ μὲν τοῦ κυρίου

---

[7] See Chapter 51 for John's discussion of "composite hypostasis."

[8] This paragraph is a creedal statement drawing principally on Cyril (from the
Doctrina Patrum, Diekamp, 8.1–7). The Chalcedonian Definition's "in two natures" is
introduced but juxtaposed with the Cyrillian "from two natures".

[9] Situating himself firmly in the apophatic tradition, John holds that all we can
know about God comes from what we can intuit from the rational order and beauty
of creation (which leads to a sense of wonder persuading us of God's existence and

divinity and humanity, in one composite hypostasis,[7] in that he was hungry and thirsty and was weary and was crucified and accepted the experience of death and burial and rose on the third day and ascended into heaven, whence he had come to us and whence he will come again at a later time. The divine Scripture and the whole choir of the saints bear witness to this.[8]

But what the essence of God is, or how it is in all things, or how God is generated by, or proceeds from, God, or how the only-begotten Son and God emptied himself and became a human being, fashioned from virginal blood by a different law than the law of nature, or how he walked on water without getting his feet wet we do not know and we are unable to say. It is therefore impossible for us to say anything about God or to form a complete concept of him beyond what has been divinely uttered to us, or said and manifested to us, by the divine texts of both the Old and the New Testaments.[9]

3 *Proof that God exists*

Now the fact that God exists is not doubted by those who accept the holy Scriptures, by which I mean the Old and the New Testaments, nor by most of the Hellenes.[1] For as we have said, the knowledge that God exists has been naturally implanted within us. The wickedness of the evil one, however, has acquired such power over human nature that it has dragged some people down to the most irrational and most utterly evil pit of perdition, which is to assert that God does not exist. Their foolishness was made manifest by David, the teacher of sacred truths, when he said, "The fool has said in his heart, 'There is no God.'"[2] Because of this, the Lord's disciples and apostles, imbued

goodness) and from what has been revealed to us in the Scriptures (specifically, God's attributes or names and his "economic" activity). Purely speculative theology is of no value.

[1]The Hellenes are the pagan Greek philosophers. Christian Greek-speakers are "Romans," even when not citizens of the Eastern Roman Empire. In Arabic sources John is referred to as Manṣūr ibn Sarjūn al-Rūmi (the Roman).

[2]Ps 13.1.

μαθηταὶ καὶ ἀπόστολοι τῷ παναγίῳ σοφισθέντες πνεύματι καὶ τῇ αὐτοῦ δυνάμει καὶ χάριτι τὰς θεοσημίας ἐργαζόμενοι τῇ τῶν θαυμάτων σαγήνῃ πρὸς τὸ φῶς τῆς θεογνωσίας ἐκ τοῦ βυθοῦ τῆς ἀγνωσίας αὐτοὺς ζωγροῦντες ἀνῆγον. Ὁμοίως καὶ οἱ τούτων τῆς χάριτος καὶ τῆς ἀξίας διάδοχοι, ποιμένες τε καὶ διδάσκαλοι, τὴν φωτιστικὴν τοῦ πνεύματος χάριν δεξάμενοι τῇ τε τῶν θαυμάτων δυνάμει τῷ τε λόγῳ τῆς χάριτος τοὺς ἐσκοτισμένους ἐφώτιζον καὶ τοὺς πεπλανημένους ἐπέστρεφον. Ἡμεῖς δὲ οἱ μηδὲ τὸ τῶν θαυμάτων μηδὲ τὸ τῆς διδασκαλίας δεξάμενοι χάρισμα, ἀναξίους γὰρ ἑαυτοὺς τῇ πρὸς τὰς ἡδονὰς προσπαθείᾳ πεποιήκαμεν, φέρε ὀλίγα τῶν παραδεδομένων ἡμῖν ὑπὸ τῶν ὑποφητῶν τῆς χάριτος περὶ τούτου διαλεξώμεθα τὸν πατέρα καὶ τὸν υἱὸν καὶ τὸ πνεῦμα τὸ ἅγιον ἐπικαλεσάμενοι.

Πάντα τὰ ὄντα ἢ κτιστά ἐστιν ἢ ἄκτιστα. Εἰ μὲν οὖν κτιστά, πάντως καὶ τρεπτά· ὧν γὰρ τὸ εἶναι ἀπὸ τροπῆς ἤρξατο, ταῦτα τῇ τροπῇ ὑποκείσεται πάντως ἢ φθειρόμενα ἢ κατὰ προαίρεσιν ἀλλοιούμενα. Εἰ δὲ ἄκτιστα, κατὰ τὸν τῆς ἀκολουθίας λόγον πάντως καὶ ἄτρεπτα· ὧν γὰρ τὸ εἶναι ἐναντίον, τούτων καὶ ὁ τοῦ πῶς εἶναι λόγος ἐναντίος ἤγουν αἱ ἰδιότητες. Τίς οὖν οὐ συνθήσεται πάντα τὰ ὄντα, ὅσα ὑπὸ τὴν ἡμετέραν αἴσθησιν, ἀλλὰ μὴν καὶ ἀγγέλους τρέπεσθαι καὶ ἀλλοιοῦσθαι καὶ πολυτρόπως κινεῖσθαι καὶ μεταβάλλεσθαι; Τὰ μὲν νοητά, ἀγγέλους φημὶ καὶ ψυχὰς καὶ δαίμονας, κατὰ προαίρεσιν τήν τε ἐν τῷ καλῷ προκοπὴν καὶ τὴν ἐκ τοῦ καλοῦ ἀποφοίτησιν, ἐπιτεινομένην τε καὶ ὑφιεμένην, τὰ δὲ λοιπὰ κατά τε γένεσιν καὶ φθορὰν αὔξησίν τε καὶ μείωσιν καὶ τὴν κατὰ ποιότητα μεταβολὴν καὶ τὴν τοπικὴν κίνησιν. Τρεπτὰ τοίνυν ὄντα πάντως καὶ κτιστά. Κτιστὰ δὲ ὄντα πάντως ὑπό τινος ἐδημιουργήθησαν. Δεῖ δὲ τὸν δημιουργὸν ἄκτιστον εἶναι· εἰ γὰρ κἀκεῖνος ἐκτίσθη, πάντως ὑπό τινος ἐκτίσθη, ἕως ἂν ἔλθωμεν εἴς τι ἄκτιστον. Ἄκτιστος οὖν ὢν ὁ δημιουργὸς πάντως καὶ ἄτρεπτός ἐστι. Τοῦτο δὲ τί ἂν ἄλλο εἴη ἢ θεός;

with wisdom by the all-holy Spirit and working miraculous signs by his power and grace, caught these people in the net of wonders and drew them up from the depths of their ignorance into the light of the knowledge of God. In a similar way, the inheritors of the grace and worth of the disciples and apostles, namely the shepherds and teachers, also received the illuminating grace of the Spirit and by the power of wonders and the word of grace enlightened those in darkness and caused the deluded to return. We, for our part, have received neither the charism of working wonders nor that of teaching, for we have made ourselves unworthy by our attachment to pleasures, but let us invoke the Father, the Son, and the Holy Spirit anyway and from what has been handed down to us by the expounders of grace, let us discuss a few things concerning this matter.

All beings are either created or uncreated. If they are created, they are necessarily subject to change, for since their being has its origin in change, they will necessarily be subject to change, altered either by decay or by deliberate choice. But if they are uncreated, it follows logically that they are also necessarily unchangeable, for if their being is the contrary, then their mode of being, or properties, will also be contrary. Who, then, will not conclude that all beings, not only those that are subject to our own perception but also angels, alter and change and in many ways move and are modified? Spiritual beings, by which I mean angels, souls, and demons, advance in goodness or fall away from goodness by deliberate choice, intensifying their efforts or slackening them, whereas the rest undergo increase and diminution in accordance with generation and decay, and change and movement with respect to place in accordance with quality. Beings that are subject to change must thus necessarily also be created. And created beings must necessarily have been created by someone. But the Creator must be uncreated. For if he were created, he would necessarily have been created by someone, until we come to something uncreated.[3] The Creator is

[3]In other words, there has to be a First Cause in order to avoid the problem of infinite regression.

Καὶ αὐτὴ δὲ ἡ τῆς κτίσεως συνοχὴ καὶ συντήρησις καὶ κυβέρνησις διδάσκει ἡμᾶς, ὅτι ἔστι θεὸς ὁ τόδε τὸ πᾶν συστησάμενος καὶ συνέχων καὶ συντηρῶν καὶ ἀεὶ προνοούμενος· πῶς γὰρ ἂν αἱ ἐναντίαι φύσεις, πυρὸς λέγω καὶ ὕδατος, ἀέρος καὶ γῆς, εἰς ἑνὸς κόσμου συμπλήρωσιν ἀλλήλοις συνεληλύθασι καὶ ἀδιάλυτοι μένουσιν, εἰ μή τις παντοδύναμος δύναμις ταῦτα καὶ συνεβίβασε καὶ ἀεὶ τηρεῖ ἀδιάλυτα;

Τί τὸ τάξαν τὰ οὐράνια καὶ ἐπίγεια, ὅσα τε δι᾽ ἀέρος καὶ ὅσα καθ᾽ ὕδατος, μᾶλλον δὲ τὰ πρὸ τούτων, οὐρανὸν καὶ γῆν καὶ ἀέρα καὶ φύσιν πυρός τε καὶ ὕδατος; Τίς ταῦτα ἔμιξε καὶ ἐμέρισε; Τί τὸ ταῦτα κινῆσαν καὶ ἄγον τὴν ἄληκτον φορὰν καὶ ἀκώλυτον; Ἆρ᾽ οὐχ ὁ τεχνίτης τούτων καὶ λόγον ἐνθεὶς πᾶσι, καθ᾽ ὃν τὸ πᾶν φέρεταί τε καὶ διεξάγεται; Τίς δὲ ὁ τεχνίτης τούτων; Ἆρ᾽ οὐχ ὁ πεποιηκὼς ταῦτα καὶ εἰς τὸ εἶναι παραγαγών; Οὐ γὰρ τῷ αὐτομάτῳ δώσομεν τοιαύτην δύναμιν. Ἔστω γὰρ τὸ γενέσθαι τοῦ αὐτομάτου· τίνος τὸ τάξαι; Καὶ τοῦτο, εἰ δοκεῖ, δῶμεν· τίνος τὸ τηρῆσαι καὶ φυλάξαι καθ᾽ οὓς πρῶτον ὑπέστη λόγους; Ἑτέρου δηλαδὴ παρὰ τὸ αὐτόματον. Τοῦτο δὲ τί ἄλλο ἐστὶν εἰ μὴ θεός;

4 Περὶ τοῦ τί ἐστι θεός; ὅτι ἀκατάληπτον

Ὅτι μὲν οὖν ἔστι θεός, δῆλον· τί δέ ἐστι κατ᾽ οὐσίαν καὶ φύσιν, ἀκατάληπτον τοῦτο παντελῶς καὶ ἄγνωστον. Ὅτι μὲν γὰρ ἀσώματον, δῆλον. Πῶς γὰρ σῶμα τὸ ἄπειρον καὶ ἀόριστον καὶ ἀσχημάτιστον καὶ ἀναφὲς καὶ ἀόρατον καὶ ἁπλοῦν καὶ ἀσύνθετον; Πῶς γὰρ σεπτόν, εἰ περιγραπτὸν καὶ παθητόν; Καὶ πῶς ἀπαθὲς τὸ ἐκ στοιχείων συγκείμενον καὶ εἰς αὐτὰ πάλιν ἀναλυόμενον;

therefore necessarily uncreated and immutable. What else could this be but God?

Moreover, the very coherence, maintenance, and governance of creation teaches us that there is a God who has formed this totality and sustains and maintains it and always exercises providential care over it. For how could contrary natures, by which I mean fire and water, air and earth, by coming together with each other constitute a single world and remain undissolved, unless some almighty power had brought them together and always keeps them undissolved?

What is it that has set the things of heaven and the things of earth in their order, all that moves through the air and all that lives in water, or rather, that which precedes them, heaven and earth, and air and the nature of fire and water? Who combined these things and divided them? What set these things in motion and keeps them in their ceaseless and unhindered course? Is there not an architect of these things, a principle inherent in all of them, by which the universe is moved and ordered? Who is the architect of these things? Is it not he who made them and brought them into being? For we cannot attribute such a power to a spontaneous process. Even if things have come into being by a spontaneous process, what has arranged it? Let us grant this too, if you wish. Then what maintains them and preserves them in accordance with the principles by which they first came to exist? Clearly something other than a spontaneous process. What else is this but God?

4   On "What is God?" That it is incomprehensible

It is clear, then, that God exists. But as to what he is in essence and nature, that is something altogether beyond our comprehension and knowledge. For it is clear that he is incorporeal. For how could that which is infinite, limitless, formless, impalpable, invisible, simple and non-composite be a body? How could it be worshiped if it were circumscribed and passible? And how could that which is composed of different elements and is resolved again into them be impassible?

Σύνθεσις γὰρ ἀρχὴ μάχης, μάχη δὲ διαστάσεως, διάστασις δὲ λύσεως· λύσις δὲ ἀλλότριον θεοῦ παντελῶς.

Πῶς δὲ καὶ σωθήσεται τὸ «διὰ πάντων ἥκειν καὶ πληροῦν τὰ πάντα θεόν», ὥς φησιν ἡ γραφή· «Οὐχὶ τὸν οὐρανὸν καὶ τὴν γῆν ἐγὼ πληρῶ, λέγει κύριος»; Ἀδύνατον γὰρ σῶμα διὰ σωμάτων διήκειν μὴ τέμνον καὶ τεμνόμενον καὶ πλεκόμενον καὶ ἀντιπαρατιθέμενον, ὥσπερ ὅσα τῶν ὑγρῶν μίγνυται καὶ συγκίρναται.

Εἰ δὲ καί τινές φασιν ἄυλον σῶμα ὡς τὸ παρὰ τοῖς τῶνἙλλήνων σοφοῖς πέμπτον σῶμα λεγόμενον, ὅπερ ἀδύνατον, κινούμενον ἔσται πάντως ὥσπερ ὁ οὐρανός· τοῦτον γὰρ πέμπτον σῶμά φασι. Τίς οὖν ὁ τοῦτον κινῶν; Πᾶν γὰρ κινούμενον ὑφ᾽ ἑτέρου κινεῖται. Κἀκεῖνον τίς; Καὶ τοῦτο ἐπ᾽ ἄπειρον, ἕως ἂν καταντήσωμεν εἴς τι ἀκίνητον· τὸ γὰρ πρῶτον κινοῦν ἀκίνητον, ὅπερ ἐστὶ τὸ θεῖον. Πῶς δὲ οὐκ ἐν τόπῳ περιγραπτὸν τὸ κινούμενον; Μόνον οὖν τὸ θεῖον ἀκίνητον, δι᾽ ἀκινησίας τὰ πάντα κινοῦν. Ἀσώματον τοίνυν ὑποληπτέον τὸ θεῖον.

Ἀλλ᾽ οὐδὲ τοῦτο τῆς οὐσίας παραστατικόν ἐστιν ὥσπερ οὐδὲ τὸ ἀγέννητον καὶ τὸ ἄναρχον καὶ τὸ ἀναλλοίωτον καὶ τὸ ἄφθαρτον καὶ ὅσα περὶ θεοῦ ἢ περὶ θεὸν εἶναι λέγεται· ταῦτα γὰρ οὐ τὸ τί ἐστι σημαίνει, ἀλλὰ τί οὐκ ἔστι. Χρὴ δὲ τὸν βουλόμενον τήν τινος οὐσίαν εἰπεῖν, τί ἐστι, φράσαι, οὐ τί οὐκ ἔστι· ὅμως ἐπὶ θεοῦ, τί ἐστιν, εἰπεῖν ἀδύνατον κατ᾽ οὐσίαν. Οἰκειότερον δὲ μᾶλλον ἐκ τῆς πάντων ἀφαιρέσεως ποιεῖσθαι τὸν λόγον· οὐδὲν γὰρ τῶν ὄντων ἐστὶν οὐχ ὡς μὴ ὤν, ἀλλ᾽ ὡς ὑπὲρ πάντα τὰ ὄντα καὶ ὑπὲρ αὐτόδε τὸ εἶναι ὤν. Εἰ γὰρ τῶν ὄντων αἱ γνώσεις, τὸ

---

[1]The text from "How could it be worshiped" to the end of the paragraph follows Gregory of Nazianzus, *Oration* 28.7 (PG 36:33BC; Moreschini, 662) very closely.
[2]Cf. Eph 1.23.
[3]Jer 23.24.
[4]This paragraph and the next follow Gregory of Nazianzus, *Oration* 28.8 (PG 36:33D–36B; Moreschini, 662–64) very closely. Gregory, and John after him, are alluding here to the Stoic concept of divinity, which interpenetrates the world in a material fashion.

For composition is the source of conflict, conflict the source of separation, and separation the source of dissolution. And dissolution is utterly alien to God.[1]

And again how would the fact be preserved that "God permeates all things and fills all things,"[2] as Scripture says, "'Do I not fill heaven and earth?' says the Lord"?[3] For it is impossible for a body to permeate other bodies without dividing and being divided, and being intermingled and coextensive with them, like those liquids that are mixed and blended.[4]

And if there are some who say that there exists an immaterial body, like that which some of the Greek philosophers call a fifth body, which is impossible, it would necessarily be in motion like the heavens, for that is what they say is a fifth body.[5] Who, then, is it who moves this? For everything that moves is moved by another. So who moves that? And so on *ad infinitum* until we come to something that is unmoved. For the first mover is unmoved, which is the divine. How will that which moves not occupy a delimited place? Therefore only the divine is unmoved, and by its absence of motion moves all things. Therefore the divine must be taken to be incorporeal.

But this is not demonstrative of the essence, just as the fact of being unbegotten, without origin, unchangeable, and incorruptible and whatever is said about God or in connection with God are not demonstrative of it either. For these signify not what he is but what he is not. Anyone who wishes to specify the essence of anything must say what it is, not what it is not. With regard to God, however, it is impossible to say what he is according to essence. It is, rather, more appropriate to discuss him in terms of abstraction from all things.

[5]A fifth essence (the "quintessence"), namely aether, was proposed by Aristotle (in addition to the four elements, fire, air, earth, and water) to account for the circular motion of the heavenly bodies, as circular movement is not characteristic of the four basic elements (Aristotle, *On the Heavens* I.2, 269a5–19; cf. Ps.-Aristotle, *On the Universe* 2, 392a6–b1). Whether the fifth essence really existed was much debated by later philosophers, particularly Neoplatonists. The Alexandrian Christian philosopher John Philoponus (*c.* 490–*c.* 574), who was known to John, argued strongly against it. See Christian Wildberg, *Philoponos, Against Aristotle on the Eternity of the World*, Ancient Commentators on Aristotle (London: Duckworth, 1987), 21–22.

ὑπὲρ γνῶσιν πάντως καὶ ὑπὲρ οὐσίαν ἔσται, καὶ τὸ ἀνάπαλιν τὸ ὑπὲρ οὐσίαν καὶ ὑπὲρ γνῶσιν ἔσται.

Ἄπειρον οὖν τὸ θεῖον καὶ ἀκατάληπτον, καὶ τοῦτο μόνον αὐτοῦ καταληπτόν, ἡ ἀπειρία καὶ ἡ ἀκαταληψία. Ὅσα δὲ λέγομεν ἐπὶ θεοῦ καταφατικῶς, οὐ τὴν φύσιν ἀλλὰ τὰ περὶ τὴν φύσιν δηλοῖ. Κἂν ἀγαθόν, κἂν δίκαιον, κἂν σοφόν, κἂν ὅ τι ἂν εἴπῃς, οὐ φύσιν λέγεις θεοῦ, ἀλλὰ τὰ περὶ τὴν φύσιν. Εἰσὶ δὲ καί τινα καταφατικῶς ἐπὶ θεοῦ λεγόμενα δύναμιν ὑπεροχικῆς ἀποφάσεως ἔχοντα, οἷον σκότος λέγοντες ἐπὶ θεοῦ οὐ σκότος νοοῦμεν, ἀλλ᾽ ὅτι οὐκ ἔστι φῶς ἀλλ᾽ ὑπὲρ τὸ φῶς.

5   Ἀπόδειξις, ὅτι εἷς ἐστι θεὸς καὶ οὐ πολλοί

Ὅτι μέν ἐστι θεός, ἱκανῶς ἀποδέδεικται, καὶ ὅτι ἀκατάληπτός ἐστιν ἡ αὐτοῦ οὐσία. Ὅτι δὲ εἷς ἐστι καὶ οὐ πολλοί, τοῖς μὲν τῇ θείᾳ πειθομένοις γραφῇ οὐκ ἀμφιβάλλεται. Φησὶ γὰρ ὁ κύριος ἐν τῇ τῆς νομοθεσίας ἀρχῇ· «Ἐγὼ κύριος ὁ θεός σου ὁ ἐξαγαγών σε ἐκ γῆς Αἰγύπτου. Οὐκ ἔσονταί σοι θεοὶ ἕτεροι πλὴν ἐμοῦ», καὶ πάλιν· «Ἄκουε, Ἰσραήλ· Κύριος ὁ θεός σου κύριος εἷς ἐστι», καὶ διὰ Ἡσαΐου τοῦ προφήτου· «Ἐγὼ γάρ, φησί, θεὸς πρῶτος καὶ ἐγὼ μετὰ ταῦτα καὶ πλὴν ἐμοῦ οὐκ ἔστι θεός. Ἔμπροσθέν μου οὐκ ἐγένετο ἄλλος θεὸς καὶ μετ᾽ ἐμὲ οὐκ ἔσται καὶ πλὴν ἐμοῦ οὐκ ἔστι», καὶ ὁ κύριος δὲ ἐν τοῖς ἱεροῖς εὐαγγελίοις οὕτω φησὶ πρὸς

---

[6]John's guide here is Dionysius the Areopagite, who speaks of ἡ ὑπὲρ τὸ εἶναι θεότης (hē hyper to einai theotēs), "the divinity that is beyond being" (Celestial Hierarchy 4.1 [PG 3:177D; Heil, 20.17]).

[7]These are three of the four God-befitting attributes that are central to Gregory of Nyssa's soteriological arguments in his Catechetical Discourse (laid out extensively in Chapter 20, and then used in Chapters 21–24 in his exposition of the ransom, the deception and the fishhook, the harrowing of Hades, etc.). (IG)

For he does not belong to the class of beings, not because he does not exist but because he transcends all beings and transcends even being itself.[6] For if knowledge concerns beings, what transcends knowledge will also necessarily transcend essence, and conversely, what transcends essence will also transcend knowledge.

Therefore the divine is infinite and incomprehensible, and this alone can be grasped about it, namely, infinity and incomprehensibility. Whatever we say about God kataphatically makes manifest not the nature but what is around the nature. Whether you talk about goodness, or justice, or wisdom,[7] or anything else, you are talking not about God's nature but about what is around the nature. There are certain things that are predicated kataphatically about God, which have the force of supreme negation. For example, when we predicate darkness of God, we do not mean darkness but that he is not light since he transcends light.

5   *Proof that God is one and not many*

That God exists has been adequately proved, and also that his essence is beyond our comprehension. Moreover, that he is one and not many is not, on the one hand, a matter of doubt for those who are persuaded by the divine Scripture.[1] For the Lord says at the beginning of the institution of the Law, "I am the Lord your God, who brought you out of the land of Egypt. You will not have other gods besides me."[2] And again, "Hear O Israel: the Lord your God is one Lord,"[3] and through Isaiah the prophet, "For I am the first God," it says, "and I am thereafter, and besides me there is no god. Before me there was no other god and after me there shall be none, and besides me there is none."[4] And the Lord in the holy Gospels says

[1] This is an echo of Gregory of Nyssa's rhetorical strategy in *Catechetical Discourse* 4, where Gregory gives scriptural arguments for Jews (though there it concerns the Word and the Spirit, not the divine unity). (IG)

[2] Ex 20.2.

[3] Dt 6.4.

[4] Is 44.6.

τὸν πατέρα· «Αὕτη ἐστὶν ἡ αἰώνιος ζωή, ἵνα γινώσκωσί σε τὸν μόνον ἀληθινὸν θεόν».

Τοῖς δὲ τῇ θείᾳ γραφῇ μὴ πειθομένοις οὕτω διαλεξόμεθα. Τὸ θεῖον τέλειόν ἐστι καὶ ἀνελλιπὲς κατά τε ἀγαθότητα κατά τε σοφίαν κατά τε δύναμιν, ἄναρχον, ἀτελεύτητον, ἀίδιον, ἀπερίγραπτον καὶ ἁπλῶς εἰπεῖν κατὰ πάντα τέλειον. Εἰ οὖν πολλοὺς ἐροῦμεν θεούς, ἀνάγκη διαφορὰν ἐν τοῖς πολλοῖς θεωρεῖσθαι. Εἰ γὰρ οὐδεμία διαφορὰ ἐν αὐτοῖς, εἷς μᾶλλόν ἐστι καὶ οὐ πολλοί. Εἰ δὲ διαφορὰ ἐν αὐτοῖς, ποῦ ἡ τελειότης; Εἴτε γὰρ κατὰ ἀγαθότητα, εἴτε κατὰ δύναμιν, εἴτε κατὰ σοφίαν, εἴτε κατὰ χρόνον, εἴτε κατὰ τόπον ὑστερήσει τοῦ τελείου, οὐκ ἂν εἴη θεός. Ἡ δὲ διὰ πάντων ταυτότης ἕνα μᾶλλον δείκνυσι καὶ οὐ πολλούς. Πῶς δὲ καὶ πολλοῖς οὖσι τὸ ἀπερίγραπτον φυλαχθήσεται; Ἔνθα γὰρ ἂν εἴη ὁ εἷς, οὐκ ἂν εἴη ὁ ἕτερος. Πῶς δὲ ὑπὸ πολλῶν κυβερνηθήσεται ὁ κόσμος καὶ οὐ διαλυθήσεται καὶ διαφθαρήσεται μάχης ἐν τοῖς κυβερνῶσι θεωρουμένης; Ἡ γὰρ διαφορὰ ἐναντίωσιν εἰσάγει. Εἰ δὲ εἴποι τις, ὅτι ἕκαστος μέρους ἄρχει, τί τὸ τάξαν καὶ τὴν διανομὴν αὐτοῖς ποιησάμενον; Ἐκεῖνο γὰρ ἂν εἴη μᾶλλον θεός. Εἷς τοίνυν ἐστὶ θεός, τέλειος, ἀπερίγραπτος, τοῦ παντὸς ποιητῆς συνοχεύς τε καὶ κυβερνήτης, ὑπερτελὴς καὶ προτέλειος.

Πρὸς δὲ καὶ φυσικὴ ἀνάγκη μονάδα εἶναι δυάδος ἀρχήν.

the following to the Father: "This is eternal life, that they may know you, the only true God."[5]

To those, on the other hand, who are not persuaded by the divine Scripture we shall argue as follows. The divine is perfect and lacking in nothing with regard to goodness, wisdom and power. It is without beginning, without end, eternal, uncircumscribed, and to put it simply, perfect in every respect. Now if we say that there are many gods, it would be necessary for us to hold that there are differences among the many. For if there were not a single difference among them, they would rather be one and not many. If there were a difference among them, where would perfection be? For if there were any lack of perfection either with regard to goodness, or with regard to power, or with regard to wisdom, or with regard to time, or with regard to place, it would not be god. An identity in every respect indicates, rather, one and not many. How, if there are many, can the attribute of non-circumscription be maintained? For in this respect, if one exists, there cannot be another. And how can the cosmos be governed by many and not fall apart and decay when conflict is discerned among those who govern? For difference entails opposition. If one should say that each rules a part, what has arranged the order and the assignment to them? For that is what would rather be God. Therefore God is one, perfect, and uncircumscribed, and the supremely perfect and more than perfect maker, upholder, and governor of the universe.[6]

Besides this, it is a natural necessity for a monad to be the source of a dyad.[7]

[5]Jn 17.3.

[6]This argument, based on the philosophical notion of the identity of indiscernibles, is drawn from Gregory of Nyssa's *Catechetical Discourse*, Prologue 4–8 (PG 45:12AD; Green, 62–63). It is not clear from whom Gregory derived this idea, but it was taken up very much later by Leibniz. (IG)

[7]Cf. Dionysius the Areopagite, *Divine Names* 5.6 (PG 3:721D; Suchla, 168).

6   *Περὶ λόγου θεοῦ*

Οὗτος τοίνυν ὁ εἷς καὶ μόνος θεὸς οὐκ ἄλογός ἐστι. Λόγον δὲ ἔχων οὐκ ἀνυπόστατον ἕξει, οὐκ ἀρξάμενον τοῦ εἶναι οὐδὲ παυσόμενον· οὐ γὰρ ἦν, ὅτε ἦν ποτε θεὸς ἄλογος. Ἀεὶ δὲ ἔχει τὸν ἑαυτοῦ λόγον ἐξ αὐτοῦ γεννώμενον, οὐ κατὰ τὸν ἡμέτερον λόγον ἀνυπόστατον καὶ εἰς ἀέρα χεόμενον, ἀλλ᾿ ἐνυπόστατον, ζῶντα, τέλειον, οὐκ ἔξω αὐτοῦ χωροῦντα, ἀλλ᾿ ἐν αὐτῷ ἀεὶ ὄντα· ποῦ γὰρ ἔσται ἔξω αὐτοῦ γινόμενος; Ἐπειδὴ γὰρ ἡ ἡμετέρα φύσις ἐπίκηρός ἐστι καὶ εὐδιάλυτος, διὰ τοῦτο καὶ ὁ λόγος ἡμῶν ἐστιν ἀνυπόστατος. Ὁ δὲ θεὸς ἀεὶ ὢν καὶ τέλειος ὢν τέλειον καὶ ἐνυπόστατον ἕξει τὸν ἑαυτοῦ λόγον καὶ ἀεὶ ὄντα καὶ ζῶντα καὶ πάντα ἔχοντα, ὅσα ὁ γεννήτωρ ἔχει. Ὥσπερ γὰρ ὁ ἡμέτερος λόγος ἐκ τοῦ νοῦ προερχόμενος οὔτε δι᾿ ὅλου ὁ αὐτός ἐστι τῷ νῷ οὔτε παντάπασιν ἕτερος—ἐκ τοῦ νοῦ μὲν γὰρ ὢν ἄλλος ἐστὶ παρ᾿ αὐτόν, αὐτὸν δὲ τὸν νοῦν εἰς τὸ ἐμφανὲς ἄγων οὐκέτι παντάπασιν ἕτερός ἐστι παρὰ τὸν νοῦν, ἀλλὰ κατὰ τὴν φύσιν ἓν ὢν ἕτερόν ἐστι τῷ ὑποκειμένῳ—οὕτως καὶ ὁ τοῦ θεοῦ λόγος, τῷ μὲν ὑφεστάναι καθ᾿ ἑαυτὸν διήρηται πρὸς ἐκεῖνον, παρ᾿ οὗ τὴν ὑπόστασιν ἔχει, τῷ δὲ ταῦτα δεικνύειν ἐν ἑαυτῷ, ἃ περὶ τὸν θεὸν καθορᾶται, ὁ αὐτός ἐστι κατὰ τὴν φύσιν ἐκείνῳ· ὥσπερ γὰρ τὸ ἐν ἅπασι τέλειον ἐπὶ τοῦ πατρὸς θεωρεῖται, οὕτως καὶ ἐπὶ τοῦ ἐξ αὐτοῦ γεγεννημένου λόγου θεωρηθήσεται.

---

[1]God is not ἄλογος (*alogos*). The word λόγος (*logos*) means "reason," either immanent as rationality or uttered as speech. In this chapter "rationality," "speech," and "word" are all renderings of the same noun λόγος (*logos*). The repetition of λόγος (*logos*) for the different aspects of rationality and speech/word makes the argument particularly compelling in Greek. Gregory of Nyssa plays on the same semantic range of λόγος (*logos*) in his *Catechetical Discourse* 1.1–11 (PG 45:13A–16D; Green, 64–67).

6   *On the Word of God*

Now this one sole God is not devoid of rationality.[1] And since he possesses rationality, this rationality will not be lacking in subsistence,[2] nor will it begin to be or cease to be. For there was no time when God was without rationality. And he always possesses his own Word begotten from him, not like our own speech, which lacks subsistence and is lost in the air, but as something subsistent, living, perfect, not going away out of him but always remaining within him, for where is there that is outside of him? Since our own nature is perishable and easily dissolved, our speech is also in consequence without subsistence. But since God exists eternally and is eternally perfect, he possesses his own Word as something perfect and subsistent, and eternally existing and living, and possessing everything that the begetter possesses. Now just as when our own speech comes forth from our mind, it is not entirely the same as the mind nor is it altogether different from it—for being from the mind it is something other than it, but by revealing the mind itself it is not altogether different from the mind, but in fact is one with it according to nature but different from it with regard to subject—so too the Word of God, with regard to his subsisting in himself, is distinguished from him from whom he derives his hypostasis, but with regard to his exhibiting within himself the same things that are perceived as pertaining to God, he is the same on the level of nature as God is. For just as perfection in all things is regarded as belonging to the Father, so too is it regarded as belonging to the Word that has been begotten by him.[3]

[2]οὐκ ἀνυπόστατον (*ouk anypostaton*). On the meaning of ἀνυπόστατος (*anypostatos*) and ἐνυπόστατος (*enypostatos*), see U. M. Lang, "Anhypostatos—enhypostatos: Church Fathers, Protestant Orthodoxy and Karl Barth," *Journal of Theological Studies* ns 49/2 (1998): 630–57.

[3]The second half of this chapter is heavily dependent on Gregory of Nyssa's *Catechetical Discourse* 1.11 (PG 45:16CD; Green, 67), with a number of phrases reproduced verbatim.

7   *Περὶ πνεύματος ἁγίου*

Δεῖ δὲ τὸν λόγον καὶ πνεῦμα ἔχειν· καὶ γὰρ καὶ ὁ ἡμέτερος λόγος οὐκ ἄμοιρός ἐστι πνεύματος. Ἀλλ' ἐφ' ἡμῶν μὲν τὸ πνεῦμα ἀλλότριον τῆς ἡμετέρας ἐστὶν οὐσίας· τοῦ ἀέρος γάρ ἐστιν ὁλκὴ καὶ φορὰ εἰσελκομένου καὶ προχεομένου πρὸς τὴν τοῦ σώματος σύστασιν, ὅπερ ἐν τῷ καιρῷ τῆς ἐκφωνήσεως φωνὴ τοῦ λόγου γίνεται τὴν τοῦ λόγου δύναμιν ἐν ἑαυτῇ φανεροῦσα. Ἐπὶ δὲ τῆς θείας φύσεως τῆς ἁπλῆς καὶ ἀσυνθέτου τὸ μὲν εἶναι πνεῦμα θεοῦ εὐσεβῶς ὁμολογητέον διὰ τὸ μὴ εἶναι τὸν τοῦ θεοῦ λόγον ἐλλιπέστερον τοῦ ἡμετέρου λόγου, οὐκ ἔστι δὲ εὐσεβὲς ἀλλότριόν τι ἔξωθεν ἐπεισερχόμενον τῷ θεῷ τὸ πνεῦμα λογίζεσθαι ὡς καὶ ἐφ' ἡμῶν τῶν συνθέτων. Ἀλλ' ὥσπερ θεοῦ λόγον ἀκούσαντες οὐκ ἀνυπόστατον οὐδὲ ἐκ μαθήσεως προσγινόμενον οὐδὲ διὰ φωνῆς προφερόμενον οὐδὲ εἰς ἀέρα χεόμενον καὶ λυόμενον ᾠήθημεν, ἀλλ' οὐσιωδῶς ὑφεστῶτα προαιρετικόν τε καὶ ἐνεργὸν καὶ παντοδύναμον, οὕτω καὶ πνεῦμα μεμαθηκότες θεοῦ τὸ συμπαρομαρτοῦν τῷ λόγῳ καὶ φανεροῦν αὐτοῦ τὴν ἐνέργειαν οὐ πνοὴν ἀνυπόστατον ἐννοοῦμεν—οὕτω γὰρ ἂν καθαιρεῖται πρὸς ταπεινότητα τὸ μεγαλεῖον τῆς θείας φύσεως, εἰ καθ' ὁμοιότητα τοῦ ἡμετέρου πνεύματος καὶ τὸ ἐν αὐτῷ πνεῦμα ὑπονοοῖτο—, ἀλλὰ δύναμιν οὐσιώδη, αὐτὴν ἐφ' ἑαυτῆς ἐν ἰδιαζούσῃ ὑποστάσει θεωρουμένην, ἐκ τοῦ πατρὸς προερχομένην καὶ ἐν τῷ λόγῳ ἀναπαυομένην καὶ αὐτοῦ οὖσαν ἐκφαντικήν, οὔτε χωρισθῆναι τοῦ θεοῦ, ἐν ᾧ ἐστι, καὶ τοῦ λόγου, ᾧ συμπαρομαρτεῖ, δυναμένην οὔτε πρὸς τὸ ἀνύπαρκτον ἀναχεομένην, ἀλλὰ καθ' ὁμοιότητα τοῦ λόγου καθ' ὑπόστασιν οὖσαν, ζῶσαν, προαιρετικήν, αὐτοκίνητον, ἐνεργόν, πάντοτε τὸ ἀγαθὸν θέλουσαν καὶ πρὸς πᾶσαν πρόθεσιν σύνδρομον ἔχουσαν τῇ βουλήσει τὴν δύναμιν, μήτε ἀρχὴν ἔχουσαν μήτε τέλος· οὔτε γὰρ ἐνέλειψέ ποτε τῷ πατρὶ λόγος οὔτε τῷ λόγῳ πνεῦμα.

7   On the Holy Spirit

Moreover, it is necessary that the Word should also have a spirit. For even our own speech is not devoid of breath.[1] Only in our case breath is something other than our own essence. For it is an indrawing and expulsion of air that is inhaled and exhaled for the sustenance of the body. In the event of speaking aloud this becomes the utterance of speech, since in the act it manifests the power of speech. In the case of the divine nature, which is simple and non-composite, on the one hand the existence of the Spirit of God is reverently to be acknowledged, so that the Word of God should not be deficient in comparison with our own speech, and on the other it is not correct that the Spirit should be considered something alien that comes into God from outside of him, as with us who are composite beings. On the contrary, when we heard about the Word of God, we did not think of it as lacking in hypostasis, or as acquired by learning, or as expressed vocally, or as diffused into the air and lost. We thought of it, rather, as subsisting essentially, as able to choose freely, and as being active and omnipotent. In the same way, when we learned about the Spirit of God that witnesses together with the Word and manifests his activity, we did not consider it a breath lacking in hypostasis—for the grandeur of the divine nature would thus be reduced to something humble, if the Spirit that is in it were to be conceived as resembling our own breath—but an essential power, contemplated as it is in itself in its own individuating hypostasis, proceeding from the Father and resting in the Word and making him manifest. Neither can it be separated from God, in whom it is, or from the Word, with whom it bears witness, nor can it be poured out into non-existence, but existing hypostatically like the Word, it is alive, capable of choosing, self-moving, active, always desiring the good, by its will possessing the power that corresponds to every

---

[1]Here again, the word play in Greek is important. "Spirit" and "breath" are both πνεῦμα (*pneuma*). For this chapter, cf. Gregory of Nyssa, *Catechetical Discourse* 2.1–3 (PG 45:17ABC; Green, 68–69), which John follows in places almost verbatim.

Οὕτως διὰ μὲν τῆς κατὰ φύσιν ἑνότητος ἡ πολύθεος τῶν Ἑλλήνων ἐξαφανίζεται πλάνη, διὰ δὲ τῆς τοῦ λόγου παραδοχῆς καὶ τοῦ πνεύματος τῶν Ἰουδαίων καθαιρεῖται τὸ δόγμα, ἑκατέρας τε αἱρέσεως παραμένει τὸ χρήσιμον, ἐκ μὲν τῆς Ἰουδαϊκῆς ὑπολήψεως ἡ τῆς φύσεως ἑνότης, ἐκ δὲ τοῦ Ἑλληνισμοῦ ἡ κατὰ τὰς ὑποστάσεις διάκρισις μόνη. Εἰ δὲ ἀντιλέγοι ὁ Ἰουδαῖος πρὸς τὴν τοῦ λόγου παραδοχὴν καὶ τοῦ πνεύματος, ὑπὸ τῆς θείας γραφῆς ἐλεγχέσθω τε καὶ ἐπιστομιζέσθω. Περὶ μὲν γὰρ τοῦ λόγου φησὶν ὁ Δαυίδ· «Εἰς τὸν αἰῶνα, κύριε, ὁ λόγος σου διαμένει ἐν τῷ οὐρανῷ», καὶ πάλιν· «Ἀπέστειλε τὸν λόγον αὐτοῦ καὶ ἰάσατο αὐτούς». Λόγος δὲ προφορικὸς οὐκ ἀποστέλλεται οὐδὲ εἰς τὸν αἰῶνα διαμένει. Περὶ δὲ τοῦ πνεύματος ὁ αὐτὸς Δαυίδ· «Ἐξαποστελεῖς τὸ πνεῦμά σου, καὶ κτισθήσονται», καὶ πάλιν· «Τῷ λόγῳ κυρίου οἱ οὐρανοὶ ἐστερεώθησαν, καὶ τῷ πνεύματι τοῦ στόματος αὐτοῦ πᾶσα ἡ δύναμις αὐτῶν», καὶ ὁ Ἰώβ· «Πνεῦμα θεῖον τὸ ποιῆσάν με, πνοὴ δὲ παντοκράτορος ἡ συνέχουσά με.» Πνεῦμα δὲ ἀποστελλόμενον καὶ ποιοῦν καὶ στερεοῦν καὶ συνέχον οὐκ ἄσθμα ἐστὶ λυόμενον, ὥσπερ οὐδὲ σωματικὸν μέλος τὸ τοῦ θεοῦ στόμα· ἀμφότερα γὰρ θεοπρεπῶς νοητέον.

8   *Περὶ τῆς ἁγίας τριάδος*

Πιστεύομεν τοιγαροῦν εἰς ἕνα θεόν, μίαν ἀρχὴν ἄναρχον, ἄκτιστον, ἀγέννητον ἀνόλεθρόν τε καὶ ἀθάνατον, αἰώνιον, ἄπειρον, ἀπερίγραπτον, ἀπεριόριστον, ἀπειροδύναμον, ἁπλῆν, ἀσύνθετον, ἀσώματον, ἄρρευστον, ἀπαθῆ, ἄτρεπτον, ἀναλλοίωτον, ἀόρατον, πηγὴν ἀγαθότητος καὶ δικαιοσύνης, φῶς νοερόν, ἀπρόσιτον,

---

[2]Cf. Gregory of Nyssa, *Catechetical Discourse* 3.2–3 (PG 45:17D–20A; Green, 69).
[3]Ps 118.89.   [4]Ps 106.20.   [5]Ps 103.30.   [6]Ps 32.6.
[7]Job 33.4. Here the divine Spirit is πνεῦμα (*pneuma*), the Breath of the Almighty is πνοή (*pnoē*).
[8]Here the puff of breath is ἄσθμα (*asthma*).

purpose, and having neither beginning nor end. For never has the Father been without Word, or the Word without Spirit.

Thus, on the one hand, the polytheistic error of the Hellenes is utterly destroyed by the unity according to nature, and, on the other, the doctrine of the Jews is demolished by the reception of the Word and the Spirit.[2] The useful part of each system of thought still stands, from the Jewish notion the unity of nature and from Hellenism only the distinction between the hypostases. If the Jew should object to the reception of the Word and the Spirit, let him be refuted and silenced by the divine Scripture. For with regard to the Word, David says: "Your word, O Lord, abides in heaven forever,"[3] and again: "He sent his word and healed them."[4] But the uttered word is not sent, nor does it abide forever. With regard to the Spirit, the same David says: "You shall send forth your Spirit and they shall be created,"[5] and again: "By the Word of the Lord the heavens were established, and all the power of them by the Breath of his mouth."[6] And Job says: "The divine Spirit is that which made me, the Breath of the Almighty is that which sustains me."[7] But the Spirit that is sent out, and makes, establishes, and sustains is not a puff of breath that is dissipated,[8] just as the mouth of the Lord is not a bodily member, for both must be understood in a manner appropriate to God.

8   *On the Holy Trinity*

We therefore believe in one God,[1] who is a single principle without beginning, uncreated, unbegotten, both indestructible and immortal, eternal, infinite, uncircumscribed, unlimited, infinitely powerful, simple, uncompounded, incorporeal, without flux, without passion, immutable, changeless, invisible, source of goodness and

---

[1]The whole of Chapter 8 is structured in accordance with the Nicene Creed in its synodal ("we believe") rather than its liturgical ("I believe") form. John gives us in effect an extended commentary on the theological clauses of the Creed—with his chief guides the *Theological Orations* of Gregory of Nazianzus (*Orations* 27–31) and *Divine Names* 2.4 of Dionysius the Areopagite—while ignoring, for the purposes of this chapter, the clauses that relate to the economy.

δύναμιν οὐδενὶ μέτρῳ γνωριζομένην, μόνῳ δὲ τῷ οἰκείῳ βουλήματι μετρουμένην—πάντα γάρ, ὅσα θέλει, δύναται—, πάντων κτισμάτων ὁρατῶν τε καὶ ἀοράτων ποιητικήν, πάντων συνεκτικὴν καὶ συντηρητικήν, πάντων προνοητικήν, πάντων κρατοῦσαν καὶ ἄρχουσαν καὶ βασιλεύουσαν ἀτελευτήτῳ καὶ ἀθανάτῳ βασιλείᾳ, μηδὲν ἐναντίον ἔχουσαν, πάντα πληροῦσαν, ὑπ᾿ οὐδενὸς περιεχομένην, αὐτὴν δὲ μᾶλλον περιέχουσαν τὰ σύμπαντα καὶ συνέχουσαν καὶ προέχουσαν, ἀχράντως ταῖς ὅλαις οὐσίαις ἐπιβατεύουσαν καὶ πάντων ἐπέκεινα καὶ πάσης οὐσίας ἐξῃρημένην ὡς ὑπερούσιον καὶ ὑπὲρ τὰ ὄντα οὖσαν, ὑπέρθεον, ὑπεράγαθον, ὑπερπλήρη, τὰς ὅλας ἀρχὰς καὶ τάξεις ἀφορίζουσαν καὶ πάσης ἀρχῆς καὶ τάξεως ὑπεριδρυμένην ὑπὲρ οὐσίαν καὶ ζωὴν καὶ λόγον καὶ ἔννοιαν, αὐτοφῶς, αὐτοαγαθότητα, αὐτοζωήν, αὐτοουσίαν ὡς μὴ παρ᾿ ἑτέρου τὸ εἶναι ἔχουσαν ἤ τι τῶν ὅσα ἐστίν, αὐτὴν δὲ πηγὴν οὖσαν τοῦ εἶναι τοῖς οὖσι, τοῖς ζῶσι τῆς ζωῆς, τοῖς λόγου μετέχουσι τοῦ λόγου, τοῖς πᾶσι πάντων ἀγαθῶν αἰτίαν, πάντα εἰδυῖαν πρὶν γενέσεως αὐτῶν, μίαν οὐσίαν, μίαν θεότητα, μίαν δύναμιν, μίαν θέλησιν, μίαν ἐνέργειαν, μίαν ἀρχήν, μίαν ἐξουσίαν, μίαν κυριότητα, μίαν βασιλείαν, ἐν τρισὶ τελείαις ὑποστάσεσι γνωριζομένην τε καὶ προσκυνουμένην μιᾷ προσκυνήσει πιστευομένην τε καὶ λατρευομένην ὑπὸ πάσης λογικῆς κτίσεως ἀσυγχύτως ἡνωμέναις καὶ ἀδιαστάτως διαιρουμέναις, ὃ καὶ παράδοξον. Εἰς πατέρα καὶ υἱὸν καὶ ἅγιον πνεῦμα, εἰς ἃ καὶ βεβαπτίσμεθα· οὕτω γὰρ ὁ κύριος τοῖς ἀποστόλοις βαπτίζειν ἐνετείλατο· «Βαπτίζοντες αὐτούς», φάσκων, «εἰς τὸ ὄνομα τοῦ πατρὸς καὶ τοῦ υἱοῦ καὶ τοῦ ἁγίου πνεύματος».

---

[2]Or "activity." The best translation of the word ἐνέργεια is disputed. The divine οὐσία is fundamentally "what God is," the divine ἐνέργεια (*energeia*) "what God does." Some scholars, such as Torstein Tollefsen, avoid the translation "energy" where possible, on the grounds that it gives the impression of being "a kind of quasi-material force" (*Activity and Participation in Late Antique and Early Christian Thought* [Oxford: Oxford University Press, 2012], 4–5). I compromise, translating ἐνέργεια usually as "energy" but sometime as "activity" or "operation."

justice, intellectual light, inaccessible, a power unknowable by any standard of measurement, but measured only by his own will—for he can do anything that he wishes—a single principle productive of all created things both visible and invisible, that sustains and preserves all things, exercises providential care over all things, exercises dominion, authority, and sovereignty over all things by an everlasting and immortal kingdom, a single principle that contains nothing contrary, that fills all things, that is not contained by anything, but rather itself contains the sum total of all things and sustains them and possesses them beforehand, that pervades all essences without suffering defilement, and transcends all things, and is detached from every essence since it is superessential and beyond beings, beyond the divine, beyond the good, beyond fullness, and is set apart from all principles and classes as a whole, and is superior to every principle and class, since it is more than essence, life, word, and concept; it is light itself, goodness itself, life itself, essence itself, since it does not have its being, or anything in the category of existents, from another, being the source itself of the being of that which exists, of the life of that which lives, of the rationality of that which participates in reason, and is the cause in all things of every good and of their form before their coming to be; it is one essence, one divinity, one power, one will, one energy,[2] one principle, one authority, one dominion, one sovereignty, known and worshiped in three perfect hypostases that are believed in and adored in a single act of worship by the whole of rational creation and that are united without confusion and divided without separation, which is also a paradox.[3] We believe in Father, Son, and Holy Spirit, in whom we have also been baptized; for it is thus that the Lord commanded the apostles to baptize, "baptizing them," he said, "in the name of the Father and of the Son and of the Holy Spirit."[4]

---

[3]On this litany of characteristics of the Godhead, cf. Gregory of Nazianzus, *Oration* 6.22 (PG 35:749B–752A; Moreschini, 246–68).

[4]Mt 28.19.

Εἰς ἕνα πατέρα, τὴν πάντων ἀρχὴν καὶ αἰτίαν, οὐκ ἔκ τινος γεννηθέντα, ἀναίτιον δὲ καὶ ἀγέννητον μόνον ὑπάρχοντα, πάντων μὲν ποιητήν, ἑνὸς δὲ μόνου πατέρα φύσει τοῦ μονογενοῦς υἱοῦ αὐτοῦ, κυρίου δὲ καὶ θεοῦ καὶ σωτῆρος ἡμῶν Ἰησοῦ Χριστοῦ, καὶ προβολέα τοῦ παναγίου πνεύματος. Καὶ εἰς ἕνα υἱὸν τοῦ θεοῦ τὸν μονογενῆ, τὸν κύριον ἡμῶν Ἰησοῦν Χριστόν, τὸν ἐκ τοῦ πατρὸς γεννηθέντα πρὸ πάντων τῶν αἰώνων, φῶς ἐκ φωτός, θεὸν ἀληθινὸν ἐκ θεοῦ ἀληθινοῦ, γεννηθέντα οὐ ποιηθέντα, ὁμοούσιον τῷ πατρί, δι' οὗ τὰ πάντα ἐγένετο. «Πρὸ πάντων τῶν αἰώνων» λέγοντες δείκνυμεν, ὅτι ἄχρονος καὶ ἄναρχος αὐτοῦ ἡ γέννησις· οὐ γὰρ ἐκ τοῦ μὴ ὄντος εἰς τὸ εἶναι παρήχθη ὁ υἱὸς τοῦ θεοῦ, τὸ ἀπαύγασμα τῆς δόξης, ὁ χαρακτὴρ τῆς τοῦ πατρὸς ὑποστάσεως, ἡ ζῶσα σοφία καὶ δύναμις, ὁ λόγος ὁ ἐνυπόστατος, ἡ οὐσιώδης καὶ τελεία καὶ ζῶσα εἰκὼν τοῦ ἀοράτου θεοῦ, ἀλλ' ἀεὶ ἦν σὺν τῷ πατρὶ καὶ ἐν αὐτῷ ἀιδίως καὶ ἀνάρχως ἐξ αὐτοῦ γεγεννημένος· οὐ γὰρ ἦν ποτε ὁ πατήρ, ὅτε οὐκ ἦν ὁ υἱός, ἀλλ' ἅμα πατήρ, ἅμα υἱὸς ἐξ αὐτοῦ γεγεννημένος· πατὴρ γὰρ ἐκτὸς υἱοῦ οὐκ ἂν κληθείη. Εἰ δὲ ἦν μὴ ἔχων υἱόν, οὐκ ἦν πατήρ, καὶ εἰ μετὰ ταῦτα ἔσχεν υἱόν, μετὰ ταῦτα ἐγένετο πατὴρ μὴ ὢν πρὸ τούτου πατὴρ καὶ ἐτράπη ἐκ τοῦ μὴ εἶναι πατὴρ εἰς τὸ γενέσθαι πατήρ, ὅπερ πάσης βλασφημίας ἐστὶ χαλεπώτερον. Ἀδύνατον γὰρ τὸν θεὸν εἰπεῖν ἔρημον τῆς φυσικῆς γονιμότητος· ἡ δὲ γονιμότης τὸ ἐξ αὐτοῦ ἤγουν ἐκ τῆς ἰδίας οὐσίας ὅμοιον κατὰ φύσιν γεννᾶν.

Ἐπὶ μὲν οὖν τῆς τοῦ υἱοῦ γεννήσεως ἀσεβὲς λέγειν χρόνον μεσιτεῦσαι ἢ μετὰ τὸν πατέρα τὴν τοῦ υἱοῦ γενέσθαι ὕπαρξιν· ἐξ αὐτοῦ γὰρ ἤγουν τῆς τοῦ πατρὸς φύσεώς φαμεν τὴν τοῦ υἱοῦ

---

[5]προβολέα τοῦ παναγίου πνεύματος (*probolea tou panagiou pneumatos*). The use of the word προβολεύς (*proboleus*, literally "emitter") applied to the Father to distinguish the Spirit's mode of origin from that of the Son, of whom the Father is γεννήτωρ (*gennētōr*, "begetter"), is derived from Gregory of Nazianzus, *Oration* 23.7 (PG 35:1157D–1160B; Moreschini, 570). Cf. also Dionysius the Areopagite, *Divine Names* 4.14 (PG 3:712C; Suchla, 160.3).

[6]This sentence reproduces the second clause of the Nicene Creed verbatim.

[7]Heb 1.3.

We believe in one Father, the principle and cause of all things, not begotten of anyone, who alone exists as uncaused and unbegotten, the maker of all things, and by nature Father of his one and single only-begotten Son, our Lord and God and Savior Jesus Christ, and originator of the all-holy Spirit.[5] And we believe in one only-begotten Son of God, our Lord Jesus Christ, who was begotten of the Father before all the ages, light from light, true God from true God, begotten not made, consubstantial with the Father, through whom all things came into being.[6] By saying "before all the ages" we indicate that his begetting was outside of time and without beginning. For the Son of God, "the radiance of glory, the stamp of the Father's hypostasis,"[7] the living wisdom and power, the enhypostatic word,[8] the substantial, perfect, and living "image of the invisible God,"[9] was not brought into being from non-being, but always was with the Father and was begotten in him eternally and from him timelessly. For the Father never existed when the Son did not exist, but at the same time there was a father and a son begotten from him, for a father cannot be called such without a son. If he existed without having a son, he would not have been a father, and if subsequently he had a son, he would subsequently have become a father, not having previously been a father, and he would have changed from not being a father into being a father, which of all blasphemy is the worst.[10] For it is impossible to say that God was bereft of his natural fecundity. And fecundity is to beget from oneself, that is to say, from one's own substance, that which is by nature similar.

Therefore with regard to the Son's generation, it is impious to say that there was an interval of time or that the existence of the Son came into being after the Father.[11] For it is from the Father's nature

---

[8]"Enhypostatic" means "subsisting in reality."

[9]Col 1.15.

[10]This is because ontological change in God can only be from perfection to imperfection, or vice versa.

[11]This refers to the Arian slogan regarding the Son, "there was once when he was not" (ἦν ποτε ὅτε οὐκ ἦν [*ēn pote hote ouk ēn*]), much attacked by Athanasius (e.g., in *De decretis* 15.4, PG 25:449B).

γέννησιν. Καὶ εἰ μὴ ἐξ ἀρχῆς δῶμεν τὸν υἱὸν συνυπάρχειν τῷ πατρὶ ἐξ αὐτοῦ γεγεννημένον, τροπὴν τῆς τοῦ πατρὸς ὑποστάσεως παρεισάγομεν, ὅτι μὴ ὢν πατὴρ ὕστερον ἐγένετο πατήρ· ἡ γὰρ κτίσις, εἰ καὶ μετὰ ταῦτα γέγονεν, ἀλλ᾽ οὐκ ἐκ τῆς τοῦ θεοῦ οὐσίας, ἐκ δὲ τοῦ μὴ ὄντος εἰς τὸ εἶναι βουλήσει καὶ δυνάμει αὐτοῦ παρήχθη, καὶ οὐχ ἅπτεται τροπὴ τῆς τοῦ θεοῦ φύσεως. Γέννησις μὲν γάρ ἐστι τὸ ἐκ τῆς οὐσίας τοῦ γεννῶντος προάγεσθαι τὸ γεννώμενον ὅμοιον κατ᾽ οὐσίαν, κτίσις δὲ καὶ ποίησις τὸ ἔξωθεν καὶ οὐκ ἐκ τῆς οὐσίας τοῦ κτίζοντος καὶ ποιοῦντος γίνεσθαι τὸ κτιζόμενον καὶ ποιούμενον ἀνόμοιον παντελῶς.

Ἐπὶ μὲν οὖν τοῦ μόνου ἀπαθοῦς καὶ ἀναλλοιώτου καὶ ἀτρέπτου καὶ ἀεὶ ὡσαύτως ἔχοντος θεοῦ καὶ τὸ γεννᾶν καὶ τὸ κτίζειν ἀπαθές· φύσει γὰρ ὢν ἀπαθὴς καὶ ἄρρευστος ὡς ἁπλοῦς καὶ ἀσύνθετος οὐ πέφυκεν ὑπομένειν πάθος ἢ ῥεῦσιν οὔτε ἐν τῷ γεννᾶν οὔτε ἐν τῷ κτίζειν οὐδέ τινος συνεργίας δεῖται, ἀλλ᾽ ἡ μὲν γέννησις ἄναρχος καὶ ἀίδιος φύσεως ἔργον οὖσα καὶ ἐκ τῆς οὐσίας αὐτοῦ προάγουσα, ἵνα τροπὴν ὁ γεννῶν μὴ ὑπομείνῃ καὶ ἵνα μὴ θεὸς πρῶτος καὶ θεὸς ὕστερος εἴη καὶ προσθήκην δέξηται. Ἡ δὲ κτίσις ἐπὶ θεοῦ θελήσεως ἔργον οὖσα οὐ συναΐδιός ἐστι τῷ θεῷ, ἐπειδὴ οὐ πέφυκε τὸ ἐκ τοῦ μὴ ὄντος εἰς τὸ εἶναι παραγόμενον συναΐδιον εἶναι τῷ ἀνάρχῳ καὶ ἀεὶ ὄντι. Ὥσπερ τοίνυν οὐχ ὁμοίως ποιεῖ ἄνθρωπος καὶ θεός—ὁ μὲν γὰρ ἄνθρωπος οὐδὲν ἐκ τοῦ μὴ ὄντος εἰς τὸ εἶναι παράγει, ἀλλ᾽ ὅπερ ποιεῖ ἐκ προϋποκειμένης ὕλης ποιεῖ, οὐ θελήσας μόνον ἀλλὰ καὶ προεπινοήσας, καὶ ἐν τῷ νῷ ἀνατυπώσας τὸ γενησόμενον, εἶτα καὶ χερσὶν ἐργασάμενος καὶ κόπον ὑπομείνας καὶ κάματον, πολλάκις δὲ καὶ ἀστοχήσας μὴ ἀποβάντος, καθὰ βούλεται τοῦ ἐπιτηδεύματος· ὁ δὲ θεὸς θελήσας μόνον ἐκ τοῦ μὴ ὄντος εἰς τὸ εἶναι τὰ πάντα παρήγαγεν—, οὕτως οὐδὲ ὁμοίως γεννᾷ θεὸς καὶ ἄνθρωπος. Ὁ μὲν γὰρ θεὸς ἄχρονος ὢν καὶ ἄναρχος καὶ ἀπαθὴς καὶ ἄρρευστος καὶ ἀσώματος καὶ μόνος καὶ ἀτελεύτητος ἀχρόνως καὶ ἀνάρχως καὶ ἀπαθῶς καὶ ἀρρεύστως γεννᾷ καὶ ἐκτὸς συνδυασμοῦ, καὶ οὔτε ἀρχὴν ἔχει ἡ ἀκατάληπτος αὐτοῦ γέννησις οὔτε τέλος. Καὶ ἀνάρχως μὲν διὰ τὸ ἄτρεπτον, ἀρρεύστως δὲ διὰ τὸ ἀπαθὲς καὶ ἀσώματον, ἐκτὸς δὲ

itself that we predicate the generation of the Son. And if we do not grant that the Son coexisted with the Father from the beginning as begotten from him, we introduce a change in the hypostasis of the Father, in that, not being a father before, he later became a father. For creation, even though it came into being subsequently, was not from the Father's substance but was brought out of non-being into being by his will and power, and so there is no question of a change in the divine nature. For generation is to produce from the substance of the one engendering that which is engendered as like in substance, whereas creation and making produce that which is created and made from what is external, not from the substance of the creator and maker, with the result that is it completely unlike.

Therefore with regard to God, who alone is impassible, unchangeable, immutable, and always the same, both begetting and creating are free from passion. For being by nature impassible and non-transient, since he is simple and non-composite, he cannot in the nature of things admit of passion or transience either in begetting or in creating, nor is he in need of any assistance. On the contrary, the begetting is without beginning and eternal, since it is a work of his nature and produces from his essence, so that the begetter should not suffer any change and so that he should not be a first God and a second God and be receptive of addition. Whereas creation, being with regard to God a work of will, is not coeternal with God, since it does not belong to the nature of that which has come into being out of nothing to be co-eternal with that which is without beginning and has always existed. Therefore just as a human being and God do not make in the same way—for humans do not bring anything out of non-being into being, but whatever they make, they make out of pre-existing matter, not only by their will but also by conceiving of it beforehand, and representing what is to be in their minds, and then working with their hands and undergoing toil and effort and frequently failing through not bringing the work to completion as they would wish, whereas God only by willing has brought everything into being from non-being—similarly, neither

συνδυασμοῦ διά τε τὸ ἀσώματον πάλιν καὶ ἕνα μόνον εἶναι θεὸν ἀπροσδεῆ ἑτέρου, ἀτελευτήτως δὲ καὶ ἀκαταπαύστως διά τε τὸ ἄναρχον καὶ ἄχρονον καὶ ἀτελεύτητον καὶ ἀεὶ ὡσαύτως ἔχειν· τὸ γὰρ ἄναρχον ἀτελεύτητον, τὸ δὲ χάριτι ἀτελεύτητον οὐ πάντως ἄναρχον ὥσπερ οἱ ἄγγελοι.

Γεννᾷ τοίνυν ὁ ἀεὶ ὢν θεὸς τὸν ἑαυτοῦ λόγον τέλειον ὄντα ἀνάρχως καὶ ἀτελευτήτως, ἵνα μὴ ἐν χρόνῳ τίκτῃ θεὸς ὁ χρόνου ἀνωτέραν ἔχων τήν τε φύσιν καὶ τὴν ὕπαρξιν. Ὁ δὲ ἄνθρωπος δῆλον ὡς ἐναντίως γεννᾷ ὑπὸ γένεσιν τελῶν καὶ φθορὰν καὶ ῥεῦσιν καὶ πληθυσμὸν καὶ σῶμα περικείμενος καὶ τὸ ἄρρεν καὶ τὸ θῆλυ ἐν τῇ φύσει κεκτημένος· ἐνδεὲς γὰρ τὸ ἄρρεν τῆς τοῦ θήλεος βοηθείας. —Ἀλλ᾽ ἵλεως εἴη ὁ πάντων ἐπέκεινα καὶ πᾶσαν νόησιν καὶ κατάληψιν ὑπερκείμενος.

Διδάσκει οὖν ἡ ἁγία καθολικὴ καὶ ἀποστολικὴ ἐκκλησία ἅμα πατέρα καὶ ἅμα τὸν μονογενῆ αὐτοῦ υἱὸν ἐξ αὐτοῦ γεγεννημένον ἀχρόνως καὶ ἀρρεύστως καὶ ἀπαθῶς καὶ ἀκαταλήπτως, ὡς μόνος ὁ τῶν ὅλων οἶδε θεός. Ὥσπερ ἅμα τὸ πῦρ καὶ ἅμα τὸ ἐξ αὐτοῦ φῶς, καὶ οὐ πρῶτον τὸ πῦρ καὶ μετὰ ταῦτα τὸ φῶς ἀλλ᾽ ἅμα, καὶ ὥσπερ τὸ φῶς ἐκ τοῦ πυρὸς ἀεὶ γεννώμενον ἀεὶ ἐν αὐτῷ ἐστι μηδαμῶς αὐτοῦ χωριζόμενον, οὕτω καὶ ὁ υἱὸς ἐκ τοῦ πατρὸς

---

[12]John's anxiety to distinguish divine begetting from human reproduction perhaps reflects contemporary Muslim polemic, which (as we may deduce from an early ninth-century text by a Christian convert to Islam, Rabban al-Tabari) argued that Christians were required by their Creed to take "Father" and "Son" in a literal sense: David Thomas, *Anti-Christian polemic in early Islam: Abū ʿĪsā al-Warrāq's "Against the Trinity"* (Cambridge: Cambridge University Press, 1992), 32. For his understanding of human reproduction, John seems to draw on Aristotle's view (one of several available theories) according to which the father imparts the form and the mother the matter, the "assistance of the female" being the supply of the material (the mother's menstrual blood) on which the male principle works to produce the embryo "as the products of art are made by means of the tools of the artist" (*Generation of Animals* 2.4, 740b21–9). On this topic and, more broadly, the theological significance of the difference between the sexes in patristic thought, see David Bradshaw, "Sexual Difference and the Difference It Makes: The Greek Fathers and Their Sources," in *The Reception of Greek Ethics in Late Antiquity and Byzantium*, ed. Sophia Xenophontos and Anna Marmodoro (Cambridge University Press, forthcoming).

do God and a human being beget in the same way. Since God is timeless and without beginning, impassible, intransient, incorporeal, single, and unending, he begets timelessly without beginning, impassibly, intransiently, and without copulation, and his incomprehensible begetting has neither beginning nor end. And since he begets timelessly because of his immutability, intransiently because of his impassibility and incorporeality, without copulation, again because of his incorporeality, he is also one God alone without need of another, begetting everlastingly and unendingly through his being without beginning, without time and without end, and ever the same. For that which is without beginning is without end, but that which by grace is without end is not necessarily without beginning, as is the case with the angels.

Accordingly, the eternally existing God begets his own perfect Word who exists without beginning and without end, so that God, whose nature and existence are superior to time, might not beget in time. Human beings, however, clearly beget in a completely different manner, since they are subject to generation, decay, transience, and increase, and are embodied and divided by nature into male and female, for the male needs the assistance of the female.[12] But far be it that this should be the case with him who is beyond all things and transcends all intellection and comprehension.[13]

Therefore the holy catholic and apostolic Church teaches the simultaneous existence of the Father and of his only-begotten Son, begotten of him timelessly without transience or passion and in a manner beyond understanding, as only the God of all knows. For just as fire and the light that comes from it are simultaneous, and it is not a case of first the fire and then subsequently the light but both simultaneously, and just as the light is always generated by the fire, is always in it, and is in no way separated from it, so too the Son is

---

[13]The ἵλεως (*hileōs*) of the opening phrase of this sentence (Ἀλλ' ἵλεως εἴη, *All' hileōs eiē*) is the Attic form of the noun ἵλαος (*hilaos*). Both Salmond and Chase take it to be the adverb ἱλέως (*hileōs*, "propitiously" or "graciously"), turning the sentence into a *non sequitur*. For the idiomatic use of ἵλεως εἴη (*hileōs eiē*, "far be it" or "God forbid"), cf. Mt 16.22.

γεννᾶται μηδαμῶς αὐτοῦ χωριζόμενος, ἀλλ' ἀεὶ ἐν αὐτῷ ἐστιν.
Ἀλλὰ τὸ μὲν φῶς ἐκ τοῦ πυρὸς γεννώμενον ἀχωρίστως, καὶ ἐν
αὐτῷ ἀεὶ μένον οὐκ ἔχει ἰδίαν ὑπόστασιν παρὰ τὸ πῦρ, ποιότης
γάρ ἐστι φυσικὴ τοῦ πυρός, ὁ δὲ υἱὸς τοῦ θεοῦ ὁ μονογενὴς ἐκ
πατρὸς γεννηθεὶς ἀχωρίστως καὶ ἀδιαστάτως καὶ ἐν αὐτῷ μένων
ἀεὶ ἔχει ἰδίαν ὑπόστασιν παρὰ τὴν τοῦ πατρός.

Λόγος μὲν οὖν καὶ ἀπαύγασμα λέγεται διὰ τὸ ἄνευ
συνδυασμοῦ καὶ ἀπαθῶς καὶ ἀχρόνως καὶ ἀρρεύστως καὶ
ἀχωρίστως γεγεννῆσθαι ἐκ τοῦ πατρός, υἱὸς δὲ καὶ χαρακτὴρ τῆς
πατρικῆς ὑποστάσεως διὰ τὸ τέλειον καὶ ἐνυπόστατον καὶ κατὰ
πάντα ὅμοιον τῷ πατρὶ εἶναι πλὴν τῆς ἀγεννησίας, μονογενὴς
δέ, ὅτι μόνος ἐκ μόνου τοῦ πατρὸς μόνως ἐγεννήθη. Οὐδὲ γὰρ
ὁμοιοῦται ἑτέρα γέννησις τῇ τοῦ υἱοῦ τοῦ θεοῦ γεννήσει, οὐδὲ
γάρ ἐστιν ἄλλος υἱὸς τοῦ θεοῦ· εἰ γὰρ καὶ τὸ πνεῦμα τὸ ἅγιον
ἐκ τοῦ πατρὸς ἐκπορεύεται, ἀλλ' οὐ γεννητῶς ἀλλ' ἐκπορευτῶς.
Ἄλλος τρόπος ὑπάρξεως οὗτος ἄληπτός τε καὶ ἄγνωστος, ὥσπερ
καὶ ἡ τοῦ υἱοῦ γέννησις. Διὸ καὶ πάντα, ὅσα ἔχει ὁ πατήρ, αὐτοῦ
εἰσι πλὴν τῆς ἀγεννησίας, ἥτις οὐ σημαίνει οὐσίας διαφορὰν οὐδὲ
ἀξίωμα, ἀλλὰ τρόπον ὑπάρξεως, ὥσπερ καὶ ὁ Ἀδὰμ ἀγέννητος ὢν
(πλάσμα γάρ ἐστι θεοῦ) καὶ ὁ Σὴθ γεννητὸς (υἱὸς γάρ ἐστιν τοῦ
Ἀδάμ) καὶ ἡ Εὔα ἐκ τῆς τοῦ Ἀδὰμ πλευρᾶς ἐκπορευθεῖσα (οὐ γὰρ
ἐγεννήθη αὕτη) οὐ φύσει διαφέρουσιν ἀλλήλων (ἄνθρωποι γάρ
εἰσιν), ἀλλὰ τῷ τῆς ὑπάρξεως τρόπῳ.

---

[14]Cf. Cyril of Alexandria, *Thesaurus* 5 (PG 75:61BC).
[15]Cf. Cyril of Alexandria, *Thesaurus* 5 (PG 75:72CD).
[16]ἀπαύγασμα (*apaugasma*, Heb 1.3).
[17]χαρακτὴρ τῆς ὑποστάσεως (*charactēr tēs hypostaseōs*, Heb 1.3).
[18]μονογενής (*monogenēs*, Heb 11.17).
[19]Ἄλλος τρόπος ὑπάρξεως οὗτος (*Allos tropos hyparxeōs houtos*). "Mode of
existence" (τρόπος ὑπάρξεως, *tropos hyparxeōs*) is a term first used in Book IV of
Against Eunomius, attributed to Basil the Great, to distinguish the Son from the

begotten of the Father without in any way being separated from him but existing eternally in him. Only whereas the light that is generated inseparably from the fire and always remains in it does not have its own hypostasis apart from the fire,[14] for it is a natural quality of the fire, the only-begotten Son of God who is begotten of the Father inseparably and without interval, and ever remains in him,[15] has his own hypostasis apart from that of the Father.

Thus the Word is also called the radiance[16] through his being begotten of the Father without copulation, impassibly, timelessly, intransiently, and inseparably; he is called Son and imprint of the Father's hypostasis[17] through his being perfect and enhypostatic and in every respect like the Father except for the Father's unbegottenness; and he is called only-begotten[18] because he has been begotten uniquely and alone from the only Father. For there is no other begetting that can be compared with the begetting of the Son by the Father, nor is there another Son of God, for if the Holy Spirit, too, proceeds from the Father, it is not by begetting but by procession. This is a different mode of existence,[19] which is beyond our apprehension and knowledge, as is also the begetting of the Son. Hence all that the Father has belongs to the Son except for unbegottenness, which does not signify a difference of essence or status but a mode of existence, just as Adam being unbegotten (for he was a being created by God) and Seth being begotten (for he was a son of Adam) and Eve proceeding from the side of Adam (for she was not begotten) differ not in nature from each other (for they were human beings) but in their mode of existence.[20]

Father with regard to unbegotten/begotten without implying two different essences: "Unbegottenness is a mode of existence not the name of an essence" (PG 29:681A); "the Father would be contrasted to the Son in term of essence if unbegottenness were an essence rather than a mode of existence" (PG 29:681C). John Damascene's formulation of this principle was to be useful to later Byzantine writers (such as Barlaam of Calabria, Joseph Bryennios, and Mark Eugenikos) in their polemics against Latin Trinitarian theology.

[20]The example is drawn from Gregory of Nazianzus, *Oration* 31.11 (PG 36:144D–145B; Moreschini, 754–56).

Χρὴ γὰρ εἰδέναι, ὅτι τὸ ἀγένητον διὰ τοῦ ἑνὸς Νῦ γραφόμενον τὸ ἄκτιστον ἤτοι τὸ μὴ γενόμενον σημαίνει, τὸ δὲ ἀγέννητον διὰ τῶν δύο Νῦ γραφόμενον δηλοῖ τὸ μὴ γεννηθέν. Κατὰ μὲν οὖν τὸ πρῶτον σημαινόμενον διαφέρει οὐσία οὐσίας· ἄλλη γὰρ οὐσία ἡ ἄκτιστος ἤτοι ἀγένητος (διὰ τοῦ ἑνὸς Νῦ), καὶ ἄλλη ἡ γενητὴ ἤτοι κτιστή. Κατὰ δὲ τὸ δεύτερον σημαινόμενον οὐ διαφέρει οὐσία οὐσίας· παντὸς γὰρ εἴδους ζώων ἡ πρώτη ὑπόστασις ἀγέννητός ἐστιν, ἀλλ᾽ οὐκ ἀγένητος· ἐκτίσθησαν μὲν γὰρ ὑπὸ τοῦ δημιουργοῦ τῷ λόγῳ αὐτοῦ παραχθέντα εἰς γένεσιν, οὐ μὴν ἐγεννήθησαν μὴ προϋπάρχοντος ἑτέρου ὁμοειδοῦς, ἐξ οὗ γεννηθῶσι.

Κατὰ μὲν οὖν τὸ πρῶτον σημαινόμενον κοινωνοῦσιν αἱ τρεῖς τῆς ἁγίας θεότητος ὑπέρθεοι ὑποστάσεις (ὁμοούσιοι γὰρ καὶ ἄκτιστοι ὑπάρχουσι), κατὰ δὲ τὸ δεύτερον σημαινόμενον οὐδαμῶς (μόνος γὰρ ὁ πατὴρ ἀγέννητος· οὐ γὰρ ἐξ ἑτέρας ἐστὶν αὐτῷ ὑποστάσεως τὸ εἶναι) καὶ μόνος ὁ υἱὸς γεννητὸς (ἐκ τῆς τοῦ πατρὸς γὰρ οὐσίας ἀνάρχως καὶ ἀχρόνως γεγέννηται) καὶ μόνον τὸ πνεῦμα τὸ ἅγιον ἐκπορευτὸν ἐκ τῆς οὐσίας τοῦ πατρός, οὐ γεννώμενον ἀλλ᾽ ἐκπορευόμενον. Οὕτω μὲν τῆς θείας διδασκούσης γραφῆς, τοῦ δὲ τρόπου τῆς γεννήσεως καὶ τῆς ἐκπορεύσεως ἀκαταλήπτου ὑπάρχοντος.

Καὶ τοῦτο δὲ ἰστέον, ὡς οὐκ ἐξ ἡμῶν μετηνέχθη ἐπὶ τὴν μακαρίαν θεότητα τὸ τῆς πατρότητος καὶ υἱότητος καὶ ἐκπορεύσεως ὄνομα, τοὐναντίον δὲ ἐκεῖθεν ἡμῖν μεταδέδοται, ὥς φησιν ὁ θεῖος ἀπόστολος· «Διὰ τοῦτο κάμπτω τὰ γόνατά μου πρὸς τὸν πατέρα, ἐξ οὗ πᾶσα πατριὰ ἐν οὐρανῷ καὶ ἐπὶ γῆς».

For one needs to know that ἀγένητον (*agenēton*, "ingenerate") written with one ν (*n*) signifies that which has not been created or has not been generated, whereas ἀγέννητον (*agennēton*, "unbegotten") written with two ν's (*n's*) indicates that which has not been begotten. Therefore in accordance with the first signification, one essence differs from another, for an uncreated or ungenerated being (written with one ν [*n*]) is one thing, and a generated or created being is another, whereas in accordance with the second signification there is no difference between one essence and another, for the first hypostasis of every species of living thing has not been begotten but is not unengendered. For they were created by the creator through his Word and brought into being; they were indeed not begotten because there was no other being of the same kind that pre-existed them and from which they were begotten.

In accordance, then, with the first signification the three superdivine hypostases of the holy Godhead are the same as each other (for they are consubstantial and uncreated), but in accordance with the second signification they are not so at all, for only the Father is unbegotten (for his being is not from another hypostasis), only the Son is begotten (for he is begotten from the substance of the Father without beginning and outside of time), and only the Holy Spirit proceeds from the substance of the Father, not begotten but brought forth by procession. That is what the divine Scripture teaches, but the mode of begottenness and of procession are beyond comprehension.[21]

One should also know this, that the terms "fatherhood," "sonship," and "procession" have not been applied to the blessed Godhead on analogy with ourselves, but on the contrary have been communicated to us from that source, as the divine Apostle says: "For this reason I bend my knees before the Father, from whom all fatherhood in heaven and on earth takes its name."[22]

---

[21]Cf. Gregory of Nazianzus, *Oration* 31.10 (PG 36:144ABC; Moreschini, 754).
[22]Eph 3.14–15.

Εἰ δὲ λέγομεν τὸν πατέρα ἀρχὴν εἶναι τοῦ υἱοῦ καὶ μείζονα, οὐ προτερεύειν αὐτὸν τοῦ υἱοῦ χρόνῳ ἢ φύσει ὑποφαίνομεν, «δι' αὐτοῦ γὰρ τοὺς αἰῶνας ἐποίησεν», οὐδὲ καθ' ἕτερόν τι, εἰ μὴ κατὰ τὸ αἴτιον, τουτέστιν ὅτι ὁ υἱὸς ἐκ τοῦ πατρὸς ἐγεννήθη καὶ οὐχ ὁ πατὴρ ἐκ τοῦ υἱοῦ καὶ ὅτι ὁ πατὴρ αἴτιός ἐστι τοῦ υἱοῦ φυσικῶς, ὥσπερ οὐκ ἐκ τοῦ φωτὸς τὸ πῦρ φαμεν προέρχεσθαι, ἀλλὰ τὸ φῶς μᾶλλον ἐκ τοῦ πυρός. Ὅτε οὖν ἀκούσωμεν ἀρχὴν καὶ μείζονα τοῦ υἱοῦ τὸν πατέρα, τῷ αἰτίῳ νοήσωμεν. Καὶ ὥσπερ οὐ λέγομεν ἑτέρας οὐσίας τὸ πῦρ καὶ ἑτέρας τὸ φῶς, οὕτως οὐχ οἷόν τε φάναι ἑτέρας οὐσίας τὸν πατέρα καὶ τὸν υἱὸν ἑτέρας, ἀλλὰ μιᾶς καὶ τῆς αὐτῆς. Καὶ καθάπερ φαμὲν διὰ τοῦ ἐξ αὐτοῦ προερχομένου φωτὸς φαίνειν τὸ πῦρ καὶ οὐ τιθέμεθα ὄργανον ὑπουργικὸν εἶναι τοῦ πυρὸς τὸ ἐξ αὐτοῦ φῶς, δύναμιν δὲ μᾶλλον φυσικήν, οὕτω λέγομεν τὸν πατέρα πάντα, ὅσα ποιεῖ, διὰ τοῦ μονογενοῦς αὐτοῦ υἱοῦ ποιεῖν οὐχ ὡς δι' ὀργάνου λειτουργικοῦ, ἀλλὰ φυσικῆς καὶ ἐνυποστάτου δυνάμεως. Καὶ ὥσπερ λέγομεν τὸ πῦρ φωτίζειν καὶ πάλιν φαμὲν τὸ φῶς τοῦ πυρὸς φωτίζειν, οὕτω πάντα, ὅσα ποιεῖ ὁ πατήρ, ὁμοίως καὶ ὁ υἱὸς ποιεῖ. Ἀλλὰ τὸ μὲν φῶς οὐκ ἰδίαν ὑπόστασιν παρὰ τὸ πῦρ κέκτηται, ὁ δὲ υἱὸς τελεία ὑπόστασίς ἐστι τῆς πατρικῆς ἀχώριστος ὑποστάσεως, ὡς ἀνωτέρω παρεστήσαμεν. Ἀδύνατον γὰρ εὑρεθῆναι ἐν τῇ κτίσει εἰκόνα ἀπαραλλάκτως ἐν ἑαυτῇ τὸν τρόπον τῆς ἁγίας τριάδος παραδεικνύουσαν. Τὸ γὰρ κτιστὸν καὶ σύνθετον καὶ ῥευστὸν καὶ τρεπτὸν καὶ περιγραπτὸν καὶ σχῆμα ἔχον καὶ φθαρτόν, πῶς σαφῶς δηλώσει τὴν πάντων τούτων ἀπηλλαγμένην ὑπερούσιον θείαν οὐσίαν; Πᾶσα δὲ ἡ κτίσις δῆλον ὡς τοῖς πλείοσι τούτων ἐνέχεται καὶ πᾶσα κατὰ τὴν ἑαυτῆς φύσιν τῇ φθορᾷ ὑπόκειται.

And if we say that the Father is the origin of the Son and greater than him, we do not imply that he precedes the Son in time or in nature, for "through him he created the aeons."[23] Nor do we imply anything else except causality, which is to say that the Son was begotten of the Father, not that the Father was begotten of the Son, and that the Father is the cause of the Son by nature, just as we do not say that a flame comes from light, but rather that light comes from a flame. So when we hear that the Father is the source of the Son and greater than him,[24] we should understand this in a causal sense. And just as we do not say that a flame is of one substance and light is of another, so too it is not appropriate to say that the Father is one of substance and the Son is of another. On the contrary, they are both of one and the same substance. And just as we say that a flame is visible on account of the light that comes from it and we do not assume that the light that comes from the flame is the flame's subordinate instrument, but rather that it is a natural power, so too we say that everything that the Father does he does through his only-begotten Son, not as if through a functional instrument but by a natural and enhypostatic power. And just as we say that the flame illuminates, and we also say that the flame's light illuminates, in a similar way all that the Father does the Son does likewise. But the light does not possess its own hypostasis apart from the flame, whereas the Son is a perfect hypostasis inseparable from the Father's hypostasis, as we have argued above. For it is impossible to find in creation an image that exactly reflects the mode of the Holy Trinity as it is in itself. For how can that which is created, composite, transient, mutable, circumscribed, and which possesses a form and is corruptible, clearly show the superessential divine essence that is clearly far removed from all these? It is evident that the whole of creation is subject to the majority of these conditions and the whole by its own nature is liable to decay.

[23]Heb 1.2.
[24]Cf. Jn 14.28.

Ὁμοίως πιστεύομεν καὶ εἰς ἓν πνεῦμα τὸ ἅγιον, τὸ κύριον καὶ ζωοποιόν, τὸ ἐκ τοῦ πατρὸς ἐκπορευόμενον καὶ ἐν υἱῷ ἀναπαυόμενον, τὸ τῷ πατρὶ καὶ υἱῷ συμπροσκυνούμενον καὶ συνδοξαζόμενον ὡς ὁμοούσιόν τε καὶ συναΐδιον, τὸ τοῦ θεοῦ πνεῦμα, τὸ εὐθές, τὸ ἡγεμονικόν, τὴν πηγὴν τῆς ζωῆς καὶ τοῦ ἁγιασμοῦ, θεὸν σὺν πατρὶ καὶ υἱῷ ὑπάρχον καὶ προσαγορευόμενον, ἄκτιστον, πλῆρες, δημιουργόν, παντοκρατορικόν, παντουργόν, παντοδύναμον, ἀπειροδύναμον, δεσπόζον πάσης τῆς κτίσεως οὐ δεσποζόμενον, πληροῦν οὐ πληρούμενον, μετεχόμενον οὐ μετέχον, ἁγιάζον οὐχ ἁγιαζόμενον, παράκλητον ὡς τὰς τῶν ὅλων παρακλήσεις δεχόμενον, κατὰ πάντα ὅμοιον τῷ πατρὶ καὶ τῷ υἱῷ, ἐκ τοῦ πατρὸς ἐκπορευόμενον καὶ δι᾽ υἱοῦ μεταδιδόμενον καὶ μεταλαμβανόμενον ὑπὸ πάσης τῆς κτίσεως καὶ δι᾽ ἑαυτοῦ κτίζον καὶ οὐσιοῦν τὰ σύμπαντα καὶ ἁγιάζον καὶ συνέχον, ἐνυπόστατον ἤτοι ἐν ἰδίᾳ ὑποστάσει ὑπάρχον, ἀχώριστον καὶ ἀνεκφοίτητον πατρὸς καὶ υἱοῦ καὶ πάντα ἔχον, ὅσα ἔχει ὁ πατὴρ καὶ ὁ υἱός, πλὴν τῆς ἀγεννησίας καὶ τῆς γεννήσεως. Ὁ μὲν γὰρ πατὴρ ἀναίτιος καὶ ἀγέννητος (οὐ γὰρ ἔκ τινος· οὐδὲ ἐξ αὐτοῦ τὸ εἶναι ἔχει οὐδέ τι τῶν ὅσα ἔχει), αὐτὸς δὲ μᾶλλόν ἐστιν ἀρχὴ καὶ αἰτία τοῦ εἶναι καὶ τοῦ πῶς εἶναι φυσικῶς τοῖς πᾶσιν. Ὁ δὲ υἱὸς ἐκ τοῦ πατρὸς γεννητῶς· τὸ δὲ πνεῦμα τὸ ἅγιον καὶ αὐτὸ μὲν ἐκ τοῦ πατρός, ἀλλ᾽ οὐ γεννητῶς ἀλλ᾽ ἐκπορευτῶς. Καὶ ὅτι μὲν ἔστι διαφορὰ γεννήσεως καὶ ἐκπορεύσεως, μεμαθήκαμεν· τίς δὲ ὁ τρόπος τῆς διαφορᾶς, οὐδαμῶς. Ἅμα δὲ καὶ ἡ υἱοῦ ἐκ τοῦ πατρὸς γέννησις, καὶ ἡ τοῦ ἁγίου πνεύματος ἐκπόρευσις.

Πάντα οὖν, ὅσα ἔχει ὁ υἱός, καὶ τὸ πνεῦμα ἐκ τοῦ πατρὸς ἔχει καὶ αὐτὸ τὸ εἶναι. Καὶ εἰ μὴ ὁ πατήρ ἐστιν, οὐδὲ ὁ υἱός ἐστιν οὐδὲ τὸ πνεῦμα. Καὶ εἰ μὴ ὁ πατὴρ ἔχει τι, οὐδὲ ὁ υἱὸς ἔχει,

---

[25]After this phrase Lequien's text (reproduced by Migne and translated by Salmond and Chase) has θεοῦν οὐ θεούμενον (*theoun ou theoumenon*, "deifying not deified"). The latter phrase is found only in three manuscripts (FHM) and is not included in Kotter's critical text. A further manuscript (C) inserts the same phrase after "filled."

We believe likewise in one Holy Spirit, the Lord and giver of life, who proceeds from the Father and rests in the Son, who is worshiped and glorified with the Father and the Son as consubstantial and coeternal with them, who is the Spirit of God, who is righteous, who is sovereign, the source of life and of sanctification, God who exists with the Father and the Son and is addressed with them, who is uncreated, complete, creator, all-sovereign, the accomplisher of all things, almighty, infinitely powerful, the Lord of all creation not its servant,[25] who fills but is not filled, is participated in but does not participate, who sanctifies but is not sanctified, who is the Paraclete because he receives the intercessions of all, who in all respects is like the Father and the Son, proceeding from the Father, being transmitted through the Son, and being participated in by the whole of creation, through whom all things are created, endowed with substance, sanctified, and sustained, who is enhypostatic, or exists in his own hypostasis, inseparable from and not departing from the Father and the Son, and having all that the Father and the Son have except for unbegottenness and begottenness. For the Father is without cause and unbegotten (for he is not from something, nor does he possess being from it,[26] or anything of whatever he possesses), but is himself, rather, the source and cause of being and of the natural mode of being in all things. The Son is from the Father by generation; the Holy Spirit is also from the Father not by generation but by procession. We have been taught that there is a difference between generation and procession, but what the manner of the difference is we have in no way been informed. Yet both the begetting of the Son from the Father and the procession of the Holy Spirit are simultaneous.

Everything, therefore, that the Son has the Holy Spirit also has from the Father, even being itself. And if the Father does not exist, neither does the Son nor the Spirit. And if the Father does not have

[26]The phrase "nor does he possess being from it" translates οὐδὲ ἐξ αὐτοῦ τὸ εἶναι ἔχει (*oude ex autou to einai echei*), which in this case Kotter has adopted from FM and many of the older codices. Other manuscripts read ἐξ ἑαυτοῦ (*ex heautou*, adopted by Lequien), which would give the translation "but derives from himself his being" (Salmond) or "has his being from himself" (Chase).

οὐδὲ τὸ πνεῦμα. Καὶ διὰ τὸν πατέρα, τουτέστιν διὰ τὸ εἶναι τὸν πατέρα, ἔστιν ὁ υἱὸς καὶ τὸ πνεῦμα. Καὶ διὰ τὸν πατέρα ἔχει ὁ υἱὸς καὶ τὸ πνεῦμα πάντα, ἃ ἔχει, τουτέστι διὰ τὸ τὸν πατέρα ἔχειν αὐτά, πλὴν τῆς ἀγεννησίας καὶ τῆς γεννήσεως καὶ τῆς ἐκπορεύσεως· ἐν ταύταις γὰρ μόναις ταῖς ὑποστατικαῖς ἰδιότησι διαφέρουσιν ἀλλήλων αἱ ἅγιαι τρεῖς ὑποστάσεις οὐκ οὐσίᾳ, τῷ δὲ χαρακτηριστικῷ τῆς οἰκείας ὑποστάσεως ἀδιαιρέτως διαιρούμεναι.

Φαμὲν δὲ ἕκαστον τῶν τριῶν τελείαν ἔχειν ὑπόστασιν, ἵνα μὴ ἐκ τριῶν ἀτελῶν μίαν σύνθετον φύσιν τελείαν γνωρίσωμεν, ἀλλ' ἐν τρισὶ τελείαις ὑποστάσεσι μίαν ἁπλῆν οὐσίαν, ὑπερτελῆ καὶ προτέλειον· πᾶν γὰρ ἐξ ἀτελῶν συγκείμενον σύνθετον πάντως ἐστίν, ἐκ δὲ τελείων ὑποστάσεων, ἀδύνατον σύνθεσιν γενέσθαι. Ὅθεν οὐδὲ λέγομεν τὸ εἶδος ἐξ ὑποστάσεων, ἀλλ' ἐν ὑποστάσεσιν. Ἀτελῶν δὲ εἴπομεν τῶν μὴ σῳζόντων τὸ εἶδος τοῦ ἐξ αὐτῶν ἀποτελουμένου πράγματος. Λίθος μὲν γὰρ καὶ ξύλον καὶ σίδηρος, ἕκαστον καθ' ἑαυτὸ τέλειόν ἐστι κατὰ τὴν ἰδίαν φύσιν, πρὸς δὲ τὸ ἐξ αὐτῶν ἀποτελούμενον οἴκημα ἀτελὲς ἕκαστον αὐτῶν ὑπάρχει· οὐδὲ γάρ ἐστιν ἕκαστον αὐτῶν καθ' ἑαυτὸ οἶκος.

Τελείας μὲν οὖν τὰς ὑποστάσεις φαμέν, ἵνα μὴ σύνθεσιν ἐπὶ τῆς θείας νοήσωμεν φύσεως· «σύνθεσις γὰρ ἀρχὴ διαστάσεως». Καὶ πάλιν ἐν ἀλλήλαις τὰς τρεῖς ὑποστάσεις λέγομεν, ἵνα μὴ πλῆθος καὶ δῆμον θεῶν εἰσαγάγωμεν. Διὰ μὲν τῶν τριῶν ὑποστάσεων τὸ ἀσύνθετον καὶ ἀσύγχυτον, διὰ δὲ τοῦ ὁμοουσίου καὶ ἐν ἀλλήλαις

[27]Gregory of Nazianzus, *Oration* 40.7 (PG 36:365C; Moreschini, 926).

[28]"Consubstantiality" (τὸ ὁμοούσιον [*to homoousion*], literally "the state of being of the same substance") was the Athanasian term adopted by the Council of Nicaea (325) to safeguard the fully divine nature of the Son.

[29]The expression "mutual indwelling" ([τὸ] ἐν ἀλλήλαις εἶναι [(*to*) *en allēlais einai*], literally "the state of being in each another"), is drawn from Dionysius the Areopagite, who in *Divine Names* 2.4 (PG 3:641A; Suchla 127.2–3) speaks of "the mutual ... abiding and grounding of the unitary hypostases in each another" (ἡ ἐν ἀλλήλαις ... τῶν ἐναρχικῶν ὑποστάσεων μονὴ καὶ ἵδρυσις, *hē en allēlais... tōn henarchikōn hypostaseōn monē kai hidrysis*). John Damascene also takes account of Dionysius' scholiast, John of Scythopolis, who in his scholion on this passage says: "Note that the phrase 'in each other' [τὸ ἐν ἀλλήλαις, *to en allēlais*] refers to the divine

something, neither does the Son nor the Spirit. And through the Father, that is, through the Father's existing, both the Son and the Spirit exist. And through the Father, the Son and the Spirit have everything that they have, that is to say, through the Father they have these things apart from unbegottenness, begottenness, and procession. For in these alone do the hypostatic properties differ from each other, the three hypostases being divided indivisibly not by essence but by that which is characteristic of its own hypostasis.

We say that each of the three has a perfect hypostasis, in order to exclude our acknowledging one perfect composite nature formed out of three imperfect natures, instead of acknowledging in three perfect hypostases one simple essence that is supremely perfect and beyond perfection. For everything compounded from imperfect hypostases is necessarily composite, but it is impossible for a composition of perfect hypostases to arise. Hence, we do not say that a form is constituted *from* hypostases but that it exists *in* hypostases. And we call imperfect those things that do not maintain the form of the thing made out of them. For in the case of stone, wood, and iron, each of them is perfect in itself in accordance with its own nature, but in relation to a building constructed out of them each of them is imperfect, for each of them is not actually a house.

We therefore call the hypostases perfect in order to exclude our attributing composition to the divine nature, for "composition is a source of separation."[27] Moreover, we say that the three hypostases are in one another in order to exclude our introducing a plurality and community of gods. By the three hypostases we acknowledge the absence of composition and confusion; by the consubstantiality[28] and mutual indwelling[29] of the hypostases and their identity of will,

hypostases with regard to their abiding and grounding, as in 'I am in the Father and the Father is in me' [cf. Jn 17.21]. The Apostle says the same about the Holy Spirit [cf. Rom 8.11]" (Suchla, *Joannis Scythopolitani prologus et scholia*, ch. 2, scholion DN 127.3). In the next paragraph but one John Damascene renders the same conception, for the first time, as τὴν ἐν ἀλλήλαις περιχώρησιν (*tēn en allēlais perichōrēsin*, "mutual perichoresis" or "interpenetration"). He returns to this formulation in Chapter 14. Cf. Chapter 52, where "perichoresis" is applied, as in Maximus the Confessor, to the relationship between Christ's two natures.

εἶναι τὰς ὑποστάσεις καὶ τῆς ταυτότητος τοῦ θελήματός τε καὶ τῆς ἐνεργείας καὶ τῆς δυνάμεως καὶ τῆς ἐξουσίας καὶ τῆς κινήσεως, ἵν' οὕτως εἴπω, τὸ ἀδιαίρετον καὶ τὸ εἶναι ἕνα θεὸν γνωρίζομεν. Εἷς γὰρ ὄντως θεὸς ὁ θεὸς καὶ ὁ λόγος καὶ τὸ πνεῦμα αὐτοῦ.

Χρὴ δὲ εἰδέναι, ὅτι ἕτερόν ἐστι τὸ πράγματι θεωρεῖσθαι καὶ ἄλλο τὸ λόγῳ καὶ ἐπινοίᾳ. Ἐπὶ μὲν οὖν πάντων τῶν κτισμάτων ἡ μὲν τῶν ὑποστάσεων διαίρεσις πράγματι θεωρεῖται· πράγματι γὰρ ὁ Πέτρος τοῦ Παύλου κεχωρισμένος θεωρεῖται. Ἡ δὲ κοινότης καὶ ἡ συνάφεια καὶ τὸ ἓν λόγῳ καὶ ἐπινοίᾳ θεωρεῖται. Νοοῦμεν γὰρ τῷ νῷ, ὅτι ὁ Πέτρος καὶ ὁ Παῦλος τῆς αὐτῆς εἰσι φύσεως καὶ κοινὴν μίαν ἔχουσι φύσιν· ἕκαστος γὰρ αὐτῶν ζῷόν ἐστι λογικὸν θνητόν, καὶ ἕκαστος σάρξ ἐστιν ἐμψυχωμένη ψυχῇ λογικῇ τε καὶ νοερᾷ. Αὕτη οὖν ἡ κοινὴ φύσις τῷ λόγῳ ἐστὶ θεωρητή. Οὐδὲ γὰρ αἱ ὑποστάσεις ἐν ἀλλήλαις εἰσίν· ἰδίᾳ δὲ ἑκάστη καὶ ἀναμέρος ἤγουν καθ' ἑαυτὴν κεχώρισται πλεῖστα τὰ διαιροῦντα αὐτὴν ἐκ τῆς ἑτέρας ἔχουσα· καὶ γὰρ καὶ τόπῳ διεστήκασι καὶ χρόνῳ διαφέρουσι καὶ γνώμῃ μερίζονται καὶ ἰσχύι καὶ μορφῇ εἴτουν σχήματι καὶ ἕξει καὶ κράσει καὶ ἀξίᾳ καὶ ἐπιτηδεύματι καὶ πᾶσι τοῖς χαρακτηριστικοῖς ἰδιώμασι, πλέον δὲ πάντων τῷ μὴ ἐν ἀλλήλαις ἀλλὰ κεχωρισμένως εἶναι. Ὅθεν καὶ δύο καὶ τρεῖς ἄνθρωποι λέγονται καὶ πολλοί.

Τοῦτο δὲ καὶ ἐπὶ πάσης ἔστιν ἰδεῖν τῆς κτίσεως. Ἐπὶ δὲ τῆς ἁγίας καὶ ὑπερουσίου καὶ πάντων ἐπέκεινα καὶ ἀλήπτου τριάδος τὸ ἀνάπαλιν. Ἐκεῖ γὰρ τὸ μὲν κοινὸν καὶ ἓν πράγματι θεωρεῖται διά τε τὸ συναΐδιον καὶ τὸ ταυτὸν τῆς οὐσίας καὶ τῆς ἐνεργείας καὶ τοῦ θελήματος καὶ τὴν τῆς γνώμης σύμπνοιαν τήν τε τῆς ἐξουσίας καὶ τῆς δυνάμεως καὶ τῆς ἀγαθότητος ταυτότητα—οὐκ εἶπον ὁμοιότητα, ἀλλὰ ταυτότητα—καὶ τὸ ἓν ἔξαλμα τῆς κινήσεως· μία γὰρ οὐσία, μία ἀγαθότης, μία δύναμις, μία θέλησις, μία ἐνέργεια,

---

[30]For detailed analyses of this and the following paragraph, see Dirk Krausmüller, "Responding to John Philoponos: Hypostases, Particular Substances and Perichoresis in the Trinity," *Journal for Late Antique Religion and Culture* 9 (2015): 13–28 (at 19–21). Idem, "A Conceptualist Turn: The Ontological Status of Created Species in Late Greek Patristic Theology," *Scrinium* 16 (2020): 233–52. On the status of universals

activity, power, authority, and, so to speak, movement we acknowledge the absence of division and the fact that they are one God. For God and his Word and his Spirit are in reality one God.

One also needs to know that it is one thing for something to be observed as an objective reality (πράγματι, *pragmati*) and another for it to be contemplated rationally and conceptually (ἐπινοίᾳ, *epinoia*). With regard to every created being the distinction between hypostases may be observed as an objective reality. For it is as an objective reality that Peter is observed to be distinct from Paul. But their community of being, relationship, and oneness is contemplated rationally and conceptually. For we apprehend by the mind that Peter and Paul are of the same nature and possess a single common nature. For each of them is a rational mortal animal, and each is flesh ensouled with a rational and intelligent soul. Therefore this common nature is contemplated in the understanding: for it is not the case that the hypostases exist within each another. Each exists individually and apart, that is to say, separately and in its own right, since each has a great many things that distinguish it from the other. They are both separated by place and differ in time, and are divided by will, power, form or shape, habit, temperament, reputation, manner of life, and all the distinctive attributes, and most of all by the fact that they exist not within each other but separately. Hence they are said to be two human beings or three or many.[30]

We see this also with regard to creation as a whole. But with regard to the holy, superessential, all-transcending, and incomprehensible Trinity, the opposite is the case. For there, that which is common and one is contemplated as an objective reality through the coeternity and identity of its essence, energy, and will, and through the unanimity of its intention and the identity of its authority, power, and goodness—I did not say similarity but identity—and through the one impulsion of its movement. For there is one essence, one

in John Damascene's thinking, Krausmüller argues that John is not fully coherent. His "distinction between common nature and individual hypostasis is misleading. In reality there are only individual natures, as John makes clear when he speaks of 'many human beings'" ("A Conceptualist Turn," 248).

μία ἐξουσία, μία καὶ ἡ αὐτὴ οὐ τρεῖς ὅμοιαι ἀλλήλαις, ἀλλὰ μία καὶ
ἡ αὐτὴ κίνησις τῶν τριῶν ὑποστάσεων. «Ἓν γὰρ ἕκαστον αὐτῶν
ἔχει πρὸς τὸ ἕτερον οὐχ ἧττον ἢ πρὸς ἑαυτό», τουτέστιν ὅτι κατὰ
πάντα ἕν εἰσιν ὁ πατὴρ καὶ ὁ υἱὸς καὶ τὸ ἅγιον πνεῦμα πλὴν τῆς
ἀγεννησίας καὶ τῆς γεννήσεως καὶ τῆς ἐκπορεύσεως· ἐπινοίᾳ
δὲ τὸ διῃρημένον. Ἕνα γὰρ θεὸν γινώσκομεν, ἐν μόναις δὲ ταῖς
ἰδιότησι τῆς τε πατρότητος καὶ τῆς υἱότητος καὶ τῆς ἐκπορεύσεως
κατά τε τὸ αἴτιον καὶ αἰτιατὸν καὶ τὸ τέλειον τῆς ὑποστάσεως ἤτοι
τὸν τῆς ὑπάρξεως τρόπον τὴν διαφορὰν ἐννοοῦμεν. Οὔτε γὰρ
τοπικὴν διάστασιν ὡς ἐφ' ἡμῶν δυνάμεθα ἐπὶ τῆς ἀπεριγράπτου
λέγειν θεότητος—ἐν ἀλλήλαις γὰρ αἱ ὑποστάσεις εἰσίν, οὐχ ὥστε
συγχεῖσθαι, ἀλλ' ὥστε ἔχεσθαι κατὰ τὸν τοῦ κυρίου λόγον· «Ἐγὼ
ἐν τῷ πατρί, καὶ ὁ πατὴρ ἐν ἐμοί», φήσαντος—οὔτε θελήματος
διαφορὰν ἢ γνώμης ἢ ἐνεργείας ἢ δυνάμεως ἤ τινος ἑτέρου,
ἅτινα τὴν πραγματικὴν καὶ δι' ὅλου ἐν ἡμῖν γεννῶσι διαίρεσιν.
Διὸ οὐδὲ τρεῖς θεοὺς λέγομεν τὸν πατέρα καὶ τὸν υἱὸν καὶ τὸ
ἅγιον πνεῦμα, ἕνα δὲ μᾶλλον θεόν, τὴν ἁγίαν τριάδα, εἰς ἓν
αἴτιον υἱοῦ καὶ πνεύματος ἀναφερομένων, οὐ συντιθεμένων οὐδὲ
συναλειφομένων κατὰ τὴν Σαβελλίου συναίρεσιν—ἑνοῦνται γάρ,
ὡς ἔφημεν, οὐχ ὥστε συγχεῖσθαι, ἀλλ' ὥστε ἔχεσθαι ἀλλήλων·

[31] Gregory of Nazianzus, *Oration* 31.16 (PG 36:152B; Moreschini, 760).
[32] ἀλλ' ὥστε ἔχεσθαι (*all' hōste echesthai*). See below, note 35.
[33] Jn 14.10.
[34] Sabellius was an early third-century theologian who apparently taught a
modalist form of Monarchianism, that is to say, that the Godhead is differentiated
only by modes of operation, which we label Father, Son, and Holy Spirit.
[35] "Coinherence" (ἔχεσθαι ἀλλήλων, *echesthai allēlōn*) and "mutual interpenetration" or "perichoresis" (τὴν ἐν ἀλλήλαις περιχώρησιν ἔχειν, *tēn en allēlais perichōrēsin
echein*) are used as equivalent expressions. This is John's first mention in the *Exact
Exposition* of "perichoresis," an expression he borrows from Maximus (e.g., *Ambig*,
17.8, 42.5), who adopted it from Gregory of Nazianzus (*Ep.* 101.31). John is the first to
apply the expression to the hypostases of the Trinity (rather than to the two natures of
Christ). Behind his introduction of "perichoresis" lies a long debate on the ontological status of the divine nature in relation to the divine hypostases. The Cappadocian
solution (three hypostases with a common nature) only raised a further problem: how
to account for the reality of the divine nature as well as the three hypostases without
introducing a fourth element into the Trinity. For John the best solution required a

goodness, one power, one will, one energy, one authority, one and the same not three similar to each other, but one and the same movement of all three hypostases. "For the oneness that each has with regard to the other is not inferior to the oneness that it has with itself,"[31] which is to say that the Father, the Son, and the Holy Spirit are one in all things except in unbegottenness, begottenness, and procession, for the separation is conceptual. For we know one God, and it is only by the properties of fatherhood, sonship, and procession, in accordance with the cause and effect and perfection of the hypostasis, or the mode of existence, that we understand the difference. For with regard to the uncircumscribed Godhead we cannot speak of a distinction in respect of place as we do in our own case—for the hypostases are in each other, not so that they are confused, but so that they coinhere,[32] in accordance with the Lord's saying: "I am in the Father and the Father is in me."[33] Nor is there a difference of will, or intention, or energy, or power, or anything else that in us gives rise to a real and complete division. Therefore neither do we call the Father, the Son, and the Holy Spirit three gods, but rather one God, the Holy Trinity, in whom the Son and the Spirit are referred to one cause, not merged or fused together as in Sabellius' contraction[34]—for they are united, as we have said, not so that they are confused, but so that they coinhere in each other, and they interpenetrate each other[35] without in the least fusing together

distinction to be made between what was objectively the case (πράγματι, *pragmati*) and what existed solely in the human mind (ἐπινοίᾳ, *epinoia*). The sixth-century Alexandrian philosopher, John Philoponus (a Monophysite), had argued that the particulars (the hypostases) were real but what they had in common (the divine nature) was a construct of our intellect. To John Damascene this smacked of tritheism. The most pressing need in his own environment was to maintain the oneness of God, i.e., the reality of the divine nature. Hence his reversal in the case of the Trinity of what obtained in the case of creation. The danger then was that instead of the nature the hypostases could be seen to exist merely conceptually. His use of "perichoresis" enables him to endow the hypostases with reality without introducing a fourth component into the Trinity. For good discussions of these issues see Krausmüller, "Responding to John Philoponos"; idem, "Under the Spell of John Philoponus: How Chalcedonian Theologians of the Late Patristic Period Attempted to Safeguard the Oneness of God," *Journal of Theological Studies* 68 (2017): 625–49.

καὶ τὴν ἐν ἀλλήλαις περιχώρησιν ἔχουσι δίχα πάσης συναλοιφῆς καὶ συμφύρσεως—οὐδὲ ἐξισταμένων ἢ κατ᾽ οὐσίαν τεμνομένων κατὰ τὴν Ἀρείου διαίρεσιν. Ἀμέριστος γὰρ ἐν μεμερισμένοις, εἰ δεῖ συντόμως εἰπεῖν, ἡ θεότης καὶ οἷον ἐν ἡλίοις τρισὶν ἐχομένοις ἀλλήλων καὶ ἀδιαστάτοις οὖσι μία τοῦ φωτὸς σύγκρασίς τε καὶ συνάφεια. Ὅταν μὲν οὖν πρὸς τὴν θεότητα βλέψωμεν καὶ τὴν πρώτην αἰτίαν καὶ τὴν μοναρχίαν καὶ τὸ ἓν καὶ ταὐτὸν τῆς θεότητος, ἵν᾽ οὕτως εἴπω, κίνημά τε καὶ βούλημα καὶ τὴν τῆς οὐσίας καὶ δυνάμεως καὶ ἐνεργείας καὶ κυριότητος ταυτότητα, ἓν ἡμῖν τὸ φανταζόμενον. Ὅταν δὲ πρὸς τὰ ἐν οἷς ἡ θεότης ᾖ, τό γε ἀκριβέστερον εἰπεῖν, ἃ ἡ θεότης καὶ τὰ ἐκ τῆς πρώτης αἰτίας ἀχρόνως ἐκεῖθεν ὄντα καὶ ὁμοδόξως καὶ ἀδιαστάτως, τουτέστι τὰς ὑποστάσεις τρία τὰ προσκυνούμενα. Εἷς πατὴρ ὁ πατὴρ καὶ ἄναρχος, τουτέστιν ἀναίτιος· οὐ γὰρ ἔκ τινος. Εἷς υἱὸς ὁ υἱὸς καὶ οὐκ ἄναρχος, τουτέστιν οὐκ ἀναίτιος· ἐκ τοῦ πατρὸς γάρ. Εἰ δὲ τὴν ἀπὸ χρόνου λάβοις ἀρχήν, καὶ ἄναρχος· ποιητὴς γὰρ χρόνων οὐχ ὑπὸ χρόνον. Ἓν πνεῦμα ἅγιον τὸ πνεῦμα, προϊὸν μὲν ἐκ τοῦ πατρός, οὐχ υἱϊκῶς δὲ ἀλλ᾽ ἐκπορευτῶς, οὔτε τοῦ πατρὸς ἐκστάντος τῆς ἀγεννησίας, διότι γεγέννηκεν, οὔτε τοῦ υἱοῦ τῆς γεννήσεως, ὅτι ἐκ τοῦ ἀγεννήτου (πῶς γάρ;), οὔτε τοῦ πνεύματος ἢ εἰς πατέρα μεταπίπτοντος ἢ εἰς υἱόν, ὅτι ἐκπεπόρευται καὶ ὅτι θεός· ἡ γὰρ ἰδιότης ἀκίνητος. Ἢ πῶς ἂν ἰδιότης μένοι, κινουμένη καὶ μεταπίπτουσα; εἰ γὰρ υἱὸς ὁ πατήρ, οὐ πατὴρ κυρίως· εἷς γὰρ κυρίως πατήρ. Καὶ εἰ πατὴρ ὁ υἱός, οὐ κυρίως υἱός· εἷς γὰρ κυρίως υἱὸς καὶ ἓν πνεῦμα ἅγιον.

Χρὴ γινώσκειν, ὅτι τὸν πατέρα οὐ λέγομεν ἔκ τινος· λέγομεν δὲ αὐτὸν τοῦ υἱοῦ πατέρα. Τὸν δὲ υἱὸν οὐ λέγομεν αἴτιον οὐδὲ πατέρα· λέγομεν δὲ αὐτὸν καὶ ἐκ τοῦ πατρὸς καὶ υἱὸν τοῦ πατρός. Τὸ δὲ πνεῦμα τὸ ἅγιον καὶ ἐκ τοῦ πατρὸς λέγομεν καὶ πνεῦμα πατρὸς ὀνομάζομεν, ἐκ τοῦ υἱοῦ δὲ τὸ πνεῦμα οὐ λέγομεν, πνεῦμα δὲ υἱοῦ ὀνομάζομεν («εἴ τις γὰρ πνεῦμα Χριστοῦ οὐκ ἔχει», φησὶν

or coalescing—nor set apart or cut up with regard to essence as in Arius' division.[36] For the Godhead, if one must put it succinctly, is undivided in the distinctions, and is like the single mingling and union of light in three suns that adhere to each other and are not separated.[37] Thus when we are focusing our attention on the Godhead and the first cause, monarchy, oneness, and identity, so to speak, of the Godhead's movement and will, and on the identity of the essence, power, energy, and sovereignty, we form a conception in ourselves of oneness. But when we turn our attention to those things in which the Godhead exists, or to put it more precisely, those things that *are* the Godhead, and those things that come from the first cause timelessly, unanimously, and without separation, that is to say, the hypostases, what we adore are three. The Father is one Father and without beginning, that is to say, without a cause, for he is not derived from anything. The Son is one Son but not without beginning, that is to say, not without a cause, for he is from the Father. But if you take a beginning to imply time, then he too is without beginning, for the creator of time is not subject to time. The Spirit is one Holy Spirit, proceeding from the Father not in the manner of sonship but by procession; the Father does not lose his unbegottenness because he has begotten, nor does the Son lose his begottenness because he has come from the unbegotten—how could that be?—nor is the Spirit changed into a father or a son because he has come forth by procession and is God. For the property is immovable. How else would it remain a property if it were movable and underwent change? For if the Father were a son, he would not properly speaking be a father; for the Father properly speaking is one. And if the Son were a father, he would not properly speaking be a son, for there is one Son properly speaking and one Holy Spirit.[38]

One needs to know that we deny that the Father is from anyone; we call him the Father of the Son. And we deny that the Son is either

[37]John takes his image of the three suns from Gregory of Nazianzus, *Oration* 31.14 (PG 36:149A; Moreschini, 758).

[38]The second half of this paragraph closely reproduces Gregory of Nazianzus, *Oration* 39.12 (PG 36:348BC; Moreschini, 910).

ὁ θεῖος ἀπόστολος) καὶ δι' υἱοῦ πεφανερῶσθαι καὶ μεταδεδόσθαι ἡμῖν ὁμολογοῦμεν («ἐνεφύσησε» γὰρ καὶ εἶπε τοῖς μαθηταῖς αὐτοῦ· «Λάβετε πνεῦμα ἅγιον»), ὥσπερ ἐκ τοῦ ἡλίου μὲν ἥ τε ἀκτὶς καὶ ἡ ἔκλαμψις (αὐτὸς γάρ ἐστιν ἡ πηγὴ τῆς τε ἀκτῖνος καὶ τῆς ἐκλάμψεως), διὰ δὲ τῆς ἀκτῖνος ἡ ἔκλαμψις ἡμῖν μεταδίδοται καὶ αὕτη ἐστὶν ἡ φωτίζουσα ἡμᾶς καὶ μετεχομένη ὑφ' ἡμῶν. Τὸν δὲ υἱὸν οὔτε τοῦ πνεύματος λέγομεν οὔτε μὴν ἐκ τοῦ πνεύματος.

9   *Περὶ τῶν ἐπὶ θεοῦ λεγομένων*

Τὸ θεῖον ἁπλοῦν ἐστι καὶ ἀσύνθετον. Τὸ δὲ ἐκ πολλῶν καὶ διαφόρων συγκείμενον σύνθετόν ἐστιν. Εἰ οὖν τὸ ἄκτιστον καὶ ἄναρχον καὶ ἀσώματον καὶ ἀθάνατον καὶ αἰώνιον καὶ ἀγαθὸν καὶ δημιουργικὸν καὶ τὰ τοιαῦτα οὐσιώδεις διαφορὰς εἴπομεν ἐπὶ θεοῦ ἐκ τοσούτων συγκείμενον, οὐχ ἁπλοῦν ἔσται, ἀλλὰ σύνθετον, ὅπερ ἐσχάτης ἀσεβείας ἐστίν. Χρὴ τοίνυν ἕκαστον τῶν ἐπὶ θεοῦ λεγομένων οὐ, τί κατ' οὐσίαν ἐστί, σημαίνειν οἴεσθαι, ἀλλ' ἤ, τί οὐκ ἔστι, δηλοῦν ἢ σχέσιν τινὰ πρός τι τῶν ἀντιδιαστελλομένων ἤ τι τῶν παρεπομένων τῇ φύσει ἢ ἐνέργειαν.

Δοκεῖ μὲν οὖν κυριώτερον πάντων τῶν ἐπὶ θεοῦ λεγομένων ὀνομάτων εἶναι ὁ ὤν, καθὼς αὐτὸς χρηματίζων τῷ Μωσεῖ ἐπὶ τοῦ ὄρους φησίν· «Εἶπον τοῖς υἱοῖς Ἰσραήλ· Ὁ ὢν ἀπέσταλκέ

---

[39]Rom 8.9.
[40]Jn 20.22.

[1]This principle, as enunciated by John Damascene, was much discussed during the fourteenth-century Hesychast Controversy. John may have derived it from Cyril of Alexandria, whose opponent in the *Dialogues on the Trinity* asks how it can

a cause or a father; we say that he is from the Father and the Son of the Father. We say that the Holy Spirit is from the Father and also call him the Spirit of the Father. But although we do not say that the Spirit is from the Son, we call him the Spirit of the Son (for the divine Apostle says: "Anyone who does not have the Spirit of Christ"[39]) and we confess that he is manifested and communicated to us through the Son (for "he breathed on them" and said to his disciples: "Receive the Holy Spirit"[40]). It is like the ray and the radiance that come from the sun (for the latter is the source of the ray and the radiance), and the radiance is communicated to us and it is that which illuminates us and which is participated in by us. But we do not say that the Son is of the Spirit nor indeed that he is from the Spirit.

9   *On what is said about God*

The divine is simple and non-composite.[1] That which is composed of many different elements is composite. So if we say with regard to God that his being uncreated, without origin, incorporeal, immortal, eternal, good, creative, and the like are essential differences, he would be composed of this number of things and would not be simple but composite, which is the height of impiety. It is therefore necessary that we should not think that each of the things we attribute to God indicates what he is essentially. On the contrary, they show either what he is not, or some relation with those things that are distinguished from him, or something that refers to the essence, or an activity.

It therefore seems that the most important of all the names attributed to God is "he who is" (ὁ ὤν, *ho ōn*), as he himself announced to Moses on the mountain, when he said: "Tell the sons of Israel, 'he

be maintained that the divine is simple and not composite if a distinction is made between the divine existence and the divine will (*Dialogue* V, PG 75:554e–555a; SC 237:290). Theodoret of Cyrus in his *On the Incarnation of the Lord* (a work until recently attributed to Cyril) regards it as axiomatic that the divine is "simple and non-composite and without form" (PG 75:1432B).

με». Ὅλον γὰρ ἐν ἑαυτῷ συλλαβὼν ἔχει τὸ εἶναι οἷόν τι πέλαγος οὐσίας ἄπειρον καὶ ἀόριστον.

Δεύτερον δὲ τὸ θεὸς ὄνομα, ὃ λέγεται ἢ ἐκ τοῦ θέειν καὶ περιέπειν τὰ σύμπαντα ἢ ἐκ τοῦ αἴθειν ὅ ἐστι καίειν («ὁ γὰρ θεὸς πῦρ καταναλίσκον» πᾶσαν κακίαν ἐστίν) ἢ ἀπὸ τοῦ θεᾶσθαι τὰ πάντα· ἀλάθητος γάρ ἐστι καὶ πάντων ἐπόπτης. Ἐθεάσατο γὰρ «τὰ πάντα πρὶν γενέσεως αὐτῶν» ἀχρόνως ἐννοήσας καὶ ἕκαστον κατὰ τὴν θελητικὴν αὐτοῦ ἄχρονον ἔννοιαν, ἥτις ἐστὶ προορισμὸς καὶ εἰκὼν καὶ παράδειγμα, ἐν τῷ προορισθέντι, καιρῷ γίνεται.

Τὸ μὲν οὖν πρότερον αὐτοῦ τοῦ εἶναι παραστατικόν ἐστι καὶ οὐ τοῦ τί εἶναι, τὸ δὲ δεύτερον ἐνεργείας· τὸ δὲ ἄναρχον καὶ ἄφθαρτον καὶ ἀγένητον ἤτοι ἄκτιστον καὶ ἀσώματον καὶ ἀόρατον καὶ τὰ τοιαῦτα, τί οὐκ ἔστι, δηλοῖ, τουτέστιν ὅτι οὐκ ἤρξατο τοῦ εἶναι οὐδὲ φθείρεται οὐδὲ ἔκτισται οὐδέ ἐστι σῶμα οὐδὲ ὁρᾶται. Τὸ δὲ ἀγαθὸν καὶ δίκαιον καὶ ὅσιον καὶ τὰ τοιαῦτα παρέπονται τῇ φύσει, οὐκ αὐτὴν δὲ τὴν οὐσίαν δηλοῖ. Τὸ δὲ κύριος βασιλεύς τε καὶ τὰ τοιαῦτα σχέσιν πρὸς τὰ ἀντιδιαστελλόμενα δηλοῖ· τῶν γὰρ κυριευομένων λέγεται κύριος καὶ τῶν βασιλευομένων βασιλεύς, τῶν δημιουργουμένων δημιουργὸς καὶ τῶν ποιμαινομένων ποιμήν.

10   Περὶ θείας ἑνώσεως καὶ διακρίσεως

Πάντα μὲν οὖν ταῦτα κοινῶς ἐπὶ πάσης τῆς θεότητος ἐκληπτέον καὶ ταυτῶς καὶ ἁπλῶς καὶ ἀμερῶς καὶ ἡνωμένως, διακεκριμένως δὲ τὸ πατὴρ καὶ τὸ υἱὸς καὶ τὸ πνεῦμα καὶ τὸ ἀναίτιον καὶ τὸ

---

[2]Ex 3.14.
[3]Cf. Dionysius the Areopagite, *Divine Names* 5.4 (PG 3:817D; Suchla, 183.4–11).
[4]Deut 4.24.
[5]On the etymology of the word "god," John follows Gregory of Nazianzus, *Oration* 30.18 (PG 36:128A; Moreschini, 740). Gregory relies in turn on etymological tra-

who is' has sent me."[2] For he gathers together and contains all being in himself like an infinite and unbounded sea.[3]

The second name is "god" (θεός, *theos*), which is derived either from the verb "to run" (θέειν, *theein*) and to pervade all things, or from the verb "to kindle" (αἴθειν, *aithein*), which means "to burn" ("for God is a fire consuming" every evil[4]), or from the verb "to see" (θεᾶσθαι, *theasthai*) all things, for nothing escapes his notice and he surveys all things.[5] For he saw "all things before they came to pass,"[6] having conceived of each of them outside of time and each comes to pass at the preordained time in accordance with the timeless intention of his will, which is a predetermination, image, and pattern.

The first name is thus indicative of his being but not of what he is. The second is indicative of his energy. The attributes of non-beginning, incorruptibility, and ingenerateness, or uncreatedness, incorporeality, and invisibility, and suchlike show what he is not, that is to say, that his being had no beginning, nor is it subject to corruption, nor was it created, nor is it a body, nor is it visible. But goodness, justice, holiness, and suchlike refer to the nature without manifesting the nature itself. The names lord, king, and suchlike manifest a relation to what is distinct from him. For he is called lord of those to whom he is master, king of those over whom he rules, creator of those whom he has created, and shepherd of those who are his flock.

10   *On divine union and distinction*

All these names, then, are to be taken as applying in common to the whole of the Godhead, identically, simply, indivisibly, and without distinction, but the names of Father, Son, and Spirit, of unoriginated and originated, and of unbegotten, begotten, and proceeding, which are indicative not of essence but of mutual relationship and mode of existence, are to be taken as applying with differentiation.

ditions going back to Plato and Aristotle. For more on etymologies of *theōria* ancient and modern, see Hannelore Rausch, *Theoria: von ihrer sakralen zur philosophischen Bedeutung* (Munich: Fink, 1982), 13–17. (IG)

[6]Dan 13(Sus).42.

αἰτιατὸν καὶ τὸ ἀγέννητον καὶ τὸ γεννητὸν καὶ ἐκπορευτόν, ἅτινα οὐκ οὐσίας εἰσὶ δηλωτικά, ἀλλὰ τῆς πρὸς ἄλληλα σχέσεως καὶ τοῦ τῆς ὑπάρξεως τρόπου.

Ταῦτα οὖν εἰδότες καὶ ἐκ τούτων ἐπὶ τὴν θείαν οὐσίαν χειραγωγούμενοι οὐκ αὐτὴν τὴν οὐσίαν καταλαμβάνομεν ἀλλὰ τὰ περὶ τὴν οὐσίαν, ὥσπερ οὐδέ, ἐὰν γνῶμεν, ὅτι ἡ ψυχὴ ἀσώματός ἐστι καὶ ἄποσος καὶ ἀσχημάτιστος, ἤδη καὶ τὴν οὐσίαν αὐτῆς κατειλήφαμεν, οὐδὲ τοῦ σώματος, εἴπερ γνῶμεν, ὅτι λευκὸν ἢ μέλαν ἐστίν, ἀλλὰ τὰ περὶ τὴν οὐσίαν. Ὁ δὲ ἀληθὴς λόγος διδάσκει ἁπλοῦν εἶναι τὸ θεῖον καὶ μίαν ἁπλῆν ἔχειν ἐνέργειαν, ἀγαθήν, πᾶσι τὰ πάντα ἐνεργοῦσαν κατὰ τὴν τοῦ ἡλίου ἀκτῖνα, ἥτις πάντα θάλπει καὶ ἐν ἑκάστῳ κατὰ τὴν φυσικὴν ἐπιτηδειότητα καὶ δεκτικὴν δύναμιν ἐνεργεῖ ἐκ τοῦ δημιουργήσαντος θεοῦ τὴν τοιαύτην εἰληφὼς ἐνέργειαν.

Διακέκριται δὲ καί, ὅσα τῆς θείας καὶ φιλανθρώπου τοῦ θεοῦ λόγου σαρκώσεως· ἐν τούτοις γὰρ οὔτε ὁ πατὴρ οὔτε τὸ πνεῦμα κατ' οὐδένα λόγον κεκοινώνηκεν εἰ μὴ κατ' εὐδοκίαν καὶ κατὰ τὴν ἄρρητον θαυματουργίαν, ἣν καὶ καθ' ἡμᾶς ἄνθρωπος ὁ θεὸς λόγος γενόμενος εἰργάζετο ὡς ἀναλλοίωτος θεὸς καὶ θεοῦ υἱός.

11 Περὶ τῶν σωματικῶς ἐπὶ θεοῦ λεγομένων

Ἐπεὶ δὲ πλεῖστα περὶ θεοῦ σωματικώτερον ἐν τῇ θείᾳ γραφῇ συμβολικῶς εἰρημένα εὑρίσκομεν, εἰδέναι χρή, ὡς ἀνθρώπους ὄντας ἡμᾶς καὶ τὸ παχὺ τοῦτο σαρκίον περικειμένους τὰς θείας καὶ ὑψηλὰς καὶ ἀύλους τῆς θεότητος ἐνεργείας νοεῖν ἢ λέγειν ἀδύνατον, εἰ μὴ εἰκόσι καὶ τύποις καὶ συμβόλοις τοῖς καθ' ἡμᾶς χρησαίμεθα. Ὅσα τοίνυν περὶ θεοῦ σωματικώτερον εἴρηται, συμβολικῶς ἐστι λελεγμένα, ἔχει δέ τινα ὑψηλοτέραν διάνοιαν· ἁπλοῦν γὰρ τὸ θεῖον καὶ ἀσχημάτιστον. Ὀφθαλμοὺς μὲν οὖν θεοῦ καὶ βλέφαρα καὶ ὅρασιν τὴν τῶν ἁπάντων ἐποπτικὴν αὐτοῦ

Therefore when we have come to know these names and have been guided by them to the divine essence, we do not grasp the essence itself but only what is "around" the essence.[1] In the same way, if we know that the soul is incorporeal, unquantifiable, and without form, we have not thereby also grasped its essence. Nor in case of the body, even if we know that it is white or black, have we thereby grasped its essence, but only what is "around" the essence. Correct reasoning teaches that the divine is simple and that it has one simple operation that is good and activates all things in all beings, like the sun's ray, which warms all beings and operates in each of them in accordance with its natural aptitude and capacity, having received such an operation from the God who created it.

Furthermore, a distinction is made in all that pertains to the divine and benevolent incarnation of the divine Word. For in these things neither the Father nor the Spirit have in any way participated, except by [the former's] gracious will and by [the latter's] ineffable miracle-working, which, when he became a human being like us, the divine Word performed as changeless God and God's Son.

11   *On what is affirmed corporeally about God*

Because we find that in the divine Scripture most things about God are stated symbolically in a rather corporeal manner, one needs to know that since we are human beings and are wrapped in this solid morsel of flesh, it is impossible for us to conceptualize or to speak of the divine, exalted, and immaterial energies of the Godhead unless we use images, types, and symbols that are familiar to us. Thus whatever is said of God in a rather corporeal manner is said symbolically and has a higher meaning. For the divine is simple and without form. Therefore we should understand the eyes of God, and his eyelids and vision as his power of exercising providential care over all things and

---

[1] "The things 'around' the essence" (τὰ περὶ τὴν οὐσίαν, *ta peri tēn ousian*) is Maximus the Confessor's way of expressing the relationship between the divine attributes and the divine essence. See esp. *Ambigua to John* 34 (PG 91:1288BC; Constas, 2:64–66).

δύναμιν καὶ τὸ ἀλάθητον τῆς αὐτοῦ γνώσεως ἐννοήσωμεν ἀπὸ τοῦ παρ' ἡμῖν διὰ ταύτης τῆς αἰσθήσεως ἐντελεστέραν γνῶσίν τε καὶ πληροφορίαν ἐγγίνεσθαι. Ὦτα δὲ καὶ ἀκοὴν τὸ ἐξιλεωτικὸν αὐτοῦ καὶ τῆς ἡμετέρας δεκτικὸν δεήσεως· καὶ γὰρ ἡμεῖς τοῖς τὰς ἱκεσίας ποιουμένοις διὰ ταύτης τῆς αἰσθήσεως εὐμενεῖς γινόμεθα γνησιώτερον αὐτοῖς τὸ οὖς ἐπικλίνοντες. Στόμα δὲ καὶ λαλιὰν τὸ ἐνδεικτικὸν τῆς βουλήσεως αὐτοῦ ἐκ τοῦ παρ' ἡμῖν διὰ στόματος καὶ λαλιᾶς σημαίνεσθαι τὰ ἐγκάρδια νοήματα. Βρῶσιν δὲ καὶ πόσιν τὴν ἡμετέραν πρὸς τὸ αὐτοῦ θέλημα συνδρομήν· καὶ γὰρ ἡμεῖς διὰ τῆς γευστικῆς αἰσθήσεως τὴν τῆς φύσεως ἀναπληροῦμεν ὄρεξιν ἀναγκαίαν. Ὄσφρησιν δέ, τὸ ἀποδεκτικὸν τῆς πρὸς αὐτὸν ἡμῶν ἐννοίας τε καὶ εὐνοίας ἐκ τοῦ παρ' ἡμῖν διὰ ταύτης αἰσθήσεως τὴν τῆς εὐωδίας ἀποδοχὴν ἐγγίνεσθαι. Πρόσωπον δὲ τὴν δι' ἔργων αὐτοῦ ἔνδειξίν τε καὶ ἐμφάνειαν ἐκ τοῦ τὴν ἡμετέραν ἐμφάνειαν διὰ προσώπου γίνεσθαι. Χεῖρας δὲ τὸ ἀνυστικὸν τῆς ἐνεργείας αὐτοῦ· καὶ γὰρ ἡμεῖς τὰ χρειώδη καὶ μάλιστα τιμιώτερα διὰ τῶν οἰκείων κατορθοῦμεν χειρῶν. Δεξιὰν δὲ τὴν ἐπὶ τοῖς αἰσίοις αὐτοῦ βοήθειαν ἐκ τοῦ καὶ ἡμᾶς μᾶλλον ἐπὶ τῶν εὐσχημοτέρων καὶ τιμιωτέρων καὶ πλείστης ἰσχύος δεομένων τῇ δεξιᾷ κεχρῆσθαι. Ψηλάφησιν δὲ τὴν ἀκριβεστέραν αὐτοῦ καὶ τῶν λίαν λεπτῶν τε καὶ κρυπτῶν διάγνωσίν τε καὶ εἴσπραξιν ἐκ τοῦ παρ' ἡμῖν μὴ δύνασθαι τοὺς ψηλαφωμένους ἐν ἑαυτοῖς τι κρύπτειν. Πόδας δὲ καὶ βάδισιν τὴν πρὸς ἐπικουρίαν τῶν δεομένων ἢ ἐχθρῶν ἄμυναν ἢ ἄλλην τινὰ πρᾶξιν ἔλευσίν τε καὶ παρουσίαν ἐκ τοῦ παρ' ἡμῖν διὰ τῆς τῶν ποδῶν χρήσεως ἀποτελεῖσθαι τὴν ἄφιξιν. Ὅρκον δὲ τὸ ἀμετάθετον τῆς βουλῆς αὐτοῦ ἐκ τοῦ παρ' ἡμῖν δι' ὅρκου τὰς πρὸς ἀλλήλους βεβαιοῦσθαι συνθήκας. Ὀργὴν δὲ καὶ θυμὸν τὴν πρὸς τὴν κακίαν ἀπέχθειάν τε καὶ ἀποστροφήν· καὶ γὰρ ἡμεῖς τὰ ἐναντία τῆς γνώμης μισοῦντες ὀργιζόμεθα. Λήθην δὲ καὶ ὕπνον καὶ νυσταγμὸν τὴν ὑπέρθεσιν τῆς κατὰ τῶν ἐχθρῶν ἀμύνης καὶ τὴν τῆς συνήθους πρὸς τοὺς οἰκείους βοηθείας ἀναβολήν. Καὶ ἁπλῶς εἰπεῖν πάντα τὰ σωματικῶς εἰρημένα ἐπὶ θεοῦ κεκρυμμένην ἔχει τινὰ ἔννοιαν ἐκ τῶν καθ' ἡμᾶς τὰ ὑπὲρ ἡμᾶς ἐκδιδάσκουσαν, εἰ μή τι περὶ τῆς

the infallibility of his knowledge on analogy with our own acquisition of more complete knowledge and assurance through the sense of sight. By his ears and hearing we should understand his readiness to be propitiated and to receive our supplication, for we too by the sense of hearing become well disposed to those who ask a kindness from us and lend a more favorable ear to them. We should understand his mouth and speech as that which is indicative of his will, on analogy with the way we express our inner thoughts in our case by mouth and speech. We should understand his food and drink as the conforming of our own will to his, for by the sense of taste we too satisfy the necessary appetite of nature. We should understand his smelling as his receiving our thinking and our affection towards him, on analogy with the way we receive a fragrance through the sense of smell. We should understand his face as the indication and manifestation of him through his works on analogy with the way we are made known through our face. We should understand his hands as the effectiveness of his energy, for we too perform what is needful and indeed what is more dignified by our own hands. We should understand his right hand as his help in things that are appropriate on analogy with our own use of our right hand in tasks that are more beautiful, more dignified, and need our full strength. We should understand his touching as his very precise discernment and drawing out of the most subtle and hidden matters on analogy with our own experience with the way people who are subjected to a body search cannot hide anything on their persons. We should understand his feet and his walking as his coming and being present for the aid of the needy, or for defence against enemies, or for any other act, on analogy with the way we bring about our own arrival by our feet. We should understand his oath as the irrevocability of his will, on analogy with our own confirmation of a contract with others by means of an oath. We should understand his wrath and anger as his hatred of evil and his aversion to it, for we too hate what opposes our will and become enraged. We should understand his forgetting and his sleep and drowsiness as his delay in defending against enemies

σωματικῆς τοῦ θεοῦ λόγου ἐπιδημίας εἴρηται· αὐτὸς γὰρ πάντα τὸν ἄνθρωπον διὰ τὴν ἡμετέραν σωτηρίαν ἀνεδέξατο, ψυχὴν νοερὰν καὶ σῶμα καὶ τὰ τῆς ἀνθρωπίνης φύσεως ἰδιώματα τά τε φυσικὰ καὶ ἀδιάβλητα πάθη.

12 Ἔτι περὶ τῶν αὐτῶν

«Ταῦτα μὲν οὖν ἐκ τῶν ἱερῶν μεμυήμεθα λογίων», ὡς ὁ θεῖος ἔφη Διονύσιος ὁ Ἀρεοπαγίτης, «ὅτι ὁ θεὸς πάντων ἐστὶν αἰτία καὶ ἀρχή, τῶν ὄντων οὐσία, τῶν ζώντων ζωή, τῶν λογικῶς ὄντων λόγος, τῶν νοερῶς ὄντων νοῦς, καὶ τῶν μὲν ἀποπιπτόντων αὐτῆς ἀνάκλησίς τε καὶ ἀνάστασις, τῶν δὲ παραφθειρόντων τὸ κατὰ φύσιν ἀνακαινισμὸς καὶ ἀναμόρφωσις, τῶν κινουμένων κατά τινα ἀνίερον σάλον ἵδρυσις ἱερὰ καὶ τῶν ἑστηκότων ἀσφάλεια καὶ τῶν ἐπ᾽ αὐτὴν ἀναγομένων ὁδὸς καὶ ἀνατατικὴ χειραγωγία. Προσθήσω δέ, ὅτι καὶ τῶν ὑπ᾽ αὐτοῦ πεποιημένων πατήρ (κυριώτερον γὰρ ὁ θεὸς ἡμῶν ἐστι πατὴρ ὁ ἐκ μὴ ὄντων εἰς τὸ εἶναι παραγαγὼν ἢ οἱ γεννήσαντες οἱ ἐξ αὐτοῦ καὶ τὸ εἶναι καὶ τὸ γεννᾶν εἰληφότες), τῶν ἑπομένων καὶ ὑπ᾽ αὐτοῦ ποιμαινομένων ποιμήν, τῶν φωτιζομένων ἔλλαμψις, τῶν τελουμένων τελεταρχία, τῶν θεουμένων θεαρχία, τῶν διεστώτων εἰρήνη καὶ τῶν ἁπλουμένων ἁπλότης καὶ τῶν ἑνιζομένων ἑνότης, ἀρχῆς ἁπάσης ὑπερούσιος καὶ ὑπάρχιος ἀρχὴ καὶ τοῦ κρυφίου ἤτοι τῆς αὐτοῦ γνώσεως κατὰ τὸ θεμιτὸν καὶ ἐφικτὸν ἑκάστῳ ἀγαθὴ μετάδοσις».

---

[1]Dionysius the Areopagite, *Divine Names* 1.4 (PG 3:589D; Suchla, 112.7) and *Divine Names* 1.3 (PG 3:589BC; Suchla, 111.12–17).

and his postponement of his customary help for his own people. And to put it simply, all that is said in physical terms about God has a hidden meaning and teaches us about that which transcends us from that which belongs to our own experience, unless it is said about the bodily dwelling among us of God's Word. For he assumed humanity in its fullness for the sake of our salvation, a rational soul, a body, the properties of human nature, and the natural, blameless passions.

12   *Further on the same*

"We have, then, been initiated into these things by the sacred oracles," as the divine Dionysius the Areopagite said, "that God is the cause and principle of all things—the essence of beings, the life of living things, the reason of rational beings, the intellect of intellectual beings—and that he is the recalling and raising up of those who fall away from this, the renewal and forming anew, in accordance with nature, of those who transgress, the holy stabilizing of those who are moved by some unholy swell, the security of those who have kept their feet, and the way and uplifting guidance of those who are raised up towards it."[1] I shall also add that he is the father of those made by him (or more precisely, our God is the father who brings forth out of non-being into being, or from whom those who are generated from him have received both being and generation), the pastor of those who follow him and are shepherded by him, "the light of those who are illuminated, the principle of consecration of those who are consecrated, the principle of deity of those who are deified, the peace of those who are at variance with each other, the simplicity of those who have been made simple, the unity of those who have been unified, the superessential and ever-existing principle of him who is hidden, or indeed the good imparting of knowledge of him insofar as is permissible and accessible to each one."[2]

---

[2]Dionysius the Areopagite, *Divine Names* 1.3 (PG 3:589C; Suchla, 111.17–112.6, modified).

12b ῎Ετι περὶ θείων ὀνομάτων ἀκριβέστερον

Τὸ θεῖον ἀκατάληπτον ὂν πάντως καὶ ἀνώνυμον ἔσται. Ἀγνοοῦντες οὖν τὴν οὐσίαν αὐτοῦ τῆς οὐσίας αὐτοῦ μὴ ἐκζητήσωμεν ὄνομα· δηλωτικὰ γὰρ τῶν πραγμάτων ἐστὶ τὰ ὀνόματα. Ἀλλ᾽ ἀγαθὸς ὢν ὁ θεὸς καὶ ἐπὶ μεθέξει τῆς ἀγαθότητος αὐτοῦ παραγαγὼν ἡμᾶς ἐκ τοῦ μὴ ὄντος εἰς τὸ εἶναι καὶ γνωστικοὺς ποιήσας ἡμᾶς ὥσπερ οὐ τῆς οὐσίας αὐτοῦ μετέδωκεν, οὕτως οὐδὲ τῆς γνώσεως τῆς οὐσίας αὐτοῦ· ἀδύνατον γὰρ φύσιν τελείως γνῶναι τὴν ὑπερκειμένην φύσιν. Εἰ δὲ καὶ τῶν ὄντων αἱ γνώσεις, τὸ ὑπερούσιον πῶς γνωσθήσεται; Δι᾽ ἄφατον οὖν ἀγαθότητα ηὐδόκησεν ἐκ τῶν καθ᾽ ἡμᾶς ὀνομάζεσθαι, ἵνα μὴ ἀμέτοχοι παντελῶς ὦμεν τῆς αὐτοῦ ἐπιγνώσεως, ἀλλ᾽ ἔχωμεν κἂν ἀμυδρὰν αὐτοῦ ἔννοιαν. Καθὸ μὲν οὖν ἀκατάληπτός ἐστι, καὶ ἀκατονόμαστος· ὡς δὲ πάντων αἴτιος καὶ πάντων τῶν ὄντων τοὺς λόγους καὶ τὰς αἰτίας ἐν ἑαυτῷ προέχων, ἐκ πάντων τῶν ὄντων κατονομάζεται, καὶ ἐκ τῶν ἐναντίων οἷον φωτὸς καὶ σκότους, ὕδατος καὶ πυρός, ἵνα γνῶμεν, ὅτι οὐ ταῦτα κατ᾽ οὐσίαν ἐστίν· ἀλλ᾽ ἔστι μὲν ὑπερούσιος, διὸ καὶ ἀκατονόμαστος, ὡς δὲ πάντων τῶν ὄντων αἴτιος ἐκ πάντων τῶν αἰτιατῶν ὀνομάζεται.— Διὸ τῶν θείων ὀνομάτων τὰ μὲν ἀποφατικῶς λέγεται δηλοῦντα τὸ ὑπερούσιον οἷον ἀνούσιος, ἄχρονος, ἄναρχος, ἀόρατος, οὐχ ὅτι τινὸς ἥττων ἐστὶν ἢ τινος ἐστέρηται (αὐτοῦ γάρ ἐστι τὰ πάντα καὶ ἐξ αὐτοῦ καὶ δι᾽ αὐτοῦ γέγονε καὶ ἐν αὐτῷ συνέστηκεν), ἀλλ᾽ ὅτι πάντων ὑπεροχικῶς τῶν ὄντων ἐξήρηται (οὐδὲν γὰρ τῶν ὄντων, ἀλλ᾽ ὑπὲρ πάντα ἐστί). Τὰ δὲ καταφατικῶς λεγόμενα ὡς αἰτίου τῶν πάντων κατηγορεῖται· ὡς γὰρ αἴτιος πάσης οὐσίας καὶ πάντων τῶν ὄντων λέγεται καὶ ὢν καὶ οὐσία, καὶ ὡς αἴτιος λόγου παντὸς καὶ σοφίας λογικοῦ τε καὶ σοφοῦ λέγεται λόγος καὶ λογικός, σοφία καὶ σοφός, ὁμοίως καὶ νοῦς καὶ νοερός, ζωὴ καὶ ζῶν, δύναμις καὶ δυνατός, καὶ ἐπὶ πάντων τῶν λοιπῶν ὁμοίως, μᾶλλον δὲ ἐκ τῶν τιμιωτέρων καὶ πλησιαζόντων αὐτῷ οἰκειοτέρως ὀνομασθήσεται.

---

[1] This chapter, which Kotter prints in the apparatus in a smaller typeface as an editorial addition, is found in manuscripts KLMN. It draws most of its material from Dionysius the Areopagite *Divine Names* 7.1–4 (PG 3:865B–873A; Suchla, 193–200).

[2] ἀνούσιος (*anousios*): without οὐσία (*ousia*), which is that which characterizes a particular existent.

12b *Further on the divine names with greater precision*[1]

The divine, being incomprehensible, is also necessarily nameless. Therefore, since we do not know its essence, we should not seek out its name, for names are indicative of actual things. But since God is good, and brought us out of non-being into being in order to share in his goodness, made us capable of knowledge, just as he did not communicate his essence, so too he did not communicate the knowledge of his essence. For it is impossible for a nature to have perfect knowledge of the nature that transcends it. And if knowledge is of beings, how will that which is beyond all being be known? Therefore out of his ineffable goodness he graciously consented to be named in accordance with what is familiar to us so that we should not be completely bereft of participation in knowledge of him, but should have some idea of him even if only a faint one. Therefore, although as incomprehensible he is also unnameable, nevertheless as causative of everything and possessing beforehand in himself the principles and causes of all beings, he may be named from all beings—even from opposites such as light and darkness, water and fire, that we might know that he is not these things essentially but is superessential, on which account he is also unnameable—since as causative of all beings he is named after all the beings that are caused.

Consequently, of the divine names some are uttered apophatically to indicate the superessential, such as without substance,[2] timeless, without beginning, and invisible, not because God is inferior to anything or lacks anything (for all things are his and came into being through him and maintain their being in him) but because he supremely transcends all beings (for he is not one among other beings but transcends all beings). Those that are uttered kataphatically are predicated of him as causative of all things.[3] For as causative of every essence and of all beings he is called both being and essence, and as causative of all rationality and wisdom in that which is rational and wise he is called reason and rational, wisdom and wise, and similarly intellect and intellectual, life and living, power and powerful, and likewise

---

[3]"Apophatic" and "kataphatic" are the two fundamental categories of theological language, the latter indicating what may be said positively about God, and the former what may only be said negatively ("what God is not") on account of his transcending all that can be expressed positively about him.

Τιμιώτερα δὲ τὰ ἄυλα τῶν ὑλικῶν καὶ τὰ καθαρὰ τῶν ῥυπαρῶν καὶ τὰ ἅγια τῶν ἐναγῶν, καὶ μᾶλλον αὐτῷ πλησιάζοντα, ἐπεὶ καὶ πλέον μετέχουσιν αὐτοῦ. Οἰκειότερον οὖν μᾶλλον ὀνομασθήσεται ἥλιος καὶ φῶς ἤπερ σκότος, καὶ ἡμέρα ἤπερ νύξ, καὶ ζωὴ ἤπερ θάνατος, καὶ πῦρ καὶ πνεῦμα καὶ ὕδωρ ὡς ζωτικὰ ἤπερ γῆ, καὶ πρὸ πάντων καὶ πλέον ἀγαθότης ἤπερ κακία, —ταὐτὸν δὲ εἰπεῖν—ὢν ἤπερ μὴ ὤν· τὸ γὰρ ἀγαθὸν ὕπαρξις καὶ ὑπάρξεως αἴτιον, τὸ δὲ κακὸν ἀγαθοῦ ἤτοι ὑπάρξεως στέρησις. Καὶ αὗται μὲν αἱ ἀποφάσεις· γλυκυτάτη δὲ καὶ ἡ ἐξ ἀμφοῖν συνάφεια οἷον ἡ ὑπερούσιος οὐσία, ἡ ὑπέρθεος θεότης, ἡ ὑπεράρχιος ἀρχὴ καὶ τὰ τοιαῦτα. Εἰσὶ δὲ καί τινα καταφατικῶς ἐπὶ θεοῦ λεγόμενα δύναμιν ὑπεροχικῆς ἀποφάσεως ἔχοντα οἷον σκότος· οὐχ ὅτι ὁ θεὸς σκότος ἐστίν, ἀλλ' ὅτι οὐκ ἔστι φῶς ἀλλ' ὑπὲρ τὸ φῶς. —Λέγεται μὲν οὖν ὁ θεὸς νοῦς καὶ λόγος καὶ πνεῦμα σοφία τε καὶ δύναμις ὡς τούτων αἴτιος καὶ ὡς ἄυλος καὶ ὡς παντουργὸς καὶ παντοδύναμος. Καὶ ταῦτα κοινῶς ἐπὶ πάσης λέγεται τῆς θεότητος τά τε ἀποφατικῶς καὶ καταφατικῶς λεγόμενα. Καὶ ἐφ' ἑκάστης τῶν τῆς ἁγίας τριάδος ὑποστάσεων ὁμοίως καὶ ὡσαύτως καὶ ἀπαραλείπτως· ὅταν γὰρ ἐννοήσω μίαν τῶν ὑποστάσεων, τέλειον θεὸν αὐτὴν οἶδα, τελείαν οὐσίαν. Ὅταν δὲ συνάψω καὶ συναριθμήσω τὰ τρία, ἕνα θεὸν οἶδα τέλειον· οὐ σύνθετόν ἐστιν ἡ θεότης, ἀλλ' ἐν τρισὶ τελείοις ἓν τέλειον ἀμερὲς καὶ ἀσύνθετον. Ὅταν δὲ τὴν πρὸς ἄλληλα σχέσιν τῶν ὑποστάσεων ἐννοήσω, οἶδα, ὅτι ἐστὶν ὁ πατὴρ ὑπερούσιος ἥλιος, πηγὴ ἀγαθότητος, ἄβυσσος οὐσίας, λόγου, σοφίας, δυνάμεως, φωτός, θεότητος, πηγὴ γεννητικὴ καὶ προβλητικὴ τοῦ ἐν αὐτῇ κρυφίου ἀγαθοῦ. Αὐτὸς μὲν οὖν ἐστι νοῦς, λόγου ἄβυσσος, λόγου γεννήτωρ καὶ διὰ λόγου προβολεὺς ἐκφαντορικοῦ πνεύματος, καὶ ἵνα μὴ πολλὰ λέγω· οὐκ ἔστι τῷ πατρὶ λόγος, σοφία, δύναμις, θέλησις, εἰ μὴ ὁ υἱός, ὅς ἐστιν ἡ μόνη δύναμις τοῦ πατρὸς ἡ προκαταρκτικὴ τῆς τῶν πάντων ποιήσεως. Οὗτος ὡς τελεία ὑπόστασις γεννωμένη, ὡς οἶδεν αὐτός, υἱός ἐστι τε καὶ λέγεται. Τὸ δὲ πνεῦμα τὸ ἅγιον ἐκφαντορικὴ τοῦ κρυφίου τῆς θεότητος δύναμις τοῦ πατρός, ἐκ πατρὸς μὲν δι' υἱοῦ ἐκπορευομένη, ὡς οἶδεν,

---

[4]On evil as the privation of good, see Chapter 18, note 2 (pp. 102–3).

[5]The Father is νοῦς (*nous*, "mind") and thus the source of λόγος (*logos*), here translated both as "reason" and as "word" because *the* Word is implied, but also

with all the rest, or rather he may be named more appropriately from those things that are held in greater esteem and are closer to him. For immaterial things are valued more than material things, pure things more than sordid things, and holy things more than polluted things, and they are closer to him because they participate more fully in him. It is therefore more appropriate that he should be named sun and light rather than darkness, day rather than night, life rather than death, fire and spirit and water, as life-giving, rather than earth, and above all and more importantly, goodness rather than evil, and—which is to say the same thing—being rather than non-being. For the good is existence and causative of existence, whereas evil is privation of goodness or existence.[4] And the negations are the same as these, but the combination of both produces the sweetest names, such as superessential essence, superdivine divinity, superoriginal source, and so on. There are some things that are affirmed of God kataphatically since they have the force of supreme negation, such as darkness, not because God is darkness but because he is not light but transcends light.

God is therefore called mind, reason, spirit, wisdom, and power as causative of these, as immaterial, and as all-working and all-powerful. And these names are applied in common to the whole of the Godhead, both those that are uttered apophatically and those that are uttered kataphatically. And they are also applied to each of the hypostases of the Holy Trinity equally, in like manner, and without exception. For when I think of one of the hypostases, I know that this hypostasis is perfect God, perfect essence. But when I take the three together and place them on the same level, I know that this is a single perfect God. The Godhead is not composite but is a single perfect subsistence, indivisible and uncompounded in three perfect subsistences. When I think of the relation of the hypostases to each other, I know that the Father is superessential sun, source of goodness, abyss of essence, of reason, of wisdom, of power, of light, of deity, begetting and emitting source of the good hidden within it. He is therefore mind, abyss of reason, begetter of Word and through word emitter of revelatory Spirit.[5] And not to speak at too great a

---

"rationality." The Father is the begetter (γεννήτωρ, *gennētōr*) of the Word and the emitter (προβολεύς, *proboleus*) of the Spirit, who are thus distinguished by two different modes of origin.

οὐ γεννητῶς· διὸ καὶ πνεῦμα ἅγιον τὸ τελεσιουργὸν τῆς τῶν ἁπάντων ποιήσεως. Ὅσα οὖν ἁρμόζει αἰτίῳ πατρί, πηγῇ, γεννήτορι, τῷ πατρὶ μόνῳ προσαρμοστέον· ὅσα δὲ αἰτιατῷ, γεννητῷ υἱῷ, λόγῳ, δυνάμει προκαταρκτικῇ, θελήσει, σοφίᾳ, τῷ υἱῷ· ὅσα δὲ αἰτιατῷ, ἐκπορευτῷ, ἐκφαντορικῷ, τελεσιουργικῇ δυνάμει, τῷ ἁγίῳ πνεύματι. Ὁ πατὴρ πηγὴ καὶ αἰτία υἱοῦ καὶ πνεύματος, πατὴρ δὲ μόνου υἱοῦ καὶ προβολεὺς πνεύματος· ὁ υἱὸς υἱός, λόγος, σοφία καὶ δύναμις, εἰκών, ἀπαύγασμα, χαρακτὴρ τοῦ πατρὸς καὶ ἐκ τοῦ πατρός, οὐχ υἱὸς δὲ τοῦ πνεύματος. Τὸ πνεῦμα τὸ ἅγιον πνεῦμα τοῦ πατρὸς ὡς ἐκ πατρὸς ἐκπορευόμενον (οὐδεμία γὰρ ὁρμὴ ἄνευ πνεύματος) καὶ υἱοῦ δὲ πνεῦμα οὐχ ὡς ἐξ αὐτοῦ, ἀλλ᾽ ὡς δι᾽ αὐτοῦ ἐκ τοῦ πατρὸς ἐκπορευόμενον· μόνος γὰρ αἴτιος ὁ πατήρ.

13   *Περὶ τόπου θεοῦ καὶ ὅτι μόνον τὸ θεῖον*
       ἀπερίγραπτον

Τόπος ἐστὶ σωματικὸς πέρας τοῦ περιέχοντος, καθ᾽ ὃ περιέχεται τὸ περιεχόμενον, οἷον ὁ ἀὴρ περιέχει τόδε τὸ σῶμα. Οὐχ ὅλος ὁ περιέχων ἀὴρ τόπος ἐστὶ τοῦ περιεχομένου σώματος, ἀλλὰ τὸ τέλος τοῦ περιέχοντος ἀέρος τὸ ἐφαπτόμενον τοῦ περιεχομένου σώματος· πάντως δέ, ὅτι τὸ περιέχον οὐκ ἔστιν ἐν τῷ περιεχομένῳ.

---

[6] Or "breath"—both "spirit" and "breath" are πνεῦμα (*pneuma*).

[7] This axiom (with an appeal to the authority of John Damascene) came to be frequently cited in works for and against the Latin doctrine of the *Filioque* (for example, by John Bekkos, Bessarion, Mark Eugenikos, and George Gennadios Scholarios).

length, there is no word, wisdom, power, or will in the Father unless it is the Son, who is the only power of the Father, the causative power of the creation of all things. The latter, as a perfect begotten hypostasis, in the manner that he himself knows, is Son and is called such. The Holy Spirit, the revelatory power of the Father's hidden deity, proceeds from the Father through the Son, in the manner that he himself knows, not by begetting. Therefore the Holy Spirit is perfective of the creation of all things. Accordingly, whatever pertains to the Father as cause, source, and begetter, is to be attributed to the Father alone. Whatever pertains to the caused, begotten Son, as word, initial power, will, and wisdom, is to be attributed to the Son. And whatever pertains to the caused, emitted, revelatory, and perfective power is to be attributed to the Holy Spirit. The Father is the source and cause of the Son and the Spirit, being the Father of the Son alone and the emitter of the Spirit. The Son is son, word, wisdom and power, image, radiance, stamp of the Father and from the Father, and is not the son of the Spirit. The Holy Spirit is spirit of the Father as proceeding from the Father (for there is no impulsion without spirit)[6] and is the Son's spirit, not as originating from him but as proceeding through him from the Father. For the Father alone is causative.[7]

13   *On the place of God and that only the divine is uncircumscribed*

Corporeal place is the limit of that which encompasses it, in accordance with which that which is encompassed is encompassed, like the air encompasses the body.[1] It is not all of the surrounding air that is the place of the body that it encompasses but the boundary of the surrounding air that touches the body that it encompasses. This is necessarily so because that which encompasses is not within that which is encompassed.

---

[1]Place (τόπος, *topos*) is one of Aristotle's categories (his main discussion is in *Physics* 4.1–5). The commentators explain place as "the limit of a container in so far as it contains what it contains" (Ammonius, *On Aristotle's Categories* 58.15–17; trans. Cohen and Matthews), or as "conceived as lying around body, and it must accompany a body, if the body is to be body" (Porphyry, *On Aristotle's Categories* 103.20–22; trans. Strange).

Ἔστι δὲ καὶ νοητὸς τόπος, ἔνθα νοεῖται καὶ ἔστιν ἡ νοητὴ καὶ ἀσώματος φύσις, ἔνθα πάρεστι καὶ ἐνεργεῖ καὶ οὐ σωματικῶς περιέχεται ἀλλὰ νοητῶς· οὐ γὰρ ἔχει σχῆμα, ἵνα σωματικῶς περισχεθῇ. Ὁ μὲν οὖν θεὸς ἄυλος ὢν καὶ ἀπερίγραπτος ἐν τόπῳ οὐκ ἔστιν· αὐτὸς γὰρ ἑαυτοῦ τόπος ἐστὶ τὰ πάντα πληρῶν καὶ ὑπὲρ τὰ πάντα ὢν καὶ αὐτὸς συνέχων τὰ πάντα. Λέγεται δὲ ἐν τόπῳ εἶναι. Καὶ λέγεται τόπος θεοῦ, ἔνθα ἔκδηλος ἡ ἐνέργεια αὐτοῦ γένηται. Αὐτὸς μὲν γὰρ διὰ πάντων ἀμιγῶς διήκει καὶ πᾶσι μεταδίδωσι τῆς ἑαυτοῦ ἐνεργείας κατὰ τὴν ἑκάστου ἐπιτηδειότητα καὶ δεκτικὴν δύναμιν, φημὶ δὴ τήν τε φυσικὴν καὶ προαιρετικὴν καθαρότητα· καθαρώτερα γὰρ τὰ ἄυλα τῶν ὑλικῶν καὶ τὰ ἐνάρετα τῶν κακίᾳ συνεζευγμένων. Λέγεται τοιγαροῦν θεοῦ τόπος ὁ πλέον μετέχων τῆς ἐνεργείας καὶ τῆς χάριτος αὐτοῦ. Διὰ τοῦτο ὁ οὐρανὸς αὐτοῦ θρόνος (ἐν αὐτῷ γάρ εἰσιν οἱ ποιοῦντες τὸ θέλημα αὐτοῦ ἄγγελοι καὶ ἀεὶ δοξάζοντες αὐτόν· αὕτη γὰρ αὐτῷ ἀνάπαυσις) καὶ ἡ γῆ ὑποπόδιον τῶν ποδῶν αὐτοῦ (ἐν αὐτῇ γὰρ διὰ σαρκὸς τοῖς ἀνθρώποις συνανεστράφη). Πποὺς δὲ θεοῦ ἡ ἁγία σὰρξ αὐτοῦ διαφόρως ὠνόμασται. Λέγεται καὶ ἡ ἐκκλησία τόπος θεοῦ· τοῦτον γὰρ εἰς δοξολογίαν αὐτοῦ ὥσπερ τι τέμενος ἀφωρίσαμεν, ἐν ᾧ καὶ τὰς πρὸς αὐτὸν ἐντεύξεις ποιούμεθα. Ὁμοίως καὶ οἱ τόποι, ἐν οἷς

---

[2]The notion of intelligible place—νοητὸς τόπος (*noētos topos*), as contrasted with τόπος σωματικός (*topos sōmatikos*)—is of Platonic origin. It is first discussed by Plotinus, who says about the soul's vision of the Good that the Good is not in any place: "but the intelligible place (νοητὸς τόπος, *noētos topos*) is in him, but he is not in another" (*Ennead* 6.7.35, lines 41–2; trans. Armstrong).

[3]The "place of God" is also found in the Septuagint in Ex 24.10–11: "And they saw the place [τὸν τόπον (*ton topon*), translating the *maqom* of the Hebrew] where the God of Israel stood.... And they appeared in the place of God." This is then taken up in the mystical tradition through Evagrius: "If then by the grace of God the intellect both turns away from these [the passions] and puts off the old man, then it will as well see its own constitution at the time of prayer like a sapphire or in the color of heaven, which recalls as well what the scripture names the place of God seen by the elders on Mount Sinai. It calls this the place and the vision of the peace by which one sees in oneself that peace which surpasses every intellect and which guards our heart. For another heaven [ἄλλος οὐρανός, *allos ouranós*—the Hebrew *maqom* also means heaven] is imprinted on a pure heart, the vision of which is both light and the spiritual place, because within it are beheld so many [great things]: the meaning of beings and the holy angels who sojourn with the worthy" (*Ep.* 39 [my trans.]). On "the

There is also intelligible place, within which a nature that is incorporeal and subject to intellectual apprehension is apprehended and exists, within which it is present and active and is encompassed not corporeally but intelligibly, for it has no shape that it might be encompassed corporeally.[2] Thus on the one hand since God is immaterial and uncircumscribed, he is not within a place. For he himself is his own place, filling all things and transcending all things and himself sustaining all things. On the other hand, he is also said to be within a place. And what is called the place of God is where his activity becomes manifest.[3] For he pervades all things without commingling with them and communicates his own energy to all according to the capacity of each and its receptive power—I mean according to the purity belonging to its nature and will.[4] For immaterial things are purer than material things and virtuous things are purer than things that are in a state of evil. Therefore the place of God is said to be that place that shares more fully in his energy and grace. For this reason heaven is his throne (for it is in heaven that the angels are who do his will and ceaselessly glorify him, for that is where his resting place is) and the earth is his footstool (for it is there that he conversed with human beings in the flesh).[5] And in scriptural terms his sacred flesh is called the foot of God.[6] A church is also said to be a place of God,[7] for we have set this place apart for

place of God" in the East Syriac tradition, see Alexander Golitzin, "The Place of the Presence of God: Aphrahat of Persia's Portrait of the Christian Holy Man," in Σύναξις εὐχαριστίας: *Studies in Honor of Archimandrite Aimilianos of Simonos Petras, Mount Athos* (Athens: Indiktos, 2003), 391–447; available online at *https://www.marquette. edu/maqom/aimilianos.html*. (IG)

[4]"Activity" and "energy" in this passage are both renderings of ἐνέργεια (*energeia*).

[5]Is 66.1.

[6]Cf. Ex 24.10 and Is 52.7; "in scriptural terms" is offered here as a translation of διαφόρως (*diaphorōs*, "in a different sense," or "pre-eminently"). John is alluding to the Christological interpretation of Isaiah's "like the feet of a messenger who announces peace."

[7]The use of ἐκκλησία (*ekklēsia*) for a church building is rare but is attested, for example, in John Chrysostom and Cyril of Jerusalem (see Lampe, s.v., section N). Elsewhere (as in Chapter 88) a church building is a ναός (*naos*, "temple").

ἔκδηλος ἡμῖν ἡ αὐτοῦ ἐνέργεια εἴτε διὰ σαρκὸς εἴτε ἄνευ σώματος γέγονε, τόποι θεοῦ λέγονται.

Ἰστέον δέ, ὅτι τὸ θεῖον ἀμερές ἐστιν, ὅλον ὁλικῶς πανταχοῦ ὂν καὶ οὐ μέρος ἐν μέρει σωματικῶς διαιρούμενον, ἀλλ᾽ ὅλον ἐν πᾶσι καὶ ὅλον ὑπὲρ τὸ πᾶν.

Ὁ δὲ ἄγγελος σωματικῶς μὲν ἐν τόπῳ οὐ περιέχεται ὥστε τυποῦσθαι καὶ σχηματίζεσθαι, ὅμως λέγεται εἶναι ἐν τόπῳ διὰ τὸ παρεῖναι νοητῶς καὶ ἐνεργεῖν κατὰ τὴν ἑαυτοῦ φύσιν καὶ μὴ εἶναι ἀλλαχοῦ, ἀλλ᾽ ἐκεῖσε νοητῶς περιγράφεσθαι, ἔνθα καὶ ἐνεργεῖ· οὐ γὰρ δύναται κατὰ ταὐτὸν ἐν διαφόροις τόποις ἐνεργεῖν, μόνου γὰρ θεοῦ ἐστι τὸ πανταχοῦ κατὰ ταὐτὸν ἐνεργεῖν. Ὁ μὲν γὰρ ἄγγελος τάχει φύσεως καὶ τῷ ἑτοίμως ἤγουν ταχέως μεταβαίνειν ἐνεργεῖ ἐν διαφόροις τόποις, τὸ δὲ θεῖον πανταχῇ ὂν καὶ ὑπὲρ τὸ πᾶν πανταχῇ κατὰ ταὐτὸν διαφόρως ἐνεργεῖ μιᾷ καὶ ἁπλῇ ἐνεργείᾳ.

Ἡ δὲ ψυχὴ συνδέδεται τῷ σώματι ὅλη ὅλῳ καὶ οὐ μέρος μέρει καὶ οὐ περιέχεται ὑπ᾽ αὐτοῦ, ἀλλὰ περιέχει αὐτὸ ὥσπερ πῦρ σίδηρον καὶ ἐν αὐτῷ οὖσα τὰς οἰκείας ἐνεργείας ἐνεργεῖ.

Περιγραπτόν ἐστι τὸ τόπῳ ἢ χρόνῳ ἢ καταλήψει περιλαμβανόμενον, ἀπερίγραπτον δὲ τὸ μηδενὶ τούτων περιεχόμενον. Ἀπερίγραπτον μὲν οὖν μόνον ἐστὶ τὸ θεῖον ἄναρχον ὂν καὶ ἀτελεύτητον καὶ πάντα περιέχον καὶ μηδεμιᾷ καταλήψει περιεχόμενον· μόνον γάρ ἐστιν ἀκατάληπτον καὶ ἀόριστον, ὑπ᾽ οὐδενὸς γινωσκόμενον, αὐτὸ δὲ μόνον ἑαυτοῦ θεωρητικόν. Ὁ δὲ ἄγγελος καὶ χρόνῳ περιγράφεται (ἤρξατο γὰρ τοῦ εἶναι) καὶ τόπῳ, εἰ καὶ νοητῶς, ὡς προείπομεν, καὶ καταλήψει (καὶ ἀλλήλων γὰρ τὴν φύσιν ἴσασι, ποσῶς καὶ ὑπὸ κτίστου ὁρίζονται τέλεον), τὰ δὲ σώματα καὶ ἀρχῇ καὶ τέλει καὶ τόπῳ σωματικῷ καὶ καταλήψει.

Ἄτρεπτον παντελῶς τὸ θεῖον καὶ ἀναλλοίωτον· πάντα γὰρ τῇ προγνώσει τὰ οὐκ ἐφ᾽ ἡμῖν προώρισεν, ἕκαστον κατὰ τὸν ἴδιον καὶ πρέποντα καιρὸν καὶ τόπον. Καὶ κατὰ τοῦτο «ὁ πατὴρ οὐδένα

giving glory to God like some sacred precinct, in which we also make our entreaties to him. Similarly, the places in which his activity has become manifest to us, either through the flesh or incorporeally, are said to be places of God.

One should also know that the divine is without parts, since the whole is wholly everywhere and is not divided into parts in a corporeal fashion. On the contrary, the whole is in all things and the whole transcends everything.

An angel is not contained corporeally in a place so that a form or shape may be attributed to it, yet it is said to be in a place through being present spiritually and acting in accordance with its own nature and not being somewhere else, but where it is spiritually circumscribed that is also where it acts. For it is not possible for it to act simultaneously in different places. It belongs only to God to act everywhere simultaneously. For an angel acts in different places by its natural swiftness and its ready, that is to say, its swift, displacement, but since the divine is everywhere and transcends everything, it acts simultaneously in different places by a single simple activity.

The soul is bound in its entirety to the whole body, not partially to a part of the body, and it is not encompassed by it, but encompasses the body like fire encompasses iron, and being in it operates by its own energy.

To be circumscribed is to be limited by place, time, or comprehension, but to be uncircumscribed is to be encompassed by none of these. Therefore to be uncircumscribed belongs only to the divine, since it is without beginning and without end and encompasses all things and is not encompassed by any comprehension.[8] For it alone is incomprehensible and infinite, known by no one; it alone can contemplate itself. An angel is circumscribed by time (for its being had a beginning), by place, even if only spiritually, as we have already said, and by comprehension (for they know each other's nature to some extent and are defined completely by the Creator), whereas bodies

---

[8]Cf. Gregory of Nazianzus, *Oration* 28.10 (PG 36:37C–40A; Moreschini, 666).

κρίνει, τὴν δὲ κρίσιν πᾶσαν δέδωκε τῷ υἱῷ»· ἔκρινε γὰρ ὁ πατὴρ
δηλονότι καὶ ὁ υἱὸς ὡς θεὸς καὶ τὸ πνεῦμα τὸ ἅγιον, αὐτὸς δὲ
ὁ υἱὸς ὡς ἄνθρωπος σωματικῶς καταβήσεται καὶ καθιεῖται ἐπὶ
θρόνου δόξης (σώματος γὰρ περιγραπτοῦ ἡ κατάβασις καὶ ἡ
καθέδρα) καὶ κρινεῖ πᾶσαν τὴν οἰκουμένην ἐν δικαιοσύνῃ.
    Πάντα ἀπέχει θεοῦ, οὐ τόπῳ ἀλλὰ φύσει. Ἐπὶ ἡμῶν φρόνησις
καὶ σοφία καὶ βουλὴ ὡς ἕξις συμβαίνει καὶ ἀποχωρεῖ, οὐ μὴν ἐπὶ
θεοῦ. Ἐπ᾽ αὐτοῦ γὰρ οὐδὲν γίνεται καὶ ἀπογίνεται· ἀναλλοίωτος
γάρ ἐστι καὶ ἄτρεπτος, καὶ οὐ χρὴ συμβεβηκὸς ἐπ᾽ αὐτοῦ λέγειν.
Τὸ ἀγαθὸν ὁ θεὸς σύνδρομον ἔχει τῇ οὐσίᾳ. Ὁ ἐπιθυμῶν ἀεὶ τοῦ
θεοῦ, οὗτος ὁρᾷ αὐτόν. Ἐν πᾶσι γάρ ἐστιν ὁ θεός· τοῦ γὰρ ὄντος
ἐξήπται τὰ ὄντα, καὶ οὐκ ἔστιν εἶναί τι, εἰ μὴ ἐν τῷ ὄντι τὸ εἶναι
ἔχοι, ὅτι πᾶσι μὲν ἐγκέκραται ὁ θεὸς ὡς συνέχων τὴν φύσιν, τῇ
δὲ ἁγίᾳ αὐτοῦ σαρκὶ ὁ θεὸς λόγος καθ᾽ ὑπόστασιν ἡνώθη καὶ
κατεμίχθη ἀσυγχύτως πρὸς τὸ ἡμέτερον. Οὐδεὶς ὁρᾷ τὸν πατέρα
εἰ μὴ ὁ υἱὸς καὶ τὸ πνεῦμα.
    Βούλησις καὶ σοφία καὶ δύναμις ὁ υἱός ἐστι τοῦ πατρός·
οὐ χρὴ γὰρ λέγειν ἐπὶ θεοῦ ποιότητα, ἵνα μὴ σύνθετον αὐτὸν
εἴπωμεν ἐξ οὐσίας καὶ ποιότητος. Ὁ υἱὸς ἐκ τοῦ πατρός ἐστι καὶ
πάντα, ὅσα ἔχει, ἐξ αὐτοῦ ἔχει. Διὸ οὐ δύναται ποιεῖν ἀφ᾽ ἑαυτοῦ
οὐδέν· οὐ γὰρ ἔχει ἰδιάζουσαν ἐνέργειαν παρὰ τὸν πατέρα.
    Ὅτι φύσει ἀόρατος ὁ θεός, ὁρατὸς ταῖς ἐνεργείαις γίνεται ἐκ
τῆς τοῦ κόσμου συστάσεως καὶ κυβερνήσεως γινωσκόμενος.
    Εἰκὼν τοῦ πατρὸς ὁ υἱός, καὶ υἱοῦ τὸ πνεῦμα, δι᾽ οὗ Χριστὸς
ἐνοικῶν ἀνθρώπῳ δίδωσιν αὐτῷ τὸ κατ᾽ εἰκόνα.
    Θεὸς τὸ πνεῦμα τὸ ἅγιον, μέσον ἀγεννήτου καὶ γεννητοῦ καὶ
δι᾽ υἱοῦ τῷ πατρὶ συναπτόμενον· πνεῦμα θεοῦ λέγεται, πνεῦμα
Χριστοῦ, νοῦς Χριστοῦ, πνεῦμα κυρίου, αὐτοκύριος, πνεῦμα

---

[9]Jn 5.22.
[10]Ps 9.9; Mt 25.31.
[11]Gregory of Nyssa, *Catechetical Discourse* 25 (PG 45:65C–68A; Green, 116–17).
Gregory, followed by John, is alluding here to God's self-declaration as ὁ ὤν (*ho ōn*),
"He who is" (Ex 3.14).

are circumscribed by their beginning and end, by their corporeal place, and by their comprehension.

The divine is utterly immutable and unchangeable, for everything that is not in our power it preordained by its foreknowledge, each according to its own proper time and place. And that is why "the Father judges no one but has given all judgement to the Son."[9] For manifestly the Father has judged, and so has the Son as God and the Holy Spirit, but the Son himself will descend corporeally as a human being and will sit on a throne of glory (for descent and sitting belong to a circumscribed body) and will judge the whole world in righteousness.[10]

All things are far from God, not by place but by nature. In our case, prudence, wisdom, and will come and go as states of mind, but this is not so with God. In his case nothing begins to be or ceases to be, for he is unchangeable and immutable and it is incorrect to speak of an accident in his case. God has the good as concomitant to his essence. Whoever always longs for God will see him. For God is in all things, "for the things that *are* depend on him who *is*,"[11] and nothing exists unless it has its being in him who is, but God penetrates all things because he sustains their nature, whereas the divine Word has been united hypostatically with his holy flesh and has been mingled without confusion with what belongs to us. No one sees the Father except the Son and the Spirit.[12]

The Son is the will, wisdom, and power of the Father. One must not attribute quality to God, in order to avoid saying that he is composite, consisting of substance and quality. The Son is from the Father and "all that he has" he has from him.[13] Therefore he can do nothing on his own account.[14] For he has no activity proper to him apart from the Father.

[12]Cf. Jn 6.46.
[13]Jn 16.15.
[14]Cf. Jn 5.30.

υἱοθεσίας, ἀληθείας, ἐλευθερίας, σοφίας (καὶ γὰρ ποιητικὸν τούτων ἁπάντων), πάντα τῇ οὐσίᾳ πληροῦν, πάντα συνέχον, πληρωτικὸν κόσμου κατὰ τὴν οὐσίαν, ἀχώρητον κόσμῳ κατὰ τὴν δύναμιν.

Θεός ἐστιν ἀίδιος οὐσία καὶ ἀπαράλλακτος, δημιουργικὴ τῶν ὄντων, εὐσεβεῖ συνειδήσει προσκυνουμένη.

Θεὸς καὶ πατὴρ ὁ ὢν ἀεὶ ἀγέννητος, ὡς μὴ ἔκ τινος γεννηθείς, γεννήσας δὲ υἱὸν συναΐδιον. Θεὸς καὶ υἱός ἐστιν ὁ ὢν ἀεὶ σὺν τῷ πατρί, ἀχρόνως καὶ ἀϊδίως καὶ ἀρρεύστως καὶ ἀπαθῶς καὶ ἀδιαστάτως ἐξ αὐτοῦ γεγεννημένος. Θεὸς τὸ πνεῦμα τὸ ἅγιόν ἐστι, δύναμις ἁγιαστική, ἐνυπόστατος, ἐκ τοῦ πατρὸς ἀδιαστάτως ἐκπορευομένη καὶ ἐν υἱῷ ἀναπαυομένη, ὁμοούσιος πατρὶ καὶ υἱῷ.

Λόγος ἐστὶν ὁ οὐσιωδῶς τῷ πατρὶ ἀεὶ συμπαρών. Λόγος πάλιν ἐστὶ καὶ ἡ φυσικὴ τοῦ νοῦ κίνησις, καθ᾿ ἣν κινεῖται καὶ νοεῖ καὶ λογίζεται οἱονεὶ φῶς αὐτοῦ ὢν καὶ ἀπαύγασμα. Λόγος πάλιν ἐστὶν ὁ ἐνδιάθετος ὁ ἐν καρδίᾳ λαλούμενος. Καὶ πάλιν λόγος ἐστὶν ἄγγελος νοήματος. Ὁ μὲν οὖν θεὸς λόγος οὐσιώδης τέ ἐστι καὶ ἐνυπόστατος, οἱ δὲ λοιποὶ τρεῖς λόγοι δυνάμεις εἰσὶ τῆς ψυχῆς οὐκ ἐν ἰδίᾳ ὑποστάσει θεωρούμενοι, ὧν ὁ μὲν πρῶτος τοῦ νοῦ φυσικόν ἐστι γέννημα ἐξ αὐτοῦ ἀεὶ φυσικῶς πηγαζόμενον, ὁ δεύτερος δὲ λέγεται ἐνδιάθετος, ὁ δὲ τρίτος προφορικός.

---

[15]Cf. Wis 13.5; Rom 1.20.
[16]2 Cor 4.4.
[17]Cf. John Damascene, *On the Divine Images* 3.18 (Louth, 96–97) and Louth's note 61 on the psychological image of the Trinity in the Byzantine tradition.
[18]1 Cor 2.11.
[19]Rom 8.9.
[20]1 Cor 2.16.
[21]Wis 1.7.
[22]2 Cor 3.17.

Seeing that God is invisible by nature, he becomes visible by his operations, being known from the ordering and government of the universe.[15]

The Father's image is the Son,[16] and the Son's is the Spirit, through whom Christ gives to human beings that which is according to the image when he dwells within them.

The Holy Spirit is God, the middle term between the Unbegotten and the Begotten and united through the Son with the Father.[17] He is called Spirit of God,[18] Spirit of Christ,[19] mind of Christ,[20] Spirit of the Lord,[21] very Lord,[22] Spirit of adoption,[23] of truth,[24] of freedom,[25] and of wisdom[26] (for he is productive of all these) who fills all things by his essence, sustains all things, fills the world with regard to essence but is uncontained by the world with regard to power.[27]

God is eternal and changeless essence, which is creative of all that exists and is worshiped with a devout mind.

He who is eternally unbegotten since he was not begotten from anyone, and who begat a coeternal Son, is God and Father. The Son, who is eternally with the Father and has been begotten from him timelessly, everlastingly, without flux, without passion, and without intermission, is also God. The Holy Spirit—a power that sanctifies, subsists as a hypostasis, proceeds from the Father without intermission, and rests in the Son, and is consubstantial with the Father and the Son—is God.

He who is essentially always present with the Father is Word. Again, a word is also the natural movement of the mind, by which it moves, thinks, and reasons, as if it were its light and radiance. Again, a word is that which is inward and is spoken in the heart. And again, a word is a messenger of thought. Now God the Word is essential

[23]Rom 8.15.
[24]Jn 14.17; 15.26.
[25]2 Cor 3.17.
[26]Is 11.2.
[27]This paragraph on the Holy Spirit summarizes Gregory of Nazianzus, *Oration* 31.29 (PG 36:165B–168B; Moreschini, 774). The expression, "middle term between the Unbegotten and the Begotten," is from *Oration* 31.8 (PG 36:141B; Moreschini, 752), where Gregory discusses the mystery of the Spirit's procession.

Τὸ πνεῦμα νοεῖται πολλαχῶς· Τὸ ἅγιον πνεῦμα· λέγονται δὲ
καὶ αἱ δυνάμεις τοῦ πνεύματος τοῦ ἁγίου πνεύματα· πνεῦμα καὶ
ὁ ἄγγελος ὁ ἀγαθός· πνεῦμα καὶ ὁ δαίμων· πνεῦμα καὶ ἡ ψυχή·
ἔστι δέ, ὅτε καὶ ὁ νοῦς πνεῦμα λέγεται· πνεῦμα καὶ ὁ ἄνεμος καὶ
ὁ ἀήρ.

14   Τὰ ἰδιώματα τῆς θείας φύσεως

Τὸ ἄκτιστον, τὸ ἄναρχον, τὸ ἀθάνατον καὶ ἀπέραντον καὶ αἰώνιον,
τὸ ἄϋλον, τὸ ἀγαθόν, τὸ δημιουργικόν, τὸ δίκαιον, τὸ φωτιστικόν,
τὸ ἄτρεπτον, τὸ ἀπαθές, τὸ ἀπερίγραπτον, τὸ ἀχώρητον,
τὸ ἀπεριόριστον, τὸ ἀόριστον, τὸ ἀσώματον, τὸ ἀόρατον, τὸ
ἀπερινόητον, τὸ ἀνενδεές, τὸ αὐτοκρατὲς καὶ αὐτεξούσιον,
τὸ παντοκρατορικόν, τὸ ζωοδοτικόν, τὸ παντοδύναμον, τὸ
ἀπειροδύναμον, τὸ ἁγιαστικὸν καὶ μεταδοτικόν, τὸ περιέχειν καὶ
συνέχειν τὰ σύμπαντα καὶ πάντων προνοεῖσθαι· πάντα ταῦτα καὶ
τοιαῦτα φύσει ἔχει οὐκ ἄλλοθεν εἰληφυῖα, ἀλλ᾽ αὐτὴ μεταδιδοῦσα
παντὸς ἀγαθοῦ τοῖς οἰκείοις ποιήμασι κατὰ τὴν ἑκάστου δεκτικὴν
δύναμιν.

Ἡ ἐν ἀλλήλαις τῶν ὑποστάσεων μονή τε καὶ ἵδρυσις·
ἀδιάστατοι γὰρ αὗται καὶ ἀνεκφοίτητοι ἀλλήλων εἰσὶν ἀσύγχυτον
ἔχουσαι τὴν ἐν ἀλλήλαις περιχώρησιν, οὐχ ὥστε συναλείφεσθαι

---

[28]This paragraph on the different senses of λόγος (*logos*) draws on Anastasius
of Sinai, *Hodēgos* 2 (PG 89:77A), some of which is reproduced in *Doctrina Patrum*,
Diekamp, 263.

[29]John now lists the different meanings of πνεῦμα (*pneuma*).

[30]This seems to refer to the "seven spirits" of Rev 1.4, 3.1, 4.5, 5.6. While one
exegetical option is to identify these seven spirits with the tradition of seven archangels, others interpret them as the Holy Spirit (in conjunction with Is 11.2–3). Andrew

and actually subsistent, whereas the other three kinds of word are powers of the soul that are not contemplated in their own hypostasis. The first of these is a natural product of the mind and always springs from it naturally. The second is called the immanent word. The third is the uttered word.[28]

Spirit is conceived of in many ways.[29] There is the Holy Spirit. The powers of the Holy Spirit are also called spirits.[30] A good angel is also a spirit, so too is a demon. The soul is also a spirit. There are also times when the mind is called spirit. The wind and the air are also spirit.

14   *The properties of the divine nature*

Uncreatedness, absence of source, immortality and boundlessness and eternity, immateriality, goodness, creativity, justice, irradiancy, immutability, impassibility, uncircumscribability, uncontainability, infinitude, indefinability, incorporeality, invisibility, incomprehensibility, self-sufficiency, independence and freedom of will, all-sovereignty, life-givingness, all-powerfulness, infinite powerfulness, the power of sanctifying and imparting, the power of containing and sustaining all things and of exercising providential care over all things—all these and similar properties the divine nature possesses naturally. It has not received them from elsewhere but itself shares every good with its own creatures according to the capacity of each to receive them.

The abiding and settling of the hypostases is in each other, for they are without separation or division from each other, their mutual interpenetration being without confusion with the result that they

of Caesarea (second half of the sixth century) allows for both interpretations: "It is possible to understand the seven spirits as the seven angels who were appointed to govern the churches. . . . By the same token, this may be understood differently . . . *the seven spirits* <meaning> the activities of the Life-giving Spirit, following Christ God, who became man for our sake." Andrew of Caesarea, *Commentary on the Apocalypse*, trans. Eugenia Scarvelis Constantinou, FOC 123 (Washington: The Catholic University of America, 2011), 57. (IG)

ἢ συγχεῖσθαι, ἀλλ᾽ ὥστε ἔχεσθαι ἀλλήλων. Υἱὸς γὰρ ἐν πατρὶ καὶ πνεύματι, καὶ πνεῦμα ἐν πατρὶ καὶ υἱῷ, καὶ πατὴρ ἐν υἱῷ καὶ πνεύματι, μηδεμιᾶς γινομένης συναλοιφῆς ἢ συμφύρσεως ἢ συγχύσεως. Καὶ τὸ ἓν καὶ ταὐτὸν τῆς κινήσεως· ἓν γὰρ ἔξαλμα καὶ μία κίνησις τῶν τριῶν ὑποστάσεων, ὅπερ ἐπὶ τῆς κτιστῆς φύσεως θεωρηθῆναι ἀδύνατον.

Καὶ ὅτι ἡ θεία ἔλλαμψις καὶ ἐνέργεια μία οὖσα καὶ ἁπλῆ καὶ ἀμερὴς καὶ ἀγαθοειδῶς ἐν τοῖς μεριστοῖς ποικιλλομένη καὶ τούτοις πᾶσι τὰ τῆς οἰκείας φύσεως συστατικὰ νέμουσα μένει ἁπλῆ, πληθυνομένη μὲν ἐν τοῖς μεριστοῖς ἀμερίστως καὶ τὰ μεριστὰ πρὸς τὴν ἑαυτῆς ἁπλότητα συνάγουσα καὶ ἐπιστρέφουσα (πάντα γὰρ αὐτῆς ἐφίεται καὶ ἐν αὐτῇ ἔχει τὴν ὕπαρξιν)· καὶ αὐτὴ τοῖς πᾶσι τὸ εἶναι καθὼς ἔχει φύσεως μεταδίδωσι· καὶ αὐτή ἐστι τῶν ὄντων τὸ εἶναι καὶ τῶν ζώντων ἡ ζωὴ καὶ τῶν λογικῶς ὄντων ὁ λόγος καὶ τῶν νοερῶς ὄντων ἡ νόησις, αὐτὴ ὑπὲρ νοῦν οὖσα καὶ ὑπὲρ λόγον καὶ ὑπὲρ ζωὴν καὶ ὑπὲρ οὐσίαν.

Ἔτι δὲ καὶ τὸ διὰ πάντων διήκειν ἀμιγῶς, δι᾽ αὐτῆς δὲ οὐδέν. Ἔτι καὶ τὸ ἁπλῇ γνώσει γινώσκειν τὰ πάντα καὶ πάντα τῷ θείῳ καὶ παντεποπτικῷ καὶ ἀύλῳ αὐτῆς ὄμματι ἁπλῶς καθορᾶν, τά τε ἐνεστῶτα τά τε παρεληλυθότα καὶ τὰ μέλλοντα πρὶν γενέσεως αὐτῶν· τὸ ἀναμάρτητον καὶ ἀφιέναι ἁμαρτίας καὶ σῴζειν· καὶ ὅτι πάντα μέν, ὅσα θέλει, δύναται, οὐχ ὅσα δὲ δύναται, θέλει· δύναται γὰρ ἀπολέσαι τὸν κόσμον, οὐ θέλει δέ.

---

[1]"Mutual interpenetration" renders τὴν ἐν ἀλλήλαις περιχώρησιν (*tēn allēlais perichōrēsin*)—"mutual perichoresis." John Damascene is the first to apply the term perichoresis to the mutual relations of the Trinity. See Chapter 8, note 35 (p. 81), above, and more fully, Richard Cross, "Perichoresis, Deification, and Christological Predication in John of Damascus," *Medieval Studies* 62 (2000): 69–124; Louth, *St John Damascene*, 112–13; Charles C. Twombly, *Perichoresis and Personhood: God, Christ,*

are not blended or confounded but that they cleave to each other.[1]
For the Son is in the Father and the Spirit, and the Spirit is in the
Father and the Son, and the Father is in the Son and the Spirit,
without there being any blending, or mixing, or confusion. And
what belongs to the movement is one and the same, for there is one
springing forth and one movement of the three hypostases, which is
something that it is impossible to observe in created nature.

And because the divine radiance and energy is one, simple, and
indivisible, even though it is benevolently varied in divisible things
and distributes to all these that which sustains their own nature, it
remains simple, multiplied indivisibly in divisible things and leading
and returning divisible things back to its own simplicity (for all things
yearn for this unity and have their existence in it). And it transmits
being to all things in accordance with their nature, and itself is the
being of what exists,[2] the life of what is alive, the rationality of what
is rational, and the intellect of what is intellectual, since it is beyond
mind, beyond rationality, beyond life, and beyond essence.

Moreover, there is the property of its pervading all things without mingling with them, whereas nothing mingles with it. And
again, there are its properties of knowing all things by a simple act of
knowledge, and seeing into all things clearly by its divine, all-survey-
ing, and immaterial eye, those that belong to the present, the past,
and the future before they come to be. And there is its property of
sinlessness and its remitting sin and saving. And it can do whatever
it wills; it does not will whatever it can do. For it is able to destroy
the world but does not will to do so.

---

and Salvation in John of Damascus, Princeton Theological Monograph Series 216
(Eugene, Oregon: Pickwick Publications, 2015).
    [2]"The being of what exists," or "the being of beings" (τῶν ὄντων τὸ εἶναι, *tōn
ontōn to einai*), is an expression previously found only in Alexander of Aphrodisias in
his commentaries on Aristotle. It could be translated as "the 'isness' of things."

15 *Περὶ αἰῶνος*

Αὐτὸς τοὺς αἰῶνας ἐποίησεν, ὁ ὑπάρχων πρὸ τῶν αἰώνων, πρὸς ὅν φησιν ὁ θεῖος Δαυίδ· «Ἀπὸ τοῦ αἰῶνος σὺ εἶ», καὶ ὁ θεῖος ἀπόστολος· «Δι' οὗ καὶ τοὺς αἰῶνας ἐποίησε».

Χρὴ τοίνυν γινώσκειν, ὅτι τὸ τοῦ αἰῶνος ὄνομα πολύσημόν ἐστι, πλεῖστα γὰρ σημαίνει· αἰὼν γὰρ λέγεται καὶ ἡ ἑκάστου τῶν ἀνθρώπων ζωή. Λέγεται πάλιν αἰὼν καὶ ὁ τῶν χιλίων ἐτῶν χρόνος. Πάλιν λέγεται αἰὼν ὅλος ὁ παρὼν βίος, καὶ αἰὼν ὁ μέλλων ὁ μετὰ τὴν ἀνάστασιν ὁ ἀτελεύτητος. Λέγεται πάλιν αἰὼν οὐ χρόνος οὐδὲ χρόνου τι μέρος ἡλίου φορᾷ καὶ δρόμῳ μετρούμενον ἤγουν δι' ἡμερῶν καὶ νυκτῶν συνιστάμενον, ἀλλὰ τὸ συμπαρεκτεινόμενον τοῖς ἀιδίοις οἷόν τι χρονικὸν κίνημα καὶ διάστημα· ὅπερ γὰρ τοῖς ὑπὸ χρόνον ὁ χρόνος, τοῦτο τοῖς ἀιδίοις ἐστὶν αἰών.

Λέγονται μὲν οὖν ἑπτὰ αἰῶνες τοῦ κόσμου τούτου ἤγουν ἀπὸ τῆς οὐρανοῦ καὶ γῆς κτίσεως μέχρι τῆς κοινῆς τῶν ἀνθρώπων συντελείας τε καὶ ἀναστάσεως. Ἔστι μὲν γὰρ συντέλεια μερικὴ ὁ ἑκάστου θάνατος· ἔστι δὲ καὶ κοινὴ καὶ παντελὴς συντέλεια, ὅτε μέλλει ἡ κοινὴ γίνεσθαι τῶν ἀνθρώπων ἀνάστασις. Ὄγδοος δὲ αἰὼν ὁ μέλλων.

Πρὸ δὲ τῆς τοῦ κόσμου συστάσεως, ὅτε οὐδὲ ἥλιος ἦν διαιρῶν ἡμέραν ἀπὸ νυκτός, οὐκ ἦν αἰὼν μετρητός, ἀλλὰ τὸ συμπαρεκτεινόμενον τοῖς ἀιδίοις οἷόν τι χρονικὸν κίνημα καὶ

---

[1] The aeons are specific ages, or in the singular, "eternity." John goes on immediately to discuss the multiple meaning of aeon.
[2] Ps 89.2.
[3] Heb 1.2.
[4] Gregory of Nazianzus, *Oration* 38.8 (PG 36:320B; Moreschini, 886).
[5] This seems to refer to the millennial day theory, a spiritual reading of the hexaemeron (the six days of creation) that goes back at least to the second-century *Epistle of Barnabas*. Drawing upon Ps 90.4 (LXX)/2 Pet 3.8 ("with the Lord one day is like a thousand years") the epistle concludes: "the Lord will complete all things in six thousand years, for with him a day indicates a thousand years" (*Barnabas* 15.4; PPS 41:79). Of course, this theory ran into trouble when chiliasm was rejected, and into even more trouble when the Byzantine Anno Mundi (AM) calendar entered the seventh

15   *On the aeon*

It is he who made the aeons,[1] he who existed before the aeons, to whom the divine David says: "From the aeon, you are,"[2] and the divine Apostle: "through whom he also made the aeons."[3]

It is therefore necessary to know that the word "aeon" is polysemic, for it signifies a great many things. For the life of each human being is called an aeon. Again, an aeon is a period of a thousand years. Again, the whole of the present life is called an aeon, and the age to come, the age after the resurrection that will have no end, is also an aeon. Again, an aeon is not time or a portion of time measured by the movement and course of the sun, constituted, that is to say, by days and nights, but is coextensive with the things that are eternal, "like some temporal movement or interval."[4] For what time is to things that are subject to time, aeon is to things that are eternal.

Thus there are said to be seven aeons of this world,[5] that is, from the creation of heaven and earth until the general consummation and resurrection of humanity. For there is a particular consummation that is the death of each human being, and there is a general and complete consummation when the general resurrection is to take place. The future aeon is the eighth.

Before the formation of the world, when there was no sun dividing day from night, there was no measurable aeon; there was only the aeon that is coextensive with the things that are eternal like

millennium. Some were anxious to get rid of such calculations. For example, the chronicler John Malalas (died in the 570s) opposed the other main dating schema—in which 1 AM (the year of the world's creation) was 5508 BC—in order to claim that the crucifixion took place in 6000 AM, and thus the much-mooted end of the sixth millennium had already passed by the time he was writing. In Damascene's time the millennium-day theory had to be modified to allow for seven days/millennia (which also had the benefit of denying chiliasm; cf. the conflation of the Origenist apocatastasis with the millennium in the following paragraph). Something similar can be found in John's contemporary, Germanus of Constantinople (patriarch 715–30), who says: "When the bishop blesses the people, it indicates the second coming of Christ in 6,500 years, through his fingers forming the sign ,ϛφ" [Greek numerals for 6,500] (*Historia mystica* 33; PPS 8:83). (IG)

διάστημα· καὶ κατὰ μὲν τοῦτο εἷς αἰών ἐστι, καθὸ καὶ λέγεται ὁ θεὸς αἰώνιος, ἀλλὰ καὶ προαιώνιος. Καὶ αὐτὸν γὰρ τὸν αἰῶνα αὐτὸς ἐποίησε· μόνος γὰρ ἄναρχος ὢν ὁ θεὸς πάντων αὐτός ἐστι ποιητής, τῶν τε αἰώνων καὶ πάντων τῶν ὄντων. Θεὸν δὲ εἰπὼν δῆλον, ὅτι τὸν πατέρα λέγω καὶ τὸν μονογενῆ αὐτοῦ υἱόν, τὸν κύριον ἡμῶν Ἰησοῦν Χριστόν, καὶ τὸ πνεῦμα αὐτοῦ τὸ πανάγιον, τὸν ἕνα θεὸν ἡμῶν.

Λέγονται δὲ αἰῶνες αἰώνων, καθότι καὶ οἱ τοῦ παρόντος κόσμου ἑπτὰ αἰῶνες πολλοὺς αἰῶνας ἤγουν ζωὰς ἀνθρώπων περιέχουσι καὶ ὁ αἰὼν ὁ εἷς πάντων τῶν αἰώνων ἐστὶ περιεκτικός. Καὶ αἰὼν αἰῶνος λέγεται ὁ νῦν καὶ ὁ μέλλων. Αἰώνιος δὲ ζωὴ καὶ αἰώνιος κόλασις τὸ ἀτελεύτητον τοῦ μέλλοντος δηλοῖ. Οὐδὲ γὰρ μετὰ τὴν ἀνάστασιν ἡμέραις καὶ νυξὶν ὁ χρόνος ἀριθμηθήσεται· ἔσται δὲ μᾶλλον μία ἡμέρα ἀνέσπερος τοῦ ἡλίου τῆς δικαιοσύνης τοῖς δικαίοις φαιδρῶς ἐπιλάμποντος, τοῖς δὲ ἁμαρτωλοῖς νὺξ βαθεῖα ἀπέραντος. Πῶς τοίνυν ὁ τῶν χιλίων ἐτῶν τῆς Ὠριγενιαστικῆς ἀποκαταστάσεως ἀριθμηθήσεται χρόνος; Πάντων οὖν τῶν αἰώνων εἷς ποιητής ἐστιν ὁ θεὸς ὁ καὶ τὰ σύμπαντα δημιουργήσας, ὁ ὑπάρχων πρὸ τῶν αἰώνων.

16 Περὶ δημιουργίας

Ἐπεὶ οὖν ὁ ἀγαθὸς καὶ ὑπεράγαθος θεὸς οὐκ ἠρκέσθη τῇ ἑαυτοῦ θεωρίᾳ, ἀλλ᾿ ὑπερβολῇ ἀγαθότητος εὐδόκησε γενέσθαι τινὰ τὰ εὐεργετηθησόμενα καὶ μεθέξοντα τῆς αὐτοῦ ἀγαθότητος, ἐκ τοῦ μὴ ὄντος εἰς τὸ εἶναι παράγει καὶ δημιουργεῖ τὰ σύμπαντα, ἀόρατά τε καὶ ὁρατά, καὶ τὸν ἐξ ὁρατοῦ καὶ ἀοράτου συγκείμενον

---

[6] Or "ages of ages," as in the liturgical doxology.

[7] The "Origenian apocatastasis," the restoration (apocatastasis) of all things, is based on Origen's exegesis of Paul's teaching that at the end of time all things will be subjected to God through Christ, "so that God may be all in all" (1 Cor 15.28). Origen accordingly held that "at the consummation and restoration of all things" "even bodily nature will receive that highest condition to which nothing more can ever be added" (*On First Principles* 3.6.9, ed. and trans. Behr). Origen's teaching, however, had

some temporal movement or interval. In this sense there is a single aeon, in accordance with which God is said to be aeonial, but also pre-aeonial, for he himself also made this aeon. For since only God is without beginning, it is he who is the maker of all things, both of the aeons and of all that exists. When I speak of God, it is clear that I mean the Father and his only-begotten Son, our Lord Jesus Christ, and his all-holy Spirit—our one God.

We also speak of "aeons of aeons."[6] Just as the seven aeons of the present world contain many aeons, that is, the lives of human beings, so too the single aeon embraces all the aeons. Moreover, now and the future are called "aeon of aeon." And "aeonial life and aeonial punishment" indicate the eternity of what is to come. For after the resurrection, time will not be reckoned by days and nights. Instead, there will be a single day without evening, with the sun of righteousness shining brightly on the righteous, but a deep and infinite night awaiting the sinful. How, therefore, will the thousand years of the Origenian apocatastasis be calculated?[7] God then, who created the universe, who exists before the aeons, is the maker of all the aeons.

16   On creation[1]

Since, then, God who is good and beyond the good was not satisfied with contemplating himself but out of a superabundance of goodness was pleased that things should come into being that would benefit from his goodness and share in it, brings the totality of things into being out of non-being and creates it, both the visible and the invisible, including humanity, which is a combination of visible and invisible. He creates by conceiving mentally, and the mental concept

undergone considerable development by the sixth century, when it was condemned in the anti-Origenist canons of 543 and 553. For a translation and judicious discussion of these canons, see Richard Price, *The Acts of the Council of Constantinople of 553* (Liverpool: Liverpool University Press, 2009), vol. 2, 270–86: Appendix I, The Anti-Origenist Canons (543 and 553).

[1]For a commentary on Chapters 16 to 44, see Louth, *St John Damascene*, 117–44.

ἄνθρωπον. Κτίζει δὲ ἐννοῶν, καὶ τὸ ἐννόημα ἔργον ὑφίσταται λόγῳ συμπληρούμενον καὶ πνεύματι τελειούμενον.

17 Περὶ ἀγγέλων

Αὐτὸς τῶν ἀγγέλων ἐστὶ ποιητὴς καὶ δημιουργὸς ἐκ τοῦ μὴ ὄντος εἰς τὸ εἶναι παραγαγὼν αὐτούς, κατ᾽ οἰκείαν εἰκόνα κτίσας αὐτοὺς φύσιν ἀσώματον, οἷόν τι πνεῦμα ἢ πῦρ ἄυλον, ὥς φησιν ὁ θεῖος Δαυίδ· «Ὁ ποιῶν τοὺς ἀγγέλους αὐτοῦ πνεύματα καὶ τοὺς λειτουργοὺς αὐτοῦ πυρὸς φλόγα,» τὸ κοῦφον καὶ διάπυρον καὶ θερμὸν καὶ τομώτατον καὶ ὀξὺ περὶ τὴν θείαν ἔφεσίν τε καὶ λειτουργίαν διαγράφων καὶ τὸ ἀνωφερὲς αὐτῶν καὶ πάσης ὑλικῆς ἐννοίας ἀπηλλαγμένον.

Ἄγγελος τοίνυν ἐστὶν οὐσία νοερά, ἀεικίνητος, αὐτεξούσιος, ἀσώματος, θεῷ λειτουργοῦσα, κατὰ χάριν ἐν τῇ φύσει τὸ ἀθάνατον εἰληφυῖα, ἧς οὐσίας τὸ εἶδος καὶ τὸν ὅρον μόνος ὁ κτίστης ἐπίσταται. Ἀσώματος δὲ λέγεται καὶ ἄυλος, ὅσον πρὸς ἡμᾶς· πᾶν γὰρ συγκρινόμενον πρὸς θεὸν τὸν μόνον ἀσύγκριτον παχύ τε καὶ ὑλικὸν εὑρίσκεται, μόνον γὰρ ὄντως ἄυλον τὸ θεῖόν ἐστι καὶ ἀσώματον.

Ἔστι τοίνυν φύσις λογικὴ νοερά τε καὶ αὐτεξούσιος, τρεπτὴ κατὰ γνώμην ἤτοι ἐθελότρεπτος· πᾶν γὰρ κτιστὸν καὶ τρεπτόν, μόνον δὲ τὸ ἄκτιστον ἄτρεπτον, καὶ πᾶν λογικὸν αὐτεξούσιον. Ὡς μὲν οὖν λογικὴ καὶ νοερὰ αὐτεξούσιός ἐστιν, ὡς δὲ κτιστὴ τρεπτή, ἔχουσα ἐξουσίαν καὶ μένειν καὶ προκόπτειν ἐν τῷ ἀγαθῷ καὶ ἐπὶ τὸ χεῖρον τρέπεσθαι.

Ἀνεπίδεκτος μετανοίας, ὅτι καὶ ἀσώματος· ὁ γὰρ ἄνθρωπος διὰ τὴν τοῦ σώματος ἀσθένειαν τῆς μετανοίας ἔτυχεν. Ἀθάνατος οὐ φύσει, ἀλλὰ χάριτι· πᾶν γὰρ τὸ ἀρξάμενον καὶ τελευτᾷ κατὰ

subsists as a work brought to completion by the Word and perfected by the Spirit.[2]

17   On angels

The same is the maker and creator of angels, bringing them out of non-being into being, having created them after his own image as an incorporeal nature, like some spirit or immaterial fire, as the divine David says: "who makes his angels spirits and his ministers a fiery flame,"[1] describing their lightness, ardor, warmth, extreme sharpness, and acuity with regard to their longing for God and ministry to him and their sublimity and deliverance from all material thought.

An angel is therefore a substance that is intellectual, always moving, possessing free will, incorporeal, ministering to God, whose nature has by grace received immortality, and the form and determining of whose essence only the Creator knows.[2] An angel is said to be incorporeal and immaterial in relation to us. For everything in comparison with God, who alone is incomparable, is dense and material, for only the divine is truly immaterial and incorporeal.

An angel, then, is a rational nature possessing intellect and free will that is mutable or changeable with regard to the will of choice. For everything created is also mutable, only that which is uncreated being immutable, and everything rational possesses free will. Therefore as rational and intellectual, the angelic nature possesses free will, but as created it is mutable, since it has the power to choose and either abide in the good and make progress in it or take a turn for the worse.

An angel is incapable of repentance because it is incorporeal, for a human being has the possibility of repentance on account of the

[2]Cf. Gregory of Nazianzus, *Oration* 38.9 (PG 36:320C–321A; Moreschini, 886) and 45.5 (PG 36:629AB; Moreschini, 1138). On the Christian tradition of creation *ex nihilo*, see George Karamanolis, *The Philosophy of Early Christianity*, 2nd ed. (London and New York: Routledge, 2021), 64–74, 84–88.

[1]Ps 103.4.
[2]The first part of the definition is from *Doctrina Patrum*, Diekamp, 250.1–2.

φύσιν. Μόνος δὲ ὁ θεὸς ἀεὶ ὤν, μᾶλλον δὲ καὶ ὑπὲρ τὸ ἀεί· οὐχ ὑπὸ χρόνον γάρ, ἀλλ' ὑπὲρ χρόνον ὁ τῶν χρόνων ποιητής.

Φῶτα δεύτερα νοερὰ ἐκ τοῦ πρώτου καὶ ἀνάρχου φωτὸς τὸν φωτισμὸν ἔχοντα, οὐ γλώσσης καὶ ἀκοῆς δεόμενα, ἀλλ' ἄνευ λόγου προφορικοῦ μεταδιδόντα ἀλλήλοις τὰ ἴδια νοήματα καὶ βουλήματα.

Διὰ τοῦ λόγου τοίνυν ἐκτίσθησαν πάντες οἱ ἄγγελοι καὶ ὑπὸ τοῦ ἁγίου πνεύματος διὰ τοῦ ἁγιασμοῦ ἐτελειώθησαν κατ' ἀναλογίαν τῆς ἀξίας καὶ τῆς τάξεως τοῦ φωτισμοῦ καὶ τῆς χάριτος μετέχοντες.

Περιγραπτοί· ὅτε γάρ εἰσιν ἐν τῷ οὐρανῷ, οὐκ εἰσὶν ἐν τῇ γῇ, καὶ εἰς τὴν γῆν ὑπὸ τοῦ θεοῦ ἀποστελλόμενοι οὐκ ἐναπομένουσιν ἐν τῷ οὐρανῷ. Οὐ περιορίζονται δὲ ὑπὸ τειχῶν καὶ θυρῶν καὶ κλείθρων καὶ σφραγίδων· ἀόριστοι γάρ. Ἀορίστους δὲ λέγω· οὐ γάρ, καθὸ εἰσιν, ἐπιφαίνονται τοῖς ἀξίοις, οἷς ὁ θεὸς φαίνεσθαι αὐτοὺς θελήσει, ἀλλ' ἐν μετασχηματισμῷ, καθὼς δύνανται οἱ ὁρῶντες ὁρᾶν. «Ἀόριστον γάρ ἐστι φύσει καὶ κυρίως μόνον τὸ ἄκτιστον· πᾶν γὰρ κτίσμα ὑπὸ τοῦ κτίσαντος αὐτὸ θεοῦ ὁρίζεται».

Ἔξωθεν τῆς οὐσίας τὸν ἁγιασμὸν ἐκ τοῦ ἁγίου πνεύματος ἔχοντες, διὰ τῆς θείας χάριτος προφητεύοντες, μὴ γάμου χρῄζοντες, ἐπειδήπερ μὴ εἰσι θνητοί.

Νόες δὲ ὄντες ἐν νοητοῖς καὶ τόποις εἰσίν, οὐ σωματικῶς περιγραφόμενοι (οὐ γὰρ σωματικῶς κατὰ φύσιν σχηματίζονται οὐδὲ τριχῇ εἰσι διαστατοί), ἀλλὰ τῷ νοητῶς παρεῖναι καὶ ἐνεργεῖν, ἔνθα ἂν προσταχθῶσι, καὶ μὴ δύνασθαι κατὰ ταὐτὸν ὧδε κἀκεῖσε εἶναι καὶ ἐνεργεῖν.

Εἴτε ἴσοι κατ' οὐσίαν εἴτε διαφέροντες ἀλλήλων, οὐκ ἴσμεν. Μόνος δὲ ὁ ποιήσας αὐτοὺς θεὸς ἐπίσταται, ὁ καὶ τὰ πάντα εἰδώς. Διαφέροντες δὲ ἀλλήλων τῷ φωτισμῷ καὶ τῇ στάσει, εἴτε πρὸς τὸν φωτισμὸν τὴν στάσιν ἔχοντες ἢ πρὸς τὴν στάσιν τοῦ φωτισμοῦ μετέχοντες, καὶ ἀλλήλους φωτίζοντες διὰ τὸ

weakness of the body. An angel is immortal not by nature but by grace, for everything that has a beginning naturally has an end. Only God exists eternally or rather, he is beyond eternity, for he who is the creator of time is not subject to time but transcends it.

The angels are secondary spiritual lights that possess their illumination from the first light that has no beginning. They have no need of speech or hearing but communicate their own thoughts and intentions to each other without verbal utterance.

All the angels, then, were created by the agency of the Word and were perfected through sanctification by the Holy Spirit in accordance with the dignity and rank of the illumination and grace in which they share.

They are circumscribed, for when they are in heaven, they are not on earth, and when they are sent to the earth by God, they do not remain in heaven. They are not confined by walls and doors, locks and seals, for they are not limited. I say not limited, because they do not appear to the worthy, to those to whom God wills them to appear, as they really are, but in a different form, in such a way that those who behold them can see them. "For properly speaking, only the uncreated is unlimited by nature, for every created thing is limited by God who created it."[3]

They have the sanctification of their essence from outside, from the Holy Spirit, prophesy by divine grace, and do not need marriage, precisely because they are not mortal.

Being intellects, they are also in intellectual places, since they are not circumscribed corporeally (for they do not have by nature a bodily form, nor are they extended three-dimensionally), but they are present and active intellectually where they are assigned to be and cannot be present and active in two different places simultaneously.

Whether they are equal or differ from each other with regard to essence we do not know. Only God who created them and who knows all things has knowledge of this. [But we do know that] they

[3] *Doctrina Patrum*, Diekamp, 252.23–24.

ὑπερέχον τῆς τάξεως ἢ φύσεως. Δῆλον δέ, ὡς οἱ ὑπερέχοντες τοῖς ὑποβεβηκόσι μεταδιδόασι τοῦ τε φωτισμοῦ καὶ τῆς γνώσεως.

Ἰσχυροὶ καὶ ἕτοιμοι πρὸς τὴν τοῦ θείου θελήματος ἐκπλήρωσιν καὶ πανταχοῦ εὐθέως εὑρισκόμενοι, ἔνθα ἂν ἡ θεία κελεύσῃ ἐπίνευσις, τάχει φύσεως, καὶ φυλάττοντες μέρη τῆς γῆς, καὶ ἐθνῶν καὶ τόπων προϊστάμενοι, καθὼς ὑπὸ τοῦ δημιουργοῦ ἐτάχθησαν, καὶ τὰ καθ᾽ ἡμᾶς οἰκονομοῦντες καὶ βοηθοῦντες ἡμῖν· πάντως δὲ ὅτι κατὰ τὸ θεῖον θέλημά τε καὶ πρόσταγμα ὑπὲρ ἡμᾶς ὄντες ἀεί τε περὶ θεὸν ὑπάρχοντες.

Δυσκίνητοι πρὸς τὸ κακὸν ἀλλ᾽ οὐκ ἀκίνητοι, νῦν δὲ καὶ ἀκίνητοι, οὐ φύσει ἀλλὰ χάριτι καὶ τῇ τοῦ μόνου ἀγαθοῦ προσεδρείᾳ. Ὁρῶντες θεὸν κατὰ τὸ ἐφικτὸν αὐτοῖς καὶ ταύτην τροφὴν ἔχοντες. Ὑπὲρ ἡμᾶς ὄντες ὡς ἀσώματοι καὶ παντὸς σωματικοῦ πάθους ἀπηλλαγμένοι, οὐ μὴν ἀπαθεῖς· μόνον γὰρ τὸ θεῖον ἀπαθές ἐστι. Μετασχηματίζονται δέ, πρὸς ὅπερ ἂν ὁ δεσπότης κελεύσῃ θεός, καὶ οὕτω τοῖς ἀνθρώποις ἐπιφαίνονται καὶ τὰ θεῖα αὐτοῖς ἀποκαλύπτουσι μυστήρια. Ἐν οὐρανῷ διατρίβουσι καὶ ἓν ἔργον ἔχουσιν ὑμνεῖν τὸν θεὸν καὶ λειτουργεῖν τῷ θείῳ αὐτοῦ θελήματι.

Καθὼς δὲ ὁ ἁγιώτατος καὶ ἱερώτατος καὶ θεολογικώτατός φησι Διονύσιος ὁ Ἀρεοπαγίτης· «Πᾶσα ἡ θεολογία ἤγουν ἡ θεία γραφὴ τὰς οὐρανίους οὐσίας ἐννέα κέκληκε, ταύτας ὁ θεῖος ἱεροτελεστὴς εἰς τρεῖς ἀφορίζει τριαδικὰς διακοσμήσεις. Καὶ πρώτην μὲν εἶναί φησι τὴν περὶ θεὸν οὖσαν ἀεὶ καὶ προσεχῶς καὶ ἀμέσως ἡνῶσθαι παραδεδομένην τὴν τῶν ἑξαπτερύγων Σεραφὶμ καὶ τῶν πολυομμάτων Χερουβὶμ καὶ τῶν ἁγιωτάτων Θρόνων, δευτέραν δὲ τὴν τῶν Κυριοτήτων καὶ τῶν Δυνάμεων καὶ τῶν Ἐξουσιῶν, τρίτην δὲ καὶ τελευταίαν τὴν τῶν Ἀρχῶν καὶ Ἀρχαγγέλων καὶ Ἀγγέλων».

Τινὲς μὲν οὖν φασιν, ὅτι πρὸ πάσης κτίσεως ἐγένοντο, ὡς ὁ θεολόγος λέγει Γρηγόριος. «Πρῶτον ἐννοεῖ τὰς ἀγγελικὰς δυνάμεις καὶ οὐρανίους, καὶ τὸ ἐννόημα ἔργον ἦν»· ἕτεροι δέ,

differ from each other in their illumination and standing, either possessing their standing in proportion to their illumination, or sharing in illumination in proportion to their standing, and they illuminate each other by the superiority of their rank or nature. And it is clear that the superior impart a share of their illumination and knowledge to the inferior.[4]

They are powerful and ready to fulfil the divine will, and by the swiftness of their nature immediately appear anywhere that the divine sign should command. They watch over parts of the earth and are set in charge of nations and places, as appointed by the Creator, and administer our affairs and help us, and being always around God they are necessarily superior to us in accordance with the divine will and command.

They are reluctant to move towards evil but are not immovable, only now they are also immovable, not by nature but by grace and their devotion to the only good. They see God so far as they are capable of doing so, and have this as their food. They are superior to us because they are incorporeal and are free of any bodily passion, though not indeed impassible for only the divine is impassible. They assume different forms, in accordance with whatever the Lord God commands them to do, and thus appear to human beings and reveal the divine mysteries to them. They occupy themselves in heaven and have one task, which is to praise God and carry out his divine will.

As the most holy, most venerable, and most theologically gifted Dionysius the Areopagite says: "The whole of theology," that is to say, the divine Scripture, "has declared the heavenly essences to be nine in number, which the divine initiator divides into three triadic ranks. And he says that the first is that which is ever around God, in which the six-winged Seraphim, the many-eyed Cherubim, and the most holy Thrones have been granted to be closely and immediately united with him, and the second rank is that of the Dominions,

---

[4]Dionysius the Areopagite, *Celestial Hierarchy* 10.2 (PG 3:273B; Heil, 40.17–22); cf. Gregory of Nazianzus, *Oration* 28.31 (PG 36:72AB; Moreschini, 692).

ὅτι μετὰ τὸ γενέσθαι τὸν πρῶτον οὐρανόν. Ὅτι δὲ πρὸ τῆς τοῦ
ἀνθρώπου πλάσεως, πάντες ὁμολογοῦσιν. Ἐγὼ δὲ τῷ θεολόγῳ
Γρηγορίῳ συντίθεμαι· ἔπρεπε γὰρ πρῶτον τὴν νοερὰν οὐσίαν
κτισθῆναι καὶ οὕτω τὴν αἰσθητὴν καὶ τότε ἐξ ἀμφοτέρων τὸν
ἄνθρωπον.

Ὅσοι δέ φασι τοὺς ἀγγέλους δημιουργοὺς τῆς οἱασδήποτε
οὐσίας, οὗτοι στόμα εἰσὶ τοῦ πατρὸς αὐτῶν, τοῦ διαβόλου· κτίσμα
γὰρ ὄντες οὔκ εἰσι δημιουργοί. Πάντων δὲ ποιητὴς καὶ προνοητὴς
καὶ συνοχεὺς ὁ θεός ἐστιν, ὁ μόνος ἄκτιστος, ὁ ἐν πατρὶ καὶ υἱῷ
καὶ ἁγίῳ πνεύματι ὑμνούμενός τε καὶ δοξαζόμενος.

18   Περὶ διαβόλου καὶ δαιμόνων

Ἐκ τούτων τῶν ἀγγελικῶν δυνάμεων πρωτοστάτης τῆς περιγείου
τάξεως καὶ τῆς γῆς τὴν φυλακὴν ἐγχειρισθεὶς παρὰ θεοῦ οὐ φύσει
πονηρὸς γεγονώς, ἀλλ᾽ ἀγαθὸς ὢν καὶ ἐπ᾽ ἀγαθῷ γενόμενος
καὶ μηδ᾽ ὅλως ἐν ἑαυτῷ παρὰ τοῦ δημιουργοῦ κακίας ἐσχηκὼς
ἴχνος, μὴ ἐνέγκας τόν τε φωτισμὸν τήν τε τιμήν, ἣν αὐτῷ ὁ
δημιουργὸς ἐδωρήσατο, αὐτεξουσίῳ προαιρέσει ἐτράπη ἐκ τοῦ
κατὰ φύσιν εἰς τὸ παρὰ φύσιν καὶ ἐπήρθη κατὰ τοῦ πεποιηκότος
αὐτὸν θεοῦ ἀντᾶραι αὐτῷ βουληθεὶς καὶ πρῶτος ἀποστὰς τοῦ
ἀγαθοῦ ἐν τῷ κακῷ ἐγένετο· οὐδὲν γὰρ ἕτερόν ἐστι τὸ κακὸν
εἰ μὴ τοῦ ἀγαθοῦ στέρησις, ὥσπερ καὶ τὸ σκότος φωτός ἐστι

[5]Dionysius the Areopagite, *Celestial Hierarchy* 6.2 (PG 3:200D–201A; Heil, 26.11–27.24, condensed).

[6]Gregory of Nazianzus, *Oration* 38.9 (PG 36:320C; Moreschini, 886).

[1]This chapter relies on Gregory of Nyssa, *Catechetical Discourse* 6.5–6 (PG 45:28ABC; Green, 78–79). (IG)

[2]That evil is the privation of good was a maxim well established in Christian

Powers, and Authorities, and the third and last rank is that of the Principalities, Archangels, and Angels."[5]

Now some say that they were brought into being before all creation. For example, Gregory the Theologian says: "First he conceived of the angelic and heavenly powers, and the conception was the accomplished work."[6] But others say that this was after the creation of the first heaven. All hold that it was before the creation of humanity. I, for my part, agree with Gregory the Theologian. For it was necessary that spiritual substance should be created first, followed by sensible substance, and then humanity from both.

Those who say that the angels are creators of any substance whatsoever are the mouthpiece of their father the devil. For since they are created beings they are not creators. The maker, controller, and sustainer of all things is God, the only uncreated one, who is hymned and glorified in the Father, Son, and Holy Spirit.

18 *On the devil and the demons*

Of these angelic powers the one who was the protector of the terrestrial order and entrusted by God with the guardianship of the earth was not wicked by nature, but was good, and was made for good, and did not have the slightest trace of evil in him from the Creator.[1] But he did not maintain within himself the luminosity and honor that the Creator had bestowed on him. By his own free choice he turned from what was in accordance with nature to what was contrary to nature and became puffed up against God who had made him. Wishing to rebel against him, and becoming the first to abandon the good, he fell into evil. For evil is nothing other than the privation of good, just as darkness is the privation of light.[2] For the good is

thought since the time of Origen (died 254), who described evil as "non-being." See Mark S. M. Scott, *Journey Back to God: Origen on the Problem of Evil* (Oxford: Oxford University Press, 2015). John would have come across this in the section of the *Catechetical Discourse* which he is drawing upon for this chapter (*Catechetical Discourse* 6.6: τὴν κακίαν ἐν τῇ τοῦ ἀγαθοῦ στερήσει θεωρεῖσθαι λέγομεν, *tēn kakian en tē tou agathou sterēsei theōreisthai legomen* [PG 45:28C; Green, 79.67]; cf. 7.3: κακόν

στέρησις. Τὸ γὰρ ἀγαθὸν φῶς ἐστι νοητόν, ὁμοίως καὶ τὸ κακὸν σκότος ἐστὶ νοητόν. Φῶς οὖν κτισθεὶς ὑπὸ τοῦ δημιουργοῦ καὶ ἀγαθὸς γεγονώς—«καὶ γὰρ εἶδεν ὁ θεὸς πάντα, ὅσα ἐποίησε, καὶ ἰδοὺ καλὰ λίαν»—αὐτεξουσίῳ θελήματι σκότος ἐγένετο. Συναπεσπάσθη δὲ καὶ ἠκολούθησεν αὐτῷ καὶ συνέπεσε πλῆθος ἄπειρον τῶν ὑπ' αὐτῷ τεταγμένων ἀγγέλων. Τῆς αὐτῆς τοιγαροῦν φύσεως τοῖς ἀγγέλοις ὑπάρχοντες κακοὶ γεγόνασι τὴν προαίρεσιν ἑκουσίως ἐκ τοῦ ἀγαθοῦ πρὸς τὸ κακὸν ἐκκλίναντες.

Οὐκ ἔχουσι τοίνυν ἐξουσίαν κατά τινος οὐδὲ ἰσχὺν εἰ μὴ ἐκ θεοῦ οἰκονομικῶς συγχωρούμενοι, ὡς ἐπὶ τοῦ Ἰώβ, καθάπερ ἐπὶ τῶν χοίρων ἐν τῷ εὐαγγελίῳ γέγραπται. Παραχωρήσεως δὲ θεοῦ γινομένης καὶ ἰσχύουσι καὶ μεταβάλλονται καὶ μετασχηματίζονται, εἰς οἷον θέλουσι σχῆμα κατὰ φαντασίαν.

Καὶ τὰ μὲν μέλλοντα οὐδὲ οἱ ἄγγελοι οὐδὲ οἱ δαίμονες οἴδασιν, ὅμως προλέγουσιν, οἱ μὲν ἄγγελοι τοῦ θεοῦ αὐτοῖς ἀποκαλύπτοντος καὶ προλέγειν κελεύοντος· ὅθεν, ὅσα λέγουσι, γίνονται. Προλέγουσι δὲ καὶ οἱ δαίμονες, ποτὲ μὲν τὰ μακρὰν γινόμενα βλέποντες, ποτὲ δὲ στοχαζόμενοι, ὅθεν καὶ τὰ πολλὰ ψεύδονται· οἷς οὐ δεῖ πιστεύειν, κἂν ἀληθεύωσι πολλάκις, οἵῳ τρόπῳ εἰρήκαμεν. Οἴδασι δὲ καὶ τὰς γραφάς.

Πᾶσα οὖν κακία ἐξ αὐτῶν ἐπενοήθη καὶ τὰ ἀκάθαρτα πάθη. Καὶ προσβάλλειν μὲν τῷ ἀνθρώπῳ συνεχωρήθησαν, βιάζεσθαι δέ τινα οὐκ ἰσχύουσιν· ἐν ἡμῖν γάρ ἐστι δέξασθαι τὴν προσβολὴν ἢ μὴ δέξασθαι. Διὸ τῷ διαβόλῳ καὶ τοῖς δαίμοσιν αὐτοῦ ἡτοίμασται

... τὸ μὴ εἶναι [τὸ ἀγαθὸν] οὕτω κατονομάζεται, kakon ... to mē einai [to agathon] houtō katonomazetai [PG 45: 32C; Green. 82.41–43]). The concept would also have been familiar to him from Dionysius (*Divine Names* 4.29, 729C) and from Maximus the Confessor (*Centuries on Love* 3.29: τὸ κακὸν στέρησίς ἐστιν ἀγαθοῦ, to kakon sterēsis estin agathou). John's formulation of it (οὐδὲν ἕτερόν ἐστι τὸ κακὸν εἰ μὴ τοῦ ἀγαθοῦ στέρησις, ouden heteron esti to kakon ei mē tou agathou sterēsis) was often quoted in late Byzantium. Discussion of the nature of privation (στέρησις) and its relationship to the contrary (τὸ ἐναντίον, to enantion) had been initiated by Aristotle (e.g., *Metaphysics* 9.2, 1046b14–15), who had confined his remarks, however, to the metaphysical or ontological level. What the principle implied on the moral level was explored by Plotinus in the eighth treatise of his first *Ennead*. For Plotinus evil comes

intellectual light, in the same way that evil is intellectual darkness. Now since light has been created by the Creator it has also been created good—"God saw everything that he had made, and indeed, it was very good"[3]—but darkness came about by free will. An infinite multitude of angels of those subordinate to him detached themselves and followed him and fell with him. Consequently, although of the same nature as the angels, they became evil in their will, since they had voluntarily turned away from good towards evil.

They therefore do not have any authority or power over anybody unless they are granted it by the dispensation of God, as in the case of Job, just as is recorded about the swine in the Gospel.[4] When God gives his permission, they have the power to change and transform themselves into whatever illusory form they wish.

With regard to what belongs to the future, neither the angels nor the demons have knowledge of it. They do, however, foretell it, in the case of God's angels when he reveals it to them and commands them to foretell it. It is thus that what they say comes to pass. The demons also foretell, sometimes by seeing what is still a long way off, and sometimes by guesswork, which means that they are generally wrong. One should not believe them, even if they frequently tell the truth in the manner that we have described. Besides, they know the Scriptures.

Therefore every evil has been devised by them, along with the unclean passions. And although they have been permitted to tempt humanity, they are not able to force anyone. For it rests with us to

from matter, which is a deficiency. It cannot be a privation in Aristotelian terms, because "if evil consists in privation, it will exist in the thing deprived of form and have no independent existence." He is aware of the position later adopted by Dionysius, Maximus, and John—"There are some lines of argument . . . which say that . . . one should not look for evil elsewhere but place it in the soul in such a way that it is simply the absence of good" (*Enn.* 1.8.11; trans. Armstrong)—but rejects it because it renders the soul deficient. Christian writers, however, on the basis of the goodness of everything God has created, cannot allow evil to be associated with matter or with some other positive contrary.

   [3]Gen 1.31.
   [4]Cf. Jn 19.11; Job 1.12; Mt 8.28–32.

τὸ πῦρ τὸ ἄσβεστον, ἡ κόλασις ἡ αἰώνιος, καὶ τοῖς ἑπομένοις αὐτῷ.

Χρὴ δὲ γινώσκειν, ὅτι, ὅπερ ἐστὶ τοῖς ἀνθρώποις ὁ θάνατος, τοῦτο τοῖς ἀγγέλοις ἡ ἔκπτωσις· μετὰ γὰρ τὴν ἔκπτωσιν οὐκ ἔστιν αὐτοῖς μετάνοια, ὥσπερ οὐδὲ τοῖς ἀνθρώποις μετὰ τὸν θάνατον.

19   Περὶ κτίσεως ὁρατῆς

Αὐτὸς ὁ θεὸς ἡμῶν ὁ ἐν τριάδι καὶ ἐν μονάδι δοξολογούμενος ἐποίησε τὸν οὐρανὸν καὶ τὴν γῆν καὶ πάντα τὰ ἐν αὐτοῖς ἐκ τοῦ μὴ ὄντος εἰς τὸ εἶναι παραγαγὼν τὰ σύμπαντα, τὰ μὲν οὐκ ἐκ προϋποκειμένης ὕλης οἷον οὐρανόν, γῆν, ἀέρα, πῦρ, ὕδωρ, τὰ δὲ ἐκ τούτων τῶν ὑπ' αὐτοῦ γεγονότων, οἷον ζῷα, φυτά, σπέρματα· ταῦτα γὰρ ἐκ γῆς καὶ ὕδατος, ἀέρος τε καὶ πυρὸς τῷ τοῦ δημιουργοῦ προστάγματι γεγόνασιν.

20   Περὶ οὐρανοῦ

Οὐρανός ἐστι περιοχὴ ὁρατῶν τε καὶ ἀοράτων κτισμάτων· ἐντὸς γὰρ αὐτοῦ αἵ τε νοεραὶ τῶν ἀγγέλων δυνάμεις καὶ πάντα τὰ αἰσθητὰ περικλείονται καὶ περιορίζονται. Μόνον δὲ τὸ θεῖον ἀπερίγραπτόν ἐστι πάντα πληροῦν καὶ πάντα περιέχον καὶ πάντα περιορίζον ὡς ὑπὲρ πάντα ὂν καὶ πάντα δημιουργῆσαν.

Ἐπεὶ τοίνυν οὐρανόν φησιν ἡ γραφὴ καὶ «οὐρανὸν τοῦ οὐρανοῦ» καὶ «οὐρανοὺς οὐρανῶν» καὶ «ἕως τρίτου οὐρανοῦ» ὁ

---

[5]Cf. Nemesius of Emesa, *On the Nature of Man* 1 (PG 40:521C–524A; Morani, 10.13–19).

[1]Ps 145.6.

[1]Ps 113.24.

[2]Ps 148.4.

[3]2 Cor 12.2.

[4]The "outer philosophers" are those of the non-Christian Greek tradition from the Pre-Socratics to the Neoplatonists. A similar distinction was made between the

accept the temptation or not to accept it. Hence the unquenchable fire, the eternal punishment, that has been prepared for the devil and his demons and those who follow them.

One also needs to know that what death is for human beings, the fall is for the angels. For after the fall there is no repentance for them, just as there is no repentance for human beings after death.[5]

19   *On the visible creation*

Our God himself, who is glorified in Trinity and in unity, made heaven and earth and all that is in them,[1] bringing everything that exists out of non-being into being, some of it from matter that had no pre-existence, such as heaven, earth, air, fire, and water, and some of it from those things that had already been brought into being by him, such as animals, plants, and seeds. For these came into being at the command of the Creator from earth and water, and from air and fire.

20   *On the vault of heaven*

Heaven is that which contains visible and invisible created beings, for within it the intelligible powers of the angels and all sensible things are enclosed and confined. Only the divine is uncircumscribed, filling all things and surrounding all things and confining all things, since it transcends all things and has created all things.

Now since Scripture speaks of heaven, "the heaven of heavens,"[1] and "the heavens of heavens,"[2] and says that blessed Paul was caught up to "the third heaven,"[3] we say that in the generation of the entire heaven we accept as creation that which the outer philosophers,[4]

"outer wisdom" and the "inner wisdom," the outer wisdom being that of the Greek philosophers, and the inner wisdom the teaching of the Scriptures and the fathers of the Church. Outer philosophers who discussed the starless sphere include the fourth-century mathematician, Theon of Alexandria (in his commentary on Ptolemy's *Almagest*, ed. Rome, 435.13), and the sixth-century commentator on Aristotle, Simplicius (in his *De Caelo* 3.32, ed. Heiberg, ii. 462.24).

μακάριος Παῦλος ἡρπάχθαι φησί, λέγομεν, ὅτι ἐν τῇ τοῦ παντὸς κοσμογενείᾳ οὐρανοῦ ποίησιν παρελάβομεν, ὃν οἱ τῶν ἔξω σοφοὶ ἄναστρον σφαῖράν φασι τὰ Μωσέως σφετερισάμενοι δόγματα. Ἔτι δὲ καὶ τὸ στερέωμα ἐκάλεσεν ὁ θεὸς οὐρανόν, ὃν ἐν μέσῳ τοῦ ὕδατος γενέσθαι προσέταξεν τάξας αὐτὸν διαχωρίζειν ἀνὰ μέσον τοῦ ὕδατος τοῦ ἐπάνω τοῦ στερεώματος καὶ ἀνὰ μέσον τοῦ ὕδατος τοῦ ὑποκάτω τοῦ στερεώματος. Τούτου τὴν φύσιν ὁ θεῖος Βασίλειος λεπτήν φησιν ὡσεὶ καπνὸν ἐκ τῆς θείας μεμυημένος γραφῆς. Ἕτεροι δὲ ὑδατώδη ὡς ἐν μέσῳ τῶν ὑδάτων γενόμενον, ἄλλοι ἐκ τῶν τεσσάρων στοιχείων, ἄλλοι πέμπτον σῶμα καὶ ἕτερον παρὰ τὰ τέσσαρα.

Τινὲς μὲν οὖν ἐδόξασαν κύκλῳ τὸ πᾶν περιέχειν τὸν οὐρανὸν σφαιροειδῆ τε ὑπάρχειν καὶ πανταχόθεν τὸ ἀνώτατον μέρος αὐτὸν εἶναι, τὸ δὲ μεσώτατον τοῦ περιεχομένου ὑπ᾽ αὐτοῦ τόπου εἶναι κατώτερον μέρος, καὶ τὰ μὲν κοῦφα καὶ ἐλαφρὰ τῶν σωμάτων τὴν ἄνω τάξιν λαχεῖν παρὰ τοῦ δημιουργοῦ, τὰ δὲ βαρέα καὶ κατωφερῆ τὴν κατωτέραν χώραν, ἥτις ἐστὶν ἡ μέση. Ἔστι μὲν οὖν κουφότερον καὶ ἀνωφερέστερον στοιχεῖον τὸ πῦρ, ὅπερ δὴ μετὰ τὸν οὐρανὸν εὐθέως τετάχθαι φασί· τοῦτον δὲ λέγουσιν τὸν αἰθέρα, μεθ᾽ ὃν κατώτερον τὸν ἀέρα. Τὴν δὲ γῆν καὶ τὸ ὕδωρ ὡς βαρύτερα καὶ κατωφερέστερα ἐν τῷ μεσωτάτῳ κρέμασθαι· ὡς εἶναι ἐξ ἐναντίας κάτω μὲν τὴν γῆν καὶ τὸ ὕδωρ—τὸ δὲ ὕδωρ κουφότερον τῆς γῆς, ὅθεν καὶ εὐκινητότερον αὐτῆς ὑπάρχει—, ἄνωθεν δὲ πανταχόθεν ὡς περιβόλαιον κύκλῳ τὸν ἀέρα καὶ περὶ τὸν ἀέρα πανταχόθεν τὸν αἰθέρα, ἔξωθεν δὲ πάντων κύκλῳ τὸν οὐρανόν.

Κυκλικῶς δέ φασι κινεῖσθαι τὸν οὐρανὸν καὶ συσφίγγειν τὰ ἐντὸς καὶ οὕτω μένειν πάγια καὶ ἀδιάπτωτα. Ἑπτὰ δὲ ζώνας φασὶ

---

[5]The second-century pagan Neopythagorean, Numenius of Apamea, famously declared: "What is Plato but Moses speaking Attic Greek?" (*Fragments*, 1.8.14). Justin Martyr, Numenius' contemporary, does not mention him but regarded it as obvious that Plato had filched his teaching on the formation of the world from Moses in view of the latter's greater antiquity (*Apology* 1.54). A little later, Clement of Alexandria specifically endorsed Numenius' aphorism (*Stromateis* 1.150.4). Origen, however, although familiar with Numenius, is more circumspect. In his apologetic work, *Against Celsus*, he mentions Moses several times (4.11; 6.43; 7.28) but only to

borrowing the teachings of Moses,[5] call the starless sphere. More-over, God called the vault of heaven "the firmament," which he appointed to be in the midst of the water, setting it to be a division between the water that is above the firmament and the water that is below the firmament.[6] The divine Basil, instructed by divine Scripture, says that the nature of this firmament is light, rather like smoke.[7] Others say that it is watery, since it has been brought into being in the midst of the waters, others that it is derived from the four elements, others that it is a fifth body and different from the four elements.[8]

Some indeed have supposed that the vault of heaven encompasses the universe and has the form of a sphere, and that everywhere is its highest point, while the innermost part of the space enclosed by it is the lowest point, and that bodies that are light and buoyant have been allotted by the Creator to the upper region, while those that are heavy and tend to sink are allotted to the lower region, which is in the middle [of the sphere].[9] Now the lightest element, most prone to move upwards, is fire, which they say is evidently placed directly after the vault of heaven. They call this the aether, after which comes the air. They say that earth and water, being heavier and more prone to sink are suspended at the central point. Consequently, in reverse order earth and water are below—water is lighter than earth and hence more mobile than the latter—and above them on all sides like an envelope is the encircling air, and around the air on all sides is the aether, and outside everything is the encircling vault of heaven.

The vault of heaven is said to move in a circular manner and compress all that is within it and so these remain stable and fixed.

---

emphasize his greater antiquity than even the Greek alphabet. Nevertheless, it soon became a received opinion among Christian writers that Plato was directly dependent on Moses.

   [6]Gen 1.6–7.
   [7]Basil of Caesarea, *Homilies on the Hexaemeron* 1.8.2 (PG 29:20C–21A; Naldini, 26).
   [8]On the fifth body (the "quintessence"), see Chapter 4, p. 65.
   [9]John refers here to the geocentric Ptolemaic system (dating from about 150).

τοῦ οὐρανοῦ, μίαν τῆς ἑτέρας ὑψηλοτέραν. Λέγουσι δὲ αὐτὸν λεπτοτάτης φύσεως ὡσεὶ καπνὸν καὶ καθ' ἑκάστην ζώνην εἶναι ἕνα τῶν πλανητῶν· ἑπτὰ γὰρ πλανήτας εἶναι ἔφησαν, Ἥλιον, Σελήνην, Δία, Ἑρμῆν, Ἄρεα, Ἀφροδίτην καὶ Κρόνον. Ἀφροδίτην δέ φασι τὸν ποτὲ μὲν Ἑωσφόρον, ποτὲ δὲ Ἕσπερον γινόμενον. Πλανήτας δὲ τούτους ἐκάλεσαν, ὅτιπερ ἐναντίως τοῦ οὐρανοῦ ποιοῦνται τὴν κίνησιν· τοῦ γὰρ οὐρανοῦ καὶ τῶν λοιπῶν ἀστέρων ἐξ ἀνατολῆς ἐπὶ δυσμὰς κινουμένων οὗτοι μόνοι ἀπὸ δυσμῶν ἐπὶ ἀνατολὰς τὴν κίνησιν ἔχουσι. Καὶ τοῦτο γνωσόμεθα ἐκ τῆς σελήνης μικρὸν καθ' ἑσπέραν ἀναποδιζούσης.

Ὅσοι τοίνυν ἔφησαν σφαιροειδῆ τὸν οὐρανόν, ἴσως λέγουσιν ἀφίστασθαι αὐτὸν καὶ ἀπέχειν τῆς γῆς, ἄνωθέν τε καὶ ἐκ πλαγίων καὶ κάτωθεν. Κάτωθεν δὲ καὶ ἐκ πλαγίων φημί, ὅσον πρὸς τὴν ἡμετέραν αἴσθησιν, ἐπεὶ κατὰ τὸν τῆς ἀκολουθίας λόγον πανταχόθεν τὸν ἄνω τόπον ὁ οὐρανὸς ἐπέχει καὶ ἡ γῆ τὸν κάτω. Καί φασι τὸν οὐρανὸν σφαιροειδῶς κυκλοῦν τὴν γῆν καὶ συμπεριφέρειν τῇ ὀξυτάτῃ κινήσει αὐτοῦ ἥλιόν τε καὶ σελήνην καὶ τοὺς ἀστέρας, καὶ ὑπὲρ μὲν γῆν ὄντος τοῦ ἡλίου ἡμέραν γίνεσθαι ἐνταῦθα, ὑπὸ δὲ τὴν γῆν νύκτα· ὑπὸ δὲ γῆν κατιόντος ἡλίου ἐνταῦθα μὲν νύκτα, ἐκεῖσε δὲ ἡμέραν.

Ἕτεροι δὲ ἡμισφαίριον τὸν οὐρανὸν ἐφαντάσθησαν ἐκ τοῦ τὸν θεηγόρον Δαυὶδ λέγειν· «Ὁ ἐκτείνων τὸν οὐρανὸν ὡσεὶ δέρριν», ὅπερ δηλοῖ τὴν σκηνήν, καὶ τὸν μακάριον Ἡσαΐαν· «Ὁ στήσας τὸν οὐρανὸν ὡσεὶ καμάραν», καὶ ὅτι δύνων ὅ τε ἥλιος καὶ ἡ σελήνη καὶ τὰ ἄστρα κυκλοῖ τὴν γῆν ἀπὸ δύσεως ἐπὶ βορρᾶν καὶ οὕτω πάλιν ἐπὶ τὴν ἀνατολὴν ἀφικνεῖται. Ὅμως, εἴτε οὕτως, εἴτε ἐκείνως, ἅπαντα τῷ θείῳ προστάγματι γέγονέ τε καὶ ἥδρασται καὶ τὸ θεῖον θέλημά τε καὶ βούλημα θεμέλιον ἀσάλευτον κέκτηται. «Αὐτὸς γὰρ εἶπε, καὶ ἐγενήθησαν· αὐτὸς

---

[10]John, of course, gives their Greek names, which are Hēlios, Selēnē, Zeus, Hermēs, Arēs, Aphroditē, and Kronos, respectively.

[11]The word "planet" (πλανήτης, planētēs) is derived from the Greek verb "to wander" (πλανάω, planaō).

There are said to be seven spheres of the vault of heaven, one higher
than the other. The vault itself is said to be of a very light nature, like
smoke, and in each sphere there is said to be one of the planets, for it
is maintained that there are seven planets: the Sun, the Moon, Jupiter, Mercury, Mars, Venus, and Saturn.[10] Venus is said sometimes to
become the morning star and sometimes the evening star. And these
are called the planets,[11] because the direction of their movement is
contrary to that of the vault of heaven, for although the vault and the
rest of the stars move from east to west, the planets alone have their
movement from west to east. This is something we know from the
moon's slight retrogression every evening.

Now those who maintain that the vault of heaven is spherical
say that it is separated from the earth by an equal distance above, to
the sides, and below. I say "below" and "to the sides" in relation to
our own senses, because it follows logically that at every point the
vault of heaven occupies the upper region and the earth the lower.
And it is said that the vault of heaven encompasses the earth like a
sphere and by its very fast motion carries round with it the sun and
the moon and the stars, and that when the sun is above the earth it
becomes day here but night below the earth, whereas when the sun
goes down below the earth it is night here but day there.

Others have imagined that the vault of heaven is hemispherical
on account of David, the singer of God, who said: "Who stretches
out the heaven like a curtain,"[12] which means "a tent,"[13] and blessed
Isaiah, who said: "Who set the heaven like a vault,"[14] and because
when the sun, the moon, and the stars set, they circle the earth from
west to north and thus arrive again at the east. However, whether one
version is correct or the other, all things came into being and were
established by the divine command and have the divine will and
purpose as their unshakable foundation.[15] "For he spoke and they

[12]Ps 103.2.

[13]As interpreted by Is 40.22.

[14]Is 40.22.

[15]Interestingly, John does not choose between the Ptolemaic geocentric system
and the biblical image of the created world, but attempts to combine the two.

ἐνετείλατο, καὶ ἐκτίσθησαν. Ἔστησεν αὐτὰ εἰς τὸν αἰῶνα καὶ εἰς τὸν αἰῶνα τοῦ αἰῶνος· πρόσταγμα ἔθετο, καὶ οὐ παρελεύσεται».

Ἔστι μὲν οὖν οὐρανὸς τοῦ οὐρανοῦ ὁ πρῶτος οὐρανός, ἐπάνω ὑπάρχων τοῦ στερεώματος. Ἰδοὺ δύο οὐρανοί· «καὶ τὸ στερέωμα γὰρ ἐκάλεσεν ὁ θεὸς οὐρανόν». Σύνηθες δὲ τῇ θείᾳ γραφῇ καὶ τὸν ἀέρα οὐρανὸν καλεῖν διὰ τὸ ὁρᾶσθαι ἄνω. «Εὐλογεῖτε» γάρ, φησί, «πάντα τὰ πετεινὰ τοῦ οὐρανοῦ», τοῦ ἀέρος λέγω. Ὁ ἀὴρ γὰρ τῶν πετεινῶν ἐστι πορεία, καὶ οὐχ ὁ οὐρανός. Ἰδοὺ τρεῖς οὐρανοί, οὓς ὁ θεῖος ἔφη ἀπόστολος. Εἰ δὲ καὶ τὰς ἑπτὰ ζώνας ἑπτὰ οὐρανοὺς ἐκλαβεῖν θελήσειας, οὐδὲν τῷ λόγῳ τῆς ἀληθείας λυμαίνεται. Σύνηθες δὲ καὶ τῇ Ἑβραΐδι φωνῇ τὸν οὐρανὸν πληθυντικῶς καλεῖν οὐρανούς. Οὐρανὸν οὐρανοῦ βουλομένη εἰπεῖν οὐρανοὺς οὐρανῶν ἔφησεν, ὅπερ δηλοῖ οὐρανὸν οὐρανοῦ τὸν ἐπάνω τοῦ στερεώματος, καὶ τὰ ὕδατα δὲ τὰ ἐπάνω τῶν οὐρανῶν ἢ τοῦ ἀέρος καὶ τοῦ στερεώματος ἢ τῶν ἑπτὰ ζωνῶν τοῦ στερεώματος ἢ τοῦ στερεώματος τῇ συνηθείᾳ τῆς Ἑβραΐδος πληθυντικῶς οὐρανῶν ὀνομαζομένου.

Πάντα μὲν οὖν τὰ κατὰ γένεσιν ὑπόκειται φθορᾷ κατὰ τὴν τῆς φύσεως ἀκολουθίαν, καὶ οἱ οὐρανοί, χάριτι δὲ θεοῦ συνέχονταί τε καὶ συντηροῦνται. Μόνον δὲ τὸ θεῖον ἄναρχόν τε φύσει καὶ ἀτελεύτητον. Διὸ καὶ εἴρηται· «Αὐτοὶ ἀπολοῦνται, σὺ δὲ διαμένεις» (ὅμως οὐκ εἰς τὸ παντελὲς ἀφανισθήσονται οἱ οὐρανοί)· «παλαιωθήσονται μὲν γὰρ καὶ ὡσεὶ περιβόλαιον εἱλιγήσονται καὶ ἀλλαγήσονται» καὶ «ἔσται οὐρανὸς καινὸς καὶ γῆ καινή».

Πολλῷ δὲ τῷ μέτρῳ ὁ οὐρανὸς μείζων ὑπάρχει τῆς γῆς. Τὴν μέντοι οὐσίαν τοῦ οὐρανοῦ οὐ δεῖ ζητεῖν ἄγνωστον ἡμῖν οὖσαν.

Μηδεὶς δὲ ἐψυχωμένους τοὺς οὐρανοὺς ἢ τοὺς φωστῆρας ὑπολαμβανέτω· ἄψυχοι γάρ εἰσι καὶ ἀναίσθητοι. Ὥστε εἰ καί φησιν

---

[16]Ps 148.5–6.
[17]Gen 1.8.
[18]Dan 3.80 (LXX).
[19]Ps 101.77.
[20]Is 65.17.

came to be; he commanded and they were created. He has established them for the aeon and for the aeon of the aeon; he established a commandment and it shall not pass away."[16]

Now there is a heaven of heaven, the first heaven, which is above the firmament. Here we have two heavens: "And God called the firmament heaven."[17] It is customary for the divine Scripture also to call the air "heaven" on account of its being seen above us. For "give praise," it says, "all you birds of heaven,"[18] by which is meant the air. For the air is where the birds fly, not the vault of heaven. Here we have three heavens, as the divine Apostle said. And if you wish to take the seven zones [of the planetary spheres] as seven heavens, no harm is done to the word of truth. It is also customary in the Hebrew language to refer to heaven in the plural as "heavens." When Hebrew wished to say "heaven of heaven," it said "heavens of heavens," which indicates the heaven of heaven that is above the firmament and the waters that are above the vault of heaven, whether it is the air and the firmament, or the seven zones of the firmament, or the firmament itself that are spoken of in the plural in accordance with Hebrew usage.

Now all things that come into being are subject to decay by a natural process, including the heavens, but are maintained and preserved by the grace of God. Only the divine is by nature without beginning and without end. That is why it is said: "They will perish but you endure"[19] (the heavens, however, will not disappear utterly). "For they will wear out like a garment and will be folded away and changed" and "there will be a new heaven and a new earth."[20]

The vault of heaven is much greater than the earth in size. But we should not investigate the essence of heaven, since it is unknowable to us.

Nor should it be assumed that the heavens or the heavenly bodies are endowed with souls, for they are inanimate and insensate.[21]

---

[21]The notion of the divinity of the heavenly bodies, taken for granted by the Greek philosophers, was first attacked on scientific grounds by John Philoponus (*c.* 490–after 567) in his *De caelo*. See S. Sambursky, *The Physical World of Late Antiquity* (London: Routledge and Kegan Paul, 1962), 159; Alan Scott, *Origen and the Life of the Stars: A History of an Idea* (Oxford: Clarendon Press, 1991), 15–21, 45, 59–60.

ἡ θεία γραφή· «Εὐφραινέσθωσαν οἱ οὐρανοί, καὶ ἀγαλλιάσθω
ἡ γῆ», τοὺς ἐν οὐρανῷ ἀγγέλους καὶ τοὺς ἐν τῇ γῇ ἀνθρώπους
πρὸς εὐφροσύνην καλεῖ· οἶδε δὲ ἡ γραφὴ καὶ προσωποποιεῖν,
καὶ ὡς ἐπὶ ἐμψύχων περὶ τῶν ἀψύχων διαλέγεσθαι, ὡς τὸ «ἡ
θάλασσα εἶδε καὶ ἔφυγεν, ὁ Ἰορδάνης ἐστράφη εἰς τὰ ὀπίσω», καὶ
«τί σοί ἐστι, θάλασσα, ὅτι ἔφυγες»; καὶ ὄρη καὶ βουνοὶ ἐρωτῶνται
λόγους σκιρτήσεως, ὥσπερ καὶ ἡμῖν σύνηθες λέγειν· συνήχθη ἡ
πόλις, οὐ τὰς οἰκοδομὰς σημαίνειν βουλομένοις, ἀλλὰ τοὺς τῆς
πόλεως οἰκήτορας· καὶ «οἱ οὐρανοὶ διηγοῦνται δόξαν θεοῦ», οὐ
φωνὴν ὠσὶν αἰσθητοῖς ἀκουομένην ἀφιέντες, ἀλλ' ἐκ τοῦ οἰκείου
μεγέθους τὴν τοῦ δημιουργοῦ δύναμιν ἡμῖν παριστάνοντες, ὧν τὸ
κάλλος κατανοοῦντες τὸν ποιητὴν ὡς ἀριστοτέχνην δοξάζομεν.

21 *Περὶ φωτός, πυρός, φωστήρων ἡλίου τε καὶ σελήνης καὶ
ἄστρων*

Τὸ πῦρ ἓν τῶν τεσσάρων στοιχείων ἐστί, κοῦφόν τε καὶ
ἀνωφερέστερον τῶν λοιπῶν καυστικόν τε καὶ φωτιστικόν, τῇ
πρώτῃ ἡμέρᾳ ὑπὸ τοῦ δημιουργοῦ κτισθέν· φησὶ γὰρ ἡ θεία
γραφή· «Καὶ εἶπεν ὁ θεός· Γενηθήτω φῶς, καὶ ἐγένετο φῶς».
Οὐχ ἕτερον γάρ ἐστι τὸ πῦρ εἰ μὴ τὸ φῶς, ὥς τινές φασιν. Ἕτεροι
δὲ τὸ κοσμικὸν πῦρ ὑπὲρ τὸν ἀέρα φασίν, ὃ καλοῦσιν αἰθέρα.
Ἐν ἀρχῇ μὲν οὖν ἐποίησεν ὁ θεὸς τὸ φῶς, ἤτοι τῇ πρώτῃ ἡμέρᾳ
καλλωπισμὸν καὶ κόσμον πάσης τῆς ὁρατῆς κτίσεως· ἄφελε γὰρ
τὸ φῶς, καὶ πάντα ἐν τῷ σκότει ἀδιάγνωστα μένουσι τὴν οἰκείαν
μὴ δυνάμενα εὐπρέπειαν ἐπιδείξασθαι. «Ἐκάλεσε δὲ ὁ θεὸς τὸ μὲν
φῶς ἡμέραν, τὸ δὲ σκότος ἐκάλεσε νύκτα». Σκότος δέ ἐστιν οὐκ
οὐσία τις, ἀλλὰ συμβεβηκός· φωτὸς γάρ ἐστι στέρησις. Ὁ γὰρ
ἀὴρ οὐκ ἐν τῇ οὐσίᾳ αὐτοῦ ἔχει τὸ φῶς. Αὐτὸ οὖν τὸ ἐστερῆσθαι

---

[22] Ps 95.11.
[23] Ps 113.5.
[24] Ps 18.2.

[1] The four elements (earth, air, fire, and water) go back to the four "roots" of

Therefore, even if the divine Scripture says: "Let the heavens rejoice and the earth exult,"[22] it is inviting the angels in heaven and human beings on earth to rejoice. Scripture knows how to personify and treat inanimate things as if they were animate, as in "the sea saw and fled, Jordan turned back," and "what is the matter with you, O sea, that you fled?" [23] And mountains and hills are asked the reason for their skipping, just as we are accustomed to saying that the city assembled, not intending to mean the buildings but the city's inhabitants. And "the heavens declare the glory of God,"[24] not by emitting a voice audible to sensible ears, but by their own magnitude representing to us the power of the Creator. By contemplating their beauty we glorify their maker as the supreme craftsman.

21 *On light, fire, and the luminary bodies of the sun, the moon, and the stars*

Fire is one of the four elements.[1] It is light and more prone to rise upwards than the others, and it both burns and illuminates. It was created by the Creator on the first day, for divine Scripture says: "And God said, 'Let there be light,' and there was light."[2] For fire is not something different from light, as some say. Others claim that the cosmic fire is above the air and call it aether. In the beginning, then, God made light, which is to say that on the first day he made that which gives beauty and order to the whole of the visible creation. For take away light and everything remains indistinguishable in darkness, incapable of displaying its own loveliness. "And God called the light day and the darkness he called night."[3] Darkness is not some kind of substance, but an accident, for it is the privation of light. Air does not have light as an integral part of its substance. Therefore this depriving the air of light God called darkness. It is not the substance of air that is darkness but the privation of light,

Empedocles (*c.* 493–*c.* 433 BCE). It was taken for granted until modern times that they were the fundamental constituents of the universe.

[2] Gen 1.3
[3] Gen 1.5.

τὸν ἀέρα φωτὸς σκότος ἐκάλεσεν ὁ θεός. Καὶ οὐχὶ ἡ οὐσία τοῦ ἀέρος ἐστὶ σκότος, ἀλλ' ἡ τοῦ φωτὸς στέρησις, ὅπερ συμβεβηκὸς μᾶλλον δηλοῖ ἤπερ οὐσίαν. Οὐκ ἐκλήθη δὲ πρώτη ἡ νύξ, ἀλλ' ἡ ἡμέρα· ὥστε πρώτη ἐστὶν ἡ ἡμέρα καὶ ἐσχάτη ἡ νύξ. Ἀκολουθεῖ οὖν ἡ νὺξ τῇ ἡμέρᾳ, καὶ ἀπ' ἀρχῆς τῆς ἡμέρας ἕως τῆς ἄλλης ἡμέρας ἓν νυχθήμερόν ἐστιν· ἔφη γὰρ ἡ γραφή· «Καὶ ἐγένετο ἑσπέρα καὶ ἐγένετο πρωί, ἡμέρα μία».

Ἐν μὲν οὖν ταῖς τρισὶν ἡμέραις ἀναχεομένου καὶ συστελλομένου τοῦ φωτὸς τῷ θείῳ προστάγματι ἥ τε ἡμέρα καὶ ἡ νὺξ ἐγίνετο. Τῇ δὲ τετάρτῃ ἡμέρᾳ ἐποίησεν ὁ θεὸς τὸν φωστῆρα τὸν μέγαν ἤτοι τὸν ἥλιον εἰς ἀρχὰς καὶ ἐξουσίας τῆς ἡμέρας (δι' αὐτοῦ γὰρ ἡ ἡμέρα συνίσταται· ἡμέρα γάρ ἐστιν ἐν τῷ τὸν ἥλιον ὑπὲρ γῆν εἶναι, καὶ διάστημα ἡμέρας ἐστὶν ὁ ἀπὸ ἀνατολῆς μέχρι δύσεως ὑπὲρ γῆν τοῦ ἡλίου δρόμος) καὶ τὸν φωστῆρα τὸν ἐλάσσω ἤτοι τὴν σελήνην καὶ τοὺς ἀστέρας εἰς ἀρχὰς καὶ ἐξουσίας τῆς νυκτὸς τοῦ φωτίζειν αὐτήν. Νὺξ δέ ἐστιν ἐν τῷ τὸν ἥλιον ὑπὸ γῆν εἶναι, καὶ διάστημα νυκτός ἐστιν ὁ ἀπὸ δύσεως μέχρις ἀνατολῆς ὑπὸ γῆν τοῦ ἡλίου δρόμος. Ἡ σελήνη τοίνυν καὶ οἱ ἀστέρες ἐτάχθησαν τὴν νύκτα φωτίζειν, οὐχ ὡς τῇ ἡμέρᾳ πάντοτε ὑπὸ γῆν ὄντες (εἰσὶ γὰρ καὶ ἐν ἡμέρᾳ ἀστέρες ἐν τῷ οὐρανῷ ὑπὲρ γῆν), ἀλλ' ὁ ἥλιος τούτους ἅμα καὶ τὴν σελήνην τῇ σφοδροτέρᾳ αἴγλῃ ἀποκρύπτων οὐκ ἐᾷ φαίνεσθαι.

Τοῖς φωστῆρσι τούτοις τὸ πρωτόκτιστον φῶς ὁ δημιουργὸς ἐναπέθετο οὐχ ὡς ἀπορῶν ἄλλου φωτός, ἀλλ' ἵνα μὴ ἀργὸν ἐκεῖνο μείνῃ τὸ φῶς· φωστὴρ γάρ ἐστιν οὐκ αὐτὸ τὸ φῶς, ἀλλὰ φωτὸς δοχεῖον.

Ἐκ τούτων τῶν φωστήρων ἑπτὰ πλανήτας φασί. Καὶ λέγουσιν αὐτοὺς ἐναντίαν τοῦ οὐρανοῦ κινεῖσθαι κίνησιν, διὸ καὶ πλανήτας αὐτοὺς ἐκάλεσαν· τὸν μὲν γὰρ οὐρανόν φασιν ἐξ ἀνατολῶν ἐπὶ δυσμὰς κινεῖσθαι, τοὺς δὲ πλανήτας ἐκ δυσμῶν ἐπὶ ἀνατολάς· συμπεριφέρειν δὲ τὸν οὐρανὸν τῇ ἑαυτοῦ κινήσει ὡς ὀξυτέρᾳ τοὺς ἑπτὰ πλανήτας. Τῶν δὲ ἑπτὰ πλανητῶν τὰ ὀνόματά ἐστι ταῦτα· Ἥλιος ☉, Σελήνη ☾, Ζεύς ♃, Ἑρμῆς ☿, Ἄρης ♂, Ἀφροδίτη ♀,

which shows it to be an accident rather than a substance. What was called "first" was not night but day, with the result that day is first and night is last. Night therefore follows day, and from the beginning of one day to that of the next is a complete twenty-four-hour period. For Scripture said, "And there was evening and there was morning, day one."[4]

Now for three days it was by the expansion and contraction of the light by divine command that day and night took place. On the fourth day God made the great luminary, which is the sun, to be the source and regulating principle of the day (for it is through the sun that the day is constituted, day being when the sun is over the earth, and the space of a day being the sun's course above the earth from east to west), and the lesser luminary, which is the moon, together with the stars, to be the source and regulating principle of the night and to illuminate it. It is night when the sun is below the earth, and the duration of a night is the sun's course below the earth from west to east. Accordingly, the moon and the stars were appointed to illuminate the night, not so that they are always below the earth during the day (for there are stars in the sky above the earth during the day as well), but the sun hides these together with the moon by its greater brilliance and does not allow them to be visible.

It was into these luminaries that the Creator infused the primordial light, not because he was at a loss for other light, but so that the primordial light should not remain idle. For the luminary is not the light itself, but the container of the light.

It is said that of these luminaries there are seven that are planets. And they say that these move in the opposite direction to the vault of heaven, which is why they are called planets. For the vault of heaven, they say, moves from east to west, whereas the planets move from west to east. The vault of heaven carries the seven planets around with it by its own motion on account of its being faster. The names of the seven planets are these: Sun ☉, Moon ☾, Jupiter ♃, Mercury ☿,

---

[4]Gen 1.5.

Κρόνος ♄. Εἶναι δὲ καθ᾽ ἑκάστης ζώνην τοῦ οὐρανοῦ ἕνα τῶν ἑπτὰ πλανητῶν·

ἐν μὲν τῇ πρώτῃ ἤτοι ἀνωτέρᾳ τὸν Κρόνον ♄,
ἐν δὲ τῇ δευτέρᾳ τὸν Δία ♃,
ἐν δὲ τῇ τρίτῃ τὸν Ἄρεα ♂,
ἐν δὲ τῇ τετάρτῃ τὸν Ἥλιον ☉,
ἐν δὲ τῇ πέμπτῃ τὴν Ἀφροδίτην ♀,
ἐν δὲ τῇ ἕκτῃ τὸν Ἑρμῆν ☿,
ἐν δὲ τῇ ἑβδόμῃ καὶ κατωτέρᾳ τὴν Σελήνην ☾.

Τρέχουσι δὲ δρόμον ἄληκτον, ὃν ὁ δημιουργὸς ἔταξεν αὐτοῖς, καὶ καθὼς ἐθεμελίωσεν αὐτά, ὥς φησιν ὁ θεῖος Δαυίδ· «Σελήνην καὶ ἀστέρας, ἃ σὺ ἐθεμελίωσας»· διὰ γὰρ τοῦ εἰπεῖν «ἐθεμελίωσας» ἐσήμανε τὸ πάγιον καὶ ἀμετάβλητον τῆς ὑπὸ θεοῦ δοθείσης αὐτοῖς τάξεώς τε καὶ εἱρμοῦ. Ἔταξε γὰρ αὐτοὺς εἰς καιροὺς καὶ εἰς ἡμέρας καὶ εἰς ἐνιαυτούς.

Διὰ μὲν γὰρ τοῦ ἡλίου αἱ τέσσαρες τροπαὶ συνίστανται. Καὶ πρώτη μὲν ἡ ἐαρινή· ἐν αὐτῇ γὰρ ἐποίησεν ὁ θεὸς τὰ σύμπαντα καὶ δηλοῖ τὸ καὶ μέχρι τοῦ νῦν ἐν αὐτῇ τῶν ἀνθῶν τὴν βλάστησιν γίνεσθαι. Ἥτις ἰσημερινὴ τροπή ἐστιν· δώδεκα γὰρ ὡρῶν τήν τε ἡμέραν καὶ τὴν νύκτα καθίστησιν. Αὕτη ἐκ τῆς μέσης ἀνατολῆς τοῦ ἡλίου συνίσταται, εὐκρὴς οὖσα, αἵματος αὐξητική, θερμὴ καὶ ὑγρὰ ὑπάρχουσα καὶ δι᾽ ἑαυτῆς μεσιτεύουσα τῷ χειμῶνί τε καὶ τῷ θέρει, τοῦ μὲν χειμῶνος θερμοτέρα καὶ ξηροτέρα, τοῦ δὲ θέρους ψυχροτέρα καὶ ὑγροτέρα. Διατείνει δὲ αὕτη ἡ ὥρα ἀπὸ Μαρτίου κα′ μέχρις Ἰουνίου κδ′. Εἶτα ὑψουμένης τῆς τοῦ ἡλίου ἀνατολῆς ἐπὶ τὰ βορειότερα μέρη ἡ θερινὴ τροπὴ διαδέχεται, μεσιτεύουσα τῷ τε ἔαρι καὶ τῷ μετοπώρῳ, ἐκ μὲν τοῦ ἔαρος τὸ θερμὸν ἔχουσα, ἐκ δὲ τοῦ μετοπώρου τὸ ξηρόν· θερμὴ γάρ ἐστι καὶ ξηρὰ καὶ τὴν ξανθὴν αὔξει χολήν. Αὕτη δὲ μεγίστην μὲν τὴν ἡμέραν ἔχει ὡρῶν πεντεκαίδεκα, τὴν δὲ νύκτα πάνυ σμικροτάτην ὡρῶν ἐννέα διάστημα ἔχουσαν. Καὶ αὕτη δὲ διατείνει ἀπὸ Ἰουνίου κδ′ μέχρι μηνὸς Σεπτεμβρίου κε′. Εἶτα πάλιν εἰς τὴν μέσην ἀνατολὴν τοῦ ἡλίου ἐπανιόντος ἡ μετοπωρινὴ τροπὴ τὴν

Mars ♂, Venus ♀, Saturn ♄.[5] And for each of the heavenly spheres there is one of the seven planets:

in the first or highest sphere is Saturn ♄;
in the second is Jupiter ♃;
in the third is Mars ♂;
in the fourth is the Sun ☉;
in the fifth is Venus ♀;
in the sixth is Mercury ☿;
in the seventh or lowest sphere is the Moon ☽.

They run the perpetual course that God has set for them, and as he established them, as the divine David says: "the moon and stars that you established."[6] For by saying "established" he meant the stability and immutability of the order and sequence given to them by God. For he set them "for seasons and for days and years."[7]

For it is by the sun that the four seasons are constituted. The first is spring, for it was in this season that God created everything, as is shown by the fact that to this day it is in spring that the flower buds develop. This is the season of the spring equinox, which makes the day and the night each consist of twelve hours. Spring is caused by the rising of the sun at its midway point, and is therefore temperate, productive of blood, warm and moist, and comes in between winter and summer, being warmer and drier than winter but cooler and moister than summer. This season extends from March 21 to June 24. Then, as the sun rises further towards the north, the summer season follows, coming in between spring and autumn, taking its warmth from spring and its dryness from autumn. For it is warm and dry and causes yellow bile to increase. Its longest day has fifteen hours, with its shortest night having a duration of nine hours. This season extends from June 24 to September 25. Then the sun returns again to the midway point of its rising and the autumn season succeeds

[5] In Greek: Hēlios, Selēnē, Zeus, Hermēs, Arēs, Aphroditē, and Kronos.
[6] Ps 8.4.
[7] Gen 1.14.

θερινὴν τροπὴν ἀμείβει μέση πως ἔχουσα ψύξεώς τε καὶ θέρμης ξηρότητός τε καὶ ὑγρότητος καὶ μεσιτεύουσα τῇ τε θερινῇ καὶ τῇ χειμερινῇ τροπῇ, ἐκ μὲν τῆς θερινῆς τὸ ξηρόν, ἐκ δὲ τῆς χειμερινῆς τὸ ψυχρὸν ἔχουσα· ψυχρὰ γάρ ἐστι καὶ ξηρὰ χολῆς τε μελαίνης αὐξητικὴ πέφυκεν. Αὕτη πάλιν ἰσημερινὴ τροπὴ ὑπάρχει δώδεκα ὡρῶν τήν τε ἡμέραν καὶ τὴν νύκτα ἔχουσα. Διατείνει δὲ αὕτη ἀπὸ Σεπτεμβρίου κε΄ μέχρι Δεκεμβρίου κε΄. Τοῦ δὲ ἡλίου ἐπὶ τὴν μικροτέραν καὶ χθαμαλωτέραν ἤτοι μεσημβρινὴν ἀνατολὴν κατιόντος ἡ χειμερινὴ ἐπιλαμβάνεται τροπή, ψυχρά τε καὶ ὑγρὰ τυγχάνουσα καὶ μεσιτεύουσα τῇ τε μετοπωρινῇ καὶ τῇ ἐαρινῇ, ἐκ μὲν τῆς μετοπωρινῆς τὸ ψυχρὸν ἔχουσα, ἐκ δὲ τῆς ἐαρινῆς τὸ ὑγρὸν κεκτημένη. Αὕτη δὲ σμικροτάτην μὲν τὴν ἡμέραν ἔχει ἐννέα ὡρῶν ὑπάρχουσαν, τὴν δὲ νύκτα μεγίστην ὡρῶν ὑπάρχουσαν πεντεκαίδεκα, φλέγματος δὲ αὕτη ὑπάρχει αὐξητική. Διατείνει δὲ ἀπὸ κε΄ Δεκεμβρίου μέχρις κα΄ Μαρτίου. Σοφῶς γὰρ ὁ δημιουργὸς προενόησατο, ὡς ἂν μὴ ἐξ ἄκρας ψυχρότητος ἢ θερμότητος ἢ ὑγρότητος ἢ ξηρότητος ἐπὶ τὴν ἄκραν ἐναντίαν ἐρχόμενοι ποιότητα χαλεποῖς περιπέσωμεν ἀρρωστήμασι· σφαλερὰς γὰρ τὰς αἰφνιδίους μεταβολὰς οἶδεν ὁ λόγος.

Οὕτω μὲν οὖν ὁ ἥλιος τὰς τροπὰς καὶ δι᾽ αὐτῶν τὸν ἐνιαυτὸν ἀπεργάζεται, καὶ τὰς ἡμέρας δὲ καὶ νύκτας, τὰς μὲν ἀνατέλλων καὶ ὑπὲρ γῆν γινόμενος, τὰς δὲ ὑπὸ γῆν δύνων καὶ τοῖς ἄλλοις φωστῆρσι, σελήνη τε καὶ ἄστρασι, τὴν φαῦσιν παραχωρῶν συνίστησι.

Φασὶ δὲ καὶ δώδεκα ζῴδια ἐξ ἀστέρων εἶναι ἐν τῷ οὐρανῷ, ἐναντίαν κίνησιν ἔχοντα τῷ τε ἡλίῳ καὶ τῇ σελήνῃ καὶ τοῖς ἄλλοις πέντε πλανήταις, καὶ διὰ τῶν δώδεκα ζῳδίων παρέρχεσθαι τοὺς ἑπτά. Ὁ μὲν οὖν ἥλιος καθ᾽ ἕκαστον ζῴδιον ἀποτελεῖ μῆνα ἕνα καὶ διὰ τῶν δώδεκα μηνῶν τὰ δώδεκα ζῴδια διέρχεται. Τῶν δὲ δώδεκα ζῳδίων τὰ ὀνόματά ἐστι ταῦτα καὶ οἱ τούτων μῆνες.

Κριὸς ♈ μηνὶ Μαρτίῳ κα΄ δέχεται τὸν ἥλιον,
Ταῦρος ♉ Ἀπριλλίῳ κγ΄,
Δίδυμοι ♊ Μαΐῳ κγ΄,

summer. This season is something of a midway point between cold and heat, dryness and moistness, and comes in between the summer and winter seasons, taking its dryness from summer and its coldness from winter. For it is cold and dry and naturally increases black bile. In this season there is again an equinox with a day and a night of twelve hours each. This season extends from September 25 to December 25. When the sun arrives at a shorter and lower, that is, more southerly, trajectory, the winter season succeeds, which is cold and moist and comes in between autumn and spring, taking its coldness from autumn and its moisture from spring. Its shortest day has nine hours and its longest night fifteen hours, and it promotes the increase of phlegm. It extends from December 25 to March 21. For the Creator wisely provided that not passing from extreme cold, or heat, or wetness, or dryness to its complete opposite we should not fall into serious illness. For reason tells us that sudden changes are dangerous.

So in this way the sun brings about the seasons and through them the year. It also brings about the days and nights, the former by rising and being above the earth, the latter by setting below the earth, and by withdrawing allows the other luminaries, the moon and the stars, to shine.

They also say that there are twelve signs of the zodiac in the vault of heaven made up of stars, which move in the opposite direction to the sun and the moon and the other five planets, and that the seven pass through the twelve signs of the zodiac. The sun spends a month in each sign of the zodiac and in the course of twelve months traverses the twelve signs. The names of the twelve signs of the zodiac and their months are these:

Aries ♈, entered by the sun on March 21,
Taurus ♉, on April 23,
Gemini ♊, on May 23,
Cancer ♋, on June 24,
Leo ♌, on July 25

Καρκῖνος ♋ Ἰουνίῳ κδ΄,
Λέων ♌ Ἰουλίῳ κε΄,
Παρθένος ♍ Αὐγούστῳ κε΄,
Ζυγὸς ♎ Σεπτεμβρίῳ κε΄,
Σκορπίος ♏ Ὀκτωβρίῳ κε΄,
Τοξότης ♐ Νοεμβρίῳ κε΄,
Αἰγόκερως ♑ Δεκεμβρίῳ κε΄,
Ὑδροχόος ♒ Ἰανουαρίῳ κ΄,
Ἰχθύες ♓ Φεβρουαρίῳ κ΄.

Ἡ δὲ σελήνη καθ᾽ ἕκαστον μῆνα τὰ δώδεκα ζῴδια διέρχεται κατωτέρα οὖσα καὶ ταχύτερον ταῦτα διοδεύουσα· ὡς γάρ, ἐὰν ποιήσῃς πόλον ἔνδον ἄλλου πόλου, ὁ ἔνδον πόλος μικρότερος εὑρεθήσεται, οὕτως καὶ ὁ δρόμος τῆς σελήνης κατωτέρας οὔσης ὀλιγώτερός ἐστι καὶ ἀνύεται τάχιον.

Οἱ μὲν οὖν Ἕλληνες διὰ τῆς τῶν ἄστρων τούτων ἡλίου τε καὶ σελήνης ἀνατολῆς καὶ δύσεως καὶ συγκρούσεώς φασι πάντα διοικεῖσθαι τὰ καθ᾽ ἡμᾶς· περὶ ταῦτα γὰρ ἡ ἀστρολογία καταγίνεται. Ἡμεῖς δέ φαμεν, ὅτι σημεῖα μὲν ἐξ αὐτῶν γίνονται, ὄμβρου καὶ ἀνομβρίας, ψύξεώς τε καὶ θέρμης, ὑγρότητος καὶ ξηρότητος καὶ ἀνέμων καὶ τῶν τοιούτων, τῶν δὲ ἡμετέρων πράξεων οὐδαμῶς· ἡμεῖς γὰρ αὐτεξούσιοι ὑπὸ τοῦ δημιουργοῦ γενόμενοι κύριοι τῶν ἡμετέρων ὑπάρχομεν πράξεων. Εἰ γὰρ ἐκ τῆς τῶν ἄστρων φορᾶς πάντα πράττομεν, κατ᾽ ἀνάγκην πράττομεν, ἃ πράττομεν· τὸ δὲ κατ᾽ ἀνάγκην γινόμενον οὔτε ἀρετὴ οὔτε κακία ἐστίν. Εἰ δὲ μήτε ἀρετὴν μήτε κακίαν κεκτήμεθα, οὔτε ἐπαίνων καὶ στεφάνων, οὔτε ψόγων ἢ κολάσεων ὑπάρχομεν ἄξιοι· εὑρεθήσεται δὲ καὶ ὁ θεὸς ἄδικος τοῖς μὲν ἀγαθά, τοῖς δὲ θλίψεις διδούς. Ἀλλ᾽ οὐδὲ κυβέρνησιν οὐδὲ τῶν ἑαυτοῦ κτισμάτων ὁ θεὸς ποιήσεται πρόνοιαν, εἰ κατ᾽ ἀνάγκην ἄγονται τὰ πάντα καὶ φέρονται. Καὶ τὸ λογικὸν δὲ περιττὸν ἐν ἡμῖν ἔσται· μηδεμιᾶς γὰρ ὄντες πράξεως κύριοι περιττῶς βουλευόμεθα. Τὸ δὲ λογικὸν πάντως τῆς βουλῆς ἡμῖν ἕνεκεν δέδοται· ὅθεν πᾶν λογικὸν καὶ αὐτεξούσιον.

Virgo ♍, on August 25,
Libra ♎, on September 25
Scorpio ♏, on October 25,
Sagittarius ♐, on November 25,
Capricorn ♑, on December 25,
Aquarius ♒, on January 20,
Pisces ♓, on February 20.

The moon passes through all twelve signs every month, since it is lower and traverses them more quickly. For if you draw a circle within another circle, the inner circle will be smaller. In the same way, since the moon's orbit is lower, it is shorter and is accomplished more quickly.

Now the Hellenes say that all our affairs are governed by the rising and setting of these stars, sun, and moon, and their conjunction, for that is what astrology deals with. But we say that signs are given by these of rain and drought, cold and heat, wetness, dryness, and winds and such things, but not at all of our own actions. For we have been endowed with free will by the Creator and are masters of our own actions. If we do everything under the influence of the stars, we do whatever we do by necessity. And that which comes about by necessity is neither virtue nor vice. If we acquire neither virtue nor vice, we are worthy neither of praise and crowns, nor of reproach or punishment. Even God will turn out to be unjust in giving good things to some and afflictions to others. Nor will God exercise government or foresight over his own creatures if everything is borne along by necessity. Even our rational faculty would be superfluous in us, for not being masters of our own actions we would be exercising our will in vain. But our rational faculty has been given to us most certainly on account of our will. Hence every rational being also has freedom of will.

We, for our part, say that these [the stars, the sun, and the moon] are not the cause of anything that comes about, neither of the origin of what comes into being, nor of the cessation of what ceases to be.

Ἡμεῖς δέ φαμεν, ὅτι οὐκ αὐτὰ αἴτιά τινός εἰσι τῶν γινομένων οὔτε γενέσεως τῶν γινομένων οὔτε τῶν φθειρομένων φθορᾶς, σημεῖα δὲ μᾶλλον ὄμβρων τε καὶ τῆς τοῦ ἀέρος μεταβολῆς. Ἴσως δ᾽ ἄν τις εἴποι, ὅτι καὶ πολέμων οὐκ αἴτια, ἀλλὰ σημεῖα, καὶ ἡ ποιότης δὲ τοῦ ἀέρος ποιουμένου ὑπὸ ἡλίου καὶ σελήνης καὶ τῶν ἀστέρων ἄλλως καὶ ἄλλως διαφόρους κράσεις καὶ ἕξεις καὶ διαθέσεις συνίστησιν. Αἱ δὲ ἕξεις τῶν ἐφ᾽ ἡμῖν· κρατοῦνται γὰρ τῷ λόγῳ καὶ ἄγονται τρεπόμεναι.

Συνίστανται δὲ πολλάκις καὶ κομῆται σημεῖά τινα θανάτων βασιλέων, ἅτινα οὔκ εἰσι τῶν ἐξ ἀρχῆς γεγενημένων ἄστρων, ἀλλὰ τῷ θείῳ προστάγματι κατ᾽ αὐτὸν τὸν καιρὸν συνίστανται καὶ πάλιν διαλύονται, ἐπεὶ καὶ ὁ κατὰ τὴν τοῦ κυρίου δι᾽ ἡμᾶς κατὰ σάρκα φιλάνθρωπον καὶ σωτήριον γέννησιν ὀφθεὶς τοῖς μάγοις ἀστὴρ οὐ τῶν ἐν ἀρχῇ γενομένων ἄστρων ἦν. Καὶ δῆλον ἐκ τοῦ ποτὲ μὲν ἐξ ἀνατολῆς ἐπὶ δύσιν ποιεῖσθαι τὸν δρόμον, ποτὲ δὲ ἐκ βορρᾶ ἐπὶ νότον, καὶ ποτὲ μὲν κρύπτεσθαι, ποτὲ δὲ φαίνεσθαι· τοῦτο γὰρ οὐκ ἔστιν ἄστρων τάξεως ἢ φύσεως.

Χρὴ δὲ γινώσκειν, ὡς ἐκ τοῦ ἡλίου φωτίζεται ἡ σελήνη οὐχ ὡς ἀπορήσαντος τοῦ θεοῦ δοῦναι αὐτῇ ἴδιον φῶς, ἀλλ᾽ ἵνα ῥυθμὸς καὶ τάξις ἐντεθῇ τῇ κτίσει ἄρχοντος καὶ ἀρχομένου καὶ παιδευθῶμεν καὶ ἡμεῖς κοινωνεῖν ἀλλήλοις καὶ μεταδιδόναι καὶ ὑποτάσσεσθαι, πρῶτον μὲν τῷ ποιητῇ καὶ δημιουργῷ θεῷ καὶ δεσπότῃ, ἔπειτα καὶ τοῖς ὑπ᾽ αὐτοῦ καθισταμένοις ἄρχουσι, καὶ μὴ ἀνακρίνειν, τίνος ἕνεκεν οὗτος ἄρχει, ἐγὼ δὲ οὔ, δέχεσθαι δὲ πάντα ἐκ θεοῦ εὐχαρίστως καὶ εὐγνωμόνως.

Ἐκλείπει δὲ ὅ τε ἥλιος καὶ ἡ σελήνη τῶν τὴν κτίσιν προσκυνούντων παρὰ τὸν κτίσαντα τὴν ἄνοιαν διελέγχοντα καὶ παιδεύοντα, ὡς τρεπτά εἰσι καὶ ἀλλοιωτά. Πᾶν δὲ τρεπτὸν οὐ θεός· κατὰ τὴν ἰδίαν γὰρ φύσιν φθαρτὸν ἅπαν τρεπτόν.

[8]Cf. Basil of Caesarea, *Homily on the Holy Birth of Christ* (PG 31:1472B).
[9]Cf. John Chrysostom, *Homily 6 on Matthew* (PG 57:64). (IG)
[10]Cf. Rom 1.25.
[11]John accepts the Platonic principle that nothing mutable is god, but applies it in a different way. For Platonists (and Aristotelians) the observable movements of the heavenly bodies had to be interpreted in such a way as to preserve the perfect

Rather, they are signs of rain and changes in the atmosphere. Some-one might perhaps say that they are not causes of wars but signs of them, and that the quality of the atmosphere produced by the sun, the moon, and the stars creates different constitutions, habits, and dispositions. But habits belong to what depends upon ourselves, for they are controlled by reason and are subject to change by us.

And often comets appear as signs of the deaths of kings.[8] They do not belong to the stars that have existed from the beginning but come into being at the appropriate time by divine command and then cease to be. And when the star was seen by the magi at the time of the Lord's benevolent and saving birth in the flesh for us, it was not one of the stars that came into being at the beginning. This is evident from the fact that their trajectory is sometimes from east to west, sometimes from north to south, and sometimes they are hidden and sometimes appear. This does not belong to the order or nature of stars.[9]

One needs to know that the moon is illuminated by the sun, not because God lacked the power to give it its own light, but so that creation might be endowed with harmony and order, with ruler and ruled, and that we too might be taught to associate with each other and share with each other and submit to each other, first to God the maker and creator and master, and then to the rulers appointed by him, and not inquire why this particular person rules and not I, but accept all things from God thankfully and in gratitude.

The sun and the moon suffer eclipse, thus censuring and cor-recting the folly of those who worship the creature rather than the Creator,[10] since they are mutable and changeable. Nothing that is mutable is god, for everything mutable is subject to decay.[11]

The sun is eclipsed when the moon's mass becomes something like a barrier and casts a shadow, and prevents the light from coming through to us. So the more fully the moon's mass conceals the sun,

regularity (and therefore divinity) of a homocentric universe, i.e., the doctrine that all the heavenly bodies maintain an unvarying distance from the earth (cf. Plato *Laws* 7, 821b–822c; Aristotle, *On the Heavens* 1.9, 277b27–9). For John, experience trumps theoretical dogmatism. The observable fact of change and irregularity disproves the divinity of the heavens.

Ἐκλείπει δὲ ὁ μὲν ἥλιος τοῦ σώματος τῆς σελήνης ὥσπερ τι μεσότοιχον γινομένου καὶ ἀποσκιάζοντος καὶ μὴ ἐῶντος διαδοθῆναι ἡμῖν τὸ φῶς. Ὅσον οὖν εὑρεθῇ τὸ σῶμα τῆς σελήνης ἀποκρύπτον τὸν ἥλιον, τοσοῦτον καὶ ἡ ἔκλειψις γίνεται. Εἰ δὲ μικρότερόν ἐστι τὸ τῆς σελήνης σῶμα, μὴ θαυμάσῃς· καὶ ὁ ἥλιος γὰρ ὑπό τινων λέγεται πολυπλασίων τῆς γῆς, ὑπὸ δὲ τῶν πατέρων ἴσος τῆς γῆς· καὶ πολλάκις μικρὸν νέφος καλύπτει αὐτὸν ἢ καὶ μικρὸς βουνὸς ἢ τοῖχος.

Ἡ δὲ τῆς σελήνης ἔκλειψις ἐκ τοῦ ἀποσκιάσματος τῆς γῆς γίνεται, ὅτε γένηται πεντεκαιδεκαταία ἡ σελήνη καὶ εὑρεθῇ ἐξ ἐναντίας κατὰ τὸ ἄκρον κέντρον, ὁ μὲν ἥλιος ὑπὸ γῆν, ἡ δὲ σελήνη ὑπὲρ γῆν· ἀποσκίασμα γὰρ ποιεῖ ἡ γῆ καὶ οὐ φθάνει τὸ ἡλιακὸν φῶς φωτίσαι τὴν σελήνην, κἀκεῖθεν ἐκλείπει.

Χρὴ δὲ γινώσκειν, ὅτι τελεία ἐκτίσθη ἡ σελήνη ὑπὸ τοῦ δημιουργοῦ ἤτοι πεντεκαιδεκαταία· ἔπρεπε γὰρ ἀπηρτισμένην γενέσθαι. Τῇ δὲ τετάρτῃ ἡμέρᾳ, ὡς ἔφημεν, ἔκτισται ὁ ἥλιος. Προέλαβεν οὖν τὸν ἥλιον ἔνδεκα ἡμέρας· ἀπὸ γὰρ τετάρτης ἡμέρας ἕως πεντεκαιδεκάτης ἔνδεκά εἰσι. Διὸ καὶ κατὰ χρόνον οἱ δώδεκα μῆνες τῆς σελήνης ἔνδεκα ἡμέρας λείπουσιν ἐκ τῶν δώδεκα μηνῶν τοῦ ἡλίου· οἱ μὲν γὰρ τοῦ ἡλίου τξε′ δ″ ἡμέρας ἔχουσιν. Διὸ τοῦ τετάρτου συντιθεμένου κατὰ τέσσαρα ἔτη μία ἀποτελεῖται ἡμέρα, ἥτις λέγεται βίσεξτον. Καὶ ὁ ἐνιαυτὸς ἐκεῖνος τξς′ ἡμέρας ἔχει. Οἱ δὲ τῆς σελήνης ἐνιαυτοὶ τνδ′ εἰσὶν ἡμερῶν·

[12]John's information on solar eclipses and (below) on lunar eclipses is accurate and is based on the reports of the great Alexandrian astronomers of the Hellenistic and early Roman periods.

[13]In fact all the great Alexandrian astronomers said that the sun was much larger than the earth. In his work On sizes and distances the first of these astronomers, Aristarchus of Samos (c. 310–230 BC), calculated, on the basis of the moon's 90-degree angle to the sun at the time of a half-moon from our terrestrial vantage-point, that "the diameter of the sun has to the diameter of the earth a ratio greater than 19 : 3 but less than 43 : 6." Benjamin Farrington, Greek Science, vol. 2 (Harmondsworth, UK: Penguin Books, 1949), 81. The true ratio is in fact 109 : 1. Aristarchus' method was not wrong, but in view of the immense distances involved, without modern instruments for measuring fractions of degrees, small errors result in very different values.

[14]It is difficult to understand on what John has based this assertion. None of the writers he would have regarded as "fathers," or indeed anyone else before his

the more complete is the eclipse.[12] Do not be surprised at this on account of the moon's mass being the smaller, for the sun is said by some to be many times larger than the earth,[13] but by the fathers to be equal to the earth,[14] and often a small cloud or a small hill or a wall hides the sun.

The eclipse of the moon takes place, as a result of the earth's shadow falling upon it, when the moon is fifteen days old and is directly opposite at its highest point, with the sun below the earth and the moon above the earth. For the earth casts a shadow and the sun's light is unable to illuminate the moon, which is therefore eclipsed.

One also needs to know that the moon was created in its full form by the Creator, that is to say, as it is at fifteen days old, for it was fitting that it should come into being in a finished state. The sun, as we have said, was created on the fourth day. The moon was therefore eleven days in advance of the sun, for it is eleven days from the fourth to the fifteenth day. Hence in the course of a year the twelve lunar months fall short of the twelve solar months by eleven days, for the solar year has 365 and a quarter days. By adding up the quarters, in four years a day is completed, which is called the bissextile.[15] And that year has 366 days. But the lunar years consist of 354 days, for from its birth or renewal the moon waxes until it becomes fourteen and three quarters days old, and then begins to wane until it is twenty-nine and a half days old and becomes completely without

own time, so far as I have been able to ascertain, held such an eccentric opinion. St Basil, for example, commenting on the two "great lights" of Gen 1.16, says that they are called such not because they are greater than the smaller stars but because, on account of their exceptional magnitude, they appear to be of the same size wherever the beholder is standing on the earth's surface, which proves just how far away they are (*Hexaemeron* 6.9). The only similar claim to John's was made in the twelfth century by Peter the Philosopher (about whom very little is known), no doubt on the basis of the statement by John himself. See Anne-Laurence Caudano, " 'Le ciel à la forme d'un cube ou a été dressé comme une peau': Pierre le Philosophe et l'orthodoxie du savoir astronomique sous Manuel Ier Comnène," *Byzantion* 81 (2011): 52–72.

[15]The bissextile day (following the reform of the calendar by an edict of Julius Caesar in 45 BC) was February 24, which in Latin system of dating was the *ante diem bis sextum* (hence "bissextile") *Kalendas Martias*, "twice the sixth day before the kalends of March."

ἡ γὰρ σελήνη, ἀφ' οὗ γεννηθῇ ἤγουν ἀνακαινισθῇ, αὔξει, ἕως
ἂν γένηται ἡμερῶν ιδ' ἡμίσεος τετάρτου, καὶ ἄρχεται λήγειν, ἕως
ἡμερῶν κθ' ἡμίσεος, καὶ τελείως γίνεται ἀφώτιστος. Καὶ πάλιν
συναπτομένη τῷ ἡλίῳ ἀναγεννᾶται καὶ ἀνακαινίζεται ὑπόμνημα
φέρουσα τῆς ἡμῶν ἀναστάσεως. Καθ' ἕκαστον οὖν ἐνιαυτὸν
τὰς ἔνδεκα ἡμέρας ἀποδίδωσι τῷ ἡλίῳ. Κατὰ οὖν τρεῖς χρόνους
ὁ ἐμβόλιμος μὴν γίνεται τοῖς Ἑβραίοις, καὶ ὁ ἐνιαυτὸς ἐκεῖνος
δεκατριῶν μηνῶν εὑρίσκεται ἐκ τῆς προσθήκης τῶν ἔνδεκα
ἡμερῶν.

Δῆλον δὲ ὡς σύνθετός ἐστιν ὅ τε ἥλιος καὶ ἡ σελήνη καὶ τὰ
ἄστρα καὶ φθορᾷ κατὰ τὴν ἰδίαν φύσιν ὑπόκεινται. Τὴν δὲ τούτων
φύσιν οὐκ ἴσμεν. Τινὲς μὲν οὖν φασι τὸ πῦρ ἐκτός τινος ὕλης
ἀφανὲς εἶναι, ὅθεν καὶ σβεννύμενον ἀφανίζεται. Ἕτεροι δὲ τοῦτο
σβεννύμενον εἰς ἀέρα φασὶ μεταβάλλεσθαι.

Ὁ ζῳδιακὸς κύκλος λοξῶς κινεῖται, διῃρημένος εἰς τμήματα
δώδεκα, ἅτινα καλεῖται ζῴδια. Τὸ δὲ ζῴδιον ἔχει δεκανοὺς τρεῖς,
μοίρας λ'· ἡ δὲ μοῖρα ἔχει λεπτὰ ξ'. Ἔχει οὖν ὁ οὐρανὸς μοίρας τξ',
τὸ ὑπὲρ γῆν ἡμισφαίριον μοίρας ρπ' καὶ τὸ ὑπὸ γῆν ρπ'.

Οἶκοι πλανητῶν· Κριὸς καὶ Σκορπίος Ἄρεως, Ταῦρος καὶ
Ζυγὸς Ἀφροδίτης, Δίδυμοι καὶ Παρθένος Ἑρμοῦ, Καρκῖνος
Σελήνης, Λέων Ἡλίου, Τοξότης καὶ Ἰχθύες Διός, Αἰγόκερως καὶ
Ὑδριχόος Κρόνου.

Ὑψώματα· Κριὸς Ἡλίου, Ταῦρος Σελήνης, Καρκῖνος Διός,
Παρθένος Ἑρμοῦ, Ζυγὸς Κρόνου, Αἰγόκερως Ἄρεως, Ἰχθύες
Ἀφροδίτης.

Τὰ σχήματα τῆς σελήνης. Σύνοδος, ὅτε γένηται ἐν τῇ μοίρᾳ,
ἐν ᾗ ἐστιν ὁ ἥλιος· †γέννα, ὅταν ἀποστῇ τοῦ ἡλίου μοίρας
ιε'· ἀνατολή, ὅτε φανῇ·† μηνοειδεῖς δύο, ὅταν ἀπέχῃ μοίρας
ξ'· διχότομοι δύο, ὅταν ἀπέχῃ μοίρας ៴'· ἀμφίκυρτοι δύο, ὅταν
ἀπέχῃ μοίρας ρκ'· πλησισέληνοι, αἵ καὶ πλησιφαεῖς, δύο, ὅταν
ἀπέχῃ μοίρας ρν'· πανσέληνος, ὅταν ἀπέχῃ μοίρας ρπ'. Δύο δὲ
εἴπομεν, μίαν αὐξούσης καὶ μίαν ληγούσης. Διὰ δύο ἥμισυ ἡμερῶν
παρέρχεται ἡ σελήνη ἕκαστον ζῴδιον.

illumination. And when it makes contact with the sun again, it is reborn and renewed, bearing a reminder of our own resurrection. So each year the moon yields eleven days to the sun. Therefore every three years an intercalary month is inserted by the Hebrews, and that year has thirteen months on account of the accumulation of the eleven days.

It is also evident that since the sun, the moon, and the stars are composite, they are subject by their own nature to decay. We do not know what their nature is. Some say that when fire is not in some kind of matter it is invisible, and hence when it is extinguished it is invisible. But others say that when it is extinguished it changes into air.[16]

The orbit of the zodiac moves obliquely. It is divided into twelve sections that are called signs. Each sign has three decans, making thirty degrees, and each degree has sixty seconds. The vault of heaven thus has 360 degrees, the hemisphere above the earth having 180 degrees, and that below the earth 180 degrees.

The planetary houses: that of Mars is Aries and Scorpio; that of Venus is Taurus and Libra; that of Mercury is Gemini and Virgo; that of the Moon is Cancer; that of the Sun is Leo; that of Jupiter is Sagittarius and Pisces; and that of Saturn is Capricorn and Aquarius.

The ascendancies: that of the Sun is Aries; that of the Moon is Taurus; that of Jupiter is Cancer; that of Mercury is Virgo; that of Saturn is Libra; that of Mars is Capricorn; that of Venus is Pisces.

The phases of the moon: it is in conjunction when it is in the same degree as the sun; it is nascent when it stands at fifteen degrees from the sun; it is ascendant when it appears; it is crescent-shaped twice when it stands at sixty degrees; it is half-full twice when it stands at ninety degrees; it is gibbous twice when it stands at 120 degrees; it is near-full twice, giving full light, when it stands at 150 degrees; it is full when it stands at 180 degrees. We say twice, once when it is waxing and once when it is waning. The moon passes through each sign of the zodiac in two and a half days.

[16]Cf. Nemesius of Emesa, *On Human Nature* 5 (PG 40:617B–629A; Morani, 49.11–53.18).

22 Περὶ ἀέρος καὶ ἀνέμων

Ἀήρ ἐστι στοιχεῖον λεπτότατον ὑγρόν τε καὶ θερμόν, τοῦ μὲν πυρὸς βαρύτερον, τῆς δὲ γῆς καὶ τῶν ὑδάτων κουφότερον, ἀναπνοῆς καὶ ἐκφωνήσεως αἴτιον, ἀχρωμάτιστον ἤτοι ἐκ φύσεως χρῶμα μὴ κεκτημένον, διειδές, διαφανές (φωτὸς γάρ ἐστι δεκτικόν) καὶ ταῖς τρισὶν αἰσθήσεσιν ἡμῶν διακονοῦν (δι' αὐτοῦ γὰρ ὁρῶμεν, ἀκούομεν, ὀσφραινόμεθα), δεκτικὸν θάλψεώς τε καὶ ψύξεως ξηρότητός τε καὶ ὑγρότητος, οὗ πᾶσαι αἱ κατὰ τόπον κινήσεις εἰσίν· ἄνω, κάτω, ἔσω, ἔξω, δεξιά, ἀριστερὰ καὶ ἡ κυκλοφορικὴ κίνησις. Οἴκοθεν μὴ κεκτημένος τὸ φῶς, ἀλλ' ὑπὸ ἡλίου καὶ σελήνης καὶ ἄστρων καὶ πυρὸς φωτιζόμενος. Καὶ τοῦτό ἐστιν, ὃ εἶπεν ἡ γραφή, ὅτι «σκότος ἦν ἐπάνω τῆς ἀβύσσου», θέλουσα δεῖξαι, ὡς οὐκ οἴκοθεν ὁ ἀὴρ τὸ φῶς κέκτηται, ἀλλ' ἄλλη τίς ἐστιν οὐσία ἡ τοῦ φωτός.

Ἄνεμος δέ ἐστι κίνησις ἀέρος. Καὶ ὁ τόπος δὲ τοῦ ἀέρος ἐστί· τόπος γάρ ἐστιν ἑκάστου σώματος ἡ τούτου περιοχή. Τί δὲ περιέχει τὰ σώματα, εἰ μὴ ἀήρ; Εἰσὶ δὲ τόποι διάφοροι, ὅθεν ἡ τοῦ ἀέρος γίνεται κίνησις, ἐξ ὧν καὶ οἱ ἄνεμοι τὰς ἐπωνυμίας ἔχουσι· δώδεκα δὲ οἱ πάντες εἰσί. Φασὶ δὲ τὸν ἀέρα σβέσιν πυρὸς ἢ ἀτμὸν ὕδατος θερμανθέντος. Ἔστι γοῦν ὁ ἀὴρ κατὰ μὲν τὴν οἰκείαν φύσιν θερμός, ψύχεται δὲ τῇ γειτνιάσει τῇ πρὸς τὸ ὕδωρ καὶ τὴν γῆν, ὡς τὰ μὲν κάτω μέρη αὐτοῦ ψυχρὰ εἶναι, τὰ δὲ ἄνω θερμά.

22b Περὶ ἀνέμων

Ἄνεμός ἐστι πλῆθος θερμῆς καὶ ξηρᾶς ἀναθυμιάσεως κινούμενον περὶ γῆν. Ἄνεμοι πνέουσιν ἀπὸ ἀνατολῆς θερινῆς καικίας, μέσης, ἀπὸ ἀνατολῆς ἰσημερινῆς ἀπηλιώτης, ἀπὸ ἀνατολῆς χειμερινῆς

---

[1]Cf. Nemesius of Emesus, *On Human Nature* 5 (PG 40:613B–629B; Morani, 47.17–54.10).

[2]Gen 1.2.

[3]The last two sentences are from Nemesius of Emesus, *On Human Nature* 5 (PG 40:620A; Morani, 49.19–21).

22   *On air and winds*

Air is a very fine moist and warm element, heavier than fire but lighter than earth and water, the cause of breathing and giving voice, colorless, that is to say, possessing no color by nature, transparent, translucent (for it is receptive of light), serving three of our sensory faculties (for it is through this element that we see, hear, and smell), receptive of heat and cold, dryness and moisture, and capable of all the spatial movements: upwards, downwards, inwards, outwards, to the right, to the left, and circular.[1] It does not possess light of itself but is illuminated by the sun, the moon, and the stars, and by fire. And this is what Scripture means when it says that "darkness was over the deep,"[2] intending to show that the air does not possess light of itself, but the essence of light is something else.

Wind is the movement of air. And there is also the place of air, for the place of every body is the limit of its extent. And what marks the limit of bodies if not air? There are various places from which air begins to flow and from which the winds take their names. There are twelve altogether. They say that the air is the cooling of fire or the vapor of heated water. At all events, the air is warm of its own nature, but is cooled by proximity to water and earth, so that its lower regions are cool but its upper regions warm.[3]

22b   *On winds*[1]

A wind is a mass of warm and dry vapor that moves round the earth. The wind blowing from the northeast is the Kaikias or Meses, from due east is the Apeliotes, from the southeast is the Euros, from the southwest is the Lips, from due west is the Zephyros, from

---

[1]This chapter, which takes its cue from the twelve winds mentioned at the end of the previous chapter, is added by four manuscripts, GHMN. H, however, inserts it before Chapter 25. For parallels to the first paragraph, Kotter draws attention to A. Diller, *The Tradition of the Minor Greek Geographers*, Philological Monographs 14 (Oxford: Oxford University Press, 1952), 34 (Agathemerus) and Strabo, *Geography* 1.29.

εὖρος, ἀπὸ δύσεως χειμερινῆς λίψ, ἀπὸ δύσεως ἰσημερινῆς ζέφυρος, ἀπὸ δύσεως θερινῆς ἀργέστης ἤτοι Ὀλυμπίας, ὁ καὶ Ἰάπυξ καὶ ἐργάστης. Εἶτα νότος καὶ ἀπαρκτίας ἀντιπνέοντες ἀλλήλοις. Ἔστι δὲ μέσος ἀπαρκτίου καὶ καικίου βορέας, εὔρου δὲ καὶ νότου μέσος Φοῖνιξ, ὁ καλούμενος εὐρόνοτος, μέσος δὲ νότου καὶ λιβὸς λιβόνοτος, ὁ καὶ λευκόνοτος, μέσος δὲ ἀπαρκτίου καὶ ἀργέστου θρασκίας ἤτοι κέρκιος ὑπὸ τῶν περιοίκων ὀνομαζόμενος.

Εἰσὶν οὖν οἱ πάντες ιβ΄, ὧν ἡ διαγραφή ἐστιν αὕτη· Ἀνατολὴ θερινή, ἀνατολὴ ἰσημερινή, ἀνατολὴ χειμερινή—καικίας, ἀπηλιώτης, εὖρος, μέσης, εὐρόνοτος, βορέας, Φοῖνιξ—ἄρκτος—ἀπαρκτίας, νότος—μεσημβρία—θρασκίας, λιβόνοτος, μέσης, λευκόνοτος, κέρκιος, λίψ—δύσις θερινή—ἀργέστης—δύσις χειμερινή—Ἰάπυξ, Ὀλυμπίας—δύσις θερινή—ἐργάστης, ζέφυρος.

23 Περὶ ὑδάτων

Καὶ τὸ ὕδωρ δὲ ἓν τῶν στοιχείων τῶν τεσσάρων ἐστί, ποίημα θεοῦ κάλλιστον. Ὕδωρ ἐστὶ στοιχεῖον ὑγρόν τε καὶ ψυχρὸν βαρύ τε καὶ κατωφερές, εὐδιάχυτον. Τούτου δὲ μνημονεύει ἡ θεία γραφὴ λέγουσα· «Καὶ σκότος ἦν ἐπάνω τῆς ἀβύσσου, καὶ πνεῦμα θεοῦ ἐπεφέρετο ἐπάνω τοῦ ὕδατος»· ἄβυσσος γὰρ οὐδὲν ἕτερόν ἐστιν, εἰ μὴ ὕδωρ πολύ, οὗ τὸ τέλος ἀκατάληπτον ἀνθρώποις. Ἐν ἀρχῇ μὲν οὖν τὸ ὕδωρ ἐπὶ πᾶσαν τὴν γῆν ἐπεπόλαζε. Καὶ πρῶτον μὲν ἐποίησεν ὁ θεὸς τὸ στερέωμα διαχωρίζον ἀναμέσον τοῦ ὕδατος τοῦ ἐπάνω τοῦ στερεώματος καὶ τοῦ ὕδατος τοῦ ὑποκάτω τοῦ στερεώματος· ἐν τῷ μέσῳ γὰρ τῆς ἀβύσσου τῶν ὑδάτων ἐστερεώθη τῷ δεσποτικῷ προστάγματι. Ὅθεν καὶ στερέωμα εἶπεν ὁ θεὸς γενέσθαι, καὶ ἐγένετο. Τίνος δὲ χάριν ἐπάνω τοῦ στερεώματος ὕδωρ ὁ θεὸς ἀπέθετο; Διὰ τὴν τοῦ ἡλίου καὶ τοῦ αἰθέρος θερμοτάτην ἔκκαυσιν· εὐθέως γὰρ μετὰ τὸ στερέωμα ὁ αἰθὴρ ἐφήπλωται. Καὶ ὁ ἥλιος δὲ σὺν τῇ σελήνῃ καὶ τοῖς ἄστροις

the northwest is the Argestes or Olympias, which is also called the Iapyx and the Ergastes. Next, the south and north winds, the Notos and the Aparktias, blow in opposite directions to each other. Midway between the Aparktias and the Kaikias is the Boreas, midway between the Euros and the Notos is the Phoinix, which is called the Euronotos, midway between the Notos and the Lips is the Libonotos, which is also called the Leukonotos, and midway between the Aparktias and the Argestes is the Thraskias, which the inhabitants of that region call the Kerkios.

The total number is therefore twelve, which may be listed as follows: northeast, due east, southeast—Kaikias, Apeliotes, Euros, Meses, Euronotos, Boreas, Phoinix; north—Aparktias, Notos; south—Thraskias, Libonotos, Meses, Leukonotos, Kerkios, Lips; northwest—Argestes; southwest—Iapyx, Olympias; northwest—Ergastes, Zephyros.

23   *On waters*

Water, too, is one of the four elements, a creation of God that is excellent. Water is an element that is wet and cold, heavy and with a tendency to sink, and easily flowing.[1] The divine Scripture mentions it when it says: "And darkness was over the abyss and the Spirit of God moved over the water."[2] For the abyss is nothing other than a great quantity of water whose full extent is beyond human comprehension. In the beginning, indeed, water covered the whole earth. And God first made the firmament that divides the water that is above the firmament from the water that is below the firmament, for it was made firm in the middle of the abyss of waters at the Lord's command. Hence God also said that a firmament should come into being and it came into being. For what reason did God set the water above the firmament? Because of the burning heat of the sun and the

---

[1]Cf. Nemesius of Emesus, *On Human Nature* 5 (PG 40:613B, 625A; Morani, 51.25–52.12, 52.14–16).

[2]Gen 1.2.

ἐν τῷ στερεώματί εἰσι· καὶ εἰ μὴ ἐπέκειτο ὕδωρ, ἐφλέχθη ἂν ὑπὸ τῆς θέρμης τὸ στερέωμα.

Εἶτα προσέταξεν ὁ θεὸς συναχθῆναι τὰ ὕδατα εἰς συναγωγὴν μίαν. Τὸ δὲ «μίαν συναγωγὴν» λέγειν οὐ δηλοῖ τὸ ἐν ἑνὶ τόπῳ συναχθῆναι αὐτά·—ἰδοὺ γὰρ μετὰ ταῦτά φησι· «Καὶ τὰ συστήματα τῶν ὑδάτων ἐκάλεσε θαλάσσας», —ἀλλὰ τὸ ὁμοῦ καθ᾽ ἑαυτὰ κεχωρισμένα τῆς γῆς γενέσθαι τὰ ὕδατα ὁ λόγος ἐδήλωσε. Συνήχθησαν τοίνυν τὰ ὕδατα «εἰς τὰς συναγωγὰς αὐτῶν, καὶ ὤφθη ἡ ξηρά». Ἐντεῦθεν αἱ δύο θάλασσαι αἱ τὴν Αἴγυπτον περιέχουσαι (μέση γὰρ αὕτη τῶν δύο κεῖται θαλασσῶν) συνέστησαν, διάφορα πελάγη καὶ ὄρη καὶ νήσους καὶ ἀγκῶνας καὶ λιμένας ἔχουσαι καὶ κόλπους διαφόρους περιέχουσαι αἰγιαλούς τε καὶ ἀκτάς— αἰγιαλὸς μὲν γὰρ ὁ ψαμμώδης λέγεται, ἀκτὴ δὲ ἡ πετρώδης καὶ ἀγχιβαθὴς ἤτοι ἡ εὐθέως ἐν τῇ ἀρχῇ βάθος ἔχουσα—, ὁμοίως καὶ ἡ κατὰ τὴν ἀνατολήν, ἥτις λέγεται Ἰνδική, καὶ ἡ βορεινή, ἥτις λέγεται Κασπία· καὶ αἱ λίμναι δὲ ἐντεῦθεν συνήχθησαν.

Ἔστιν οὖν ὁ μὲν Ὠκεανὸς οἷόν τις ποταμὸς κυκλῶν πᾶσαν τὴν γῆν, περὶ οὗ εἴρηκεν, ὡς ἐμοὶ δοκεῖ, ἡ γραφή, ὅτι «ποταμὸς ἐκπορεύεται ἐκ τοῦ παραδείσου» πότιμον καὶ γλυκὺ ὕδωρ ἔχων. Οὗτος χορηγεῖ τὸ ὕδωρ ταῖς θαλάσσαις, ὅπερ ἐν ταῖς θαλάσσαις χρονίζον καὶ ἑστὼς ἀκίνητον πικρὸν γίνεται τοῦ ἡλίου ἀεὶ τὸ λεπτότερον ἀνιμωμένου καὶ τῶν σιφώνων, ὅθεν καὶ τὰ νέφη συνίστανται καὶ οἱ ὄμβροι γίνονται διὰ τῆς διηθήσεως γλυκαινομένου τοῦ ὕδατος.

Οὗτος καὶ εἰς τέσσαρας ἀρχὰς ἤτοι εἰς τέσσαρας ποταμοὺς διαιρεῖται. «Ὄνομα τῷ ἑνὶ Φεισών», τουτέστι Γάγγης ὁ Ἰνδικός. «Καὶ ὄνομα τῷ ἄλλῳ Γηών»· οὗτός ἐστιν ὁ Νεῖλος ὁ ἀπὸ Αἰθιοπίας εἰς Αἴγυπτον κατερχόμενος. Καὶ ὄνομα τῷ τρίτῳ Τίγρις. Καὶ ὄνομα τῷ τετάρτῳ Εὐφράτης. Εἰσὶ δὲ καὶ ἕτεροι πλεῖστοι καὶ μέγιστοι ποταμοί, ὧν οἱ μὲν εἰς τὴν θάλασσαν κενοῦνται, οἱ δὲ καὶ ἐν τῇ γῇ ἀναλίσκονται. Ὅμως καὶ πᾶσα ἡ γῆ διάτρητός

aether. For the aether is spread out immediately after the firmament. And the sun with the moon and the stars are in the firmament. If there were no layer of water the firmament would be set on fire by the heat.[3]

Then God commanded that the waters should be gathered together into a single mass.[4] Saying "a single mass" does not mean that they were gathered into one place, for note that after this it says: "And the groupings of the waters he called seas"[5]—what the phrase actually means is that the waters were separated from the earth by themselves all together. Therefore the waters were gathered together "into their masses and dry land appeared."[6] Thus were constituted the two thalassic seas that surround Egypt (for Egypt lies between two seas), which have various pelagic seas, mountains, islands, headlands and various bays containing beaches (αἰγιαλοί, *aigialoi*) and rockbound coasts (ἀκταί, *aktai*)—for a sandy beach is called an αἰγιαλός (*aigialos*) and an ἀκτή (*aktē*) is a littoral that is rocky and deep inshore or quickly becomes deep—and constituted in the same way was the eastern sea, which is called the Indian, and the northern, which is called the Caspian, and then the lakes.

Then there is the Ocean, which is like a river encircling the whole earth. Scripture, in my opinion, refers to this when it says that "a river flows out of Paradise,"[7] which has drinkable fresh water. The Ocean supplies the seas with their water, which through standing still for a long time in the seas becomes brackish, since the sun and waterspouts are constantly drawing up the lighter part, with the result that clouds are formed and rains occur, the water having been sweetened by the filtration.

The Ocean is divided into four branches, "The name of the first is Phison,"[8] that is, the Indian Ganges. "And the name of the second is Geon."[9] This is the Nile, which comes down from Ethiopia into Egypt. And the name of the third is Tigris. And the name of the

[3]Cf. Basil of Caesarea, *Hexaemeron* 3.5.3–4 (PG 29:64C–65A; Naldini, 86).
[4]Gen 1.9.   [5]Gen 1.10.   [6]Gen 1.9.
[7]Gen 2.10.   [8]Gen 2.11.   [9]Gen 2.13.

ἐστι καὶ ὑπόνομος ὥσπερ τινὰς φλέβας ἔχουσα, δι' ὧν ἐκ τῆς θαλάσσης δεχομένη τὰ ὕδατα τὰς πηγὰς ἀνίησι. Πρὸς οὖν τὴν ποιότητα τῆς γῆς καὶ τὸ τῶν πηγῶν ὕδωρ γίνεται. Διηθεῖται μὲν γὰρ διὰ τῆς γῆς τὸ θαλάττιον ὕδωρ καὶ οὕτω γλυκαίνεται. Εἰ δὲ ὁ τόπος, ὅθεν ἡ πηγὴ ἀναδίδοται, τύχοι πικρὸς ἢ ἁλμυρός, πρὸς τὴν γῆν καὶ τὸ ὕδωρ ἀνάγεται. Στενούμενον δὲ πολλάκις τὸ ὕδωρ καὶ βίᾳ ῥηγνύμενον θερμαίνεται, κἀντεῦθεν τὰ αὐτοφυῆ θερμὰ ἀνάγονται ὕδατα. Τῷ οὖν θείῳ προστάγματι κοιλώματα ἐν τῇ γῇ γεγόνασι, καὶ οὕτως εἰς τὰς συναγωγὰς αὐτῶν συνήχθη τὰ ὕδατα· ἐντεῦθεν καὶ τὰ ὄρη γεγόνασι.

Πρώτῳ τοίνυν τῷ ὕδατι προσέταξεν ὁ θεὸς ἐξαγαγεῖν ψυχὴν ζῶσαν, ἐπειδὴ ἤμελλε δι' ὕδατος καὶ τοῦ ἐν ἀρχῇ ἐπιφερομένου τοῖς ὕδασιν ἁγίου πνεύματος ἀνακαινίζειν τὸν ἄνθρωπον· τοῦτο γὰρ ὁ θεῖος ἔφη Βασίλειος. Ἐξήγαγε δὲ ζῷα μικρά τε καὶ μεγάλα, κήτη, δράκοντας, ἰχθύας ἐν τοῖς ὕδασιν ἕρποντας καὶ πετεινὰ πτερωτά. Διὰ τῶν πετεινῶν οὖν συνάπτεται τό τε ὕδωρ καὶ ἡ γῆ καὶ ὁ ἀήρ· ἐξ ὑδάτων μὲν γὰρ ταῦτα γέγονεν, ἐν τῇ γῇ δὲ διατρίβει καὶ ἐν ἀέρι ἵπταται. Κάλλιστον δὲ στοιχεῖον τὸ ὕδωρ καὶ πολύχρηστον καὶ ῥύπου καθάρσιον, μόνον μὲν σωματικοῦ, καὶ ψυχικοῦ δέ, εἰ προσλάβοι τὴν χάριν τοῦ πνεύματος.

23b *Περὶ πελαγῶν*

Διαδέχεται τὸ Αἰγαῖον πέλαγος Ἑλλήσποντος λῆγον εἰς Ἄβυδον καὶ Σηστόν· εἶτα ἡ Προποντὶς λήγουσα εἰς Χαλκηδόνα καὶ Βυζάντιον· ἔνθα τὰ στενά, ἀφ' ὧν ὁ Πόντος ἄρχεται· εἶτα ἡ Μαιῶτις λίμνη. Πάλιν δὲ ἀπ' ἀρχῆς Εὐρώπης καὶ Λιβύης Ἰβηρικὸν

[10]Cf. Basil of Caesarea, *Hexaemeron* 4.6.3 (PG 29:92C; Naldini, 124–26).

[11]Cf. Gen 1.20: ἑρπετὰ ψυχῶν ζωσῶν (*herpeta psychōn zōsōn*), literally, "creeping things of living souls." John modifies the Septuagint text, dropping ἑρπετὰ and making ψυχῶν ζωσῶν singular because this better suits his symbolic exegesis.

[12]Cf. Basil of Caesarea, *Hexaemeron* 2.6 (PG 29:42C–44B; Naldini, 56–58) and 8.2 (PG 29:165D–169B; Naldini, 240–44).

[1]This chapter is added by manuscripts HKLMN. On the seas, cf. Basil, *Hexaemeron* 4.3–4 (PG 29:81D–88B; Naldini, 114–20).

fourth is Euphrates. There are also many other great rivers, some of which empty out into the sea, while others are absorbed into the ground. After all, the whole earth is perforated with underground channels, as if it had veins, through which it receives waters from the sea and sends them up as springs. Now, the water of the springs takes its quality from that of the earth. For the sea water is filtered through the earth and thus becomes sweet.[10] If the place where the spring gushes happens to be bitter or salty, the water also comes out like the earth. Often when the water is compressed and bursts out with force it becomes heated, and for that reason natural hot springs occur. Then by the divine command hollows were formed in the land and it was thus that the waters accumulated in their expanses. It is also how mountains came about.

Then God commanded the first water to bring forth living soul,[11] because he intended to renew humanity through water and the Holy Spirit that in the beginning moved over the waters. For this is what the divine Basil said.[12] And it brought forth animals small and great, whales, serpents, fish swimming in the waters, and winged fowl. In fact, it is through the birds that water, earth, and air are connected with each other, for they came into being from water, spend their time on land, and fly in the air. Water is an excellent element with multiple uses. It cleanses away filth, not only the filth of the body but also, if in addition it receives the grace of the Spirit, that of the soul.

23b *On seas*[1]

The Aegean Sea is succeeded by the Hellespont, which ends at Abydus and Sestus. Then comes the Propontis,[2] which ends at Chalcedon and Byzantium. Then come the straits,[3] after which the Pontic Sea begins,[4] and then comes Lake Maiotis.[5] From the opposite

[2]Today the Sea of Marmara.
[3]The Bosphorus.
[4]Today the Black Sea.
[5]Today the Sea of Azov.

τὸ ἀπὸ Στηλῶν εἰς Πυρήνην τὸ ὄρος· Λιγυστικὸν δὲ τὸ ἕως τῶν
τῆς Τυρρηνίας περάτων· Σαρδώνιον δὲ τὸ ὑπὲρ τὴν Σαρδὼ νεῦον
πρὸς τὴν Λιβύην κάτω· Τυρρηνικὸν δὲ τὸ μέχρι Σικελίας λῆγον,
ἀρχόμενον ἀπὸ Λιγυστικῆς ἄκρων· εἶτα Λιβυκόν· εἶτα Κρητικὸν
καὶ Σικελικὸν καὶ Ἰώνιον καὶ Ἄδριον, τὸ δὲ ἀνακεχυμένον ἐκ
τοῦ Σικελικοῦ πελάγους, ὃν καλοῦσιν Κορινθιακὸν κόλπον ἤτοι
Ἀλκυονίδα θάλασσαν. Τῷ δὲ Σουνίῳ καὶ Σκυλλαίῳ περιεχόμενον
πέλαγος Σαρωνικόν· εἶτα Μυρτῷον καὶ Ἰκάριον, ἐν ᾧ αἱ Κυκλάδες·
εἶτα Καρπάθιον καὶ Παμφύλιον. καὶ Αἰγύπτιον. Ὑπὲρ δὲ τὸ Ἰκάριον
ἑξῆς ἀναχεῖται τὸ Αἰγαῖον. Ἔστι δὲ ὁ τῆς Εὐρώπης παράπλους ἀπὸ
Τανάιδος ποταμοῦ ἐκβολῶν ἕως Ἡρακλέους στηλῶν στάδια ς,
θψθ΄· τῆς δὲ Λιβύης ἀπὸ Τίγας ἕως στόματος Κανωβικοῦ στάδια
β, θσνβ΄, τῆς δὲ Ἀσίας ἀπὸ Κανώβου ἕως Τανάιδος ποταμοῦ μετὰ
τῶν κόλπων ὁ παράπλους στάδια δ, ρια΄. Ὁμοῦ παράλιος σὺν
κόλποις τῆς καθ᾽ ἡμᾶς οἰκουμένης στάδια ϊγ, θοβ΄.

24 Περὶ γῆς καὶ τῶν ἐξ αὐτῆς

Ἡ γῆ ἓν τῶν τεσσάρων στοιχείων ἐστὶ ξηρόν τε καὶ ψυχρὸν καὶ
βαρὺ καὶ ἀκίνητον, ὑπὸ τοῦ θεοῦ ἐκ τοῦ μὴ ὄντος εἰς τὸ εἶναι
τῇ πρώτῃ ἡμέρᾳ παρηγμένον. «Ἐν ἀρχῇ» γάρ, φησίν, «ἐποίησεν
ὁ θεὸς τὸν οὐρανὸν καὶ τὴν γῆν». Ἧς τὴν ἕδραν καὶ τὴν βάσιν
οὐδεὶς ἀνθρώπων εἰπεῖν δεδύνηται· οἱ μὲν γὰρ ἐπὶ ὑδάτων φασὶν
ἡδράσθαι καὶ πεπῆχθαι αὐτήν, ὥς φησιν ὁ θεῖος Δαυίδ· «Τῷ
στερεώσαντι τὴν γῆν ἐπὶ τῶν ὑδάτων», οἱ δὲ ἐπὶ τοῦ ἀέρος.
Ἄλλος δέ φησιν· «Ὁ ἑδράσας τὴν γῆν ἐπ᾽ οὐδενός». Καὶ πάλιν
ὁ θεηγόρος Δαυὶδ ὡς ἐκ προσώπου τοῦ δημιουργοῦ· «Ἐγώ»,

---

[6]The Pillars of Hercules, today the Straits of Gibraltar.
[7]The Roman stade was 185 meters (almost 300 yards). The length of the coastline from the estuary of the Tanais (the River Don) to the Pillars of Hercules (the Straits of Gibraltar) is therefore about 12,900 km (8,000 miles).
[8]The length given of the coastline from Tingis (Tangier, in Morocco) to the Canopic mouth (the westernmost branch of the Nile Delta, in Egypt) is equivalent to about 5,400 km (3,360 miles).
[9]About 7,400 km (4,600 miles).

end, at the beginning of Europe and Libya, the Iberian Sea extends from the Pillars[6] to the mountains of the Pyrenees. The Ligurian Sea extends to the limits of the Tyrrhenian. The Sardinian Sea goes round from above Sardinia down towards Libya. The Tyrrhenian Sea that ends at the Sicilian Sea begins at the limits of the Ligurian. Then comes the Libyan Sea, then the Cretan, the Sicilian, the Ionian, and the Adriatic. The latter empties out from the Sicilian Sea and is called the Corinthian Gulf or the Alcyonian Sea. Between Sunium and Scyllaeum is the Saronic Sea. Then come the Myrtoan and the Icarian Seas, in which lie the Cyclades. Then come the Carpathian, Pamphylian, and Egyptian Seas. Above the Icarian Sea there extends the Aegean. The length of the coastline of Europe from the Tanais estuary to the Pillars of Hercules is 69,709 stades.[7] That of the coastline of Libya from Tingis to the Canopic mouth is 29,252 stades.[8] That of Asia from the Canopus to the River Tanais, with its gulfs, is 40,111 stades.[9] Altogether the length of the coastline of our inhabited world, including the gulfs, is 139,072 stades.[10]

24   *On the earth and its products*

Earth is one of the four elements. Dry, cold, heavy, and immobile, it was brought into being by God out of nothing on the first day. For "in the beginning," it says, "God made the heaven and the earth."[1] What its foundation and base is, no human being is able to say. Some say that it is founded and set fast upon the waters, since the divine David says: "Who established the earth upon the waters."[2] Others say that it is founded and set upon the air. Another says: "He established the earth upon nothing."[3] And again David, who utters

---

[10]The total, which comes to 25,700 km (almost 16,000 miles), is only half the figure calculated from satellite images today (50,000 km, or 31,000 miles), which take in every indentation of the coastline, but represents the ancient sailing distances quite well.

[1]Gen 1.1.
[2]Ps 135.6.
[3]Job 26.7.

φησίν, «ἐστερέωσα τοὺς στύλους αὐτῆς», τὴν συνεκτικὴν αὐτῆς δύναμιν στύλους ὀνομάσας. Τὸ δὲ «ἐπὶ θαλασσῶν ἐθεμελίωσεν αὐτὴν» δηλοῖ τὸ πανταχόθεν περικεχύσθαι τῇ γῇ τὴν τοῦ ὕδατος φύσιν. Κἂν οὖν ἐφ᾽ ἑαυτῆς, κἂν ἐπὶ ἀέρος, κἂν ἐπὶ ὑδάτων, κἂν ἐπ᾽ οὐδενὸς δῶμεν ἡδράσθαι αὐτήν, χρὴ μὴ ἀφίστασθαι τῆς εὐσεβοῦς ἐννοίας, ἀλλὰ πάντα ὁμοῦ συγκρατεῖσθαι, ὁμολογεῖν καὶ συνέχεσθαι τῇ δυνάμει τοῦ κτίσαντος.

Ἐν ἀρχῇ μὲν οὖν, καθώς φησιν ἡ γραφή, ὑπὸ ὑδάτων ἐκεκάλυπτο καὶ ἀκατασκεύαστος ἤτοι ἀκόσμητος ἦν. Τοῦ δὲ θεοῦ προστάξαντος τὰ τῶν ὑδάτων δοχεῖα γεγόνασι, καὶ τότε τὰ ὄρη ὑπῆρξαν, τῷ τε θείῳ προστάγματι τὸν οἰκεῖον ἀπειλήφει κόσμον παντοδαπέσι χλόαις καὶ φυτοῖς ὡραϊσθεῖσα, οἷς τὸ θεῖον ἐνέθηκε πρόσταγμα δύναμιν αὐξητικήν τε καὶ θρεπτικὴν καὶ σπερματικὴν ἤτοι ὁμοίου γεννητικήν. Ἐξήγαγε δὲ τοῦ δημιουργοῦ κελεύσαντος καὶ παντοῖα γένη ζῴων ἑρπετῶν τε καὶ θηρίων καὶ κτηνῶν. Πάντα μὲν πρὸς τὴν τοῦ ἀνθρώπου εὔκαιρον χρῆσιν, ἀλλὰ τούτων τὰ μὲν πρὸς βρῶσιν οἷον ἐλάφους, πρόβατα, δορκάδας καὶ τὰ τοιαῦτα, τὰ δὲ πρὸς διακονίαν οἷον καμήλους, βόας, ἵππους, ὄνους καὶ τὰ τοιαῦτα, τὰ δὲ πρὸς τέρψιν οἷον πιθήκους· καὶ τῶν ὀρνέων κίσσας τε καὶ ψιττακοὺς καὶ τὰ τοιαῦτα, καὶ τῶν φυτῶν δὲ καὶ βοτανῶν τὰ μὲν κάρπιμα καὶ ἐδώδιμα, τὰ δὲ εὐώδη καὶ ἀνθηρὰ πρὸς τέρψιν ἡμῖν δεδομένα οἷον τὸ ῥόδον καὶ τὰ τοιαῦτα, τὰ δὲ πρὸς νοσημάτων ἴασιν. Οὐκ ἔστι γὰρ οὐδὲν ζῷον οὐδὲ φυτόν, ἐν ᾧ οὐκ ἐνέργειάν τινα τῇ τῶν ἀνθρώπων χρείᾳ χρησιμεύουσαν ὁ δημιουργὸς ἐναπέθετο· ὁ γὰρ τὰ πάντα πρὶν γενέσεως αὐτῶν ἐπιστάμενος εἰδώς, ὡς μέλλει ἐν αὐτεξουσίῳ παραβάσει ὁ ἄνθρωπος γενέσθαι καὶ τῇ φθορᾷ παραδίδοσθαι, πάντα πρὸς εὔκαιρον χρῆσιν αὐτοῦ, τά τε ἐν τῷ στερεώματι ἔν τε τῇ γῇ καὶ τὰ ἐν ὕδασιν ἔκτισε.

Πρὸ μὲν οὖν τῆς παραβάσεως, πάντα ὑποχείρια τῷ ἀνθρώπῳ ἦν· ἄρχοντα γὰρ αὐτὸν κατέστησεν ὁ θεὸς πάντων τῶν ἐν τῇ γῇ καὶ τῶν ἐν τοῖς ὕδασι. Καὶ ὁ ὄφις δὲ συνήθης τῷ ἀνθρώπῳ ἦν μᾶλλον τῶν ἄλλων αὐτῷ προσερχόμενος καὶ τερπνοῖς

divine words as if in the person of the Creator: "I have established," he says, "its pillars,"[4] meaning by "pillars" its power of cohesion. The phrase "he founded it upon the seas"[5] signifies that the nature of water was poured out on every side. Therefore whether we concede that the earth is founded upon itself, or upon air, or upon the waters, or upon nothing, it is necessary not to stray from orthodox thinking but confess that all things are held together and maintained in being by the power of the Creator.

In the beginning, then, as Scripture says, the earth was covered by waters and was chaotic or disordered.[6] When God commanded, the receptacles of the waters came into being, and then the mountains came to exist, and at the divine command the earth received its proper order and was made beautiful with all kinds of verdure and plants. Into these the divine command introduced the power of development, and growth, and producing seed for reproducing itself. And at the Creator's bidding the earth brought forth every species of animal, reptiles, and both wild and domestic beasts. All things were suitable for human use, some for consumption such as deer, sheep, gazelles, and the like, other for service, such as camels, oxen, horses, donkeys, and the like, and others for pleasure such as monkeys. And of species of birds it brought forth jays and parrots and the like, and of plants and herbs, some fruit-bearing and edible, others fragrant flowering, given to us for our pleasure, such as roses and the like, and others given to us for the healing of maladies. For there is no animal or plant in which the Creator has not instilled some active property useful for human needs. For knowing all things before their creation, because he saw that humankind would enter into a voluntary state of transgression and incur corruption, he created everything in the heavens and on earth and in the waters for humanity's use at the appropriate time.

Thus before the transgression, all things were subject to man, for God made him ruler of everything on the land and in the waters. Even the serpent was accustomed to man more than the

<hr />

[4]Ps 74.4.   [5]Ps 23.2.   [6]Gen 1.2.

προσομιλῶν τοῖς κινήμασιν. Ὅθεν δι' αὐτοῦ τὴν κακίστην ὁ ἀρχέκακος διάβολος ὑποθήκην τοῖς προπάτορσιν εἰσηγήσατο. Καὶ ἡ γῆ δὲ αὐτομάτη τοὺς καρποὺς ἔφερε πρὸς χρείαν τῶν ὑποχειρίων αὐτῷ ζώων, καὶ οὔτε ὄμβρος ἦν τῇ γῇ οὔτε χειμών. Μετὰ δὲ τὴν παράβασιν, ἡνίκα «παρασυνεβλήθη τοῖς κτήνεσι τοῖς ἀνοήτοις καὶ ὡμοιώθη αὐτοῖς», ἄρχειν ἐν ἑαυτῷ τὴν ἄλογον ἐπιθυμίαν τοῦ λογικοῦ νοῦ παρασκευάσας, παρήκοος τῆς τοῦ δεσπότου ἐντολῆς γενόμενος, ἐπανέστη τῷ ὑπὸ τοῦ δημιουργοῦ χειροτονηθέντι ἄρχοντι ἡ ὑποχείριος κτίσις, ἐν ἱδρῶτι ἐργάζεσθαι τὴν γῆν, ἐξ ἧς ἐλήφθη.

Ἀλλ' οὐδὲ νῦν ἄχρηστος ἡ τῶν θηρίων χρῆσις ἐκφοβοῦσα καὶ πρὸς ἐπίγνωσιν καὶ ἐπίκλησιν τοῦ πεποιηκότος φέρουσα θεοῦ. Καὶ ἡ ἄκανθα δὲ μετὰ τὴν παράβασιν ἐξεφύη τῆς γῆς κατὰ τὴν τοῦ κυρίου ἀπόφασιν, μεθ' ἣν συνεζεύχθη καὶ τῇ ἀπολαύσει τοῦ ῥόδου ἡ ἄκανθα εἰς ὑπόμνησιν τῆς παραβάσεως ἡμᾶς ἄγουσα, δι' ἣν ἀκάνθας καὶ τριβόλους ἡ γῆ ἀνατέλλειν ἡμῖν κατεδικάσθη.

Ὅτι μὲν ταῦτα οὕτως ἔχει, πιστευτέον ἐκ τοῦ καὶ μέχρι τοῦ νῦν τὴν τούτων διαμονὴν ἐνεργεῖν τὸν τοῦ κυρίου λόγον· ἔφη γάρ· «Αὐξάνεσθε καὶ πληθύνεσθε καὶ πληρώσατε τὴν γῆν».

Σφαιροειδῆ δέ τινές φασι τὴν γῆν, ἕτεροι δὲ κωνοειδῆ. Ἥττων δὲ καὶ πάνυ σμικροτέρα ἐστὶ τοῦ οὐρανοῦ ὥσπερ τις στιγμὴ ἐν μέσῳ τούτου κρεμαμένη. Καὶ αὐτὴ δὲ παρελεύσεται καὶ ἀλλαγήσεται. Μακάριος δέ ἐστιν ὁ τὴν τῶν πραέων γῆν κληρονομῶν· ἡ γὰρ μέλλουσα τοὺς ἁγίους ὑποδέχεσθαι γῆ ἀθάνατός ἐστι. Τίς οὖν ἀξίως τὴν ἄπειρόν τε καὶ ἀκατάληπτον τοῦ δημιουργοῦ σοφίαν θαυμάσειεν; Ἢ τίς τῆς πρεπούσης εὐχαριστίας ἐφίκοιτο τοῦ δοτῆρος τῶν τοσούτων ἀγαθῶν;

others, approaching him and keeping him company with pleasant conversations. Hence it was through him that the devil, the originator of evil, made the most evil proposal to our first ancestors. And the earth brought forth its fruits of its own accord for the use of the animals that were subject to man, and there were neither violent storms nor wintry weather in the land. But after the transgression, when "he was compared to the mindless beasts and became like them,"[7] and had contrived that irrational desire within himself should rule over his rational mind, since he had become disobedient to the divine command, the creation that had been made subject to the ruler appointed by the Creator rose up in rebellion, and he was to work with sweat the earth from which he had been taken.

But not even now is the usefulness of wild animals nullified for they cause fear and bring us to know and invoke God the Creator. And the thorn that grew up out of the earth after the transgression in accordance with the Lord's judgement was subsequently united with the pleasure of the rose, the thorn prompting us to recall the transgression, on account of which the earth was condemned to bring forth thorns and thistles for us.

That this is the case is to be believed by the fact that their persistence to this day is effected by the Lord's word, for he said: "Be fruitful and multiply and fill the earth."[8]

Some say that the earth is spherical, others that it is conical. It is inferior to the vault of heaven and much smaller, like a dot suspended in the midst of it.[9] And this earth will pass away and be changed. Blessed is he who inherits the earth of the meek, for the earth which is to receive the saints is everlasting. Who, then, could worthily wonder at the Creator's infinite and incomprehensible wisdom? Or who could give adequate thanks to the giver of such blessings?

[7]Ps 48.13.

[8]Gen 3.19.

[9]The word translated here as "dot" (στιγμή, *stigmē*) can mean a geometrical point, which in Ptolemy's *Almagest* is a σημεῖον (*sēmeion*). If John intends the latter meaning, he may have in mind Ptolemy's theory of the sun's movement in an eccentric circle around a geometrical point (see Farrington, *Greek Science* ii, 91–2), which in John's view would be the earth.

24b

Εἰσὶ δὲ αἱ γνωσθεῖσαι ἐπαρχίαι τῆς γῆς ἤτοι σατραπίαι αὖται·
Εὐρώπης μὲν ἐπαρχίαι λδ', πίνακες ι'· α' Ἰουβερνία, νῆσος
Βρετανική β' Ἀλουίωνος νῆσος Βρετανική γ' Ἰσπανία Βαιτική δ'
Ἰσπανία Λουσιτανία ε'Ἰσπανία Ταρακωνησία ϛ' Γαλλία Ἀκουιτανία
ζ' Γαλλία Λουγδονησία η' Γαλλία Κελτική θ' Γαλλία Ναρβωνησία
ι' Γερμανία μεγάλη ια' Ῥαιτία καὶ Οὐινδελικία ιβ' Νωρικόν ιγ'
Παννονία ἡ ἄνω ιδ' Παννονία ἡ κάτω ιε' Ἰλλυρίς ιϛ' Δελματία
ιζ' Ἰταλία ιη' Κύρνος νῆσος ιθ' Σαρδὼ νῆσος κ' Σικελία νῆσος
κα' Σαρματία ἡ ἐν Εὐρώπῃ κβ' Ταυρικὴ Χερσόνησος κγ' Ἰάζυγες
Μετανάσται κδ' Δακία κε' Μυσία ἡ ἄνω κϛ' Μυσία ἡ κάτω κζ'
Θρᾴκη κη' Χερσόνησος κθ' Μακεδονία λ'Ἤπειρος λα' Ἀχαῖα λβ'
Εὔβοια νῆσος λγ' Πελοπόννησος λδ' Κρήτη νῆσος.

Λιβύης ἐπαρχίαι ιβ', πίνακες η'· α' Μαυριτανία Τιγγιτανή
β' Μαυριτανία Καισαρηνσία γ' Νουμιδία δ' Ἀφρικὴ ὅλη ε'
Κυρηναϊκὴ πεντάπολις ϛ' Μαρμαρική ζ' Λιβύη η' Αἴγυπτος ἡ κάτω
θ' Αἴγυπτος Θηβαῖς ι' ἡ ἐντὸς Ἀφρικῆς Λιβύη ια' ἡ ἄνω Αἰγύπτου
Αἰθιοπία ιβ' ἡ ἐντὸς τούτων πάντων νωτιωτάτη Αἰθιοπία.

Ἀσίας ἠπείρου μεγάλης ἐπαρχίαι μη', κανόνες ιβ'· α' Βιθυνία
Πόντου β' Ἀσία ἡ ἰδίως, πρὸς τῇ Ἐφέσῳ γ' Φρυγία μεγάλη δ'
Λυκία ε' Γαλατία ϛ' Παφλαγονία ζ' Παμφυλία η' Καππαδοκία θ'
Ἀρμενία μικρά ι' Κιλικία ια' Σαρματία ἡ ἐντὸς Ἀσίας ιβ' Κολχίς ιγ'
Ἰβηρία ιδ' Ἀλβανία ιε' Ἀρμενία μεγάλη ιϛ' Κύπρος νῆσος ιζ' Συρία
κοίλη ιη' Συρία Φοινίκη ιθ' Συρία Παλαιστίνη κ' Ἀραβία Πετραία
κα' Μεσοποταμία κβ' Ἀραβία ἔρημος κγ' Βαβυλωνία κδ' Ἀσσυρία

---

[1]This chapter on the known world in late antiquity is added by manuscripts
EMN. Kotter identifies its sources as mainly Book 8 of Ptolemy's *Geographia*, which
dates from about 150 AD, and, for the last paragraph, the third-century AD Alexandrian geographer, Agathemerus (for these passages, see Diller, *The Tradition of the
Minor Greek Geographers*, 35 and 34).

[2]The tables (πίνακες) are lists, or perhaps maps (Book 8 of Ptolemy's *Geographia*
contained the maps).

[3]The Jazyges were a Sarmatian tribe who migrated (hence "Metanastae") from
Central Asia to present-day Hungary.

24b *(Untitled)*[1]

The earth's known provinces or satrapies are the following: Europe has thirty-four provinces, ten tables:[2] 1. British Island of Hibernia; 2. British Island of Albion; 3. Hispania Baetica; 4. Hispania Lusitania; 5. Hispania Tarraconensis; 6. Gallia Aquitania; 7. Gallia Lugdunensis; 8. Gallia Belgica; 9. Gallia Narbonensis; 10. Germania Magna; 11. Rhaetia and Vindelicia; 12. Noricum; 13. Pannonia Superior; 14. Pannonia Inferior; 15. Illyricum; 16. Dalmatia; 17. Italy; 18. Island of Corsica; 19. Island of Sardinia; 20. Island of Sicily; 21. European Sarmatia; 22. Taurica Chersonesus; 23. Jazyges Metanastae;[3] 24. Dacia; 25. Moesia Superior; 26. Moesia Inferior; 27. Thrace; 28. Chersonesus; 29. Macedonia; 30. Epeirus; 31. Achaea; 32. Island of Euboea; 33. Peloponnese; 34. Island of Crete.

Libya has twelve provinces, eight tables: 1. Mauretania Tingitana; 2. Mauretania Caesariensis; 3. Numidia; 4. Africa Proconsularis; 5. Cyrenaican Pentapolis; 6. Marmarica; 7. Libya;[4] 8. Lower Egypt; 9. Egypt Thebaidis; 10. Libya in Africa;[5] 11. Ethiopia of Upper Egypt; 12. Ethiopia, the southernmost among all these.

The continent of greater Asia has forty-eight provinces, twelve canons:[6] 1. Bithynia of Pontus; 2. Asia proper by Ephesus; 3. Greater Phrygia; 4. Lycia; 5. Galatia; 6. Paphlagonia; 7. Pamphylia; 8. Cappadocia; 9. Lesser Armenia; 10. Cilicia; 11. Sarmatia in Asia; 12. Colchis; 13. Iberia;[7] 14. Albania;[8] 15. Greater Armenia; 16. Island of Cyprus; 17. Coele Syria; 18. Phoenician Syria; 19. Palestinian Syria; 20. Arabia Petraea; 21. Mesopotamia; 22. Arabia Deserta; 23. Babylonia; 24. Assyria; 25. Susa; 26. Media; 27. Persis; 28. Parthia; 29. Carmania Deserta; 30. Carmania Secunda;[9] 31. Arabia Felix; 32. Hyrcania;[10]

---

[4]Libya is both a province and the continent of Africa as a whole.
[5]Modern Tunisia.
[6]The canons (κανόνες, *kanones*) are tables.
[7]The eastern Iberia, modern Georgia.
[8]The Caucasian Albania, between Armenia and the Caspian Sea.
[9]The modern Kerman province of Iran.
[10]South of the Caspian Sea in modern Iran.

κε′ Σουσιανή κς′ Μηδία κζ′ Περσίς κη′ Παρθία κθ′ Καρμανία
ἔρημος λ′ Καρμανία ἑτέρα λα′ Ἀραβία εὐδαίμων λβ′ Ὑρκανία λγ′
Μαργιανή λδ′ Βακτριανή λε′ Σογδιανή λς′ Σακῶν λζ′ Σκυθία ἡ
ἐντὸς Ἰμάου ὄρους λη′ Σκυθία ἡ ἐκτὸς Ἰμάου ὄρους λθ′ Σηρική
μ′ Ἀρεία μα′ Παροπανισάδαι μβ′ Δραγγιανή μγ′ Ἀραχωσία μδ′
Γεδρωσία με′ Ἰνδικὴ ἡ ἐντὸς Γάγγου τοῦ ποταμοῦ μς′ Ἰνδικὴ ἡ
ἐκτὸς Γάγγου τοῦ ποταμοῦ μζ′ Σῖναι μη′ Ταπροβάνη νῆσος.

Ὁμοῦ γίνονται

Εὐρώπης μὲν πίνακες ι′, ἐπαρχίαι λδ′, πόλεις ἐπίσημοι ριη′
Λιβύης δὲ πίνακες μὲν η′, χῶραι δὲ ιβ′, πόλεις ἐπίσημοι νβ′ Ἀσίας
δὲ μεγάλης πίνακες μὲν ιβ′, ἐπαρχίαι δὲ μη′, πόλεις ἐπίσημοι ρπ′ αἱ
πᾶσαι τῆς οἰκουμένης χῶραι ϟδ′, πόλεις τν′.

Ἔθνη δὲ οἰκεῖ τὰ πέρατα· κατ᾽ ἀπηλιώτην Βακτριανοί, κατ᾽
εὖρον Ἰνδοί, κατὰ Φοίνικα Ἐρυθρὰ θάλασσα καὶ Αἰθιοπία, κατὰ
λευκόνοτον οἱ ὑπὲρ Σύρτιν Γεράμαντες, κατὰ λίβα Αἰθίοπες καὶ
δυσμικοὶ Ὑπέρμαυροι, κατὰ ζέφυρον Στῆλαι καὶ ἀρχαὶ Λιβύης καὶ
Εὐρώπης, κατὰ ἀργέστην Ἰβηρία ἡ νῦν Ἰσπανία, κατὰ δὲ θρασκίαν
Κελτοὶ καὶ τὰ ὅμορα, κατὰ ἀπαρκτίαν οἱ ὑπὲρ Θράκην Σκύθαι,
κατὰ βορρᾶν Πόντος Μαιῶτις καὶ Σαρμάται, κατὰ καικίαν Κασπία
θάλασσα καὶ Σάκες.

25   Περὶ παραδείσου

Ἐπειδὴ δὲ ἔμελλεν ὁ θεὸς ἐξ ὁρατῆς τε καὶ ἀοράτου κτίσεως
πλαστουργεῖν τὸν ἄνθρωπον κατ᾽ οἰκείαν εἰκόνα τε καὶ ὁμοίωσιν
ὥσπερ τινὰ βασιλέα καὶ ἄρχοντα πάσης τῆς γῆς καὶ τῶν ἐν αὐτῇ

---

[11]An ancient Persian province centered on the oasis of Merv in Central Asia.

[12]Bactriana was another Persian province covering the area of modern Afghanistan and Tajikistan.

[13]North of Bactriana, on the Silk Road to China. Sogdiana's main cities were Samarkand and Bokhara.

[14]The Sakas inhabited the Tarim Basin in Central Asia.

[15]Mount Imeon is the Central Asian mountain system comprising the Hindu Kush, the Pamirs, and the Tian Shan range.

33. Margiana;[11] 34. Bactriana;[12] 35. Sogdiana;[13] 36. Of the Sakas;[14] 37. Scythia this side of Mount Imeon;[15] 38. Scythia beyond Mount Imeon; 39. Serica;[16] 40. Areia;[17] 41. Paropanisadae; 42. Drangania; 43. Arachosia; 44. Gedrosia; 45. India this side of the River Ganges; 46. India beyond the River Ganges; 47. Sinae;[18] 48. Island of Taprobane.[19]

All together, they come to:

Europe	10 tables	34 provinces	118 notable cities
Libya	8 tables	12 countries	52 notable cities
Greater Asia	12 tables	48 provinces	180 notable cities
The whole inhabited world		94 countries	350 cities

The nations inhabiting the extreme boundaries are: towards the Apeliotes,[20] the Bactrians; towards the Euros, the Indians; towards the Phoinix, the Red Sea and Ethiopia; towards the Leukonotos, the Geramantes beyond Syrtis; towards the Lips, the Ethiopians and the western Moors; towards the Zephyros, the Pillars and the starting-points of Libya and Europe; towards the Argestes, Iberia,[21] which is now Hispania; towards the Thraskias, the Celts and their neighbors; towards the Aparktias, the Scythians beyond Thrace; towards the Boreas, Pontus Maeotis and the Sarmatians; towards the Kaikias, the Caspian Sea and the Sakas.

25 On paradise

Since God intended to fashion man out of visible and invisible creation in accordance with his image and likeness like a king and ruler of the whole earth and everything in it, he appointed for him

[16]"The land of silk"—China as approached by the overland Silk Road.

[17]Areia and the following four provinces were Persian satrapies on the far side of the Hindu Kush.

[18]China as approached by the sea route.

[19]Today Sri Lanka.

[20]Starting due east and going in a clockwise direction.

[21]The western Iberia, modern Spain and Portugal.

προκαθίστησιν αὐτῷ οἷόν τι βασίλειον, ἐν ᾧ διαιτώμενος μακαρίαν καὶ πανολβίαν ἕξει ζωήν. Οὗτός ἐστιν ὁ θεῖος παράδεισος θεοῦ χερσὶν ἐν Ἐδὲμ πεφυτευμένος, εὐφροσύνης καὶ θυμηδίας ἁπάσης ταμιεῖον. Ἐδὲμ γὰρ τρυφὴ ἑρμηνεύεται. Ἐν τῇ ἀνατολῇ μὲν πάσης τῆς γῆς ὑψηλότερος κείμενος, εὔκρατος δὲ καὶ ἀέρι λεπτῷ καὶ καθαρωτάτῳ περιλαμπόμενος, φυτοῖς ἀειθαλέσι κομῶν, εὐωδίας πλήρης, φωτὸς ἔμπλεως, ὥρας ἁπάσης αἰσθητῆς καὶ κάλλους ὑπερβαίνων ἐπίνοιαν, θεῖον ὄντως χωρίον καὶ ἄξιον τοῦ κατ' εἰκόνα θεοῦ ἐνδιαίτημα, ἐν ᾧ οὐδὲν τῶν ἀλόγων ηὐλίζετο, μόνος δὲ ὁ ἄνθρωπος, τῶν θείων χειρῶν τὸ πλαστούργημα.

Ἐν μέσῳ τούτου ξύλον ζωῆς ὁ θεὸς ἐφύτευσεν καὶ ξύλον τῆς γνώσεως. Τὸ μὲν ξύλον τῆς γνώσεως ἀπόπειράν τινα καὶ δοκιμὴν καὶ γυμνάσιον τῆς τοῦ ἀνθρώπου ὑπακοῆς καὶ παρακοῆς. Διὸ καὶ ξύλον τοῦ γινώσκειν καλὸν καὶ πονηρὸν κέκληται, ἢ ὅτι δύναμιν ἐδίδου γνωστικὴν τοῖς μεταλαμβάνουσι τῆς οἰκείας φύσεως, ὅπερ καλὸν μὲν τοῖς τελείοις, κακὸν δὲ τοῖς ἀτελεστέροις, ἔτι καὶ τὴν αἴσθησιν λιχνοτέροις, ὥσπερ στερεὰ τροφὴ τοῖς ἔτι δεομένοις γάλακτος· οὐκ ἐβούλετο γὰρ ὁ κτίσας ἡμᾶς θεὸς μεριμνᾶν καὶ περὶ πολλὰ τυρβάζεσθαι οὐδὲ φροντιστὰς καὶ προνοητὰς τῆς ἰδίας ζωῆς γενέσθαι. Ὅπερ δὴ καὶ πέπονθεν ὁ Ἀδάμ· γευσάμενος γὰρ ἔγνω, ὅτι γυμνὸς ἦν, καὶ περίζωμα ἑαυτῷ περιεποιεῖτο· φύλλα γὰρ συκῆς λαβὼν περιεζώσατο. Πρὸ δὲ τῆς γεύσεως «γυμνοὶ ἦσαν ἀμφότεροι, ὅ τε Ἀδὰμ καὶ ἡ Εὔα, καὶ οὐκ ᾐσχύνοντο». Τοιούτους δὲ ἀπαθεῖς ἐβούλετο εἶναι ἡμᾶς ὁ θεός (ἀπαθείας γὰρ ἄκρας τοῦτό ἐστιν), ἔτι δὲ καὶ ἀμερίμνους, ἓν ἔργον ἔχοντας τὸ τῶν ἀγγέλων, ὑμνεῖν ἀλήκτως καὶ ἀδιαλείπτως τὸν κτίσαντα, καὶ τῆς αὐτοῦ κατατρυφᾶν θεωρίας καὶ αὐτῷ ἐπιρρίπτειν τὴν ἑαυτῶν μέριμναν. Ὅπερ καὶ διὰ τοῦ προφήτου Δαυὶδ πρὸς ἡμᾶς ἀπεφθέγξατο· «Ἐπίρριψον ἐπὶ κύριον τὴν μέριμνάν σου», λέγων, «καὶ αὐτός σε διαθρέψει», καὶ ἐν τοῖς ἱεροῖς εὐαγγελίοις τοὺς οἰκείους μαθητὰς διδάσκων φησί· «Μὴ μεριμνήσητε τῇ ψυχῇ

a kind of kingdom in which he would dwell and lead a blessed and wholly happy life. This is the divine paradise planted by God's hands in Eden, a storehouse of every joy and delight. For "Eden" translated is "felicity." It lay in the east higher than all the earth, with a mild climate and resplendent with a light and very pure air. It was thick with evergreen plants, full of fragrance, flooded with light, and surpassing any conceivable sensible loveliness and beauty. It was truly a divine place and worthy habitation for him who was in God's image. In it nothing that was irrational had its dwelling-place, only man, fashioned by the divine hands.

In the middle of it God planted the tree of life and the tree of knowledge. The tree of knowledge was a kind of testing and trial and exercise of man's obedience and disobedience. It was for this reason that it was called the tree of the knowledge of good and evil, or else because it gave to those who partook of it the power of knowing their own nature, which is good for the perfect but evil for those who are less developed and still more indulgent of their senses, like solid food is for those who still need milk. For God who created us did not want us to be "worried and distracted by many things,"[1] or to be concerned about providing for our own life. Indeed, this is what Adam suffered. For when he tasted, he knew that he was naked and made himself a loin-cloth, for he took some fig leaves and put them round himself. Before they tasted, "Adam and Eve were both naked, and were not ashamed."[2] God wanted us to be dispassionate in the same way (for this belongs to the highest dispassion), and also free from care, having one task, that of the angels, which is to praise the Creator ceaselessly and uninterruptedly, and to enjoy his contemplation and cast all our cares on him. That is what he told us through the prophet David, saying, "Cast your care upon the Lord, and he will sustain you,"[3] and in the holy Gospels when he taught his own disciples and said: "Do not worry about your life, what you will eat, or about your body, what you will wear."[4] And again, strive for "the kingdom of God and his righteousness, and all these things will be

[1]Lk 10.41.   [2]Gen 2.25.   [3]Ps 54.23.   [4]Lk 12.22.

ὑμῶν, τί φάγητε, καὶ τῷ σώματι ὑμῶν, τί ἐνδύσησθε», καὶ πάλιν·
«Αἰτεῖτε τὴν βασιλείαν τοῦ θεοῦ καὶ τὴν δικαιοσύνην αὐτοῦ,
καὶ ταῦτα πάντα προστεθήσεται ὑμῖν», καὶ πρὸς τὴν Μάρθαν·
«Μάρθα, Μάρθα, μεριμνᾷς καὶ τυρβάζῃ περὶ πολλά, ἑνὸς δέ
ἐστι χρεία· Μαρία γὰρ τὴν ἀγαθὴν μερίδα ἐξελέξατο, ἥτις οὐκ
ἀφαιρεθήσεται ἀπ᾽ αὐτῆς», τὸ καθῆσθαι δηλονότι παρὰ τοὺς
πόδας αὐτοῦ καὶ ἀκούειν τῶν λόγων αὐτοῦ.

Τὸ δὲ τῆς ζωῆς ξύλον ἢ ξύλον ἔχον ἐνέργειαν ζωῆς παρεκτικὴν
ἢ τοῖς τῆς ζωῆς ἀξίοις καὶ τῷ θανάτῳ οὐχ ὑποκειμένοις μόνοις
ἐδώδιμον. Τινὲς μὲν οὖν αἰσθητὸν τὸν παράδεισον ἐφαντάσθησαν,
ἕτεροι δὲ νοητόν. Πλὴν ἔμοιγε δοκεῖ, ὅτι ὥσπερ ὁ ἄνθρωπος
αἰσθητὸς ἅμα καὶ νοητὸς δεδημιούργητο, οὕτω καὶ τὸ τούτου
ἱερώτατον τέμενος αἰσθητὸν ἅμα καὶ νοητὸν καὶ διπλῆν ἔχον τὴν
ἔμφασιν· τῷ γὰρ σώματι ἐν τῷ θειοτάτῳ χώρῳ καὶ ὑπερκαλλεῖ,
καθὼς ἱστορήσαμεν, αὐλιζόμενος, τῇ ψυχῇ ἐν ὑπερτέρῳ καὶ
ἀσυγκρίτῳ καὶ περικαλλεστέρῳ τόπῳ διέτριβε θεὸν ἔχων οἶκον
τὸν ἔνοικον καὶ αὐτὸν ἔχων εὐκλεὲς περιβόλαιον καὶ τὴν αὐτοῦ
περιβεβλημένος χάριν καὶ τοῦ μόνου γλυκυτάτου καρποῦ τῆς
αὐτοῦ θεωρίας κατατρυφῶν οἷά τις ἄγγελος ἄλλος καὶ ταύτῃ
τρεφόμενος. Ὅπερ δὴ καὶ ξύλον ζωῆς ἀξίως ὠνόμασται· ζωῆς
γὰρ θανάτῳ μὴ διακοπτομένης ἡ γλυκύτης τῆς θείας μεθέξεως
τοῖς μεταλαμβάνουσι μεταδίδωσιν. Ὃ δὴ καὶ πᾶν ξύλον ὁ θεὸς
ἐκάλεσεν· «Ἀπὸ παντὸς ξύλου τοῦ ἐν τῷ παραδείσῳ βρώσει»,
φησί, «φάγεσθε·» αὐτὸς γάρ ἐστι τὸ πᾶν, ἐν ᾧ καὶ δι᾽ οὗ τὸ πᾶν.

Τὸ δὲ τῆς τοῦ καλοῦ τε καὶ κακοῦ γνώσεως ξύλον ἡ τῆς
πολυσχεδοῦς θεωρίας διάγνωσις. Αὕτη δέ ἐστιν ἡ τῆς οἰκείας
ἐπίγνωσις φύσεως, ἥτις καλὴ μὲν τοῖς τελείοις καὶ ἐν τῇ θείᾳ
θεωρίᾳ βεβιωκόσιν, ἐξ ἑαυτῆς τὴν τοῦ δημιουργοῦ μεγαλουργίαν
δημοσιεύουσα, τοῖς μὴ δεδιόσι μετάπτωσιν διὰ τὸ ἐκ τοῦ χρόνου
εἰς ἕξιν τινὰ τῆς τοιαύτης ἐληλακέναι θεωρίας, οὐ καλὴ δὲ τοῖς

given to you as well,"[5] and to Martha: "Martha, Martha, you are worried and distracted by many things; there is need of only one thing. Mary has chosen the better part, which will not be taken away from her,"[6] that is to say, to sit at his feet and listen to his words.

The tree of life was either a tree possessing the active power of providing life, or else a tree edible only by those worthy of life and not subject to death. Some have imagined paradise as sensible, others as intelligible. It seems to me, however, that just as man was created at the same time both sensible and intelligible, so too his most sacred precinct was at the same time both sensible and intelligible and had a dual aspect. For whereas in the body, as we have related, he dwelt in a most divine and supremely beautiful spot, in the soul he spent his time in a more sublime and incomparably more beautiful place, where he had the indwelling God as his dwelling and had him as a glorious covering, and was clothed with his grace, and delighted in the most sweet fruit of his contemplation alone like another angel and was nourished by this contemplation. Hence it was rightly called the tree of life, for the sweetness of participation in the divine communicates to those who partake of it a life uninterrupted by death. Indeed, this is what God called the "whole tree." It says: "You may eat from the whole tree in paradise,"[7] for he is the whole, in whom and through whom the whole exists.

The tree of the knowledge of good and evil is the multifaceted discernment of contemplation. This is the knowledge of one's own nature, which is good for those who are perfectly mature and have spent their life in divine contemplation, thereby making known publicly the magnificent work of the Creator, those who do not fear a lapse because through the passage of time they have forged a habit of such contemplation, but is not good for those who are still young and more greedy in their appetites, who are naturally

[5] Mt 6.33.
[6] Lk 10.41–42.
[7] Gen 2.16. The "whole tree" (πᾶν ξύλον) may equally be translated as "every tree," the more natural meaning in the context (as in all the English translations of Genesis). John uses the opportunity of the dual meaning of πᾶν to make a theological point.

νέοις ἔτι καὶ τὴν ἔφεσιν λιχνοτέροις, οὓς διὰ τὸ ἀβέβαιον τῆς ἐν τῷ κρείττονι διαμονῆς καὶ τὸ μήπω παγίως ἐνεδρασθῆναι τῇ τοῦ μόνου καλοῦ προσεδρείᾳ ἡ τοῦ οἰκείου κηδεμονία σώματος πρὸς ἑαυτὴν ἀνθέλκειν καὶ περισπᾶν πέφυκεν. Οὕτω διπλοῦν οἶμαι τὸν θεῖον παράδεισον. Καὶ ἀληθῶς οἱ θεοφόροι πατέρες παρέδωκαν οἵ τε οὕτως, οἵ τε ἐκείνως διδάξαντες. Δυνατὸν δὲ νοῆσαι πᾶν ξύλον τὴν ἐκ πάντων τῶν κτισμάτων τῆς θείας δυνάμεως γινομένην ἐπίγνωσιν, ὥς φησιν ὁ θεῖος ἀπόστολος· «Τὰ γὰρ ἀόρατα αὐτοῦ ἀπὸ κτίσεως κόσμου τοῖς ποιήμασι νοούμενα καθορᾶται». —Πασῶν δὲ τῶν ἐννοιῶν καὶ θεωριῶν τούτων ἡ καθ᾽ ἡμᾶς ὑψηλοτέρα πέφυκεν, ἡ τῆς ἡμετέρας φημὶ συστάσεως, ὥς φησιν ὁ θεῖος Δαυίδ· «Ἐθαυμαστώθη ἡ γνῶσίς σου ἐξ ἐμοῦ», τουτέστιν ἐκ τῆς ἐμῆς κατασκευῆς. Ἐπισφαλὴς δὲ αὕτη τῷ Ἀδὰμ ὑπῆρχε νεοπαγεῖ ὄντι, δι᾽ ἃς εἴπομεν αἰτίας—ἢ ξύλον μὲν ζωῆς τὴν ἐκ πάντων τῶν αἰσθητῶν ἐγγινομένην θειοτέραν ἔννοιαν καὶ τὴν δι᾽ αὐτῶν ἐπὶ τὸν ἁπάντων γενεσιουργόν τε καὶ δημιουργὸν καὶ αἴτιον ἀναγωγήν, ὅπερ καὶ πᾶν ξύλον ὠνόμασε τὸ πλῆρες καὶ ἀδιαίρετον μόνην τε τοῦ καλοῦ φέρων τὴν μέθεξιν, ξύλον δὲ γνώσεως καλοῦ καὶ πονηροῦ τὴν αἰσθητὴν καὶ ἐνήδονον βρῶσιν, τὴν τῷ δοκεῖν μὲν γλυκαίνουσαν, τῷ ὄντι δὲ ἐν μετουσίᾳ κακῶν τὸν μετέχοντα καθιστῶσαν· φησὶ γὰρ ὁ θεός· «Ἀπὸ παντὸς ξύλου τοῦ ἐν τῷ παραδείσῳ βρώσει φαγῇ», διὰ πάντων, οἶμαι, τῶν κτισμάτων ἐπ᾽ ἐμὲ τὸν ποιητὴν ἀναβιβάσθητι, λέγων, καὶ ἕνα καρπὸν ἐκ πάντων κάρπωσαι, ἐμὲ τὴν ὄντως ζωήν. Πάντα σοι ζωὴν καρποφορείτωσαν, καὶ τὴν ἐμὴν μέθεξιν ποιοῦ τῆς οἰκείας ὑπάρξεως σύστασιν· οὕτω γὰρ ἔσῃ ἀθάνατος. «Ἀπὸ δὲ τοῦ ξύλου τοῦ γινώσκειν καλὸν καὶ πονηρόν, οὐ φάγεσθε ἀπ᾽ αὐτοῦ. Ἧι δ᾽ ἂν ἡμέρᾳ φάγητε ἀπ᾽ αὐτοῦ, θανάτῳ ἀποθανεῖσθε»· φυσικῶς γὰρ ἡ αἰσθητὴ βρῶσις τοῦ ὑπεκρεύσαντός ἐστιν ἀναπλήρωσις καὶ εἰς

drawn and distracted by solicitude for their own bodies, through the uncertainty of their stability in what is better and their as yet unconsolidated perseverance in the only good.

Thus I think that the divine paradise was twofold. And truly, the God-bearing fathers have handed this down to us, some teaching it in one way and others in another. It is possible to understand the "whole tree" as the knowledge that comes from all the things created by the power of God, as the divine Apostle says: "Ever since the creation of the world his eternal power and divine nature, invisible though they are, have been understood and seen through the things he has made."[8] Of all these thoughts and speculations the loftiest is that which concerns ourselves—I mean our own being—as the divine David says: "The knowledge of you that comes from me"— that is, from my own constitution—"has been declared wonderful."[9] But this was precarious for Adam, since he was newly formed, for reasons we have already stated. Or the tree of life may be taken as the more divine understanding that comes from all sensible things and through them the ascent to the generator, creator, and cause of all things, which is also why he called the full and undivided tree that brings the only participation in the good "the whole tree," whereas the tree of the knowledge of good and evil is the sensible and pleasurable food, which while appearing to be sweet in reality makes anyone who partakes of it a participant in evil. For God says: "From the whole tree which in is paradise you may eat,"[10] saying, I think, that from created things you should ascend to me their maker, and from all of them enjoy one fruit, which is myself, the true life. May all of them bear the fruit of life for you, and may you make participation in me the basis of your own existence, for in this way you will be immortal. "But of the tree of the knowledge of good and evil, you shall not eat of it. On whichever day you eat of it, you will

[8]Rom 1.20.
[9]Ps 138.6.
[10]Gen 2.16, taking παντὸς ξύλου (*pantos xylou*, "of every tree" in most English translations) in John's preferred sense.

ἀφεδρῶνα χωρεῖ καὶ φθοράν· καὶ ἀμήχανον ἄφθαρτον διαμένειν τὸν αἰσθητῆς βρώσεως ἐν μετουσίᾳ γινόμενον.

(25b) Ἡ ξύλον μὲν ζωῆς ἡ μετοχὴ τοῦ θεοῦ, δι' ἧς καὶ οἱ ἄγγελοι τρέφονται, δι' ἧς τὴν ἀφθαρσίαν λαμβάνειν ἠμέλλομεν· ἔδει γὰρ ἡμᾶς πρῶτον ἀδιακρίτως ὑποταγῆναι τῷ νόμῳ τοῦ θεοῦ, ἕως εἰς τελείαν ἕξιν τῆς ἀρετῆς ἤλθομεν, καὶ οὕτως δῶρον παρὰ θεοῦ λαβεῖν τὴν διάκρισιν καλοῦ τε καὶ κακοῦ, ὅπερ ἐστὶ ξύλον τοῦ γινώσκειν καλὸν καὶ κακόν. Οὐκ ἀσφαλὴς γὰρ τῷ ἀρτιπαγεῖ ἡ διάκρισις τῶν λογισμῶν καὶ τὸ ἀντιρρητικὸν διὰ τὸ ἐμπαθῆ ἔτι καὶ ἡδυπαθῆ ἔχειν τὸν λογισμόν. Ξύλον μὲν οὖν ζωῆς φημι τὴν ἐκ θεοῦ δεδομένην ἐντολήν—ξύλον γὰρ ζωῆς ἐστιν ἡ δικαιοσύνη πᾶσι τοῖς ἀντεχομένοις αὐτῆς. Καὶ ηὐλόγηται ξύλον, δι' οὗ δικαιοσύνη πεφύτευται, φησὶ Σολομών—ξύλον δὲ γνώσεως τὴν διάκρισιν καλοῦ τε καὶ κακοῦ. Ἔδει οὖν τὸν Ἀδὰμ διὰ τῆς ἀδιακρίτου ὑπακοῆς ἑνωθῆναι θεῷ καὶ πλουτῆσαι τῇ ἑνώσει τὴν θέωσιν ἐν καιρῷ, ὅτε ὁ φύσει θεὸς ηὐδόκει, καὶ πάντων τὴν ἀληθῆ γνῶσίν τε καὶ διάκρισιν καὶ τὴν ἀπέραντον ζωήν. Ἔδει δὲ ἀπόπειραν γενέσθαι τῆς ἀδιακρίτου ὑπακοῆς. Δίδωσι τοίνυν ἐντολὴν ὁ θεός, μὴ γεύσασθαι τοῦ ξύλου τῆς γνώσεως, μὴ πιστεῦσαι τῇ ἰδίᾳ διακρίσει μηδὲ φαγεῖν ἀπὸ ξύλου τινὸς ἔχοντος φυσικὴν ἐνέργειαν ἐμποιητικὴν τῆς ἐπιγνώσεως ἑαυτοῦ ἤτοι τῆς ἰδίας φύσεως. Προσβαλόντος οὖν τοῦ πονηροῦ διὰ τοῦ ὄφεως καὶ εἰπόντος· «ἔσεσθε ὡς θεοὶ γινώσκοντες καλὸν καὶ πονηρόν», ἐὰν φάγητε, ἐπίστευσε τῇ ἰδίᾳ διακρίσει, καὶ ἔδοξεν αὐτῷ καλὸν ἡ θέωσις καὶ ἡ γνῶσις. Καὶ οὐκ ἐλογίσατο, ὅτι πάντα καλὰ ἐν καιρῷ αὐτῶν καὶ οὐ καλὸν τὸ καλόν, εἰ μὴ καλῶς γένηται, καὶ ὡς οὐ χρὴ προαρπάζειν τὸ δοθησόμενον παρὰ γνώμην τοῦ διδόντος τὸ εἶναι καὶ τὸ εὖ εἶναι. Καὶ εἶδεν, ὡς καλόν, καὶ ἔφαγεν καὶ ἐγυμνώθη τῆς πρὸς θεὸν ἐκστάσεως, καὶ διηνοίχθησαν οἱ ὀφθαλμοὶ οἱ σωματικοί, καὶ τὰ πάθη ἐκινήθησαν, καὶ ἔγνωσαν, ὅτι γυμνοί εἰσι, καὶ ᾐσχύνθησαν. Καὶ περιεσπάσθησαν ἀπὸ θεοῦ

die.''[11] For sensible food is naturally the replenishment of what has been excreted and passes into the latrine and decomposes. And it is impossible for someone who partakes of sensible food to remain incorruptible.

Or the tree of life is the participation in God by which the angels too are nourished and by which we are to receive incorruption. For it was necessary for us first to be subject unreservedly to the law of God until we arrive at a perfect habit of virtue, and thus receive as a gift from God the distinction between good and evil, which is the tree of the knowledge of good and evil. For in the newly-formed human being the ability to distinguish thoughts and to refute a thought because it is impassioned or voluptuous was not yet secure. I therefore say that the tree of life is the commandment given by God—for the tree of life is righteousness for all who adhere to this. And the tree through which righteousness was implanted is blessed, says Solomon[12]—and the tree of knowledge is the distinction between good and evil. What was therefore needed was that through unreserved obedience Adam should be united to God and should enrich the union with deification at the appropriate time when he who is by nature God should see fit, and with the true knowledge and distinction of all things and eternal life. It was also needed that a test should be made of unreserved obedience. God therefore gave the commandment not to taste the tree of knowledge, not to have faith in one's own judgement, and not to eat of any tree that possesses a natural energy productive of knowledge of itself or of its own nature. Therefore when the evil one approached him through the serpent and said: "You shall be like gods, knowing good and evil,"[13] if you eat, he had confidence in his own judgement and it seemed to him that deification and knowledge were good. And he did not reflect that all things are good at their appropriate time, and the good is not good if it is not brought about in a good way, and that it was not necessary

[11]Gen 2.17.
[12]Prov 11.30.
[13]Gen 3.5.

καὶ ὡς νήπιοι ἐλιχνεύθησαν πρὸς τὴν ἡδονὴν καὶ ἐξωρίσθησαν ἐκ τοῦ ξύλου τῆς ζωῆς καὶ θνητοὶ γεγόνασιν.Ἤιδει δὲ ὁ ἐχθρὸς ἐκ τῆς πείρας, ὅτι τὸ προσεδρεύειν θεῷ θεώσεως καὶ ζωῆς αἰωνίου γίνεται πρόξενον.

26 Περὶ ἀνθρώπου

Οὕτω μὲν οὖν τὴν νοητὴν οὐσίαν ὑπεστήσατο ὁ θεός, ἀγγέλους φημὶ καὶ πάντα τὰ κατ᾽ οὐρανὸν τάγματα,—ταῦτα γὰρ ἀριδήλως νοερᾶς ἐστι καὶ ἀσωμάτου φύσεως· «ἀσωμάτου» δέ φημι συγκρινομένης πρὸς τὴν τῆς ὕλης παχύτητα· μόνον γὰρ ὄντως τὸ θεῖον ἄυλόν τε καὶ ἀσώματον—ἔτι δὲ καὶ τὴν αἰσθητήν, οὐρανόν τε καὶ γῆν καὶ τὰ τούτων ἐν μέσῳ κείμενα, καὶ τὴν μὲν οἰκείαν (οἰκεία γὰρ θεῷ ἡ λογικὴ φύσις καὶ νῷ μόνῳ ληπτή), τὴν δὲ πάντη που πορρωτάτω κειμένην, ὡς ὑπὸ τὴν αἴσθησιν δηλαδὴ πίπτουσαν. Ἔδει δὲ ἐξ ἀμφοτέρων μίξιν γενέσθαι καὶ «σοφίας μείζονος γνώρισμα καὶ τῆς περὶ τὰς φύσεις πολυτελείας», ὥς φησιν ὁ θεηγόρος Γρηγόριος, οἷόν τινα σύνδεσμον «τῆς ὁρατῆς τε καὶ ἀοράτου φύσεως». Τὸ δὲ «ἔδει» φημὶ τὴν τοῦ δημιουργοῦ ὑπεμφαίνων βούλησιν· αὕτη γὰρ θεσμὸς καὶ νόμος πρεπωδέστατος, καὶ οὐδεὶς ἐρεῖ τῷ πλαστουργῷ· «Τί με ἐποίησας οὕτως»; Ἐξουσίαν γὰρ ἔχει ὁ κεραμεὺς ἐκ τοῦ ἰδίου πηλοῦ διάφορα κατασκευάζειν σκεύη πρὸς ἔνδειξιν τῆς ἑαυτοῦ σοφίας.

---

[14]The terms "being" (τὸ εἶναι, to einai) and "well-being" (τὸ εὖ εἶναι, to eu einai) distinguish between existence as such and the (moral) quality of existence. The distinction was developed by the commentators on Aristotle and is found in Gregory of Nazianzus (Oration 38.3 [PG 36:313C; Moreschini, 880]), Dionysius the Areopagite (e.g., Divine Names 4.2 [PG 3:696A; Suchla, 144.14–15], and 5.8 [PG 3:821D; Suchla, 186.10]), Nemesius of Emesa (On Human Nature 18 [PG 40:680C; Morani 77.14]), and Maximus the Confessor (e.g., Ambigua to John 7.10, 10.12, 10.119, and 42.12 [PG

to snatch in advance what was to be given, and against the will of the giver of being and well-being.[14] And he saw it as good and ate and was stripped of his ecstasy towards God, and their bodily eyes were opened, and the passions were set in motion, and they knew that they were naked and were ashamed. And they were drawn away from God and like infants greedily desired pleasure, and they were exiled from the tree of life and became mortal. But the adversary sang from experience that what procures deification and eternal life is to wait upon God.[15]

26   *On man*

In this way, then, God created the noetic reality,[1] meaning angels and all the heavenly orders, for these are clearly of a spiritual and incorporeal nature—by "incorporeal" I mean in comparison with the coarseness of matter, for only the divine is truly immaterial and incorporeal—and also the sensible reality, the heavens and the earth and the things that lie within them. The former is akin to him (for rational nature is akin to God and apprehensible only by the intellect), but the latter lies at the farthest extreme from him, since it manifestly falls under the senses. Moreover, it was necessary that a combination of the two should take place and become "a mark of greater wisdom and of the divine magnificence regarding the natures," as the theologian Gregory says, as a kind of binding together "of the visible and invisible natures."[2] I use the expression "it was necessary" (ἔδει, *edei*) to indicate the Creator's will. For this is the most fitting law and rule, and nobody will ask the Creator: "Why did you make me like this?"[3] For the potter has the right to

91:1073C, 1116C, 1204C, and 1325B; Constas, 1:86, 168, and 340, and 2:142]). Maximus adds a further category, "eternal well-being" (τὸ ἀεὶ εὖ εἶναι, *to aei eu einai*), but this is not used by John Damascene.

[15]This paragraph is added by manuscripts GMN.

[1]τὴν νοητὴν οὐσίαν (*tēn noētēn ousian*), literally, "the intelligible substance."
[2]Gregory of Nazianzus, *Oration* 38.11 (PG 36:321C; Moreschini, 888).
[3]Rom 9.20.

Ἐπεὶ δὲ ταῦτα οὕτως εἶχεν, ἐξ ὁρατῆς τε καὶ ἀοράτου φύσεως δημιουργεῖ τὸν ἄνθρωπον οἰκείαις χερσὶ κατ' εἰκόνα τε καὶ ὁμοίωσιν, ἐκ γῆς μὲν τὸ σῶμα διαπλάσας, ψυχὴν δὲ λογικὴν καὶ νοερὰν διὰ τοῦ οἰκείου ἐμφυσήματος δοὺς αὐτῷ, ὅπερ δὴ θείαν εἰκόνα φαμέν· τὸ μὲν γὰρ «κατ' εἰκόνα» τὸ νοερὸν δηλοῖ καὶ αὐτεξούσιον, τὸ δὲ «καθ' ὁμοίωσιν» τὴν τῆς ἀρετῆς κατὰ τὸ δυνατὸν ὁμοίωσιν.

Ἅμα δὲ τὸ σῶμα καὶ ἡ ψυχὴ πέπλασται, οὐ τὸ μὲν πρῶτον, τὸ δὲ ὕστερον κατὰ τὰ Ὠριγένους ληρήματα.

Ἐποίησεν οὖν ὁ θεὸς τὸν ἄνθρωπον ἄκακον, εὐθῆ, ἐνάρετον, ἄλυπον, ἀμέριμνον, πάσῃ ἀρετῇ κατηγλαϊσμένον, πᾶσιν ἀγαθοῖς κομῶντα, οἷόν τινα κόσμον δεύτερον, ἐν μεγάλῳ μικρόν, ἄγγελον ἄλλον, προσκυνητὴν μικτόν, ἐπόπτην τῆς ὁρατῆς κτίσεως, μύστην τῆς νοουμένης, βασιλέα τῶν ἐπὶ γῆς, βασιλευόμενον ἄνωθεν, ἐπίγειον καὶ οὐράνιον, πρόσκαιρον καὶ ἀθάνατον, ὁρατὸν καὶ νοούμενον, μέσον μεγέθους καὶ ταπεινότητος, τὸν αὐτὸν πνεῦμα καὶ σάρκα, σάρκα διὰ τὴν ἔπαρσιν, πνεῦμα διὰ τὴν χάριν, τὸ μὲν ἵνα πάσχῃ καὶ πάσχων ὑπομιμνήσκηται καὶ παιδεύηται, τὸ δὲ ἵνα μένῃ καὶ δοξάζῃ τὸν εὐεργέτην, τῷ μεγέθει φιλοτιμούμενον, ζῷον ἐνταῦθα οἰκονομούμενον τουτέστιν ἐν τῷ παρόντι βίῳ, καὶ ἀλλαχοῦ μεθιστάμενον ἐν τῷ αἰῶνι τῷ μέλλοντι, καί—πέρας τοῦ μυστηρίου—τῇ πρὸς θεὸν νεύσει θεούμενον, θεούμενον δὲ τῇ μετοχῇ τῆς θείας ἐλλάμψεως καὶ οὐκ εἰς τὴν θείαν μεθιστάμενον οὐσίαν.

Ἐποίησε δὲ αὐτὸν φύσιν ἀναμάρτητον καὶ θέλησιν αὐτεξούσιον. Ἀναμάρτητον δέ φημι οὐχ ὡς μὴ ἐπιδεχόμενον ἁμαρτίαν (μόνον γὰρ τὸ θεῖον ἁμαρτίας ἐστὶν ἀνεπίδεκτον), ἀλλ' οὐκ ἐν τῇ φύσει τὸ ἁμαρτάνειν ἔχοντα, ἐν τῇ προαιρέσει δὲ μᾶλλον, ἤτοι ἐξουσίαν ἔχοντα μένειν καὶ προκόπτειν ἐν τῷ ἀγαθῷ τῇ θείᾳ συνεργούμενον χάριτι, ὡσαύτως καὶ τρέπεσθαι ἐκ τοῦ

make various vessels from the same clay as a demonstration of his personal skill.

Since this was the case, he created man by his own hands from visible and invisible nature according to his image and likeness: he fashioned the body from the earth, but he gave it a rational and intelligent soul by his own inbreathing, which is what we call the divine image. For the expression "according to the image" indicates what belongs to the intellect and to free will, whereas the expression "according to the likeness" indicates likeness in virtue so far as is possible.

The body and the soul were formed at the same time, not one first and the other later, as the ravings of Origen would have it.[4]

Therefore God made man innocent, upright, virtuous, free from pain, free from concern, resplendent with every virtue, rich in every good thing, "like a second world, a small one within a large one, another angel, a mixed worshiper, a contemplator of the visible creation, an initiate into the creation that is apprehended by the mind, ruler of all that is on earth but ruled from above, earthly and heavenly, transient and immortal, visible and apprehended mentally, intermediate between greatness and insignificance, at the same time spirit and flesh, flesh through pride, spirit through grace, the one that he may suffer and through suffering may be reminded and instructed, the other that he may stand fast and glorify his benefactor, endowed with greatness, here, that is to say, in the present life, an animal that is disciplined but elsewhere transferred to the future age, and—the height of the mystery—deified by his inclination towards God,"[5] deified by participation in the divine radiance, not transferred into the divine essence.

And he made him sinless in his nature and independent in his will. By sinless I mean not because he is incapable of sinning (for only the divine is incapable of sin), but because he has the power

[4]Cf. Canon 1 of 543 and Canon 1 of 553 (Price, *The Acts of Constantinople 553*, 2.281 and 284).

[5]Gregory of Nazianzus, *Oration* 38.11 (PG 36:324A; Moreschini, 890), a famous and much-quoted passage.

καλοῦ καὶ ἐν τῷ κακῷ γίνεσθαι τοῦ θεοῦ παραχωροῦντος διὰ τὸ αὐτεξούσιον· οὐκ ἀρετὴ γὰρ τὸ βίᾳ γινόμενον.

Ψυχὴ τοίνυν ἐστὶν οὐσία ζῶσα ἁπλῆ, ἀσώματος, σωματικοῖς ὀφθαλμοῖς κατ' οἰκείαν φύσιν ἀόρατος, λογική τε καὶ νοερά, ἀσχημάτιστος, ὀργανικῷ κεχρημένη σώματι καὶ τούτῳ ζωῆς αὐξήσεώς τε καὶ αἰσθήσεως καὶ γεννήσεως παρεκτική, οὐχ ἕτερον ἔχουσα παρ' ἑαυτὴν τὸν νοῦν, ἀλλὰ μέρος αὐτῆς τὸ καθαρώτατον (ὥσπερ γὰρ ὀφθαλμὸς ἐν σώματι, οὕτως ἐν ψυχῇ νοῦς), αὐτεξούσιος, θελητική τε καὶ ἐνεργητική, τρεπτὴ ἤτοι ἐθελότρεπτος, ὅτι καὶ κτιστή, πάντα ταῦτα κατὰ φύσιν ἐκ τῆς τοῦ δημιουργήσαντος αὐτὴν χάριτος εἰληφυῖα, ἐξ ἧς καὶ τὸ εἶναι καὶ τὸ φύσει οὕτως εἶναι εἴληφεν.

Ἀσώματα δὲ καὶ ἀόρατα καὶ ἀσχημάτιστα κατὰ δύο τρόπους νοοῦμεν· τὰ μὲν κατ' οὐσίαν, τὰ δὲ κατὰ χάριν, καὶ τὰ μὲν φύσει ὄντα, τὰ δὲ πρὸς τὴν τῆς ὕλης παχύτητα. Ἐπὶ θεοῦ μὲν οὖν φύσει, ἐπὶ δὲ ἀγγέλων καὶ δαιμόνων καὶ ψυχῶν χάριτι, καὶ ὡς πρὸς τὴν τῆς ὕλης παχύτητα λέγεται.

Σῶμά ἐστι τὸ τριχῇ διαστατὸν ἤγουν τὸ ἔχον μῆκος καὶ πλάτος καὶ βάθος ἤτοι πάχος. Πᾶν δὲ σῶμα ἐκ τῶν τεσσάρων στοιχείων συνίσταται, τὰ δὲ τῶν ζῴων σώματα ἐκ τῶν τεσσάρων χυμῶν.

Χρὴ εἰδέναι, ὅτι τέσσαρα στοιχεῖά ἐστι· γῆ, ξηρὰ καὶ ψυχρά· ὕδωρ, ψυχρὸν καὶ ὑγρόν· ἀήρ, ὑγρὸς καὶ θερμός· πῦρ, θερμὸν καὶ ξηρόν. Ὁμοίως καὶ χυμοὶ τέσσαρες ἀναλογοῦντες τοῖς τέσσαρσι στοιχείοις· μέλαινα χολὴ ἀναλογοῦσα τῇ γῇ (ξηρὰ γάρ ἐστι καὶ ψυχρά), φλέγμα ἀναλογοῦν τῷ ὕδατι (ψυχρὸν γάρ ἐστι καὶ ὑγρόν), αἷμα ἀναλογοῦν τῷ ἀέρι (ὑγρὸν γάρ ἐστι καὶ θερμόν), ξανθὴ χολὴ ἀναλογοῦσα τῷ πυρί (θερμὴ γάρ ἐστι καὶ ξηρά). Οἱ

[6]John takes this point (the unity of the soul and the intellect) from the opening paragraph of Nemesius of Emesa's *On Human Nature* 1 (PG 40:504A; Morani, 1), where Nemesius goes on to argue against Plotinus' tripartite division of intellect, soul, and body. From here until Chapter 44, John relies heavily on Nemesius (late fourth century), on whom see Karamanolis, *Philosophy of Early Christianity*, 157–59, 185–87.

of sinning not in his nature but rather in his freedom of choice; or else because he has the power of remaining in the good and making progress in it by the cooperation of divine grace, and equally the power of turning away from the good and abiding in evil, which God allows through the power of free will. For virtue is not brought about by force.

The soul, then, is a living substance, which is simple, incorporeal, invisible in its own nature to corporeal eyes, rational and intelligent, without form, using the body as an instrument and able to supply it with the powers of growth, sensation, and reproduction, without having the intellect as something other than itself but having it as the most pure part of itself (for what the eye is to the body, the intellect is to the soul),[6] as endowed with free will, volition, and the power to act, mutable or changeable with regard to will because it is also created, having received all these by nature from the grace of him who created it, from which grace it has received both its being and its being in the way that it is.

We think of incorporeal, invisible, and formless things in two ways, some in accordance with essence, others in accordance with grace, the former being what they are by nature, the latter in comparison with the coarseness of matter. In the case of God, of course, incorporeality is said to be by nature; in the case of angels, demons, and souls it is said to be by grace and in comparison with the coarseness of matter.[7]

A body is that which has three dimensions,[8] namely, length, breadth, and depth or thickness. Each body is formed from the four elements, and the bodies of living beings from the four humors.

One needs to know that the four elements are earth, which is dry and cold, water, which is moist and cold, air, which is moist and

---

[7]*Doctrina Patrum*, Diekamp, 253.4–7, unattributed. The incorporeality of angels and souls has been discussed before (of angels at the beginning of Chapter 17 and in the first sentence of the present chapter, of souls in the previous paragraph) but this is the first time that incorporeality is characterized specifically as a gift of grace.

[8]Cf. Nemesius of Emesa, *On Human Nature* 2 (PG 40:540B; Morani, 18.15–16).

μὲν οὖν καρποὶ ἐκ τῶν στοιχείων συνίστανται, οἱ δὲ χυμοὶ ἐκ τῶν καρπῶν, τὰ δὲ τῶν ζῴων σώματα ἐκ τῶν χυμῶν καὶ εἰς τὰ αὐτὰ ἀναλύεται· πᾶν γὰρ συντιθέμενον εἰς τὰ αὐτὰ ἀναλύεται, ἐξ ὧν συνετέθη.

Χρὴ γινώσκειν, ὅτι ὁ ἄνθρωπος καὶ τοῖς ἀψύχοις κοινωνεῖ καὶ τῆς τῶν ἀλόγων μετέχει ζωῆς καὶ τῆς τῶν λογικῶν μετείληφε νοήσεως. Κοινωνεῖ γὰρ τοῖς μὲν ἀψύχοις κατὰ τὸ σῶμα καὶ τὴν ἀπὸ τῶν τεσσάρων στοιχείων κρᾶσιν, τοῖς δὲ φυτοῖς κατά τε ταῦτα καὶ τὴν θρεπτικὴν καὶ αὐξητικὴν καὶ σπερματικὴν ἤγουν γεννητικὴν δύναμιν, τοῖς δὲ ἀλόγοις καὶ ἐν τούτοις μέν, ἐξ ἐπιμέτρου δὲ κατὰ τὴν ὄρεξιν ἤγουν θυμὸν καὶ ἐπιθυμίαν καὶ κατὰ τὴν αἴσθησιν καὶ κατὰ τὴν καθ᾽ ὁρμὴν κίνησιν.

Αἰσθήσεις μὲν οὖν εἰσι πέντε· ὅρασις, ἀκοή, ὄσφρησις, γεῦσις, ἁφή. Τῆς δὲ καθ᾽ ὁρμὴν κινήσεώς ἐστι τὸ ἀπὸ τόπου εἰς τόπον μεταβατικὸν καὶ τὸ κινητικὸν ὅλου τοῦ σώματος καὶ τὸ φωνητικὸν καὶ ἀναπνευστικόν· ταῦτα γὰρ ἐν ἡμῖν ἐστι ποιεῖν καὶ μὴ ποιεῖν.

Συνάπτεται δὲ διὰ τοῦ λογικοῦ ταῖς ἀσωμάτοις καὶ νοεραῖς φύσεσι λογιζόμενος καὶ νοῶν καὶ κρίνων ἕκαστα καὶ τὰς ἀρετὰς μεταδιώκων καὶ τῶν ἀρετῶν τὸν κολοφῶνα, τὴν εὐσέβειαν, ἀσπαζόμενος· διὸ καὶ μικρὸς κόσμος ὁ ἄνθρωπός ἐστιν.

Χρὴ δὲ εἰδέναι, ὡς ἴδια μὲν τοῦ σώματος μόνου τομὴ καὶ ῥεῦσις καὶ μεταβολή. Μεταβολὴ μὲν ἡ κατὰ ποιότητα ἤγουν θερμασίαν καὶ ψύξιν καὶ τὰ τοιαῦτα. Ῥεῦσις δὲ ἡ κατὰ κένωσιν· κενοῦται γὰρ ξηρὰ καὶ ὑγρὰ καὶ πνεύματα, ὧν χρῄζει τῆς ἀναπληρώσεως· ὥστε φυσικά εἰσι πάθη ἥ τε πεῖνα καὶ ἡ δίψα.

Ἴδια δὲ τῆς ψυχῆς ἡ εὐσέβεια καὶ ἡ νόησις. Κοινὰ δὲ ψυχῆς καὶ σώματος αἱ ἀρεταί, ἐχουσῶν καὶ τούτων ἐπὶ τὴν ψυχὴν τὴν ἀναφοράν, οἷον ψυχῆς προσχρωμένης σώματι.

⁹Nemesius of Emesa, *On Human Nature* 1 (PG 40:505B–508A; Morani, 2.13–20).

¹⁰Nemesius of Emesa, *On Human Nature* 26 (PG 40:704B; Morani 87.20–22).

¹¹Cf. Nemesius of Emesa, *On Human Nature* 1 (PG 40:508A; Morani 2.21–23). Note that the term used here for "religion" is εὐσέβεια (*eusebeia*, "piety"), which

warm, and fire, which is warm and dry. There are also four humors corresponding to the four elements: black bile, which corresponds to earth (for it is dry and cold), phlegm, which corresponds to water (for it is cold and moist), blood, which corresponds to air (for it is moist and warm), yellow bile, which corresponds to fire (for it is warm and dry). Now fruits are formed from the elements, humors from the fruits, and the bodies of animals from the humors, and they are resolved back into them. For everything that is composite breaks down into the same things from which it was formed.

One needs to know that man "has things in common with inanimate beings, and also shares life with irrational beings, and intellect with rational beings. For with inanimate beings he shares corporeality and composition from the four elements; with plants he shares the same things plus the power of nourishment, growth, and fertilization or reproduction; and with irrational beings he shares these and in addition to them appetite (namely, anger and desire), sensation, and spontaneous movement."[9]

Then there are five senses: sight, hearing, smell, taste, and touch. "What belongs to spontaneous movement is the power of passing from one place to another, the power of moving any part of the body and the powers of utterance and breathing. For with these it depends upon us whether we do them or not."[10]

Through his rationality man is also connected with incorporeal and intellectual natures, since he reasons, and thinks, and judges each thing and pursues the virtues and embraces the summit of the virtues, which is religion.[11] Wherefore man is also a microcosm.[12]

One needs to know that division, flow, and change are properties of the body alone. Change relates to quality, that is, to heating, cooling, and the like. Flow relates to evacuation, for solids, liquids,

---

means specifically the Christian religion. When pagan religion is meant (as at the beginning of the third paragraph of Chapter 77), it is called θρησκεία (*thrēskeia*, "religion" or "cult").

[12]Cf. Gregory of Nazianzus, *Oration* 28.22 (PG 36:56A–57A; Moreschini, 680).

Χρὴ γινώσκειν, ὅτι τὸ λογικὸν φύσει κατάρχει τοῦ ἀλόγου·
διαιροῦνται γὰρ αἱ δυνάμεις τῆς ψυχῆς εἰς λογικὸν καὶ ἄλογον.
Τοῦ δὲ ἀλόγου μέρη εἰσὶ δύο· τὸ μὲν ἀνήκοόν ἐστι λόγου ἤγουν οὐ
πείθεται λόγῳ, τὸ δὲ κατήκοόν ἐστι καὶ ἐπιπειθὲς λόγῳ. Ἀνήκοον
μὲν οὖν καὶ μὴ πειθόμενον λόγῳ ἐστὶ τὸ ζωτικόν, ὃ καὶ σφυγμικὸν
καλεῖται, καὶ τὸ σπερματικὸν ἤγουν γεννητικὸν καὶ τὸ φυτικόν,
ὃ καὶ θρεπτικὸν καλεῖται· τούτου δέ ἐστι καὶ τὸ αὐξητικόν, τὸ
καὶ διαπλάσσον τὰ σώματα. Ταῦτα γὰρ οὐ λόγῳ κυβερνῶνται,
ἀλλὰ τῇ φύσει. Τὸ δὲ κατήκοον καὶ ἐπιπειθὲς λόγῳ διαιρεῖται
εἰς ἐπιθυμίαν καὶ θυμόν. Καλεῖται δὲ κοινῶς τὸ ἄλογον μέρος
τῆς ψυχῆς παθητικὸν καὶ ὀρεκτικόν. Χρὴ δὲ γινώσκειν, ὅτι τοῦ
ἐπιπειθοῦς λόγῳ ἐστὶ καὶ ἡ καθ᾽ ὁρμὴν κίνησις.

Δεῖ γινώσκειν, ὅτι τῶν πραγμάτων τὰ μέν ἐστιν ἀγαθά, τὰ
δὲ φαῦλα. Προσδοκώμενον μὲν οὖν ἀγαθὸν ἐπιθυμίαν συνιστᾷ,
παρὸν δὲ ἡδονήν· ὁμοίως δὲ προσδοκώμενον κακὸν φόβον,
παρὸν δὲ λύπην. Δεῖ δὲ εἰδέναι, ὅτι ἀγαθὸν ἐνταῦθα εἰπόντες ἢ τὸ
ὄντως ἀγαθὸν ἢ τὸ δοκοῦν ἀγαθὸν εἴπομεν, ὁμοίως καὶ κακόν.

and gases are evacuated and need to be replenished. Hence hunger and thirst are natural experiences.[13]

Religion and intellection are properties of the soul. The virtues are common to the body and the soul, although these too are referred to the soul, in that the soul makes use of the body.

One needs to know that the rational element naturally rules the irrational. For the soul's faculties are divided into rational and irrational. The irrational element has two parts. The one is unheeding to reason, that is to say, does not obey reason; the other gives heed and is obedient to reason. The faculties that indeed do not give heed to reason and do not obey it are the vital, which is also called the pulsative, the spermatic or generative, and the vegetative, which is also called the nutritive. To the last-named belongs the principle of the growth and formation of bodies. For these are governed not by reason but by nature. The part that is heedful and obedient to reason is divided into desire and anger. The irrational part of the soul is commonly called the passible and appetitive. And one should know that impulsive movement also belongs to the part that is subject to reason.[14]

One needs to know that among realities some are good and others bad. Thus when something good is expected, it creates desire, and when present, pleasure. Similarly when something evil is expected it creates fear, and when present, sorrow. One should know that when we speak of good in this context, we mean either what is really good or what only appears to be good, and likewise with regard to evil.[15]

[13]Cf. Nemesius of Emesa, *On Human Nature* 1 (PG 40:516C–517A; Morani, 7.16–21).

[14]Cf. Nemesius of Emesa, *On Human Nature* 15 (PG 40:668C–672B; Morani, 72.4–21).

[15]Cf. Nemesius of Emesa, *On Human Nature* 17 (PG 40:676BC; Morani, 75.8–27).

27   Περὶ ἡδονῶν

Τῶν ἡδονῶν αἱ μέν εἰσι ψυχικαί, αἱ δὲ σωματικαί. Καὶ ψυχικαὶ μέν, ὅσαι μόνης εἰσὶ τῆς ψυχῆς αὐτῆς καθ᾽ αὑτὴν ὡς αἱ περὶ τὰ μαθήματα καὶ τὴν θεωρίαν. Σωματικαὶ δὲ αἱ μετὰ κοινωνίας τῆς ψυχῆς καὶ τοῦ σώματος γινόμεναι καὶ διὰ τοῦτο σωματικαὶ καλούμεναι ὡς αἱ περὶ τροφὰς καὶ συνουσίας καὶ τὰ τοιαῦτα. Μόνου δὲ τοῦ σώματος οὐκ ἂν εὕροι τις ἡδονάς.

Πάλιν τῶν ἡδονῶν αἱ μέν εἰσιν ἀληθεῖς, αἱ δὲ ψευδεῖς, καὶ αἱ μὲν τῆς διανοίας μόνης κατ᾽ ἐπιστήμην καὶ θεωρίαν, αἱ δὲ μετὰ σώματος κατ᾽ αἴσθησιν. Καὶ τῶν μετὰ σώματος ἡδονῶν αἱ μέν εἰσι φυσικαὶ ἅμα καὶ ἀναγκαῖαι, ὧν χωρὶς ζῆν ἀδύνατον, ὡς αἱ τροφαὶ τῆς ἐνδείας ἀναπληρωτικαὶ καὶ τὰ ἐνδύματα ἀναγκαῖα, αἱ δὲ φυσικαὶ μέν, οὐκ ἀναγκαῖαι δέ, ὡς αἱ κατὰ φύσιν καὶ κατὰ νόμον μίξεις (αὗται γὰρ εἰς μὲν τὴν διαμονὴν τοῦ παντὸς γένους συντελοῦσι, δυνατὸν δὲ καὶ χωρὶς αὐτῶν ἐν παρθενίᾳ ζῆν), αἱ δὲ οὔτε ἀναγκαῖαι οὔτε φυσικαὶ ὡς μέθη καὶ λαγνεία καὶ πλησμοναὶ τὴν χρείαν ὑπερβαίνουσαι· οὔτε γὰρ εἰς σύστασιν τῆς ζωῆς ἡμῶν συντελοῦσιν οὔτε εἰς διαδοχὴν τοῦ γένους, ἀλλὰ καὶ προσβλάπτουσιν. Τὸν τοίνυν κατὰ θεὸν ζῶντα δεῖ μετέρχεσθαι τὰς ἀναγκαίας ἅμα καὶ φυσικάς, ἐν δευτέρᾳ δὲ τάξει τὰς φυσικὰς καὶ οὐκ ἀναγκαίας τίθεσθαι μετὰ τοῦ προσήκοντος καιροῦ καὶ τρόπου καὶ μέτρου γινομένας, τὰς δὲ ἄλλας χρὴ πάντως παραιτεῖσθαι.

Καλὰς δὲ ἡδονὰς χρὴ ἡγεῖσθαι τὰς μὴ συμπεπλεγμένας λύπῃ μήτε μεταμέλειαν ἐμποιούσας μηδὲ ἑτέρας βλάβης γεννητικάς, μήτε τοῦ μέτρου πέρα χωρούσας μήτε τῶν σπουδαίων ἔργων ἡμᾶς ἀφελκούσας ἐπὶ πολὺ ἢ καταδουλούσας.

---

[1]Nemesius of Emesa, *On Human Nature* 18 (PG 40:677B; Morani, 76.6–11, condensed).
[2]Nemesius of Emesa, *On Human Nature* 18 (PG 40:677C; Morani, 76.14–17).

27   On pleasures

"Among the pleasures some are psychological and others physical. Psychological pleasures are those which belong to the soul alone in its own right such as those to do with study and contemplation. Physical pleasures arise from the communion of the soul with the body and are called physical for that reason, such as those to do with food, sex, and suchlike. One would not be able to find pleasures belonging to the body alone."[1]

Again, "some pleasures are genuine, others are spurious, and some belong to the intellect alone, like knowledge and contemplation, others to the intellect with the body, like sensation."[2] And of those pleasures which involve the body, some are natural and necessary, without which it would be impossible to live, such as food to satisfy hunger and necessary clothing, others are natural but not necessary, such as sexual relations in accordance with nature and the law (for while these contribute to the perpetuation of the human race as a whole, it is also possible to live without them in virginity), and others are neither necessary nor natural, such as drunkenness, lewdness, and stuffing oneself beyond what one needs, for those contribute neither to the maintenance of our life nor to the perpetuation of the human race, but actually harm us. Furthermore, someone who lives in accordance with God must relegate even necessary and natural pleasures to second place, and reckon those that are natural but not necessary as to be enjoyed at the appropriate time and in a suitable manner and measure. But the others must be renounced altogether.[3]

Good pleasures should be considered "those that are not bound up with sorrow, do not give rise to remorse, do not cause other harm, do not exceed the bounds of moderation, do not distract us for long from more important work, and do not enslave us."[4]

---

[3]Cf. Nemesius of Emesa, *On Human Nature* 18 (PG 40:677C–680B; Morani, 76.6–25).
    [4]Nemesius of Emesa, *On Human Nature* 18 (PG 40:680B; Morani, 77.8–11).

28 Περὶ λύπης

Τῆς δὲ λύπης εἴδη τέσσαρα· ἄχος, ἄχθος, φθόνος, ἔλεος. Ἄχος μὲν οὖν ἐστι λύπη ἀφωνίαν ἐμποιοῦσα, ἄχθος δὲ λύπη βαρύνουσα, φθόνος δὲ λύπη ἐπὶ ἀλλοτρίοις ἀγαθοῖς, ἔλεος δὲ λύπη ἐπὶ ἀλλοτρίοις κακοῖς.

29 Περὶ φόβου

Διαιρεῖται δὲ καὶ ὁ φόβος εἰς ἕξ· εἰς ὄκνον, εἰς αἰδῶ, εἰς αἰσχύνην, εἰς κατάπληξιν, εἰς ἔκπληξιν, εἰς ἀγωνίαν. Ὄκνος μὲν οὖν ἐστι φόβος μελλούσης ἐνεργείας. Αἰδὼς δὲ φόβος ἐπὶ προσδοκίᾳ ψόγου· κάλλιστον δὲ τοῦτο τὸ πάθος. Αἰσχύνη δὲ φόβος ἐπὶ αἰσχρῷ πεπραγμένῳ· οὐδὲ τοῦτο δὲ ἀνέλπιστον εἰς σωτηρίαν. Κατάπληξις δὲ φόβος ἐκ μεγάλης φαντασίας. Ἔκπληξις δὲ φόβος ἐξ ἀσυνήθους φαντασίας. Ἀγωνία δὲ φόβος διαπτώσεως ἤγουν ἀποτυχίας· φοβούμενοι γὰρ ἀποτυχεῖν τῆς πράξεως ἀγωνιῶμεν.

30 Περὶ θυμοῦ

Θυμὸς δέ ἐστι ζέσις τοῦ περὶ καρδίαν αἵματος ἐξ ἀναθυμιάσεως τῆς χολῆς ἢ ἀναθολώσεως γινομένη. Διὸ καὶ χολὴ λέγεται καὶ χόλος. Ἔστι δέ, ὅτε ὁ θυμὸς καὶ ὄρεξίς ἐστιν ἀντιτιμωρήσεως· ἀδικούμενοι γὰρ ἢ νομίζοντες ἀδικεῖσθαι θυμούμεθα, καὶ γίνεται τότε μικτὸν τὸ πάθος ἐξ ἐπιθυμίας καὶ θυμοῦ.

Εἴδη δὲ τοῦ θυμοῦ τρία· ὀργή, ἥτις καλεῖται χολὴ καὶ χόλος, καὶ μῆνις καὶ κότος. Θυμὸς μὲν γὰρ ἀρχὴν καὶ κίνησιν ἔχων ὀργὴ καὶ χολὴ καὶ χόλος λέγεται. Μῆνις δὲ χολὴ ἐπιμένουσα ἤγουν μνησικακία· εἴρηται δὲ παρὰ τὸ μένειν καὶ τῇ μνήμῃ

28   *On pain*

"The varieties of pain are four: grief, sorrow, envy, compassion. Grief is a pain that strikes one dumb. Sorrow is a pain that oppresses one. Envy is pain at other people's good fortune. Compassion is pain at other people's misfortune."[1]

29   *On fear*

Fear is divided into six varieties: apprehension, nervousness, shame, terror, consternation, anxiety. Apprehension is fear of something that is about to happen. Nervousness is fear of an expected reproach—this is the best kind of fear. Shame is fear of some disgraceful act that has been committed—not even this is without hope of salvation. Terror is fear arising out of some forceful mental image. Consternation is fear arising from some unaccustomed mental image. Anxiety is fear of stumbling or failing, for if we are afraid of failing in something we do, we are anxious.[1]

30   *On anger*

"Anger is the heat of the blood around the heart that comes about when the bile fumes or becomes turbid. For this reason it is also called bile or gall. There are times when anger is also an appetite for revenge, for we become angry when we are wronged or think we are wronged, and then the passion becomes a mixture of desire and anger."[1]

"There are three kinds of anger: bitterness, which is called bile and gall, and wrath and rancor. For when anger is first set in motion, it is called bitterness, bile, and gall. Wrath, or the remembrance

[1]Nemesius of Emesa, *On Human Nature* 19 (PG 40:688A; Morani 80.13–15).

[1]Cf. Nemesius of Emesa, *On Human Nature* 20 (PG 40:688B–689A; Morani, 81.15–82.3).

[1]Nemesius of Emesa, *On Human Nature* 20 (PG 40:692A; Morani, 81.2–6).

παραδίδοσθαι. Κότος δὲ ὀργὴ ἐπιτηροῦσα καιρὸν εἰς τιμωρίαν· εἴρηται δὲ καὶ οὗτος παρὰ τὸ κεῖσθαι. Ἔστι δὲ ὁ θυμὸς τὸ δορυφορικὸν τοῦ λογισμοῦ, ἔκδικος τῆς ἐπιθυμίας· ὅταν γὰρ ἐπιθυμήσωμεν πράγματος καὶ κωλυθῶμεν ὑπό τινος, θυμούμεθα κατ᾽ αὐτοῦ ὡς ἀδικηθέντες, τοῦ λογισμοῦ δηλονότι κρίναντος ἄξιον ἀγανακτήσεως τὸ γινόμενον ἐπὶ τῶν φυλαττόντων κατὰ φύσιν τὴν οἰκείαν τάξιν.

Τοῦ δὲ μὴ πειθομένου λόγῳ ἐστὶ τὸ θρεπτικὸν καὶ γεννητικὸν καὶ σφυγμικόν· καλεῖται δὲ αὐξητικὸν μὲν τὸ θρεπτικὸν καὶ γεννητικόν, ζωτικὸν δὲ τὸ σφυγμικόν.

Τοῦ μὲν οὖν θρεπτικοῦ δυνάμεις εἰσὶ τέσσαρες· ἑλκτικὴ ἡ ἕλκουσα τὴν τροφήν, καθεκτικὴ ἡ κατέχουσα τὴν τροφὴν καὶ μὴ ἐῶσα αὐτὴν εὐθέως ἐκκριθῆναι, ἀλλοιωτικὴ ἡ ἀλλοιοῦσα τὴν τροφὴν εἰς τοὺς χυμούς, ἀποκριτικὴ ἡ τὸ περίττωμα διὰ τοῦ ἀφεδρῶνος ἐκκρίνουσα καὶ ἐκβάλλουσα.

Χρὴ δὲ εἰδέναι, ὅτι τῶν κατὰ τὸ ζῷον δυνάμεων αἱ μέν εἰσιν ψυχικαί, αἱ δὲ φυσικαί, αἱ δὲ ζωτικαί. Καὶ ψυχικαὶ μὲν αἱ κατὰ προαίρεσιν ἤγουν ἡ καθ᾽ ὁρμὴν κίνησις καὶ ἡ αἴσθησις. Τῆς δὲ καθ᾽ ὁρμὴν κινήσεώς ἐστι τό τε κατὰ τόπον μεταβατικὸν καὶ κινητικὸν ὅλου τοῦ σώματος καὶ φωνητικὸν καὶ ἀναπνευστικόν· ἐν ἡμῖν γάρ ἐστι ποιῆσαι ταῦτα καὶ μὴ ποιῆσαι. Φυσικαὶ δὲ καὶ ζωτικαὶ αἱ ἀπροαίρετοι. Καὶ φυσικαὶ μὲν ἡ θρεπτικὴ καὶ αὐξητικὴ καὶ σπερματική, ζωτικὴ δὲ ἡ σφυγμική· αὗται γὰρ καὶ θελόντων καὶ μὴ θελόντων ἐνεργοῦσι.

---

[2]Nemesius of Emesa, *On Human Nature* 20 (PG 40:692AB; Morani, 81.6–10).

[3]Nemesius of Emesa, *On Human Nature* 20 (PG 40:692B; Morani, 81.10–11).

[4]The following paragraphs to the end of the chapter, which are drawn from Nemesius of Emesa, *On Human Nature* 22, 23 and 26, are not in the manuscripts used by Lequien (and therefore not in the Salmond and Casey translations).

[5]Cf. Nemesius of Emesa, *On Human Nature* 22 (PG 40:692B; Morani, 82.20–22).

[6]Nemesius of Emesa, *On Human Nature* 23 (PG 40:693A; Morani, 83.2–5), slightly expanded.

[7]The three divisions are the ψυχικαί (*psychikai*), the φυσικαί (*physikai*), and the ζωτικαί (*zōtikai*).

of a wrong, is bile that endures. It derives its name (μνησικακία, *mnēsikakia*) from remaining (μένειν, *menein*) and being handed over to the memory (μνήμη, *mnēmē*). Rancor is bitterness on the watch for an opportunity for revenge. This too derives its name (κότος, *kotos*) from being put on deposit (κεῖσθαι, *keisthai*)."[2]

"Anger is the bodyguard of reasoning,"[3] the champion of desire. For when we desire something and are thwarted by someone, we become angry against him as people who have been wronged, evidently because our reasoning judges what has happened as worthy of censure in the case of those who naturally guard their own position.[4]

The functions that are not controlled by reason are the nutritive, the reproductive, and the pulsative. The nutritive and reproductive functions are called the augmentative function, the pulsative function is called the vital function.[5]

"The powers of the nutritive function are four. The ingestive power is that which draws in food. The retentive power is that which retains the food and does not allow it to be evacuated quickly. The transformative power is that which transforms the food in the digestive juices. The excretive power is that which evacuates the waste through the anus and expels it."[6]

One needs to know that "of the powers concerning the living organism, some are spiritual, others are natural, and others vital.[7] The spiritual are those connected with free choice, that is to say, the powers of deciding to move and of sensation. That which belongs to the power of deciding to move is going from one place to another, moving the whole body, uttering speech, and breathing. For it belongs to us to do them or not to do them. The natural and vital powers are those which are not subject to the will. And the natural powers are the nutritive, the augmentative, and the spermatic, while the vital power is the pulsative," for these operate both voluntarily and involuntarily.[8]

[8]Nemesius of Emesa, *On Human Nature* 26 (PG 40:704B–705A; Morani, 87.17–25).

31 Περὶ τοῦ φανταστικοῦ

Φανταστικόν ἐστι δύναμις τῆς ἀλόγου ψυχῆς διὰ τῶν αἰσθητηρίων ἐνεργοῦσα, ἥτις λέγεται αἴσθησις. Φανταστὸν δὲ καὶ αἰσθητὸν τὸ τῇ φαντασίᾳ καὶ τῇ αἰσθήσει ὑποπῖπτον· ὡς ὅρασις μὲν αὐτὴ ἡ ὀπτικὴ δύναμις, ὁρατὸν δὲ τὸ ὑποπῖπτον τῇ ὁράσει, λίθος τυχὸν ἤ τι τῶν τοιούτων. Φαντασία δέ ἐστι πάθος τῆς ἀλόγου ψυχῆς ὑπὸ φανταστοῦ τινος γινόμενον, φάντασμα δὲ πάθος διάκενον ἐν τοῖς ἀλόγοις τῆς ψυχῆς ἀπ᾽ οὐδενὸς φανταστοῦ γινόμενον. Ὄργανον δὲ τοῦ φανταστικοῦ ἡ ἐμπρόσθιος κοιλία τοῦ ἐγκεφάλου.

32 Περὶ αἰσθήσεως

Αἴσθησίς ἐστι δύναμις τῆς ψυχῆς ἀντιληπτικὴ τῶν ὑλῶν ἤγουν διαγνωστική· αἰσθητήρια δὲ τὰ ὄργανα ἤγουν τὰ μέλη, δι᾽ ὧν αἰσθανόμεθα· αἰσθητὰ δὲ τὰ τῇ αἰσθήσει ὑποπίπτοντα· αἰσθητικὸν δὲ τὸ ζῷον τὸ ἔχον τὴν αἴσθησιν. Εἰσὶ δὲ αἰσθήσεις πέντε, ὁμοίως καὶ αἰσθητήρια πέντε.

Πρώτη αἴσθησις ὅρασις. Αἰσθητήρια δὲ καὶ ὄργανα τῆς ὁράσεως τὰ ἐξ ἐγκεφάλου νεῦρα καὶ οἱ ὀφθαλμοί. Αἰσθάνεται δὲ ἡ ὄψις κατὰ πρῶτον μὲν λόγον τοῦ χρώματος, συνδιαγινώσκει δὲ τῷ χρώματι καὶ τὸ κεχρωσμένον σῶμα καὶ τὸ μέγεθος αὐτοῦ καὶ τὸ σχῆμα καὶ τὸν τόπον, ἔνθα ἐστί, καὶ τὸ διάστημα τὸ μεταξὺ καὶ τὸν ἀριθμὸν κίνησίν τε καὶ στάσιν καὶ τὸ τραχὺ καὶ λεῖον καὶ ὁμαλὸν καὶ ἀνώμαλον καὶ τὸ ὀξὺ καὶ τὸ ἀμβλὺ καὶ τὴν σύστασιν, εἴτε ὑδατώδης, εἴτε γεώδης ἤγουν ὑγρὰ ἢ ξηρά.

Δευτέρα αἴσθησίς ἐστιν ἀκοὴ τῶν φωνῶν καὶ τῶν ψόφων οὖσα αἰσθητική. Διαγινώσκει δὲ αὐτῶν τὴν ὀξύτητα καὶ τὴν βαρύτητα λειότητά τε καὶ τραχύτητα καὶ μέγεθος. Ὄργανα δὲ

31 *On the imagination*

"The ability to imagine is a power of the irrational soul activated by the senses, an activation that is called sensation. What is imagined and sensed falls under imagination and sensation, just as vision is itself the power of seeing, whereas what is seen, for example a stone or some such thing, falls under vision. Imagination is a passion of the irrational soul brought about by something imagined. An illusion is an empty passion that is brought about in the irrational parts of the soul but not out of anything imagined. The organ of the ability to imagine is the brain's front ventricle."[1]

32 *On sense-perception*

Sense-perception is the soul's power of apprehending or discerning material things. Sense-organs are the instruments or members by which we sense. Sensible things are those things that come within the range of the senses. A sensitive thing is a living being that possesses sense-perception. There are five senses with five corresponding sense-organs.[1]

The first sense is that of sight. The organs and instruments of sight are the eyes and the nerves that come from the brain. "What is sensed in the first instance is the aspect of color, and perceived along with the color is also the colored body, its size, its shape, the place it occupies, the distance that intervenes, its number, whether it is in motion or at rest, its roughness or smoothness, its regularity or irregularity, its sharpness or bluntness, and its consistency, whether it is watery or earthy, that is to say, wet or dry."[2]

The second sense is that of hearing, "which is the perception of voices and sounds. It distinguishes between their high and low pitch,

---

[1]Nemesius of Emesa, *On Human Nature* 6 (PG 40:632B–633B; Morani, 55.9–56.4), abbreviated.

[1]Cf. Nemesius of Emesa, *On Human Nature* 6 (PG 40:636A; Morani, 56.5–6).
[2]Nemesius of Emesa, *On Human Nature* 7 (PG 40:644A; Morani, 59.19–60.1).

αὐτῆς τὰ νεῦρα τὰ ἐξ ἐγκεφάλου τὰ μαλακὰ καὶ τῶν ὤτων ἡ κατασκευή. Μόνος δὲ ἄνθρωπος καὶ πίθηκος οὐ κινοῦσι τὰ ὦτα.

Τρίτη αἴσθησις ὄσφρησις, ἥτις γίνεται μὲν διὰ τῶν ῥινῶν ἀναπεμπουσῶν τοὺς ἀτμοὺς ἐπὶ τὸν ἐγκέφαλον, περαίνεται δὲ εἰς τὰ πέρατα τῶν προσθίων κοιλιῶν τοῦ ἐγκεφάλου. Ἔστι δὲ αἰσθητικὴ καὶ ἀντιληπτικὴ τῶν ἀτμῶν. Τῶν δὲ ἀτμῶν ἡ γενικωτάτη διαφορά ἐστιν εὐωδία καὶ δυσωδία καὶ τὸ μέσον τούτων, ὃ μήτε εὐῶδές ἐστι μήτε δυσῶδες. Γίνεται δὲ εὐωδία τῶν ὑγρῶν τῶν ἐν τοῖς σώμασιν ἀκριβῶς πεφθέντων, μέσως δὲ μέση διάθεσις· καταδεέστερον δὲ ἢ μηδὲ ὅλως πεφθέντων ἡ δυσωδία γίνεται.

Τετάρτη αἴσθησις ἡ γεῦσις. Ἔστι δὲ τῶν χυμῶν ἀντιληπτικὴ ἤγουν αἰσθητική. Ὄργανα δὲ αὐτῆς ἡ γλῶσσα καὶ ταύτης πλέον τὸ ἄκρον καὶ ἡ ὑπερῴα, ἣν καλοῦσί τινες οὐρανίσκον· ἐν οἷς ἐστι τὰ ἐξ ἐγκεφάλου φερόμενα νεῦρα πεπλατυσμένα καὶ ἀπαγγέλλοντα τῷ ἡγεμονικῷ τὴν γενομένην ἀντίληψιν ἤγουν αἴσθησιν. Αἱ δὲ καλούμεναι γευστικαὶ ποιότητες τῶν χυμῶν εἰσιν αὗται· γλυκύτης, δριμύτης, ὀξύτης, στρυφνότης, αὐστηρότης, πικρότης, ἁλμυρότης, λιπαρότης, γλισχρότης· τούτων γάρ ἐστιν ἡ γεῦσις διαγνωστική. Τὸ δὲ ὕδωρ ἄποιόν ἐστι κατὰ ταύτας τὰς ποιότητας· οὐδεμίαν γὰρ αὐτῶν ἔχει. Ἡ δὲ στρυφνότης ἐπίτασις καὶ πλεονασμός ἐστι τῆς αὐστηρότητος.

Πέμπτη αἴσθησίς ἐστιν ἡ ἁφή, ἥτις κοινή ἐστι πάντων τῶν ζῴων· ἥτις γίνεται ἐκ τοῦ ἐγκεφάλου πεμπομένων νεύρων εἰς ὅλον τὸ σῶμα. Διὸ καὶ ὅλον τὸ σῶμα, ἀλλὰ καὶ τὰ ἄλλα αἰσθητήρια τὴν τῆς ἁφῆς ἔχουσιν αἴσθησιν. Ὑπόκειται δὲ τῇ ἁφῇ τὸ ψυχρὸν καὶ θερμόν, τό τε μαλακὸν καὶ σκληρὸν καὶ γλίσχρον καὶ κραῦρον, βαρύ τε καὶ κοῦφον· διὰ μόνης γὰρ ἁφῆς ταῦτα γνωρίζεται. Κοινὰ δὲ ἁφῆς καὶ ὄψεως τό τε τραχὺ καὶ λεῖον, τό τε ξηρὸν καὶ ὑγρόν, παχύ τε καὶ λεπτόν, ἄνω τε καὶ κάτω καὶ ὁ τόπος καὶ τὸ μέγεθος, ὅταν εἴη τοιοῦτο ὡς κατὰ μίαν προσβολὴν τῆς

³Nemesius of Emesa, *On Human Nature* 10 (PG 40:657AB; Morani, 67.5–11).
⁴Nemesius of Emesa, *On Human Nature* 11 (PG 40:657B–660A; Morani, 67.13–68.2), modified.

their softness and harshness and their loudness. The organs of this sense are the soft nerves coming from the brain and the construction of the ears. Only human beings and apes do not move their ears."[3]

The third sense is that of smell, "which takes place when vapors are drawn up through the nostrils towards the brain and ends at the limits of the brain's front ventricles. It is the faculty by which vapors are perceived and apprehended. Among vapors, the most general difference is between fragrant smells and foul smells and what lies between them, which is neither fragrant nor foul. A fragrant smell is produced from the liquids in bodies when they are digested efficiently, a middling digestion produces an intermediate smell, poor digestion or none at all produces a foul smell."[4]

The fourth sense is that of taste. "It is the power of perceiving or sensing flavors. The organs of this sense are the tongue, especially its tip, and the palate, which some call the roof of the mouth. In these the nerves coming from the brain broaden out and report back to the intellect the perception or sensation that has taken place. What are called the taste qualities of the flavors are these: sweetness, pungency, acidity, sourness, tartness, bitterness, saltiness, fattiness, and stickiness. For taste distinguishes between these. But water is tasteless with regard to these qualities, for it possesses none of them. Sourness is an intensified and excessive tartness."[5]

The fifth sense is that of touch, which is common to all animals.[6] It takes place through the nerves that go out from the brain to all parts of the body.[7] Thus the whole body and even the other sense-organs have the sense of touch. Subject to the sense of touch are "cold and heat, softness and hardness, stickiness and crumbliness, heaviness and lightness, for these are known only by the sense of touch. Common to touch and sight are roughness and smoothness, dryness and wetness, thickness and thinness, right way up and wrong way up, and also position and size, when these can be taken in by a

[5]Nemesius of Emesa, *On Human Nature* 9 (PG 40:656BC; Morani, 66.6–11). John adds the vernacular term for "palate."

[6]Cf. Nemesius of Emesa, *On Human Nature* 8 (PG 40:649B; Morani, 63.14).

[7]Cf. Nemesius of Emesa, *On Human Nature* 8 (PG 40:652A; Morani, 64.1–15).

ἁφῆς περιλαμβάνεσθαι, καὶ τὸ πυκνόν τε καὶ μανὸν ἤγουν ἀραιὸν καὶ τὸ στρογγύλον, ὅταν εἴη μικρόν, καὶ ἄλλα τινὰ σχήματα. Ὁμοίως δὲ καὶ τοῦ πλησιάζοντος σώματος αἰσθάνεται, σὺν τῇ μνήμῃ δὲ καὶ τῇ διανοίᾳ, ὡσαύτως δὲ καὶ ἀριθμοῦ μέχρι δύο ἢ τριῶν καὶ τούτων μικρῶν καὶ ῥᾳδίως περιλαμβανομένων. Τούτων δὲ μᾶλλον τῆς ἁφῆς ἡ ὅρασις ἀντιλαμβάνεται.

Χρὴ γινώσκειν, ὡς ἕκαστον τῶν ἄλλων αἰσθητηρίων διπλοῦν ὁ δημιουργὸς κατεσκεύασεν, ἵνα τοῦ ἑνὸς βλαπτομένου τὸ ἕτερον ἀναπληροῖ τὴν χρείαν· δύο γὰρ ὀφθαλμοὺς καὶ δύο ὦτα καὶ δύο πόρους τῆς ῥινὸς καὶ δύο γλώσσας, ἀλλ᾽ ἐν τοῖς μὲν τῶν ζῴων διῃρημένας ὡς ἐν τοῖς ὄφεσιν, ἐν τοῖς δὲ ἡνωμένας ὡς ἐν τῷ ἀνθρώπῳ· τὴν δὲ ἁφὴν ἐν ὅλῳ τῷ σώματι πλὴν ὀστέων καὶ νεύρων ὀνύχων τε καὶ κεράτων καὶ τριχῶν καὶ συνδέσμων καὶ ἄλλων τινῶν τοιούτων.

Χρὴ γινώσκειν, ὅτι ἡ μὲν ὄψις κατ᾽ εὐθείας γραμμὰς ὁρᾷ, ἡ δὲ ὄσφρησις καὶ ἡ ἀκοὴ οὐ κατ᾽ εὐθεῖαν μόνον, ἀλλὰ πανταχόθεν. Ἡ δὲ ἁφὴ καὶ ἡ γεῦσις οὐδὲ κατ᾽ εὐθεῖαν οὐδὲ πανταχόθεν γνωρίζουσιν, ἀλλὰ τότε μόνον, ὅταν αὐτοῖς πλησιάσωσι τοῖς ἰδίοις αἰσθητοῖς.

33 Περὶ τοῦ διανοητικοῦ

Τοῦ δὲ διανοητικοῦ εἰσιν αἵ τε κρίσεις καὶ αἱ συγκαταθέσεις καὶ αἱ ὁρμαὶ πρὸς τὴν πρᾶξιν καὶ αἱ ἀφορμαὶ καὶ αἱ ἀποφυγαὶ τῆς πράξεως, ἰδικῶς δὲ αἵ τε νοήσεις τῶν νοητῶν καὶ αἱ ἀρεταὶ καὶ αἱ ἐπιστῆμαι καὶ τῶν τεχνῶν οἱ λόγοι καὶ τὸ βουλευτικὸν καὶ τὸ προαιρετικόν. Τούτου δέ ἐστι τὸ καὶ διὰ τῶν ὀνείρων θεσπίζον ἡμῖν τὸ μέλλον, ἥνπερ μόνην ἀληθῆ μαντείαν οἱ Πυθαγορικοὶ λέγουσιν εἶναι τοῖς Ἑβραίοις ἀκολουθήσαντες. Ὄργανον δὲ καὶ τούτου ἡ μέση κοιλία τοῦ ἐγκεφάλου καὶ τὸ ψυχικὸν πνεῦμα τὸ ἐν αὐτῇ.

single act of touching, and also compactness and looseness, or soft-ness and roundness, when they are of small size, and other shapes. Similarly touch also perceives the approach of a body, together with memory and the intellect, and equally numbers up to two or three, when the objects are small and easily grasped. But these are better apprehended by sight than by touch."[8]

One needs to know that "the Creator formed each of the other sense-organs in pairs, so that if one was damaged the other might supply the function. For he formed two eyes, two ears, two nasal passages, and two tongues (but divided in certain animals, such as snakes, and united in others, such as man). He formed touch, how-ever, in the whole body apart from the bones, tendons, nails, horns, hair, ligaments, and suchlike."[9]

One needs to know that "whereas sight functions in straight lines, smell and hearing do not function in one direction only but from all sides. Touch and taste function neither in straight lines nor from all sides but only when they are in contact with the sensible objects proper to them."[10]

33   *On the faculty of thinking*

"To the faculty of thinking belong judgements, assents, impulses towards action, cessations or avoidances of action, and especially the forming of concepts, the virtues, the sciences, the principles of the arts, and the capacities for deliberation and free will. Also belonging to the faculty of thinking is the intimation of the future to us through dreams, which the Pythagoreans, following the Hebrews, say is the only true divination. The organ of the faculty of thinking is the mid-dle ventricle of the brain and the spirit of life that is found there."[1]

[8]Nemesius of Emesa, *On Human Nature* 8 (PG 40:652B–653A; Morani, 64.15–25).

[9]Nemesius of Emesa, *On Human Nature* 8 (PG 40:649ABC; Morani, 63.2–19), condensed.

[10]Nemesius of Emesa, *On Human Nature* 9 (PG 40:656A; Morani, 66.2–5).

[1]Nemesius of Emesa, *On Human Nature* 12 (PG 40:660B; Morani, 68.6–13).

34 Περὶ τοῦ μνημονευτικοῦ

Τὸ δὲ μνημονευτικόν ἐστι μνήμης καὶ ἀναμνήσεως αἴτιόν τε καὶ ταμιεῖον· μνήμη γάρ ἐστι φαντασία ἐγκαταλελειμμένη ἀπό τινος αἰσθήσεως τῆς κατ' ἐνέργειαν φαινομένης ἢ σωτηρία αἰσθήσεώς τε καὶ νοήσεως. Ἡ γὰρ ψυχὴ τῶν μὲν αἰσθητῶν διὰ τῶν αἰσθητηρίων ἀντιλαμβάνεται ἤγουν αἰσθάνεται, καὶ γίνεται δόξα, τῶν δὲ νοητῶν διὰ τοῦ νοῦ, καὶ γίνεται νόησις· ὅταν οὖν τοὺς τύπους, ὧν τε ἐδόξασεν, ὧν τε ἐνόησεν, διασῴζῃ, μνημονεύειν λέγεται.

Δεῖ δὲ γινώσκειν, ὅτι ἡ τῶν νοητῶν ἀντίληψις οὐ γίνεται, εἰ μὴ ἐκ μαθήσεως ἢ φυσικῆς ἐννοίας, οὐ γὰρ ἐξ αἰσθήσεως· τὰ μὲν γὰρ αἰσθητὰ καθ' ἑαυτὰ μνημονεύεται· τὰ δὲ νοητά, εἴ τι μὲν ἐμάθομεν, μνημονεύομεν, τῆς δὲ οὐσίας αὐτῶν μνήμην οὐκ ἔχομεν.

Ἀνάμνησις δὲ λέγεται μνήμης ἀπολλυμένης ὑπὸ λήθης ἀνάκτησις. Λήθη δέ ἐστι μνήμης ἀποβολή. Τὸ μὲν οὖν φανταστικὸν διὰ τῶν αἰσθήσεων ἀντιλαμβανόμενον τῶν ὑλῶν παραδίδωσι τῷ διανοητικῷ ἢ διαλογιστικῷ (ταὐτὸν γὰρ ἀμφότερα)· ὃ παραλαβὸν καὶ κρῖναν παραπέμπει τῷ μνημονευτικῷ. Ὄργανον δὲ τοῦ μνημονευτικοῦ ἡ ὄπισθεν κοιλία τοῦ ἐγκεφάλου, ἣν καὶ παρεγκεφαλίδα καλοῦσι, καὶ τὸ ἐν αὐτῇ ψυχικὸν πνεῦμα.

34   *On the faculty of memory*

"The faculty of memory is both the cause and repository of remembrance and recollection. For the memory is the image left behind by some sense-perception that has actually occurred or the preservation of a sense-perception or a thought. For the soul apprehends or perceives, on the one hand, sensible objects by the sense-organs and a conjecture arises, and on the other, intelligible objects by the mind and a concept arises. Therefore, when it preserves the impressions, both those of which it has formed a conjecture and those of which it has formed a concept, it is said to remember."[1]

One also needs to know that the apprehension of intelligible objects takes place only by learning or innate thinking, not as a result of sensation. Sensible objects are remembered as they are in themselves, whereas with regard to intelligible objects, unless we learn them and commit them to memory, we have no remembrance of what they are.[2]

"The recovery of a memory lost through forgetting is called recollection. Forgetting is the shedding of memory. Once the faculty of imagination has apprehended material objects through the senses, it transmits them to the cognitive or reasoning faculty (for both are the same thing). When the latter has received them and judged them, it sends them on to the faculty of memory. The organ of the faculty of memory is the brain's posterior ventricle, which is also called the cerebellum, and the spirit of life that is found there."[3]

[1]Nemesius of Emesa, *On Human Nature* 13 (PG 40:660B–661A; Morani, 68.15–21). John omits Nemesius' attribution of the definition "the image left behind by some sense-perception that has actually occurred" to Origen, and of the definition "the preservation of a sense perception or a thought" to Plato.

[2]Cf. Nemesius of Emesa, *On Human Nature* 13 (PG 40:661AB; Morani, 68.21–69.4).

[3]Nemesius of Emesa, *On Human Nature* 13 (PG 40:661B–664A: Morani, 69.9–20). After "Forgetting is the shedding of memory," John omits a brief discussion by Nemesius referring to Plato.

35 Περὶ ἐνδιαθέτου λόγου καὶ προφορικοῦ

Πάλιν δὲ διαιρεῖται τὸ λογικὸν τῆς ψυχῆς εἴς τε τὸν ἐνδιάθετον λόγον καὶ εἰς τὸν προφορικόν. Ἔστι δὲ ἐνδιάθετος μὲν λόγος κίνημα ψυχῆς ἐν τῷ διαλογιστικῷ γινόμενον ἄνευ τινὸς ἐκφωνήσεως· ὅθεν πολλάκις σιωπῶντες λόγον ὅλον παρ᾿ ἑαυτοῖς διεξερχόμεθα καὶ ἐν τοῖς ὀνείροις διαλεγόμεθα. Κατὰ τοῦτο δὲ μάλιστα λογικοὶ πάντες ἐσμέν· καὶ γὰρ οἱ ἐκ γεννετῆς κωφοὶ ἢ καὶ οἱ διά τι νόσημα ἢ πάθος τὴν φωνὴν ἀποβαλόντες οὐδὲν ἧττον λογικοί εἰσιν. Ὁ δὲ προφορικὸς λόγος ἐν τῇ φωνῇ καὶ ταῖς διαλέκτοις τὴν ἐνέργειαν ἔχει, ἤγουν ὁ διὰ γλώσσης καὶ στόματος προφερόμενος λόγος· διὸ καὶ προφορικὸς λέγεται. Ἔστι δὲ ἄγγελος νοήματος. Κατὰ τοῦτο καὶ λαλητικοὶ λεγόμεθα.

36 Περὶ πάθους καὶ ἐνεργείας

Τὸ πάθος ὁμωνύμως λέγεται· λέγεται γὰρ πάθος καὶ τὸ σωματικὸν ὡς τὰ νοσήματα καὶ τὰ ἕλκη, λέγεται πάλιν πάθος καὶ τὸ ψυχικόν, ἥ τε ἐπιθυμία καὶ ὁ θυμός. Ἔστι δὲ κοινῶς μὲν καὶ γενικῶς πάθος ζῴου, ᾧ ἕπεται ἡδονὴ καὶ λύπη· ἕπεται γὰρ τῷ πάθει λύπη. Καὶ οὐκ αὐτὸ τὸ πάθος ἐστὶ λύπη· τὰ γὰρ ἀναίσθητα πάσχοντα οὐκ ἀλγεῖ. Οὐκ ἄρα τὸ πάθος ἐστὶν ἄλγημα, ἀλλ᾿ ἡ τοῦ πάθους αἴσθησις. Δεῖ δὲ τοῦτο ἀξιόλογον εἶναι ἤγουν μέγα, ἵνα τῇ αἰσθήσει ὑποπέσῃ.

Τῶν δὲ ψυχικῶν παθῶν ὅρος ἐστὶν οὗτος· Πάθος ἐστὶ κίνησις τῆς ὀρεκτικῆς δυνάμεως αἰσθητὴ ἐπὶ φαντασίᾳ ἀγαθοῦ ἢ κακοῦ. Καὶ ἄλλως· Πάθος ἐστὶ κίνησις ἄλογος τῆς ψυχῆς δι᾿ ὑπόληψιν καλοῦ ἢ κακοῦ. Ἡ μὲν ὑπόληψις τοῦ καλοῦ τὴν ἐπιθυμίαν κινεῖ, ἡ δὲ τοῦ κακοῦ ὑπόληψις τὸν θυμόν. Τὸ δὲ γενικὸν ἤγουν κοινὸν πάθος οὕτως ὁρίζονται· Πάθος ἐστὶ κίνησις ἐν ἑτέρῳ ἐξ ἑτέρου.

35   *On the immanent and the uttered word*

The soul's rational faculty may be divided further into the immanent word and the uttered word. "The immanent word is a movement of the soul in the reasoning faculty without any vocal expression. Thus we frequently go through a whole discourse silently in our own minds and we hold conversations in our dreams. In this respect we are all indeed reasoning beings, for those who are deaf and dumb from birth, or through some illness or accident have lost their voice are not less capable of reasoning. The uttered word is made operative by the voice and by language."[1] That is to say, the uttered word is brought about by the tongue and the mouth, which is also why it is called "uttered." It is also a messenger of thought. In this respect we are said to be beings endowed with speech.

36   *On passion and energy*

"Passion is a term that is used equivocally. For what is experienced by the body is called passion, such as illnesses and injuries, and moreover, what is experienced by the soul is also called passion, referring to desire and anger. In the common and general sense, passion is what is experienced by a living being and is followed by pleasure or pain, for pain follows passion. Pain is not the passion itself, for beings lacking sensation experience passion but do not suffer pain. Therefore passion is not the pain actually felt but is the sensation of the passion. This should be considered worth noting, that is to say, important, for it to come under sensation."[1]

"The definition of the passions experienced by the soul is as follows: Passion is a sensory movement of the appetitive faculty prompted by a mental impression of good or bad. Alternatively, passion is an irrational movement of the soul through forming an

[1]Nemesius of Emesa, *On Human Nature* 14 (PG 40:666A; Morani, 71.9–15).

[1]Nemesius of Emesa, *On Human Nature* 16 (PG 40:673A; Morani, 73.20–74.3), abbreviated.

Ἐνέργεια δέ ἐστι κίνησις δραστική· δραστικὸν δὲ λέγεται τὸ ἐξ αὐτοῦ κινούμενον. Οὕτως καὶ ὁ θυμὸς ἐνέργεια μέν ἐστι τοῦ θυμοειδοῦς, πάθος δὲ τῶν δύο μερῶν, τῆς ψυχῆς καὶ προσέτι παντὸς τοῦ σώματος, ὅταν ὑπὸ τοῦ θυμοῦ βιαίως ἄγηται πρὸς τὰς πράξεις· ἐξ ἑτέρου γὰρ ἐν ἑτέρῳ γέγονεν ἡ κίνησις, ὅπερ λέγεται πάθος. Καὶ καθ᾽ ἕτερον δὲ τρόπον ἡ ἐνέργεια πάθος λέγεται· ἐνέργεια μὲν γάρ ἐστι κατὰ φύσιν κίνησις, πάθος δὲ παρὰ φύσιν. Κατὰ τοῦτον οὖν τὸν λόγον ἡ ἐνέργεια πάθος λέγεται, ὅταν μὴ κατὰ φύσιν κινῆται, εἴτε ἐξ ἑαυτοῦ, εἴτε ἐξ ἑτέρου. Τῆς οὖν καρδίας ἡ μὲν κατὰ τοὺς σφυγμοὺς κίνησις φυσικὴ οὖσα ἐνέργειά ἐστιν, ἡ δὲ κατὰ τοὺς παλμοὺς ἄμετρος οὖσα καὶ οὐ κατὰ φύσιν πάθος ἐστὶ καὶ οὐκ ἐνέργεια.

Οὐ πᾶσα δὲ κίνησις τοῦ παθητικοῦ πάθος καλεῖται, ἀλλ᾽ αἱ σφοδρότεραι καὶ εἰς αἴσθησιν προβαίνουσαι· αἱ γὰρ μικραὶ καὶ ἀνεπαίσθητοι οὐδέπω πάθη εἰσί· δεῖ γὰρ ἔχειν τὸ πάθος καὶ μέγεθος ἀξιόλογον. Διὸ πρόσκειται τῷ ὅρῳ τοῦ πάθους κίνησις αἰσθητή· αἱ γὰρ μικραὶ κινήσεις λανθάνουσαι τὴν αἴσθησιν οὐ ποιοῦσι πάθος.

Χρὴ γινώσκειν, ὅτι ἡ ἡμετέρα ψυχὴ διττὰς ἔχει τὰς δυνάμεις, τὰς μὲν γνωστικάς, τὰς δὲ ζωτικάς. Καὶ γνωστικαὶ μέν εἰσι νοῦς, διάνοια, δόξα, φαντασία, αἴσθησις, ζωτικαὶ δὲ ἤγουν ὀρεκτικαὶ βούλησις καὶ προαίρεσις. Ἵνα δὲ σαφέστερον γένηται τὸ λεγόμενον, λεπτολογήσωμεν τὰ περὶ τούτων. Καὶ πρῶτον περὶ τῶν γνωστικῶν εἴπωμεν.

Περὶ μὲν οὖν φαντασίας καὶ αἰσθήσεως ἱκανῶς ἤδη ἐν τοῖς προλελεγμένοις εἴρηται. Διὰ τῆς αἰσθήσεως τοίνυν ἐν τῇ ψυχῇ συνίσταται πάθος, ὃ καλεῖται φαντασία· ἐκ δὲ τῆς φαντασίας γίνεται δόξα. Εἶτα ἡ διάνοια ἀνακρίνασα τὴν δόξαν, εἴτε ἀληθής ἐστιν εἴτε ψευδής, κρίνει τὸ ἀληθές· ὅθεν καὶ διάνοια λέγεται ἀπὸ

assumption that something is good or bad. The assumption of 'good' stimulates desire; the assumption of 'bad' provokes anger. Passion in the general and common sense is defined as follows: Passion is a movement in one thing that arises out of another. Energy is an efficacious movement. Efficacious means that which moves of itself. Thus anger is on the one hand an energy of the irascible faculty, and on the other, a passion of the two parts, of the soul and in addition of the whole body, when the latter is led forcibly by anger towards action. For the movement has taken place in one thing but has arisen out of another, which is what is called passion. Yet from another point of view, an energy is called a passion. For an energy is a movement in accordance with nature; a passion is a movement contrary to nature. Therefore in this sense an energy is called a passion when it does not move in accordance with nature, either of its own accord or as a result of another. Thus in the case of the heart, its regular beat is an energy since it is a natural movement, whereas its palpitation is a passion and not an energy, since it is irregular and not in accordance with nature."[2]

"Not every movement of the passible part of the soul is called a passion, but only those that are more vehement and result in perception. For the small and imperceptible movements are not yet passions. Passion must also have an intensity worth noting. Consequently, perceptible movement is added to the definition of passion. For minor movements that escape perception do not constitute passion."[3]

One needs to know that the faculties our soul possesses are twofold, some being cognitive, others vital. The cognitive faculties are mind, discursive reason, opinion, imagination, and perception, whereas the vital or appetitive faculties are will and freedom of choice. To make what has been said clearer, let us discuss what

[2]Nemesius of Emesa, *On Human Nature* 16 (PG 40:673B–676A; Morani, 74.3–18), with some omissions, and a comment by John: "The assumption of 'good' stimulates desire; the assumption of 'bad' provokes anger."

[3]Nemesius of Emesa, *On Human Nature* 16 (PG 40:676AB; Morani, 75.1–6), with some omissions.

τοῦ διανοεῖν καὶ διακρίνειν. Τὸ οὖν κριθὲν καὶ ὁρισθὲν ἀληθὲς νοῦς λέγεται.

Ἄλλως δέ· Χρὴ γινώσκειν, ὅτι ἡ μὲν πρώτη τοῦ νοῦ κίνησις νόησις λέγεται. Ἡ δὲ περί τι νόησις ἔννοια λέγεται, ἥτις ἐπιμείνασα καὶ τυπώσασα τὴν ψυχὴν πρὸς τὸ νοούμενον ἐνθύμησις προσαγορεύεται. Ἡ δὲ ἐνθύμησις ἐν ταὐτῷ μείνασα καὶ ἑαυτὴν βασανίσασα καὶ ἀνακρίνασα φρόνησις ὀνομάζεται. Ἡ δὲ φρόνησις πλατυνθεῖσα ποιεῖ τὸν διαλογισμὸν ἐνδιάθετον λόγον ὀνομαζόμενον, ὃν ὁριζόμενοί φασι· κίνημα ψυχῆς πληρέστατον, ἐν τῷ διαλογιστικῷ γινόμενον ἄνευ τινὸς ἐκφωνήσεως, ἐξ οὗ τὸν προφορικὸν λόγον φασὶ προέρχεσθαι διὰ γλώσσης λαλούμενον. Εἰπόντες τοίνυν περὶ τῶν γνωστικῶν δυνάμεων εἴπωμεν καὶ περὶ τῶν ζωτικῶν ἤγουν ὀρεκτικῶν.

Χρὴ γινώσκειν, ὅτι τῇ ψυχῇ ἐνέσπαρται φυσικῶς δύναμις ὀρεκτικὴ τοῦ κατὰ φύσιν ὄντος καὶ πάντων τῶν οὐσιωδῶς τῇ φύσει προσόντων συνεκτική, ἥτις λέγεται θέλησις· ἡ μὲν γὰρ οὐσία τοῦ τε εἶναι καὶ ζῆν καὶ κινεῖσθαι κατὰ νοῦν τε καὶ αἴσθησιν ὀρέγεται τῆς οἰκείας ἐφιεμένη φυσικῆς καὶ πλήρους ὀντότητος. Διόπερ καὶ οὕτως ὁρίζονται τοῦτο τὸ φυσικὸν θέλημα· Θέλημά ἐστιν ὄρεξις λογική τε καὶ ζωτικὴ μόνων ἠρτημένη τῶν φυσικῶν. Ὥστε ἡ μὲν θέλησίς ἐστιν αὐτὴ ἡ φυσικὴ καὶ λογικὴ ὄρεξις, ἡ ἁπλῆ δύναμις· ἡ γὰρ τῶν ἀλόγων ὄρεξις μὴ οὖσα λογικὴ οὐ λέγεται θέλησις.

Βούλησις δέ ἐστι ποιὰ φυσικὴ θέλησις ἤγουν φυσικὴ καὶ λογικὴ ὄρεξίς τινος πράγματος. Ἔγκειται μὲν γὰρ τῇ τοῦ ἀνθρώπου ψυχῇ δύναμις τοῦ λογικῶς ὀρέγεσθαι. Ὅτε οὖν φυσικῶς κινηθῇ αὕτη

---

[4]John now turns to Maximus the Confessor as his main source, reproducing a number of passages verbatim from Maximus' *Opuscula*. In John's time, only a little more than forty years since Maximus' death in exile in 662, the Confessor had not yet become a patristic authority. Indeed John seems to have been a pioneer in establishing him as one. As Andrew Louth says, "The real beginnings of Maximus' theological reception are to be found in Palestine, where commitment to the conciliar Orthodoxy of the empire had deep roots." Andrew Louth, "Maximus the Confessor's Influence

this is about in detail. And first let us speak about the cognitive faculties.

Imagination and sensation have already been sufficiently treated in what has been said above. Thus it is through sensation that the passion is constituted in the soul that is called imagination, and from imagination comes opinion. Then the intellect, by scrutinizing opinion to see whether it is true or false, judges what is true. Hence the word for discursive reasoning (διάνοια, *dianoia*) is derived from "turning over in the mind" (διάνοεῖν, *dianoein*) and "examining" (διακρίνειν, *diakrinein*). Therefore what has been judged and determined to be true is called mind (νοῦς, *nous*).

Looking at it in another way,[4] one needs to know that "the primary movement of the mind is called thinking (νόησις, *noēsis*). What thinking is about is called a notion (ἔννοια, *ennoia*). When this has lingered in the soul and has formed an impression on it with regard to what has been apprehended, it is called a reflection (ἐνθύμησις, *enthymēsis*). When the reflection has lingered in the mind and has itself been tested and scrutinized, it is called a considered judgement (φρόνησις, *phronēsis*). When the considered judgement is drawn out, it produces a weighing up of arguments which is called the immanent word (ἐνδιάθετος λόγος, *endiathetos logos*), which they define as a complete movement of the soul that takes place in the reasoning faculty without any vocal expression, from which the uttered word (προφορικὸς λόγος, *prophorikos logos*), they say, comes forth through being expressed linguistically."[5] Having spoken of the cognitive faculties, let us now speak of the vital or appetitive faculties.

One needs to know that there is a faculty naturally implanted in the soul that is appetitive of what is in accordance with nature and

and Reception in Byzantine and Modern Orthodoxy," in *The Oxford Handbook of Maximus the Confessor*, edited by Pauline Allen and Bronwen Neil (Oxford: Oxford University Press, 2015), 500–15, at 501. It was through Maximus, moreover, that John was introduced to Nemesius of Emesa. Louth, "Maximus the Confessor's Influence and Reception," 501.

[5]Maximus the Confessor, *Opusculum 1, To Marinus* (PG 91:21A).

ἡ λογικὴ ὄρεξις πρός τι πρᾶγμα, λέγεται βούλησις· βούλησις γάρ
ἐστιν ὄρεξις καὶ ἔφεσίς τινος πράγματος λογική.

Λέγεται δὲ βούλησις καὶ ἐπὶ τῶν ἐφ᾽ ἡμῖν καὶ ἐπὶ τῶν οὐκ
ἐφ᾽ ἡμῖν, τουτέστι καὶ ἐπὶ τῶν δυνατῶν καὶ ἐπὶ τῶν ἀδυνάτων.
Βουλόμεθα γὰρ πολλάκις πορνεῦσαι ἢ σωφρονῆσαι ἢ ὑπνῶσαι ἤ τι
τῶν τοιούτων· καὶ ταῦτα τῶν ἐφ᾽ ἡμῖν εἰσι καὶ δυνατά. Βουλόμεθα
δὲ καὶ βασιλεῦσαι· τοῦτοοὐκ ἔστι τῶν ἐφ᾽ ἡμῖν. Βουλόμεθα δὲ
τυχὸν καὶ μηδέποτε ἀποθανεῖν· τοῦτο τῶν ἀδυνάτων ἐστίν.

Ἔστι δὲ ἡ βούλησις τοῦ τέλους, οὐ τῶν πρὸς τὸ τέλος. Τέλος
μὲν οὖν ἐστι τὸ βουλητὸν ὡς τὸ βασιλεῦσαι, ὡς τὸ ὑγιᾶναι· πρὸς
τὸ τέλος δὲ τὸ βουλευτὸν ἤγουν ὁ τρόπος, δι᾽ οὗ ὀφείλομεν
ὑγιᾶναι ἢ βασιλεῦσαι· εἶτα μετὰ τὴν βούλησιν ζήτησις καὶ
σκέψις. Καὶ μετὰ ταῦτα, εἰ τῶν ἐφ᾽ ἡμῖν ἐστι, γίνεται βουλὴ
ἤγουν βούλευσις. Βουλὴ δέ ἐστιν ὄρεξις ζητητικὴ περὶ τῶν ἐφ᾽
ἡμῖν πρακτῶν γινομένη· βουλεύεται γάρ, εἰ ὤφειλε μετελθεῖν
τὸ πρᾶγμα ἢ οὔ. Εἶτα κρίνει τὸ κρεῖττον, καὶ λέγεται κρίσις.
Εἶτα διατίθεται καὶ ἀγαπᾷ τὸ ἐκ τῆς βουλῆς κριθέν, καὶ λέγεται
γνώμη· ἐὰν γὰρ κρίνῃ καὶ μὴ διατεθῇ πρὸς τὸ κριθὲν ἤγουν
ἀγαπήσῃ αὐτό, οὐ λέγεται γνώμη. Εἶτα μετὰ τὴν διάθεσιν γίνεται
προαίρεσις ἤγουν ἐπιλογή· προαίρεσις γάρ ἐστι δύο προκειμένων
τὸ αἱρεῖσθαι καὶ ἐκλέγεσθαι τοῦτο πρὸ τοῦ ἑτέρου. Εἶτα ὁρμᾷ
πρὸς τὴν πρᾶξιν, καὶ λέγεται ὁρμή. Εἶτα κέχρηται, καὶ λέγεται
χρῆσις. Εἶτα παύεται τῆς ὀρέξεως μετὰ τὴν χρῆσιν.

Ἐπὶ μὲν οὖν τῶν ἀλόγων ὄρεξις γίνεταί τινος, καὶ εὐθέως
ὁρμὴ πρὸς τὴν πρᾶξιν· ἄλογος γάρ ἐστιν ἡ ὄρεξις τῶν ἀλόγων,
καὶ ἄγονται ὑπὸ τῆς φυσικῆς ὀρέξεως. Διὸ οὐδὲ θέλησις λέγεται
ἡ τῶν ἀλόγων ὄρεξις οὐδὲ βούλησις· θέλησις γάρ ἐστι λογικὴ καὶ
αὐτεξούσιος φυσικὴ ὄρεξις. Ἐπὶ δὲ τῶν ἀνθρώπων λογικῶν ὄντων

---

[6]For a discussion of John's view of how the will operates, see Frede, "John of
Damascus on Human Action, the Will, and Human Freedom."

[7]Cf. Maximus the Confessor, *Opusculum 1, To Marinus* (PG 91:12C).

[8]Cf. Maximus the Confessor, *Opusculum 1, To Marinus* (PG 91:13A), and *Opusculum 26b/Additamentum 24* (PG 91:276C).

embraces everything that is essentially characteristic of nature.[6] This is called the capacity for willing (θέλησις, *thelēsis*). For the essence of being and living and moving, both mentally and sensibly, has an appetency directed towards its own natural and full realization.[7] For that reason, this natural will (θέλημα, *thelēma*) is also defined as follows: Will is a rational and vital appetency that depends solely on what belongs to nature. Consequently, the capacity for willing is the natural and rational appetency itself, the simple faculty, for since the appetency of irrational beings is not rational, it is not called a capacity for willing.[8]

Actual willing or wishing (βούλησις, *boulēsis*) is a natural capacity for willing of a particular kind, that is to say, a natural and rational appetency in relation to some specific thing. For there lies within the human soul a faculty of reaching out in a rational manner. Therefore when this rational appetency in relation to some specific thing is set in motion in a natural manner, it is called wishing. For wishing is an appetency and yearning for some rational specific thing.[9]

Wishing is also attributed to what lies within our power and to what does not lie within our power, that is to say, to both possible and impossible things. For we often wish to have sex, or to be chaste, or to go to sleep, or some such thing, and these are within our power and possible. We can also wish to become a king, but this is not within our power. We might perhaps wish never to die, but this belongs to the class of impossibilities.[10]

Wishing belongs to the end, not to the means to the end. The end is the thing willed (τὸ βουλητόν, *to boulēton*), such as becoming a king or being in good health, whereas the means to the end is the thing deliberated (τὸ βουλευτόν, *to bouleuton*), or the steps we need to take in order to be in good health or become a king. Next after wishing come search (ζήτησις, *zētēsis*) and consideration (σκέψις, *skepsis*). And after these comes counsel or deliberation (βουλή or βούλευσις, *boulē* or *bouleusis*). Counsel is a searching appetency

---

[9]Cf. Maximus the Confessor, *Opusculum 1, To Marinus* (PG 91:13B).
[10]Cf. Maximus the Confessor, *Opusculum 1, To Marinus* (PG 91:13C).

ἄγεται μᾶλλον ἡ φυσικὴ ὄρεξις ἥπερ ἄγει· αὐτεξουσίως γὰρ καὶ
μετὰ λόγου κινεῖται, ἐπειδὴ συνεζευγμέναι εἰσὶν αἱ γνωστικαὶ
καὶ ζωτικαὶ δυνάμεις ἐν αὐτῷ. Αὐτεξουσίως οὖν ὀρέγεται καὶ
αὐτεξουσίως βούλεται καὶ αὐτεξουσίως ζητεῖ καὶ σκέπτεται καὶ
αὐτεξουσίως βουλεύεται καὶ αὐτεξουσίως κρίνει καὶ αὐτεξουσίως
διατίθεται καὶ αὐτεξουσίως προαιρεῖται καὶ αὐτεξουσίως ὁρμᾷ καὶ
αὐτεξουσίως πράττει ἐπὶ τῶν κατὰ φύσιν ὄντων.

Χρὴ δὲ γινώσκειν, ὅτι ἐπὶ θεοῦ βούλησιν μὲν λέγομεν,
προαίρεσιν δὲ κυρίως οὐ λέγομεν· οὐ γὰρ βουλεύεται ὁ θεός.
Ἀγνοίας γάρ ἐστι τὸ βουλεύεσθαι· περὶ γὰρ τοῦ γινωσκομένου
οὐδεὶς βουλεύεται. Εἰ δὲ ἡ βουλὴ ἀγνοίας, πάντως καὶ ἡ
προαίρεσις. Ὁ δὲ θεὸς πάντα εἰδὼς ἁπλῶς οὐ βουλεύεται.

Οὔτε δὲ ἐπὶ τῆς τοῦ κυρίου ψυχῆς φαμεν βουλὴν ἢ προαίρεσιν·
οὐ γὰρ εἶχεν ἄγνοιαν. Εἰ γὰρ καὶ τῆς ἀγνοούσης τὰ μέλλοντα
φύσεως ἦν, ἀλλ᾽ ὅμως καθ᾽ ὑπόστασιν ἑνωθεῖσα τῷ θεῷ λόγῳ
πάντων τὴν γνῶσιν εἶχεν οὐ χάριτι, ἀλλ᾽, ὡς εἴρηται, διὰ τὴν καθ᾽
ὑπόστασιν ἕνωσιν· ὁ αὐτὸς γὰρ ἦν καὶ θεὸς καὶ ἄνθρωπος. Διὸ
οὐδὲ γνωμικὸν εἶχε θέλημα. Θέλησιν μὲν γὰρ εἶχε τὴν φυσικήν,
τὴν ἁπλῆν, τὴν ἐν πάσαις ταῖς ὑποστάσεσι τῶν ἀνθρώπων ὁμοίως
θεωρουμένην, τὴν δὲ γνώμην ἤγουν τὸ θελητὸν οὐκ εἶχεν ἡ
ἁγία αὐτοῦ ψυχὴ ἐναντίον τοῦ θείου αὐτοῦ θελήματος οὐδὲ
ἄλλο παρὰ τὸ θεῖον αὐτοῦ θέλημα. Ἡ γὰρ γνώμη συνδιαιρεῖται
ταῖς ὑποστάσεσι πλὴν τῆς ἁγίας καὶ ἁπλῆς καὶ ἀσυνθέτου καὶ
ἀδιαιρέτου θεότητος· ἐκεῖ γὰρ τῶν ὑποστάσεων μὴ εἰς ἅπαν
διαιρουμένων καὶ διισταμένων οὐδὲ τὸ θελητὸν διαιρεῖται. Κἀκεῖ
μέν, ἐπειδὴ μία ἡ φύσις, μία καὶ ἡ φυσικὴ θέλησις· ἐπειδὴ δὲ
καὶ αἱ ὑποστάσεις ἀδιάστατοί εἰσιν, ἓν καὶ τὸ θελητὸν καὶ μία ἡ
κίνησις τῶν τριῶν ὑποστάσεων. Ἐπὶ δὲ τῶν ἀνθρώπων, ἐπειδὴ μὲν
ἡ φύσις μία, μία καὶ ἡ φυσικὴ θέλησις· ἐπειδὴ δὲ αἱ ὑποστάσεις

(ὄρεξις ζητητική, *orexis zētētikē*) that functions with regard to things that lie within our power to bring into effect. For what is deliberated is whether one should pursue a matter or not. Next one judges what is best, and this is called judgement (κρίσις, *krisis*). Next one becomes inclined towards, and fond of, what has been judged as a result of deliberation, and this is called a disposition (γνώμη, *gnōmē*). For if one judges and does not become inclined towards what has been judged, or fond of it, that is not called a disposition. Next after the inclination comes choice or selection (προαίρεσις or ἐπιλογή, *proairesis* or *epilogē*). For choice is choosing between two things set before one and selecting one rather than the other. Then one is impelled to action, and this is called impulse (ὁρμή, *hormē*). Then one has enjoyment of it and this is called use (χρῆσις, *chrēsis*). Then after use the appetency ceases.[11]

In the case of irrational animals, however, when some appetency arises it is quickly followed by an impulse towards action. For the appetency of irrational animals is irrational, and they are led by their natural appetency (φυσικὴ ὄρεξις, *physikē orexis*). Therefore the appetency of irrational animals is called neither a capacity for willing (θέλησις, *thelēsis*) nor actual willing (βούλησις, *boulēsis*). For the capacity for willing is a rational and self-determining natural appetency. In the case of human beings, the natural appetency, since they are rational animals, is led rather than leads. It moves in a voluntary manner and by the use of reason because in human beings the cognitive and vital faculties are harnessed together. Thus human beings exercise their appetency voluntarily, wish voluntarily, search and consider voluntarily, deliberate voluntarily, judge voluntarily, weigh up voluntarily, choose voluntarily, are impelled voluntarily, and act voluntarily with regard to natural beings.[12]

---

[11]Cf. Maximus the Confessor, *Opusculum 1, To Marinus* (PG 91:13C–16B, 21D–24A).

[12]I.e., always by the use of *autexousion*. Cf. Maximus the Confessor, *Opusculum 1, To Marinus* (PG 91:17C–20A).

κεχωρισμέναι εἰσὶ καὶ διεστήκασιν ἀλλήλων κατά τε τόπον καὶ χρόνον καὶ τὴν πρὸς τὰ πράγματα διάθεσιν καὶ ἕτερα πλεῖστα, τούτου ἕνεκα διάφορα τὰ θελήματα καὶ αἱ γνῶμαι. Ἐπὶ δὲ τοῦ κυρίου ἡμῶν Ἰησοῦ Χριστοῦ, ἐπειδὴ μὲν διάφοροι αἱ φύσεις, διάφοροι καὶ αἱ θελήσεις αἱ φυσικαὶ τῆς αὐτοῦ θεότητος καὶ τῆς αὐτοῦ ἀνθρωπότητος ἤγουν αἱ θελητικαὶ δυνάμεις· ἐπειδὴ δὲ μία ἡ ὑπόστασις καὶ εἷς ὁ θέλων, ἓν καὶ τὸ θελητὸν ἤγουν τὸ γνωμικὸν θέλημα, τῆς ἀνθρωπίνης αὐτοῦ θελήσεως ἑπομένης δηλαδὴ τῇ θείᾳ αὐτοῦ θελήσει καὶ ταῦτα θελούσης, ἃ ἡ θεία αὐτοῦ ἤθελε θέλησις.

Χρὴ δὲ γινώσκειν, ὡς ἕτερον μέν ἐστιν ἡ θέλησις, ἕτερον δὲ βούλησις, ἕτερον δὲ τὸ θελητὸν καὶ ἕτερον τὸ θελητικὸν καὶ ἕτερον ὁ θέλων. Θέλησις μὲν γάρ ἐστιν αὐτὴ ἡ ἁπλῆ δύναμις τοῦ θέλειν, βούλησις δὲ ἡ περί τι θέλησις, θελητὸν δὲ τὸ ὑποκείμενον τῇ θελήσει πρᾶγμα ἤγουν ὅπερ θέλομεν (οἷον κινεῖται ἡ ὄρεξις πρὸς βρῶσιν· ἡ μὲν ἁπλῶς ὄρεξις ἡ λογικὴ θέλησίς ἐστιν, ἡ δὲ πρὸς βρῶσιν ὄρεξις βούλησίς ἐστιν, αὐτὴ δὲ ἡ βρῶσις θελητόν ἐστι), θελητικὸν δὲ τὸ ἔχον τὴν θελητικὴν δύναμιν οἷον ὁ ἄνθρωπος, θέλων δὲ αὐτὸς ὁ κεχρημένος τῇ θελήσει. Δεῖ εἰδέναι, ὡς τὸ θέλημα ποτὲ μὲν τὴν θέλησιν δηλοῖ ἤτοι τὴν θελητικὴν δύναμιν καὶ λέγεται θέλημα φυσικόν, ποτὲ δὲ τὸ θελητὸν καὶ λέγεται θέλημα γνωμικόν.

One needs to know that in the case of God we attribute actual willing (βούλησις, *boulēsis*) to him but not, properly speaking, free choice (προαίρεσις, *proairesis*). God does not deliberate, for deliberation belongs to ignorance. Nobody deliberates about what is known. If counsel belongs to ignorance, so necessarily does free choice. Since God knows all things absolutely, he does not deliberate.

Nor do we speak of counsel or free choice in the case of the Lord's soul. For there was no ignorance in him. Even though he was of a nature that was ignorant of what belonged to the future, nevertheless, because that nature was hypostatically united to God the Word, he had knowledge of all things, not by grace, but, as I have said, through the hypostatic union. For the same was both God and man. Hence he did not possess a gnomic will (γνωμικὸν θέλημα, *gnōmikon thelēma*) either. He did possess the natural, the simple, capacity for willing (θέλησις, *thelēsis*) that may be observed in all human hypostases without exception, but his holy soul did not possess a human intention (γνώμη, *gnōmē*), or something willed, that was opposed to his divine will, nor anything other than that which was his divine will.[13] For the gnomic will varies according to the hypostases, with the exception of the holy, simple, uncompounded, and undivided Godhead. For in this case, since the hypostases are in no way divided or set apart, neither is what is willed divided. In the same case, too, because the nature is one, the natural will is also one, and because the hypostases are not separated, what is willed is one and the activity of the three hypostases is also one. In the case of human beings, however, because the nature is one, the natural will is also one, but because the hypostases are separated and set apart from each other both in place and in time, and also with regard to their attitude towards material things and in many other respects too, on this account there are differences in what they will and what they intend. In the case of our Lord Jesus Christ, however, because the natures are different, the natural wills of his divinity and of his humanity, that is to say, the volitional facilities (θελητικαὶ δυνάμεις,

[13]Cf. Maximus the Confessor, *Opusculum 1, To Marinus* (PG 91:29CD).

37   Περὶ ἐνεργείας

Χρὴ γινώσκειν, ὡς πᾶσαι αἱ δυνάμεις αἱ προειρημέναι, αἵ τε γνωστικαὶ αἵ τε ζωτικαὶ καὶ αἱ φυσικαὶ καὶ αἱ τεχνικαί, ἐνέργειαι λέγονται· ἐνέργεια γάρ ἐστιν ἡ φυσικὴ ἑκάστης οὐσίας δύναμίς

---

[1]Ἐνέργειαι (*energeiai*), translated here as "activities," are what an essence *does* rather than *is*. It is not a term that is easily translated on every occasion by the same English word. At other times I use "operations" and sometimes "energies," where the latter word has become familiar through the seventh-century Monothelete (one will)

thelētikai dynameis), are also different. But because the hypostasis is one and the one who wills is one, that which is willed, namely, the gnomic will, is also one, seeing that his human will manifestly follows his divine will and wills the same things that his divine will wishes.

One needs to know that the capacity for willing (θέλησις, *thelēsis*) is one thing and actual willing (βούλησις, *boulēsis*) is another, and that what is willed (τὸ θελητόν, *to thelēton*) is one thing, the faculty of volition (τὸ θελητικόν, *to thelētikon*) is another, and the agent of willing (ὁ θέλων, *ho thelōn*) is another. For the capacity for willing is the simple power itself of willing. Actual willing is the direction of the capacity of willing towards something. What is willed is the matter that is subject to the will, namely, that which we will. (For example, appetency is oriented towards food. Appetency on its own is a rational capacity for willing but when appetency is directed towards food it is actual willing, and the food itself is what is willed.) The faculty of willing is that which possesses the power to will, such as a human being, and the agent of willing is the one who exercises the capacity for willing.

One should be aware that the will (τὸ θέλημα, *to thelēma*) sometimes denotes the capacity for willing, or the faculty of volition, and is called "natural will" (θέλημα φυσικόν, *thelēma physikon*), and sometimes denotes what is willed and is called "gnomic will" (θέλημα γνωμικόν, *thelēma gnōmikon*).

37 On activity

One needs to know that all the powers that have been discussed, both the cognitive and the vital, and also the natural and the acquired, are called "activities" (ἐνέργειαι, *energeiai*).[1] For activity is the natural power and movement of each essence. And again:

Christological controversy, in which one of the solutions proposed (and rejected) was "Monenergism." For a succinct account of the Monothelete heresy, see Demetrios Bathrellos, *The Byzantine Christ: Person, Nature, and Will in the Christology of St Maximus the Confessor* (Oxford: Oxford University Press, 2004), 60–98.

τε καὶ κίνησις. Καὶ πάλιν· Ἐνέργειά ἐστι φυσικὴ ἡ πάσης οὐσίας
ἔμφυτος κίνησις. Ὅθεν δῆλον, ὅτι, ὧν ἡ οὐσία ἡ αὐτή, τούτων
καὶ ἡ ἐνέργεια ἡ αὐτή, ὧν δὲ αἱ φύσεις διάφοροι, τούτων καὶ αἱ
ἐνέργειαι διάφοροι· ἀμήχανον γὰρ οὐσίαν ἄμοιρον εἶναι φυσικῆς
ἐνεργείας.
    Ἐνέργεια πάλιν ἐστὶ φυσικὴ ἡ δηλωτικὴ ἑκάστης οὐσίας
δύναμις. Καὶ πάλιν· Ἐνέργειά ἐστι φυσικὴ καὶ πρώτη ἡ ἀεικίνητος
δύναμις τῆς νοερᾶς ψυχῆς, τουτέστιν ὁ ἀεικίνητος αὐτῆς λόγος
φυσικῶς ἐξ αὐτῆς ἀεὶ πηγαζόμενος. Ἐνέργειά ἐστι φυσικὴ ἡ
ἑκάστης οὐσίας δύναμίς τε καὶ κίνησις, ἧς χωρὶς μόνον τὸ μὴ ὄν.
    Λέγονται δὲ ἐνέργειαι καὶ αἱ πράξεις ὡς τὸ λαλεῖν, τὸ
περιπατεῖν, τὸ ἐσθίειν καὶ πίνειν καὶ τὰ τοιαῦτα. Καὶ τὰ πάθη
δὲ τὰ φυσικὰ πολλάκις ἐνέργειαι λέγονται οἷον πεῖνα, δίψα
καὶ τὰ τοιαῦτα. Λέγεται πάλιν ἐνέργεια καὶ τὸ ἀποτέλεσμα τῆς
δυνάμεως. Διττῶς δὲ λέγεται καὶ τὸ δυνάμει καὶ τὸ ἐνεργείᾳ.
Λέγομεν γὰρ τὸν παῖδα τὸν θηλάζοντα δυνάμει γραμματικόν· ἔχει
γὰρ ἐπιτηδειότητα διὰ μαθήσεως γενέσθαι γραμματικός. Λέγομεν
πάλιν τὸν γραμματικὸν καὶ δυνάμει γραμματικὸν καὶ ἐνεργείᾳ·
ἐνεργείᾳ μέν, ὅτι ἔχει τὴν γνῶσιν τῆς γραμματικῆς, δυνάμει δέ,
ὅτι δύναται ἐξηγεῖσθαι, οὐκ ἐνεργεῖ δὲ τὴν ἐξήγησιν. Λέγομεν
πάλιν ἐνεργείᾳ γραμματικόν, ὅτε ἐνεργεῖ ἤγουν ἐξηγεῖται.
    Χρὴ οὖν γινώσκειν, ὅτι ὁ δεύτερος τρόπος κοινός ἐστι τοῦ
δυνάμει καὶ τοῦ ἐνεργείᾳ, δεύτερος μὲν τοῦ δυνάμει, πρῶτος δὲ
τοῦ ἐνεργείᾳ.
    Ἐνέργεια φύσεώς ἐστι πρώτη καὶ μόνη καὶ ἀληθὴς ἡ
αὐθαίρετος ἤτοι λογικὴ καὶ αὐτεξούσιος ζωὴ καὶ τοῦ καθ' ἡμᾶς
εἴδους συστατική· ἧς ἀποστεροῦντες τὸν κύριον, οὐκ οἶδα, ὅπως

²This definition is drawn from Ps.-Alexander of Alexandria, as given by Maximus the Confessor (if Maximus is indeed the author) in *Opusculum 27/Additamentum 25* (PG 91:280D): Ἐνέργεια φυσική ἐστιν ἡ πάσης οὐσίας ἔμφυτος κίνησις (*Energeia physikē estin hē pasēs ousias emphytos kinēsis*). On this opusculum, which is a florilegium on the two energies of the Lord compiled at around the time of the Lateran Council of 649, see Marek Jankowiak and Phil Booth, "A New Date-List of the Works of Maximus the Confessor," in Allen and Neil, *The Oxford Handbook of Maximus the Confessor*, 19–83, at 67.

Natural activity is the innate movement of every essence.[2] It is therefore clear that those things that have the same essence also have the same activity, and those things that have different natures also have different activities. For it is impossible for an essence to be without a natural activity.

Natural activity, again, is the power that makes each essence manifest.[3] And again: Natural and primary activity is the ever-moving power of the intellectual soul, that is to say, its ever-moving reason flowing out naturally from it. Natural activity is the power and movement of each essence; only non-being is without it.[4]

Actions such as speaking, walking, eating, drinking, and suchlike are also called activities. And the natural passions such as hunger, thirst, and suchlike are also frequently called activities. Again, the result of the capacity is also called activity.

There are two ways of speaking about something, either as in potentiality or as in actuality. For we call the child at the breast potentially a scholar. For it has the aptitude through education to become learned. Again, we say that a scholar is learned both in potentiality and in actuality, in actuality because he has a knowledge of grammar, but in potentiality because he is able to expound texts but is not actually expounding them. Again, we speak of an actual scholar when he is in action, that is to say, when he is actively teaching.

One should know that the second way embraces both potentiality and actuality, for on the one hand, the latter is in potentiality, on the other, the former is in actuality.

The natural activity that alone is primary and true is the independent—that is to say, rational and free—life that constitutes our own species. I do not understand how those who deprive the Lord of this can say that he is God who has become man. Activity

[3] Again from Ps.-Alexander of Alexandria via Maximus the Confessor, *Opusculum 27/Additamentum 25* (PG 91:280D).

[4] Anastasius of Sinai, *Hodēgos* 2 (PG 89:65BC). The definition of ἐνέργεια (*energeia*)—"Natural activity is the power and movement of each essence"—is taken by Anastasius from Gregory of Nyssa, *Tractate to Xenodorus*, which has perished except for this fragment.

αὐτὸν θεὸν ἐνανθρωπήσαντα λέγουσιν. Ἐνέργειά ἐστι φύσεως κίνησις δραστική· δραστικὸν δὲ λέγεται τὸ ἐξ ἑαυτοῦ κινούμενον.

38   Περὶ ἑκουσίου καὶ ἀκουσίου

Ἐπειδὴ τὸ ἑκούσιον ἐν πράξει τινί ἐστι καὶ τὸ νομιζόμενον δὲ ἀκούσιον ἐν πράξει τινί ἐστι, πολλοὶ δέ τινες καὶ τὸ ὄντως ἀκούσιον οὐ μόνον ἐν τῷ πάσχειν ἀλλὰ καὶ ἐν τῷ πράττειν τίθενται, δεῖ εἰδέναι, ὅτι πρᾶξίς ἐστιν ἐνέργεια λογική. Ταῖς δὲ πράξεσιν ἕπεται ἔπαινος ἢ ψόγος, καὶ αἱ μὲν αὐτῶν μεθ' ἡδονῆς, αἱ δὲ μετὰ λύπης πράττονται, καὶ αἱ μὲν αὐτῶν εἰσιν αἱρεταὶ τῷ πράττοντι, αἱ δὲ φευκταί, καὶ τῶν αἱρετῶν αἱ μὲν ἀεὶ αἱρεταί, αἱ δὲ κατά τινα χρόνον, ὁμοίως καὶ τῶν φευκτῶν. Καὶ πάλιν αἱ μὲν τῶν πράξεων ἐλεοῦνται, αἱ δὲ συγγνώμης ἀξιοῦνται, αἱ δὲ μισοῦνται καὶ κολάζονται. Τῷ μὲν οὖν ἑκουσίῳ πάντως ἐπακολουθεῖ ἔπαινος ἢ ψόγος καὶ τὸ μεθ' ἡδονῆς πράττεσθαι καὶ τὸ αἱρετὰς εἶναι τὰς πράξεις τοῖς πράττουσιν ἢ ἀεὶ ἢ τότε, ὅτε πράττονται, τῷ δὲ ἀκουσίῳ τὸ συγγνώμης ἢ ἐλέους ἀξιοῦσθαι καὶ τὸ μετὰ λύπης πράττεσθαι καὶ τὸ μὴ εἶναι αἱρετὰς μηδὲ δι' ἑαυτοῦ τελεῖν τὸ πραττόμενον, εἰ καὶ βιάζοιτο.

Τοῦ δὲ ἀκουσίου τὸ μέν ἐστι κατὰ βίαν, τὸ δὲ δι' ἄγνοιαν· κατὰ βίαν μέν, ὅταν ἡ ποιητικὴ ἀρχὴ ἤγουν αἰτία ἔξωθέν ἐστιν ἤγουν ὅταν ὑφ' ἑτέρου βιαζώμεθα, μηδ' ὅλως πειθόμενοι μηδὲ συμβαλλώμεθα κατ' οἰκείαν ὁρμὴν μηδὲ ὅλως συμπράττωμεν ἢ δι' ἑαυτῶν τὸ βιασθὲν ποιῶμεν, ὃ καὶ ὁριζόμενοί φαμεν· Οὗ ἡ ἀρχὴ ἔξωθεν μηδὲν συμβαλλομένου κατ' οἰκείαν ὁρμὴν τοῦ βιασθέντος. Ἀρχὴν δέ φαμεν τὴν ποιητικὴν αἰτίαν. Τὸ δὲ δι' ἄγνοιαν ἀκούσιόν ἐστιν, ὅταν μὴ αὐτοὶ παρέχωμεν αἰτίαν τῆς ἀγνοίας, ἀλλ' οὕτω συμβῇ. Εἰ γὰρ μεθύων τις φόνον ποιήσει,

---

[5]John draws his definition from Maximus the Confessor, *Opusculum 27/Additamentum 25* (PG 91:281A), who has culled it, he says, from Gregory of Nyssa: Ἐνέργειά ἐστι κίνησις δραστική (*Energeia esti kinēsis drastikē*).

(ἐνέργεια, *energeia*) is an active natural movement.[5] The term "active" (δραστικόν, *drastikon*) is applied to that which moves of its own accord.

38   *On voluntary and involuntary*

Since what is voluntary (τὸ ἑκούσιον, *to ekousion*) involves some action and what is considered involuntary (τὸ ἀκούσιον, *to akousion*) also involves some action, and many classify what is truly involuntary not only among passive experiences but also among acts, one needs to know that "action is a rational activity."[1] Actions are followed by praise or blame. Some of them are accompanied by pleasure, others by distress. Some of them are to be chosen by the actor, others are to be avoided, and of those that are to be chosen, some are always to be chosen, others at particular times, and similarly with actions that are to be avoided. Moreover, some actions call for mercy, others deserve forgiveness, and others are to be detested and punished. Thus what is voluntary is inevitably followed by praise or blame, with regard both to its accomplishment with pleasure and to the fact that the actions are to be chosen by those who do them, either always or at the time when they are done, whereas what is involuntary deserves forgiveness or mercy, with regard both to what is done with distress and to what is not to be chosen or accomplished of one's own accord, even under duress.[2]

With regard to what is involuntary, sometimes it occurs as a result of compulsion and sometimes through ignorance. It occurs as a result of compulsion when the efficient principle or cause is external, that is to say, when we are compelled by another person but are in no way persuaded, nor do we concur with it of our own impulse, nor do we collaborate with it, or do what we are forced to do of our

---

[1] The definition (πρᾶξίς ἐστιν ἐνέργεια λογική, *praxis estin energeia logikē*) is cited from Nemesius of Emesa, *On Human Nature* 29 (PG 40:717C; Morani, 94.3).

[2] This paragraph paraphrases Nemesius of Emesa, *On Human Nature* 29 (PG 40:717B–720A; Morani, 93.20–94.13).

ἀγνοῶν ἐφόνευσεν, οὐ μὴν ἀκουσίως· τὴν γὰρ αἰτίαν τῆς ἀγνοίας ἤγουν τὴν μέθην αὐτὸς ἔπραξεν. Εἰ δέ τις ἐν τῷ συνήθει τόπῳ τοξεύων τὸν πατέρα παριόντα ἀπέκτεινε, δι' ἄγνοιαν λέγεται ἀκουσίως τοῦτο πεποιηκέναι.

Τοῦ οὖν ἀκουσίου διττοῦ ὄντος, τοῦ μὲν κατὰ βίαν, τοῦ δὲ δι' ἄγνοιαν, τὸ ἑκούσιον ἀμφοτέροις ἀντίκειται· ἔστι γὰρ ἑκούσιον τὸ μήτε κατὰ βίαν μήτε δι' ἄγνοιαν γινόμενον. Ἑκούσιον τοίνυν ἐστίν, οὗ ἡ ἀρχὴ τουτέστιν ἡ αἰτία ἐν αὐτῷ εἰδότι τὰ καθ' ἕκαστα, δι' ὧν καὶ ἐν οἷς ἡ πρᾶξις. «Καθ' ἕκαστα» δέ ἐστιν, ἃ καλεῖται παρὰ τοῖς ῥήτορσι περιστατικὰ μόρια, οἷον τίς ἤγουν ὁ πράξας, τίνα ἤγουν τὸν παθόντα, τί ἤγουν αὐτὸ τὸ πραχθέν, τυχὸν ἐφόνευσε· τίνι ἤγουν ὀργάνῳ, ποῦ ἤγουν τόπῳ, πότε ἤγουν ἐν ποίῳ χρόνῳ, πῶς ὁ τρόπος τῆς πράξεως, διὰ τί ἤγουν διὰ ποίαν αἰτίαν.

Ἰστέον, ὥς εἰσί τινα μέσα ἑκουσίων καὶ ἀκουσίων, ἅτινα ἀηδῆ καὶ λυπηρὰ ὄντα διὰ μεῖζον κακὸν καταδεχόμεθα, ὡς διὰ ναυάγιον ἀποβάλλομεν τὰ ἐν τῷ πλοίῳ.

Ἰστέον, ὡς τὰ παιδία καὶ τὰ ἄλογα ἑκουσίως μὲν ποιεῖ, οὐ μὴν δὲ καὶ προαιρούμενα, καὶ ὅσα διὰ θυμὸν πράττομεν μὴ προβουλευσάμενοι, ἑκουσίως ποιοῦμεν, οὐ μὴν καὶ κατὰ προαίρεσιν. Καὶ ὁ φίλος αἰφνιδίως ἐπέστη ἑκουσίως μὲν ἡμῖν, οὐ μὴν καὶ προαιρούμενος. Καὶ ὁ θησαυρῷ ἀνελπίστως περιτυχὼν ἑκουσίως περιέτυχεν, οὐ μὴν καὶ προαιρούμενος. Πάντα ταῦτα ἑκούσια μὲν διὰ τὸ ἐπ' αὐτοῖς ἥδεσθαι, οὐ μὴν καὶ κατὰ προαίρεσιν, διότι οὐκ ἀπὸ βουλῆς. Δεῖ δὲ πάντως βουλὴν προηγεῖσθαι τῆς προαιρέσεως, καθὼς εἴρηται.

---

[3]The definition is cited from Nemesius of Emesa, *On Human Nature* 30 (PG 40:720B; Morani, 94.24–25).

[4]Cf. Nemesius of Emesa, *On Human Nature* 31 (PG 40:725AB; Morani, 96.26–97.10).

[5]Cf. Nemesius of Emesa, *On Human Nature* 32 (PG 40:728B; Morani, 98.5–10).

[6]Cf. Nemesius of Emesa, *On Human Nature* 31 (PG 40:725B–728A; Morani, 97.14–17).

[7]Cf. Nemesius of Emesa, *On Human Nature* 31 (PG 40:720B–721A; Morani, 94.24–95.2).

own accord. And that is how we define it: An involuntary act is "an act the principle of which is external, with the one under compulsion not concurring in any way whatsoever of his own accord."[3] The "principle" is what we call the efficient cause. What is done in ignorance, on the other hand, is involuntary when we ourselves do not contribute the cause of the ignorance, but it simply happens that way. For if someone commits a murder in a drunken state, he has murdered in ignorance but not involuntarily, for the cause of the ignorance, namely, the drunkenness, is something he has brought about himself. But if someone is practicing archery in the usual place and kills his father who happens to be passing by, he is said to have done this in ignorance and involuntarily.[4]

Thus while what is involuntary has a dual aspect, one aspect depending on compulsion, the other on ignorance, what is voluntary is the opposite in both respects, for it is accomplished neither under compulsion nor under ignorance. What is voluntary, then, is an act the principle of which, that is to say, the cause, is in the actor who knows the particulars on account of which and by which the act takes place.[5] "The particulars" are what teachers of rhetoric call the circumstantial elements, such as *who*, or the agent of the act, *whom*, or the one affected by the act, *what*, or the act itself, such as a murder, *by what*, or the instrument, *where*, or the place, *when*, or at what time, *how*, or the way in which the act was accomplished, *why*, or for what reason.[6]

Note that there are certain acts that come in between the voluntary and the involuntary. These are unpleasant and painful but we accept them in order to avoid a greater evil, such as when we jettison a ship's cargo in order to avoid shipwreck.[7]

Note that just like children and irrational animals, who do things voluntarily but not because they have freely chosen to do them, whatever we do in anger without previous deliberation we do voluntarily but certainly not also by deliberate choice.[8] Similarly,

[8]Cf. Nemesius of Emesa, *On Human Nature* 33 (PG 40:732A; Morani, 99.16–19).

39 Περὶ τοῦ ἐφ᾽ ἡμῖν, τουτέστι τοῦ αὐτεξουσίου

Ὁ περὶ τοῦ αὐτεξουσίου λόγος τουτέστι τοῦ ἐφ᾽ ἡμῖν πρώτην μὲν ἔχει ζήτησιν, εἰ ἔστι ἐφ᾽ ἡμῖν· πολλοὶ γὰρ οἱ πρὸς τοῦτο ἀντιβαίνοντες. Δευτέραν δέ, τίνα ἐστὶ τὰ ἐφ᾽ ἡμῖν καὶ τίνων ἐξουσίαν ἔχομεν. Τρίτην τὴν αἰτίαν ἐξετάσαι, δι᾽ ἣν ὁ ποιήσας ἡμᾶς θεὸς αὐτεξουσίους ἐποίησεν. Ἀναλαβόντες οὖν περὶ τοῦ πρώτου, πρῶτον εἴπωμεν ἀποδεικνύντες, ὅτι ἔστι τινὰ ἐφ᾽ ἡμῖν, ἐκ τῶν παρ᾽ ἐκείνοις ὁμολογουμένων καὶ εἴπωμεν οὕτως·

Τῶν γινομένων πάντων ἢ θεόν φασιν αἴτιον εἶναι ἢ ἀνάγκην ἢ εἱμαρμένην ἢ φύσιν ἢ τύχην ἢ τὸ αὐτόματον. Ἀλλὰ τοῦ μὲν θεοῦ ἔργον οὐσία καὶ πρόνοια· τῆς δὲ ἀνάγκης τῶν ἀεὶ ὡσαύτως ἐχόντων ἡ κίνησις· τῆς δὲ εἱμαρμένης τὸ ἐξ ἀνάγκης τὰ δι᾽ αὐτῆς ἐπιτελεῖσθαι (καὶ γὰρ αὕτη τῆς ἀνάγκης ἐστί)· τῆς δὲ φύσεως γένεσις, αὔξησις, φθορά, φυτὰ καὶ ζῷα· τῆς δὲ τύχης τὰ σπάνια καὶ ἀπροσδόκητα (ὁρίζονται γὰρ τὴν τύχην σύμπτωσιν καὶ συνδρομὴν δύο αἰτίων ἀπὸ προαιρέσεως τὴν ἀρχὴν ἐχόντων, ἄλλο τι, παρ᾽ ὃ πέφυκεν, ἀποτελούντων, ὡς τάφρον ὀρύσσοντα θησαυρὸν

---

[9]Cf. Nemesius of Emesa, *On Human Nature* 33 (PG 40:733B; Morani, 100.25–101.5).

[1]This chapter faithfully reproduces Nemesius of Emesa, *On Human Nature* 39 (PG 40:761A–764C; Morani, 112.8–113.16), omitting only the last paragraph, which discusses Aristotle. On the context of Christian discussions of free will and divine providence, see Karamanolis, *Philosophy of Early Christianity*, 130–65.

when a friend turns up unexpectedly, we accept it willingly although certainly not also by deliberate choice. And someone who comes across a treasure while not actually looking for it also accepts it willingly although certainly not also by deliberate choice. All these things are voluntary because they give pleasure although they have certainly not also come about by deliberate choice on account of their not resulting from counsel.[9] Counsel must necessarily precede deliberate choice, as we have stated.

39   *On what lies within our power, that is, on free will*[1]

"The first consideration in a discussion on free will (τὸ αὐτεξούσιον, *to autexousion*), that is, on what lies within our power, is whether we possess it, for there are many who deny that we do.[2] The second relates to what lies within our power and what are the things over which we have control. The third relates to the examination of the cause, the reason why God who created us endowed us with free will. So taking up the first point, let us first prove from what is admitted by them that there are things within our power" and proceed as follows.[3]

"They say that the cause of everything that happens is either God, or necessity, or fate, or nature, or chance, or spontaneity. But what belong to the work of God are essence and providence. What belongs to the work of necessity is the movement of those things whose state is always invariable. What belongs to the work of fate is what has necessarily been brought about by it (for fate too belongs to necessity). What belong to the work of nature are generation, growth, decay, plants, and animals. What belong to the work of chance are rare and unexpected events (for chance is defined as the coincidence and concurrence of two causes that have their origin in deliberate choice but result in something other than intended, such

[2]On the αὐτεξούσιον (*autexousion*), see Frede, "John of Damascus on Human Action, the Will, and Human Freedom," 79–82; Karamanolis, *Philosophy of Early Christianity*, 143–48.

[3]Nemesius of Emesa, *On Human Nature* 39 (PG 40:761AB; Morani, 112.8–13).

εὑρεῖν· οὔτε γὰρ ὁ θεὶς τὸν θησαυρὸν οὕτως ἔθηκεν, ὥστε τοῦτον
εὑρεῖν, οὔτε ὁ εὑρὼν οὕτως ὤρυξεν, ὡς εὑρεῖν θησαυρόν, ἀλλ᾽
ὁ μὲν ἵν᾽ ὅταν θέλῃ, ἀνέληται, ὁ δὲ ἵνα τάφρον ὀρύξῃ· συνέπεσε
δὲ ἄλλο τι, παρ᾽ ὃ προηροῦντο ἀμφότεροι)· τοῦ δὲ αὐτομάτου
τὰ τῶν ἀψύχων ἢ ἀλόγων συμπτώματα ἄνευ φύσεως καὶ τέχνης.
Οὕτως αὐτοί φασι. Τίνι τοίνυν τούτων ὑπαγάγωμεν τὰ διὰ τῶν
ἀνθρώπων, εἴπερ ὁ ἄνθρωπος οὐκ ἔστιν αἴτιος καὶ ἀρχὴ πράξεως;
Οὐδὲ γὰρ θεῷ θεμιτὸν ἐπιγράφειν αἰσχρὰς ἔσθ᾽ ὅτε πράξεις καὶ
ἀδίκους οὐδὲ ἀνάγκη (οὐ γὰρ τῶν ἀεὶ ὡσαύτως ἐχόντων ἐστίν)
οὐδὲ εἱμαρμένη (οὐ γὰρ τῶν ἐνδεχομένων, ἀλλὰ τῶν ἀναγκαίων
τὰ τῆς εἱμαρμένης λέγουσιν) οὔτε φύσει (φύσεως γὰρ ἔργα ζῷα
καὶ φυτά) οὐδὲ τύχῃ (οὐ γὰρ σπάνιοι καὶ ἀπροσδόκητοι τῶν
ἀνθρώπων αἱ πράξεις) οὔτε τῷ αὐτομάτῳ (ἀψύχων γὰρ λέγουσιν
ἢ ἀλόγων συμπτώματα τοῦ αὐτομάτου). Λείπεται δὴ αὐτὸν τὸν
πράττοντα καὶ ποιοῦντα ἄνθρωπον ἀρχὴν εἶναι τῶν ἰδίων ἔργων
καὶ αὐτεξούσιον.

Ἔτι, εἰ μηδεμιᾶς ἐστιν ἀρχὴ πράξεως ὁ ἄνθρωπος, περιττῶς
ἔχει τὸ βουλεύεσθαι· εἰς τί γὰρ χρήσεται τῇ βουλῇ μηδεμιᾶς
ὢν κύριος πράξεως; Πᾶσα γὰρ βουλὴ πράξεως ἕνεκα. Τὸ δὲ
κάλλιστον καὶ τιμιώτατον τῶν ἐν ἀνθρώπῳ περιττὸν ἀποφαίνειν
τῶν ἀτοπωτάτων ἂν εἴη. Εἰ τοίνυν βουλεύεται, πράξεως ἕνεκα
βουλεύεται· πᾶσα γὰρ βουλὴ πράξεως ἕνεκα καὶ διὰ πρᾶξιν.

as when someone digging a trench finds a treasure. Neither did the person who deposited the treasure do it in such a way that the other would find it, nor did the person who found it by digging at that spot do it so as to find it, but the one did it so that he could take it away when he wanted, and the other in order to dig a trench. What resulted was different from what either intended.) And what belong to spontaneity are the coincidences of inanimate or irrational beings without the intervention of nature or art."[4] That is their argument. "To which of these categories, then, are we to assign what is done by human beings, if human beings are not the cause and principle of their own action? For it is not permissible to attribute any kind of shameful or unjust act to God, or to necessity (for the two are not always the same), or to fate (for they say that what concerns fate belongs not to contingencies but to necessities), or to nature (for the works of nature are animals and plants), or to chance (for the acts of human beings are not rare and unexpected), or to spontaneity (for they say that the coincidences of inanimate or irrational beings belong to spontaneity). What of course remains is that the acting and doing human person is himself or herself the principle and free agent of his or her own actions."[5]

"Furthermore, if the human person is not the principle of any act at all, it is superfluous for him or her to possess the power of deliberation. For what use is counsel if one is not master of one's own actions? For all counsel is for the sake of action. It would be absurd in the extreme to prove that the most beautiful and most honorable human faculty was superfluous. If the human person deliberates he or she deliberates for the sake of action. For all counsel is for the sake of action and on account of action."[6]

[4]Nemesius of Emesa, *On Human Nature* 39 (PG 40:761B–764A; Morani, 112.13–113.1).

[5]Nemesius of Emesa, *On Human Nature* 39 (PG 40:764AB; Morani, 1113.1–17).

[6]Nemesius of Emesa, *On Human Nature* 39 (PG 40:764B; Morani, 113.9–15). The statement, "For all counsel is for the sake of action," is not in the text as printed by Migne but appears in Morani's critical text after the sentence immediately following (Morani, 113.13–14).

40 Περὶ τῶν γινομένων

Τῶν γινομένων τὰ μέν εἰσιν ἐφ᾽ ἡμῖν, τὰ δὲ οὐκ ἐφ᾽ ἡμῖν. Ἐφ᾽ ἡμῖν μὲν οὖν εἰσιν, ὧν ἡμεῖς ἐσμεν αὐτεξούσιοι ποιεῖν τε καὶ μὴ ποιεῖν, τουτέστι πάντα τὰ δι᾽ ἡμῶν ἑκουσίως πραττόμενα (οὐ γὰρ ἑκουσίως ἐλέγετο πράττεσθαι τῆς πράξεως οὐκ οὔσης ἐφ᾽ ἡμῖν) καὶ ἁπλῶς, οἷς ἕπεται ψόγος ἢ ἔπαινος καὶ ἐφ᾽ οἷς ἐστι προτροπὴ καὶ νόμος. Κυρίως δὲ ἐφ᾽ ἡμῖν ἐστι τὰ ψυχικὰ πάντα καὶ περὶ ὧν βουλευόμεθα· ἡ δὲ βουλὴ τῶν ἐπίσης ἐνδεχομένων ἐστίν. Ἐπίσης δὲ ἐνδεχόμενόν ἐστιν, ὃ αὐτό τε δυνάμεθα, καὶ τὸ ἀντικείμενον αὐτῷ· ποιεῖται δὲ τούτου τὴν αἵρεσιν ὁ νοῦς ὁ ἡμέτερος, καὶ οὗτός ἐστιν ἀρχὴ πράξεως. Ταῦτα τοίνυν ἐστὶ τὰ ἐφ᾽ ἡμῖν, τὰ ἐπίσης ἐνδεχόμενα, οἷον τὸ κινεῖσθαι καὶ μὴ κινεῖσθαι, ὁρμᾶν καὶ μὴ ὁρμᾶν, ὀρέγεσθαι τῶν μὴ ἀναγκαίων καὶ μὴ ὀρέγεσθαι, ψεύδεσθαι καὶ μὴ ψεύδεσθαι, διδόναι καὶ μὴ διδόναι, χαίρειν ἐφ᾽ οἷς δεῖ καὶ μὴ χαίρειν ὁμοίως καὶ ἐφ᾽ οἷς οὐ δεῖ, καὶ ὅσα τοιαῦτα, ἐν οἷς ἐστι τὰ τῆς ἀρετῆς καὶ τῆς κακίας ἔργα· τούτων γάρ ἐσμεν αὐτεξούσιοι. Τῶν δὲ ἐπίσης ἐνδεχομένων εἰσὶ καὶ αἱ τέχναι· ἐφ᾽ ἡμῖν γάρ ἐστι μετελθεῖν, ἢν ἂν θελήσωμεν, καὶ μὴ μετελθεῖν.

Χρὴ δὲ γινώσκειν, ὡς ἡ μὲν αἵρεσις τῶν πρακτῶν ἀεὶ ἐφ᾽ ἡμῖν ἐστιν· ἡ δὲ πρᾶξις πολλάκις κωλύεται κατά τινα τρόπον τῆς προνοίας.

41 Διὰ ποίαν αἰτίαν αὐτεξούσιοι γεγόναμεν

Φαμὲν τοίνυν εὐθέως τῷ λογικῷ συνεισέρχεσθαι τὸ αὐτεξούσιον. Πᾶν γὰρ γεννητὸν καὶ τρεπτόν ἐστιν. Ὧν γὰρ ἡ ἀρχὴ τῆς γενέσεως ἀπὸ τροπῆς ἤρξατο, ἀνάγκη ταῦτα τρεπτὰ εἶναι. Τροπὴ δέ ἐστι

40 *On what comes about*

Among the things that come about, some depend on us, others do not depend on us. Those that depend on us are those that we are free to do or not to do, that is to say, all the things that are done voluntarily by us "(for an act that does not depend on us would not be said to be done voluntarily) and, to put it simply, which incur blame or praise and which are subject to exhortation and law [. . .]. Properly speaking, what depends on us is everything to do with the soul and about which we deliberate [. . .]. And counsel concerns equally balanced contingencies. An equally balanced contingency is that which we have the ability to do and its opposite. Our own mind makes the choice to do it, and that is the beginning of action. These then are the equally balanced contingencies that depend on us, contingencies such as moving or not moving, following an impulse or not following it, reaching out after things that are not necessary or not reaching out after them, lying or not lying, giving or not giving, rejoicing when one ought to, or conversely not rejoicing when one ought not to, and similar situations that concern matters of virtue and vice, for with regard to these we have freedom of choice. Among balanced contingencies are also the arts,"[1] for it depends on us whether we pursue them, if we so wish, or do not pursue them.

One also needs to know that the choice of what is to be done always depends on us, but its accomplishment is often prevented by some kind of providence.

41 *Why we were created with free will*

"We therefore maintain that free will (τὸ αὐτεξούσιον, *to autexousion*) came into being at the same time as the faculty of reason."[1] For everything that has been engendered is also mutable. For whatever

[1]Nemesius of Emesa, *On Human Nature* 40 (PG 40:768AB; Morani, 114.15–115.4).

[1]Nemesius of Emesa, *On Human Nature* 41 (PG 40:773A; Morani, 117.8).

τὸ ἐκ μὴ ὄντων εἰς τὸ εἶναι παραχθῆναι καὶ τὸ ἐξ ὑποκειμένης ὕλης ἕτερόν τι γενέσθαι. Τὰ μὲν οὖν ἄψυχα καὶ ἄλογα τρέπονται κατὰ τὰς προειρημένας σωματικὰς ἀλλοιώσεις, τὰ δὲ λογικὰ κατὰ προαίρεσιν· τοῦ γὰρ λογικοῦ τὸ μέν ἐστι θεωρητικόν, τὸ δὲ πρακτικόν, θεωρητικὸν μὲν τὸ κατανοοῦν, ὡς ἔχει τὰ ὄντα, πρακτικὸν δὲ τὸ βουλευτικόν, τὸ ὁρίζον τοῖς πρακτοῖς τὸν ὀρθὸν λόγον. Καὶ καλοῦσι τὸ μὲν θεωρητικὸν νοῦν, τὸ δὲ πρακτικὸν λόγον, καὶ τὸ μὲν θεωρητικὸν σοφίαν, τὸ δὲ πρακτικὸν φρόνησιν. Πᾶς οὖν ὁ βουλευόμενος ὡς ἐπ᾽ αὐτῷ τῆς αἱρέσεως οὔσης τῶν πρακτῶν βουλεύεται, ἵνα τὸ προκριθὲν ἐκ τῆς βουλῆς ἕληται καὶ ἑλόμενος πράξῃ· εἰ δὲ τοῦτο, ἐξ ἀνάγκης παρυφίσταται τῷ λογικῷ τὸ αὐτεξούσιον· ἢ γὰρ οὐκ ἔσται λογικόν, ἢ λογικὸν ὂν κύριον ἔσται πράξεων καὶ αὐτεξούσιον. Ὅθεν καὶ τὰ ἄλογα οὔκ εἰσιν αὐτεξούσια· ἄγονται γὰρ μᾶλλον ὑπὸ τῆς φύσεως ἤπερ ἄγουσι· διὸ οὐδὲ ἀντιλέγουσι τῇ φυσικῇ ὀρέξει, ἀλλ᾽, ἅμα ὀρεχθῶσί τινος, ὁρμῶσι πρὸς τὴν πρᾶξιν. Ὁ δὲ ἄνθρωπος λογικὸς ὢν ἄγει μᾶλλον τὴν φύσιν, ἤπερ ἄγεται· διὸ καὶ ὀρεγόμενος, εἴπερ ἐθέλοι, ἐξουσίαν ἔχει τὴν ὄρεξιν ἀναχαιτίσαι ἢ ἀκολουθῆσαι αὐτῇ. Ὅθεν τὰ μὲν ἄλογα οὐδὲ ἐπαινεῖται οὐδὲ ψέγεται, ὁ δὲ ἄνθρωπος καὶ ἐπαινεῖται καὶ ψέγεται.

Χρὴ δὲ γινώσκειν, ὅτι καὶ οἱ ἄγγελοι λογικοὶ ὄντες αὐτεξούσιοι ὑπάρχουσι καὶ ὡς κτιστοὶ καὶ τρεπτοί. Καὶ ἔδειξεν ὁ μὲν διάβολος ἀγαθὸς ὑπὸ τοῦ δημιουργοῦ γενόμενος, αὐτεξουσίως δὲ τῆς κακίας εὑρετὴς γεγονώς, καὶ αἱ σὺν αὐτῷ ἀποστατήσασαι δυνάμεις ἤγουν οἱ δαίμονες, τὰ δὲ λοιπὰ τάγματα τῶν ἀγγέλων ἐν τῷ ἀγαθῷ διαμείναντα.

originated in change is necessarily liable to change. Change means to be brought from non-being into being and also to become something other than the previously existing matter. Inanimate and irrational beings change according to the corporeal changes just mentioned, but rational beings change by choice, "for the rational faculty has a contemplative side and a practical side, the contemplative side being the power of cognition, of apprehending how things are, and the practical side being the power of deliberation, which determines correct reasoning in practical matters. And they call the contemplative side mind, and the practical side reasoning, the contemplative side wisdom and the practical side prudence. Everyone therefore who deliberates does so because the choice of what is to be done depends on him, so that he might choose what he has judged beforehand as a result of counsel and having chosen it might put it into practice."[2] But if this is the case, "free will was necessarily brought into existence along with the faculty of reason. A being will be either irrational or rational, and if rational will be master of its actions and endowed with free will."[3] It follows that irrational animals do not have free will. For they are led by nature rather than lead it themselves. Therefore neither do they deny their natural appetency, but as soon as they form an appetite for something, they are impelled to act. Human beings, however, being rational, lead their nature rather than being led by it. Therefore when an appetite arises, they have the power, if they wish, either to rein in the appetite or to follow it. Therefore irrational animals are not subject either to praise or to blame, whereas human beings are subject both to praise and to blame.

One needs to know that since the angels are rational, they too have free will and as created beings are also mutable. This is indicated by the fact that the devil, although created good by the Creator, of his own free will became the inventor of evil, and the powers that rebelled with him, namely, the demons, whereas the remaining orders of angels persevered in the good.

---

[2]Nemesius of Emesa, *On Human Nature* 41 (PG 40:773BC; Morani, 117.17–22).
[3]Nemesius of Emesa, *On Human Nature* 41 (PG 40:773C; Morani, 117.25–118.1).

42   Περὶ τῶν οὐκ ἐφ' ἡμῖν

Τῶν δὲ οὐκ ἐφ' ἡμῖν τὰ μὲν ἐκ τῶν ἐφ' ἡμῖν ἔχει τὰς ἀρχὰς ἤτοι τὰς αἰτίας, τουτέστιν αἱ ἀμοιβαὶ τῶν πράξεων ἡμῶν ἔν τε τῷ παρόντι καὶ ἐν τῷ μέλλοντι αἰῶνι, τὰ δὲ λοιπὰ πάντα τῆς θείας βουλῆς ἐξήρτηται. Ἡ μὲν γὰρ γένεσις πάντων ἐκ τοῦ θεοῦ, ἡ δὲ φθορὰ διὰ τὴν ἡμετέραν κακίαν ἐπήχθη πρὸς τιμωρίαν καὶ ὠφέλειαν. «Θεὸς γὰρ θάνατον οὐκ ἐποίησεν οὐδὲ τέρπεται ἐπ' ἀπωλείᾳ ζώντων» δι' ἀνθρώπου δὲ μᾶλλον θάνατος, τουτέστι τῆς τοῦ Ἀδὰμ παραβάσεως, ὁμοίως καὶ αἱ λοιπαὶ τιμωρίαι. Τὰ δὲ λοιπὰ πάντα τῷ θεῷ ἀναθετέον· ἤ τε γὰρ γένεσις ἡμῶν τῆς δημιουργικῆς αὐτοῦ δυνάμεώς ἐστι, καὶ ἡ διαμονὴ τῆς συνεκτικῆς δυνάμεως αὐτοῦ, καὶ ἡ κυβέρνησις τῆς προνοητικῆς αὐτοῦ δυνάμεως.

Ἐπειδὴ δέ τινες ἀντιλέγουσι τῇ προνοίᾳ, εἴπωμεν λοιπὸν ὀλίγα καὶ περὶ προνοίας.

43   Περὶ προνοίας

Πρόνοια τοίνυν ἐστὶν ἐκ θεοῦ εἰς τὰ ὄντα γινομένη ἐπιμέλεια. Καὶ πάλιν· Πρόνοιά ἐστι βούλησις θεοῦ, δι' ἣν πάντα τὰ ὄντα τὴν πρόσφορον διεξαγωγὴν λαμβάνει. Εἰ δὲ θεοῦ βούλησίς ἐστιν ἡ πρόνοια, πᾶσα ἀνάγκη πάντα τὰ τῇ προνοίᾳ γινόμενα κατὰ τὸν ὀρθὸν λόγον κάλλιστά τε καὶ θεοπρεπέστατα γίνεσθαι καὶ ὡς οὐκ ἔνι κρείττω γενέσθαι. Ἀνάγκη γὰρ τὸν αὐτὸν εἶναι ποιητὴν τῶν ὄντων καὶ προνοητήν· οὔτε γὰρ πρέπον οὔτε ἀκόλουθον ἄλλον μὲν ποιητὴν εἶναι τῶν ὄντων, ἄλλον δὲ προνοητήν· οὕτω γὰρ ἐν ἀσθενείᾳ πάντως εἰσὶν ἀμφότεροι, ὁ μὲν τοῦ ποιεῖν, ὁ δὲ τοῦ προνοεῖν. Ὁ θεὸς τοίνυν ἐστὶν ὅ τε ποιητὴς καὶ προνοητής, καὶ ἡ ποιητικὴ δὲ αὐτοῦ δύναμις καὶ ἡ συνεκτικὴ καὶ ἡ προνοητικὴ ἡ ἀγαθὴ αὐτοῦ θέλησίς ἐστι· «πάντα γάρ, ὅσα ἠθέλησεν, ὁ κύριος

42   *On what does not depend on us*

Of the things that do not depend on us, some have their principle or cause in what does depend on us. These are the recompenses for our deeds both in this age and in the age to come. The rest are all dependent on the divine will. For the origin of all things is from God but their decay was imposed subsequently, on account of our evil, for our punishment and benefit. "For God did not make death, nor does he delight in the destruction of the living."[1] Rather, death came about through man, that is to say, through Adam's transgression and so did the rest of the punishments.[2] Everything else is to be attributed to God, for our origin belongs to his creative power, our continuance to his power of maintaining in being, and our governance to his providential power.

But since some deny providence, let us say a few words on this subject.

43   *On providence*

"Providence, then, is the care exercised by God over that which exists."[1] And again: "Providence is the will of God by which all beings receive the direction appropriate to them. If providence is God's will, logically it is absolutely necessary that everything that has come into being as a result of providence should have been brought about in the way that is best and most befits God, and that it could not have been brought about in any better way. For it is necessary that the same should be the maker of existing things and the one who foresees and provides for them. For it is neither appropriate nor consistent that one should be the maker of that which exists and another should be the one who foresees and provides for it. For in that case, both of them would necessarily be in a state of

[1]Wis 1.13.
[2]Cf. Rom 5.12.

[1]Nemesius of Emesa, *On Human Nature* 43 (PG 40:792B; Morani, 125.5).

ἐποίησεν», καὶ τῷ θελήματι αὐτοῦ οὐδεὶς ἀνθέστηκεν. Ἠθέλησε γενέσθαι τὰ πάντα, καὶ γέγονε· θέλει συνίστασθαι τὸν κόσμον, καὶ συνίσταται, καὶ πάντα, ὅσα θέλει, γίνεται.

Ὅτι δὲ προνοεῖ καὶ ὅτι καλῶς προνοεῖ, ὀρθότατα σκοπήσειεν ἄν τις οὕτως· Μόνος ὁ θεός ἐστι φύσει ἀγαθὸς καὶ σοφός· ὡς οὖν ἀγαθὸς προνοεῖ (ὁ γὰρ μὴ προνοῶν οὐκ ἀγαθός· καὶ γὰρ καὶ οἱ ἄνθρωποι καὶ τὰ ἄλογα τῶν οἰκείων τέκνων προνοοῦνται φυσικῶς, καὶ ὁ μὴ προνοῶν ψέγεται), ὡς δὲ σοφὸς ἄριστα τῶν ὄντων ἐπιμελεῖται.

Χρὴ τοίνυν τούτοις προσέχοντας πάντα θαυμάζειν, πάντα ἐπαινεῖν, πάντα ἀνεξετάστως ἀποδέχεσθαι τὰ τῆς προνοίας ἔργα, κἂν φαίνηται τοῖς πολλοῖς ἄδικα διὰ τὸ ἄγνωστον καὶ ἀκατάληπτον εἶναι τοῦ θεοῦ τὴν πρόνοιαν. Πάντα δὲ λέγω τὰ οὐκ ἐφ᾽ ἡμῖν· τὰ γὰρ ἐφ᾽ ἡμῖν οὐ τῆς προνοίας ἐστίν, ἀλλὰ τοῦ ἡμετέρου αὐτεξουσίου.

Τῆς δὲ προνοίας τὰ μὲν κατ᾽ εὐδοκίαν ἐστί, τὰ δὲ κατὰ συγχώρησιν· Κατ᾽ εὐδοκίαν μέν, ὅσα ἀναντιρρήτως εἰσὶν ἀγαθά, κατὰ συγχώρησιν δὲ <εἴδη πολλά>. Συγχωρεῖ γὰρ πολλάκις καὶ τὸν δίκαιον περιπεσεῖν συμφοραῖς, ἵνα τὴν ἐν αὐτῷ λανθάνουσαν ἀρετὴν δείξῃ τοῖς ἄλλοις ὡς ἐπὶ τοῦ Ἰώβ. Ἄλλοτε συγχωρεῖ τῶν ἀτόπων τι πραχθῆναι, ἵνα διὰ τῆς πράξεως τῆς δοκούσης ἀτόπου μέγα τι καὶ θαυμαστὸν κατορθωθῇ ὡς διὰ τοῦ σταυροῦ τὴν σωτηρίαν τῶν ἀνθρώπων. Κατ᾽ ἄλλον τρόπον συγχωρεῖ τὸν ὅσιον πάσχειν κακῶς, ἵνα μὴ ἐκ τοῦ ὀρθοῦ συνειδότος ἐκπέσῃ ἢ καὶ ἐκ τῆς δοθείσης αὐτῷ δυνάμεώς τε καὶ χάριτος εἰς ἀλαζονείαν ἐκπέσῃ ὡς ἐπὶ τοῦ Παύλου. Ἐγκαταλείπεται τις πρὸς καιρὸν πρὸς διόρθωσιν ἄλλου, ἵνα τὸ κατ᾽ αὐτὸν σκοποῦντες οἱ ἄλλοι

[2]Nemesius of Emesa, *On Human Nature* 43 (PG 40:792B–793A; Morani, 125.6–12).
[3]Ps 134.6.
[4]Cf. Rom 9.19.
[5]Cf. Ps 148.5.

weakness, both the one who creates and the one who foresees and provides."[2] Therefore God is both the creator and the one who foresees and provides, and his creative, preservative, and providential powers are his good will. For "whatever the Lord pleased to do he did,"[3] and no one has resisted his will.[4] He willed everything to come into being and it came into being.[5] He wills to preserve the world and it is preserved. And everything that he wills comes to pass.

That he exercises foresight and provides well, one may very rightly observe in the following way. Only God is good and wise by nature. Therefore as good he exercises foresight (for one who does not exercise foresight is not good; both human beings and irrational animals naturally provide for their own young, and one who does not provide incurs blame), and as wise he cares for all that exists in the best way.[6]

Therefore when we give our attention to these things, we ought to admire all the works of providence, praise them all, and accept them all without examination, even though they might appear unjust to most people on account of the fact that God's providence is beyond our knowledge and comprehension. I mean by "all" the things that do not depend on us, for the things that do depend on us do not belong to providence but to our own free will.[7]

Of those things that belong to providence, some are by God's good pleasure, others are by his permission. Those that are by his good pleasure are those that are incontrovertibly good. Those that are by his permission are of many kinds. "For frequently he allows even the just man to encounter misfortunes so that he might show the virtue concealed in him to others, as in the case of Job.[8] At other times he allows something outrageous to be done, so that through the act of what appears to be outrageous something great and wonderful might be achieved, such as the salvation of humankind through

[6]Cf. Nemesius of Emesa, *On Human Nature* 43 (PG 40:813AB; Morani, 135.8–10).

[7]Cf. Nemesius of Emesa, *On Human Nature* 43 (PG 40:809C–812A; Morani, 135.9–18).

[8]Cf. Job 1.12.

παιδεύωνται, ὡς ἐπὶ τοῦ Λαζάρου καὶ τοῦ πλουσίου· φυσικῶς
γὰρ ὁρῶντές τινας πάσχοντας συστελλόμεθα. Ἐγκαταλείπεταί
τις καὶ εἰς ἄλλου δόξαν, οὐ δι’ οἰκείας ἢ γονέων ἁμαρτίας ὡς
ὁ ἐκ γενετῆς τυφλὸς εἰς δόξαν τοῦ υἱοῦ τοῦ ἀνθρώπου. Πάλιν
συγχωρεῖταί τις παθεῖν εἰς ἄλλου ζῆλον, ἵνα τῆς δόξης τοῦ
παθόντος μεγαλυνθείσης ἄοκνον τὸ πάθος τοῖς ἄλλοις γένηται
ἐλπίδι τῆς μελλούσης δόξης καὶ ἐπιθυμίᾳ τῶν μελλόντων ἀγαθῶν
ὡς ἐπὶ τῶν μαρτύρων. Παραχωρεῖταί τις καὶ εἰς αἰσχρὰν ἐμπεσεῖν
πρᾶξιν ἐνίοτε εἰς διόρθωσιν ἑτέρου χείρονος πάθους, οἷον
ἔστι τις ἐπαιρόμενος ἐπὶ ταῖς ἀρεταῖς καὶ τοῖς κατορθώμασιν
αὐτοῦ, παραχωρεῖ τοῦτον ὁ θεὸς εἰς πορνείαν ἐμπεσεῖν, ὅπως
διὰ τοῦ πτώματος εἰς συναίσθησιν τῆς οἰκείας ἀσθενείας ἐλθὼν
ταπεινωθῇ καὶ προσελθὼν ἐξομολογήσηται τῷ κυρίῳ.

Χρὴ δὲ γινώσκειν, ὅτι ἡ μὲν αἵρεσις τῶν πρακτῶν ἐφ’ ἡμῖν
ἐστι, τὸ δὲ τέλος τῶν μὲν ἀγαθῶν τῆς τοῦ θεοῦ συνεργίας
δικαίως συνεργοῦντος τοῖς προαιρουμένοις τὸ ἀγαθὸν ὀρθῷ
τῷ συνειδότι κατὰ τὴν πρόγνωσιν αὐτοῦ, τῶν δὲ πονηρῶν τῆς
ἐγκαταλείψεως τοῦ θεοῦ πάλιν κατὰ τὴν πρόγνωσιν αὐτοῦ
δικαίως ἐγκαταλιμπάνοντος.

Τῆς δὲ ἐγκαταλείψεώς εἰσιν εἴδη δύο· ἔστι γὰρ ἐγκατάλειψις
οἰκονομικὴ καὶ παιδευτικὴ καὶ ἔστιν ἐγκατάλειψις τελεία
ἀπογνωστική. Οἰκονομικὴ μὲν καὶ παιδευτικὴ ἡ πρὸς διόρθωσιν
καὶ σωτηρίαν καὶ δόξαν τοῦ πάσχοντος γινομένη ἢ καὶ πρὸς
ἄλλων ζῆλον καὶ μίμησιν ἢ καὶ πρὸς δόξαν θεοῦ· ἡ δὲ τελεία
ἐγκατάλειψις, ὅτε τοῦ θεοῦ πάντα πρὸς σωτηρίαν πεποιηκότος
ἀνεπαίσθητος καὶ ἀνιάτρευτος, μᾶλλον δὲ ἀνίατος ἐξ οἰκείας
προθέσεως διαμείνῃ ὁ ἄνθρωπος· τότε παραδίδοται εἰς τελείαν
ἀπώλειαν ὡς ὁ Ἰούδας. Φείσεται ἡμῶν ὁ θεὸς καὶ ἐξελεῖται τῆς
τοιαύτης ἐγκαταλείψεως.

9Cf. 2 Cor 12.7.
10Cf. Lk 16.19–31.
11Cf. Jn 9.1–3.
12Nemesius of Emesa, *On Human Nature* 43 (PG 40:812AB; Morani, 134.4–19),

the cross. In a different way he allows a saint to suffer unfairly that he might not lapse from a correct conscience or fall into conceit through the power and grace granted to him, as in case of Paul.[9] Someone may be abandoned for a time for the correction of another, that by observing what has happened to him the others might be instructed, as in the case of Lazarus and the rich man,[10] for naturally when we see people suffering we pull ourselves together. Someone may also be abandoned for the glory of another, not because of his own sins or the sins of his parents, like the man born blind for the glory of the Son of Man.[11] Again, someone may be allowed to suffer to encourage the zeal of another, that when the glory of the sufferer has been exalted, suffering resolutely borne might become for others a source of hope for future glory and desire for future blessings, as in the case of the martyrs."[12] Someone may also be allowed at times to commit some disgraceful act for the correction of another worse passion, as for example when someone who preens himself on his virtues and achievements is allowed by God to fall into fornication, so that by the fall he might come to an awareness of his own weakness and learn humility and make his confession to the Lord.

One needs to know that whereas "the choice of what is to be done depends on us,"[13] the accomplishment of good choices takes place through the help of God, who in accordance with his foreknowledge justly assists those who choose the good with an upright conscience, but the accomplishment of evil choices takes place through the abandonment of God, who, again in accordance with his foreknowledge, justly abandons those who choose evil.

There are two kinds of abandonment, for there is an abandonment that is providential and disciplinary and there is an abandonment of final rejection. The providential and disciplinary kind is that which comes about for the correction, salvation, and glory of the one who experiences it, or else for the sake of encouraging zeal and

---

omitting a line quoted from Menander (341/2 BC–*c.* 290 BC), the leading playwright of the New Comedy, on one's own suffering being a cause for others to fear the divine.

[13]Nemesius of Emesa, *On Human Nature* 38 (PG 40:749B; Morani, 109.23).

Χρὴ δὲ εἰδέναι, ὡς πολλοί εἰσιν οἱ τρόποι τῆς τοῦ θεοῦ προνοίας καὶ μήτε λόγῳ ἑρμηνευθῆναι μήτε νῷ περιληφθῆναι δυνάμενοι.

Δεῖ γινώσκειν, ὡς πᾶσαι αἱ σκυθρωπαὶ ἐπιφοραὶ τοῖς μετ' εὐχαριστίας δεχομένοις πρὸς σωτηρίαν ἐπάγονται καὶ πάντως ὠφελείας γίνονται πρόξενοι.

Χρὴ εἰδέναι, ὡς ὁ θεὸς προηγουμένως θέλει πάντας σωθῆναι καὶ τῆς βασιλείας αὐτοῦ τυχεῖν· οὐ γὰρ ἐπὶ τὸ κολάσαι ἔπλασεν ἡμᾶς, ἀλλὰ πρὸς τὸ μετασχεῖν τῆς ἀγαθότητος αὐτοῦ ὡς ἀγαθός. Ἁμαρτάνοντας δὲ θέλει κολάζεσθαι δικαίως.

Λέγεται οὖν τὸ μὲν πρῶτον προηγούμενον θέλημα καὶ εὐδοκία ἐξ αὐτοῦ ὄν, τὸ δὲ δεύτερον ἑπόμενον θέλημα καὶ παραχώρησις ἐξ ἡμετέρας αἰτίας. Καὶ αὕτη διττή· ἡ μὲν οἰκονομικὴ καὶ παιδευτικὴ πρὸς σωτηρίαν, ἡ δὲ ἀπογνωστικὴ πρὸς τελείαν κόλασιν, ὡς εἰρήκαμεν. Ταῦτα δὲ ἐπὶ τῶν οὐκ ἐφ' ἡμῖν.

Τῶν δὲ ἐφ' ἡμῖν τὰ μὲν ἀγαθὰ προηγουμένως θέλει καὶ εὐδοκεῖ, τὰ δὲ πονηρὰ καὶ ὄντως κακὰ οὔτε προηγουμένως οὔτε ἑπομένως θέλει. Παραχωρεῖ δὲ τῷ αὐτεξουσίῳ· τὸ γὰρ κατὰ βίαν γινόμενον οὐ λογικὸν οὐδὲ ἀρετή. Προνοεῖ δὲ ὁ θεὸς πάσης τῆς κτίσεως καὶ διὰ πάσης τῆς κτίσεως εὐεργετῶν καὶ παιδεύων καὶ δι' αὐτῶν πολλάκις τῶν δαιμόνων ὡς ἐπὶ τοῦ Ἰὼβ καὶ τῶν χοίρων.

imitation in others, or else for the glory of God. The abandonment of final rejection is that which comes about when God has done everything for someone's salvation yet that person remains obdurate and incurable, or rather incorrigible through his own free choice. In that event, he is handed over to final perdition, as in the case of Judas. May God spare us and deliver us from such abandonment.

One needs also to know that the ways of God's providence are many and can neither be explained in words nor grasped by the mind.

One should know that when they are accepted with thanksgiving, all the vexatious things that happen to us are laid upon us for our salvation and most certainly become occasions of benefit for us.

One should know that God principally "wishes that all should be saved"[14] and attain to his kingdom. For he created us not with a view to our being punished, but so that we might share in his goodness since he is good. But those who are sinners he will punish justly.

It is therefore said that his first antecedent will and approval is from him, but his second consequent will and permission has its cause in us. And the latter is twofold. On the one hand it is providential and disciplinary with a view to our salvation; on the other, it involves rejection with a view to our consummate punishment, as we have said. That completes our discussion of what does not depend on us.

With regard to what does depend on us, those that are good God wills and approves antecedently, those that are wicked and truly evil he wills neither antecedently nor consequently. But he permits them to the exercise of free will, for what takes place under compulsion is neither rational nor a matter of virtue. God exercises providential care over the whole of creation and uses the whole of creation to do good and to instruct, frequently even using the demons themselves, as in the cases of Job and the [Gadarene] swine.[15]

---

[14]1 Tim 2.4.
[15]Cf. Job 1.12 and Mt 8.30–32.

44 Περὶ προγνώσεως καὶ προορισμοῦ

Χρὴ γινώσκειν, ὡς πάντα μὲν προγινώσκει ὁ θεός, οὐ πάντα δὲ προορίζει· προγινώσκει γὰρ καὶ τὰ ἐφ᾽ ἡμῖν, οὐ προορίζει δὲ αὐτά· οὐ γὰρ θέλει τὴν κακίαν γενέσθαι οὐδὲ βιάζεται τὴν ἀρετήν. Ὥστε τῆς θείας προγνωστικῆς κελεύσεως ἔργον ἐστὶν ὁ προορισμός. Προορίζει δὲ τὰ οὐκ ἐφ᾽ ἡμῖν κατὰ τὴν πρόγνωσιν αὐτοῦ· ἤδη γὰρ κατὰ τὴν πρόγνωσιν αὐτοῦ προέκρινε πάντα ὁ θεὸς κατὰ τὴν ἀγαθότητα καὶ τὴν δικαιοσύνην αὐτοῦ.

Χρὴ δὲ γινώσκειν, ὅτι ἡ μὲν ἀρετὴ ἐκ τοῦ θεοῦ ἐδόθη ἐν τῇ φύσει καὶ αὐτός ἐστι παντὸς ἀγαθοῦ ἀρχὴ καὶ αἰτία καὶ ἐκτὸς τῆς αὐτοῦ συνεργίας καὶ βοηθείας ἀδύνατον ἀγαθὸν θελῆσαι ἢ πρᾶξαι ἡμᾶς. Ἐφ᾽ ἡμῖν δέ ἐστιν ἢ ἐμμεῖναι τῇ ἀρετῇ καὶ ἀκολουθῆσαι τῷ θεῷ πρὸς ταύτην καλοῦντι ἢ ἀποφοιτῆσαι τῆς ἀρετῆς, ὅπερ ἐστὶν ἐν τῇ κακίᾳ γενέσθαι καὶ ἀκολουθῆσαι τῷ διαβόλῳ πρὸς ταύτην καλοῦντι ἀβιάστως· ἡ γὰρ κακία οὐδὲν ἕτερόν ἐστιν εἰ μὴ ἀναχώρησις τοῦ ἀγαθοῦ, ὥσπερ καὶ τὸ σκότος τοῦ φωτός ἐστιν ἀναχώρησις. Μένοντες οὖν ἐν τῷ κατὰ φύσιν ἐν τῇ ἀρετῇ ἐσμεν, ἐκκλίνοντες δὲ ἐκ τοῦ κατὰ φύσιν παρὰ φύσιν ἐρχόμεθα καὶ ἐν τῇ κακίᾳ γινόμεθα.

Μετάνοιά ἐστιν ἐκ τοῦ παρὰ φύσιν εἰς τὸ κατὰ φύσιν καὶ ἐκ τοῦ διαβόλου πρὸς τὸν θεὸν ἐπάνοδος δι᾽ ἀσκήσεως καὶ πόνων.

Τοῦτον τοίνυν τὸν ἄνθρωπον ὁ δημιουργὸς ἄρρενα κατεσκεύασε μεταδοὺς αὐτῷ τῆς ἑαυτοῦ θείας χάριτος καὶ ἐν κοινωνίᾳ ἑαυτοῦ διὰ ταύτης αὐτὸν ποιησάμενος· ὅθεν καὶ τὴν τῶν ζῴων ὀνομασίαν προφητικῶς ὡς δούλων αὐτῷ δοθέντων δεσποτικῶς ἐποιήσατο. Κατ᾽ εἰκόνα γὰρ θεοῦ λογικός τε καὶ νοερὸς καὶ αὐτεξούσιος γενόμενος εἰκότως τὴν τῶν ἐπιγείων ἀρχὴν ἐνεχειρίζετο ὑπὸ τοῦ κοινοῦ τῶν ἀπάντων δημιουργοῦ τε καὶ δεσπότου.

Εἰδὼς δὲ ὁ προγνώστης θεός, ὡς ἐν παραβάσει γενήσεται καὶ τῇ φθορᾷ ὑποπεσεῖται, ἐποίησεν ἐξ αὐτοῦ τὸ θῆλυ, «βοηθὸν

44   *On foreknowledge and predestination*

One needs to know that although God has foreknowledge of all things, he does not predetermine all things, for he has foreknowledge of what depends upon us, but he does not predetermine it. For he does not will that evil should come about, but neither does he compel virtue. Thus predetermination is a work of the command of God's foreknowledge. He predetermines the things that do not depend on us in accordance with his foreknowledge. For God has already pre-judged all things in accordance with his goodness and justice.

One also needs to know that virtue is a gift from God implanted in our nature, and he himself is the principle and cause of every good, and without his cooperation and help it is impossible for us to will it or to put it into practice, whereas it depends on us whether we persevere in virtue and follow God, who calls us to it, or whether we turn away from virtue, which is to fall into evil and follow the devil, who calls us to it without forcing us. For evil is nothing other than a privation of good, just as darkness is a privation of light. Therefore by persevering in what is according to nature we are in a state of virtue, but by turning away from what is according to nature we arrive at a state contrary to nature and fall into evil.

Repentance is a return from what is contrary to nature to what is according to nature, a return from the devil to God, through ascetic struggle and toil.

This human being, then, God fashioned as male, giving him a share of his own divine grace, and through this grace putting him in communion with himself. It was thus that with the authority of a master he gave names to the animals in the style of a prophet, as if they were slaves given to him. For since he had been made rational, intelligent, and in possession of free will, in the image of God, it was appropriate that he should be entrusted with authority over the creatures of the earth by the common Creator and master of all.

But since God in his foreknowledge knew that he would enter into transgression and become subject to decay, he made the female

αὐτῷ κατ' αὐτόν», βοηθὸν δὲ πρὸς τὴν διὰ γεννήσεως μετὰ τὴν παράβασιν τοῦ γένους ἐκ διαδοχῆς σύστασιν. Ἡ γὰρ πρώτη πλάσις γένεσις λέγεται καὶ οὐ γέννησις· γένεσις μὲν γάρ ἐστιν ἡ ἐκ θεοῦ πρώτη πλάσις, γέννησις δὲ ἡ ἐκ καταδίκης τοῦ θανάτου διὰ τὴν παράβασιν ἐξ ἀλλήλων διαδοχή.

Τοῦτον ἔθετο ἐν τῷ παραδείσῳ τῷ τε νοητῷ καὶ τῷ αἰσθητῷ· ἐν μὲν γὰρ τῷ αἰσθητῷ ἐπὶ γῆς σωματικῶς διαιτώμενος ψυχικῶς τοῖς ἀγγέλοις συνανεστρέφετο θείας γεωργῶν ἐννοίας καὶ ταύταις τρεφόμενος, γυμνὸς τῇ ἁπλότητι καὶ ἀτέχνῳ ζωῇ πρὸς μόνον τὸν δημιουργὸν διὰ τῶν κτισμάτων ἐναγόμενος καὶ τῇ αὐτοῦ θεωρίᾳ ἐνηδυνόμενός τε καὶ εὐφραινόμενος.

Ἐπειδὴ τοίνυν αὐτὸν αὐτεξουσίῳ θελήματι φυσικῶς κατεκόσμησε, δίδωσι νόμον αὐτῷ μὴ γεύσασθαι τοῦ ξύλου τῆς γνώσεως. Περὶ οὗ ξύλου αὐταρκῶς ἐν τῷ περὶ παραδείσου κεφαλαίῳ κατά γε τὴν ἡμετέραν εἰρήκαμεν δύναμιν. Ταύτην τὴν ἐντολὴν αὐτῷ δίδωσιν ἐπαγγειλάμενος, ὡς, εἰ μὲν φυλάξοι τὸ τῆς ψυχῆς ἀξίωμα τῷ λόγῳ τὴν νίκην διδούς, ἐπιγινώσκων τὸν κτίσαντα καὶ τούτου φυλάττων τὸ πρόσταγμα, τῆς ἀιδίου μεθέξει μακαριότητος καὶ ζήσεται εἰς τὸν αἰῶνα κρείττων θανάτου γενόμενος. Εἰ δέ γε τὴν ψυχὴν ὑποτάξει τῷ σώματι καὶ τὰ τοῦ σώματος προτιμήσει τερπνὰ τὴν οἰκείαν τιμὴν ἀγνοήσας καὶ τοῖς ἀνοήτοις παρεικασθεὶς κτήνεσι, τοῦ πεποιηκότος τὴν ζεύγλην ἀποσεισάμενος καὶ τὸ θεῖον αὐτοῦ παριδὼν ἐπίταγμα, θανάτῳ ἔσται ὑπεύθυνος καὶ φθορᾷ καὶ πόνῳ καθυποβληθήσεται τὸν ταλαίπωρον ἕλκων βίον. Οὐ γὰρ ἦν λυσιτελὲς ἀπείραστον ἔτι τυγχάνοντα καὶ ἀδόκιμον τῆς ἀφθαρσίας τυχεῖν, ἵνα μὴ εἰς τῦφον ἐμπέσῃ καὶ κρῖμα τοῦ διαβόλου. Ἐκεῖνος διὰ τὸ ἄφθαρτον μετὰ τὴν ἐκ προαιρέσεως ἔκπτωσιν τὴν ἐν τῷ κακῷ ἀμεταμέλητον

---

[1]Gen 2.19.

[2]John accepts the view, well established by his own time, that although human procreation was one of the consequences of the Fall, the division of the sexes had been providentially arranged by God from the beginning in his foreknowledge of

from him, a "helper of his own kind,"[1] a helper for the maintenance of the race by succession through the process of childbirth after the transgression.[2] For the original formation is called creation (γένεσις, *genesis*) not generation (γέννησις, *gennēsis*). For creation is the original formation by God, whereas generation is the succession from one to another that has resulted from the sentence of death incurred by the transgression.

This man was set by God in the Paradise that was both intelligible and sensible. For while he was living corporeally on earth in the sensible Paradise, spiritually he kept company with the angels, cultivating divine thoughts and being nourished by them, naked in simplicity and in the artlessness of his life, raised up to God alone through his creatures and finding pleasure and delight in the contemplation of him.

Furthermore, since he had endowed him naturally with free will, he gave him a law not to taste of the tree of knowledge. We have spoken of this tree sufficiently, to the best of our ability, in the chapter on Paradise. He gave him this injunction with the promise that if he should preserve the dignity of his soul by giving victory to reason, knowing the Creator and keeping his commandment, he would share in eternal beatitude and live forever, having become stronger than death. But if, on the other hand, he should subordinate the soul to the body and prefer the pleasures of the body, and ignoring his own dignity make himself like the senseless beasts,[3] and shake off the yoke of his maker and neglect his divine ordinance, he would be liable to death and corruption and would be assigned to dragging out his wretched existence in toil. For it was not to his advantage, since he was still inexperienced and untested, to arrive at incorruption, for fear he should fall into pride and incur the judgement of the devil. For after his freely chosen fall the latter became irrevocably fixed in evil and acquired an immutable steadfastness

the transgression. On this topic, see Bradshaw, "Sexual Difference and the Difference It Makes."

[3]Cf. Ps 48.13, 21.

ἔσχε καὶ ἄτρεπτον παγιότητα ὥσπερ αὖ πάλιν καὶ οἱ ἄγγελοι μετὰ
τὴν ἐκ προαιρέσεως τῆς ἀρετῆς ἐκλογὴν τὴν ἐν τῷ καλῷ διὰ τῆς
χάριτος ἀμετακίνητον ἵδρυσιν.

Ἔδει τοίνυν πρότερον δοκιμασθέντα τὸν ἄνθρωπον καὶ τῇ
πείρᾳ διὰ τῆς τηρήσεως τῆς ἐντολῆς τελειωθέντα οὕτω τὴν
ἀφθαρσίαν ἀρετῆς κομίσασθαι ἔπαθλον· μέσος γὰρ θεοῦ καὶ
ὕλης γενόμενος διὰ μὲν τῆς τηρήσεως τῆς ἐντολῆς μετὰ τὴν
ἀπαλλαγὴν τῆς πρὸς τὰ ὄντα φυσικῆς σχέσεως ἑνωθεὶς τῷ θεῷ
καθ᾽ ἕξιν τὴν περὶ τὸ καλὸν παγιότητα λαμβάνειν ἀμετακίνητον
ἔμελλε, διὰ δὲ τῆς παραβάσεως πρὸς τὴν ὕλην μᾶλλον κινηθεὶς
καὶ τῆς αὐτοῦ αἰτίας, τοῦ θεοῦ φημι, ἀποσπάσας τὸν νοῦν τῇ
φθορᾷ προσοικειοῦσθαι· καὶ παθητὸς ἀντὶ ἀπαθοῦς καὶ θνητὸς
ἀντὶ ἀθανάτου γίνεσθαι καὶ συνδυασμοῦ καὶ ῥευστῆς γεννήσεως
ἐπιδέεσθαι καὶ τῇ ἐφέσει τῆς ζωῆς τῶν μὲν ἡδέων ὡς δῆθεν ταύτην
συνιστώντων ἀντέχεσθαι, πρὸς δὲ τοὺς τούτων προμηθουμένους
τὴν στέρησιν ἀδεῶς ἀπεχθάνεσθαι καὶ τὴν μὲν ἔφεσιν ἐκ θεοῦ
πρὸς τὴν ὕλην, τὸν δὲ θυμὸν ἐκ τοῦ τῆς σωτηρίας ὄντως ἐχθροῦ
μεταφέρειν πρὸς τὸ ὁμόφυλον. Φθόνῳ τοίνυν διαβόλου ἡττήθη
ὁ ἄνθρωπος· οὐ γὰρ ἔφερεν ὁ φθονερὸς καὶ μισόκαλος δαίμων
αὐτὸς διὰ τὴν ἔπαρσιν κάτω γενόμενος ἡμᾶς τῶν ἄνω τυχεῖν,
ὅθεν καὶ θεότητος ἐλπίδι ὁ ψεύστης δελεάζει τὸν ἄθλιον καὶ πρὸς
τὸ ἴδιον τῆς ἐπάρσεως ὕψος ἀναγαγὼν πρὸς τὸ ὅμοιον καταφέρει
τῆς πτώσεως βάραθρον.

on account of his incorruptibility, just as conversely, after their free choice of virtue, the angels acquired an immovable stability in good as a result of grace.

It was therefore necessary for man to be first tested, and once he had been perfected by the trial through keeping the injunction, to win in this way the prize for virtue, which is incorruption. For since he had been brought into being half way between God and matter, it was intended that after having been delivered from his natural relationship with material things through keeping the injunction and been united with God as a habitual state, he was to receive an irrevocable steadfastness with regard to the good. But since through the transgression he moved instead towards matter, and detached his mind from its cause—I mean God—he was to assimilate himself to corruption and become passible rather than impassible, mortal rather than immortal, and in need of sexual relations and transient generation and through the desire for life cling to the pleasures as supposedly constituting life, but hate those unrestrainedly who would deprive them of these pleasures, and transfer his desire from God to matter and his anger from the true enemy of salvation to his fellow human beings. Man was therefore defeated "by the envy of the devil."[4] For that envious demon, that hater of the good, once he had been brought low by his conceit, could not bear to see us attain to higher things. Therefore the liar ensnared the wretched one with the hope of divinity,[5] and drawing him up to the same height of conceit as himself, dragged him down to an equal pit of humiliation.

---

[4]Wis 2.24. In the Greek patristic tradition, the emphasis given to demonic envy as the cause of the Fall tended to mitigate the weight of guilt incurred as a result. In the West the emphasis from the time of Augustine was rather on Adam's free decision to transgress, resulting in a personal guilt transmitted to subsequent generations.

[5]Cf. Gen 3.5. Deification (sharing in the life of God) was the goal of creation from the beginning. Eve's sin, followed by that of Adam, was essentially an attempt to seize this as a personal possession before the appointed time.

45   *Περὶ τῆς θείας οἰκονομίας καὶ περὶ τῆς δι' ἡμᾶς*
     κηδεμονίας καὶ τῆς ἡμῶν σωτηρίας

Ταύτῃ τοίνυν τῇ προσβολῇ τοῦ ἀρχεκάκου δαίμονος δελεασθέντα
τὸν ἄνθρωπον καὶ τὴν τοῦ δημιουργοῦ ἐντολὴν οὐ φυλάξαντα
καὶ γυμνωθέντα τῆς χάριτος καὶ τὴν πρὸς θεὸν παρρησίαν
ἀπεκδυσάμενον καὶ σκεπασθέντα τῇ τοῦ μοχθηροῦ βίου
τραχύτητι (τοῦτο γὰρ τὰ φύλλα τῆς συκῆς) καὶ περιβληθέντα τὴν
νέκρωσιν ἤτοι τὴν θνητότητα καὶ παχύτητα τῆς σαρκός (τοῦτο
γὰρ ἡ τῶν νεκρῶν δερμάτων ἀμφίασις) καὶ τοῦ παραδείσου κατὰ
τὴν τοῦ θεοῦ δικαιοκρισίαν γεγονότα ἐξόριστον καὶ θανάτῳ
κατάκριτον καὶ φθορᾷ ὑποχείριον οὐ παρεῖδεν ὁ συμπαθὴς ὁ
τὸ εἶναι δοὺς καὶ τὸ εὖ εἶναι χαρισάμενος, ἀλλὰ πολλοῖς
πρότερον παιδαγωγήσας καὶ πρὸς ἐπιστροφὴν καλέσας στόνῳ
καὶ τρόμῳ, ὕδατος κατακλυσμῷ καὶ παντὸς τοῦ γένους μικροῦ
δεῖν πανωλεθρίᾳ, συγχύσει καὶ διαιρέσει γλωσσῶν, ἀγγέλων
ἐπιστασίᾳ, πόλεων ἐμπρησμῷ, τυπικαῖς θεοφανείαις, πολέμοις,
νίκαις, ἥτταις, σημείοις καὶ τέρασι καὶ ποικίλαις δυνάμεσι, νόμῳ,
προφήταις, δι' ὧν τὸ σπουδαζόμενον ἦν ἡ τῆς ἁμαρτίας ἀναίρεσις
πολυσχεδῶς χεθείσης καὶ καταδουλωσαμένης τὸν ἄνθρωπον
καὶ πᾶν εἶδος κακίας ἐπισωρευσάσης τῷ βίῳ καὶ ἡ πρὸς τὸ εὖ
εἶναι τοῦ ἀνθρώπου ἐπάνοδος. Ἐπειδὴ δι' ἁμαρτίας ὁ θάνατος
εἰς τὸν κόσμον εἰσῆλθεν ὥσπερ τι θηρίον ἄγριον καὶ ἀνήμερον
τὸν ἀνθρώπινον λυμαινόμενος βίον, ἔδει δὲ τὸν λυτροῦσθαι
μέλλοντα ἀναμάρτητον εἶναι καὶ μὴ τῷ θανάτῳ διὰ τῆς ἁμαρτίας
ὑπεύθυνον, ἔτι δὲ νευρωθῆναι καὶ ἀνακαινισθῆναι τὴν φύσιν
καὶ ἔργῳ παιδαγωγηθῆναι καὶ διδαχθῆναι ἀρετῆς ὁδὸν τῆς μὲν

---

[1] For a discussion of John's teaching on the divine economy, see Louth, *St John Damascene*, 144–79.

[2] God's making "leather tunics" (χιτῶνας δερματίνους, *chitōnas dermatinous*) for Adam and Eve (Gen 3.21) had been interpreted by Philo (*Quaest. in Gen.* I, 55) as the creation of physical bodies—in effect a second phase of creation subsequent to the Fall. This was taken up by Origen (*Selecta in Genesim*, PG 12:101AB) as a possible spiritual interpretation but was not well received in later exegesis, except possibly by Gregory of Nyssa (cf. *On the Making of Man* 17.4, PG 44:189D). The more usual

45   On the divine economy, and on God's care for us and our salvation[1]

And so man was ensnared by the assault of the demon, the author of evil, and did not keep the Creator's commandment, and was stripped of grace, and deprived of the free access he had to God, and was covered with the roughness of a life of toil (for that is the meaning of the fig leaves), and was clothed with perishability, that is to say, with mortality and the coarseness of the flesh (for that is the meaning of the garments of dead skins),[2] and was exiled from Paradise in accordance with God's just judgement and was condemned to death and made subject to corruption. Yet the compassionate giver of being and bestower of well-being did not abandon him, but at first educated him in many ways and called on him to return in groaning and trembling, by a deluge of water and near destruction of the whole race, by a confusion and division of tongues, by angelic visitation, by a wholesale burning of cities, by theophanies in symbolic form, by wars, victories, defeats, signs and wonders, and various acts of power, by the law and the prophets, the deliberate purpose of which was the eradication of sin, which had become diffused in many ways and had enslaved humanity and heaped up every kind of evil on human life, and the return of humanity to well-being. Since it was through sin that death came into the world like a ferocious wild animal to ravage human life, it was necessary that the humanity that was to be redeemed should be sinless and not subject to death through sin,[3] and moreover that it should be strengthened and renewed in its nature and guided in deed and taught the way of virtue that leads away from corruption and towards eternal life. Finally, it is shown the great sea of God's

opinion was that of John Chrysostom (*Homilies on Genesis* 18.1, PG 53:149), who saw the garments of skin as a sign of God's providence and compassion in the altered conditions after the Fall. For the history of the exegesis of Genesis 3.21 see *The Brill Dictionary of Gregory of Nyssa*, edited by L. F. Mateo-Seco and G. Maspero (Leiden: Brill, 2010), 768–70, and for a theological discussion of the text, Panayiotis Nellas, *Deification in Christ: The Nature of the Human Person* (Crestwood, NY: St Vladimir's Seminary Press, 1987), 43–91.

[3]Cf. Rom 5.12–19.

φθορᾶς ἀπάγουσαν, πρὸς δὲ τὴν ζωὴν ποδηγοῦσαν τὴν αἰώνιον· τέλος τὸ μέγα περὶ αὐτὸν τῆς φιλανθρωπίας ἐνδείκνυται πέλαγος· αὐτὸς γὰρ ὁ δημιουργός τε καὶ κύριος τὴν ὑπὲρ τοῦ οἰκείου πλάσματος ἀναδέχεται πάλην καὶ ἔργῳ διδάσκαλος γίνεται· καὶ ἐπειδὴ θεότητος ἐλπίδι ὁ ἐχθρὸς δελεάζει τὸν ἄνθρωπον, σαρκὸς προβλήματι δελεάζεται καὶ δείκνυται ἅμα τὸ ἀγαθὸν καὶ τὸ σοφόν, τὸ δίκαιόν τε καὶ τὸ δυνατὸν τοῦ θεοῦ· τὸ μὲν ἀγαθόν, ὅτι οὐ παρεῖδε τοῦ οἰκείου πλάσματος τὴν ἀσθένειαν, ἀλλ᾽ ἐσπλαγχνίσθη ἐπ᾽ αὐτῷ πεσόντι καὶ χεῖρα ὤρεξε· τὸ δίκαιον, ὅτι ἀνθρώπου ἡττηθέντος οὐχ ἕτερον ποιεῖ νικῆσαι τὸν τύραννον οὐδὲ βίᾳ ἐξαρπάζει τοῦ θανάτου τὸν ἄνθρωπον, ἀλλ᾽ ὃν πάλαι διὰ τῆς ἁμαρτίας καταδουλοῦται ὁ θάνατος, τοῦτον ὁ ἀγαθὸς καὶ δίκαιος νικητὴν πάλιν πεποίηκε καὶ τῷ ὁμοίῳ τὸν ὅμοιον ἀνεσώσατο, ὅπερ ἄπορον ἦν· τὸ δὲ σοφόν, ὅτι εὗρε τοῦ ἀπόρου λύσιν εὐπρεπεστάτην· εὐδοκίᾳ γὰρ τοῦ θεοῦ καὶ πατρὸς ὁ μονογενὴς υἱὸς καὶ λόγος τοῦ θεοῦ καὶ θεὸς ὁ ὢν εἰς τὸν κόλπον τοῦ πατρός, ὁ ὁμοούσιος τῷ πατρὶ καὶ τῷ ἁγίῳ πνεύματι, ὁ προαιώνιος, ὁ ἄναρχος, ὁ ἐν ἀρχῇ ὢν καὶ πρὸς τὸν θεὸν καὶ πατέρα ὢν καὶ θεὸς ὤν, ὁ ἐν μορφῇ θεοῦ ὑπάρχων κλίνας οὐρανοὺς κατέρχεται, τουτέστιν τὸ ἀταπείνωτον αὐτοῦ ὕψος ἀταπεινώτως ταπεινώσας συγκαταβαίνει τοῖς ἑαυτοῦ δούλοις συγκατάβασιν ἄφραστόν τε καὶ ἀκατάληπτον (τοῦτο γὰρ δηλοῖ ἡ κατάβασις) καὶ θεὸς ὢν τέλειος ἄνθρωπος τέλειος γίνεται καὶ ἐπιτελεῖται τὸ πάντων καινῶν καινότατον, τὸ μόνον καινὸν ὑπὸ τὸν ἥλιον, δι᾽ οὗ ἡ ἄπειρος τοῦ θεοῦ ἐμφανίζεται δύναμις. Τί γὰρ μεῖζον τοῦ γενέσθαι τὸν θεὸν ἄνθρωπον; Καὶ ὁ λόγος σὰρξ ἀτρέπτως ἐγένετο ἐκ πνεύματος ἁγίου καὶ Μαρίας τῆς ἁγίας ἀειπαρθένου καὶ θεοτόκου καὶ μεσίτης θεοῦ καὶ ἀνθρώπων χρηματίζει ὁ μόνος φιλάνθρωπος, οὐκ ἐκ θελήματος ἢ ἐπιθυμίας ἢ συναφείας ἀνδρὸς ἢ γεννήσεως ἐνηδόνου ἐν τῇ ἀχράντῳ μήτρᾳ τῆς παρθένου συλληφθείς, ἀλλ᾽ ἐκ πνεύματος ἁγίου καὶ τῆς πρώτης τοῦ Ἀδὰμ γενέσεως· καὶ γίνεται ὑπήκοος τῷ πατρὶ τῷ καθ᾽ ἡμᾶς καὶ ἐξ ἡμῶν προσλήμματι τὴν ἡμετέραν παρακοὴν

benevolent love that surrounds it, for the Creator and Lord himself
takes up the struggle for his own creation and becomes its teacher
in deed. And seeing that the adversary ensnares man by the hope of
divinity, he is ensnared himself by the screen of the flesh[4] and reveals
at the same time the goodness and wisdom, the justice and power, of
God: goodness, because he did not overlook the weakness of his own
creature but had compassion on him when he fell and extended his
hand to him; justice, because when man suffered defeat, he did not
make another victorious over the tyrant nor did he snatch man from
death by force, but he who is good and just made him, whom death
had formerly enslaved through sin again victorious, and restored like
through like, which was difficult; wisdom, because he found the most
appropriate solution to the problem, for by the good pleasure of God
the Father, the only-begotten Son and Word of God and God, "who
is in the bosom of the Father," who is consubstantial with the Father
and the Holy Spirit, who is before the ages, who is eternal, who is
"in the beginning" and is "with God" the Father and "is God," who
"being in the form of God" "bent down the heavens and descends,"
that is to say, humbling his most unabased sublimity without humiliation, he condescends to his own servants with an inexpressible and
incomprehensible condescension (for that is what descent signifies)
and being perfect God he becomes perfect man and accomplishes the
newest of all new things, the only "new thing under the sun," by which
the infinite power of God becomes apparent.[5] For what is greater than
God becoming man? And the Word became flesh, without incurring
change, from the Holy Spirit and Mary, the holy Ever-Virgin and Theotokos, and the only lover of mankind is called a mediator between
God and humanity, conceived in the immaculate womb of the Virgin
not by the will or desire of a man or by sexual union or pleasurable
engendering, but from the Holy Spirit and the first creation of Adam.
And he becomes obedient to the Father in that addition which is our
own and has been received from us, and heals our disobedience and

[4]Cf. Gregory of Nyssa, *Catechetical Discourse* 26.4 (PG 45:68CD; Green, 119).
[5]Cf. Jn 1.18; Jn 1.1; Phil 2.6; Ps 17.10; Eccl 1.9 (etc.).

ἰώμενος καὶ ὑπογραμμὸς ἡμῖν ὑπακοῆς γινόμενος, ἧς ἐκτὸς οὐκ
ἔστι σωτηρίας τυχεῖν.

46 *Περὶ τοῦ τρόπου τῆς συλλήψεως τοῦ θεοῦ λόγου καὶ τῆς
θείας αὐτοῦ σαρκώσεως*

Ἄγγελος γὰρ κυρίου ἀπεστάλη πρὸς τὴν ἁγίαν παρθένον ἐκ
δαυιτικοῦ φύλου καταγομένην· «πρόδηλον γὰρ ὡς ἐξ Ἰούδα
ἀνατέταλκεν ὁ κύριος», «ἐξ ἧς φυλῆς οὐδεὶς προσέσχηκε τῷ
θυσιαστηρίῳ», ὡς ὁ θεῖος ἔφη ἀπόστολος· περὶ οὗ ὕστερον ἐροῦμεν
ἀκριβέστερον. Ἦν εὐαγγελιζόμενος ἔλεγε· «Χαῖρε, κεχαριτωμένη,
ὁ κύριος μετὰ σοῦ. Ἡ δὲ διεταράχθη ἐπὶ τῷ λόγῳ» καί φησι πρὸς
αὐτὴν ὁ ἄγγελος· «Μὴ φοβοῦ, Μαριάμ· εὗρες γὰρ χάριν παρὰ
κυρίῳ καὶ τέξῃ υἱὸν καὶ καλέσεις τὸ ὄνομα αὐτοῦ Ἰησοῦν. Αὐτὸς
γὰρ σώσει τὸν λαὸν αὐτοῦ ἀπὸ τῶν ἁμαρτιῶν αὐτῶν.» Ὅθεν τὸ
«Ἰησοῦς» σωτὴρ ἑρμηνεύεται. Τῆς δὲ διαπορούσης·

«Πῶς ἔσται μοι τοῦτο, ἐπεὶ ἄνδρα οὐ γινώσκω;» Πάλιν φησὶ
πρὸς αὐτὴν ὁ ἄγγελος· «Πνεῦμα ἅγιον ἐπελεύσεται ἐπὶ σέ, καὶ
δύναμις ὑψίστου ἐπισκιάσει σοι. Διὸ καὶ τὸ γεννώμενον ἅγιον
κληθήσεται υἱὸς θεοῦ». Ἡ δὲ πρὸς αὐτόν· «Ἰδοὺ ἡ δούλη κυρίου·
γένοιτό μοι κατὰ τὸ ῥῆμά σου».

Μετὰ οὖν τὴν συγκατάθεσιν τῆς ἁγίας παρθένου πνεῦμα
ἅγιον ἐπῆλθεν ἐπ᾽ αὐτὴν κατὰ τὸν τοῦ κυρίου λόγον, ὃν εἶπεν ὁ
ἄγγελος, καθαῖρον αὐτὴν καὶ δύναμιν δεκτικὴν τῆς τοῦ λόγου
θεότητος παρέχον, ἅμα δὲ καὶ γεννητικήν. Καὶ τότε ἐπεσκίασεν ἐπ᾽
αὐτὴν ἡ τοῦ θεοῦ τοῦ ὑψίστου ἐνυπόστατος σοφία καὶ δύναμις,
ὁ υἱὸς τοῦ θεοῦ ὁ τῷ πατρὶ ὁμοούσιος, οἱονεὶ θεῖος σπόρος
καὶ συνέπηξεν ἑαυτῷ ἐκ τῶν ἁγνῶν καὶ καθαρωτάτων αὐτῆς
αἱμάτων σάρκα ἐψυχωμένην ψυχῇ λογικῇ τε καὶ νοερᾷ, ἀπαρχὴν
τοῦ ἡμετέρου φυράματος, οὐ σπερματικῶς ἀλλὰ δημιουργικῶς

becomes an example to us of obedience, without which it is not possible to attain salvation.

46   *On the manner of the conception of God the Word and on his divine incarnation*

For an angel of the Lord was sent to the holy Virgin descended from the tribe of David. "For it is evident that the Lord was of the line of Judah,"[1] "from which no one has ever served at the altar,"[2] as the divine Apostle said. We shall speak of this in more detail later. Bringing good tidings, the angel said: "Hail, O full of grace! The Lord is with you. She was startled by this address," and the angel said to her: "Do not be afraid, Mary, for you have found favor with God and you will bear a son and call his name Jesus. He will save his people from their sins." For that reason "Jesus" is interpreted as "savior." But she was perplexed. "How will this happen to me, since I have no knowledge of a man?" Again, the angel said to her: "The Holy Spirit will come upon you, and the power of the Most High will overshadow you. Therefore the child to be born will be called Son of God." She said to him: "Behold, the handmaid of the Lord; let it be to me according to your word."[3]

And so, after the consent of the holy Virgin, the Holy Spirit came upon her in accordance with the Lord's word, which the angel spoke to her, purifying her and granting her the power to receive the divinity of the Word and at the same time to give birth to it. It was then that the enhypostatic wisdom and power of the Most High God overshadowed her, the Son of God who is consubstantial with the Father, like a divine sowing, and from her chaste and most pure blood formed for himself flesh ensouled with a rational and intelligent soul, the firstfruit of our human substance,[4] not from semen but by a creative act

[1]Heb 7.14.   [2]Heb 7.13.   [3]Lk 1.28–38.
[4]The word translated here as "human substance" is φύραμα (*phyrama*), the basic meaning of which, according to Lampe (s.v.), is "paste" or "an undifferentiated mass" like potter's clay. It comes to be used metaphorically for the human substance from the early fourth century.

διὰ τοῦ ἁγίου πνεύματος, οὐ ταῖς κατὰ μικρὸν προσθήκαις
ἀπαρτιζομένου τοῦ σχήματος, ἀλλ᾽ ὑφ᾽ ἓν τελειωθέντος. Αὐτὸς
ὁ τοῦ θεοῦ λόγος χρηματίσας τῇ σαρκὶ ὑπόστασις· οὐ γὰρ
προϋποστάσῃ καθ᾽ ἑαυτὴν σαρκὶ ἡνώθη ὁ θεὸς λόγος, ἀλλ᾽
ἐνοικήσας τῇ γαστρὶ τῆς ἁγίας παρθένου ἀπεριγράπτως ἐν τῇ
ἑαυτοῦ ὑποστάσει ἐκ τῶν ἁγνῶν τῆς παρθένου αἱμάτων σάρκα
ἐψυχωμένην ψυχῇ λογικῇ τε καὶ νοερᾷ ὑπεστήσατο ἀπαρχὴν
προσλαβόμενος τοῦ ἀνθρωπίνου φυράματος, αὐτὸς ὁ λόγος
γενόμενος τῇ σαρκὶ ὑπόστασις. Ὥστε ἅμα σάρξ, ἅμα θεοῦ
λόγου σάρξ, ἅμα σὰρξ ἔμψυχος λογική τε καὶ νοερά, ἅμα θεοῦ
λόγου σὰρξ ἔμψυχος λογική τε καὶ νοερά. Διὸ οὐκ ἄνθρωπον
ἀποθεωθέντα λέγομεν, ἀλλὰ θεὸν ἐνανθρωπήσαντα· ὢν γὰρ
φύσει τέλειος θεὸς γέγονε φύσει τέλειος ἄνθρωπος ὁ αὐτὸς οὐ
τραπεὶς τὴν φύσιν οὐδὲ φαντάσας τὴν οἰκονομίαν, ἀλλὰ τῇ ἐκ
τῆς ἁγίας παρθένου ληφθείσῃ λογικῶς τε καὶ νοερῶς ἐψυχωμένῃ
σαρκὶ καὶ ἐν αὐτῷ τὸ εἶναι λαχούσῃ ἑνωθεὶς καθ᾽ ὑπόστασιν
ἀσυγχύτως καὶ ἀναλλοιώτως καὶ ἀδιαιρέτως, μὴ μεταβαλὼν τὴν
τῆς θεότητος αὐτοῦ φύσιν εἰς τὴν τῆς σαρκὸς οὐσίαν μήτε μὴν
τὴν οὐσίαν τῆς σαρκὸς αὐτοῦ εἰς τὴν φύσιν τῆς αὐτοῦ θεότητος
οὐδὲ ἐκ τῆς θείας αὐτοῦ φύσεως καί, ἧς προσελάβετο ἀνθρωπίνης
φύσεως, μίαν φύσιν ἀποτελέσας σύνθετον.

47   Περὶ τῶν δύο φύσεων

Ἀτρέπτως γὰρ καὶ ἀναλλοιώτως ἡνώθησαν ἀλλήλαις αἱ φύσεις
μήτε τῆς θείας φύσεως ἐκστάσης τῆς οἰκείας ἁπλότητος μήτε μὴν
τῆς ἀνθρωπίνης ἢ τραπείσης εἰς θεότητος φύσιν ἢ εἰς ἀνυπαρξίαν

---

[5]John has borrowed this locution from Ps.-Chrysostom's *Homily on Psalm 76.4*,
"*I remembered God and rejoiced*" (PG 61:697). The Greek neatly balances the phrases:
οὐκ ἄνθρωπον ἀποθεωθέντα ... ἀλλὰ θεὸν ἐνανθρωπήσαντα (*ouk anthrōpon
apotheōthenta ... alla theon enanthrōpēsanta*).

[1]Kotter draws attention to the closeness of the whole of this chapter to Maximus

through the Holy Spirit, the form not being completed by small increments but perfected in a single operation. The Word of God himself is reckoned the hypostasis with regard to the flesh, for God the Word was not united to flesh that already existed in itself, but came to dwell in the womb of the holy Virgin without being circumscribed in his own hypostasis, and gave substance to flesh from the chaste blood of the Virgin, flesh that was ensouled with a rational and intelligent soul, and, assuming what is representative of the human substance, the Word himself became the hypostasis with regard to the flesh. As a result, he was at the same time flesh, at the same time flesh of God the Word, at the same time rational and intelligent ensouled flesh, at the same time rational and intelligent ensouled flesh of God the Word. Therefore we do not speak of a human being who has been deified but of God who has been inhominated.[5] For being by nature perfect God, he became by nature perfect man, the same not changing his nature or creating an illusion of the dispensation [of the incarnation], but united hypostatically without confusion, change, or division with the rationally and intelligently ensouled flesh assumed from the holy Virgin and possessing its being in him, neither transforming the nature of his Godhead into the substance of the flesh, nor the substance of his flesh into the nature of the Godhead, and not producing a single composite nature out of his divine nature and the human nature that he assumed.

47   *On the two natures*[1]

For the natures were united with each other without change and without alteration. Neither did the divine nature abandon the simplicity proper to it, nor indeed did the human nature either change into the divine nature or end up in non-existence, nor was a single

the Confessor's Christological treatise addressed to John Cubicularius (*Letter* 12, PG 91:460A–509B), although John does not reproduce any of Maximus' text. On the relationship of John's Christology to that of Leontius of Byzantium and Maximus the Confessor, see Brian E. Daley, SJ, *God Visible: Patristic Christology Reconsidered* (Oxford: Oxford University Press, 2018), 200–31.

χωρησάσης μήτε ἐκ τῶν δύο μιᾶς γεγενημένης συνθέτου φύσεως· ἡ γὰρ σύνθετος φύσις οὐδ᾽ ὁποτέρας τῶν, ἐξ ὧν συνετέθη, φύσεων ὁμοούσιος ὑπάρχειν δύναται ἐξ ἑτέρων ἀποτελεσθεῖσα ἕτερον. Οἷον τὸ σῶμα τὸ ἐκ τῶν τεσσάρων στοιχείων συντεθειμένον οὐδὲ τῷ πυρὶ λέγεται ὁμοούσιον οὔτε πῦρ ὀνομάζεται οὔτε ἀὴρ λέγεται οὔτε ὕδωρ οὔτε γῆ οὐδέ τινι τούτων ἐστὶν ὁμοούσιον. Εἰ τοίνυν κατὰ τοὺς αἱρετικοὺς μιᾶς συνθέτου φύσεως ὁ Χριστὸς μετὰ τὴν ἕνωσιν ἐχρημάτισεν, ἐξ ἁπλῆς φύσεως ἐτράπη εἰς σύνθεσιν καὶ οὔτε τῷ πατρὶ ἁπλῆς φύσεως ὄντι ἐστὶν ὁμοούσιος οὔτε τῇ μητρί (οὐ γὰρ ἐκ θεότητος καὶ ἀνθρωπότητος αὕτη συντέθειται) οὔτε μὴν ἐν θεότητί ἐστι καὶ ἀνθρωπότητι, οὔτε δὲ θεὸς ὀνομασθήσεται οὐδὲ ἄνθρωπος, ἀλλὰ Χριστὸς μόνον. Καὶ ἔσται τὸ Χριστὸς οὐ τῆς ὑποστάσεως αὐτοῦ ὄνομα, ἀλλὰ τῆς μιᾶς κατ᾽ αὐτοὺς φύσεως.

Ἡμεῖς δὲ οὐ μιᾶς συνθέτου φύσεως τὸν Χριστὸν δογματίζομεν οὐδὲ ἐξ ἑτέρων ἕτερον ὥσπερ ἐκ ψυχῆς καὶ σώματος ἄνθρωπον ἢ ὡς ἐκ τεσσάρων στοιχείων σῶμα, ἀλλ᾽ ἐξ ἑτέρων τὰ αὐτά· ἐκ θεότητος μὲν γὰρ καὶ ἀνθρωπότητος θεὸν τέλειον καὶ ἄνθρωπον τέλειον τὸν αὐτὸν καὶ εἶναι καὶ λέγεσθαι ἐκ δύο τε καὶ ἐν δυσὶ φύσεσιν ὁμολογοῦμεν. Τὸ δὲ Χριστὸς ὄνομα τῆς ὑποστάσεως λέγομεν, οὐ μονοτρόπως λεγόμενον, ἀλλὰ τῶν δύο φύσεων ὑπάρχον σημαντικόν· αὐτὸς γὰρ ἑαυτὸν ἔχρισε, χρίων μὲν ὡς θεὸς τὸ σῶμα τῇ θεότητι αὐτοῦ, χριόμενος δὲ ὡς ἄνθρωπος· αὐτὸς γάρ ἐστι τοῦτο κἀκεῖνο. Χρίσις δὲ ἡ θεότης τῆς ἀνθρωπότητος. Εἰ γὰρ μιᾶς φύσεως συνθέτου ὢν ὁ Χριστὸς ὁμοούσιός ἐστι τῷ πατρί, ἔσται ἄρα καὶ ὁ πατὴρ σύνθετος καὶ τῇ σαρκὶ ὁμοούσιος, ὅπερ ἄτοπον καὶ πάσης βλασφημίας ἀνάπλεον.

composite nature brought into being out of the two. For a composite nature cannot be consubstantial with either of the natures from which it has been composed, since it has resulted in something other out of different things. For example, the body, which has been constituted out of the four elements, is not said to be consubstantial with fire nor is it called fire, or air, or water, or earth, or said to be consubstantial with any of these. So if, according to the heretics, Christ formed one composite nature after the union, he was changed from a simple nature into a composite one and is consubstantial neither with the Father, who is of a simple nature, nor with his mother (for she herself is not composed of divinity and humanity), nor indeed is he in a state both of divinity and humanity, nor could he be called God or man, but only Christ. And Christ would not be the name of his hypostasis but, in their view, the name of the one nature.

But we do not teach that Christ is of a single composite nature, nor do we hold that he is something other formed from different things, like a human being formed from soul and body or like the body formed from the four elements, but he is from different things with the same persisting. For we confess that being from divinity and humanity the same is, and is said to be, perfect God and perfect man, from two and in two natures.[2] We say that "Christ" is the name of the hypostasis, not applying it only in one way but indicating that which exists of the two natures. For he anointed himself,[3] anointing the body by his divinity in that he is God, and being anointed in that he is man. For he is both the one and the other. The anointing is the divinity of the humanity. For since Christ is consubstantial with the Father, if he were of a single composite nature, the Father too would be composite and consubstantial with the flesh, which is absurd and the height of blasphemy.

[2]John combines Cyril of Alexandria's "from two" with the Council of Chalcedon's "in two." The neo-Chalcedonian argument against the Monophysites always insists on the identity of Chalcedon's Christology ("in two natures") with Cyril's ("from two natures").

[3]"Christ" (like "Messiah," which it translates) means the "anointed one."

Πῶς δὲ καὶ μία φύσις τῶν ἐναντίων οὐσιωδῶν διαφορῶν δεκτικὴ γενήσεται; Πῶς γὰρ δυνατὸν τὴν αὐτὴν φύσιν κατὰ ταὐτὸν κτιστὴν εἶναι καὶ ἄκτιστον, θνητὴν καὶ ἀθάνατον, περιγραπτὴν καὶ ἀπερίγραπτον; Εἰ δὲ καὶ μιᾶς λέγοντες τὸν Χριστὸν φύσεως ἁπλῆν ταύτην εἴποιεν, ἢ γυμνὸν αὐτὸν θεὸν ὁμολογήσουσι καὶ φαντασίαν εἰσάξουσιν τὴν ἐνανθρώπησιν ἢ ψιλὸν ἄνθρωπον κατὰ Νεστόριον. Καὶ ποῦ τὸ τέλειον ἐν θεότητι καὶ τὸ ἐν ἀνθρωπότητι τέλειον; Πότε δὲ καὶ δύο τὸν Χριστὸν λέξουσι φύσεων μιᾶς συνθέτου φύσεως αὐτὸν μετὰ τὴν ἕνωσιν λέγοντες; Ὅτι γὰρ μιᾶς ὁ Χριστὸς φύσεως πρὸ τῆς ἑνώσεως, παντί που δῆλον.

Ἀλλὰ τοῦτό ἐστι τὸ ποιοῦν τοῖς αἱρετικοῖς τὴν πλάνην, τὸ ταὐτὸν λέγειν τὴν φύσιν καὶ τὴν ὑπόστασιν. Ἐπειδὴ δὲ μίαν τῶν ἀνθρώπων φύσιν φαμέν, ἰστέον, ὡς οὐκ ἀφορῶντες εἰς τὸν τῆς ψυχῆς καὶ τοῦ σώματος λόγον τοῦτο λέγομεν· ἀδύνατον γὰρ μιᾶς φύσεως λέγειν τὴν ψυχὴν καὶ τὸ σῶμα πρὸς ἄλληλα συγκρινόμενα. Ἀλλ' ἐπειδὴ πλεῖσται ὑποστάσεις τῶν ἀνθρώπων εἰσί, πάντες δὲ τὸν αὐτὸν ἐπιδέχονται λόγον τῆς φύσεως (πάντες γὰρ ἐκ ψυχῆς εἰσι συντεθειμένοι καὶ σώματος καὶ πάντες τῆς φύσεως τῆς ψυχῆς μετειλήφασι καὶ τὴν οὐσίαν τοῦ σώματος κέκτηνται) τὸ κοινὸν εἶδος τῶν πλείστων καὶ διαφόρων ὑποστάσεων μίαν φύσιν φαμέν, ἑκάστης δηλαδὴ ὑποστάσεως δύο φύσεις ἐχούσης καὶ ἐν δυσὶ τελούσης ταῖς φύσεσι, ψυχῆς λέγω καὶ σώματος.

Ἐπὶ δὲ τοῦ κυρίου ἡμῶν Ἰησοῦ Χριστοῦ οὐκ ἔστι κοινὸν εἶδος λαβεῖν· οὔτε γὰρ ἐγένετο οὐδὲ ἔστιν οὔτε ποτὲ γενήσεται ἄλλος Χριστὸς ἐκ θεότητος καὶ ἀνθρωπότητος, ἐν θεότητι καὶ ἀνθρωπότητι θεὸς τέλειος ὁ αὐτὸς καὶ ἄνθρωπος τέλειος. Ἀλλὰ καὶ πάσης συνθέτου φύσεως τὰ μέρη ἅμα τὴν ἐκ τοῦ μὴ ὄντος εἰς τὸ εἶναι παραγωγὴν ἔσχηκε πρὸς συμπλήρωσιν τοῦ παντός. Καὶ δυνατὸν τὰ ὁμόχρονα μίαν φύσιν ἀποτελεῖν σύνθετον, τοιοῦτον ὅρον καὶ φυσικὸν

[4]Nestorius, patriarch of Constantinople from 428 until his deposition in 431, objected to the "natural union" (ἕνωσις φυσική, henōsis physikē) of the Alexandrian tradition, preferring the moral or "prosopic" union conveyed by Mary's title of Christotokos, "Christ-bearer." This seemed to Cyril and the bishops who condemned

Moreover, how could one nature become receptive of opposing essential differences? For how is it possible for the same nature to be at the same time both created and uncreated, mortal and immortal, circumscribed and uncircumscribed?

If those who say that Christ is of a single nature should claim that this nature is simple, they would either be confessing him as only God and would be presenting the incarnation as an illusion, or they would be confessing him as a mere man in the manner of Nestorius.[4] Where, then, is the perfection in divinity and the perfection in humanity? And when would they say that Christ is of two natures, seeing that they claim that after the union he is of one composite nature? That Christ was of one nature before the union is obvious to anybody.

Now what causes the heretics to fall into error is their saying that nature and hypostasis are the same thing. When we say that human nature is one, it should be understood that we do not say this with reference to the definition of the soul and the body. For it is impossible to say that the soul and the body when compared to each other are of one nature. But since there are very many hypostases of human beings, and to all of them the same definition of nature is applicable (for all of them are composed of soul and body, and all of them share in the soul's nature and possess the body's substance), we say that the common species of the very numerous and different hypostases is one nature, each hypostasis clearly possessing two natures and operating in the two natures, by which I mean the natures of soul and body.

In the case of our Lord Jesus Christ, it is not possible to establish a common species. For there has not been, nor will there ever be, another Christ out of divinity and humanity, the same being perfect God and perfect man in divinity and humanity.[5] Moreover,

Nestorius at Ephesus in 431 to be teaching that Christ was a mere man with only a parallel existence to the divine Word.

[5]The passage that follows in smaller type (from "Moreover" to "a single nature") is attested by only two manuscripts, MN.

νόμον παρὰ τοῦ δημιουργοῦ δεχόμενα, ὥστε φύσεως νόμῳ κατὰ διαδοχὴν ὅμοια ἐξ ὁμοίων γεννᾶσθαι. Ἐπὶ δὲ τοῦ κυρίου τῶν ἑνωθεισῶν φύσεων ἡ μὲν ἄναρχός ἐστι καὶ ἄχρονος, ἡ δὲ ἠργμένη καὶ ὑπὸ χρόνον· καὶ οὐ γέγονεν εἶδος πρὸς συμπλήρωσιν τοῦ παντός (ἐπεὶ οὐ κατέπαυσεν ὁ θεὸς ἀπὸ τῶν ἔργων αὐτοῦ τῇ ἡμέρᾳ τῇ ἑβδόμῃ) οὔτε δύο φυσικῶς ἡνώθησαν, ἀλλὰ παραδόξως καὶ ὑπερφυῶς. Τὰ δὲ παράδοξα καὶ ὑπερφυῆ οὐ φύσιν ἀποτελεῖ· οὐ γάρ φαμεν βάτου φύσιν προσομιλοῦσαν πυρὶ καὶ μὴ φλεγομένην οὐδὲ φύσιν ἀνθρώπου μεταρσίου γενομένου ὡς (ὡς] ὢν Ν) εἰς τὸν οὐρανὸν οὔτε φύσιν σώματος ἀνθρωπείου δροσιζομένην ἐν πυρί, ἀλλὰ παράδοξα ταῦτά φαμεν περὶ μίαν ὑπόστασιν. Οὕτω καὶ τὴν σάρκωσιν τοῦ κυρίου ἐν μιᾷ ὑποστάσει τῶν τῆς θεότητος ὑποστάσεων οὐ νόμῳ φύσεως, ἀλλ' ὑπερφυεῖ οἰκονομίᾳ τὴν ἕνωσιν τῶν φύσεων γεγενῆσθαί φαμεν καὶ οὔτε ὑπὸ φύσεως ὅρον, ὥστε ἀπὸ Χριστοῦ Χριστὸν γεννᾶσθαι καὶ εἶδος ἀποτελεῖσθαι Χριστῶν περιεκτικὸν πολλῶν ὑποστάσεων, ἀλλὰ μίαν ὑπόστασιν σύνθετον ἐκ δύο φύσεων καὶ ἐν δύο φύσεσι καὶ δύο φύσεις, ἑκάστης φύσεως καὶ μετὰ τὴν ἕνωσιν φυλαττούσης τὸν οἰκεῖον ὅρον τε καὶ νόμον καὶ τὴν πρὸς ἄλληλα διαφοράν. Ἐπὶ μὲν γὰρ τοῦ ἀνθρώπου, καθὸ μὲν θεωρεῖται πρὸς ἄλληλα διαφορὰ ψυχῆς τε καὶ σώματος, δύο φύσεις φαμέν· καθὸ δὲ οὐ θεωρεῖται φυσικὴ διαφορὰ ὑποστάσεων ἐξ ὑποστάσεως μιᾶς, καὶ μιᾶς μὲν φύσεως λέγονται τὰ καθ' ὑπόστασιν διαφέροντα ὁμοειδῆ, μιᾶς δὲ ὑποστάσεως τὰ κατ' οὐσίαν διαφέροντα καὶ καθ' ὑπόστασιν ἡνωμένα. Αἱ οὖν ἑτεροειδεῖς ὑποστάσεις οὐχ ὑποστατικῶς συγκρίνονται ἢ διακρίνονται, ἀλλὰ φυσικῶς· καὶ αἱ ὁμοειδεῖς ὑποστάσεις οὐ φυσικῶς συγκρίνονται ἢ διακρίνονται. Καὶ ὥσπερ ἀδύνατον τὰ ὑποστατικῇ διαφορᾷ διαφέροντα μιᾶς εἶναι ὑποστάσεως, οὕτως ἀδύνατον τὰ φυσικῇ διαφορᾷ (φυσικὰ διάφορα Ν) διαφέροντα μιᾶς εἶναι φύσεως. Ἐντεῦθεν οὐκ ἔστιν εἰπεῖν μίαν φύσιν ἐπὶ τοῦ κυρίου ἡμῶν Ἰησοῦ Χριστοῦ. Διὸ δὴ ἐκ δύο φύσεων τελείων, θείας τε καὶ ἀνθρωπίνης, φαμὲν γεγενῆσθαι τὴν ἕνωσιν οὐ κατὰ φυρμὸν ἢ σύγχυσιν ἢ ἀνάκρασιν, ὡς ὁ θεήλατος ἔφη Διόσκορος Σευῆρός τε καὶ ἡ τούτων ἐναγὴς συμμορία, οὐδὲ

he had control of the parts of every composite nature at the same time as their being brought into being out of non-being for the completion of the universe. It is possible for things that are contemporaneous to constitute a single composite nature, seeing that they have received this rule and natural law from the Creator, so that by the law of nature they would be generated successively as like from like. But in the case of the Lord's united natures, one is without beginning and timeless, and the other had a beginning and is subject to time. And no species came into being for the completion of the universe (since God did not cease from his works on the seventh day), nor were two united naturally, but miraculously and supernaturally. Things that are miraculous and supernatural do not constitute a nature. For we do not call a bush brought into contact with fire but not burning a nature, nor do we call a person caught up into heaven a nature, nor do we call a human body refreshed by fire a nature, but we call these miracles concerning a single hypostasis.[6] So, too, we do not say that the incarnation of the Lord in a single hypostasis of the hypostases of the Godhead took place by a law of nature but that the union of the natures took place by a supernatural dispensation and not by a rule of nature, so that a Christ could be generated from Christ and a species of Christs be constituted embracing many hypostases. No, we say that there is one composite hypostasis from two natures and in two natures, each nature after the union preserving its own rule and law and its difference with regard to the other. In the case of human beings, seeing that the difference between soul and body is observable, we say that there are two natures. But seeing that no natural difference is observable between one hypostasis and another, they are said to belong to one uniform nature though differing hypostatically, whereas those things that differ essentially but are united hypostatically are said to belong to a single hypostasis. Therefore hypostases of different species are compared or distinguished not by hypostasis but by nature, and hypostases of the same species are not compared or distinguished by nature. And just as it is impossible for things that differ by a hypostatic difference to be of a single hypostasis, so it is impossible for things that differ by a natural difference to be of a single nature. Consequently, it is not possible to speak of a

[6]Cf. Ex 3; 4 Kg 2.11; Dan 3.

προσωπικὴν ἢ σχετικὴν ἢ κατ' ἀξίαν ἢ ταυτοβουλίαν ἢ ὁμοτιμίαν ἢ ὁμωνυμίαν ἢ εὐδοκίαν, ὡς ὁ θεοστυγὴς ἔφη Νεστόριος Διόδωρός τε καὶ ὁ Μομψουεστίας Θεόδωρος καὶ ἡ τούτων δαιμονιώδης ὁμήγυρις, ἀλλὰ κατὰ σύνθεσιν ἤτοι καθ' ὑπόστασιν ἀτρέπτως καὶ ἀσυγχύτως καὶ ἀναλλοιώτως καὶ ἀδιαιρέτως καὶ ἀδιασπάστως καὶ ἐν δυσὶ φύσεσι τελείως ἐχούσαις μίαν ὑπόστασιν ὁμολογοῦμεν τοῦ υἱοῦ τοῦ θεοῦ καὶ σεσαρκωμένου, τὴν αὐτὴν ὑπόστασιν λέγοντες τῆς θεότητος καὶ τῆς ἀνθρωπότητος αὐτοῦ καὶ τὰς δύο φύσεις ὁμολογοῦντες σῴζεσθαι ἐν αὐτῷ μετὰ τὴν ἕνωσιν, οὐκ ἰδίᾳ καὶ ἀναμέρος τιθέντες ἑκάστην, ἀλλ' ἡνωμένας ἀλλήλαις ἐν τῇ μιᾷ συνθέτῳ ὑποστάσει. Οὐσιώδη γάρ φαμεν τὴν ἕνωσιν, τουτέστιν ἀληθῆ καὶ οὐ κατὰ φαντασίαν· οὐσιώδη δέ, οὐχ ὡς τῶν δύο φύσεων ἀποτελεσασῶν μίαν σύνθετον φύσιν, ἀλλ' ἑνωθεισῶν ἀλλήλαις κατὰ ἀλήθειαν εἰς μίαν ὑπόστασιν σύνθετον τοῦ υἱοῦ τοῦ θεοῦ. Καὶ σῴζεσθαι αὐτῶν τὴν οὐσιώδη διαφορὰν ὁριζόμεθα· τὸ γὰρ κτιστὸν μεμένηκε κτιστὸν καὶ τὸ ἄκτιστον ἄκτιστον, καὶ τὸ θνητὸν ἔμεινε θνητὸν καὶ ἀθάνατον τὸ ἀθάνατον καὶ τὸ περιγραπτὸν περιγραπτὸν καὶ τὸ ἀπερίγραπτον ἀπερίγραπτον, τὸ ὁρατὸν ὁρατὸν καὶ τὸ ἀόρατον ἀόρατον· «Τὸ μὲν διαλάμπει τοῖς θαύμασι, τὸ δὲ ταῖς ὕβρεσιν ὑποπέπτωκεν».

---

[7]Dioscorus (d. 454), Cyril's successor on the patriarchal throne of Alexandria, was deposed and anathematized by the Council of Chalcedon (451) for having supported Eutyches, an archimandrite of Constantinople, whose Christological teaching denied Christ's full humanity. Severus (d. 538), patriarch of Antioch from 512, was the leader in the early part of the sixth century of those dubbed monophysites, who were opposed to Chalcedon on the grounds that its two-nature Christology was too close to that of Nestorius.

[8]Πρόσωπον (prosōpon; "person") is a relational term. It is the "face" a hypostasis presents to other hypostases, or the "role" it plays. A "prosopic" union is therefore a union of roles that does not entail a single hypostasis as the subject of the union.

[9]Nestorius was condemned by the Council of Ephesus (431) for driving too strong a wedge between Christ's humanity and his divinity. Diodore of Tarsus (d. before 394) and his pupil Theodore of Mopsuestia (d. 428) were the leading theologians of the Antiochene tradition to which Nestorius belonged. Theodore was condemned at the Fifth Ecumenical Council (Constantinople II, 553).

single nature in the case of our Lord Jesus Christ. On that account, then, we say that the union from two complete natures, the divine and the human, took place not by blending or confusion or mixing, as the God-deluded Dioscorus said and Severus and their accursed faction,[7] nor by a prosopic,[8] or relative union, or a union in terms of dignity, or by identity of will, or by equality of honor, or by verbal identity, or by good pleasure, as the God-hated Nestorius said, and Diodore, and Theodore of Mopsuestia, and their demonic band,[9] but we confess that the union took place by composition, that is to say, hypostatically, immutably, without confusion, change, division, or separation,[10] and having perfectly in two natures a single hypostasis of the Son of God made flesh, and we declare that the hypostasis of his divinity and of his humanity is the same, and confess that the two natures are preserved in him after the union, not setting each apart on its own but holding them to be united with each other in the one composite hypostasis. For we say that the union is substantial, that is to say, true and not illusory. And it is substantial not as a single composite nature formed out of two natures, but with the two natures truly united with each other in one composite hypostasis of the Son of God. And we define that the essential difference of these natures is preserved. For what was created remained created and what was uncreated remained uncreated, what was mortal remained mortal and what was immortal remained immortal, what was circumscribed remained circumscribed and was uncircumscribed remained uncircumscribed, what was visible remained visible and what was invisible remained invisible. "The one shines with miracles, while the other has succumbed to outrages."[11]

[10]"Immutably, without confusion, change, division, or separation" (ἀτρέπτως καὶ ἀσυγχύτως καὶ ἀναλλοιώτως καὶ ἀδιαιραίτως καὶ ἀδιασπάστως, *atreptōs kai asynchytōs kai analloiōtōs kai adiairaitōs kai adiaspastōs*) reproduces the first three of the famous "Chalcedonian adverbs" (ἀσυγχύτως, ἀτρέπτως, ἀδιαιραίτως; *asynchytōs, atreptōs, adiairaitōs*) from the Definition of 451, and paraphrases the fourth (ἀχωρίστως, *achōristōs*).

[11]Leo I, *Letter* 28 (the Tome of Leo), 14.29 (excerpted in *Doctrina Patrum*, Diekamp, 83.12). John defends Leo's rather crude dyophysite language, which without further qualification sounds to Eastern ears distinctly Nestorian.

Οἰκειοῦται δὲ τὰ ἀνθρώπινα ὁ λόγος (αὐτοῦ γάρ εἰσι τὰ
τῆς ἁγίας αὐτοῦ σαρκὸς ὄντα) καὶ μεταδιδοῖ τῇ σαρκὶ τῶν
ἰδίων κατὰ τὸν τῆς ἀντιδόσεως τρόπον διὰ τὴν εἰς ἄλληλα τῶν
μερῶν περιχώρησιν καὶ τὴν καθ᾽ ὑπόστασιν ἕνωσιν, καὶ ὅτι εἷς
ἦν καὶ ὁ αὐτὸς ὁ καὶ τὰ θεῖα καὶ τὰ ἀνθρώπινα «ἐνεργῶν ἐν
ἑκατέρᾳ μορφῇ μετὰ τῆς θατέρου κοινωνίας». Διὸ δὴ καὶ ὁ
κύριος τῆς δόξης ἐσταυρῶσθαι λέγεται καίτοι τῆς θείας αὐτοῦ
μὴ παθούσης φύσεως, καὶ ὁ υἱὸς τοῦ ἀνθρώπου πρὸ τοῦ πάθους
ἐν τῷ οὐρανῷ εἶναι ὡμολόγηται, ὡς αὐτὸς ὁ κύριος ἔφησεν. Εἷς
γὰρ ἦν καὶ ὁ αὐτὸς κύριος τῆς δόξης ὁ φύσει καὶ ἀληθείᾳ υἱὸς
ἀνθρώπου ἤτοι ἄνθρωπος γενόμενος, καὶ αὐτοῦ τά τε θαύματα
καὶ τὰ πάθη γινώσκομεν, εἰ καὶ κατ᾽ ἄλλο ἐθαυματούργει καὶ κατ᾽
ἄλλο τὰ πάθη ὁ αὐτὸς ὑπέμεινεν. Ἴσμεν γάρ, ὥσπερ μίαν αὐτοῦ
τὴν ὑπόστασιν, οὕτω καὶ τὴν τῶν φύσεων οὐσιώδη διαφορὰν
σῴζεσθαι. Πῶς δὲ σωθείη διαφορὰ μὴ σῳζομένων τῶν τὴν
διαφορὰν ἐχόντων πρὸς ἄλληλα; Διαφορὰ γὰρ διαφερόντων ἐστὶ
διαφορά. Τῷ μὲν οὖν λόγῳ, ᾧ διαφέρουσιν ἀλλήλων αἱ φύσεις τοῦ
Χριστοῦ τουτέστι τῷ λόγῳ τῆς οὐσίας, φαμὲν συνάπτεσθαι αὐτὸν
τοῖς ἄκροις, κατὰ μὲν τὴν θεότητα τῷ τε πατρὶ καὶ τῷ πνεύματι,
κατὰ δὲ τὴν ἀνθρωπότητα τῇ τε μητρὶ καὶ ἡμῖν· ὁμοούσιος γάρ
ἐστιν ὁ αὐτός, κατὰ μὲν τὴν θεότητα τῷ τε πατρὶ καὶ τῷ πνεύματι,
κατὰ δὲ τὴν ἀνθρωπότητα τῇ τε μητρὶ καὶ πᾶσι τοῖς ἀνθρώποις.
Ὧι δὲ λόγῳ συνάπτονται αἱ φύσεις αὐτοῦ, διαφέρειν αὐτὸν φαμεν
τοῦ τε πατρὸς καὶ τοῦ πνεύματος, τῆς τε μητρὸς καὶ τῶν λοιπῶν
ἀνθρώπων· συνάπτονται γὰρ αἱ φύσεις αὐτοῦ τῇ ὑποστάσει μίαν
ὑπόστασιν σύνθετον ἔχουσαι, καθ᾽ ἣν διαφέρει τοῦ τε πατρὸς καὶ
τοῦ πνεύματος, τῆς τε μητρὸς καὶ ἡμῶν.

---

[12]Leo I, *Letter* 28 (the Tome of Leo), 14.27. It is this phrase correlating Christ's
human and divine activities that made Leo's Tome acceptable to the fathers of Chalcedon. John qualifies Leo's generally rather strong dyophysite language by invoking the
principle of the reciprocal interpenetration, or perichoresis (διὰ τὴν εἰς ἄλληλα τῶν
μερῶν περιχώρησιν, *dia tēn eis allēla tōn merōn perichōrēsin*), of the two natures.
[13]1 Cor 2.8.

Moreover, the Word appropriates what is human (for what belongs to his holy flesh is his) and communicates his own attributes to the flesh by the method of exchange on account of the parts coinhering in each other and the hypostatic union, and because he was one and the same who "performs what is proper to both the divine and the human in each form in communion with the other."[12] Indeed that is how the Lord of glory is said to have been crucified[13] even though his divine nature did not suffer, and it is confessed that the Son of Man was in heaven before his passion, as the Lord himself said.[14] For the same Lord of glory was one with him who was by nature and in truth the Son of Man, that is to say, who became man, and we recognize that the miracles and the passion were of the same Lord, even though the same performed his miracles in one capacity and underwent his passion in another. For we know that just as his hypostasis is one, so too that the essential difference of the natures is preserved. How would the difference be preserved unless the things that differ from each other are preserved? For "difference is the difference between things that differ."[15] Therefore by the principle by which Christ's natures differ from each other, that is to say, by the principle of essence, we say that he is joined to the two terms, by the divinity to the Father and the Spirit, and by the humanity to his mother and us. For the same is consubstantial, with respect to the divinity with the Father and the Spirit, and with respect to the humanity with his mother and all human beings.[16] But by the principle by which his natures are joined, we say that he differs from the Father and the Spirit, and from his mother and the rest of humanity. For his natures are joined in the hypostasis, since they have one composite hypostasis by which he differs from the Father and the Spirit, and from his mother and us.

[14]Jn 3.13 (long ending, cited below in Chapter 91, p. 272).

[15]*Doctrina Patrum*, Diekamp, 159.35.

[16]John echoes the Definition of Chalcedon: "consubstantial with the Father in respect of the Godhead, and the same consubstantial with us in respect of the manhood" (trans. Price, in Richard Price and Michael Gaddis, *The Acts of the Council of Chalcedon* (Liverpool: Liverpool University Press, 2005), vol. 2, 204).

48 Περὶ τοῦ τρόπου τῆς ἀντιδόσεως

Ὅτι μὲν οὖν ἕτερόν ἐστιν οὐσία καὶ ἕτερον ὑπόστασις, πλειστάκις εἰρήκαμεν, καὶ ὅτι ἡ μὲν οὐσία τὸ κοινὸν καὶ περιεκτικὸν εἶδος τῶν ὁμοειδῶν ὑποστάσεων σημαίνει οἷον θεός, ἄνθρωπος, ἡ δὲ ὑπόστασις ἄτομον δηλοῖ ἤτοι πατέρα, υἱόν, πνεῦμα ἅγιον, Πέτρον, Παῦλον. Ἰστέον τοίνυν, ὅτι τὸ μὲν τῆς θεότητος καὶ τῆς ἀνθρωπότητος ὄνομα τῶν οὐσιῶν ἤτοι φύσεών ἐστι παραστατικόν, τὸ δὲ θεὸς καὶ ἄνθρωπος καὶ ἐπὶ τῆς φύσεως τάττεται, ὁπόταν λέγωμεν· Θεός ἐστιν ἀκατάληπτος οὐσία, καὶ ὅτι εἷς ἐστι θεός· λαμβάνεται δὲ καὶ ἐπὶ τῶν ὑποστάσεων ὡς τοῦ μερικωτέρου δεχομένου τὸ τοῦ καθολικωτέρου ὄνομα, ὡς ὅταν φησὶν ἡ γραφή· «Διὰ τοῦτο ἔχρισέ σε ὁ θεὸς ὁ θεός σου» (ἰδοὺ γὰρ τὸν πατέρα καὶ τὸν υἱὸν ἐδήλωσε), καὶ ὡς ὅταν λέγῃ· «Ἄνθρωπός τις ἦν ἐν χώρᾳ τῇ Αὐσίτιδι» (τὸν γὰρ Ἰὼβ μόνον ἐδήλωσεν).

Ἐπὶ οὖν τοῦ κυρίου ἡμῶν Ἰησοῦ Χριστοῦ, ἐπειδὴ δύο μὲν τὰς φύσεις γινώσκομεν, μίαν δὲ τὴν ὑπόστασιν ἐξ ἀμφοτέρων σύνθετον, ὅτε μὲν τὰς φύσεις ἀναθεωροῦμεν, θεότητα καὶ ἀνθρωπότητα καλοῦμεν, ὅτε δὲ τὴν ἐκ τῶν φύσεων συντεθεῖσαν ὑπόστασιν, ποτὲ μὲν ἐκ τοῦ συναμφοτέρου Χριστὸν ὀνομάζομεν καὶ θεὸν καὶ ἄνθρωπον κατ' αὐτὸ καὶ θεὸν σεσαρκωμένον, ποτὲ δὲ ἐξ ἑνὸς τῶν μερῶν θεὸν μόνον καὶ υἱὸν θεοῦ καὶ ἄνθρωπον μόνον καὶ υἱὸν ἀνθρώπου, καὶ ποτὲ μὲν ἐκ τῶν ὑψηλῶν μόνον, ποτὲ δὲ ἐκ τῶν ταπεινῶν μόνον· εἷς γάρ ἐστιν ὁ κἀκεῖνο καὶ τοῦτο ὁμοίως ὑπάρχων, τὸ μὲν ὢν ἀεὶ ἀναιτίως ἐκ πατρός, τὸ δὲ γενόμενος ὕστερον διὰ φιλανθρωπίαν.

Θεότητα μὲν οὖν λέγοντες οὐ κατονομάζομεν αὐτῆς τὰ τῆς ἀνθρωπότητος ἰδιώματα (οὐ γὰρ φαμεν θεότητα παθητὴν ἢ κτιστήν) οὔτε δὲ τῆς σαρκὸς ἤτοι τῆς ἀνθρωπότητος κατηγοροῦμεν τὰ τῆς θεότητος ἰδιώματα (οὐ γὰρ φαμεν σάρκα ἤτοι ἀνθρωπότητα ἄκτιστον). Ἐπὶ δὲ τῆς ὑποστάσεως, κἂν ἐκ

48 *On the manner of the exchange*

That the essence, then, is one thing and the hypostasis another we have stated very often, and also that the essence signifies the common and comprehensive species of hypostases of the same kind, such as man or God, whereas the hypostasis indicates an individual, such as Father, Son, Holy Spirit, Peter, or Paul. One should therefore know that the nouns "divinity" and "humanity" are indicative of essences, that is to say, of natures, whereas the nouns "God" and "man" are also predicated of a nature, as when we say: "God is an incomprehensible essence" and "God is one." They are, moreover, predicated of hypostases, as when the more particular receives the name of the more general, for example, when Scripture says: "Therefore God, your God, has anointed you"[1] (note that this indicates the Father and the Son), and when it says: "There was a certain man in the land of Ausitis"[2] (which indicates Job alone).

In the case of our Lord Jesus Christ, since we acknowledge two natures, but one hypostasis composed from both, when we are considering the natures, we call them divinity and humanity, but when we are considering the hypostasis composed from the natures, sometimes because of the combination we call Christ both God and man at the same time, or God made flesh, sometimes because of one of the parts we call him God alone and Son of God, or man alone and Son of Man, and sometimes we refer to him by his sublime attributes alone, while at others by his humble attributes alone. For he who exists equally both as the former and as the latter is one, the former existing eternally and without causation from the Father, the latter having come into being subsequently through divine love for humanity.

Therefore, when we are speaking of the divinity, we do not attribute to it the properties of the humanity (for we do not say that divinity is passible or created), nor do we attribute to the flesh, that is to say, to the humanity, the properties of the divinity (for we do not

[1] Ps 44.8.
[2] Job 1.1.

τοῦ συναμφοτέρου, κἂν ἐξ ἑνὸς τῶν μερῶν ταύτην ὀνομάσωμεν, ἀμφοτέρων τῶν φύσεων τὰ ἰδιώματα αὐτῇ ἐπιτίθεμεν. Καὶ γὰρ ὁ Χριστός, ὅπερ ἐστὶ τὸ συναμφότερον, καὶ θεὸς καὶ ἄνθρωπος λέγεται καὶ κτιστὸς καὶ ἄκτιστος καὶ παθητὸς καὶ ἀπαθής. Καὶ ὅταν ἐξ ἑνὸς τῶν μερῶν καὶ υἱὸς θεοῦ καὶ θεὸς ὀνομάζηται, δέχεται τὰ τῆς συνυφεστηκυίας φύσεως ἰδιώματα ἤτοι τῆς σαρκός, θεὸς παθητὸς ὀνομαζόμενος καὶ κύριος τῆς δόξης ἐσταυρωμένος, οὐ καθὸ θεὸς ἀλλὰ καθὸ καὶ ἄνθρωπος ὁ αὐτός· καὶ ὅταν ἄνθρωπος καὶ υἱὸς ἀνθρώπου ὀνομάζηται, δέχεται τὰ τῆς θείας οὐσίας ἰδιώματα καὶ αὐχήματα παιδίον προαιώνιον καὶ ἄνθρωπος ἄναρχος, οὐ καθὸ παιδίον καὶ ἄνθρωπος, ἀλλὰ καθὸ θεὸς ὢν προαιώνιος γέγονεν ἐπ' ἐσχάτων παιδίον. Καὶ οὗτός ἐστιν ὁ τρόπος τῆς ἀντιδόσεως ἑκατέρας φύσεως ἀντιδιδούσης τῇ ἑτέρᾳ τὰ ἴδια διὰ τὴν τῆς ὑποστάσεως ταυτότητα καὶ τὴν εἰς ἄλληλα αὐτῶν περιχώρησιν. Κατὰ τοῦτο δυνάμεθα εἰπεῖν περὶ Χριστοῦ· «Οὗτος ὁ θεὸς ἡμῶν ἐπὶ τῆς γῆς ὤφθη», καί· Ὁ ἄνθρωπος οὗτος ἄκτιστός ἐστι καὶ ἀπαθὴς καὶ ἀπερίγραπτος.

49 Περὶ ἀριθμοῦ τῶν φύσεων

Ὥσπερ δὲ ἐπὶ τῆς θεότητος μίαν φύσιν ὁμολογοῦμεν, τρεῖς δὲ ὑποστάσεις κατὰ ἀλήθειαν οὔσας φαμὲν καὶ πάντα μὲν τὰ φυσικὰ καὶ οὐσιώδη ἁπλᾶ φαμεν, τὴν δὲ διαφορὰν τῶν ὑποστάσεων ἐν μόναις ταῖς τρισὶν ἰδιότησι, τῇ ἀναιτίῳ καὶ πατρικῇ καὶ τῇ αἰτιατῇ καὶ υἱκῇ καὶ ἐκπορευτῇ ἐπιγινώσκομεν· ἀνεκφοιτήτους δὲ αὐτὰς καὶ ἀδιαστάτους ἀλλήλων καὶ ἡνωμένας καὶ ἐν ἀλλήλαις ἀσυγχύτως περιχωρούσας ἐπιστάμεθα, καὶ ἡνωμένας

say that flesh, that is to say, humanity, is uncreated). But in the case of the hypostasis, whether we are speaking of it in terms of the combination, or whether we are speaking of it in terms of one of its parts, we attribute the properties of both natures to it. For Christ—the name that expresses the combination of the two—is called both God and man, both created and uncreated, both passible and impassible. But when he is named from one of the parts and is called Son of God and God, he receives the properties of the nature that forms a unity with the other part, that is to say, the properties of the flesh, and is named passible God and crucified Lord of glory, not in respect of being God but in respect of the same being also human. And when he is named as Man and Son of Man, he receives the properties and glorious distinctions of the divine essence, eternal child and human being without beginning, not in respect of being a child and a human being but in respect of being eternal God, yet becoming a child in these latter days. And this is the manner of the exchange, each nature exchanging with the other its own properties through the identity of the hypostasis and the mutual interpenetration of the natures.[3] It is in this way that we can say of Christ: "This God of ours was seen on earth,"[4] and: This human being is uncreated and impassible and uncircumscribed.

49   *On the number of the natures*

Just as we confess one nature with regard to the Godhead, but say that there are three hypostases actually existing and that all natural and essential things are simple, so too we acknowledge the difference of the hypostases only in the three properties of uncaused and paternal, and caused and filial, and proceeding. We know for certain that these are inseparable from each other and undivided and united with each other and interpenetrating each other without confusion,

---

[3]The technical term for this is "the communication of idioms" (*communicatio idiomatum*).

[4]Bar 3.36, 38.

μὲν ἀσυγχύτως (τρεῖς γάρ εἰσιν, εἰ καὶ ἥνωνται), διαιρουμένας δὲ ἀδιαστάτως. Εἰ γὰρ καὶ ἑκάστη καθ' ἑαυτὴν ὑφέστηκεν ἤγουν τελεία ἐστὶν ὑπόστασις καὶ τὴν οἰκείαν ἰδιότητα ἤτοι τὸν τῆς ὑπάρξεως τρόπον διάφορον κέκτηται, ἀλλ' ἥνωνται τῇ τε οὐσίᾳ καὶ τοῖς φυσικοῖς ἰδιώμασι καὶ τῷ μὴ διίστασθαι μηδὲ ἐκφοιτᾶν τῆς πατρικῆς ὑποστάσεως καὶ εἷς θεός εἰσί τε καὶ λέγονται.

Τὸν αὐτὸν τρόπον καὶ ἐπὶ τῆς θείας καὶ ἀπορρήτου καὶ πάντα νοῦν καὶ κατάληψιν ὑπερεχούσης οἰκονομίας τοῦ ἑνὸς τῆς ἁγίας τριάδος θεοῦ λόγου κυρίου τε ἡμῶν Ἰησοῦ Χριστοῦ δύο μὲν φύσεις ὁμολογοῦμεν, θείαν τε καὶ ἀνθρωπίνην, συνεληλυθυίας ἀλλήλαις καὶ καθ' ὑπόστασιν ἑνωθείσας, μίαν δὲ ὑπόστασιν ἐκ τῶν δύο φύσεων ἀποτελεσθεῖσαν σύνθετον. Σῴζεσθαι δέ φαμεν τὰς δύο φύσεις καὶ μετὰ τὴν ἕνωσιν ἐν τῇ μιᾷ συνθέτῳ ὑποστάσει ἤγουν ἐν τῷ ἑνὶ Χριστῷ καὶ κατὰ ἀλήθειαν αὐτὰς εἶναι καὶ τὰ τούτων φυσικὰ ἰδιώματα, ἡνωμένας μέντοι ἀσυγχύτως καὶ ἀδιαιρέτως διαφερούσας τε καὶ ἀριθμουμένας. Καὶ ὥσπερ αἱ τρεῖς ὑποστάσεις τῆς ἁγίας τριάδος ἀσυγχύτως ἥνωνται καὶ ἀδιαστάτως διῄρηνται καὶ ἀριθμοῦνται, καὶ ὁ ἀριθμὸς διαίρεσιν ἢ διάστασιν ἢ ἀλλοτρίωσιν καὶ διατομὴν ἐν αὐταῖς οὐκ ἐργάζεται (ἕνα γὰρ θεὸν ἐπιγινώσκομεν τὸν πατέρα καὶ τὸν υἱὸν καὶ τὸ πνεῦμα τὸ ἅγιον), τὸν αὐτὸν τρόπον καὶ αἱ τοῦ Χριστοῦ φύσεις, εἰ καὶ ἥνωνται, ἀλλ' ἀσυγχύτως ἥνωνται, καὶ εἰ ἐν ἀλλήλαις περιχωροῦσιν, ἀλλὰ τὴν εἰς ἀλλήλας τροπήν τε καὶ μεταβολὴν οὐ προσίενται· φυλάττει γὰρ ἑκατέρα φύσις τὴν ἑαυτῆς φυσικὴν ἰδιότητα ἀμετάβλητον. Διὸ καὶ ἀριθμοῦνται, καὶ ὁ ἀριθμὸς οὐκ εἰσάγει διαίρεσιν. Εἷς γάρ ἐστιν ὁ Χριστὸς ἐν θεότητι καὶ ἀνθρωπότητι τέλειος· ὁ γὰρ ἀριθμὸς οὐ διαιρέσεως ἢ ἑνώσεως αἴτιος πέφυκεν, ἀλλὰ τῆς ποσότητος τῶν ἀριθμουμένων σημαντικός, εἴτε ἡνωμένων εἴτε διῃρημένων· ἡνωμένων μέν, ὅτι πεντήκοντα λίθους ἔχει ὁ τοῖχος οὗτος, διῃρημένων δέ, ὅτι πεντήκοντα λίθοι κεῖνται ἐν τῷ πεδίῳ τούτῳ· καὶ ἡνωμένων μέν, ὅτι δύο φύσεις εἰσὶν ἐν τῷ ἄνθρακι, πυρὸς λέγω καὶ ξύλου, διῃρημένων δέ, ὅτι ἡ φύσις τοῦ πυρὸς ἑτέρα ἐστὶ καὶ ἡ τοῦ ξύλου ἑτέρα, ἄλλου τρόπου ἑνοῦντος καὶ διαιροῦντος αὐτὰ καὶ οὐ τοῦ ἀριθμοῦ. Ὥσπερ τοίνυν ἀδύνατον

and that on the one hand they are united without confusion (for they are three even though they are united) and on the other hand are divided without discontinuity. For although each subsists in itself, that is to say, is a complete hypostasis, and possesses its own distinctive character or different mode of existence, they are nevertheless united in essence and natural properties and by the fact of not being separated or departing from the Father's hypostasis, and are one God both in reality and in name. In the same way, in the case also of the divine and ineffable economy transcending all thought and comprehension, of one of the Holy Trinity, our Lord Jesus Christ, we confess two natures, a divine and a human, that have come together and been united hypostatically to form one composite hypostasis from two natures. We say that the two natures are preserved even after the union in the one composite hypostasis, that is to say, in the one Christ, and that these exist in reality along with their natural properties, which are united without confusion and differ and are enumerated without division. And just as the three hypostases of the Holy Trinity are united without confusion and are divided and enumerated without interval, and number does not produce division, or separation, or alienation, or partition in them (for we acknowledge the Father, the Son, and the Holy Spirit as one God), in the same way, although Christ's natures are united, they are united without confusion, and although they interpenetrate each other, they do not change or mutate into each other, for each nature preserves its own natural property unaltered. Hence they are also enumerated, but number does not introduce division. For Christ is one, perfect in divinity and humanity. Number is not by nature the cause of either division or union, but is indicative of the quantity of the things that are enumerated, whether they are united or divided. They are united when a wall, for example, contains fifty stones, but divided when fifty stones lie in a field. And they are united when two natures are in a piece of charcoal, I mean fire and wood, but divided because the nature of fire is one thing and the nature of wood another, these things being united and divided in a different manner and not by

τὰς τρεῖς ὑποστάσεις τῆς θεότητος, εἰ καὶ ἥνωνται ἀλλήλαις, μίαν ὑπόστασιν εἰπεῖν διὰ τὸ μὴ σύγχυσιν καὶ ἀφανισμὸν τῆς τῶν ὑποστάσεων διαφορᾶς ἐργάσασθαι, οὕτω καὶ τὰς δύο φύσεις τοῦ Χριστοῦ τὰς καθ᾽ ὑπόστασιν ἡνωμένας ἀδύνατον μίαν φύσιν εἰπεῖν, ἵνα μὴ ἀφανισμὸν καὶ σύγχυσιν καὶ ἀνυπαρξίαν τῆς αὐτῶν διαφορᾶς ἐργασώμεθα.

50 Ὅτι πᾶσα ἡ θεία φύσις ἐν μιᾷ τῶν αὐτῆς ὑποστάσεων ἡνώθη πάσῃ τῇ ἀνθρωπίνῃ φύσει καὶ οὐ μέρος μέρει

Τὰ κοινὰ καὶ καθολικὰ κατηγοροῦνται τῶν αὐτοῖς ὑποκειμένων μερικῶν. Κοινὸν τοίνυν ἡ οὐσία, μερικὸν δὲ ἡ ὑπόστασις. Μερικὸν δέ, οὐχ ὅτι μέρος τῆς φύσεως ἔχει, μέρος δὲ οὐκ ἔχει, ἀλλὰ μερικὸν τῷ ἀριθμῷ ὡς ἄτομον· ἀριθμῷ γὰρ καὶ οὐ φύσει διαφέρειν λέγονται αἱ ὑποστάσεις. Κατηγορεῖται δὲ ἡ οὐσία τῆς ὑποστάσεως, διότι ἐν ἑκάστῃ τῶν ὁμοειδῶν ὑποστάσεων τελεία ἡ οὐσία ἐστί. Διὸ οὐδὲ διαφέρουσιν ἀλλήλων αἱ ὑποστάσεις κατ᾽ οὐσίαν, ἀλλὰ κατὰ συμβεβηκότα, ἅτινά εἰσι τὰ χαρακτηριστικὰ ἰδιώματα, χαρακτηριστικὰ δὲ ὑποστάσεως καὶ οὐ φύσεως· καὶ γὰρ τὴν ὑπόστασιν ὁρίζονται οὐσίαν μετὰ συμβεβηκότων. Ὥστε τὸ κοινὸν μετὰ τοῦ ἰδιάζοντος ἔχει ἡ ὑπόστασις· ἡ οὐσία δέ, καθ᾽ ἑαυτὴν οὐχ ὑφίσταται, ἀλλ᾽ ἐν ταῖς ὑποστάσεσι θεωρεῖται. Πασχούσης τοίνυν μιᾶς τῶν ὑποστάσεων πᾶσα ἡ οὐσία, καθ᾽ ἣν ἡ ὑπόστασις, πεπονθέναι λέγεται ἐν μιᾷ τῶν αὐτῆς ὑποστάσεων. Οὐ μέντοιγε ἀνάγκη καὶ πάσας τὰς ὁμοειδεῖς ὑποστάσεις συμπάσχειν τῇ πασχούσῃ ὑποστάσει.

Οὕτω τοίνυν ὁμολογοῦμεν τὴν τῆς θεότητος φύσιν πᾶσαν τελείως εἶναι ἐν ἑκάστῃ τῶν αὐτῆς ὑποστάσεων, πᾶσαν ἐν πατρί,

¹For the whole chapter, cf. Leontius of Byzantium, *Epilyseis* (*Solutions to the Argument Proposed by Severus*), PG 86/2:1920–25; critical ed. and English trans., Brian E. Daley, SJ, *Leontius of Byzantium: Complete Works* (Oxford Oxford University Press, 2017), 274.1–282.15.

number. Therefore just as one cannot say that the three hypostases of the Godhead, even if they are united with each other, are one hypostasis without entailing the confusion of the hypostases and the disappearance of the difference between them, so too one cannot call the two natures of Christ, which are united hypostatically, one nature without entailing the disappearance, confusion, and annihilation of the difference between them.[1]

50   *That the whole of the divine nature has been united in one of its hypostases with the whole of human nature and not a part with a part of it*

Elements that are common and universal are predicated of the particulars subordinate to them. An essence, accordingly, is common, whereas a hypostasis is a particular. It is a particular not because it possesses a part of the nature, for it does not possess a part but is a particular in number as an individual. For hypostases are said to differ in number but not in nature. An essence is predicated of a hypostasis because the essence is complete in each of the hypostases of the same species. For that reason hypostases differ from one another not by essence but by accidents, which are the characteristic properties, but characteristic of the hypostasis, not of the nature.[1] This is because a hypostasis is defined as an essence with accidents. As a result, a hypostasis possesses that which is common along with that which is individuating. The essence does not subsist in itself, but is perceived in the hypostases. Thus when one hypostasis suffers, the whole of the essence individuated in the hypostasis is said to suffer in one of its hypostases. It is not, of course, necessary that all the hypostases of the same species should suffer along with the hypostasis that does suffer.

   Thus, then, we confess that the whole nature of the deity is in each of its hypostases, the whole in the Father, the whole in the Son,

[1]Cf. Leontius of Byzantium, *Epilyseis* (*Solutions to the Argument Proposed by Severus*), PG 86/2:1945B; Daley, *Leontius of Byzantium*, 308.21–310.1.

πᾶσαν ἐν υἱῷ, πᾶσαν ἐν ἁγίῳ πνεύματι. Διὸ καὶ τέλειος θεὸς ὁ
πατήρ, τέλειος θεὸς ὁ υἱός, τέλειος θεὸς τὸ πνεῦμα τὸ ἅγιον.
Οὕτω καὶ ἐν τῇ ἐνανθρωπήσει τοῦ ἑνὸς τῆς ἁγίας τριάδος θεοῦ
λόγου φαμὲν πᾶσαν καὶ τελείαν τὴν φύσιν τῆς θεότητος ἐν μιᾷ
τῶν αὐτῆς ὑποστάσεων ἑνωθῆναι τῇ ἀνθρωπίνῃ φύσει πάσῃ
καὶ οὐ μέρος μέρει. Φησὶ γοῦν ὁ θεῖος ἀπόστολος, ὅτι «ἐν αὐτῷ
κατοικεῖ πᾶν τὸ πλήρωμα τῆς θεότητος σωματικῶς», τουτέστιν
ἐν τῇ σαρκὶ αὐτοῦ, καὶ ὁ τούτου φοιτητὴς ὁ θεοφόρος καὶ τὰ θεῖα
πολὺς Διονύσιος, «ὅτι ὁλικῶς ἡμῖν ἐν μιᾷ τῶν ἑαυτῆς ἐκοινώνησεν
ὑποστάσεων». Οὐ μὴν λέγειν ἀναγκασθησόμεθα, πάσας τὰς
ὑποστάσεις τῆς ἁγίας θεότητος ἤτοι τὰς τρεῖς πάσαις ταῖς τῆς
ἀνθρωπότητος ὑποστάσεσι καθ᾽ ὑπόστασιν ἡνῶσθαι· κατ᾽ οὐδένα
γὰρ κεκοινώνηκε λόγον ὁ πατὴρ καὶ τὸ πνεῦμα τὸ ἅγιον τῇ
σαρκώσει τοῦ θεοῦ λόγου εἰ μὴ κατ᾽ εὐδοκίαν καὶ βούλησιν. Πάσῃ
δὲ τῇ ἀνθρωπίνῃ φύσει φαμὲν ἑνωθῆναι πᾶσαν τὴν τῆς θεότητος
οὐσίαν. Οὐδὲν γάρ, ὧν ἐνεφύτευσε τῇ ἡμετέρᾳ φύσει ὁ θεὸς λόγος
ἀρχῆθεν πλάσας ἡμᾶς, ἐνέλιπεν, ἀλλὰ πάντα ἀνέλαβε, σῶμα,
ψυχὴν νοερὰν καὶ λογικὴν καὶ τὰ τούτων ἰδιώματα (τὸ γὰρ ἑνὸς
τούτων ἀμοιροῦν ζῷον οὐκ ἄνθρωπος)· ὅλον γὰρ ὅλος ἀνέλαβέ
με, καὶ ὅλος ὅλῳ ἡνώθη, ἵνα ὅλῳ τὴν σωτηρίαν χαρίσηται· «τὸ
γὰρ ἀπρόσληπτον ἀθεράπευτον».
     Ἥνωται τοίνυν σαρκὶ διὰ μέσου νοῦ ὁ λόγος τοῦ θεοῦ
μεσιτεύοντος θεοῦ καθαρότητι καὶ σαρκὸς παχύτητι. Ἡγεμονικὸν
μὲν γὰρ ψυχῆς τε καὶ σαρκὸς νοῦς, τῆς ψυχῆς τὸ καθαρώτατον,
ἀλλὰ καὶ νοῦ ὁ θεός· καὶ ὅτε μὲν παραχωρεῖται ὑπὸ τοῦ
κρείττονος, τὴν οἰκείαν ὁ νοῦς ἡγεμονίαν ἐνδείκνυται. Ἐκνικᾶται
δὲ καὶ ἕπεται τῷ κρείττονι καὶ ταῦτα ἐνεργεῖ, ἃ ἡ θεία βούλεται
θέλησις.

and the whole in the Holy Spirit. Hence the Father is perfect God, the Son is perfect God, and the Holy Spirit is perfect God. Thus, too, we say that in the incarnation of the one divine Word of the Holy Trinity the whole and perfect nature of the deity in one of its hypostases was united with the whole of human nature, and not a part of the deity with a part of human nature. Therefore the divine Apostle says: "In him the whole fullness of deity dwells bodily,"[2] that is to say, in his flesh, and the apostle's disciple, the God-bearing Dionysius, mighty in matters divine, says "because [the thearchy] participated wholly in us in one of its hypostases."[3] We are certainly not obliged to hold that all the hypostases of the holy Godhead, that is to say, all three, are united hypostatically with all the hypostases of the human race. For by no reckoning did the Father and the Holy Spirit participate in the incarnation of God the Word except by good pleasure and will. And we say that the whole of the essence of the Godhead was united with the whole of human nature. For God the Word lacked nothing of what he implanted in our nature when he created us. On the contrary, he assumed all of it, body, intelligent and rational soul, and their properties (for the animal that lacks one of these is not human). For the whole of him assumed the whole of me, and the whole of him was united with the whole of me, that salvation may be granted to the whole,[4] "for what has not been assumed cannot be healed."[5]

The Word of God, then, is united to flesh by means of mind, which mediates between the purity of God and the materiality of flesh. For the principal element governing both soul and flesh is mind, the purest part of the soul, but God is also the principal element governing mind. And indeed when it is permitted by its superior, the mind demonstrates its own authority. But it is prevailed upon by its superior and follows it, doing that which the divine will wishes.

[2]Col 2.9.

[3]Dionysius the Areopagite, *Divine Names* 1.3.4 (PG 3:592A; Suchla, 113); reproduced in *Doctrina Patrum* (Diekamp, 69.13).

[4]Cf. Gregory of Nazianzus, *Ep.* 101 (PG 37:177B).

[5]Gregory of Nazianzus, *Ep.* 101 (PG 37:181C).

Χωρίον ὁ νοῦς γέγονε τῆς καθ' ὑπόστασιν αὐτῷ ἡνωμένης θεότητος ὥσπερ δηλαδὴ καὶ ἡ σάρξ, οὐ σύνοικος, ὡς ἡ τῶν αἱρετικῶν ἐναγὴς πλανᾶται οἴησις· «οὐ γὰρ ἂν μεδιμναῖον», λέγουσα, «χωρήσει διμέδιμνον». σωματικῶς τὰ ἄυλα κρίνουσα.

Πῶς δὲ θεὸς τέλειος καὶ ἄνθρωπος τέλειος καὶ ὁμοούσιος τῷ τε πατρὶ καὶ ἡμῖν ὁ Χριστὸς λεχθήσεται, εἰ μέρος τῆς θείας φύσεως μέρει τῆς ἀνθρωπίνης ἐν αὐτῷ ἥνωται φύσεως;

Λέγομεν δὲ τὴν φύσιν ἡμῶν ἐγηγέρθαι ἐκ τῶν νεκρῶν καὶ ἀνεληλυθέναι καὶ κεκαθικέναι ἐκ δεξιῶν τοῦ πατρός, οὐ καθὸ πᾶσαι αἱ τῶν ἀνθρώπων ὑποστάσεις ἀνέστησαν καὶ ἐκάθισαν ἐκ δεξιῶν τοῦ πατρός, ἀλλὰ πᾶσα ἡ φύσις ἐν τῇ τοῦ Χριστοῦ ὑποστάσει. Φησὶ γοῦν ὁ θεῖος ἀπόστολος· «Συνήγειρε καὶ συνεκάθισεν ἡμᾶς ἐν τῷ Χριστῷ».

Καὶ τοῦτο δέ φαμεν, ὅτι ἐκ κοινῶν οὐσιῶν ἡ ἔνωσις γέγονε· πᾶσα γὰρ οὐσία κοινή ἐστι πασῶν τῶν ὑπ' αὐτῆς περιεχομένων ὑποστάσεων, καὶ οὐκ ἔστιν εὑρεῖν μερικὴν καὶ ἰδιάζουσαν φύσιν ἤτοι οὐσίαν, ἐπεὶ ἀνάγκη τὰς αὐτὰς ὑποστάσεις καὶ ὁμοουσίους καὶ ἑτεροουσίους λέγειν καὶ τὴν ἁγίαν τριάδα καὶ ὁμοούσιον καὶ ἑτεροούσιον κατὰ τὴν θεότητα λέγειν. Ἡ αὐτὴ τοίνυν φύσις ἐν ἑκάστῃ τῶν ὑποστάσεων θεωρεῖται. Καὶ ὅτε εἴπωμεν τὴν φύσιν τοῦ λόγου σεσαρκῶσθαι κατὰ τοὺς μακαρίους Ἀθανάσιόν τε καὶ Κύριλλον, τὴν θεότητα λέγομεν ἡνῶσθαι σαρκί. Διὸ οὐ δυνάμεθα εἰπεῖν· Ἡ φύσις τοῦ λόγου ἔπαθεν (οὐ γὰρ ἔπαθεν ἡ θεότης ἐν αὐτῷ), λέγομεν δὲ τὴν ἀνθρωπίνην φύσιν πεπονθέναι ἐν τῷ Χριστῷ, οὐ μὴν δὲ πάσας τὰς ὑποστάσεις τῶν ἀνθρώπων ἐμφαίνοντες, καὶ τῇ ἀνθρωπίνῃ φύσει πεπονθέναι ὁμολογοῦμεν τὸν Χριστόν. Ὥστε φύσιν τοῦ λόγου λέγοντες αὐτὸν τὸν λόγον σημαίνομεν. Ὁ δὲ λόγος καὶ τὸ κοινὸν τῆς οὐσίας κέκτηται καὶ τὸ ἰδιάζον τῆς ὑποστάσεως.

The mind became the seat of the divinity united hypostatically with it, just as the flesh obviously did too, not in the sense of cohabiting with it, as the abominable conceit of the heretics erroneously puts it, saying, "a corn-measure could not hold a double measure,"[6] judging immaterial things by material standards. How can Christ be said to be perfect God and perfect man, consubstantial both with the Father and with us, if a part of the divine nature is united in him with a part of the human nature?[7]

We say that our nature has been raised from the dead and has ascended and been seated at the right hand of the Father, not in the sense that all human hypostases have risen from the dead and have sat at the right hand of the Father, but that the whole of human nature has done so in the hypostasis of Christ. For the divine Apostle says: "he raised us up with him and seated us with him in Christ."[8]

And we say this, too, that the union took place from common essences. For every essence is common to all the hypostases included under it, and it is not possible to find a nature or essence that is partial and individual, since it would then be necessary to say that the same hypostases were both of the same essence and of a different essence and that the Holy Trinity is both of the same essence and of a different essence with regard to deity. Therefore the same nature is contemplated in each of the hypostases. And when we say in accordance with the blessed Athanasius and Cyril that the nature of the Word became incarnate, we are saying that the divinity was united with flesh. Hence we cannot say "the nature of the Word suffered" (for the divinity did not suffer in him). But we say that the human nature suffered in Christ, without implying that every human hypostasis did, and we confess that Christ suffered in his human nature. Consequently, when we say "the nature of the Word," we mean the Word himself. The Word possesses both what is common to the essence and what is particular to the hypostasis.

---

[6]Gregory of Nazianzus, *Ep.* 101 (PG 37:184B).
[7]For the whole paragraph, cf. PG 37:184BC.
[8]Eph 2.6.

51   *Περὶ τῆς μιᾶς τοῦ θεοῦ λόγου συνθέτου ὑποστάσεως*

Προεῖναι μὲν οὖν ἀχρόνως καὶ ἀιδίως φαμὲν τὴν θείαν τοῦ θεοῦ
λόγου ὑπόστασιν ἁπλῆν καὶ ἀσύνθετον, ἄκτιστον, ἀσώματον,
ἀόρατον, ἀναφῆ, ἀπερίγραπτον, πάντα ἔχουσαν ὅσα ἔχει ὁ
πατὴρ ὡς αὐτῷ ὁμοούσιον, τῷ τῆς γεννήσεως τρόπῳ καὶ σχέσει
τῆς πατρικῆς ὑποστάσεως διαφέρουσαν, τελείως ἔχουσαν,
οὐδέποτε τῆς πατρικῆς ἐκφοιτῶσαν ὑποστάσεως, ἐπ᾽ ἐσχάτων
δὲ τῶν ἡμερῶν τῶν πατρικῶν κόλπων οὐκ ἀποστάντα τὸν λόγον
(ἀπεριγράπτως γάρ) ἐνῳκηκέναι τῇ γαστρὶ τῆς ἁγίας παρθένου
ἀσπόρως καὶ ἀπεριλήπτως, ὡς οἶδεν αὐτός, καὶ ἐν αὐτῇ τῇ
προαιωνίῳ αὐτοῦ ὑποστάσει ὑποστήσασθαι ἑαυτῷ σάρκα ἐκ τῆς
ἁγίας παρθένου.

  Ἐν πᾶσι μὲν οὖν καὶ ὑπὲρ τὰ πάντα ἦν καὶ ἐν τῇ γαστρὶ
ὑπάρχων τῆς ἁγίας θεοτόκου, ἀλλ᾽ ἐν αὐτῇ ἐνεργείᾳ σαρκώσεως.
Σεσάρκωται τοίνυν ἐξ αὐτῆς προσλαβόμενος τὴν ἀπαρχὴν τοῦ
ἡμετέρου φυράματος, σάρκα ἐψυχωμένην ψυχῇ λογικῇ τε καὶ
νοερᾷ, ὥστε αὐτὴν χρηματίσαι τῇ σαρκὶ ὑπόστασιν τὴν τοῦ θεοῦ
λόγου ὑπόστασιν καὶ σύνθετον γενέσθαι τὴν πρότερον ἁπλῆν
οὖσαν τοῦ λόγου ὑπόστασιν, σύνθετον δὲ ἐκ δύο τελείων φύσεων
θεότητός τε καὶ ἀνθρωπότητος, καὶ φέρειν αὐτὴν τῆς θείας
τοῦ θεοῦ λόγου υἱότητος τὸ χαρακτηριστικὸν καὶ ἀφοριστικὸν
ἰδίωμα, καθ᾽ ὃ διακέκριται τοῦ πατρὸς καὶ τοῦ πνεύματος, τά τε
τῆς σαρκὸς χαρακτηριστικὰ καὶ ἀφοριστικὰ ἰδιώματα, καθ᾽ ἃ
διαφέρει τῆς τε μητρὸς καὶ τῶν λοιπῶν ἀνθρώπων, φέρειν δὲ καὶ
τὰ τῆς θείας φύσεως ἰδιώματα, καθ᾽ ἃ ἥνωται τῷ πατρὶ καὶ τῷ
ἁγίῳ πνεύματι, καὶ τὰ τῆς ἀνθρωπίνης φύσεως γνωρίσματα, καθ᾽
ἃ ἥνωται τῇ τε μητρὶ καὶ ἡμῖν. Ἔτι δὲ διαφέρει τοῦ τε πατρὸς καὶ

---

[1]The Fourth Ecumenical Council (Chalcedon, 451) had avoided the expression
"hypostatic union" (from the second of Cyril of Alexandria's "Twelve Chapters"
appended to his Third Letter to Nestorius) but the expression had been adopted by
the Fifth Ecumenical Council (Constantinople II, 553), where in the fourth of the
anathemas against the "Three Chapters" (i.e., Theodore of Mopsuestia and certain
writings of Theodoret of Cyrus and Ibas of Edessa) "hypostatic" union (ἕνωσις

51   On the one composite hypostasis of God the Word[1]

We say, then, that the divine hypostasis of God the Word has pre-existed timelessly and eternally as simple, non-composite, uncreated, incorporeal, invisible, intangible, uncircumscribed, possessing all that the Father has since it is consubstantial with him, differing in its mode of generation and its relationship with the Father's hypostasis, but possessing all that the Father has perfectly, and never departing from the Father's hypostasis. Yet in these last days, without abandoning the bosom of the Father (because he exists in an uncircumscribed manner) the Word came to dwell within the womb of the holy Virgin without seed and without conception, in the manner that he himself knows, and in his same eternal hypostasis fashioned flesh for himself out of the holy Virgin.

Thus he was in all things and beyond all things and also existed in the womb of the holy Theotokos, but in her by the operation (ἐνέργεια, *energeia*) of enfleshment. And so he became enfleshed, taking from her a representative portion of our clay, flesh ensouled by a rational and intelligent soul, with the result that the hypostasis of God the Word was designated by the hypostasis in the flesh and the hypostasis of the Word that was previously simple became composite from two perfect natures of divinity and humanity, itself bearing the characteristic and distinguishing property of the divine sonship of God the Word, by which he is distinct from the Father and the Spirit, and also the characteristic and distinguishing properties of the flesh, by which he is distinct from his mother and the rest of humankind, and moreover the properties of the divine nature by which he is united with the Father and the Holy Spirit, and the marks of the human nature by which he is united to his mother and to us. Furthermore, he differs both from the Father and the Spirit and from

καθ' ὑπόστασιν, *henōsis kath' hypostasin*) is expressly equated with "composite" or "synthetic" union (ἕνωσις κατὰ σύνθεσιν, *henōsis kata synthesin*) without comment. In this chapter, John Damascene explains how the two are related, the hypostatic union forming a synthesis of the Word with the flesh without confusion of which the hypostasis is the Word of God.

τοῦ πνεύματος τῆς τε μητρὸς καὶ ἡμῶν κατὰ τὸ ὑπάρχειν θεόν τε ὁμοῦ καὶ ἄνθρωπον τὸν αὐτόν· τοῦτο γὰρ τῆς τοῦ Χριστοῦ ὑποστάσεως ἰδιαίτατον ἰδίωμα γινώσκομεν.

Τοιγαροῦν ὁμολογοῦμεν αὐτὸν ἕνα υἱὸν τοῦ θεοῦ καὶ μετὰ τὴν ἐνανθρώπησιν καὶ υἱὸν ἀνθρώπου τὸν αὐτόν, ἕνα Χριστόν, ἕνα κύριον, τὸν μόνον μονογενῆ υἱὸν καὶ λόγον τοῦ θεοῦ, Ἰησοῦν, τὸν κύριον ἡμῶν. Δύο αὐτοῦ τὰς γεννήσεις σέβοντες—Οὐ γὰρ πέπονθεν σαρκωθείς—πῶς γὰρ ἂν πάθοι τὸ φύσει ἀπαθές; —οὐδὲ ἐτράπη ὁ ἁπλοῦς σύνθετος γενόμενος· ἡ γὰρ τροπὴ πάθος ἐστί, τὸ δὲ ἀπαθὲς πάντως καὶ ἄτρεπτον. Ἐνήργησε τοιγαροῦν σαρκωθείς, οὐκ ἔπαθεν· οὔτε γὰρ ἡ φύσις αὐτοῦ ἡ θεία ἐτράπη ἢ προσθήκην ἐδέξατο, οὐδὲ τὸ τῆς ὑποστάσεως αὐτοῦ ἰδίωμα, τουτέστιν ἡ υἱότης, ἐτράπη· ἔμεινε γὰρ υἱὸς τοῦ θεοῦ καὶ υἱὸς ἀνθρώπου γενόμενος. Οὐκ ἔπαθεν οὖν, ἀλλ᾽ ἐνήργησε δημιουργήσας ἑαυτῷ σάρκα ἐψυχωμένην ψυχῇ λογικῇ τε καὶ νοερᾷ καὶ δοὺς αὐτῇ ἑαυτὸν ὑπόστασιν καὶ ἐν ἑαυτῷ αὐτὴν ὑποστήσας. —Ἰστέον γάρ, ὡς ἐπὶ τῆς πυρώσεως δύο χρὴ ἐννοεῖν. Πεπυρῶσθαι γὰρ λέγεται τὸ πυρούμενον καθ᾽ ἕνα μὲν τρόπον, ὅτι ὁ σίδηρος τυχὸν ἢ τὸ ξύλον εἰς πῦρ προϋφεστὼς εἰσερχόμενον λαμβάνει ἐξ αὐτοῦ πῦρ μήπω καθ᾽ αὐτὸ προϋποστὰν καὶ γίνεται αὐτῷ ὑπόστασις (ἐν αὐτῷ γὰρ τῷ ξύλῳ προϋπάρχοντι καὶ προϋφεστῶτι ὑφίσταται τὸ πῦρ, ὃ λαμβάνει ἐκ τοῦ προϋφεστῶτος πυρός) καὶ γίνεται ἡ τοῦ σιδήρου ὑπόστασις καὶ τοῦ ἐν αὐτῷ θεωρουμένου πυρὸς ὑπόστασις μία ὑπόστασις τοῦ τε ξύλου καὶ τοῦ ἐν αὐτῷ πυρός (οὐ γὰρ ὑπέστη καθ᾽ αὐτὸ τὸ ἐν τῷ ξύλῳ πῦρ, ἀλλ᾽ αἰτίαν τῆς ὑποστάσεως καὶ τῆς ἀναμερος κεχωρισμένης ἐκ τῶν λοιπῶν πυρῶν ὑπάρξεως καὶ συμπήξεως τὸ ξύλον ἔσχε) καὶ ἔστι μία ὑπόστασις τοῦ τε ξύλου καὶ τοῦ ἐν αὐτῷ ὑποστάντος πυρός, προηγουμένως μὲν τοῦ ξύλου, ἑπομένως δὲ τοῦ πυρός· προϋπάρχουσα γὰρ τοῦ ξύλου μετὰ ταῦτα ἐγένετο καὶ τοῦ πυρός. Λέγεται δὲ καὶ καθ᾽ ἕτερον τρόπον πύρωσις ὡς τοῦ πυρουμένου ξύλου δεχομένου τὴν τοῦ πυρὸς ἐνέργειαν· τὸ γὰρ λεπτότερον μεταδίδωσι τῷ παχυτέρῳ τῆς οἰκείας ἐνεργείας. Ἐπὶ μὲν οὖν τῆς πυρώσεως τὸ ξύλον ἐστὶ τὸ πυρούμενον, καὶ λέγεται πύρωσις τοῦ ξύλου καὶ οὐ ξύλωσις τοῦ πυρός· τὸ γὰρ ξύλον προϋπάρχει τε καὶ ὑπόστασις τῷ πυρὶ γίνεται καὶ τὴν τοῦ

his mother and us by being at the same time both God and man. For we acknowledge this to be the most clearly distinguishing property of Christ's hypostasis.

Accordingly, we confess him as one Son of God and the same also as Son of Man, after the inhomination, one Christ, one Lord, the sole only-begotten Son and Word of God, Jesus our Lord. We venerate his double generation[2]—For he did not suffer when he was enfleshed—for how can that which is impassible by nature suffer?—nor was he who is simple changed when he became composite. For change is a passion, but the impassible is necessarily immutable. That is why when he was in the flesh he performed actions, but did not suffer. Nor did his divine nature change or receive any augmentation, nor did the property of his hypostasis, that is to say, his sonship, change. For he remained Son of God even when he became Son of Man. Therefore he did not suffer, but operated through having created for himself flesh ensouled by a rational and intelligent soul, and having given himself to it as its hypostasis and having made it subsist in him.—For one should know that as in the case of setting on fire one should conceive of two elements. For what is set on fire is said to become fire in a certain sense, because when iron, say, or wood is thrust into an already existing fire, it takes fire from it that has not yet already existed in its own right and becomes a hypostasis for it (for the fire that has been taken from the already existing fire subsists in the very wood that has already existed and subsisted before it) and the hypostasis of the iron and the hypostasis of the fire that is observed in it become a single hypostasis of the wood and the fire in it (for the fire in the wood did not subsist in itself, but had the wood as the cause of its hypostasis and its separate existence and coming to be apart from all other fires) and is a single hypostasis of the wood and the fire that subsists in it, the wood previously existing and the fire being subsequent. For the hypostasis of the wood existed already and that of the fire came afterwards. Being set on fire is also spoken of in a different way as the burning of the wood set alight that has received the fire's energy. For the more subtle communicated its own energy to the coarser. In the case, then, of burning, the wood is the thing burnt, and is

[2]The long passage in smaller type that follows is an insertion in manuscripts MN.

πυρὸς ἐνέργειαν δέχεται. Ἐπὶ δὲ τοῦ κυρίου ἡμῶν Ἰησοῦ Χριστοῦ οὐχ οὕτως, ἀλλὰ σάρκωσις μὲν τοῦ λόγου λέγεται ὡς τοῦ λόγου γενομένου τῇ σαρκὶ ὑποστάσεως (προϋπῆρχε γὰρ ἡ ὑπόστασις τοῦ λόγου, καὶ ἐν αὐτῇ ὑπέστη ἡ σάρξ), θέωσις δὲ τῆς σαρκός· αὕτη γὰρ μετέσχε τῶν τῆς θεότητος, καὶ οὐχ ἡ θεότης τῶν αὐτῆς παθῶν· διὰ γὰρ τῆς σαρκὸς ἡ θεότης ἐνήργει ὡς τὸ πῦρ διὰ τοῦ ξύλου, οὐχ ἡ σὰρξ διὰ τοῦ λόγου. Οὐκ ἔπαθε τοίνυν σαρκωθεὶς ὁ λόγος, ἀλλ᾽ ἐνήργησε τὴν σάρκωσιν μεταδοὺς τῇ σαρκὶ τῆς τε ὑποστάσεως καὶ τῆς θεώσεως. Θεώσεως δὲ λέγω οὐχὶ τραπείσης εἰς θεότητος φύσιν, ἀλλὰ τῆς μεθέξεως τῆς ὑπὸ τῶν τῆς θεότητος αὐχημάτων· ἐζωοποίει γὰρ οὐ κατ᾽ οἰκείαν φύσιν, ἀλλὰ τῇ ἑνώσει τῇ πρὸς τὴν θεότητα. Καὶ ἐν Θαβὼρ ἤστραψε καὶ ἀπαστράπτει οὐ διὰ τὴν ἰδίαν φύσιν, ἀλλὰ διὰ τὴν τῆς καθ᾽ ὑπόστασιν ἡνωμένης αὐτῇ θεότητος ἐνέργειαν, ὡς τὸ ξύλον λάμπει καὶ καίει οὐ κατὰ τὴν οἰκείαν φυσικὴν ἐνέργειαν, ἀλλὰ διὰ τὴν τοῦ καθ᾽ ὑπόστασιν ἡνωμένου αὐτῷ πυρὸς τῆς ἐνεργείας μέθεξιν.—μίαν τὴν ἐκ πατρὸς προαιώνιον ὑπὲρ αἰτίαν καὶ λόγον καὶ χρόνον καὶ φύσιν καὶ μίαν τὴν ἐπ᾽ ἐσχάτων δι᾽ ἡμᾶς καὶ καθ᾽ ἡμᾶς καὶ ὑπὲρ ἡμᾶς—«δι᾽ ἡμᾶς» ὅτι διὰ τὴν ἡμετέραν σωτηρίαν, «καθ᾽ ἡμᾶς» ὅτι γενόμενος ἄνθρωπος ἐκ γυναικὸς καὶ χρόνῳ κυήσεως, «ὑπὲρ ἡμᾶς» ὅτι οὐκ ἐκ σπορᾶς, ἀλλ᾽ ἐξ ἁγίου πνεύματος καὶ τῆς ἁγίας παρθένου ὑπὲρ νόμον κυήσεως—, οὐ θεὸν αὐτὸν μόνον κηρύττοντες γυμνὸν τῆς καθ᾽ ἡμᾶς ἀνθρωπότητος οὐδὲ μὴν ἄνθρωπον μόνον ψιλοῦντες αὐτὸν τῆς θεότητος, οὐκ ἄλλον καὶ ἄλλον, ἀλλ᾽ ἕνα καὶ τὸν αὐτὸν ὁμοῦ θεόν τε καὶ ἄνθρωπον, θεὸν τέλειον καὶ ἄνθρωπον τέλειον, ὅλον θεὸν καὶ ὅλον ἄνθρωπον, τὸν αὐτὸν ὅλον θεὸν καὶ μετὰ τῆς σαρκὸς αὐτοῦ καὶ ὅλον ἄνθρωπον καὶ μετὰ τῆς ὑπερθέου αὐτοῦ θεότητος, διὰ τοῦ εἰπεῖν «τέλειον θεὸν καὶ τέλειον ἄνθρωπον» τὸ πλῆρες καὶ ἀνελλιπὲς δηλοῦντες τῶν φύσεων, διὰ δὲ τοῦ εἰπεῖν

[3]The linguistic neatness of the argument is rather lost in English. In Greek the comparison is between two nouns of the same form, πύρωσις (*pyrōsis*, "endowing with fire," here translated as "setting on fire" or "burning") and σάρκωσις (*sarkōsis*, "endowing with flesh, here translated as "enfleshment").

spoken of as the exposure of the wood to fire, not the exposure of fire to wood. For the wood already exists and becomes a hypostasis for the fire and receives the fire's energy. In the case of our Lord Jesus Christ, the situation is different. Here we speak of the enfleshment of the Word,[3] since the Word has become a hypostasis for the flesh (for the hypostasis of the Word already existed, and the flesh came to subsist in it), and the deification of the flesh.[4] For the flesh came to participate in what pertains to the divinity, not the divinity in the passions of the flesh. For the divinity operates through the flesh as fire does through the wood; it is not that the flesh operates through the Word. The Word therefore did not suffer as incarnate, but brought about the incarnation by imparting to the flesh a sharing in its hypostasis and deification. By deification I do not mean a change [of the flesh] into the nature of divinity; I mean [its] participation in the glorious attributes of the divinity. For it endows with life not by virtue of its own nature, but by its union with the divinity. On Tabor it became brilliant and flashed forth not through its own nature, but through the energy of the divinity hypostatically united with it, just as wood gives light and burns not by its own natural energy but through participation in the energy of the fire hypostatically united with it—one from the Father before the ages,[5] beyond cause and reason and time and nature, and one in these latter days for us and like us and beyond us—"for us" because for our salvation, "like us" because he became a human being from a woman and by conception in time, "beyond us" because he did not come from semen but from the Holy Spirit and the holy Virgin by a conception transcending the law [of nature]—and we do not proclaim him God alone, without our humanity, or man alone, depriving him of his divinity, not two distinct entities but one and the same God and man simultaneously, perfect God and perfect man, wholly God and wholly man, the same wholly God even with his flesh and wholly man even with his supremely divine divinity, manifesting the fullness and lack of deficiency of the natures through

---

[4]"Deification" here is θέωσις (*theōsis*), a noun of the same form as πύρωσις (*pyrōsis*, "burning") and σάρκωσις (*sarkōsis*, "enfleshment").

[5]The sense follows on from "We venerate his double generation" above, before the insertion.

«ὅλον θεὸν καὶ ὅλον ἄνθρωπον» τὸ μοναδικὸν καὶ ἄτμητον δεικνύντες τῆς ὑποστάσεως.

Καὶ «μίαν φύσιν τοῦ θεοῦ λόγου σεσαρκωμένην» ὁμολογοῦμεν διὰ τοῦ εἰπεῖν «σεσαρκωμένην» τὴν τῆς σαρκὸς οὐσίαν σημαίνοντες κατὰ τὸν μακάριον Κύριλλον. Καὶ σεσάρκωται τοίνυν ὁ λόγος καὶ τῆς οἰκείας ἀυλότητος οὐκ ἐξέστηκε καὶ ὅλος σεσάρκωται καὶ ὅλος ἐστὶν ἀπερίγραπτος. Σμικρύνεται σωματικῶς καὶ συστέλλεται καὶ θεϊκῶς ἐστιν ἀπερίγραπτος οὐ συμπαρεκτεινομένης τῆς σαρκὸς αὐτοῦ τῇ ἀπεριγράπτῳ αὐτοῦ θεότητι.

Ὅλος μὲν οὖν ἐστι θεὸς τέλειος, οὐχ ὅλον δὲ θεός (οὐ γὰρ μόνον θεός, ἀλλὰ καὶ ἄνθρωπος), καὶ ὅλος ἄνθρωπος τέλειος, οὐχ ὅλον δὲ ἄνθρωπος (οὐ μόνον γὰρ ἄνθρωπος, ἀλλὰ καὶ θεός). Τὸ μὲν «ὅλον» φύσεως ἐστι παραστατικόν, τὸ «ὅλος» δὲ ὑποστάσεως, ὥσπερ τὸ μὲν «ἄλλο» φύσεως, τὸ «ἄλλος» δὲ ὑποστάσεως.

Ἰστέον δέ, ὡς, εἰ καὶ περιχωρεῖν ἐν ἀλλήλαις τὰς τοῦ κυρίου φύσεις φαμέν, ἀλλ' οἴδαμεν, ὡς ἐκ τῆς θείας φύσεως ἡ περιχώρησις γέγονεν· αὕτη μὲν γὰρ διὰ πάντων διήκει, καθὼς βούλεται, καὶ περιχωρεῖ, δι' αὐτῆς δὲ οὐδέν. Καὶ αὐτὴ μὲν τῶν οἰκείων αὐχημάτων τῇ σαρκὶ μεταδίδωσι μένουσα αὐτὴ ἀπαθὴς καὶ τῶν τῆς σαρκὸς παθῶν ἀμέτοχος· εἰ γὰρ ὁ ἥλιος ἡμῖν τῶν οἰκείων ἐνεργειῶν μεταδιδοὺς μένει τῶν ἡμετέρων ἀμέτοχος, πόσῳ μᾶλλον ὁ τοῦ ἡλίου ποιητής τε καὶ κύριος.

---

[6]The reference here is to the Apollinarian phrase (μία φύσις τοῦ θεοῦ λόγου σεσαρκωμένη, *mia physis tou theou logou sesarkōmenē*) from Apollinarius' *Letter to Jovianus* 251.1–2, which was adopted by Cyril of Alexandria (in a perfectly orthodox sense) under the mistaken impression that it derived from Athanasius. Understood in a miaphysite sense excluding the flesh as another nature, it became the chief slogan of the Cyrillian anti-Chalcedonians.

saying "perfect God and perfect man" and indicating the singleness and absence of division of the hypostasis through saying "wholly God and wholly man."

We also confess "one enfleshed nature of God the Word," indicating by saying "enfleshed," in accordance with the blessed Cyril, the essence of the flesh.[6] And further, the Word became flesh and yet did not abandon his own proper immateriality, became wholly enfleshed and yet remains wholly uncircumscribed. He humbles himself in bodily terms and contracts himself, yet in divine terms remains uncircumscribed and non-coextensive with his flesh by reason of his uncircumscribed divinity.

And so the whole of him (ὅλος, *holos*) is perfect God, but he is not entirely (ὅλον, *holon*) God (for he is not only God but also man), and the whole of him is perfect man, but he is not entirely man (for he is not only man but also God). The word "entirely" is indicative of nature, whereas "the whole" is indicative of hypostasis, just as "other" in the neuter (ἄλλο, *allo*) refers to a nature, whereas "other" in the masculine (ἄλλος, *allos*) refers to a hypostasis.[7]

One should also note that although we say that the Lord's natures interpenetrate each other, we know that the interpentration comes from the divine nature. For this nature permeates all things, just as it wills, but is itself permeated by nothing. And it communicates its own splendors to the flesh while remaining itself dispassionate and without a share in the passions of the flesh. For if the sun communicates its own energies to us but remains without a share in our own energies, how much more so does the sun's Maker and Lord.

---

[7]Daley sees the language of this paragraph as deliberately provocative (*God Visible*, 227)—the distinction between perfect God but not entirely God pushes logic to its limits. John is exploiting here the possibilities offered to him by the structure of the Greek language (with its three genders, masculine feminine and neuter) to make his Christological point, as Daley says, with a new clarity.

52 Πρὸς τοὺς λέγοντας· Ὑπὸ τὸ συνεχὲς ποσὸν ἀνάγονται αἱ τοῦ κυρίου φύσεις ἢ ὑπὸ τὸ διωρισμένον

Εἰ δέ τις ἐρωτῶν περὶ τῶν τοῦ κυρίου φύσεων, εἰ ὑπὸ τὸ συνεχὲς ποσὸν ἀναφέροιντο ἢ ὑπὸ τὸ διωρισμένον, ἐροῦμεν, ὅτι αἱ τοῦ κυρίου φύσεις οὔτε ἓν σῶμά εἰσιν οὔτε μία ἐπιφάνεια οὔτε μία γραμμή, οὐ χρόνος, οὐ τόπος, ἵνα ὑπὸ τὸ συνεχὲς ἀναχθῶσι ποσόν· ταῦτα γάρ εἰσι τὰ συνεχῶς ἀριθμούμενα.

Ἰστέον δέ, ὡς ὁ ἀριθμὸς τῶν διαφερόντων ἐστὶ καὶ ἀδύνατον ἀριθμεῖσθαι τὰ κατὰ μηδὲν διαφέροντα· καθ᾽ ὃ δὲ διαφέρουσι, κατὰ τοῦτο καὶ ἀριθμοῦνται. Οἷον ὁ Πέτρος καὶ ὁ Παῦλος, καθ᾽ ὃ μὲν ἥνωνται, οὐκ ἀριθμοῦνται· τῷ λόγῳ γὰρ τῆς οὐσίας ἑνούμενοι δύο φύσεις οὐ δύνανται λέγεσθαι, καθ᾽ ὑπόστασιν δὲ διαφέροντες δύο ὑποστάσεις λέγονται. Ὥστε ὁ ἀριθμὸς τῶν διαφερόντων ἐστί, καὶ ᾧ τρόπῳ διαφέρουσι τὰ διαφέροντα, τούτῳ τῷ τρόπῳ καὶ ἀριθμοῦνται.

Ἥνωνται μὲν αἱ τοῦ Χριστοῦ φύσεις ἀσυγχύτως καθ᾽ ὑπόστασιν, διῄρηνται δὲ ἀδιαιρέτως λόγῳ καὶ τρόπῳ τῆς διαφορᾶς. Καὶ ᾧ μὲν τρόπῳ ἥνωνται, οὐκ ἀριθμοῦνται· οὐ γὰρ καθ᾽ ὑπόστασιν δύο εἶναί φαμεν τὰς φύσεις τοῦ Χριστοῦ. Ὧι δὲ τρόπῳ ἀδιαιρέτως διῄρηνται, ἀριθμοῦνται; δύο γάρ εἰσιν αἱ φύσεις τοῦ Χριστοῦ λόγῳ καὶ τρόπῳ τῆς διαφορᾶς. Ἡνωμέναι γὰρ καθ᾽ ὑπόστασιν καὶ τὴν ἐν ἀλλήλαις περιχώρησιν ἔχουσαι ἀσυγχύτως ἥνωνται, τὴν οἰκείαν ἑκάστη φυσικὴν διαφορὰν διασῴζουσα. Τῷ τρόπῳ τοιγαροῦν τῆς διαφορᾶς καὶ μόνῳ ἀριθμούμεναι ὑπὸ τὸ διωρισμένον ποσὸν ἀναχθήσονται.

Εἷς τοίνυν ἐστὶν ὁ Χριστός, θεὸς τέλειος καὶ ἄνθρωπος τέλειος, ὃν προσκυνοῦμεν σὺν πατρὶ καὶ πνεύματι μιᾷ προσκυνήσει μετὰ τῆς ἀχράντου σαρκὸς αὐτοῦ οὐκ ἀπροσκύνητον τὴν σάρκα λέγοντες (προσκυνεῖται γὰρ ἐν τῇ μιᾷ τοῦ λόγου ὑποστάσει, ἥτις αὐτῇ ὑπόστασις γέγονεν), οὐ τῇ κτίσει λατρεύοντες (οὐ γὰρ ὡς ψιλῇ σαρκὶ προσκυνοῦμεν ἀλλ᾽ ὡς ἡνωμένῃ θεότητι καὶ ὡς εἰς ἓν πρόσωπον καὶ μίαν ὑπόστασιν τοῦ θεοῦ λόγου τῶν δύο αὐτοῦ ἀναγομένων φύσεων). Δέδοικα τοῦ ἄνθρακος ἅψασθαι διὰ τὸ τῷ

52   *To those who ask whether the Lord's natures refer to a
continuous or to a divided quantity*

If anyone asks concerning the Lord's natures whether they refer to
a continuous quantity or to a divided one, we reply that the Lord's
natures are neither a single body, nor a single surface, nor a single
line, nor time, nor place, so as to refer to continuity. For these are the
things that are numbered continuously.

One should also note that number belongs to things that differ
and that it is impossible for things that do not differ in any way to be
numbered; it is their difference that enables them to be numbered.
Take, for example, Peter and Paul. With regard to what unites them
they are not numerable, for united as they are on account of their
essence, they cannot be said to be two natures, but differing as they
do hypostatically, they are said to be two hypostases. Thus number
belongs to things that differ, and the manner in which different
things differ is the manner in which they are counted.

Christ's natures are on the one hand united without confusion by
virtue of the hypostasis, and on the other divided indivisibly by reason of, and in the mode of, the difference. And because of the mode
in which they are united, they are not numerable, for we do not say
that Christ's natures are two hypostatically. But because of the mode
in which they are divided indivisibly, they are numerable, for Christ's
natures are two by reason of, and in the mode of, the difference. For
they are united hypostatically and are unified through penetrating
each other reciprocally without confusion, each preserving its own
natural difference. Consequently, they are referable to divided quantity only when they are numbered by the mode of difference.

Therefore Christ is one, perfect God and perfect man, whom
we worship with the Father and the Spirit in a single act of worship
together with his immaculate flesh, not saying that the flesh is not to
be worshiped (for it is worshiped in the one hypostasis of the Word,
which became a hypostasis for it), not adoring creation (for we do
not worship it as mere flesh but as united to the divinity and because

ξύλῳ συνημμένον πῦρ. Προσκυνῶ τοῦ Χριστοῦ τὸ συναμφότερον διὰ τὴν τῇ σαρκὶ ἡνωμένην θεότητα· οὐ γὰρ τέταρτον παρεντίθημι πρόσωπον ἐν τῇ τριάδι—μὴ γένοιτο—, ἀλλ' ἓν πρόσωπον ὁμολογῶ τοῦ θεοῦ λόγου καὶ τῆς σαρκὸς αὐτοῦ. Τριὰς γὰρ ἔμεινεν ἡ τριὰς καὶ μετὰ τὴν τοῦ λόγου σάρκωσιν.

53   Πρὸς τό, εἰ οὐκ ἔστι φύσις ἀνυπόστατος, ἀπάντησις

Εἰ γὰρ καὶ μή ἐστι φύσις ἀνυπόστατος ἢ οὐσία ἀπρόσωπος (ἐν ὑποστάσεσι γὰρ καὶ προσώποις ἥ τε οὐσία καὶ ἡ φύσις θεωρεῖται), ἀλλ' οὐκ ἀνάγκη τὰς ἀλλήλαις ἑνωθείσας φύσεις καθ' ὑπόστασιν ἑκάστην ἰδίαν κεκτῆσθαι ὑπόστασιν· δύνανται γὰρ εἰς μίαν συνδραμοῦσαι ὑπόστασιν μήτε ἀνυπόστατοι εἶναι μήτε ἰδιάζουσαν ἑκάστη ἔχειν ὑπόστασιν, ἀλλὰ μίαν καὶ τὴν αὐτὴν ἀμφότεραι. Ἡ αὐτὴ γὰρ τοῦ λόγου ὑπόστασις ἀμφοτέρων τῶν φύσεων ὑπόστασις χρηματίσασα οὔτε ἀνυπόστατον μίαν αὐτῶν εἶναι συγχωρεῖ οὔτε μὴν ἑτεροϋποστάτους ἀλλήλων εἶναι παραχωρεῖ, οὐδὲ ποτὲ μὲν τῆσδε ποτὲ δὲ ἐκείνης, ἀλλ' ἀεὶ ἀμφοτέρων ἀδιαιρέτως καὶ ἀχωρίστως ὑπάρχει ὑπόστασις, οὐ μεριζομένη καὶ διαιρουμένη καὶ μέρος μὲν αὐτῆς τῇδε, μέρος δὲ τῇδε διανέμουσα, ἀλλὰ πᾶσα ταύτης καὶ πᾶσα ἐκείνης ἀμερῶς καὶ ὁλοσχερῶς ὑπάρχουσα. Οὐ γὰρ ἰδιοσυστάτως ὑπέστη ἡ τοῦ θεοῦ λόγου σὰρξ οὐδὲ ἑτέρα ὑπόστασις γέγονε παρὰ τὴν τοῦ θεοῦ λόγου ὑπόστασιν, ἀλλ' ἐν αὐτῇ ὑποστᾶσα ἐνυπόστατος μᾶλλον καὶ οὐ καθ' αὑτὴν ἰδιοσύστατος ὑπόστασις γέγονε. Διὸ οὐδὲ ἀνυπόστατός ἐστιν οὐδὲ ἑτέραν ἐν τῇ τριάδι παρεισφέρει ὑπόστασιν.

his two natures are referred to one person and one hypostasis of God the Word). I am afraid to touch the piece of coal because of the fire combined with the wood. I worship Christ's "both together" because of the divinity united with the flesh. For I do not add a fourth person to the Trinity—God forbid!—but confess one person of God the Word and his flesh. For the Trinity remained a Trinity even after the incarnation of the Word.

53 *A reply to the question whether there is any nature without hypostasis*

For even if there is no nature without hypostasis or essence without individual expression (for essence and nature are contemplated in hypostases and individual existences), it is not necessary that the natures that have been united hypostatically to each other should each possess its own hypostasis. For it is possible for them to concur in a single hypostasis without being either anhypostatic or each having its own distinct hypostasis, but both together having one and the same [hypostasis]. For when the same hypostasis of the Word is called the hypostasis of both natures, this [statement] neither admits that one of them is anhypostatic, nor does it concede that they are distinct hypostatically from each other, nor is it a case of sometimes the one and sometimes the other, but [the statement affirms] that a hypostasis exists that always belongs to both without division and without separation, not shared and divided, with one part being apportioned to this and another to that, but the whole belonging to this and the whole belonging to that without division and in its entirety. For the flesh of God the Word did not subsist as a distinct entity, nor did a different hypostasis come into being other than the hypostasis of God the Word, but rather, [the flesh] became enhypostatic through being caused to exist within [the hypostasis of God the Word], and did not become a hypostasis subsisting independently in itself. Hence it is neither anhypostatic nor does it introduce another hypostasis into the Trinity.

54 Περὶ τοῦ τρισαγίου

Ἐντεῦθεν καὶ τὴν ἐν τῷ τρισαγίῳ προσθήκην ὑπὸ τοῦ
ματαιόφρονος Πέτρου τοῦ κναφέως γεγενημένην βλάσφημον
ὁριζόμεθα ὡς τέταρτον παρεισάγουσαν πρόσωπον καὶ ἀναμέρος
τιθεῖσαν τὸν τοῦ θεοῦ υἱὸν τὴν τοῦ πατρὸς ἐνυπόστατον δύναμιν
καὶ ἀναμέρος τὸν ἐσταυρωμένον ὡς ἄλλον ὄντα παρὰ τὸν ἰσχυρὸν
ἢ παθητὴν τὴν ἁγίαν τριάδα δοξάζουσαν καὶ συσταυροῦσαν
τῷ υἱῷ τὸν πατέρα καὶ τὸ πνεῦμα τὸ ἅγιον. Ἄπαγε ταύτην τὴν
βλάσφημον καὶ παρέγγραπτον φλυαρίαν. Ἡμεῖς γὰρ τὸ «ἅγιος
ὁ θεὸς» ἐπὶ τοῦ πατρὸς ἐκλαμβάνομεν οὐκ αὐτῷ μόνῳ τὸ τῆς
θεότητος ἀφορίζοντες ὄνομα, ἀλλὰ καὶ τὸν υἱὸν θεὸν εἰδότες καὶ
τὸ πνεῦμα τὸ ἅγιον, καὶ τὸ «ἅγιος ἰσχυρὸς» ἐπὶ τοῦ υἱοῦ τίθεμεν
οὐκ ἀπαμφιεννύντες τῆς ἰσχύος τὸν πατέρα καὶ τὸ πνεῦμα τὸ
ἅγιον, καὶ τὸ «ἅγιος ἀθάνατος» ἐπὶ τοῦ ἁγίου πνεύματος τάττομεν
οὐκ ἔξω τῆς ἀθανασίας τιθέντες τὸν πατέρα καὶ τὸν υἱόν, ἀλλ᾽
ἐφ᾽ ἑκάστης τῶν ὑποστάσεων πάσας τὰς θεωνυμίας ἁπλῶς καὶ
ἀπολύτως ἐκλαμβάνοντες καὶ τὸν θεῖον ἀπόστολον ἐκμιμούμενοι
φάσκοντα· «Ἡμῖν δὲ εἷς θεὸς ὁ πατήρ, ἐξ οὗ τὰ πάντα καὶ ἡμεῖς
ἐξ αὐτοῦ, καὶ εἷς κύριος Ἰησοῦς Χριστός, δι᾽ οὗ τὰ πάντα καὶ
ἡμεῖς δι᾽ αὐτοῦ», οὐ μὴν ἀλλὰ καὶ τὸν θεολόγον Γρηγόριον,
ὧδέ πη λέγοντα· «Ἡμῖν δὲ εἷς θεὸς ὁ πατήρ, ἐξ οὗ τὰ πάντα,
καὶ εἷς κύριος Ἰησοῦς Χριστός, δι᾽ οὗ τὰ πάντα, καὶ ἓν πνεῦμα
ἅγιον, ἐν ᾧ τὰ πάντα᾽, τοῦ ‘ἐξ οὗ’ καὶ ‘δι᾽ οὗ’ καὶ ‘ἐν ᾧ’ μὴ φύσεις
τεμνόντων (οὐδὲ γὰρ ἂν μετέπιπτον αἱ προθέσεις ἢ αἱ τάξεις τῶν
ὀνομάτων), ἀλλὰ χαρακτηριζόντων μιᾶς καὶ ἀσυγχύτου φύσεως
ἰδιότητας· καὶ τοῦτο δῆλον· ἐξ ὧν εἰς ἓν συνάγονται πάλιν, εἴ τῳ
μὴ παρέργως ἐκεῖνο ἀναγινώσκεται παρὰ τῷ ἀποστόλῳ, τὸ ‘ἐξ
αὐτοῦ καὶ δι᾽ αὐτοῦ καὶ εἰς αὐτὸν τὰ πάντα· αὐτῷ ἡ δόξα εἰς τοὺς
αἰῶνας. Ἀμήν᾽».

---

[1]The Trisagion ("Holy God, Holy Mighty, Holy Immortal, have mercy on us")
was generally understood to be addressed to the Trinity, but in Syria it was thought
to be addressed to Christ. Peter the Fuller (d. 488), the first anti-Chalcedonian patriarch of Antioch, made some controversial liturgical innovations, among them the

54   *On the Trisagion*

It follows from this that we define as blasphemous the addition to
the Trisagion made by the empty-headed Peter the Fuller,[1] since it
introduces a fourth person by treating the Son of God, who is the
enhypostatic power of the Father, separately from the crucified one as
if it considered him other than mighty, or considered the Holy Trinity
passible, and crucified the Father and the Holy Spirit along with the
Son. Away with this blasphemous and interpolated nonsense! For we
take the words "Holy God" to refer to the Father, not assigning the
name of divinity to him alone, but knowing that the Son is God as is
also the Holy Spirit. And we reckon the words "Holy Mighty" to apply
to the Son without stripping the Father and the Holy Spirit of might.
And we allot the word "Holy Immortal" to the Holy Spirit without
placing the Father and the Son outside of immortality. No, we take
all the divine names as applying simply and absolutely to each of the
hypostases, and imitate the divine Apostle, who says: "But for us there
is one God, the Father, from whom are all things and from whom we
exist, and one Lord Jesus Christ, through whom are all things and
through whom we exist,"[2] and also Gregory the Theologian, where
he says: "'But for us there is one God, the Father, from whom are all
things, and one Lord Jesus Christ, through whom are all things, and
in whom are all things,' the 'from whom' and 'through whom' and 'in
whom' not dividing the natures (for one may not change round the
prepositions or the order of the names), but indicating the properties
of a single unconfused nature. And this is clear. From these they come
together again into one if the Apostle's text that says 'From him and
through him and to him are all things. To him be the glory forever.
Amen'"[3] is not read perversely.

That the Trisagion is not addressed to the Son alone but to the
Holy Trinity, the divine and holy Athanasius bears witness, together

addition of the theopaschite formula ("who was crucified for us") to the third clause
of the Trisagion.

  [2]1 Cor 8.6.

  [3]Gregory of Nazianzus, *Oration* 39.12 (PG 36:348AB; Moreschini, 910).

Ὅτι γὰρ οὐκ εἰς τὸν υἱὸν μόνον λέλεκται τὸ τρισάγιον, ἀλλ᾽ εἰς τὴν ἁγίαν τριάδα, μάρτυς ὁ θεῖος καὶ ἱερὸς Ἀθανάσιος Βασίλειός τε καὶ Γρηγόριος καὶ πᾶς ὁ τῶν θεοφόρων πατέρων χορός, ὅτιπερ διὰ τῆς τρισσῆς ἁγιότητος τὰς τρεῖς τῆς ὑπερουσίου θεότητος ὑποστάσεις τὰ ἅγια Σεραφὶμ ἡμῖν ὑπεμφαίνουσι. Διὰ δὲ τῆς μιᾶς κυριότητος τὴν μίαν τῆς θεαρχικῆς τριάδος οὐσίαν τε καὶ βασιλείαν γνωρίζουσι. Φησὶ γοῦν ὁ θεολόγος Γρηγόριος· «Οὕτω μὲν οὖν τὰ ἅγια τῶν ἁγίων, ἃ καὶ τοῖς Σεραφὶμ συγκαλύπτεται καὶ δοξάζεται τρισὶν ἁγιασμοῖς εἰς μίαν συνιοῦσι κυριότητα καὶ θεότητα· ὃ καὶ ἄλλῳ τινὶ πρὸ ἡμῶν πεφιλοσόφηται κάλλιστά τε καὶ ὑψηλότατα».

Φασὶ μὲν οὖν οἱ τὴν ἐκκλησιαστικὴν ἱστορίαν συντάξαντες λιτανεύοντος τοῦ ἐν Κωνσταντινουπόλει λαοῦ διά τινα θεήλατον ἀπειλὴν ἐπὶ Πρόκλου τοῦ ἀρχιεπισκόπου γεγενημένην, ἀφαρπαχθῆναι παιδίον τοῦ λαοῦ καὶ οὕτω μυηθῆναι ὑπ᾽ ἀγγελικῆς τινος διδασκαλίας τὸν τρισάγιον ὕμνον «ἅγιος ὁ θεός, ἅγιος ἰσχυρός, ἅγιος ἀθάνατος, ἐλέησον ἡμᾶς» καὶ αὖθις ἐπιστραφέντος τοῦ παιδίου καὶ τὸ μυηθὲν ἀπαγγείλαντος ᾆσαι τὸν ὕμνον ἅπαν τὸ πλῆθος καὶ οὕτω κοπάσαι τὴν ἀπειλήν. Καὶ ἐν τῇ ἁγίᾳ δὲ καὶ μεγάλῃ τῇ οἰκουμενικῇ τετάρτῃ συνόδῳ, τῇ ἐν Χαλκηδόνι φημί, οὕτως ὑμνηθῆναι ὁ τρισάγιος οὗτος ὕμνος παραδέδοται· οὕτω γὰρ τοῖς πεπραγμένοις τῆς αὐτῆς ἁγίας συνόδου ἐμφέρεται. Γέλως οὖν ὄντως καὶ παίγνιον τὴν δι᾽ ἀγγέλων μυηθεῖσαν καὶ τῇ τῆς ἐπαγωγῆς λήξει πιστωθεῖσαν καὶ τῇ τοσῶνδε ἁγίων πατέρων συνόδῳ κυρωθεῖσαν καὶ βεβαιωθεῖσαν καὶ πρότερον ὑπὸ τῶν Σεραφὶμ ὑμνηθεῖσαν τὴν τρισάγιον ᾠδὴν ὡς τῆς τρισυποστάτου θεότητος ἐμφαντικὴν τῇ τοῦ κναφέως οἷον καταπατηθῆναι ἀλόγῳ οἰήσει καὶ δῆθεν διορθωθῆναι ὡς τῶν Σεραφὶμ ὑπερβάλλοντος. Ἀλλ᾽ ὦ τῆς αὐθαδείας, ἵνα μὴ λέγω τῆς ἀνοίας. Ἡμεῖς δὲ οὕτω φαμέν, κἂν δαίμονες διαρρήγνυνται· «Ἅγιος ὁ θεός, ἅγιος ἰσχυρός, ἅγιος ἀθάνατος, ἐλέησον ἡμᾶς».

---

[4]Gregory of Nazianzus, *Oration* 38.8 (PG 36:320BC; Moreschini, 886).
[5]Proclus was archbishop of Constantinople from 434 to 446. John mentions him in connection with the first time the Trisagion was sung, but perhaps also has in mind

with Basil, Gregory, and the whole choir of the God-bearing fathers, that through the threefold holiness the holy seraphim indicate to us the three hypostases of the superessential divinity. But through the single dominion they acknowledge the single essence and kingdom of the thearchic Trinity. Gregory the Theologian therefore says: "Thus, then, the Holy of Holies, which is both veiled by the seraphim and glorified by the threefold repetition of 'holy,' comes together as a single dominion and divinity, as discussed by somebody else before us in a most beautiful and sublime manner."[4]

Those, then, who have composed the history of the Church say that once in the time of Archbishop Proclus,[5] when the people of Constantinople were holding a procession to avert some threat sent by God, a child in the crowd went into an ecstasy and in this state was initiated by some angelic teaching into the Trisagion hymn, "Holy God, Holy Mighty, Holy Immortal, have mercy on us." And when the child came back to its senses again and announced what it had been taught, the whole crowd sang the hymn and so averted the threat.[6] And it has been handed down to us that at the holy and great Fourth Ecumenical Council, I mean the Council of Chalcedon, the Trisagion hymn was sung in this way, for that is what is recorded in the acts of this holy council.[7] It is therefore truly ridiculous and comical that the Trisagion hymn, which has been taught by angels, and attested by the cessation of the attack, and ratified and confirmed by the council of so many holy fathers, and was previously sung by the seraphim as revelatory of the trihypostatic Godhead, should, as it were, be trampled down and supposedly corrected by the foolish Fuller as if he were superior to the seraphim. What arrogance, not to say stupidity! What we say, even if the demons should burst, is: "Holy God, Holy Mighty, Holy Immortal, have mercy on us."

his statement in his *Tome to the Armenians* that one of the Trinity became incarnate, which was taken by some in a theopaschite sense.

    [6]The legend, as recorded in the Greek *Menologion*, attributes the threat to a series of earthquakes.

    [7]In the acclamations after the condemnation and deposition of Dioscorus of Alexandria, ACO 2.1.1, p. 195.30.

55 Περὶ τῆς ἐν εἴδει καὶ ἐν ἀτόμῳ θεωρουμένης φύσεως καὶ διαφορᾶς, ἑνώσεως καὶ σαρκώσεως, καὶ πῶς ἐκληπτέον «τὴν μίαν φύσιν τοῦ θεοῦ λόγου σεσαρκωμένην»

Ἡ φύσις ἢ ψιλῇ θεωρίᾳ κατανοεῖται (καθ᾽ αὑτὴν γὰρ οὐχ ὑφέστηκεν), ἢ κοινῶς ἐν πάσαις ταῖς ὁμοειδέσιν ὑποστάσεσι ταύτας συνάπτουσα καὶ λέγεται ἐν τῷ εἴδει θεωρουμένη φύσις, ἢ ὁλικῶς ἡ αὐτὴ ἐν προσλήψει συμβεβηκότων ἐν μιᾷ ὑποστάσει καὶ λέγεται ἐν ἀτόμῳ θεωρουμένη φύσις. Ὁ οὖν θεὸς λόγος σαρκωθεὶς οὔτε τὴν ἐν ψιλῇ θεωρίᾳ κατανοουμένην φύσιν ἀνέλαβεν (οὐ γὰρ σάρκωσις τοῦτο, ἀλλ᾽ ἀπάτη καὶ πλάσμα σαρκώσεως) οὔτε τὴν ἐν τῷ εἴδει θεωρουμένην (οὐ γὰρ πάσας τὰς ὑποστάσεις ἀνέλαβεν), ἀλλὰ τὴν ἐν ἀτόμῳ τὴν αὐτὴν οὖσαν τῷ εἴδει (ἀπαρχὴν γὰρ ἀνέλαβε τοῦ ἡμετέρου φυράματος), οὐ καθ᾽ αὑτὴν ὑποστᾶσαν καὶ ἄτομον χρηματίσασαν πρότερον καὶ οὕτως ὑπ᾽ αὐτοῦ προσληφθεῖσαν, ἀλλ᾽ ἐν τῇ αὐτοῦ ὑποστάσει ὑπάρξασαν. Αὐτὴ γὰρ ἡ ὑπόστασις τοῦ θεοῦ λόγου ἐγένετο τῇ σαρκὶ ὑπόστασις, καὶ κατὰ τοῦτο «ὁ λόγος σὰρξ ἐγένετο», ἀτρέπτως δηλαδή, καὶ ἡ σὰρξ λόγος ἀμεταβλήτως, καὶ ὁ θεὸς ἄνθρωπος· θεὸς γὰρ ὁ λόγος, καὶ ὁ ἄνθρωπος θεὸς διὰ τὴν καθ᾽ ὑπόστασιν ἕνωσιν. Ταὐτὸν οὖν ἐστιν εἰπεῖν φύσιν τοῦ λόγου καὶ τὴν ἐν ἀτόμῳ φύσιν· οὔτε γὰρ τὸ ἄτομον ἤγουν τὴν ὑπόστασιν κυρίως καὶ μόνως δηλοῖ οὔτε τὸ κοινὸν τῶν ὑποστάσεων, ἀλλὰ τὴν κοινὴν φύσιν ἐν μιᾷ τῶν ὑποστάσεων θεωρουμένην καὶ ἐξεταζομένην.

---

[1]See Krausmüller's interesting discussion of this sentence in "A Conceptualist Turn," 248–49. The first two options follow Basil and Gregory of Nyssa in affirming the reality of universals only in their instantiations. The third option is "decidedly odd" because according to the classic expression of Trinitarian theology it appears to be unnecessary (p. 248). Krausmüller accounts for it by arguing that there is no distinction between the "as common" (κοινῶς, koinōs) and the "wholly" (ὁλικῶς, holikōs) of the second and third options. The logical contrast with "as common" (or "commonly") is "individually" (ἰδικῶς, idikōs), but to have introduced this would have been to make an unacceptable contrast between a common nature and an

55   *On the nature and difference observable in the species and the individual, on union and incarnation, and on how the expression "one enfleshed nature of God the Word" is to be taken*

Nature is apprehended either as a pure concept (for in itself it has no subsistence), or as that which unites what is common to all hypostases of the same species and is called a nature observable in the species, or as that which with the addition of accidents exists wholly in a single hypostasis and is called a nature observable in the individual.[1] Thus when God the Word was enfleshed, he did not assume nature in the purely conceptual sense (for that would not be [a true] incarnation but a fraudulent and fictitious one), or the nature observable in the species (for he did not assume all the hypostases [in the species]), but the nature observable in the individual that is the same as that in the species (for he assumed what was representative of our clay), which did not subsist in itself and previously have the status of an individual and was thus assumed by him, but on the contrary, attained existence in his own hypostasis. For this same hypostasis of God the Word became the hypostasis of the flesh, and in this sense "the Word became flesh,"[2] that is to say, without change, and the flesh became Word without alteration, and God became a human being. For the Word was God and the human being was God through the hypostatic union. Therefore the expressions "the nature of the Word" and "the nature in the individual" are identical in meaning. For properly speaking [these expressions] do not signify exclusively either the individual, that is to say, the hypostasis, or what is common to the hypostases, but the common nature observed and examined in one of the hypostases.

individual nature. It is for this reason that John speaks of "a nature with the addition of accidents." Krausmüller, however, is not impressed. He concludes: "John's reference to the hypostatic idioms, which is rather clumsily inserted into the text, provides no solution because it is not the common but the individual nature to which these idioms accede" (p. 249).

[2] Jn 1.14.

Ἄλλο μὲν οὖν ἐστιν ἕνωσις, καὶ ἕτερον σάρκωσις· ἡ μὲν γὰρ ἕνωσις μόνην δηλοῖ τὴν συνάφειαν, πρὸς τί δὲ γέγονεν ἡ συνάφεια, οὐκέτι. Ἡ δὲ σάρκωσις, ταὐτὸν δ' ἐστὶν εἰπεῖν καὶ ἐνανθρώπησις, τὴν πρὸς σάρκα ἤτοι πρὸς ἄνθρωπον συνάφειαν δηλοῖ, καθάπερ καὶ ἡ πύρωσις τὴν πρὸς τὸ πῦρ ἕνωσιν. Αὐτὸς μὲν οὖν ὁ μακάριος Κύριλλος ἐν τῇ πρὸς Σούκενσον δευτέρᾳ ἐπιστολῇ ἑρμηνεύων τὸ «μίαν φύσιν τοῦ θεοῦ λόγου σεσαρκωμένην» οὕτω φησίν· «Εἰ μὲν γὰρ μίαν εἰπόντες τοῦ λόγου φύσιν σεσιγήκαμεν, οὐκ ἐπενεγκόντες τὸ ʽσεσαρκωμένηνʼ, ἀλλ' οἷον ἔξω τιθέντες τὴν οἰκονομίαν, ἦν αὐτοῖς τάχα που καὶ οὐκ ἀπίθανος ὁ λόγος προσποιουμένοις ἐρωτᾶν· Εἰ μία φύσις τὸ ὅλον, ποῦ τὸ τέλειον ἐν ἀνθρωπότητι; Ἢ πῶς ὑφέστηκεν ἡ καθ' ἡμᾶς οὐσία; Ἐπειδὴ δὲ καὶ ἡ ἐν ἀνθρωπότητι τελειότης καὶ τῆς καθ' ἡμᾶς οὐσίας ἡ δήλωσις εἰσκεκόμισται διὰ τοῦ λέγειν ʽσεσαρκωμένηνʼ, παυσάσθωσαν καλαμίνην ῥάβδον ἑαυτοῖς ὑποστήσαντες». Ἐνταῦθα μὲν οὖν τὴν φύσιν τοῦ λόγου ἐπὶ τῆς φύσεως ἔταξεν. Εἰ γὰρ ἀντὶ ὑποστάσεως τὴν φύσιν παρείληφεν, οὐκ ἄτοπον ἦν, καὶ δίχα τοῦ «σεσαρκωμένην» τοῦτο εἰπεῖν· μίαν γὰρ ὑπόστασιν τοῦ θεοῦ λόγου ἀπολύτως λέγοντες οὐ σφαλλόμεθα. Ὁμοίως δὲ καὶ Λεόντιος ὁ Βυζάντιος ἐπὶ τῆς φύσεως τὸ ῥητὸν ἐνόησεν, οὐκ ἀντὶ τῆς ὑποστάσεως. Ἐν δὲ τῇ πρὸς τὰς Θεοδωρήτου μέμψεις τοῦ δευτέρου ἀναθεματισμοῦ οὕτω φησὶν ὁ μακάριος Κύριλλος· «Ἡ φύσις τοῦ λόγου ἤγουν ἡ ὑπόστασις, ὅ ἐστιν αὐτὸς ὁ λόγος». Ὥστε τὸ εἰπεῖν «φύσιν τοῦ λόγου» οὔτε τὴν ὑπόστασιν μόνην σημαίνει οὔτε τὸ κοινὸν τῶν ὑποστάσεων, ἀλλὰ τὴν κοινὴν φύσιν ἐν τῇ τοῦ λόγου ὑποστάσει ὁλικῶς θεωρουμένην.

Ὅτι μὲν οὖν ἡ φύσις τοῦ λόγου ἐσαρκώθη ἤτοι ἡνώθη σαρκί, εἴρηται. Φύσιν δὲ τοῦ λόγου παθοῦσαν σαρκὶ οὐδέπω καὶ νῦν ἀκηκόαμεν, Χριστὸν δὲ παθόντα σαρκὶ ἐδιδάχθημεν· ὥστε οὐ τὴν

---

[3]Cyril of Alexandria, *Second Letter to Succensus* 4 (Wickham, 88–90; trans. Wickham, 89–91, modified).

[4]See Leontius of Byzantium, *Epaporēmata* (*Thirty Chapters against Severus*) 24 (Daley, *Leontius of Byzantium*, 326.6–16).

Union, then, is one thing and enfleshment is another. For union indicates only the conjunction; it does not yet indicate in relation to what the conjunction has taken place. Enfleshment (σάρκωσις, *sarkōsis*), which is the same as saying inhomination (ἐνανθρώπησις, *enanthrōpēsis*), indicates the conjunction with flesh, that is, with human nature, just as ignition indicates union with fire. The blessed Cyril himself, when interpreting the phrase "one enfleshed nature of God the Word" in his *Second Letter to Succensus*, says the following: "If we had spoken of the one nature of the Word without making the overt addition 'enfleshed,' to the exclusion apparently of the divine plan, there might have been some plausibility to their pretended question about the complete humanity or the possibility of our substance's continued existence. In view, though, of the fact that the introduction of the word 'enfleshed' expresses completeness in manhood and our nature, they should cease leaning on that broken reed."[3] In this passage, then, he interpreted "nature" as the nature of the Word. For if he had taken "nature" in the sense of "hypostasis," it would not have been absurd to have uttered the phrase without the word "enfleshed." For if we say simply "one hypostasis of God the Word," we are not wrong. Moreover, Leontius of Byzantium understood the expression in the same way as referring to nature, but not to nature instead of hypostasis.[4] And in his response to Theodoret's complaints against the second of the anathemas, the blessed Cyril uses the following expression: "The nature of the Word, namely, the hypostasis, which is the Word himself."[5] So to say "the nature of the Word" signifies neither the hypostasis on its own nor what is common to the hypostases, but the common nature contemplated wholly in the hypostasis of the Word.

It is said, then, that the nature of the Word became flesh, that is, was united with the flesh. Never until now have we heard that the nature of the Word suffered in the flesh. We have been taught that

[5]Cyril, *Against Theodoret*, ACO 1.1.6, p. 115.2. The anathemas are the "Twelve Chapters," the anathematized propositions that Cyril appended to his *Third Letter to Nestorius* (trans. Wickham, 29–33).

ὑπόστασιν δηλοῖ τὸ εἰπεῖν «φύσιν τοῦ λόγου». Λείπεται τοίνυν εἰπεῖν, ὅτι τὸ σεσαρκῶσθαι μὲν ἡνῶσθαί ἐστι σαρκί, τὸ δὲ σάρκα γενέσθαι τὸν λόγον αὐτὴν τὴν τοῦ λόγου ὑπόστασιν ἀτρέπτως γενέσθαι τῆς σαρκὸς ὑπόστασιν. Καὶ ὅτι μὲν ὁ θεὸς ἄνθρωπος γέγονε καὶ ὁ ἄνθρωπος θεός, εἴρηται. Θεὸς γὰρ ὁ λόγος, γέγονεν δὲ ἀμεταβλήτως ἄνθρωπος. Ὅτι δὲ ἡ θεότης ἄνθρωπος γέγονεν ἢ ἐσαρκώθη ἢ ἐνηνθρώπησεν, οὐδαμῶς ἀκηκόαμεν. Ὅτι δὲ ἡ θεότης ἡνώθη τῇ ἀνθρωπότητι ἐν μιᾷ τῶν αὐτῆς ὑποστάσεων, μεμαθήκαμεν. Καὶ ὅτι ὁ θεὸς μορφοῦται ἤτοι οὐσιοῦται τὸ ἀλλότριον ἤτοι τὸ καθ' ἡμᾶς, εἴρηται. Ἐφ' ἑκάστης γὰρ τῶν ὑποστάσεων τὸ θεὸς ὄνομα τάττεται, θεότητα δὲ ἐπὶ ὑποστάσεως εἰπεῖν οὐ δυνάμεθα. Θεότητα γὰρ τὸν πατέρα μόνον ἢ τὸν υἱὸν μόνον ἢ μόνον τὸ πνεῦμα τὸ ἅγιον οὐκ ἀκηκόαμεν· θεότης μὲν γὰρ τὴν φύσιν δηλοῖ, τὸ δὲ πατὴρ τὴν ὑπόστασιν, ὥσπερ καὶ ἀνθρωπότης τὴν φύσιν, Πέτρος δὲ τὴν ὑπόστασιν. Θεὸς δὲ καὶ τὸ κοινὸν τῆς φύσεως σημαίνει καὶ ἐφ' ἑκάστη τῶν ὑποστάσεων τάττεται παρωνύμως ὥσπερ καὶ ἄνθρωπος· θεὸς γάρ ἐστιν ὁ θείαν ἔχων φύσιν, καὶ ἄνθρωπος ὁ ἀνθρωπίνην.

Ἐπὶ πᾶσι τούτοις ἰστέον, ὡς ὁ πατὴρ καὶ τὸ πνεῦμα τὸ ἅγιον κατ' οὐδένα λόγον τῇ σαρκώσει τοῦ λόγου κεκοινώνηκεν εἰ μὴ κατὰ τὰς θεοσημίας καὶ κατ' εὐδοκίαν καὶ βούλησιν.

56 Ὅτι θεοτόκος ἡ ἁγία παρθένος

Θεοτόκον δὲ κυρίως καὶ ἀληθῶς τὴν ἁγίαν παρθένον κηρύττομεν· ὡς γὰρ θεὸς ἀληθὴς ὁ ἐξ αὐτῆς γεννηθείς, ἀληθὴς θεοτόκος ἡ τὸν ἀληθινὸν θεὸν ἐξ αὐτῆς σεσαρκωμένον γεννήσασα. Θεὸν γὰρ

---

[1]Θεοτόκος (*Theotokos*), literally "God-birthing," often translated as "Mother of God" (which I have reserved for θεομήτωρ [*theomētōr*] and θεοῦ μήτηρ [*theou mētēr*]), and sometimes as "God-bearing" (which I have reserved for θεοφόρος

it was Christ who suffered in the flesh. Consequently, to say "the nature of the Word" does not indicate the hypostasis. What therefore remains to be said is that on the one hand to be enfleshed means to be united with the flesh, and on the other the Word's becoming flesh means that the hypostasis of the Word itself became without change the hypostasis of the flesh. Moreover, it may be said that God became man and man God. For God the Word became man without alteration. That the Godhead became man or was enfleshed or inhominated, we have in no way heard said. What we have been taught is that the Godhead in one of its hypostases was united to humanity. And that God assumed a form or substance that was alien to him, that is to say, our own nature, is also said. For the name "God" (θεός, *theos*) is applied to each of the hypostases, but we cannot say "Godhead" (θεότης, *theotēs*) of a hypostasis. For we have not heard of "Godhead" as the Father alone, or the Son alone, or the Holy Spirit alone. "Godhead" indicates the nature, and "Father" the hypostasis, just as humanity indicates the nature and Peter the hypostasis. "God" signifies both what is common to the nature and, derivatively, what applies to each of the hypostases, just as "man" does. For "God" is that which possesses a divine nature, and "man" that which possesses a human nature.

With regard to all these points one should know that the Father and the Holy Spirit in no sense participated in the enfleshment of the Word except with regard to the miracles and with regard to good pleasure and counsel.

56 *That the holy Virgin is Theotokos*

We proclaim the holy Virgin literally and truly Theotokos,[1] for since he who was born from her was truly God, she who gave birth to the true God who became incarnate from her was truly God-birthing. For we say that God was born from her, not that the divinity of the

---

[*theophoros*], a term often applied to the saints, to which John strongly objects as a term applicable to the Virgin in relation to Christ).

φαμεν ἐξ αὐτῆς γεγεννῆσθαι, οὐχ ὡς τῆς θεότητος τοῦ λόγου
ἀρχὴν τοῦ εἶναι λαβούσης ἐξ αὐτῆς, ἀλλ᾽ ὡς αὐτοῦ τοῦ θεοῦ
λόγου τοῦ πρὸ αἰώνων ἀχρόνως ἐκ τοῦ πατρὸς γεννηθέντος καὶ
ἀνάρχως καὶ ἀιδίως ὑπάρχοντος σὺν τῷ πατρὶ καὶ τῷ πνεύματι ἐπ᾽
ἐσχάτων τῶν ἡμερῶν διὰ τὴν ἡμετέραν σωτηρίαν ἐν τῇ γαστρὶ
αὐτῆς ἐνοικήσαντος καὶ ἐξ αὐτῆς ἀμεταβλήτως σαρκωθέντος
καὶ γεννηθέντος. Οὐ γὰρ ἄνθρωπον ψιλὸν ἐγέννησεν ἡ ἁγία
παρθένος, ἀλλὰ θεὸν ἀληθινόν, οὐ γυμνὸν ἀλλὰ σεσαρκωμένον,
οὐκ οὐρανόθεν τὸ σῶμα καταγαγόντα καὶ ὡς διὰ σωλῆνος
δι᾽ αὐτῆς παρελθόντα, ἀλλ᾽ ἐξ αὐτῆς ὁμοούσιον ἡμῖν σάρκα
ἀναλαβόντα καὶ ἐν ἑαυτῷ ὑποστήσαντα. Εἰ γὰρ οὐρανόθεν τὸ
σῶμα κεκόμισται καὶ οὐκ ἐκ τῆς καθ᾽ ἡμᾶς φύσεως εἴληπται, τίς
χρεία τῆς ἐνανθρωπήσεως; Ἡ γὰρ ἐνανθρώπησις τοῦ θεοῦ λόγου
διὰ τοῦτο γέγονεν, ἵνα αὐτὴ ἡ ἁμαρτήσασα καὶ πεσοῦσα καὶ
φθαρεῖσα φύσις νικήσῃ τὸν ἀπατήσαντα τύραννον καὶ οὕτω τῆς
φθορᾶς ἐλευθερωθῇ, καθώς φησιν ὁ θεῖος ἀπόστολος· «Ἐπειδὴ
δι᾽ ἀνθρώπου ὁ θάνατος, καὶ δι᾽ ἀνθρώπου ἀνάστασις νεκρῶν»· εἰ
τὸ πρῶτον ἀληθῶς, καὶ τὸ δεύτερον.

Εἰ δὲ καὶ λέγει· «Ὁ πρῶτος Ἀδὰμ ἐκ γῆς χοϊκός, ὁ δεύτερος
Ἀδάμ, ὁ κύριος, ἐξ οὐρανοῦ», οὐ τὸ σῶμά φησιν ἐξ οὐρανοῦ, ἀλλὰ
δηλῶν ὡς οὐ ψιλὸς ἄνθρωπός ἐστιν. Ἰδοὺ γὰρ καὶ Ἀδὰμ αὐτὸν
ὠνόμασε καὶ κύριον τὸ συναμφότερον σημαίνων. Ἀδὰμ μὲν γὰρ
ἑρμηνεύεται γηγενής· γηγενὴς δὲ δῆλον, ὡς ἔστιν ἡ ἀνθρώπου
φύσις ἡ ἐκ χοὸς πλασθεῖσα· κύριος δὲ τῆς θείας οὐσίας ἐστὶ
παραστατικόν.

Πάλιν δέ φησιν ὁ ἀπόστολος· «Ἐξαπέστειλεν ὁ θεὸς τὸν υἱὸν
αὐτοῦ τὸν μονογενῆ γεννώμενον ἐκ γυναικός». Οὐκ εἶπε διὰ
γυναικός, ἀλλ᾽ «ἐκ γυναικός». Ἐσήμανεν οὖν ὁ θεῖος ἀπόστολος,
ὡς αὐτός ἐστιν ὁ μονογενὴς υἱὸς τοῦ θεοῦ καὶ θεὸς ὁ ἐκ τῆς
παρθένου γενόμενος ἄνθρωπος καὶ αὐτός ἐστιν ὁ ἐκ τῆς παρθένου
γεννηθεὶς ὁ υἱὸς τοῦ θεοῦ καὶ θεός, γεννηθεὶς δὲ σωματικῶς, καθὸ

Word received the beginning of its being from her, but that the very Word of God, who before the ages was timelessly begotten of the Father and exists without beginning and eternally with the Father and the Spirit, in the last days for our salvation came to dwell in her womb and was made flesh and was born from her without undergoing any change. For the holy Virgin did not give birth to a mere human being, but to true God, not unclothed but enfleshed, not bringing down his body from heaven and passing through her as if through a tube,[2] but receiving flesh from her of the same substance as ours and subsisting in himself. For if he brought down his body from heaven and did not receive it from our own nature, what use would there have been for the inhomination? For the inhomination of God the Word took place for this reason, so that this nature that has sinned and fallen and become corrupted should vanquish the tyrant that deceived it and thus be freed from corruption, as the divine Apostle says: "For since death came through a human being, the resurrection of the dead has also come through a human being."[3] If the first is true, so is the second.

And although the Apostle also says: "The first Adam was from the earth, the second Adam, the Lord, is from heaven,"[4] he does not say that his body was from heaven but shows that he was not a mere human being. For note how he named him both Adam and Lord, meaning the two together. For Adam, when translated means "earthborn," and earthborn signifies that human nature was formed out of dust. But "Lord" is indicative of the divine essence.

Moreover, the Apostle says: "God sent his only-begotten Son born of a woman."[5] He did not say "through a woman" but "of a woman." Therefore the divine Apostle indicated that the only-begotten Son of God and God is the same as him who became a human being from the Virgin, and that he who was born from the Virgin is the same as the Son of God and God, who was born corporeally,

---

[2] A Valentinian notion rejected by John Damascene (following Epiphanius of Salamis, *Panarion* 1.388) in *On Heresies* 31.

[3] 1 Cor 15.21.   [4] 1 Cor 15.47.   [5] Gal 4.4.

γέγονεν ἄνθρωπος, οὐ προδιαπλασθέντι ἀνθρώπῳ ἐνοικήσας
ὡς ἐν προφήτῃ, ἀλλ' αὐτὸς οὐσιωδῶς καὶ ἀληθῶς γενόμενος
ἄνθρωπος ἤτοι ἐν τῇ ὑποστάσει αὐτοῦ ἐψυχωμένην σάρκα ψυχῇ
λογικῇ τε καὶ νοερᾷ ὑποστήσας, αὐτὸς γεγονὼς αὐτῇ ὑπόστασις·
τοῦτο γὰρ σημαίνει τὸ «γενόμενον ἐκ γυναικός». Πῶς γὰρ ἂν
αὐτὸς ὁ τοῦ θεοῦ λόγος ὑπὸ νόμον γέγονεν, εἰ μὴ ἄνθρωπος ἡμῖν
ὁμοούσιος γέγονεν;
    Ὅθεν δικαίως καὶ ἀληθῶς θεοτόκον τὴν ἁγίαν Μαρίαν
ὀνομάζομεν· τοῦτο γὰρ τὸ ὄνομα ἅπαν τὸ μυστήριον τῆς
οἰκονομίας συνίστησι. Εἰ γὰρ θεοτόκος ἡ γεννήσασα, πάντως
θεὸς ὁ ἐξ αὐτῆς γεννηθείς, πάντως δὲ καὶ ἄνθρωπος. Πῶς γὰρ ἂν
ἐκ γυναικὸς γεννηθείη θεὸς ὁ πρὸ αἰώνων ἔχων τὴν ὕπαρξιν, εἰ μὴ
ἄνθρωπος γέγονεν; Ὁ γὰρ υἱὸς ἀνθρώπου ἄνθρωπος δηλονότι.
Εἰ δὲ αὐτὸς ὁ γεννηθεὶς ἐκ γυναικὸς θεός ἐστιν, εἷς ἐστι δηλονότι
ὁ ἐκ θεοῦ πατρὸς γεννηθεὶς κατὰ τὴν θείαν καὶ ἄναρχον οὐσίαν
καὶ ἐπ' ἐσχάτων τῶν χρόνων ἐκ τῆς παρθένου τεχθεὶς κατὰ τὴν
ἠργμένην καὶ ὑπὸ χρόνον οὐσίαν ἤτοι τὴν ἀνθρωπίνην. Τοῦτο δὲ
μίαν ὑπόστασιν καὶ δύο φύσεις καὶ δύο γεννήσεις σημαίνει τοῦ
κυρίου ἡμῶν Ἰησοῦ Χριστοῦ.
    Χριστοτόκον δὲ οὔ φαμεν τὴν ἁγίαν παρθένον, διότι ἐπ'
ἀναιρέσει τῆς θεοτόκος φωνῆς ὁ μιαρὸς καὶ βδελυρὸς καὶ
ἰουδαιόφρων Νεστόριος, τὸ σκεῦος τῆς ἀτιμίας, καὶ ἐπὶ ἀτιμίᾳ
τῆς μόνης ὄντως τετιμημένης ὑπὲρ πᾶσαν κτίσιν θεοτόκου, κἂν
αὐτὸς διαρρήγνυται σὺν τῷ πατρὶ αὐτοῦ τῷ σατανᾷ, ἐξηύρατο
ὡς ἐπηρεαζομένην· χριστὸς γὰρ καὶ Δαυὶδ ὁ βασιλεὺς καὶ Ἀαρὼν
ὁ ἀρχιερεύς (ταῦτα γὰρ τὰ χριόμενα, βασιλεία τε καὶ ἱερωσύνη)
καὶ πᾶς θεοφόρος ἄνθρωπος Χριστὸς λέγεσθαι δύναται, ἀλλ'
οὐ θεὸς φύσει, ὡς καὶ Νεστόριος ὁ θεήλατος τὸν ἐκ παρθένου

---

[6]The turn of phrase here alludes to Arius and beyond him to Judas. Athanasius reports that Arius (the archetypal heretic for the fourth-century fathers) died
suddenly in Constantinople in 336, apparently after collapsing while sitting on the
lavatory. "Falling face first," says Athanasius, "he burst in the middle" (Letter 54.3,
in *Athanasius Werke*, vol. 2.1, ed. H. G. Opitz [Berlin: De Gruyter, 1940], 178–80),

in that he became man, not coming to dwell in an already existing human being, as if in a prophet, but the same essentially and truly became man, that is to say, gave substance in his own hypostasis to ensouled flesh endowed with a rational and intelligent soul, the same having become himself a hypostasis for it. For this is what the phrase "became [a human being] of a woman" means. For how would the Word of God himself have become subject to the law, if he had not become a human being of the same substance as ourselves?

Consequently, we rightly and truly call the holy Mary "Theotokos," for this name encapsulates the entire mystery of the economy. For if she who gave birth to him was Theotokos, he who was born of her was necessarily God, and was also necessarily human. For how could God, who has his existence before the ages, have been born of a woman unless he became human? For the Son of Man was clearly a human being. If he who was born of a woman is God, then clearly he who was born of God the Father with regard to his divine and eternal essence and in the last years was born of the Virgin in accordance with that nature that had a beginning and is subject to time, namely, human nature, is one and the same. This [word "Theotokos"] indicates the one hypostasis and two natures and double generation of our Lord Jesus Christ.

We do not call the holy Virgin Christotokos because the foul and loathsome and Jewish-minded Nestorius, the vessel of dishonor, invented this as a term of abuse, even if he himself would burst with Satan, his father,[6] in order to do away with the title of Theotokos and bring dishonor on the Theotokos, who alone has truly been honored above all creation.[7] For David the king and Aaron the high priest (for the anointed offices are these: kingship and priesthood) and every God-bearing human being may be called Christ but is not God by

alluding to Judas, of whom it is reported by the evangelist Luke that "falling headlong, he burst open in the middle and all his bowels gushed out" (Acts 1.18). (IG)

[7]Nestorius had proposed that the term Christotokos should be used instead of Theotokos in order to exclude any idea of passibility in the Godhead. This was the issue that sparked the controversy between him and Cyril of Alexandria that led to his condemnation at the Council of Ephesus (431).

τεχθέντα θεοφόρον εἰπεῖν ἐφρυάξατο. Ἡμᾶς δὲ μὴ γένοιτο
θεοφόρον αὐτὸν εἰπεῖν ἢ νοῆσαι, ἀλλὰ θεὸν σεσαρκωμένον.
Αὐτὸς γὰρ ὁ λόγος σὰρξ ἐγένετο, κυηθεὶς μὲν ἐκ τῆς παρθένου,
προελθὼν δὲ θεὸς μετὰ τῆς προσλήψεως, ἤδη καὶ αὐτῆς ὑπ'
αὐτοῦ θεωθείσης ἅμα τῇ εἰς τὸ εἶναι ταύτης παραγωγῇ, ὡς ὁμοῦ
γενέσθαι τὰ τρία, τὴν πρόσληψιν, τὴν ὕπαρξιν, τὴν θέωσιν αὐτῆς
ὑπὸ τοῦ λόγου, καὶ οὕτω νοεῖσθαι καὶ λέγεσθαι θεοτόκον τὴν
ἁγίαν παρθένον οὐ μόνον διὰ τὴν φύσιν τοῦ λόγου, ἀλλὰ καὶ διὰ
τὴν θέωσιν τοῦ ἀνθρωπίνου, ὧν ἅμα ἡ σύλληψις καὶ ἡ ὕπαρξις
τεθαυματούργηται, ἡ μὲν σύλληψις τοῦ λόγου, τῆς δὲ σαρκὸς
ἡ ἐν αὐτῷ τῷ λόγῳ ὕπαρξις, αὐτῆς τῆς θεομήτορος ὑπερφυῶς
χορηγούσης τὸ πλασθῆναι τῷ πλάστῃ καὶ τὸ ἀνθρωπισθῆναι τῷ
θεῷ καὶ ποιητῇ τοῦ παντὸς θεοῦντι τὸ πρόσλημμα, σῳζούσης
τῆς ἑνώσεως τὰ ἑνωθέντα τοιαῦτα, οἷα καὶ ἥνωνται· οὐ τὸ θεῖον
λέγω μόνον, ἀλλὰ καὶ τὸ ἀνθρώπινον τοῦ Χριστοῦ τὸ ὑπὲρ ἡμᾶς
καὶ καθ' ἡμᾶς. Οὔτε γὰρ γενόμενος πρότερον καθ' ἡμᾶς ὕστερον
γέγονεν ὑπὲρ ἡμᾶς, ἀλλ' ἢ ἐκ πρώτης ὑπάρξεως ἄμφω ὑπῆρξε διὰ
τὸ ἐξ ἄκρας συλλήψεως ἐν αὐτῷ τῷ λόγῳ τὴν ὕπαρξιν ἐσχηκέναι·
ἀνθρώπινον μὲν οὖν ἐστι κατὰ τὴν οἰκείαν φύσιν, θεοῦ δὲ καὶ
θεῖον ὑπερφυῶς. Ἔτι δὲ καὶ τῆς ἐμψύχου σαρκὸς τὰ ἰδιώματα
ἔσχε· κατεδέξατο γὰρ αὐτὰ ὁ λόγος οἰκονομίας λόγῳ, φυσικῆς
κινήσεως τάξει κατὰ ἀλήθειαν φυσικῶς γινόμενα.

57   Περὶ τῶν ἰδιωμάτων τῶν δύο φύσεων

Τέλειον δὲ θεὸν ὁμολογοῦντες τὸν αὐτὸν καὶ τέλειον ἄνθρωπόν
φαμεν τὸν αὐτὸν πάντα ἔχειν, ὅσα ὁ πατήρ, πλὴν τῆς ἀγεννησίας,
καὶ πάντα ἔχειν, ὅσα ὁ Ἀδὰμ ὁ πρῶτος, δίχα μόνης ἁμαρτίας,

nature, yet the accursed Nestorius in his arrogance tried to call the one born of a virgin "God-bearing" (θεοφόρος, *theophoros*). God forbid that we should speak of him or think of him as "God-bearing," instead of as God incarnate. For the Word himself became flesh, conceived of the Virgin, and born as God together with his assumed flesh, which itself was already deified by him at the very time of its coming into being, with the result that the three came into being simultaneously, its assumption, its existence, and its deification by the Word. And thus the holy Virgin is to be spoken of and thought of as Theotokos, not only on account of the nature of the Word, but also on account of the deification of the human element. Both the conception and the existence of these was brought about wonderfully at the same time by divine action, that is, the conception of the Word, the existence of the flesh in the Word himself, the Mother of God herself in a manner transcending nature providing the means by which the Fashioner was fashioned and the God and Creator of the universe was inhominated, deifying that which he assumed, while the union preserves what was united just as they were at the time they were united—I do not mean Christ's divine element alone but also his human element, that which is more than us and that which is like us. For he did not first become like us and then afterwards more than us, but from the beginning of his existence existed as both, in virtue of possessing from the earliest moment of conception an existence in the Word himself. Thus he is human in accordance with our own nature, and of God and divine in a manner transcending us. Moreover, he possessed the properties of the ensouled flesh. For the Word accepted these on account of the economy, when by the order of natural movement they came into being naturally in reality.

57   *On the properties of the two natures*

Confessing the same to be perfect God and perfect man, we say that he has everything that the Father has, except unbegottenness, and everything that the first Adam had, with the exception only of

ἅτινά ἐστι σῶμα καὶ ψυχὴ λογική τε καὶ νοερά· ἔχειν δὲ αὐτὸν καταλλήλως ταῖς δύο φύσεσι διπλᾶ τὰ τῶν δύο φύσεων φυσικά· δύο θελήσεις φυσικάς, τήν τε θείαν καὶ τὴν ἀνθρωπίνην, καὶ ἐνεργείας δύο φυσικάς, θείαν τε καὶ ἀνθρωπίνην, καὶ αὐτεξούσια δύο φυσικά, θεῖόν τε καὶ ἀνθρώπινον, καὶ σοφίαν καὶ γνῶσιν, θείαν τε καὶ ἀνθρωπίνην. Ὁμοούσιος γὰρ ὢν τῷ θεῷ καὶ πατρὶ αὐτεξουσίως θέλει καὶ ἐνεργεῖ ὡς θεός, ὁμοούσιος δὲ ὢν καὶ ἡμῖν αὐτεξουσίως θέλει καὶ ἐνεργεῖ ὡς ἄνθρωπος ὁ αὐτός· αὐτοῦ γὰρ τὰ θαύματα, αὐτοῦ καὶ τὰ παθήματα.

58 *Περὶ θελημάτων καὶ αὐτεξουσίων τοῦ κυρίου ἡμῶν Ἰησοῦ Χριστοῦ*

Ἐπειδὴ μὲν οὖν δύο φύσεις τοῦ Χριστοῦ, δύο αὐτοῦ καὶ τὰ φυσικὰ θελήματα καὶ τὰς φυσικὰς ἐνεργείας φαμέν. Ἐπειδὴ δὲ μία τῶν δύο αὐτοῦ φύσεων ἡ ὑπόστασις, ἕνα καὶ τὸν αὐτόν φαμεν θέλοντά τε καὶ ἐνεργοῦντα φυσικῶς κατ' ἄμφω, ἐξ ὧν καὶ ἐν αἷς καὶ ἅπερ ἐστὶ Χριστὸς ὁ θεὸς ἡμῶν, θέλειν δὲ καὶ ἐνεργεῖν οὐ διῃρημένως, ἀλλ' ἡνωμένως· θέλει γὰρ καὶ «ἐνεργεῖ ἑκατέρα μορφὴ μετὰ τῆς θατέρου κοινωνίας».[1] Ὧν γὰρ ἡ οὐσία ἡ αὐτή, τούτων καὶ ἡ θέλησις καὶ ἡ ἐνέργεια ἡ αὐτή· ὧν δὲ διάφορος ἡ οὐσία, τούτων διάφορος καὶ ἡ θέλησις καὶ ἡ ἐνέργεια. Καὶ τὸ ἀνάπαλιν, ὧν ἡ θέλησις καὶ ἡ ἐνέργεια ἡ αὐτή, τούτων καὶ ἡ οὐσία ἡ αὐτή· ὧν δὲ διάφορος ἡ θέλησις καὶ ἡ ἐνέργεια, τούτων καὶ ἡ οὐσία διάφορος.

Διὸ δὴ ἐπὶ μὲν πατρὸς καὶ υἱοῦ καὶ ἁγίου πνεύματος ἐκ τῆς ταυτότητος τῆς τε ἐνεργείας καὶ τοῦ θελήματος τὴν ταυτότητα τῆς φύσεως ἐπιγινώσκομεν. Ἐπὶ δὲ τῆς θείας οἰκονομίας ἐκ τῆς διαφορᾶς τῶν ἐνεργειῶν καὶ τῶν θελημάτων καὶ τὴν τῶν φύσεων διαφορὰν ἐπιγινώσκομεν καὶ τὴν τῶν φύσεων διαφορὰν εἰδότες συνομολογοῦμεν καὶ τὸ τῶν θελημάτων καὶ ἐνεργειῶν διάφορον.

---

[1] This phrase (ἐνεργεῖ ἑκατέρα μορφὴ μετὰ τῆς θατέρου κοινωνίας, *energei hekatera morphē meta tēs thaterou koinōnias*) is from the Definition of Christ's Two Wills promulgated by the Sixth Ecumenical Council (Constantinople III, 680–81).

sin, that is to say, a body and a rational and intelligent soul. And we say that corresponding to the two natures, the same has a double set of the natural properties belonging to the two natures: two natural wills, the divine and the human, and two natural energies, both divine and human, and two natural volitions, both divine and human, and wisdom and knowledge, both divine and human. For being consubstantial with God the Father, he wills and acts of his own volition as God; and being consubstantial with us, the same wills and acts of his own volition as a human being. For the miracles belong to the same and the sufferings also belong to the same.

58   *On the wills and volitions of our Lord Jesus Christ*

Therefore because Christ has two natures, we say that he also has two natural wills and two natural energies. But because the hypostasis of these two natures is one, we also say that he who wills and operates naturally in accordance with both is one. Christ our God is from these natures and in these natures and they are precisely what Christ is, not willing and operating in a divided manner but in a united manner. For "each form" wills and "operates in communion with the other."[1] When things are of the same essence, their will and energy is also the same, but when their essence is different, their will and energy is also different. And conversely, when things have the same will and energy, their essence is the same, and when things have a different will and energy, their essence is also different.

Therefore in the case of the Father and Son and Holy Spirit, we acknowledge the identity of the nature from the identity of the energy and the will. But in the case of the divine economy we acknowledge the difference of the natures from the difference of the energies and wills, and knowing the difference of the natures we also confess at the same time the difference of the wills and the energies. The number

It is the Greek translation of Pope Leo's *agit enim utraque forma cum alterius communione* from his Tome that had been adopted by the Fourth Ecumenical Council (Chalcedon, 451).

Ὥσπερ γὰρ τῶν τοῦ αὐτοῦ ἑνὸς φύσεων Χριστοῦ ὁ ἀριθμὸς εὐσεβῶς νοούμενός τε καὶ λεγόμενος οὐ διαιρεῖ τὸν ἕνα Χριστόν, ἀλλὰ σῳζομένην καὶ ἐν τῇ ἑνώσει παρίστησι τῶν φύσεων τὴν διαφοράν, οὕτω καὶ ὁ ἀριθμὸς τῶν οὐσιωδῶς προσόντων ταῖς αὐτοῦ φύσεσι θελημάτων καὶ ἐνεργειῶν (κατ᾽ ἄμφω γὰρ τὰς φύσεις θελητικὸς ἦν καὶ ἐνεργητικὸς τῆς ἡμῶν σωτηρίας) οὐ διαίρεσιν εἰσάγει—μὴ γένοιτο—, ἀλλὰ τὴν αὐτῶν δηλοῖ καὶ μόνον, κἂν τῇ ἑνώσει, φυλακὴν καὶ σωτηρίαν· φυσικὰ γὰρ καὶ οὐχ ὑποστατικά φαμεν τὰ θελήματα καὶ τὰς ἐνεργείας. Λέγω δὲ αὐτὴν τὴν θελητικὴν καὶ ἐνεργητικὴν δύναμιν, καθ᾽ ἣν θέλει καὶ ἐνεργεῖ τά τε θέλοντα καὶ ἐνεργοῦντα. Εἰ γὰρ ὑποστατικὰ δῶμεν αὐτά, ἑτεροθελεῖς καὶ ἑτεροενεργεῖς τὰς τρεῖς ὑποστάσεις τῆς ἁγίας τριάδος εἰπεῖν ἀναγκασθησόμεθα.

Ἰστέον γάρ, ὡς οὐ ταὐτόν ἐστι, θέλειν καὶ πῶς θέλειν· τὸ μὲν γὰρ θέλειν φύσεως ὥσπερ καὶ τὸ ὁρᾶν (πᾶσι γὰρ ἀνθρώποις πρόσεστι), τὸ δὲ πῶς θέλειν οὐ φύσεως, ἀλλὰ τῆς ἡμετέρας γνώμης ὥσπερ καὶ τὸ πῶς ὁρᾶν, καλῶς ἢ κακῶς (οὐ γὰρ πάντες ἄνθρωποι ὁμοίως θέλουσιν οὐδ᾽ ὁμοίως ὁρῶσι). Τοῦτο καὶ ἐπὶ τῶν ἐνεργειῶν δώσομεν· τὸ γὰρ πῶς θέλειν, πῶς ὁρᾶν, πῶς ἐνεργεῖν τρόπος ἐστὶ τῆς τοῦ θέλειν καὶ ὁρᾶν καὶ ἐνεργεῖν χρήσεως, μόνῳ τῷ κεχρημένῳ προσὸν καὶ τῶν ἄλλων αὐτὸν κατὰ τὴν κοινῶς λεγομένην διαφορὰν χωρίζον.

Λέγεται οὖν τὸ μὲν ἁπλῶς θέλειν θέλησις ἤτοι ἡ θελητικὴ δύναμις λογικὴ οὖσα ὄρεξις καὶ θέλημα φυσικόν· τὸ δὲ πῶς θέλειν ἤτοι τὸ τῇ θελήσει ὑποκείμενον θελητὸν καὶ θέλημα γνωμικόν· θελητικὸν δέ ἐστι τὸ πεφυκὸς θέλειν, οἷον θελητική ἐστιν ἡ θεία φύσις, ὡσαύτως καὶ ἡ ἀνθρωπίνη· θέλων δέ ἐστιν ὁ κεχρημένος τῇ θελήσει ἤτοι ἡ ὑπόστασις οἷον ὁ Πέτρος.

---

²Cf. Anastasius of Sinai, *Hodēgos* 2.4 (PG 89:64D–65A); Maximus the Confessor, *Disputation with Pyrrhus* 22–23 (PG 91:292D–293A). The paragraph numbers are not in the Greek text but are supplied by the English translator of the *Disputation*: Joseph P. Farrell, *The Disputation with Pyrrhus of our Father among the Saints, Maximus the*

of the natures of the one and the same Christ, when understood and spoken of correctly, does not divide the one Christ, but presents the difference of the natures as preserved even in the unity. Similarly, the number of wills and energies belonging essentially to his natures (for he exercised will and activity in both of his natures for the sake of our salvation) does not introduce division—God forbid!—but simply manifests the maintenance and preservation of the two natures even in the union. For we say that the wills and the energies are natural, not hypostatic. I am referring to the faculty itself of willing and acting by which he wills and brings about that which he wants and does. If we grant these to be hypostatic, we shall be obliged to say that the three hypostases of the Holy Trinity have different wills and different activities.

For one should know that willing and how we will are not the same thing. On the one hand, willing, like seeing, belongs to our nature (for all people are endowed with will); on the other, how we will belongs not to our nature but to our own deliberation, as does how we see, whether correctly or wrongly (for not all people will in the same way or see in the same way). We grant this also to the energies. For how we will, how we see, and how we act are each a mode of exercising the faculties of willing, seeing, and acting, which belongs to the user alone and divides him or her from others in accordance with the commonly agreed difference.[2]

Thus the ability simply to will is called the capacity for willing or the volitional power, since it is a rational appetency and natural will. But the manner of willing or what falls under the will is what is wished for and the will of choice. The volitional is the natural act of willing, that is to say, the divine nature is volitional, as also is human nature. And one who wills is one who exercises the will, namely, a hypostasis such as Peter.

Confessor (Waymart, PA: St Tikhon's Seminary Press, 1990). I give them for ease of reference to Farrell's translation. Despite his extraordinary decision to cast his translation in pseudo-seventeenth-century English, his text is not unhelpful.

Ἐπειδὴ τοίνυν εἷς μέν ἐστιν ὁ Χριστὸς καὶ μία αὐτοῦ ἡ ὑπόστασις, εἷς καὶ ὁ αὐτός ἐστιν ὁ θέλων καὶ ἐνεργῶν θεϊκῶς τε καὶ ἀνθρωπίνως. Ἐπειδὴ δὲ δύο φύσεις ἔχει θελητικὰς ὡς λογικάς (πᾶν γὰρ λογικὸν θελητικόν τε καὶ αὐτεξούσιον), δύο θελήσεις ἤτοι θελήματα φυσικὰ ἐπ᾽ αὐτοῦ ἐροῦμεν. Θελητικὸς γάρ ἐστιν ὁ αὐτὸς κατ᾽ ἄμφω ταῖς αὐτοῦ φύσεσιν· τὴν γὰρ φυσικῶς ἐνυπάρχουσαν ἡμῖν θελητικὴν δύναμιν ἀνέλαβε. Καὶ ἐπειδὴ εἷς ἐστιν ὁ Χριστὸς καὶ ὁ αὐτὸς ὁ θέλων καθ᾽ ἑκατέραν φύσιν, τὸ αὐτὸ θελητὸν λέξομεν ἐπ᾽ αὐτοῦ οὐχὶ μόνα θέλοντος, ἃ φυσικῶς ὡς θεὸς ἤθελεν (οὐ γὰρ θεότητος τὸ θέλειν φαγεῖν, πιεῖν καὶ τὰ τοιαῦτα), ἀλλὰ καὶ τὰ συστατικὰ τῆς ἀνθρωπίνης φύσεως, οὐκ ἐναντιότητι γνώμης, ἀλλ᾽ ἐν ἰδιότητι τῶν φύσεων· τότε γὰρ ταῦτα φυσικῶς ἤθελεν, ὅτε ἡ θεία αὐτοῦ θέλησις ἤθελε καὶ παρεχώρει τῇ σαρκὶ πάσχειν καὶ πράττειν τὰ ἴδια.

Ὅτι δὲ φυσικῶς πρόσεστι τῷ ἀνθρώπῳ ἡ θέλησις, ἐντεῦθεν δῆλον. Ὑπεξαιρουμένης τῆς θείας τρία εἴδη ζωῆς εἰσιν· ἡ φυτική, ἡ αἰσθητική, ἡ νοερά. Τῆς μὲν οὖν φυτικῆς ἴδιον ἡ θρεπτική, ἡ αὐξητική, ἡ γεννητικὴ κίνησις· τῆς δὲ αἰσθητικῆς ἡ καθ᾽ ὁρμὴν κίνησις· τῆς δὲ λογικῆς καὶ νοερᾶς ἡ αὐτεξούσιος. Εἰ οὖν κατὰ φύσιν πρόσεστι τῇ φυτικῇ ἡ θρεπτικὴ καὶ τῇ αἰσθητικῇ ἡ καθ᾽ ὁρμὴν κίνησις, κατὰ φύσιν ἄρα πρόσεστι καὶ τῇ λογικῇ καὶ νοερᾷ ἡ αὐτεξούσιος· αὐτεξουσιότης δὲ οὐδὲν ἕτερόν ἐστιν εἰ μὴ ἡ θέλησις· γεγονὼς τοίνυν ὁ λόγος σὰρξ ἔμψυχος, νοερὰ καὶ αὐτεξούσιος, γέγονε καὶ θελητικός.

Ἔτι δὲ καὶ ἀδίδακτά εἰσι τὰ φυσικά· οὐδεὶς γὰρ λογίζεσθαι ἢ ζῆν ἢ πεινῆν ἢ διψῆν ἢ ὑπνοῖν μανθάνει. Οὔτε δὲ θέλειν μανθάνομεν· ὥστε φυσικὸν τὸ θέλειν.

Καὶ πάλιν· Εἰ ἐν τοῖς ἀλόγοις ἄγει μὲν ἡ φύσις, ἄγεται δὲ ἐν τῷ ἀνθρώπῳ ἐξουσιαστικῶς κατὰ θέλησιν κινουμένῳ, ἄρα φύσει θελητικὸς ὁ ἄνθρωπος.

Now, because Christ is one and his hypostasis is one, he who wills and acts in both a divine manner and a human manner is one and the same. But because he has two natures which are volitional (θελητικαί, *thelētikai*) in as much as they are rational (for every rational being is volitional and endowed with free will) we shall say of him that he has two capacities for willing or natural wills. For the same is volitional in both of his natures, for he assumed the volitional power that naturally exists within us. And because Christ who wills in either nature is one and the same, we shall say of him that what is wished for is the same, since he did not wish only for the things which he naturally willed as God (for it does not belong to divinity to wish to eat, drink, and suchlike) but also the things that go to make up human nature, not in opposition to the will of choice (γνώμη, *gnōmē*), but in the specific character of the natures. For he willed these things naturally when his divine capacity for willing willed and ceded to the flesh the power to suffer and do what belonged properly to it.[3]

From this it is obvious that the capacity for willing (θέλησις, *thelēsis*) belongs naturally to human beings. With the exception of the divine, there are three kinds of life: the vegetative, the sensory, and the intelligent. Proper to vegetative life are the powers of nutrition, growth, and reproduction. Proper to sensory life is impulsive movement. Proper to rational and intelligent life is the movement of free will. Therefore if the power of nutrition is naturally attached to vegetative life, and impulsive movement to sensory life, it follows that free will is also naturally attached to rational and intelligent life. Freedom of will (αὐτεξουσιότης, *autexousiotēs*) is nothing other than the capacity for willing. Thus the Word's becoming flesh endowed with soul, intelligence, and free will means that he was also endowed with volition.[4]

Moreover, natural properties are not taught, for no one learns how to think, or live, or be hungry or thirsty, or how to sleep. Nor do we learn how to will. Therefore willing is natural.

[3] Cf. Maximus the Confessor, *Disputation with Pyrrhus* 10–13 (PG 91:289AB).
[4] Cf. Maximus the Confessor, *Disputation with Pyrrhus* 40–55 (PG 91:301ABC).

Καὶ πάλιν· Εἰ κατ' εἰκόνα τῆς μακαρίας καὶ ὑπερουσίου θεότητος ὁ ἄνθρωπος γεγένηται, αὐτεξούσιος δὲ φύσει καὶ θελητικὴ ἡ θεία φύσις, ἄρα καὶ ὁ ἄνθρωπος ὡς αὐτῆς εἰκὼν αὐτεξούσιος φύσει καὶ θελητικός. Τὸ γὰρ αὐτεξούσιον θέλησιν ὡρίσαντο οἱ πατέρες.

Ἔτι δὲ εἰ πᾶσιν ἀνθρώποις ἐνυπάρχει τὸ θέλειν καὶ οὐ τοῖς μὲν ὑπάρχει, τοῖς δὲ οὐκ ἐνυπάρχει, τὸ δὲ κοινῶς πᾶσιν ἐνθεωρούμενον φύσιν χαρακτηρίζει ἐν τοῖς ὑπ' αὐτὸ ἀτόμοις, ἄρα φύσει θελητικὸς ὁ ἄνθρωπος.

Καὶ αὖθις· Εἰ τὸ μᾶλλον καὶ ἧττον ἡ φύσις οὐκ ἐπιδέχεται, ἐπίσης δὲ πᾶσιν ἐνυπάρχει τὸ θέλειν καὶ οὐ τοῖς μὲν πλέον, τοῖς δὲ ἔλαττον, ἄρα φύσει θελητικὸς ὁ ἄνθρωπος· ὥστε εἰ φύσει θελητικὸς ὁ ἄνθρωπος, καὶ ὁ κύριος, οὐ μόνον καθὸ θεός, ἀλλὰ καὶ καθὸ ἄνθρωπος γέγονε, φύσει θελητικός ἐστιν. Ὥσπερ γὰρ τὴν ἡμετέραν φύσιν ἀνέλαβεν, οὕτω καὶ τὸ ἡμέτερον θέλημα φύσει ἀνείληφεν, καὶ κατὰ τοῦτο οἱ πατέρες τὸ ἡμέτερον ἐν αὐτῷ τυπῶσαι αὐτὸν ἔφησαν θέλημα.

Εἰ φυσικὸν οὐκ ἔστι τὸ θέλημα, ἢ ὑποστατικὸν ἔσται ἢ παρὰ φύσιν· ἀλλ' εἰ μὲν ὑποστατικόν, ἑτερόβουλος οὕτω γε ἔσται ὁ υἱὸς τῷ πατρί· μόνης γὰρ ὑποστάσεως χαρακτηριστικὸν τὸ ὑποστατικόν· εἰ δὲ παρὰ φύσιν, ἔκπτωσις τῆς φύσεως ἔσται τὸ θέλημα· φθαρτικὰ γὰρ τῶν κατὰ φύσιν τὰ παρὰ φύσιν.

Ὁ τῶν ὅλων θεὸς καὶ πατὴρ καθὸ πατὴρ θέλει ἢ καθὸ θεός. Ἀλλ' εἰ μὲν καθὸ πατήρ, ἄλλο αὐτοῦ ἔσται παρὰ τὸ τοῦ υἱοῦ θέλημα· οὐ γὰρ πατὴρ ὁ υἱός. Εἰ δὲ καθὸ θεός, θεὸς δὲ ὁ υἱός, θεὸς δὲ καὶ τὸ πνεῦμα τὸ ἅγιον· ἄρα τὸ θέλημα φύσεως ἤγουν φυσικόν.

Ἔτι εἰ κατὰ τοὺς πατέρας, ὧν τὸ θέλημα ἕν, τούτων καὶ ἡ οὐσία μία, ἓν δὲ θέλημα τῆς θεότητος τοῦ Χριστοῦ καὶ τῆς ἀνθρωπότητος αὐτοῦ, ἄρα μία καὶ ἡ αὐτὴ τούτων ἔσται καὶ ἡ οὐσία.

And again, whereas among irrational beings nature is in control, among human beings it is itself controlled, because human beings move of their own accord in accordance with their capacity for willing. Therefore human beings are naturally volitional.

And again, if human beings were created in the image of the blessed and superessential Godhead, and the divine nature is naturally free and volitional, it follows that human beings, as the image of this nature, are also free and naturally volitional. For the fathers have defined free will (τὸ αὐτεξούσιον, *to autexousion*) as the capacity for willing.

Furthermore, if the ability to will exists in all human beings—it is not found in some but not in others—and what is observed commonly in all is characteristic of the nature of the individuals of that class, it follows that human beings are naturally volitional.[5]

And again, if nature is not susceptible of more and less, and also the ability to will exists in all, and not more in some and less in others, it follows that human beings are volitional by nature. Consequently, if human beings are volitional by nature, the Lord also, not only as God but also in that he became man, is volitional by nature. For just as he assumed our nature, so too did he naturally assume our will, and in accordance with this the fathers said that he impressed our own will within him.

If the will (τὸ θέλημα, *to thelēma*) is not natural, it is either hypostatic or contrary to nature. But if it is hypostatic, the Son will be different in will from the Father, for what is hypostatic is only characteristic of the hypostasis. But if it is contrary to nature, the will will be a falling away from nature, for what is contrary to nature is corruptive of what is according to nature.

The God and Father of all wills (θέλει, *thelei*) either as Father or as God. But if he wills as Father, his will will be other than that of the Son. For the Son is not the Father. But if he wills as God, the Son is God and the Holy Spirit is also God. Therefore the will belongs to nature, that is to say, it is natural.

[5] Cf. Maximus the Confessor, *Disputation with Pyrrhus* 58–61 (PG 91:304BCD).

Καὶ πάλιν· Εἰ κατὰ τοὺς πατέρας ἡ τῆς φύσεως διαφορὰ τῷ ἑνὶ θελήματι οὐ διαφαίνεται, ἀνάγκη ἢ ἓν θέλημα λέγοντας φυσικὴν ἐν Χριστῷ μὴ λέγειν διαφορὰν ἢ φυσικὴν λέγοντας διαφορὰν ἓν θέλημα μὴ λέγειν.

Καὶ αὖθις· Εἰ, καθώς φησι τὸ θεῖον εὐαγγέλιον, ἐλθὼν ὁ κύριος εἰς τὰ μέρη Τύρου καὶ Σιδῶνος «καὶ εἰσελθὼν εἰς οἶκον οὐδένα ἠθέλησε γνῶναι καὶ οὐκ ἠδυνήθη λαθεῖν», εἰ τὸ θεῖον αὐτοῦ θέλημα παντοδύναμον, θελήσας δὲ λαθεῖν οὐ δεδύνηται, ἄρα καθὸ ἄνθρωπος θελήσας οὐκ ἠδυνήθη καὶ θελητικὸς ἦν καὶ καθὸ ἄνθρωπος.

Καὶ πάλιν· «Ἐλθών», φησίν, «εἰς τὸν τόπον» «εἶπε· Διψῶ». «Καὶ ἔδωκαν αὐτῷ οἶνον μετὰ χολῆς μεμιγμένον, καὶ γευσάμενος οὐκ ἠθέλησε πιεῖν». Εἰ μὲν οὖν καθὸ θεὸς ἐδίψησε καὶ γευσάμενος οὐκ ἠθέλησε πιεῖν, ἐμπαθὴς ἄρα καθὸ θεός· πάθος γὰρ ἥ τε δίψα καὶ ἡ γεῦσις. Εἰ δὲ οὐ καθὸ θεός, πάντως καθὸ ἄνθρωπος θελητικὸς ἦν.

Καὶ ὁ μακάριος δὲ Παῦλος ὁ ἀπόστολος· «Γενόμενος», φησίν, «ὑπήκοος μέχρι θανάτου, θανάτου δὲ σταυροῦ». Ἡ ὑπακοὴ τοῦ ὄντος θελήματός ἐστιν ὑποταγή, οὐ τοῦ μὴ ὄντος· οὐ γὰρ τὸ ἄλογον ὑπήκοον ἢ παρήκοον λέξομεν· ὑπήκοος δὲ γενόμενος τῷ πατρὶ ὁ κύριος οὐ καθὸ θεὸς γέγονεν, ἀλλὰ καθὸ ἄνθρωπος. «Καθὸ γὰρ θεὸς οὔτε ὑπήκοος οὔτε παρήκοος· τῶν ὑπὸ χεῖρα γὰρ ταῦτα», καθὼς ὁ θεηγόρος ἔφη Γρηγόριος. Θελητικὸς ἄρα καὶ καθὸ ἄνθρωπος ὁ Χριστός.

Φυσικὸν δὲ τὸ θέλημα λέγοντες, οὐκ ἠναγκασμένον τοῦτό φαμεν, ἀλλ᾽ αὐτεξούσιον· εἰ γὰρ λογικόν, πάντως καὶ αὐτεξούσιον. Οὐ μόνον γὰρ ἡ θεία καὶ ἄκτιστος φύσις οὐδὲν ἠναγκασμένον ἔχει, ἀλλ᾽ οὐδὲ ἡ νοερὰ καὶ κτιστή. Τοῦτο δὲ δῆλον· φύσει γὰρ ὢν ἀγαθὸς ὁ θεὸς καὶ φύσει δημιουργὸς καὶ φύσει θεὸς οὐκ ἀνάγκῃ ταῦτά ἐστι. Τίς γὰρ ὁ τὴν ἀνάγκην ἐπάγων;

Moreover, if according to the fathers those things that have one will also have one essence, and the will of Christ's divinity and of his humanity is one, it would follow that the essence of these too would be one and the same.

And again, if according to the fathers the difference in nature is not conveyed by a single will, it necessarily follows that either by affirming a single natural will in Christ we deny the difference, or by affirming a natural difference we deny a single will.[6]

And furthermore, if, as the divine Gospel says, the Lord came to the district of Tyre and Sidon and "on entering a house did not want anyone to know he was there, but could not escape notice,"[7] if his divine will was all-powerful and he wished to escape notice but could not do so, it follows that it was because he willed as a human being that he could not do so, and also that as a human being he was volitional.

And again, it says "On coming to the place," he said "I am thirsty."[8] "And they gave him wine mixed with gall, but when he tasted it, he did not want to drink it."[9] Now if it was as God that he was thirsty and tasted and did not want to drink, it would follow that as God he was subject to passion, for thirsting and tasting are passions. But if he was not volitional as God, he must have been volitional as a human being.

And blessed Paul the apostle says: "He became obedient to the point of death, even death on a cross."[10] Obedience is the submission of a real will, not of an unreal one. For we would not call an irrational being either obedient or disobedient. The Lord became obedient to the Father not as God but as a human being. "For as God he was neither obedient nor disobedient, for these belong to those who are subject to others," as the theologian Gregory said.[11] Therefore it was as a human being that Christ was volitional.[12]

---

[6]Cf. Maximus the Confessor, *Disputation with Pyrrhus* 106–10 (PG 91:313C–316A).
[7]Mk 7.24.   [8]Jn 19.28.   [9]Mt 27.34.   [10]Phil 2.8.
[11]Gregory of Nazianzus, *Oration* 30.6 (PG 36:109C; Moreschini, 724).
[12]Cf. Maximus the Confessor, *Disputation with Pyrrhus* 135–36 (PG 91:324AB).

Δεῖ δὲ εἰδέναι, ὡς αὐτεξουσιότης ὁμωνύμως λέγεται, ἄλλως μὲν ἐπὶ θεοῦ, ἄλλως δὲ ἐπὶ ἀγγέλων, καὶ ἄλλως ἐπὶ ἀνθρώπων. Ἐπὶ θεοῦ μὲν γὰρ ὑπερουσίως, ἐπὶ δὲ ἀγγέλων ὡς συντρεχούσης τῇ ἕξει τῆς προχειρήσεως καὶ παρενθήκην ὅλως χρόνου μὴ παραδεχομένης (ἔχων γὰρ φυσικῶς τὸ αὐτεξούσιον ἀπαρεμποδίστως τούτῳ κέχρηται, μηδὲ τὴν ἐκ σωμάτων ἀντιπάθειαν ἔχων μηδὲ τὸν προσβάλλοντα), ἐπὶ δὲ ἀνθρώπων ὡς χρονικῶς τῆς ἕξεως προεπινοουμένης τῆς ἐγχειρήσεως· αὐτεξούσιος μὲν γάρ ἐστιν ὁ ἄνθρωπος καὶ φυσικῶς ἔχει τὸ αὐτεξούσιον, ἔχει δὲ καὶ τὴν ἐκ τοῦ διαβόλου προσβολὴν καὶ τὴν τοῦ σώματος κίνησιν. Διὰ οὖν τὴν προσβολὴν καὶ τὸ βάρος τοῦ σώματος ἐφυστερίζει ἡ προχείρησις τῆς ἕξεως.

Εἰ οὖν θέλων ὁ Ἀδὰμ ὑπήκουσε καὶ θελήσας ἔφαγεν, ἄρα πρωτοπαθὴς ἐν ἡμῖν ἡ θέλησις· εἰ δὲ πρωτοπαθὴς ἡ θέλησις, ταύτην δὲ μετὰ τῆς φύσεως ὁ λόγος σαρκωθεὶς οὐκ ἀνέλαβεν, οὐκ ἄρα ἔξω τῆς ἁμαρτίας γεγόναμεν.

Ἔτι δὲ εἰ ἔργον αὐτοῦ ἡ αὐτεξούσιος τῆς φύσεως ὑπάρχει δύναμις, ταύτην δὲ οὐκ ἀνέλαβεν, ἢ καταγνοὺς τῆς οἰκείας δημιουργίας ὡς οὐ καλῆς ἢ φθονήσας ἡμῖν τῆς κατ᾽ αὐτὴν θεραπείας, ἡμᾶς μὲν τῆς παντελοῦς ἀποστερῶν θεραπείας, ἑαυτὸν δὲ ὑπὸ πάθος ὄντα δεικνὺς τῷ μὴ θέλειν ἢ τῷ μὴ δύνασθαι τελείως σῴζειν.

Ἀδύνατον δὲ ἕν τι σύνθετον ἐκ τῶν δύο θελημάτων λέγειν ὥσπερ ἐκ τῶν φύσεων σύνθετον τὴν ὑπόστασιν. Πρῶτον μὲν ὅτι αἱ συνθέσεις τῶν ἐν ὑποστάσει ὄντων καὶ οὐ τῶν ἑτέρῳ λόγῳ καὶ οὐκ ἰδίῳ θεωρουμένων εἰσί· δεύτερον δέ, ὅτι, εἰ τῶν θελημάτων καὶ ἐνεργειῶν σύνθεσιν λέξομεν, καὶ τῶν ἄλλων φυσικῶν ἰδιωμάτων σύνθεσιν εἰπεῖν ἀναγκασθησόμεθα, τοῦ ἀκτίστου καὶ κτιστοῦ, τοῦ ἀοράτου καὶ ὁρατοῦ καὶ τῶν τοιούτων. Πῶς δὲ καὶ τὸ ἐκ τῶν θελημάτων σύνθετον θέλημα προσαγορευθήσεται (ἀδύνατον γὰρ

In saying that the will is natural we mean that it is not constrained but is free. For if it is rational, it is necessarily free. For it is not only the divine and uncreated nature that is in no way constrained, but also intelligent created nature. This is obvious. For since God is good by nature and Creator by nature and God by nature, these things do not exist by necessity. For who is there to impose necessity?[13]

One should also know that the expression "freedom of will" (αὐτεξουσιότης, *autexousiotēs*) is used equivocally. It is used in one way in relation to God, in another way in relation to angels, and in another way in relation to human beings. For in relation to God, it is used in a superessential sense. In relation to angels the execution of the intention is concurrent with its formation, there being absolutely no interval of time between the two (for since free will is possessed by nature, it is exercised without any hindrance arising either out of the opposition of corporeality or from anyone impeding them). In relation to human beings there is a delay between forming an intention and executing it. For although human beings are free and possess freedom of will by nature, they are impeded by the devil and the movement of the body. Therefore as a result of the impact and weight of the body the execution of an intention comes after its formation.

If, then, Adam willingly succumbed, and after willing, ate, it follows that the first to suffer in us was the will. And if the will was the first to suffer, yet when the Word was enfleshed he did not assume the will along with our nature, then we have not been freed from sin.

Furthermore, if the faculty of free will that belongs to our nature is his work, yet he did not assume it, either he condemned his own creation as not good, or else, begrudging us its healing, he deprived us of complete healing and showed himself to be subject to passion in not being willing or not being able to save us fully.

It is also impossible to speak of a composite unity formed out of two wills in the same way that the hypostasis is composed from two natures. First because compositions are of entities that exist

---

[13]Cf. Maximus the Confessor, *Disputation with Pyrrhus* 25 (PG 91:293BC).

τὸ σύνθετον τῇ τῶν συντεθέντων ὀνομάζεσθαι προσηγορίᾳ), ἐπεὶ καὶ τὸ ἐκ τῶν φύσεων σύνθετον φύσιν προσαγορεύσομεν καὶ οὐχ ὑπόστασιν· Ἔτι δὲ καὶ εἰ ἓν σύνθετον θέλημα ἐπὶ Χριστοῦ λέξομεν, θελήματι τοῦ πατρὸς αὐτὸν χωρίζομεν· οὐ γὰρ σύνθετον τὸ τοῦ πατρὸς θέλημα. Λείπεται τοίνυν εἰπεῖν μόνην τὴν ὑπόστασιν τοῦ Χριστοῦ σύνθετον καὶ κοινὴν ὥσπερ τῶν φύσεων, οὕτω καὶ τῶν φυσικῶν αὐτοῦ.

Γνώμην δὲ καὶ προαίρεσιν ἐπὶ τοῦ κυρίου λέγειν ἀδύνατον, εἴπερ κυριολεκτεῖν βουλόμεθα. Ἡ γνώμη γὰρ μετὰ τὴν περὶ τοῦ ἀγνοουμένου ζήτησιν καὶ βούλευσιν ἤτοι βουλὴν καὶ κρίσιν πρὸς τὸ κριθέν ἐστι διάθεσις. Μεθ᾽ ἣν ἡ προαίρεσις ἐκλεγομένη καὶ αἱρουμένη πρὸ τοῦ ἑτέρου τὸ ἕτερον. Ὁ δὲ κύριος οὐ φιλὸς ὢν ἄνθρωπος ἀλλὰ καὶ θεὸς καὶ πάντα εἰδὼς ἀνενδεὴς σκέψεως καὶ ζητήσεως καὶ βουλῆς ὑπῆρχε καὶ κρίσεως καὶ φυσικῶς τήν τε πρὸς τὸ καλὸν εἶχεν οἰκείωσιν καὶ τὴν πρὸς τὸ κακὸν ἀλλοτρίωσιν. Οὕτω γοῦν καὶ Ἡσαΐας φησίν, ὅτι «πρὶν ἢ γνῶναι τὸ παιδίον ἢ προελέσθαι πονηρά, ἐκλέξεται τὸ ἀγαθόν· διότι πρὶν ἢ γνῶναι τὸ παιδίον ἀγαθὸν ἢ κακόν, ἀπειθεῖ πονηρίᾳ τοῦ ἐκλέξασθαι τὸ ἀγαθόν». Τὸ γὰρ «πρὶν» δηλοῖ, ὅτι οὐ καθ᾽ ἡμᾶς ζητήσας καὶ βουλευσάμενος ἀλλὰ θεὸς ὢν καὶ θεϊκῶς καὶ τὸ κατὰ σάρκα ὑποστάς, τουτέστι καθ᾽ ὑπόστασιν ἡνωμένος τῇ σαρκί, αὐτῷ τῷ εἶναι καὶ τὸ πάντα εἰδέναι τὸ ἐκ φύσεως εἶχεν ἀγαθόν· φυσικαὶ γάρ εἰσιν αἱ ἀρεταὶ καὶ φυσικῶς καὶ ἐπίσης πᾶσιν ἐνυπάρχουσιν, εἰ καὶ μὴ πάντες ἐπίσης ἐνεργοῦμεν τὰ τῆς φύσεως. Ἐκ τοῦ κατὰ φύσιν γὰρ εἰς τὸ παρὰ φύσιν διὰ τῆς παραβάσεως ἠλάσαμεν. Ὁ δὲ κύριος ἐκ τοῦ παρὰ φύσιν εἰς τὸ κατὰ φύσιν ἡμᾶς ἐπανήγαγε· τοῦτο γάρ ἐστι τὸ κατ᾽ εἰκόνα καὶ καθ᾽ ὁμοίωσιν. Καὶ ἡ ἄσκησις δὲ καὶ οἱ ταύτης πόνοι οὐ πρὸς τὸ ἐπικτήσασθαι τὴν ἀρετὴν ἔξωθεν ἐπείσακτον οὖσαν ἐπενοήθησαν, ἀλλὰ πρὸς τὸ τὴν ἐπείσακτον καὶ παρὰ φύσιν κακίαν ἀποβαλέσθαι, ὥσπερ καὶ τὸν τοῦ σιδήρου ἰὸν οὐ φυσικὸν ὄντα, ἀλλ᾽ ἐξ ἀμελείας ἐπιγενόμενον

hypostatically and are not regarded as existing by virtue of a different principle than their own. And second, because if we spoke of a composition of wills and energies we would be obliged to speak also of a composition of the other natural properties, uncreated and created, invisible and visible, and so forth. And what would a will composed of two wills be called (for it is impossible for a composite entity to be called by the name of the things that compose it), because then we would call the composition from the natures a nature and not a hypostasis? Moreover, if we said that in Christ there is one composite will, we would be distinguishing it from the will of the Father, for the Father's will is not composite. What remains is to say that only the hypostasis of Christ is composite and common. Just as in the case of the natures, the same is true for what belongs to the natures.[14]

It is strictly speaking impossible to attribute the formation of an opinion (γνώμη, *gnōmē*) and freedom of choice (προαίρεσις, *proairesis*) to the Lord. For an opinion, which is formed after enquiry and deliberation, or counsel and judgement, with regard to what is not known, is a disposition towards what has been judged. After the formation of the opinion comes the free choice that chooses and selects one thing in preference to another. But since the Lord was not a mere human being but was also God and omniscient, he had no need of reflection and enquiry and counsel and judgement and naturally had a propensity towards the good and an aversion to evil. It is therefore thus that Isaiah says: "Before the child knows or chooses evil, it will choose the good; because before the child knows what is good or evil, it rejects evil by choosing the good."[15] The word "before" indicates that he did not make enquiry and take counsel as we do, but that since he was God and subsisted in a divine manner in the flesh, that is to say was united hypostatically to the flesh, through his very being and omniscience he possessed goodness by nature. For the virtues belong to our nature and also naturally inhere in all

[14] Cf. Maximus the Confessor, *Disputation with Pyrrhus* 26–27 (PG 91:296ABC).
[15] Is 7.15–16.

διὰ μόχθου ἀποβάλλοντες τὴν φυσικὴν τοῦ σιδήρου λαμπρότητα ἐμφανίζομεν.

Ἰστέον δέ, ὡς τὸ τῆς γνώμης ὄνομα πολύτροπον καὶ πολυσήμαντόν ἐστι. Ποτὲ μὲν γὰρ δηλοῖ τὴν παραίνεσιν, ὥς φησιν ὁ θεῖος ἀπόστολος· «Περὶ δὲ τῶν παρθένων ἐπιταγὴν κυρίου οὐκ ἔχω, γνώμην δὲ δίδωμι·» ποτὲ δὲ βουλήν, ὡς ὅταν φησὶν ὁ προφήτης Δαυίδ· «Ἐπὶ τὸν λαόν σου κατεπανουργεύσαντο γνώμην», ποτὲ δὲ ψῆφον, ὡς ὁ Δανιήλ· «Περὶ τίνος ἐξῆλθεν ἡ γνώμη ἡ ἀναιδὴς αὕτη;», ποτὲ δὲ ἐπὶ πίστεως ἢ δόξης ἢ φρονήματος, καὶ ἁπλῶς εἰπεῖν, κατὰ εἴκοσιν ὀκτὼ σημαινόμενα λαμβάνεται τὸ τῆς γνώμης ὄνομα.

59 *Περὶ ἐνεργειῶν τῶν ἐν τῷ κυρίῳ ἡμῶν Ἰησοῦ Χριστῷ*

Δύο δὲ καὶ τὰς ἐνεργείας φαμὲν ἐπὶ τοῦ κυρίου ἡμῶν Ἰησοῦ Χριστοῦ· εἶχε γὰρ ὡς μὲν θεὸς καὶ τῷ πατρὶ ὁμοούσιος τὴν θείαν ἐνέργειαν καὶ ὡς ἄνθρωπος γενόμενος καὶ ἡμῖν ὁμοούσιος τῆς ἀνθρωπίνης φύσεως τὴν ἐνέργειαν.

Ἰστέον δέ, ὡς ἄλλο ἐστὶν ἐνέργεια καὶ ἄλλο ἐνεργητικὸν καὶ ἄλλο ἐνέργημα καὶ ἄλλο ἐνεργῶν. Ἐνέργεια μὲν οὖν ἐστιν ἡ

[16]Cf. Maximus the Confessor, *Disputation with Pyrrhus* 82–97 (PG 91:308C–312C).
[17]1 Cor 7.25.
[18]Ps 82.4.

human beings, even if not all of us act in accordance with nature. For through the fall, we passed from what is in accordance with nature to what is contrary to nature. But the Lord led us back from what is contrary to nature to what is in accordance with nature. For this is what "in the image and likeness" means. Asceticism and its labors were not devised in order to acquire virtue as something external added on to us, but in order to get rid of evil that has been added and is contrary to nature, just like rust, which does not belong to the nature of iron but has occurred through neglect, is removed by us laboriously to reveal the natural brightness of the iron.[16]

One should also note that the word "opinion" (γνώμη, *gnōmē*) has many different meanings. Sometimes it implies exhortation, as when the divine Apostle says: "Now concerning virgins, I have no command of the Lord, but I give my opinion,"[17] sometimes counsel, as when the prophet David says: "Against your people they have devised villainous counsel,"[18] sometimes a decree, as when Daniel says: "For what reason has this shameless decree been issued,"[19] and sometimes it is used in respect of belief, or intention, or purpose. In short, the word "opinion" is taken in twenty-eight senses.[20]

59　*On the activities (ἐνέργειαι,* energeiai) *in our Lord Jesus Christ*

We say that in the case of our Lord Jesus Christ there are also two activities (ἐνέργειαι, *energeiai*). For as God and consubstantial with the Father, he possessed the divine activity and as having become human and consubstantial with us, he possessed the activity that belongs to human nature.

And one should note that activity (ἐνέργεια, *energeia*) is one thing and having a capacity for activity (ἐνεργητικόν, *energētikon*) is

[19]Dan 2.15.
[20]On the multiple meanings of γνώμη in Maximus (John's principal source here), see Lars Thunberg, *Microcosm and Mediator*, 2nd ed. (Chicago and La Salle, IL: Open Court, 1995), 213–18.

δραστικὴ καὶ οὐσιώδης τῆς φύσεως κίνησις· ἐνεργητικὸν δὲ ἡ φύσις, ἐξ ἧς ἡ ἐνέργεια πρόεισιν· ἐνέργημα δὲ τὸ τῆς ἐνεργείας ἀποτέλεσμα· ἐνεργῶν δὲ ὁ κεχρημένος τῇ ἐνεργείᾳ ἤτοι ἡ ὑπόστασις. Λέγεται δὲ καὶ ἡ ἐνέργεια ἐνέργημα, καὶ τὸ ἐνέργημα ἐνέργεια, ὡς καὶ τὸ κτίσμα κτίσις. Οὕτω φαμέν· πᾶσα ἡ κτίσις, τὰ κτίσματα δηλοῦντες.

Ἰστέον, ὡς ἡ ἐνέργεια κίνησίς ἐστι καὶ ἐνεργεῖται μᾶλλον ἢ ἐνεργεῖ, καθώς φησιν ὁ θεηγόρος Γρηγόριος ἐν τῷ περὶ τοῦ ἁγίου πνεύματος λόγῳ· «Εἰ δὲ ἐνέργειά ἐστιν, ἐνεργηθήσεται δηλονότι καὶ οὐκ ἐνεργήσει καὶ ὁμοῦ τῷ ἐνεργηθῆναι παύσεται».

Δεῖ δὲ γινώσκειν, ὅτι αὐτὴ ἡ ζωὴ ἐνέργειά ἐστι καὶ ἡ τροπὴ τοῦ ζώου ἐνέργεια, καὶ πᾶσα ἡ τοῦ ζώου οἰκονομία ἥ τε θρεπτικὴ καὶ αὐξητικὴ ἤγουν φυτικὴ καὶ ἡ καθ᾽ ὁρμὴν κίνησις ἤγουν αἰσθητικὴ καὶ ἡ νοερὰ καὶ αὐτεξούσιος κίνησις. Δυνάμεως δὲ ἀποτέλεσμα ἡ ἐνέργεια. Εἰ οὖν ταῦτα πάντα θεωροῦμεν ἐν τῷ Χριστῷ, ἄρα καὶ ἀνθρωπίνην ἐνέργειαν ἐπ᾽ αὐτοῦ φήσομεν. Ἐνέργεια λέγεται τὸ πρῶτον ἐν ἡμῖν συνιστάμενον νόημα· καὶ ἔστιν ἁπλῆ καὶ ἄσχετος ἐνέργεια τοῦ νοῦ καθ᾽ αὐτὸν ἀφανῶς τὰ ἴδια νοήματα προβαλλομένου, ὧν χωρὶς οὐδὲ νοῦς ἂν κληθείη δικαίως. Λέγεται δὲ πάλιν ἐνέργεια καὶ ἡ διὰ τῆς προφορᾶς τοῦ λόγου φανέρωσις καὶ ἐξάπλωσις τῶν νενοημένων. Αὕτη δὲ οὐκέτι ἄσχετός ἐστι καὶ ἁπλῆ, ἀλλ᾽ ἐν σχέσει θεωρουμένη ἐκ νοήματος καὶ λόγου συντεθειμένη. Καὶ αὐτὴ δὲ ἡ σχέσις, ἣν ἔχει ὁ ποιῶν πρὸς τὸ γινόμενον, ἐνέργειά ἐστι· καὶ αὐτὸ τὸ ἀποτελούμενον ἐνέργεια λέγεται. Καὶ τὸ μέν ἐστι ψυχῆς μόνης, τὸ δὲ ψυχῆς σώματι κεχρημένης, τὸ δὲ σώματος νοερῶς ἐψυχωμένου, τὸ δὲ ἀποτέλεσμα· ὁ νοῦς γὰρ προθεωρήσας τὸ ἐσόμενον οὕτω διὰ τοῦ σώματος ἐργάζεται. Τῆς ψυχῆς τοίνυν ἐστὶν ἡ ἡγεμονία· κέχρηται γὰρ ὡς ὀργάνῳ τῷ σώματι, ἄγουσα τοῦτο καὶ ἰθύνουσα. Ἑτέρα δέ ἐστιν ἡ τοῦ σώματος ἐνέργεια ἀγομένου ὑπὸ τῆς ψυχῆς καὶ κινουμένου. Τὸ δὲ ἀποτέλεσμα τοῦ μὲν σώματος ἡ ἁφὴ καὶ ἡ κράτησις καὶ ἡ τοῦ ποιουμένου οἱονεὶ περιένεξις, τῆς δὲ ψυχῆς ἡ

another, and an accomplished act (ἐνέργημα, *energēma*) is another, and one who acts (ἐνεργῶν, *energōn*) is another. Activity, then, is the efficacious and essential movement of nature; that which has a capacity for activity is the nature from which the activity derives; an accomplished act is the result of the activity; one who acts is one who carries out the activity, namely, a hypostasis. It is also the case that an activity is called an accomplished act, and an accomplished act is called an activity, as when we call the creature a creation. It is thus that we say "all creation" when we mean created beings.

One should note that activity is movement and is the result rather than the cause of acting. As Gregory the Theologian says in his oration on the Holy Spirit: "If there is an activity, clearly it is the result of action, not the cause, and ceases at the same time as that which causes it."[1]

One also needs to know that life itself is an activity and the mode of a living being is an activity, as is also the whole economy of a living being, namely, its capacity for nourishment and growth, or vegetative activity, and its impulsive movement, or sensory activity, and its intelligent and freely-willed movement. Activity is also the actuality of a potentiality. Therefore if we observe all these in Christ, we may conclude that he also has a human activity.

The first thought formed in us is called an activity. And it is a simple and unqualified activity of the mind by which the mind of itself invisibly projects its own thoughts without which the mind could not rightly be called such. Again, the manifestation and unfolding of what has been thought in uttered speech is also called an activity. This is no longer unqualified and simple, but is contemplated in relation [to other things] since it is composed of thought and word. And the relation itself that the one who makes has to the thing made is an activity. And the accomplishment itself is called an activity. And the one belongs to the soul alone, the other to the soul operating through a body, the other to the body endowed with an intelligent soul, and the other is the accomplishment. For the mind

[1]Gregory of Nazianzus, *Oration* 31.6 (PG 36:140A; Moreschini, 750).

τοῦ γινομένου οἱονεὶ μόρφωσις καὶ σχηματισμός. Οὕτω καὶ περὶ τοῦ κυρίου ἡμῶν Ἰησοῦ Χριστοῦ ἡ μὲν τῶν θαυμάτων δύναμις τῆς θεότητος αὐτοῦ ὑπῆρχεν ἐνέργεια, ἡ δὲ χειρουργία καὶ τὸ θελῆσαι καὶ τὸ εἰπεῖν «θέλω, καθαρίσθητι» τῆς ἀνθρωπότητος αὐτοῦ ὑπῆρχεν ἐνέργεια. Ἀποτέλεσμα δὲ τῆς μὲν ἀνθρωπίνης ἡ τῶν ἄρτων κλάσις, τὸ ἀκοῦσαι τὸν λεπρὸν τὸ «θέλω», τῆς δὲ θείας ὁ τῶν ἄρτων πληθυσμὸς καὶ ἡ τοῦ λεπροῦ κάθαρσις· δι᾿ ἀμφοτέρων γάρ, διά τε τῆς ψυχικῆς ἐνεργείας καὶ τοῦ σώματος, μίαν καὶ τὴν αὐτὴν συγγενῆ καὶ ἴσην ἐνεδείκνυτο αὐτοῦ τὴν θείαν ἐνέργειαν. Ὥσπερ γὰρ τὰς φύσεις ἡνωμένας γινώσκομεν καὶ τὴν ἐν ἀλλήλαις ἐχούσας περιχώρησιν καὶ τὴν τούτων διαφορὰν οὐκ ἀρνούμεθα, ἀλλὰ καὶ ἀριθμοῦμεν καὶ ἀδιαιρέτους αὐτὰς γινώσκομεν, οὕτω καὶ τῶν θελημάτων καὶ τῶν ἐνεργειῶν καὶ τὸ συναφὲς γινώσκομεν καὶ τὸ διάφορον ἐπιγινώσκομεν καὶ ἀριθμοῦμεν καὶ διαίρεσιν οὐκ εἰσάγομεν. Ὃν τρόπον γὰρ ἡ σὰρξ καὶ τεθέωται καὶ μεταβολὴν τῆς οἰκείας οὐ πέπονθε φύσεως, τὸν αὐτὸν τρόπον καὶ τὸ θέλημα καὶ ἡ ἐνέργεια καὶ τεθέωνται καὶ τῶν οἰκείων οὐκ ἐξίστανται ὅρων· εἷς γάρ ἐστιν ὁ τοῦτο κἀκεῖνο ὢν καὶ οὕτως κἀκείνως ἤτοι θεϊκῶς τε καὶ ἀνθρωπίνως θέλων καὶ ἐνεργῶν.

Δύο τοίνυν τὰς ἐνεργείας ἐπὶ Χριστοῦ λέγειν ἀναγκαῖον διὰ τὸ διττὸν τῆς φύσεως· ὧν γὰρ ἡ φύσις παρηλλαγμένη, τούτων διάφορος ἡ ἐνέργεια, καὶ ὧν ἡ ἐνέργεια παρηλλαγμένη, τούτων ἡ φύσις διάφορος. Καὶ τὸ ἀνάπαλιν· Ὧν ἡ φύσις ἡ αὐτή, τούτων καὶ ἡ ἐνέργεια ἡ αὐτή, καὶ ὧν ἡ ἐνέργεια μία, τούτων καὶ ἡ οὐσία μία, κατὰ τοὺς θεηγόρους πατέρας. Ἀνάγκη τοίνυν δυοῖν θάτερον ἢ μίαν ἐνέργειαν ἐπὶ Χριστοῦ λέγοντας μίαν λέγειν καὶ τὴν οὐσίαν ἤ, εἴπερ τῆς ἀληθείας ἐχόμεθα καὶ δύο τὰς οὐσίας εὐαγγελικῶς τε καὶ πατρικῶς ὁμολογοῦμεν, δύο καὶ τὰς ἐνεργείας καταλλήλως αὐτοῖς ἑπομένους συνομολογεῖν· ὁμοούσιος γὰρ ὢν τῷ θεῷ καὶ πατρὶ κατὰ τὴν θεότητα ἴσος ἔσται καὶ κατὰ τὴν ἐνέργειαν. Ὁμοούσιος δὲ ὢν ἡμῖν ὁ αὐτὸς κατὰ τὴν ἀνθρωπότητα ἴσος

first contemplates what is to be done and thus acts through the body. The leading role belongs to the soul, for it uses the body as its instrument, which it leads and directs. The activity of the body is different, because it is led and moved by the soul. And the accomplishment for the body is the touching and holding of what has been made as if embracing it, but for the soul is like the shaping and forming of what has come to be. So it was, too, with regard to our Lord Jesus Christ. His power of performing miracles was an activity of his divinity, whereas his gesture, and his willing, and his saying: "I do choose. Be made clean!"[2] was an activity of his humanity. And an accomplishment of his humanity was the breaking of the bread, the leper's hearing "I do choose," whereas the accomplishment of his divinity was the multiplication of the loaves and the cleansing of the leper. For through both, through the activity of his soul as well as his body, he showed his divine energy to be one and the same, cognate and equal. For just as we know that the natures are united and interpenetrate each other yet do not deny their difference but number them and know that they are indivisible, so too we both acknowledge the union of the wills and the activities and recognize and number the difference but do not introduce any division. For the manner in which the flesh was deified and yet did not suffer any change in its proper nature is the same manner in which the will and the activity were deified and yet did not go beyond their proper boundaries. For he who is both one thing and the other and wills and acts in both one way and the other, that is, both divinely and humanly, is a single being.[3]

It is therefore necessary to say that in Christ's case there are two activities on account of the duality of the nature. Things that are of a dissimilar nature will also have a different activity, and things that are of a dissimilar activity will also have a different nature. And conversely, things that are of the same nature will also have the same activity and things that have one activity will also have one nature,

[2]Mt 8.3.
[3]Cf. Anastasius of Sinai, frag. 94 (PG 94:1049BCD).

ἔσται καὶ κατὰ τὴν ἐνέργειαν. Φησὶ γοῦν ὁ μακάριος Γρηγόριος, ὁ Νυσαέων ἐπίσκοπος· «Ὧν δὲ ἡ ἐνέργεια μία, τούτων πάντως καὶ ἡ δύναμις ἡ αὐτή· πᾶσα γὰρ ἐνέργεια δυνάμεώς ἐστιν ἀποτέλεσμα». Ἀδύνατον δὲ ἀκτίστου καὶ κτιστῆς φύσεως μίαν φύσιν ἢ δύναμιν ἢ ἐνέργειαν εἶναι. Εἰ δὲ μίαν Χριστοῦ τὴν ἐνέργειαν εἴποιμεν, τῇ τοῦ λόγου θεότητι προσάψομεν τῆς νοερᾶς ψυχῆς τὰ πάθη, φόβον φημὶ καὶ λύπην καὶ ἀγωνίαν.

Εἰ δὲ λέγοιεν, ὡς περὶ τῆς ἁγίας τριάδος διαλεγόμενοι οἱ πατέρες οἱ ἅγιοι ἔφασαν· Ὧν ἡ οὐσία μία, τούτων καὶ ἡ ἐνέργεια, καὶ ὧν διάφορος ἡ οὐσία, τούτων διάφορος καὶ ἡ ἐνέργεια, καὶ ὡς οὐ χρὴ τὰ τῆς θεολογίας ἐπὶ τὴν οἰκονομίαν μετάγειν, ἐροῦμεν· Εἰ ἐπὶ τῆς θεολογίας μόνον εἴρηται τοῖς πατράσι, καὶ οὐκ ἔτι μετὰ τὴν σάρκωσιν τῆς αὐτῆς ἐνεργείας ὁ υἱὸς τῷ πατρὶ οὐδὲ τῆς αὐτῆς ἔσται οὐσίας. Τίνι δὲ ἀπονεμοῦμεν τὸ «ὁ πατήρ μου ἕως ἄρτι ἐργάζεται, κἀγὼ ἐργάζομαι», καὶ «ἃ βλέπει τὸν πατέρα ποιοῦντα, ταῦτα καὶ ὁ υἱὸς ὁμοίως ποιεῖ», καὶ «εἰ ἐμοὶ οὐ πιστεύετε, τοῖς ἔργοις μου πιστεύσατε», καὶ «τὰ ἔργα, ἃ ἐγὼ ποιῶ, μαρτυρεῖ περὶ ἐμοῦ», καὶ «ὥσπερ ὁ πατὴρ ἐγείρει τοὺς νεκροὺς καὶ ζωοποιεῖ, οὕτω καὶ ὁ υἱός, οὓς θέλει, ζωοποιεῖ»; Ταῦτα γὰρ πάντα οὐ μόνον ὁμοούσιον καὶ μετὰ σάρκωσιν τῷ πατρὶ δείκνυσιν αὐτόν, ἀλλὰ καὶ τῆς αὐτῆς ἐνεργείας.

Καὶ πάλιν· Εἰ ἡ περὶ τὰ ὄντα πρόνοια οὐ μόνον πατρὸς καὶ ἁγίου πνεύματος, ἀλλὰ καὶ τοῦ υἱοῦ ἐστι καὶ μετὰ σάρκωσιν, ἐνέργεια δὲ τοῦτό ἐστιν· ἄρα καὶ μετὰ σάρκωσιν τῆς αὐτῆς ἐστιν ἐνεργείας τῷ πατρί.

---

[4]The fathers St John has in mind appear to be the fathers of the Sixth Ecumenical Council (Constantinople III, 680–81), who defined the two natural operations or energies in Christ, the human and the divine.
[5]Cf. Maximus the Confessor, *Disputation with Pyrrhus* 187 (PG 91:344D–345A).

according to the fathers who speak of God.[4] It is therefore necessary of two positions to maintain one or the other: either by holding that there is one activity in Christ to say that the essence is also one, or, if we stick to the truth and confess two essences in the manner of the gospels and the fathers, to acknowledge also two activities appropriately corresponding to them. For being consubstantial with God the Father with regard to his divinity, he must also be equal to him with regard to his activity.[5] And the same being consubstantial with us with regard to his humanity, he must also be equal to us with regard to his activity. It is thus that blessed Gregory, the bishop of Nyssa, says: "Those things of which the activity is one necessarily also have the same power, for every activity is characteristic of a power."[6] It is impossible that uncreated and created nature should have a single nature, power, or activity. If we were to say that Christ's activity is simply one, we would be attributing to the divinity of the Word the passions of the intelligent soul, by which I mean fear and sorrow and anguish.

But if they were to say that in their discussions of the Holy Trinity the holy fathers said: Things that are of one essence are also of one activity, and when the essence is different the activity is also different, and we must not transfer to the economy what belongs to the level of theology, we would reply: If this is said by the fathers only with regard to theology, then after the enfleshment the Son would no longer have the same activity as the Father nor would he be of the same essence. To whom should we assign the sayings: "My Father is still working, and I also am working,"[7] and "what he sees the Father doing, these the Son does likewise,"[8] and "even though you do not believe me, believe my works,"[9] and "the works that I do testify to me,"[10] and "just as the Father raises the dead and gives them life, so also the Son gives life to whomsoever he wishes"?[11] All these not only

---

[6]Gregory of Nyssa, *On the Lord's Prayer*, Oration 3, PG 44:1160A (= *Doctrina Patrum*, Diekamp, 76.10).

[7]Jn 5.17.   [8]Jn 5.19.   [9]Jn 10.38.
[10]Jn 10.25.   [11]Jn 5.21.

Εἰ ἐκ τῶν θαυμάτων τῆς αὐτῆς οὐσίας ὄντα τῷ πατρὶ τὸν Χριστὸν ἔγνωμεν, ἐνέργεια δὲ θεοῦ τυγχάνει τὰ θαύματα, ἄρα καὶ μετὰ σάρκωσιν τῆς αὐτῆς ἐνεργείας ἐστὶ τῷ πατρί.

Εἰ δὲ μία ἐνέργεια τῆς θεότητος αὐτοῦ καὶ τῆς σαρκὸς αὐτοῦ, σύνθετος ἔσται, καὶ ἔσται ἢ ἑτέρας ἐνεργείας παρὰ τὸν πατέρα ἢ καὶ ὁ πατὴρ συνθέτου ἐνεργείας ἔσται. Εἰ δὲ συνθέτου ἐνεργείας, δῆλον ὅτι καὶ φύσεως.

Εἰ δὲ εἴποιεν, ὅτι τῇ ἐνεργείᾳ πρόσωπον συνεισάγεται, ἐροῦμεν, ὅτι, εἰ τῇ ἐνεργείᾳ πρόσωπον συνεισάγεται, κατὰ τὴν εὔλογον ἀντιστροφὴν καὶ τῷ προσώπῳ ἐνέργεια συνεισαχθήσεται, καὶ ἔσονται, ὥσπερ τρία πρόσωπα ἤτοι ὑποστάσεις τῆς ἁγίας τριάδος, οὕτω καὶ τρεῖς ἐνέργειαι, ἢ ὥσπερ μία ἡ ἐνέργεια, οὕτω καὶ ἓν πρόσωπον καὶ μία ὑπόστασις. Οἱ δὲ ἅγιοι πατέρες συμφώνως εἰρήκασι τὰ τῆς αὐτῆς οὐσίας καὶ τῆς αὐτῆς εἶναι ἐνεργείας.

Ἔτι δέ, εἰ τῇ ἐνεργείᾳ πρόσωπον συνεισάγεται, οἱ μήτε μίαν μήτε δύο Χριστοῦ τὰς ἐνεργείας λέγειν θεσπίσαντες οὔτε ἓν πρόσωπον αὐτοῦ λέγειν οὔτε δύο προσέταξαν.

Καὶ ἐπὶ τῆς πεπυρακτωμένης μαχαίρας ὥσπερ αἱ φύσεις σῴζονται τοῦ τε πυρὸς καὶ τοῦ σιδήρου, οὕτω καὶ αἱ δύο ἐνέργειαι καὶ τὰ τούτων ἀποτελέσματα. Ἔχει γὰρ ὁ μὲν σίδηρος τὸ τμητικόν, τὸ δὲ πῦρ τὸ καυστικόν, καὶ ἡ τομὴ μὲν τῆς τοῦ σιδήρου ἐνεργείας ἐστὶν ἀποτέλεσμα, ἡ δὲ καῦσις τοῦ πυρός· καὶ σῴζεται τὸ τούτων διάφορον ἐν τῇ κεκαυμένῃ τομῇ καὶ ἐν τῇ τετμημένῃ καύσει, εἰ καὶ μήτε ἡ καῦσις τῆς τομῆς δίχα γίγνοιτο μετὰ τὴν ἕνωσιν μήτε ἡ τομὴ δίχα τῆς καύσεως· καὶ οὔτε διὰ τὸ διττὸν τῆς φυσικῆς ἐνεργείας δύο πεπυρακτωμένας μαχαίρας φαμὲν οὔτε διὰ τὸ μοναδικὸν τῆς πεπυρακτωμένης μαχαίρας σύγχυσιν τῆς οὐσιώδους αὐτῶν διαφορᾶς ἐργαζόμεθα. Οὕτω καὶ ἐν τῷ Χριστῷ

---

[12]Cf. Maximus the Confessor, *Disputation with Pyrrhus* 195–206 (PG 91:348B–349B).

[13]Cf. Maximus the Confessor, *Opusculum* 5 (PG 91:64D).

show him to be consubstantial with the Father even after enfleshment but also show him to have the same activity.

And again, if providential care for the things that are belongs not
only to the Father and the Holy Spirit but also to the Son even after
enfleshment, this is an activity, too. Therefore even after enfleshment
his activity was the same as that of the Father.

If as a result of the miracles we perceive Christ to be of the same
essence as the Father, and the miracles occur through the activity of
God, it follows that even after enfleshment he had the same activity
as the Father.[12]

And if the activity of his divinity and that of his flesh were one,
he would be composite, and either he would have a different activity
than the Father has or else the Father would have a composite activity. If the activity is composite, so is the nature.[13]

And if they were to say that a person is introduced by the activity,
we would reply that if a person is introduced by the activity, logic
requires that conversely an activity is introduced by the person, and
just as there are three persons or hypostases in the Holy Trinity, so
also there would be three activities, or just as there is one activity,
so also there would be one person and one hypostasis. But the holy
fathers have declared unanimously that things with the same essence
also have the same activity.

Moreover, if a person is introduced by the activity, those who
decreed that there should be no discussion either of one activity or
of two activities in Christ, commanded that neither should there be
any talk either of one person or of two persons in him.[14]

Take the case of a sword made red-hot in a fire.[15] Just as the
natures of both the fire and the iron are preserved, so also are the two
activities and their effects. For the iron has the property of cutting
and the fire of burning, the cut being the effect of the activity of the

---

[14]Cf. Maximus the Confessor, *Disputation with Pyrrhus* 165–69 (PG
91:336D–337B).

[15]The image comes from Maximus the Confessor, *Disputation with Pyrrhus* 170
(PG 91:341B).

τῆς μὲν θεότητος αὐτοῦ ἡ θεία καὶ παντοδύναμος ἐνέργεια, τῆς δὲ ἀνθρωπότητος αὐτοῦ ἡ καθ' ἡμᾶς. Ἀποτέλεσμα δὲ τῆς μὲν ἀνθρωπίνης τὸ κρατηθῆναι τὴν χεῖρα τῆς παιδὸς καὶ ἑλκυσθῆναι, τῆς δὲ θείας ἡ ζωοποίησις· ἄλλο γὰρ τοῦτο, κἀκεῖνο ἕτερον, εἰ καὶ ἀλλήλων ἀχώριστοι ὑπάρχουσιν ἐν τῇ θεανδρικῇ ἐνεργείᾳ. Εἰ διὰ τὸ μίαν εἶναι τὴν τοῦ κυρίου ὑπόστασιν μία ἔσται καὶ ἡ ἐνέργεια, διὰ τὴν μίαν ὑπόστασιν μία ἔσται καὶ ἡ οὐσία.

Καὶ πάλιν· Εἰ μίαν ἐνέργειαν ἐπὶ τοῦ κυρίου εἴποιμεν, ἢ θείαν ταύτην λέξομεν ἢ ἀνθρωπίνην ἢ οὐδετέραν. Ἀλλ' εἰ μὲν θείαν, θεὸν αὐτὸν μόνον γυμνὸν τῆς καθ' ἡμᾶς ἀνθρωπότητος λέξομεν. Εἰ δὲ ἀνθρωπίνην, ψιλὸν αὐτὸν ἄνθρωπον βλασφημήσομεν. Εἰ δὲ οὐδὲ θείαν οὐδὲ ἀνθρωπίνην, οὐδὲ θεὸν οὐδὲ ἄνθρωπον, οὐδὲ τῷ πατρὶ οὐδὲ ἡμῖν ὁμοούσιον· ἐκ γὰρ τῆς ἑνώσεως ἡ καθ' ὑπόστασιν ταυτότης γέγονεν, οὐ μὴν δὲ καὶ ἡ διαφορὰ τῶν φύσεων ἀνῄρηται. Τῆς δὲ διαφορᾶς σῳζομένης τῶν φύσεων, σωθήσονται δηλαδὴ καὶ αἱ τούτων ἐνέργειαι· οὐ γάρ ἐστι φύσις ἀνενέργητος.

Εἰ μία τοῦ δεσπότου Χριστοῦ ἡ ἐνέργεια, ἢ κτιστὴ ἔσται ἢ ἄκτιστος· μέσον γὰρ τούτων οὐκ ἔστιν ἐνέργεια ὥσπερ οὐδὲ φύσις. Εἰ οὖν κτιστή, κτιστὴν μόνην δηλώσει φύσιν· εἰ δὲ ἄκτιστος, ἄκτιστον μόνην χαρακτηρίσει οὐσίαν. Δεῖ γὰρ πάντως κατάλληλα ταῖς φύσεσιν εἶναι τὰ φυσικά· ἀδύνατον γὰρ ἐλλιποῦς φύσεως ὕπαρξιν εἶναι. Ἡ δὲ κατὰ φύσιν ἐνέργεια οὐ τῶν ἐκτὸς ὑπάρχει, καὶ δῆλον, ὅτι οὔτε εἶναι οὔτε γινώσκεσθαι τὴν φύσιν δυνατὸν ἐνεργείας δίχα· δι' ὧν γὰρ ἐνεργεῖ ἕκαστον, τὴν οἰκείαν φύσιν πιστοῦται, ὅπερ ἐστὶ μὴ τρεπόμενον.

Εἰ μία Χριστοῦ ἡ ἐνέργεια, ἡ αὐτὴ τῶν θείων καὶ τῶν ἀνθρωπίνων ποιητική. Οὐδὲν δὲ τῶν ὄντων ἐν τοῖς κατὰ φύσιν μένον τὰ ἐναντία ποιεῖν δύναται· οὐ γὰρ τὸ πῦρ ψύχει καὶ

---

¹⁶Cf. Mt 9.25; Mk 5:40–42.
¹⁷Cf. Maximus the Confessor, *Disputation with Pyrrhus* 193–94 (PG 91:348AB). The expression "theandric activity"(θεανδρικὴ ἐνέργεια) was problematic for Chalcedonian Christology because it seemed to lend strong support to miaphysites and monotheletes, yet at the same time had near-apostolic authority (as was thought)

iron, and the burn that of the fire. And the difference between these is preserved in the burning cut and in the cutting burn, even though the burning does not take place apart from the cut, after the union of the two, nor does the cut take place apart from the burn. And we do not say that there are two red-hot swords on account of the double effect of their natural activity, nor do we contrive a confusion of their essential difference on account of the red-hot sword's being a single entity. In the same way in the case of Christ, his divine and all-powerful activity belongs to his divinity and what is characteristic of us belongs to his humanity. It was a characteristic of his human nature to take hold of the child's hand and draw her up, but of his divine nature to restore her to life.[16] For the two are different even though they are inseparable from each other in the theandric activity.[17] If because the Lord's hypostasis is one his activity is also one, on account of the one hypostasis there would only be one essence.

And again, if we attribute only one activity to the Lord, we would have to say that it is either divine, or human, or neither. But if it is divine, we would be saying that he is God alone, bereft of what belongs to our humanity. If it is human we would be blasphemously calling him a mere human being. If it is neither divine nor human, the Lord would be neither God nor man, consubstantial neither with the Father nor with us. For his hypostatic identity was brought about as a result of the union yet the difference of the nature was not by any means destroyed. When the difference of the natures is preserved, clearly the difference of their activities is also preserved, for there is no nature that is devoid of activity.

If the activity of Christ the Master is a single one, it is either created or uncreated, for between these there is no activity, just as there is no nature. Therefore if it is created, it will manifest a created nature alone, but if it is uncreated it will indicate an uncreated nature alone.[18] Natural properties are necessarily always correlative

through its use by Dionysius the Areopagite. John returns to it in Chapter 63, where he discusses it at some length.

[18]Cf. Maximus the Confessor, *Disputation with Pyrrhus* 177–82 (PG 91:340C–341A).

θερμαίνει, οὐδὲ ξηραίνει καὶ ὑγραίνει τὸ ὕδωρ. Πῶς οὖν ὁ φύσει ὢν θεὸς καὶ φύσει γενόμενος ἄνθρωπος τά τε θαύματα καὶ τὰ πάθη μιᾷ ἐνεργείᾳ ἐπετέλεσεν;

Εἰ οὖν ἔλαβεν ὁ Χριστὸς νοῦν ἀνθρώπινον ἤγουν ψυχὴν νοεράν τε καὶ λογικήν, διανοηθήσεται πάντως καὶ ἀεὶ διανοηθήσεται· ἐνέργεια δὲ νοῦ ἡ διάνοια. Ἄρα καὶ καθὸ ἄνθρωπος ἐνεργὴς ὁ Χριστὸς καὶ ἀεὶ ἐνεργής.

Ὁ δὲ ἅγιος Ἰωάννης ὁ Χρυσόστομος ἐν τῇ ἑρμηνείᾳ τῶν Πράξεων δευτέρῳ λόγῳ οὕτω φησίν· «Οὐκ ἂν δέ τις ἁμάρτοι καὶ τὸ πάθος αὐτοῦ πρᾶξιν καλέσας· ἐν τῷ γὰρ τὰ πάντα παθεῖν ἐποίησε τὸ μέγα καὶ θαυμαστὸν ἐκεῖνο ἔργον τὸν θάνατον καταλύσας καὶ τὰ ἄλλα πάντα ἐργασάμενος».

Εἰ πᾶσα ἐνέργεια φύσεώς τινος οὐσιώδης ὁρίζεται κίνησις, ὡς οἱ περὶ ταῦτα δεινοὶ διειλήφασι, ποῦ φύσιν τις εἶδεν ἀκίνητον ἢ παντελῶς ἀνενέργητον ἢ ἐνέργειαν εὕρηκεν οὐ φυσικῆς δυνάμεως ὑπάρχουσαν κίνησιν; «Μίαν δὲ φυσικὴν τὴν ἐνέργειαν θεοῦ καὶ ποιήματος» οὐκ ἄν τις εὖ φρονῶν δοίη κατὰ τὸν μακάριον Κύριλλον· οὐδὲ ζωοποιεῖ τὸν Λάζαρον ἡ ἀνθρωπίνη φύσις, οὐδὲ δακρύει ἡ θεϊκὴ ἐξουσία· τὸ μὲν γὰρ δάκρυον τῆς ἀνθρωπότητος ἴδιον, ἡ δὲ ζωὴ τῆς ἐνυποστάτου ζωῆς. Ἀλλ᾽ ὅμως κοινῶς ἀμφοτέρων ἑκάτερα διὰ τὸ ταὐτὸν τῆς ὑποστάσεως. Εἷς μὲν γάρ ἐστιν ὁ Χριστὸς καὶ ἓν αὐτοῦ τὸ πρόσωπον ἤτοι ἡ ὑπόστασις, ἀλλ᾽ ὅμως ἔχει δύο φύσεις, τῆς θεότητος καὶ τῆς ἀνθρωπότητος αὐτοῦ. Ἐκ μὲν οὖν τῆς θεότητος ἡ δόξα φυσικῶς προϊοῦσα ἑκατέρου κοινὴ διὰ τὴν τῆς ὑποστάσεως ἐγένετο ταυτότητα, ἐκ δὲ τῆς σαρκὸς τὰ ταπεινὰ ἑκατέρῳ κοινά· εἷς γάρ ἐστι καὶ ὁ αὐτὸς ὁ τοῦτό τε κἀκεῖνο ὢν ἤτοι θεὸς καὶ ἄνθρωπος, καὶ τοῦ αὐτοῦ, τά τε τῆς θεότητος καὶ τὰ τῆς ἀνθρωπότητος· τὰς

---

[19]Cf. Maximus the Confessor, *Disputation with Pyrrhus* 184 (PG 91:341CD).

[20]John Chrysostom, *Homily 1 on Acts* 18.17–20 (reproduced in the *Doctrina Patrum*, Diekamp, 86.14–16).

[21]The "experts" John perhaps has in mind are the commentators on the philosophers, such as John Philoponus, and scholars such as the sixth-century grammarian, John of Caesarea, who in his *Disputation with a Manichaean* takes it as axiomatic that

to the natures, for the existence of a defective nature is impossible. A natural activity does not come from anything exterior, and it is obvious that no nature can be without activity or can be known to be such. For it is through the activities of each that its proper nature is confirmed. This is incontrovertible.[19]

If the activity of Christ is one, then the same activity is productive of both divine and human operations. But no being that remains in its natural condition is capable of performing what is opposite to it. For fire does not chill and warm, nor does water desiccate and moisten. How, then, did he who is God by nature and became human by nature accomplish his miracles and his passion by a single activity?

Now if Christ assumed a human mind, that is to say, a soul that was both spiritual and rational, he will assuredly have the capacity to think and will always have the capacity to think. The activity of the mind is thinking. Therefore since Christ was active as a human being he was always active.

In the second homily of his exegesis of the Acts of the Apostles, St John Chrysostom says the following: "One would not be mistaken in also calling his passion an act (πρᾶξις, *praxis*), for by suffering all things he brought about that great and wonderful work which abolished death and performed all the other things."[20]

If every activity of any given nature is defined as a movement intrinsic to its essence, as the experts in these matters have determined,[21] where has anyone seen a nature that is without motion or utterly devoid of activity, or has come across an activity that is not a movement of a natural power? Nobody in his right mind, according to the blessed Cyril, would grant that "the activity of God and the creature is a single natural activity."[22] Neither does the human nature restore life to Lazarus, nor does the divine power shed tears.[23] For

"every activity is the activity of an essence." *Disputatio cum Manichaeo* 33, ed. Marcel Richard, *Joannis Caesariensis presbyteri et grammatici opera quae supersunt*, CCSG 1 (Turnhout: Brepols, 1977), 121.157.

[22]Cyril of Alexandria, *Thesaurus* 32 (PG 75:453B).

[23]Cf. Jn 11.35.

μὲν γὰρ θεοσημίας ἡ θεότης εἰργάζετο, ἀλλ᾽ οὐ δίχα τῆς σαρκός, τὰ δὲ ταπεινὰ ἡ σάρξ, ἀλλ᾽ οὐ χωρὶς τῆς θεότητος. Καὶ πασχούσῃ γὰρ τῇ σαρκὶ συνημμένη ἦν ἡ θεότης ἀπαθὴς διαμένουσα καὶ τὰ πάθη ἐκτελοῦσα σωτήρια, καὶ ἐνεργούσῃ τῇ τοῦ λόγου θεότητι συνημμένος ἦν ὁ ἅγιος νοῦς νοῶν καὶ εἰδὼς τὰ τελούμενα.

Τῶν μὲν οὖν οἰκείων αὐχημάτων ἡ θεότης τῷ σώματι μεταδίδωσιν, αὐτὴ δὲ τῶν τῆς σαρκὸς παθῶν διαμένει ἀμέτοχος. Οὐ γάρ, ὥσπερ διὰ τῆς σαρκὸς ἡ θεότης τοῦ λόγου ἐνήργει, οὕτω καὶ διὰ τῆς θεότητος ἡ σὰρξ αὐτοῦ ἔπασχεν· ὄργανον γὰρ ἡ σὰρξ τῆς θεότητος ἐχρημάτισεν. Εἰ καὶ τοίνυν ἐξ ἄκρας συλλήψεως οὐδ᾽ ὁτιοῦν διηρημένον ἦν τῆς ἑκατέρας μορφῆς, ἀλλ᾽ ἑνὸς προσώπου αἱ τοῦ παντὸς χρόνου πράξεις ἑκατέρας μορφῆς γεγόνασιν, ὅμως αὐτά, ἅπερ ἀχωρίστως γεγένηνται, κατ᾽ οὐδένα τρόπον συγχέομεν, ἀλλά, τί ποίας εἴη μορφῆς, ἐκ τῆς τῶν ἔργων ποιότητος αἰσθανόμεθα.

Ἐνεργεῖ τοίνυν ὁ Χριστὸς καθ᾽ ἑκατέραν αὐτοῦ τῶν φύσεων, καὶ «ἐνεργεῖ ἑκατέρα φύσις ἐν αὐτῷ μετὰ τῆς θατέρου κοινωνίας», τοῦ μὲν λόγου κατεργαζομένου, ἅπερ ἐστὶ τοῦ λόγου, διὰ τὴν αὐθεντίαν καὶ ἐξουσίαν τῆς θεότητος, ὅσα ἐστὶν ἀρχικὰ καὶ βασιλικά, τοῦ δὲ σώματος ἐκτελοῦντος, ὅσα ἐστὶ τοῦ σώματος, πρὸς τὸ βούλημα τοῦ ἑνωθέντος αὐτῷ λόγου, οὗ καὶ γέγονεν ἴδιον. Οὐ γὰρ ἀφ᾽ ἑαυτοῦ πρὸς τὰ φυσικὰ πάθη τὴν ὁρμὴν ἐποιεῖτο οὐδ᾽ αὐτὴν ἐκ τῶν λυπηρῶν ἀφορμὴν καὶ παραίτησιν ἢ τὰ ἔξωθεν προσπίπτοντα ἔπασχεν, ἀλλ᾽ ἐκινεῖτο κατὰ τὴν ἀκολουθίαν τῆς φύσεως τοῦ λόγου θέλοντος καὶ παραχωροῦντος οἰκονομικῶς πάσχειν αὐτὸ καὶ πράττειν τὰ ἴδια, ἵνα διὰ τῶν ἔργων τῆς φύσεως πιστωθῇ ἡ ἀλήθεια.

Ὥσπερ δὲ ὑπὲρ οὐσίαν οὐσιώθη ἐκ παρθένου κυηθείς, οὕτω καὶ ὑπὲρ ἄνθρωπον τὰ ἀνθρώπων ἐνήργει ἐπὶ ἀστάτου ὕδατος γηΐνοις ποσὶ πορευόμενος οὐ γεωθέντος τοῦ ὕδατος, ἀλλὰ τῆς θεότητος ὑπερφυεῖ δυνάμει συνισταμένου πρὸς τὸ ἀδιάχυτον

tears are a property of humanity, whereas life is a property of life that has hypostatic existence. Through the identity of the hypostasis, however, each of the two is common to both natures. For Christ is one, and his person or hypostasis is one, yet he has two natures, that of his divinity and that of his humanity. Therefore the glory that naturally emanates from the divinity became common to each of the two natures through the identity of the hypostasis, and the humble characteristics of the flesh became common to each of the two. For he is one and the same since he is both the former and the latter, that is to say, God and man, and what belongs to the divinity and what belongs to the humanity are both his. The miracles were worked by the divinity, but not without the flesh; the humble things were done by the flesh but not without the divinity. And when the flesh suffered, the divinity was united with it, but remained dispassionate and rendered the sufferings salvific, and when the divinity of the Word was operating the holy mind was united with it, apprehending spiritually and knowing what was being effected.

Whereas the divinity communicated its own splendors to the body, the former remained without a share in the sufferings of the flesh. It was not a case of just as the divinity of the Word operated through the flesh, so also his flesh suffered through the divinity, for the flesh served as an instrument of the divinity. Therefore even though from the first moment of conception there was no division whatsoever between either form, but the actions of each form at all times belonged to a single person, nevertheless we do not in any way confuse those things that took place without separation, but perceive what belongs to each form from the quality of the works.

Christ therefore operates in each of his two natures and "each nature works in him in communion with the other,"[24] the Word executing what belongs to the Word, through the authority and power of the divinity, those things that pertain to sovereignty and

---

[24]From Leo I, *Letter* 28 (Tome of Leo), 14.27, quoted in the Definition of the Fourth Ecumenical Council (Chalcedon, 451) and repeated in the Definition of the Sixth Ecumenical Council (Constantinople III, 680–81).

καὶ βάρει ὑλικῶν ποδῶν μὴ ὑπείκοντος. Οὐκ ἀνθρωπίνως γὰρ ἔπραττε τὰ ἀνθρώπινα (οὐ γὰρ ἄνθρωπος μόνον, ἀλλὰ καὶ θεός· ὅθεν καὶ τὰ τούτου πάθη ζωοποιὰ καὶ σωτήρια) οὐδὲ θεϊκῶς ἐνήργει τὰ θεῖα (οὐ γὰρ θεὸς μόνον, ἀλλὰ καὶ ἄνθρωπος· ὅθεν δι᾽ ἁφῆς καὶ λόγου καὶ τῶν τοιούτων τὰς θεοσημίας εἰργάζετο).

Εἰ δὲ λέγοι τις, ὡς «οὐκ ἐπ᾽ ἀναιρέσει τῆς ἀνθρωπίνης ἐνεργείας μίαν ἐνέργειαν ἐπὶ Χριστοῦ λέγομεν, ἀλλ᾽ ἐπειδὴ ἀντιδιαστελλομένη τῇ θείᾳ ἐνεργείᾳ πάθος λέγεται ἡ ἀνθρωπίνη ἐνέργεια, κατὰ τοῦτο μίαν ἐνέργειαν ἐπὶ Χριστοῦ λέγομεν, ἐροῦμεν· Κατὰ τοῦτον τὸν λόγον καὶ οἱ μίαν φύσιν λέγοντες οὐκ ἐπ᾽ ἀναιρέσει τῆς ἀνθρωπίνης ταύτην λέγουσιν, ἀλλ᾽ ἐπειδὴ ἀντιδιαστελλομένη ἡ ἀνθρωπίνη φύσις πρὸς τὴν θείαν φύσιν παθητικὴ λέγεται. Ἡμᾶς δὲ μὴ γένοιτο τῇ πρὸς τὴν θείαν ἐνέργειαν διαστολῇ πάθος τὴν ἀνθρωπίνην προσαγορεῦσαι κίνησιν· οὐδενὸς γάρ, καθόλου φάναι, ὕπαρξις ἐκ παραθέσεως ἢ ἐκ συγκρίσεως γινώσκεται ἢ ὁρίζεται. Οὕτω γὰρ ἀλληλαίτια εὑρεθήσονται τὰ ὄντα πράγματα. Εἰ γὰρ διὰ τὸ ἐνέργειαν εἶναι τὴν θείαν κίνησιν ἡ ἀνθρωπίνη πάθος ἐστί, πάντως καὶ διὰ τὸ ἀγαθὴν εἶναι τὴν θείαν φύσιν πονηρὰ ἔσται ἡ ἀνθρωπίνη, καὶ κατὰ τὴν σὺν ἀντιθέσει ἀντιστροφὴν διὰ τὸ πάθος λέγεσθαι τὴν ἀνθρωπίνην κίνησιν ἡ θεία κίνησις ἐνέργεια λέγεται, καὶ διὰ τὸ πονηρὰν εἶναι τὴν ἀνθρωπίνην φύσιν ἀγαθὴ ἔσται ἡ θεία». Καὶ πάντα δὲ τὰ κτίσματα οὕτως ἔσται πονηρά, καὶ ψεύσεται ὁ εἰπών· «Καὶ εἶδεν ὁ θεὸς πάντα, ὅσα ἐποίησε, καὶ ἰδοὺ καλὰ λίαν».

Ἡμεῖς δέ φαμεν, ὅτι «οἱ ἅγιοι πατέρες πολυτρόπως τὴν ἀνθρωπίνην ὠνόμασαν κίνησιν πρὸς τὰς ὑποκειμένας ἐννοίας. Προσηγόρευσαν γὰρ αὐτὴν καὶ δύναμιν καὶ ἐνέργειαν καὶ διαφορὰν καὶ κίνησιν καὶ ἰδιότητα καὶ ποιότητα καὶ πάθος· οὐ κατὰ ἀντιδιαστολὴν τῆς θείας, ἀλλ᾽ ὡς συνεκτικὴν μὲν καὶ ἀναλλοίωτον δύναμιν, ἐνέργειαν δὲ ὡς χαρακτηριστικὴν καὶ τὴν ἐν πᾶσι τοῖς ὁμοειδέσιν ἀπαραλλαξίαν ἐμφαίνουσαν, διαφορὰν δὲ ὡς ἀφοριστικήν, κίνησιν δὲ ὡς ἐνδεικτικήν, ἰδιότητα δὲ ὡς

royal power, whereas the body performs what belongs to the body, in keeping with the will of the Word united to it, to which it has come to belong. For it did not feel impelled of its own accord to accept physical suffering, nor did it experience this impulse through aversion to painful things and withdrawal from them or the events that befell it externally, but it moved following the process of its own nature with the Word willing it and allowing it to suffer and do what was proper to it in accordance with the dispensation of the incarnation, that through its works the truth of its nature might be confirmed.

And just as he was invested with substance in a manner transcending substance when he was conceived of a virgin, so also he operated as a human being in a manner transcending the human when he walked on unstable water with earthly feet,[25] not because the water had been turned into land but because by the supernatural power of the divinity it had been made compact with respect to its fluidity and did not give way to the weight of material feet. For he did not perform human actions in a human manner (since he was not only man but also God, hence even his sufferings were life-giving and salvific), nor did he perform divine actions in a divine manner (since he was not only God but also man, hence he worked the miracles by touch and word and such things).

If anyone were to say: "We attribute one energy to Christ not to abolish the human energy but because the human energy, as distinguished from the divine energy, is called a passion, and it is in this sense that we attribute one energy to Christ," we would reply: "By this argument those also who maintain one nature do not do so to abolish the human nature but because the human nature as distinct from the divine nature is said to be passible. God forbid that we should call the human movement a passion because of its distinction from the divine energy. For, generally speaking, the existence of nothing is known or defined through juxtaposition or comparison. If that were so, existing things would be the cause of each other. For if human motion is a passion on account of divine motion being

[25]Cf. Mt 14.25.

συστατικὴν καὶ μόνῃ αὐτῇ καὶ οὐκ ἄλλῃ προσοῦσαν, ποιότητα
δὲ ὡς εἰδοποιόν, πάθος δὲ ὡς κινουμένην· πάντα γὰρ τὰ ἐκ θεοῦ
καὶ μετὰ θεὸν πάσχει τῷ κινεῖσθαι ὡς μὴ ὄντα αὐτοκίνησις ἢ
αὐτοδύναμις, οὐ κατὰ ἀντιδιαστολὴν οὖν, ὡς εἴρηται, ἀλλὰ τὸν
δημιουργικῶς αὐτοῖς ἐντεθέντα παρὰ τῆς τὸ πᾶν συστησαμένης
αἰτίας λόγον· ὅθεν καὶ μετὰ τῆς θείας συνεκφωνοῦντες αὐτὴν
ἐνέργειαν προσηγόρευσαν. Ὁ γὰρ εἰπών· ῾Ενεργεῖ γὰρ ἑκατέρα
μορφὴ μετὰ τῆς θατέρου κοινωνίας᾽, τί ἕτερον πεποίηκεν ἢ ὁ
εἰπών· ῾Καὶ γὰρ τεσσαράκοντα ἡμέρας ἄποσιτος μείνας ὕστερον
ἐπείνασεν᾽ (ἔδωκε γὰρ τῇ φύσει, ὅτε ἤθελε, τὰ ἴδια ἐνεργεῖν) ἢ οἱ
διάφορον ἐν αὐτῷ φήσαντες ἐνέργειαν ἢ οἱ διπλῆν ἢ οἱ ἄλλην καὶ
ἄλλην;» Ταῦτα γὰρ δι᾽ ἀντωνυμίας δύο τὰς ἐνεργείας σημαίνουσι·
καὶ δι᾽ ἀντωνυμίας γὰρ πολλάκις ὁ ἀριθμὸς ἐνδείκνυται καὶ διὰ
τοῦ εἰπεῖν θεῖόν τε καὶ ἀνθρώπινον. «Ἡ γὰρ διαφορὰ διαφερόντων
ἐστὶ διαφορά»· τὰ δὲ μὴ ὄντα, πῶς διοίσουσιν;

---

[26]Cf. Maximus the Confessor, *Disputation with Pyrrhus* 205–10 (PG 91:349BCD).
[27]Gen 1.31.

an energy, it would follow that the human nature would be evil on account of the divine nature being good, and by the conversion of the opposite terms of the argument by which the divine motion is called energy on account of the human motion being called passion, the divine nature would be good on account of the human nature being evil."[26] And in this way all creatures would be evil, and he who said: "And God saw all the things that he had made, and behold, they were very good"[27] would be proved a liar.

But we say that "the holy fathers named the human motion in different ways in relation to the underlying concepts. For they called it power, and energy, and difference, and movement, and property, and quality, and passion, not in contradistinction to the divine motion but power when it is comprehensive and unchanging, and energy when it defines the character and manifests the invariability in all things of the same species, and difference when it distinguishes, and movement when it indicates, and property when it is constitutive and belongs to this alone and no other, and quality when it specifies, and passion when it is moved. For everything that is from God and after God experiences being moved since it is not the principle of movement or the principle of power itself, therefore not in virtue of contradistinction, as has been said, but in virtue of the principle inserted creatively in them by the cause that constituted the universe. Hence they called this 'energy' even when they designated it together with the divine motion. For what else did he who said 'Each of the two forms is in action in communion with the other'[28] do that was different from him who says 'He fasted for forty days and forty nights, and afterwards was famished'[29] (for when he wished he allowed the nature to effect what was proper to it), or from those who said that there was a different energy at work within him, or those who held that it was double, or those who said that it was two different motions?" For through the pronoun these indicate

[28]Leo I, *Letter* 28 (Tome of Leo), 14.27, cited by the Definitions of the Fourth (Chalcedon, 451) and Sixth (Constantinople III, 680–81) Ecumenical Councils.
[29]Mt 4.2.

60   Πρὸς τοὺς λέγοντας· Εἰ δύο φύσεων καὶ ἐνεργειῶν
ὁ ἄνθρωπος, ἀνάγκη ἐπὶ Χριστοῦ τρεῖς φύσεις καὶ
τοσαύτας λέγειν τὰς ἐνεργείας

Ὁ μὲν καθ᾿ ἕκαστα ἄνθρωπος ἐκ δύο συγκείμενος φύσεων, ψυχῆς
τε καὶ σώματος, καὶ ταύτας ἀμεταβλήτους ἔχων ἐν ἑαυτῷ δύο
φύσεις εἰκότως λεχθήσεται· σῴζει γὰρ ἑκατέρων καὶ μετὰ τὴν
ἕνωσιν τὴν φυσικὴν ἰδιότητα. Οὔτε γὰρ τὸ σῶμα ἀθάνατον ἀλλὰ
φθαρτόν, οὔτε ἡ ψυχὴ θνητὴ ἀλλ᾿ ἀθάνατος, οὔτε τὸ σῶμα
ἀόρατον οὔτε ἡ ψυχὴ σωματικοῖς ὀφθαλμοῖς ὁρατή, ἀλλ᾿ ἡ μὲν
λογικὴ καὶ νοερὰ καὶ ἀσώματος, τὸ δὲ παχύ τε καὶ ὁρατὸν καὶ
ἄλογον. Οὐ μιᾶς δὲ φύσεως τὰ κατ᾿ οὐσίαν ἀντιδιαιρούμενα· οὐ
μιᾶς ἄρα οὐσίας ψυχή τε καὶ σῶμα.

Καὶ πάλιν· Εἰ ζῷον λογικὸν θνητὸν ὁ ἄνθρωπος, πᾶς δὲ ὅρος
τῶν ὑποκειμένων φύσεών ἐστι δηλωτικός, οὐ ταὐτὸν δὲ κατὰ
φύσεως λόγον τὸ λογικὸν τῷ θνητῷ· οὐκ ἄρα μιᾶς φύσεως εἴη ὁ
ἄνθρωπος κατὰ τὸν τοῦ οἰκείου ὁρισμοῦ κανόνα.

Εἰ δὲ λέγοιτό ποτε μιᾶς φύσεως ὁ ἄνθρωπος, ἀντὶ τοῦ εἴδους
τὸ τῆς φύσεως παραλαμβάνεται ὄνομα λεγόντων ἡμῶν, ὅτι οὐ
διαλλάττει ἄνθρωπος ἀνθρώπου κατά τινα φύσεως διαφοράν,
ἀλλὰ τὴν αὐτὴν σύστασιν ἔχοντες πάντες οἱ ἄνθρωποι καὶ
ἐκ ψυχῆς συντεθειμένοι καὶ σώματος καὶ δύο ἕκαστος φύσεις
τελοῦντες ὑφ᾿ ἕνα πάντες ὁρισμὸν ἀνάγονται. Καὶ οὐ παράλογον
τοῦτο, ὁπότε καὶ πάντων τῶν κτιστῶν ὡς γενητῶν μίαν φύσιν

---

[30]*Doctrina Patrum*, Diekamp, 159.35.

[1]A definition (in its fuller form, "a human being is a rational mortal animal
capable of receiving mind and knowledge"), going back in its essentials to Aristotle,

two operations, and through the pronoun the number is frequently indicated and also through saying divine and human. "For difference is the difference of things that differ."[30] And when things do not exist how could they differ?

60 *To those who say: If a human being consists of two natures and activities, it would be necessary to say in the case of Christ that there are three natures and the same number of activities*

Certainly, as each human being consists of two natures, soul and body, and possesses these unchanged in its own being, it may rightly be said that a human being has two natures. For a human being preserves the natural property of each of the two even after the union. For neither is the body immortal but mortal, nor is the soul mortal but immortal; nor is the body invisible, nor is the soul visible to corporeal eyes, but on the contrary the one is rational and intelligent and incorporeal, whereas the other is coarse and visible and irrational. For those things that are distinct in essence do not belong to a single nature. Therefore soul and body do not belong to a single nature.

And again, if a human being is a rational mortal animal,[1] and every definition is indicative of the underlying natures, and the rational, according to the law of nature, is not the same as the mortal, it follows that a human being by its own definition is not of a single nature.

But if it is sometimes said that a human being is of one nature, the word "nature" is being taken in the sense of "species," as when we say that one human being does not differ from another by any difference of nature, but since all human beings have the same constitution and are composed of soul and body, and each one consists of two natures, all of them come under a single definition. And this is

Topics 1.5, 128b35, and much quoted in the fuller form by the commentators on Aristotle and the church fathers.

ὁ ἱερὸς Ἀθανάσιος ἔφησεν ἐν τῷ κατὰ τῶν βλασφημούντων
τὸ πνεῦμα τὸ ἅγιον οὑτωσὶ λέγων· «Ὅτι δὲ ἄνω τῆς κτίσεώς
ἐστι τὸ πνεῦμα τὸ ἅγιον καὶ ἄλλο μὲν παρὰ τὴν τῶν γενητῶν
φύσιν, ἴδιον δὲ τῆς θεότητος, ἔξεστι πάλιν συνιδεῖν». «Πᾶν γάρ,
ὃ κοινῶς καὶ ἐν πολλοῖς θεωρεῖται, οὐ τινὶ μὲν πλέον, τινὶ δὲ
ἔλαττον ὑπάρχον, οὐσία ὀνομάζεται». Ἐπεὶ οὖν πᾶς ἄνθρωπος
ἐκ ψυχῆς ἐστι συντεθειμένος καὶ σώματος, κατὰ τοῦτο μία φύσις
τῶν ἀνθρώπων λέγεται. Ἐπὶ δὲ τῆς ὑποστάσεως τοῦ κυρίου οὐ
λέγειν δυνάμεθα μίαν φύσιν· αἵ τε γὰρ φύσεις σῴζουσι καὶ μετὰ
τὴν ἕνωσιν ἑκάστη τὴν φυσικὴν ἰδιότητα, καὶ εἶδος Χριστῶν οὐκ
ἔστι εὑρεῖν. Οὐ γὰρ ἐγένετο ἄλλος Χριστὸς ἐκ θεότητός τε καὶ
ἀνθρωπότητος, θεός τε καὶ ἄνθρωπος ὁ αὐτός.

Καὶ πάλιν· Οὐ ταὐτόν ἐστι τὸ κατ᾽ εἶδος τοῦ ἀνθρώπου ἓν
καὶ τὸ κατ᾽ οὐσίαν ψυχῆς καὶ σώματος ἕν. Τὸ μὲν γὰρ κατ᾽ εἶδος
τοῦ ἀνθρώπου ἓν τὴν ἐν πᾶσι τοῖς ἀνθρώποις ἀπαραλλαξίαν
ἐνδείκνυται· τὸ δὲ κατ᾽ οὐσίαν ψυχῆς καὶ σώματος ἓν αὐτὸ τὸ
εἶναι αὐτῶν λυμαίνεται εἰς ἀνυπαρξίαν αὐτὰ παντελῆ ἄγον·
ἢ γὰρ τὸ ἓν εἰς τὴν τοῦ ἑτέρου μεταποιηθήσεται οὐσίαν ἢ ἐξ
ἑτέρων ἕτερον γενήσεται καὶ ἀμφότερα τραπήσονται ἢ ἐπὶ τῶν
ἰδίων ὅρων μένοντα δύο φύσεις ἔσονται. Οὐ γὰρ ταὐτὸν κατ᾽
οὐσίας λόγον τὸ σῶμα τῷ ἀσωμάτῳ. Οὐκ ἀνάγκη τοίνυν ἐπὶ τοῦ
ἀνθρώπου μίαν φύσιν λέγοντας (οὐ διὰ τὸ ταὐτὸν τῆς οὐσιώδους
ποιότητος ψυχῆς τε καὶ σώματος, ἀλλὰ διὰ τὸ ἀπαράλλακτον τῶν
ὑπὸ τὸ εἶδος ἀναγομένων ἀτόμων) μίαν καὶ ἐπὶ Χριστοῦ φύσιν
λέγειν, ἔνθα εἶδος περιεκτικὸν πολλῶν ὑποστάσεων οὐκ ἔστιν.

Ἔτι δὲ πᾶσα σύνθεσις ἐκ τῶν προσεχῶς συντεθέντων
συντεθεῖσθαι λέγεται· οὐ γὰρ λέγομεν τὸν οἶκον ἐκ γῆς καὶ
ὕδατος συντεθεῖσθαι, ἀλλ᾽ ἐκ πλίνθου καὶ ξύλων. Ἐπεὶ ἀνάγκη
καὶ τὸν ἄνθρωπον λέγειν ἐκ πέντε συγκεῖσθαι φύσεων, ἔκ τε

not strange when the holy Athanasius said that all created things, in virtue of their having come into being have a single nature, and says in his treatise against those who blaspheme the Holy Spirit: "That the Holy Spirit is superior to creation and other than the nature of things that have come into being, and belongs properly to the Godhead, is again something that it is possible to comprehend."[2] "For everything that may be observed commonly and in many, not existing more in one and less in another, is called an essence."[3] Therefore since every human being is composed of soul and body, on this account the nature of human beings is said to be single. But in the case of the Lord's hypostasis we cannot say that there is a single nature. For the natures are preserved even after the union, each with its natural property, and it is not possible to identify a species of Christs. For no other Christ has come into being out of divinity and humanity, the same both God and man.

And again, the unity of human beings according to species and the unity of soul and body according to essence are not the same thing. For the unity of human beings according to species is indicated by the invariability of all human beings, whereas the unity of soul and body according to essence violates their being and reduces them to utter non-existence. For either one would be transformed into the essence of the other, or from two different things a third would come into being and both would be changed, or by remaining within their own limits, they would be two natures. For the corporeal is not the same as the incorporeal on the level of essence. It is therefore not necessary because we speak of one nature in the case of human beings (not on account of the identity of the essential quality of soul and body, but on account of the invariability of individuals belonging to the species) also to say in Christ's case that he has one nature, where there is no species that includes many hypostases.

[2] Athanasius of Alexandria, *Letters to Serapion* 1.26 (PG 26:589C), reproduced in *Doctrina Patrum*, Diekamp, 205.11–15.

[3] A dogmatic fragment from Eulogius of Alexandria (PG 86/2:2944), reproduced in *Doctrina Patrum*, Diekamp, 205.20–21.

τῶν τεσσάρων στοιχείων καὶ ψυχῆς. Οὕτω καὶ ἐπὶ τοῦ κυρίου
ἡμῶν Ἰησοῦ Χριστοῦ οὐ τὰ μέρη τῶν μερῶν σκοποῦμεν, ἀλλὰ τὰ
προσεχῶς συντεθέντα, θεότητά τε καὶ ἀνθρωπότητα.

Ἔτι δὲ εἰ δύο φύσεις τὸν ἄνθρωπον λέγοντες τρεῖς φύσεις ἐπὶ
Χριστοῦ λέγειν ἀναγκασθησόμεθα, καὶ ὑμεῖς ἐκ δύο φύσεων τὸν
ἄνθρωπον λέγοντες ἐκ τριῶν τὸν Χριστὸν δογματίζετε φύσεων·
ὁμοίως καὶ περὶ ἐνεργειῶν· κατάλληλον γὰρ ἀνάγκη τῇ φύσει
τὴν ἐνέργειαν εἶναι. Ὅτι δὲ δύο φύσεων ὁ ἄνθρωπος λέγεταί τε
καὶ ἔστι, μάρτυς ὁ θεολόγος Γρηγόριος· «Φύσεις μὲν γὰρ δύο»
φάσκων «θεὸς καὶ ἄνθρωπος· ἐπεὶ καὶ ψυχὴ καὶ σῶμα». Καὶ ἐν
τῷ περὶ βαπτίσματος δὲ λόγῳ τοιάδε φησί· «Διττῶν δὲ ὄντων
ἡμῶν ἐκ ψυχῆς καὶ σώματος, καὶ τῆς μὲν ὁρατῆς τῆς δὲ ἀοράτου
φύσεως, διττὴ καὶ ἡ κάθαρσις δι' ὕδατος καὶ πνεύματος».

61 *Περὶ τοῦ τεθεῶσθαι τὴν φύσιν τῆς τοῦ κυρίου σαρκὸς
        καὶ τὸ θέλημα*

Χρὴ εἰδέναι, ὡς οὐ κατὰ μεταβολὴν φύσεως ἢ τροπὴν ἢ ἀλλοίωσιν
ἢ σύγχυσιν ἡ σὰρξ τοῦ κυρίου τεθεῶσθαι λέγεται καὶ ὁμόθεος
καὶ θεὸς γενέσθαι, ὥς φησιν ὁ θεολόγος Γρηγόριος· «Ὧν τὸ
μὲν ἐθέωσε, τὸ δὲ ἐθεώθη», καὶ «θαρρῶ λέγειν ὁμόθεον», καὶ
«ἄνθρωπον γενέσθαι τὸ χρῖσαν καὶ θεὸν τὸ χριόμενον». Ταῦτα

---

[4]Cf. a fragment of Heraclianus of Chalcedon preserved in *Doctrina Patrum*,
Diekamp, 207.19–208.27.
    [5]Gregory of Nazianzus, *Letter* 101.19 (PG 37:180A) reproduced in *Doctrina
Patrum*, Diekamp, 11.I; 207.VI.
    [6]Gregory of Nazianzus, *Oration* 40.8 (PG 36:368A; Moreschini, 928), reproduced
in *Doctrina Patrum*, Diekamp, 207.VII.

Moreover, every complex whole is said to be constructed out of the things that directly compose it. For we do not say that a house is constructed out of earth and water, but out of bricks and timber. Otherwise, we would also have to say that a human being is composed of five natures, of the four elements and a soul. The same applies to our Lord Jesus Christ. We do not focus on the parts of the parts, but on what directly composes him, divinity and humanity.[4]

And furthermore, if by saying that human beings have two natures we should be obliged to say that in Christ's case there are three natures, then you too, by saying that human beings are composed of two natures, are declaring as dogma that Christ is composed of three natures. The same is true with regard to the activities, for it is necessary that the activity should correspond to the nature. That human beings are said to have two natures and actually do have them, is attested by Gregory the Theologian, who says, "God and man are two natures, as indeed are soul and body."[5] And in his oration on baptism he says the following: "Since we are formed of two natures, of soul and body, the one being visible and the other invisible, the purification by water and the Spirit is also of a dual nature."[6]

61 On the deification of the nature of the Lord's flesh and will

One needs to know that it is not by a transformation, or change, or modification, or confusion of nature that the Lord's flesh is said to have been deified and become wholly one with God and God, as Gregory the Theologian says: "Of which the one deified, while the other was deified,"[1] and "I would venture to say, wholly one with God,"[2] and "that which anointed became man and that which was

---

[1]Gregory of Nazianzus, *Oration* 38.13 (PG 36:325BC; Moreschini, 892) (= *Oration* 45.9).

[2]Gregory of Nazianzus, *Oration* 45.13 (PG 36:641A; Moreschini, 1150). "Wholly one with God" translates ὁμόθεον (*homotheon.* literally "identically god"), a word coined by Gregory of Nazianzus on the lines of *homoousion.* John uses it again in Chapter 91 (2) (c), where it is rendered "equally divine as." Reproduced in *Doctrina Patrum*, Diekamp, 127.16.

γὰρ οὐ κατὰ μεταβολὴν φύσεως, ἀλλὰ κατὰ τὴν οἰκονομικὴν
ἕνωσιν, τὴν καθ᾽ ὑπόστασιν λέγω, καθ᾽ ἣν ἀδιασπάστως τῷ θεῷ
λόγῳ ἥνωται, καὶ τὴν ἐν ἀλλήλαις τῶν φύσεων περιχώρησιν,
ὥς φαμεν καὶ τὴν τοῦ σιδήρου πύρωσιν· ὥσπερ γὰρ τὴν
ἐνανθρώπησιν χωρὶς μεταβολῆς καὶ τροπῆς ὁμολογοῦμεν,
οὕτω καὶ τὴν θέωσιν γενέσθαι τῆς σαρκὸς δοξάζομεν. Οὔτε
γὰρ διότι ὁ λόγος σὰρξ ἐγένετο, τῶν ὅρων ἐξέστη τῆς οἰκείας
θεότητος οὔτε τῶν προσόντων αὐτῇ θεοπρεπῶν αὐχημάτων,
οὔτε μὴν ἡ σὰρξ θεωθεῖσα τῆς οἰκείας ἐτράπη φύσεως ἢ τῶν
αὐτῆς φυσικῶν ἰδιωμάτων. Μεμενήκασι γὰρ καὶ μετὰ τὴν ἕνωσιν
αἱ φύσεις ἀσύμφυρτοι καὶ αἱ τούτων ἰδιότητες ἀλώβητοι. Ἡ δὲ
τοῦ κυρίου σὰρξ τὰς θείας ἐνεργείας ἐπλούτησε διὰ τὴν πρὸς
τὸν λόγον ἀκραιφνεστάτην ἕνωσιν ἤτοι τὴν καθ᾽ ὑπόστασιν
οὐδαμῶς τῶν κατὰ φύσιν ἰδίων ὑποστᾶσα ἔκπτωσιν· οὐ γὰρ
κατ᾽ οἰκείαν ἐνέργειαν, ἀλλὰ διὰ τὸν ἡνωμένον αὐτῇ λόγον τὰ
θεῖα ἐνήργει τοῦ λόγου δι᾽ αὐτῆς τὴν οἰκείαν ἐνδεικνυμένου
ἐνέργειαν. Καίει μὲν γὰρ ὁ πεπυρακτωμένος σίδηρος, οὐ φυσικῷ
δὲ λόγῳ τὴν καυστικὴν κεκτημένος ἐνέργειαν, ἀλλ᾽ ἐκ τῆς πρὸς
τὸ πῦρ ἑνώσεως τοῦτο κτησάμενος.

Ἡ αὐτὴ τοιγαροῦν θνητή τε ἦν δι᾽ ἑαυτὴν καὶ ζωοποιὸς διὰ
τὴν πρὸς τὸν λόγον καθ᾽ ὑπόστασιν ἕνωσιν. Ὁμοίως καὶ τὴν τοῦ
θελήματος θέωσιν οὐχ ὡς μεταβληθείσης τῆς φυσικῆς κινήσεως
λέγομεν, ἀλλ᾽ ὡς ἡνωμένης τῷ θείῳ αὐτοῦ καὶ παντοδυνάμῳ
θελήματι, καὶ γεγονότος θεοῦ ἐνανθρωπήσαντος θέλημα· ὅθεν
θέλων μὲν λαθεῖν οὐκ ἠδυνήθη δι᾽ ἑαυτοῦ εὐδοκήσαντος τοῦ
θεοῦ λόγου δειχθῆναι ἐν αὐτῷ ἀληθῶς ὑπάρχον τὸ ἀσθενὲς τοῦ
ἀνθρωπίνου θελήματος, θέλων δὲ τὴν τοῦ λεπροῦ ἐνήργησε
κάθαρσιν διὰ τὴν πρὸς τὸ θεῖον θέλημα ἕνωσιν.

Ἰστέον δέ, ὡς ἡ θέωσις τῆς φύσεως καὶ τοῦ θελήματος
ἐμφαντικώτατον καὶ δεικτικώτατόν ἐστι τῶν τε δύο φύσεων καὶ

anointed became God."[3] For these things took place not by a transformation of nature but by the union pertaining to the dispensation
of the incarnation, I mean the hypostatic union by which the flesh
was inseparably united to God the Word, and the mutual interpenetration of the natures, as we also say in the case of red-hot iron.
For just as we confess that the inhomination took place without
transformation or change, so also we believe that the deification of
the flesh took place in the same manner. For neither did the Word
step outside the boundaries of his proper divinity, or outside the
honorable distinctions befitting God that belong to it, on account of
his becoming flesh, nor indeed did the flesh abandon its own nature
or change its natural properties when it was deified. For even after
the union the natures remained distinct from each other with their
properties unimpaired. For the Lord's flesh was enriched with the
divine energies through the most perfect, that is to say, the hypostatic, union with the Word, without suffering the least diminution
of its own natural properties. For it was not by its own energy but
by the Word united with it that it performed the divine acts of the
Word, who through it demonstrated his own energy. For the red-hot
iron burns not because it possesses the power to burn on account
of its own nature, but because it has acquired it as a result of being
united with fire.[4]

That is why the flesh was both mortal in itself and life-giving
through its hypostatic union with the Word. In the same way we
also say that the deification of the will takes place not because its
natural movement has been changed but because it was united with
his divine and almighty will and became the will of God made man.
It was thus that when he wished to escape notice he could not of
himself do so, because it pleased God the Word to show that the
weakness of the human will really did exist within him, but when he

---

[3]Gregory of Nazianzus, *Oration* 30.21 (PG 36:132BC; Moreschini, 744), reproduced in *Doctrina Patrum*, Diekamp, 127.20; cf. Maximus the Confessor, *Opusculum*
9, 120A.

[4]Cf. Theodotus of Ancyra, in *Doctrina Patrum*, Diekamp, 126–28.

τῶν δύο θελημάτων· ὥσπερ γὰρ ἡ πύρωσις οὐ μεταβάλλει τὴν τοῦ πυρωθέντος φύσιν εἰς τὴν τοῦ πυρός, ἀλλὰ δηλοῖ τό τε πυρωθὲν καὶ τὸ πυρῶσαν, καὶ οὐχ ἑνός, ἀλλὰ δύο ἐστὶ δηλωτικόν, οὕτω καὶ ἡ θέωσις οὐ μίαν φύσιν ἀποτελεῖ σύνθετον, ἀλλὰ τὰς δύο καὶ τὴν καθ᾽ ὑπόστασιν ἕνωσιν. Φησὶ γοῦν ὁ θεολόγος Γρηγόριος· «Ὧν τὸ μὲν ἐθέωσε, τὸ δὲ ἐθεώθη·» «ὧν» γὰρ εἰπὼν καὶ «τὸ μὲν» καὶ «τὸ δὲ» δύο ἔδειξεν.

62 Ἔτι περὶ θελημάτων καὶ αὐτεξουσίων νοῶν τε καὶ γνώσεων καὶ σοφιῶν

Θεὸν τέλειον καὶ ἄνθρωπον τέλειον λέγοντες τὸν Χριστὸν πάντως πάντα δώσομεν τά τε τοῦ πατρὸς φυσικὰ τά τε τῆς μητρός· γέγονε γὰρ ἄνθρωπος ἵνα τὸ νικηθὲν νικήσῃ. Οὐκ ἀδύνατος γὰρ ἦν ὁ τὰ πάντα δυνάμενος καὶ τῇ παντοδυνάμῳ αὐτοῦ ἐξουσίᾳ καὶ δυνάμει ἐξελέσθαι τοῦ τυραννοῦντος τὸν ἄνθρωπον, ἀλλ᾽ ἦν ἐγκλήματος τῷ τυραννοῦντι ὑπόθεσις ἄνθρωπον νικήσαντι καὶ ὑπὸ θεοῦ βιασθέντι. Αὐτὸν οὖν τὸν πεσόντα νικητὴν ἀναδεῖξαι βουληθεὶς ὁ συμπαθὴς θεὸς καὶ φιλάνθρωπος, ἄνθρωπος γίνεται τῷ ὁμοίῳ τὸ ὅμοιον ἀνακαλούμενος.

Ὅτι δὲ λογικὸν καὶ νοερὸν ζῷον ὁ ἄνθρωπος, οὐδεὶς ἀντερεῖ. Πῶς οὖν ἄνθρωπος γέγονεν, εἰ σάρκα ἄψυχον ἢ ψυχὴν ἄνουν ἀνέλαβεν; Οὐ τοῦτο γὰρ ἄνθρωπος. Τί δὲ καὶ τῆς ἐνανθρωπήσεως

---

[5]Cf. Maximus the Confessor, *Disputation with Pyrrhus*, 113–16 (PG 91:316CD).

[1]Or "perfect God and perfect man." John's phraseology (θεὸν τέλειον καὶ ἄνθρωπον τέλειον, *theon teleion kai anthrōpon teleion*) echoes that of Definition of Chalcedon: "the same perfect in Godhead, and the same perfect in manhood" (τέλειον τὸν αὐτὸν ἐν θεότητι καὶ τέλειον τὸν αὐτὸν ἐν ἀνθρωπότητι, *teleion ton*

wished to bring about the cleansing of the leper, he did so through the union of the human with the divine will.

One should note that the deification of the nature and the will is supremely revelatory and indicative of the two natures and the two wills. For just as bringing to red heat does not change the nature of what is heated into that of fire but manifests both that which is heated and that which heats, and is indicative not of one thing but of two, so too deification does not produce a single compound nature but the two and their hypostatic union.[5] It is thus that Gregory the Theologian says: "of which the one deified, while the other was deified." By saying "of which" in the plural and "the one" and "the other," he made it clear that there were two.

62 *A further discussion of wills and of minds possessing free will, and of different knowledges and wisdoms*

When we say that Christ is fully God and fully man,[1] we are assuredly attributing to him all the natural properties that belong to his Father and to his mother. For he became a man so that what had been defeated should prove victorious. For he who can do everything did not lack the power to release humanity from the tyrant by his omnipotent authority and might, but there would have been grounds for complaint for the tyrant if he had defeated humanity but been compelled by God. Since God in his compassion and love for humanity wished to make the one who had been defeated victorious, he became a human being to call back like by like.

No one would dispute that a human being is a rational and intelligent animal.[2] How, then, could [God] have become a human being if he had assumed flesh that was without soul, or a soul that

auton en theotēti kai teleion ton auton en anthrōpotēti) (trans. Richard Price, *Acts of the Council of Chalcedon*, vol.2, 204).

[2]The definition of man as "rational and intelligent" (λογικὸν καὶ νοερόν, *logikon kai noeron*) was commonly assumed by the Neoplatonic commentators on Aristotle (Aristotle himself having only said, in *Posterior Analytics* 92a1, that man is a mortal animal).

ἀπωνάμεθα τοῦ πρωτοπαθήσαντος μὴ σεσωσμένου μηδὲ τῇ συναφείᾳ τῆς θεότητος ἀνακεκαινισμένου τε καὶ νενευρωμένου; «Τὸ γὰρ ἀπρόσληπτον ἀθεράπευτον». Ἀναλαμβάνει τοίνυν ὅλον τὸν ἄνθρωπον καὶ τὸ τούτου κάλλιστον ὑπὸ ἀρρωστίαν πεσόν, ἵνα ὅλῳ τὴν σωτηρίαν χαρίσηται. Νοῦς δὲ ἄσοφος ἐστερημένος τε γνώσεως οὐκ ἂν εἴη ποτέ· εἰ γὰρ ἀνενέργητος καὶ ἀκίνητος, καὶ ἀνύπαρκτος πάντως. Τὸ κατ᾽ εἰκόνα ἀνακαινίσαι βουλόμενος ὁ θεὸς λόγος γέγονεν ἄνθρωπος. Τί δὲ τὸ κατ᾽ εἰκόνα εἰ μὴ ὁ νοῦς; Τὸ κρεῖττον οὖν παρεὶς τὸ χεῖρον ἀνέλαβε; Νοῦς γὰρ ἐν μεταιχμίῳ ἐστὶ θεοῦ καὶ σαρκός, τῆς μὲν ὡς σύνοικος, τοῦ θεοῦ δὲ ὡς εἰκών. Νοῦς οὖν νοΐ μίγνυται, καὶ μεσιτεύει νοῦς θεοῦ καθαρότητι καὶ σαρκὸς παχύτητι· εἰ γὰρ ψυχὴν ἄνουν ὁ κύριος ἀνέλαβεν, ἀλόγου ζῴου ψυχὴν ἀνέλαβεν.

Εἰ δέ, ὅτι σάρκα γεγενῆσθαι τὸν λόγον, ἔφη ὁ εὐαγγελιστής, ἰστέον ὡς παρὰ τῇ ἁγίᾳ γραφῇ ποτὲ μὲν ψυχὴ λέγεται ὁ ἄνθρωπος ὡς τὸ «ἐν ἑβδομήκοντα πέντε ψυχαῖς εἰσῆλθεν Ἰακὼβ εἰς Αἴγυπτον», ποτὲ δὲ σὰρξ ὡς τὸ» ὄψεται πᾶσα σὰρξ τὸ σωτήριον τοῦ θεοῦ». Οὐ σὰρξ τοίνυν ἄψυχος οὐδὲ ἄνους, ἀλλ᾽ ἄνθρωπος γέγονεν ὁ κύριος. Φησὶ γοῦν αὐτός· «Τί με δέρεις ἄνθρωπον, ὃς τὴν ἀλήθειαν ὑμῖν λελάληκα;» Ἀνέλαβε τοίνυν σάρκα ἐψυχωμένην ψυχῇ λογικῇ τε καὶ νοερᾷ, ἡγεμονικὴ μὲν τῆς σαρκός, ἡγεμονευομένη δὲ ὑπὸ τῆς τοῦ λόγου θεότητος.

Εἶχε μὲν οὖν φυσικῶς καὶ ὡς θεὸς καὶ ὡς ἄνθρωπος τὸ θέλειν, εἴπετο δὲ καὶ ὑπετάσσετο τῷ αὐτοῦ θελήματι μὴ κινούμενον γνώμῃ ἰδίᾳ, ἀλλὰ ταῦτα θέλον, ἃ τὸ θεῖον αὐτοῦ ἤθελε θέλημα. Παραχωρούσης γὰρ τῆς θείας θελήσεως ἔπασχε τὰ ἴδια φυσικῶς. Ὅτε μὲν γὰρ παρῃτεῖτο τὸν θάνατον, φυσικῶς τῆς θείας αὐτοῦ θελησάσης θελήσεως καὶ παραχωρησάσης παρῃτήσατο τὸν θάνατον, ἠγωνίασέ τε καὶ ἐδειλίασε. Καὶ ὅτε ἤθελεν ἡ θεία αὐτοῦ θέλησις αἱρεῖσθαι τὴν ἀνθρωπίνην αὐτοῦ θέλησιν τὸν θάνατον, ἑκούσιον αὐτῇ τὸ πάθος ἐγίνετο· οὐ γὰρ καθὸ θεὸς

was without a mind? For such a being would not have been human. And what benefit would have been obtained from the incarnation if that which had suffered originally had not been saved or renewed and strengthened by the union with the divinity? "For what was not assumed was not healed."[3] He therefore took on himself the whole of what it is to be human, and the best part of it that had fallen sick, in order that he might grant salvation to the whole. A mind could never be without wisdom or devoid of knowledge, for if it were without activity and without movement it would also most certainly be without existence. Since God the Word wished to renew that which was in the image, he became a human being. What is that which is in the image if not the mind? Did he then disregard what was superior and assume what was inferior? For the mind comes in the middle between God and flesh as the companion of the latter and as being in the image of God. Mind therefore mingles with mind and mind also mediates between the purity of God and the coarseness of the flesh. For if the Lord had assumed a soul without mind, he would have assumed the soul of an irrational animal.

Since the Evangelist said that the Word became flesh,[4] you should also know that in Holy Scripture a human being is sometimes called a soul, as in the phrase "Jacob entered into Egypt, a total of seventy-five souls,"[5] and sometimes flesh, as in the phrase "all flesh shall see the salvation of God."[6] Now the Lord was not without soul or without mind but became a human being. And so he himself says: "Why do you strike me, a man who has told you the truth?"[7] Therefore he assumed flesh endowed with a rational and intelligent soul, which on the one hand governed the flesh and on the other was governed by the divinity of the Word.

Indeed, he possessed the faculty of willing naturally both as God and as a human being, and it followed his will and was subordinate to it, not being moved by a personal opinion but always willing that which his divine will willed. For by the concession of the divine will

---

[3]Gregory of Nazianzus, *Letter* 101.32 (PG 37:181C).
[4]Jn 1.14.   [5]Acts 7.14.   [6]Is 40.5; Lk 3.6.   [7]Jn 18.23, Jn 8.40.

μόνον ἑκουσίως ἑαυτὸν παρέδωκεν εἰς θάνατον, ἀλλὰ καὶ καθὸ ἄνθρωπος. Ὅθεν τὴν κατὰ τοῦ θανάτου τόλμαν καὶ ἡμῖν ἐχαρίσατο. Οὕτω γοῦν πρὸ τοῦ σωτηρίου πάθους φησί· «Πάτερ, εἰ δυνατόν, παρελθέτω ἀπ᾽ ἐμοῦ τὸ ποτήριον τοῦτο»· δηλονότι ὡς ἄνθρωπος τὸ ποτήριον πίνειν ἔμελλεν, οὐ γὰρ ὡς θεός. Ὡς ἄνθρωπος τοίνυν θέλει τὸ ποτήριον παρελθεῖν· ταῦτα τῆς φυσικῆς δειλίας τὰ ῥήματα. «Πλὴν μὴ τὸ ἐμὸν γινέσθω θέλημα» ἤτοι καθ᾽ ὅ σου ἑτεροούσιός εἰμι, «ἀλλὰ τὸ σὸν» ἤτοι τὸ ἐμὸν καὶ σόν, καθ᾽ ὅ σου πέφυκα ὁμοούσιος· ταῦτα τῆς εὐτολμίας τὰ ῥήματα. Πρότερον γὰρ τῆς φυσικῆς ἀσθενείας πειραθεῖσα κατ᾽ αἴσθησιν τὴν ἐπὶ τῷ χωρισμῷ τοῦ σώματος καὶ φυσικὴν συμπάθειαν παθοῦσα ἡ τοῦ κυρίου ψυχὴ ὡς ἀληθῶς ἀνθρώπου γενομένου κατ᾽ εὐδοκίαν αὐτοῦ, αὖθις τῷ θείῳ νευρωθεῖσα θελήματι τοῦ θανάτου καταθαρρύνεται. Ἐπειδὴ γὰρ ὁ αὐτὸς ὅλος ἦν θεὸς μετὰ τῆς ἀνθρωπότητος αὐτοῦ καὶ ὅλος ἄνθρωπος μετὰ τῆς αὐτοῦ θεότητος, αὐτὸς ὡς ἄνθρωπος ἐν ἑαυτῷ καὶ δι᾽ ἑαυτοῦ ὑπέταξε τὸ ἀνθρώπινον τῷ θεῷ καὶ πατρὶ τύπον ἡμῖν ἑαυτὸν ἄριστον καὶ ὑπογραμμὸν διδοὺς καὶ ὑπήκοος τῷ πατρὶ γέγονεν.

Αὐτεξουσίως δὲ ἤθελε τῷ τε θείῳ καὶ τῷ ἀνθρωπίνῳ θελήματι· πάσῃ γὰρ λογικῇ φύσει πάντως ἐμπέφυκε τὸ αὐτεξούσιον θέλημα. Εἰς τί γὰρ ἕξει τὸ λογικὸν μὴ αὐτεξουσίως λογιζομένη; Τὴν μὲν γὰρ φυσικὴν ὄρεξιν καὶ τοῖς ἀλόγοις ζῴοις δημιουργὸς ἐνέσπειρε πρὸς σύστασιν τῆς οἰκείας φύσεως αὐτὰ ἄγουσαν· λόγου γὰρ ἀμοιροῦντα οὐ δύναται ἄγειν, ἀλλ᾽ ἄγεται ὑπὸ τῆς φυσικῆς ὀρέξεως. Ὅθεν ἅμα ἡ ὄρεξις γένηται, εὐθέως καὶ ἡ πρὸς τὴν πρᾶξιν ὁρμή· οὐ γὰρ λόγῳ ἢ βουλῇ ἢ σκέψει ἢ κρίσει κέχρηται. Ὅθεν οὔτε ὡς ἀρετὴν μετιόντα ἐπαινεῖται καὶ μακαρίζεται οὔτε ὡς κακίαν πράττοντα κολάζεται. Ἡ δὲ λογικὴ φύσις ἔχει μὲν τὴν φυσικὴν ὄρεξιν κινουμένην, ὑπὸ δὲ τοῦ λόγου ἀγομένην τε καὶ ῥυθμιζομένην ἐπὶ τῶν φυλασσόντων τὸ κατὰ φύσιν· τοῦ γὰρ

it naturally experienced what was proper to it. For when he begged to be spared death, he did so naturally, his divine will having willed it and conceded it, and he suffered anguish and fear. And when his divine will willed that his human will should choose death, the suffering was voluntarily accepted by it. For it was not only as God that he voluntarily surrendered himself to death, but also as a human being. As a result, he granted courage in the face of death to us too. Thus before his saving passion he said: "Father, if it is possible, let this cup pass from me,"[8] clearly because he was to drink the cup as a human being not as God. As a human being, of course, he wished to avoid the cup—these were the words of natural fear. "Yet let not my will be done"—which is to say, insofar as I am of a different substance—"but yours"—which is to say, mine and yours insofar as I am of the same substance as you.[9] These are the words of courage. For although the Lord's soul was first tempted by natural weakness on account of a sense of separation from the body and feeling a natural attachment to it because he had truly become human by his own good pleasure, again it was strengthened by the divine will and received the courage to face death. Since the same was wholly God along with his humanity and wholly human along with his divinity, the same as a human being in himself and through himself subjected the human to God the Father and, giving himself to us as an excellent model and example, became obedient to the Father.[10]

In acting freely he willed with both his divine and his human wills. For free will (τὸ αὐτεξούσιον, *to autexousion*) is most certainly innate in all rational nature. For what is the point of the rational faculty if it does not reason freely? The Creator implanted a natural appetency even in irrational animals for the maintenance of their own nature and this leads them, for what has no share in reason cannot lead, but is led by its natural appetency. Hence as soon as an appetite arises the impulse to satisfy it also arises immediately,

[8] Mt 26.39.
[9] Lk 22.42.
[10] For the whole paragraph cf. Gregory of Nazianzus, *Oration* 30.12 (PG 36:117C–120A; Moreschini, 732).

λόγου τὸ προτέρημα τοῦτό ἐστιν, ἡ αὐτεξούσιος θέλησις, ἥντινα φυσικὴν ἐν τῷ λογικῷ φαμεν κίνησιν. Διὸ καὶ ὡς ἀρετὴν μετιοῦσα ἐπαινεῖται καὶ μακαρίζεται καὶ ὡς κακίαν μετιοῦσα κολάζεται.

Ὥστε ἤθελε μὲν αὐτεξουσίως κινουμένη ἡ τοῦ κυρίου ψυχή, ἀλλ᾽ ἐκεῖνα αὐτεξουσίως ἤθελεν, ἃ ἡ θεία αὐτοῦ θέλησις ἤθελε θέλειν αὐτήν· οὐ γὰρ νεύματι τοῦ λόγου ἡ σὰρξ ἐκινεῖτο (καὶ Μωσῆς γὰρ καὶ πάντες οἱ ἅγιοι νεύματι θείῳ ἐκινοῦντο), ἀλλ᾽ ὁ αὐτὸς εἷς ὢν θεός τε καὶ ἄνθρωπος κατά τε τὴν θείαν καὶ τὴν ἀνθρωπίνην ἤθελε θέλησιν. Διὸ οὐ γνώμῃ, φυσικῇ δὲ μᾶλλον δυνάμει αἱ δύο τοῦ κυρίου θελήσεις διέφερον ἀλλήλων. Ἡ μὲν γὰρ θεία αὐτοῦ θέλησις ἄναρχός τε ἦν καὶ παντουργός, ἑπομένην ἔχουσα τὴν δύναμιν καὶ ἀπαθής, ἡ δὲ ἀνθρωπίνη αὐτοῦ θέλησις ἀπὸ χρόνου τε ἤρξατο καὶ αὐτὴ τὰ φυσικὰ καὶ ἀδιάβλητα πάθη ὑπέμεινε καὶ φυσικῶς οὐ παντοδύναμος ἦν, ὡς δὲ τοῦ θεοῦ λόγου ἀληθῶς καὶ κατὰ φύσιν γενομένη καὶ παντοδύναμος.

63 *Περὶ τῆς θεανδρικῆς ἐνεργείας*

Ὁ μακάριος Διονύσιος «καινήν τινα θεανδρικὴν ἐνέργειαν» φήσας τὸν Χριστὸν «ἡμῖν πεπολιτευμένον», οὐκ ἀναιρῶν τὰς φυσικὰς ἐνεργείας μίαν ἐνέργειαν ἔκ τε τῆς ἀνθρωπίνης καὶ τῆς θείας γεγενημένην φησίν—οὕτω γὰρ ἂν καὶ μίαν φύσιν εἴποιμεν καινήν, ἐκ θείας τε καὶ ἀνθρωπίνης φύσεως γεγενημένην· «ὧν γὰρ ἡ

---

[11]Cf. Maximus the Confessor, *Disputation with Pyrrhus* 32–33 (PG 91:297AB).

[1]Dionysius the Areopagite, *Letter* 4 (PG 3:1072C; Ritter, 161). Dionysius' phrase is

for there is no exercise of reason, or will, or thought, or judgement. Consequently, irrational animals are neither praised nor deemed blessed on account of participating in virtue, nor are they punished on account of doing evil. But although rational nature experiences an arousal of its natural appetency, this is led and kept in order in cases when what is in accordance with nature is maintained. For the advantage of reason is this, free will (ἡ αὐτεξούσιος θέλησις, *hē autexousios thelēsis*), which we call a natural movement in the rational faculty. Therefore it is praised and deemed blessed on account of participating in virtue, and punished on account of participating in evil.

As a result, the Lord's soul willed freely when it acted, but it freely willed to will the same as those things which his divine will willed. For it was not at the bidding of the Word that the flesh acted (for Moses too and all the saints acted at God's bidding), but since the same was one, both God and man, he willed in accordance with his divine and his human will.[11] Therefore the Lord's two wills differed from each other not by virtue of opinion but rather by virtue of natural power. For his divine will was without beginning and omnipotent, possessing a consequent power, and was impassible, whereas his human will began in time and was subject to natural and blameless passions, and although naturally not omnipotent, became so truly and by nature since it belonged to God the Word.

63   *On the theandric activity*

When the blessed Dionysius spoke of Christ as "a new theandric activity living among us,"[1] he was not abolishing the natural operations and saying that a single operation had come into being derived from the human and the divine. For in that case we should also say that a single nature had come into being derived from the divine and the human natures, "for what has a single operation also has a

καινή τις θεανδρικὴ ἐνέργεια. John devotes a chapter to it because Dionysius' phrase was a strong weapon in the armory of the Monophysites.

ἐνέργεια μία, τούτων καὶ ἡ οὐσία μία» κατὰ τοὺς ἁγίους πατέρας—, ἀλλὰ θέλων δεῖξαι τὸν καινὸν καὶ ἀπόρρητον τρόπον τῆς τῶν φυσικῶν τοῦ Χριστοῦ ἐνεργειῶν ἐκφάνσεως τῷ ἀπορρήτῳ τρόπῳ τῆς εἰς ἄλληλα τῶν Χριστοῦ φύσεων περιχωρήσεως προσφόρως καὶ τὴν κατὰ ἄνθρωπον αὐτοῦ πολιτείαν ξένην καὶ παράδοξον καὶ τῇ φύσει τῶν ὄντων ἄγνωστον καὶ τὸν τρόπον τῆς κατὰ τὴν ἀπόρρητον ἕνωσιν ἀντιδόσεως· οὐ διῃρημένας γάρ φαμεν τὰς ἐνεργείας οὐδὲ διῃρημένως ἐνεργούσας τὰς φύσεις, ἀλλ᾽ ἡνωμένας, ἑκάστην μετὰ τῆς θατέρου κοινωνίας ἐνεργοῦσαν τοῦθ᾽, ὅπερ ἴδιον ἔσχηκεν. Οὔτε γὰρ τὰ ἀνθρώπινα ἀνθρωπίνως ἐνήργησεν (οὐ γὰρ ψιλὸς ἦν ἄνθρωπος) οὐδὲ τὰ θεῖα κατὰ θεὸν μόνον (οὐ γὰρ ἦν γυμνὸς θεός), ἀλλὰ θεὸς ὁμοῦ ὑπάρχων καὶ ἄνθρωπος. Ὥσπερ γὰρ τῶν φύσεων τὴν ἕνωσιν καὶ τὴν φυσικὴν διαφορὰν ἐπιστάμεθα, οὕτω καὶ τῶν φυσικῶν θελημάτων τε καὶ ἐνεργειῶν.

Ἰστέον τοιγαροῦν, ὡς ἐπὶ τοῦ κυρίου ἡμῶν Ἰησοῦ Χριστοῦ ποτὲ μὲν ὡς ἐπὶ δύο φύσεων τὸν λόγον ποιούμεθα, ποτὲ δὲ ὡς ἐφ᾽ ἑνὸς προσώπου, καὶ τοῦτο δὲ κἀκεῖνο εἰς μίαν ἀναφέρεται ἔννοιαν· αἱ γὰρ δύο φύσεις εἷς ἐστι Χριστός, καὶ ὁ εἷς Χριστὸς δύο φύσεις ἐστί. Ταὐτὸν οὖν ἐστιν εἰπεῖν· Ἐνεργεῖ ὁ Χριστὸς καθ᾽ ἑκατέραν τῶν αὐτοῦ δύο φύσεων, καὶ «ἐνεργεῖ ἑκατέρα φύσις ἐν τῷ Χριστῷ μετὰ τῆς θατέρου κοινωνίας». Κοινωνεῖ τοίνυν ἡ μὲν θεία φύσις τῇ σαρκὶ ἐνεργούσῃ διὰ τὸ εὐδοκίᾳ τῆς θείας θελήσεως παραχωρεῖσθαι πάσχειν καὶ πράττειν τὰ ἴδια καὶ διὰ τὸ τὴν ἐνέργειαν τῆς σαρκὸς πάντως εἶναι σωτήριον, ὅπερ οὐ τῆς ἀνθρωπίνης ἐνεργείας ἐστίν, ἀλλὰ τῆς θείας. Ἡ δὲ σὰρξ τῇ θεότητι τοῦ λόγου ἐνεργούσῃ διά τε τὸ ὡς δι᾽ ὀργάνου τοῦ σώματος τὰς θείας ἐκτελεῖσθαι ἐνεργείας καὶ διὰ τὸ ἕνα εἶναι τὸν ἐνεργοῦντα θεϊκῶς τε ἅμα καὶ ἀνθρωπίνως.

single essence" according to the holy fathers.[2] On the contrary, he wished to indicate the new and ineffable mode of the manifestation of Christ's natural operations in a manner that was appropriate to the ineffable mode of the mutual interpenetration of Christ's natures in each other and his strange and miraculous life as a human being, which is not found in the nature of beings, and the mode of the exchange that occurred in the ineffable union.[3] For we say that the operations are not separated nor do the natures operate in a separate fashion, but in union with each other, each doing what was proper to it in communion with the other. Nor did he do what was human in a human fashion (for he was not a mere man) nor did do what was divine only as God (for he was not God plain and simple), but he existed simultaneously as both God and man. For just as we have sure knowledge of the union and natural difference of the natures, so also we have sure knowledge of the union and natural difference of the natural wills and operations.

For that very reason one should note that in the case of our Lord Jesus Christ we sometimes talk about two natures, and sometimes about one person, but both the one and the other refer to a single concept. For the two natures are one Christ, and the one Christ is two natures. The two expressions, Christ operates in each of his two natures, and "each nature operates in Christ in communion with the other,"[4] therefore have the same meaning. On the one hand, then, the divine nature is in communion with the flesh because the latter is operative on account of being allowed by the good pleasure of the divine will to suffer and do what is proper to it and also on account of the operation of the flesh being most assuredly salvific, which does not belong to the human operation but to the divine. And on the other hand the flesh is in communion with the divinity of the Word, because the latter is operative on account of performing the

[2]The holy fathers of the Sixth Ecumenical Council (Constantinople III, 680–81), who defined Christ's two natural wills and operations.

[3]Cf. Maximus the Confessor, *Disputation with Pyrrhus* 189–92 (PG 91:345C–348A).

[4]Leo I, *Letter* 28 (Tome of Leo), 14.27.

Εἰδέναι γὰρ χρή, ὡς ὁ ἅγιος αὐτοῦ νοῦς καὶ τὰς φυσικὰς αὐτοῦ ἐνεργεῖ ἐνεργείας, νοῶν καὶ γινώσκων, ὅτι ἐστὶ θεοῦ νοῦς καὶ ὅτι ὑπὸ πάσης προσκυνεῖται τῆς κτίσεως, καὶ μεμνημένος τῶν ἐπὶ τῆς γῆς αὐτοῦ διατριβῶν τε καὶ παθῶν, κοινωνεῖ δὲ ἐνεργούσῃ τῇ τοῦ λόγου θεότητι καὶ διεπούσῃ καὶ κυβερνώσῃ τὸ πᾶν, νοῶν καὶ γινώσκων καὶ διέπων οὐχ ὡς ψιλὸς ἀνθρώπου νοῦς, ἀλλ᾽ ὡς θεῷ καθ᾽ ὑπόστασιν ἡνωμένος καὶ θεοῦ νοῦς χρηματίσας.

Τοῦτο οὖν δηλοῖ ἡ θεανδρικὴ ἐνέργεια, ὅτι ἀνδρωθέντος θεοῦ ἤγουν ἐνανθρωπήσαντος καὶ ἡ ἀνθρωπίνη αὐτοῦ ἐνέργεια θεία ἦν ἤγουν τεθεωμένη καὶ οὐκ ἄμοιρος τῆς θείας αὐτοῦ ἐνεργείας καὶ ἡ θεία αὐτοῦ ἐνέργεια οὐκ ἄμοιρος τῆς ἀνθρωπίνης αὐτοῦ ἐνεργείας, ἀλλ᾽ ἑκατέρα σὺν τῇ ἑτέρᾳ θεωρουμένη. Λέγεται δὲ ὁ τρόπος οὗτος περίφρασις, ὅταν τις δύο τινὰ διὰ μιᾶς περιλάβῃ λέξεως. Ὥσπερ γὰρ μίαν τὴν τετμημένην καῦσιν λέγομεν καὶ τὴν κεκαυμένην τομὴν τῆς πεπυρακτωμένης μαχαίρας, ἄλλην δὲ ἐνέργειάν φαμεν τὴν τομὴν καὶ ἄλλην τὴν καῦσιν καὶ ἄλλης καὶ ἄλλης φύσεως, τοῦ μὲν πυρὸς τὴν καῦσιν, τοῦ δὲ σιδήρου τὴν τομήν, οὕτω μίαν τοῦ Χριστοῦ θεανδρικὴν ἐνέργειαν λέγοντες δύο τὰς ἐνεργείας νοοῦμεν τῶν δύο φύσεων αὐτοῦ, τῆς μὲν θεότητος αὐτοῦ τὴν θείαν καὶ τῆς ἀνθρωπότητος αὐτοῦ τὴν ἀνθρωπίνην ἐνέργειαν.

64 Περὶ τῶν φυσικῶν καὶ ἀδιαβλήτων παθῶν

Ὁμολογοῦμεν δέ, ὅτι πάντα τὰ φυσικὰ καὶ ἀδιάβλητα πάθη τοῦ ἀνθρώπου ἀνέλαβεν. Ὅλον γὰρ τὸν ἄνθρωπον καὶ πάντα τὰ τοῦ ἀνθρώπου ἀνέλαβε πλὴν τῆς ἁμαρτίας· αὕτη γὰρ οὐ φυσική ἐστιν οὐδὲ ὑπὸ τοῦ δημιουργοῦ ἡμῖν ἐνσπαρεῖσα, ἀλλ᾽ ἐκ τῆς τοῦ διαβόλου ἐπισπορᾶς ἐν τῇ ἡμετέρᾳ αὐτεξουσίῳ προαιρέσει

divine operations as if using the body as an instrument and also on account of the fact that he who is operating in a divine mode at the same time as in a human mode is a single being.

For one needs to know that his holy mind both performs its natural operations, apprehending and knowing that it is the mind of God and that it is worshiped by the whole of creation, and remembering his life on earth and what he suffered, and it also shares in the divinity of the Word that activates, administers, and governs the universe, apprehending and knowing and administering not as the mere mind of a human being but as united hypostatically with God and called the mind of God.

The theandric activity therefore means this: that when God was made man, that is to say, when he became a human being, his human activity was divine, that is to say, was deified and was not without a share in his divine activity, and his divine activity was not without a share in his human activity, but each is contemplated along with the other. This figure of speech is called "periphrasis," when one encapsulates two things in a single word. For in the case of the red-hot sword, we call the cutting burn and the burning cut a single thing, but we say that the cut is one activity and the burn another and they belong to two different natures, the burning belonging to the fire and the cutting to the iron.[5] In the same way, when we speak of a single theandric activity of Christ we understand by this the two activities of his two natures, the divine activity of his divinity and the human activity of his humanity.

64   *On natural and blameless passions*

We confess, too, that he assumed all the natural and blameless passions that belong to humanity. For he assumed the whole human being and everything that belongs to human beings apart from sin. For the latter is not natural, nor was it sown in us by the Creator. On the contrary, it was constituted voluntarily in our faculty of free will

[5]Cf. Maximus the Confessor, *Disputation with Pyrrhus* 183–84 (PG 91:341B).

ἑκουσίως συνισταμένη, οὐ βίᾳ ἡμῶν κρατοῦσα. Φυσικὰ δὲ καὶ ἀδιάβλητα πάθη εἰσὶ τὰ οὐκ ἐφ' ἡμῖν, ὅσα ἐκ τῆς ἐπὶ τῇ παραβάσει κατακρίσεως εἰς τὸν ἀνθρώπινον εἰσῆλθε βίον· οἷον πεῖνα, δίψα, κόπος, πόνος, τὸ δάκρυον, ἡ φθορά, ἡ τοῦ θανάτου παραίτησις, ἡ δειλία, ἡ ἀγωνία (ἐξ ἧς οἱ ἱδρῶτες, οἱ θρόμβοι τοῦ αἵματος), ἡ διὰ τὸ ἀσθενὲς τῆς φύσεως ὑπὸ τῶν ἀγγέλων βοήθεια καὶ τὰ τοιαῦτα, ἅτινα πᾶσι τοῖς ἀνθρώποις φυσικῶς ἐνυπάρχουσι.

Πάντα τοίνυν ἀνέλαβεν, ἵνα πάντα ἁγιάσῃ. Ἐπειράσθη καὶ ἐνίκησεν, ἵνα ἡμῖν τὴν νίκην πραγματεύσηται καὶ δῷ τῇ φύσει δύναμιν νικᾶν τὸν ἀντίπαλον, ἵνα ἡ φύσις ἡ πάλαι νικηθεῖσα, δι' ὧν προσβολῶν ἐνικήθη, διὰ τούτων νικήσῃ τὸν πάλαι νικήσαντα.

Ὁ μὲν οὖν πονηρὸς ἔξωθεν προσέβαλεν οὐ διὰ λογισμῶν ὥσπερ καὶ τῷ Ἀδάμ· κἀκείνῳ γὰρ οὐ διὰ λογισμῶν, ἀλλὰ διὰ τοῦ ὄφεως. Ὁ δὲ κύριος τὴν προσβολὴν ἀπεκρούσατο καὶ ὡς καπνὸν διέλυσεν, ἵνα προσβαλόντα αὐτῷ τὰ πάθη καὶ νικηθέντα καὶ ἡμῖν εὐκαταγώνιστα γένηται καὶ οὕτως ὁ νέος Ἀδὰμ τὸν παλαιὸν ἀνασώσηται.

Ἀμέλει τὰ φυσικὰ ἡμῶν πάθη κατὰ φύσιν καὶ ὑπὲρ φύσιν ἦσαν ἐν τῷ Χριστῷ. Κατὰ φύσιν μὲν γὰρ ἐκινεῖτο ἐν αὐτῷ, ὅτε παρεχώρει τῇ σαρκὶ πάσχειν τὰ ἴδια· ὑπὲρ φύσιν δέ, οὐ γὰρ προηγεῖτο ἐν τῷ κυρίῳ τῆς θελήσεως τὰ φυσικά· οὐδὲν γὰρ ἠναγκασμένον ἐπ' αὐτοῦ θεωρεῖται, ἀλλὰ πάντα ἑκούσια· θέλων γὰρ ἐπείνασε, θέλων ἐδίψησε, θέλων ἐδειλίασε, θέλων ἀπέθανεν.

as a result of a second sowing by the devil, and it does not gain control over us by force. The natural and blameless passions are those that do not depend on our own will but have entered into human life as a result of the condemnation following the transgression, such as hunger, thirst, weariness, toil, the shedding of tears, the experience of decay, the shunning of death, the fear, the agony (hence the sweats and the drops of blood), the help given by the angels on account of the weakness of nature, which naturally exist in all human beings.

So then, he assumed everything that he might sanctify everything. He was tempted and was victorious, that he might gain the victory for us and give to human nature the power to defeat the adversary, so that the human nature that was formerly defeated might defeat the former victor by the very means that were used to defeat it.

In fact the evil one attacked from outside, not through thoughts, just as he also did in the case of Adam, for with him too he attacked not through thoughts but through the serpent. The Lord for his part repelled the attack and dissolved it like smoke, so that through his being attacked by the passions and overcoming them they might also be easily destroyed by us, and thus the new Adam would rescue the old.

And indeed, our natural passions also existed in Christ in accordance with nature and beyond nature. For it was in accordance with nature that they were operative within him when he allowed the flesh to suffer what was proper to it. And it was beyond nature because in the Lord that which was natural did not take precedence over the will. For nothing in his case is regarded as forced by necessity; on the contrary, everything is voluntary. For it was by willing that he was hungry, by willing that he was thirsty, by willing that he was afraid, by willing that he died.

65   *Περὶ ἀγνοίας καὶ δουλείας*

Δεῖ γινώσκειν, ὅτι τὴν μὲν ἀγνοοῦσαν καὶ δούλην ἀνέλαβεν φύσιν· καὶ γὰρ δούλη ἐστὶν ἡ ἀνθρώπου φύσις τοῦ ποιήσαντος αὐτὴν θεοῦ καὶ οὐκ ἔχει τὴν τῶν μελλόντων γνῶσιν. «Ἐὰν οὖν» κατὰ τὸν θεολόγον Γρηγόριον «χωρίσῃς τὸ ὁρώμενον τοῦ νοουμένου», δούλη τε λέγεται καὶ ἀγνοοῦσα ἡ σάρξ, διὰ δὲ τὴν τῆς ὑποστάσεως ταυτότητα καὶ τὴν ἀδιάσπαστον ἕνωσιν κατεπλούτησεν ἡ τοῦ κυρίου ψυχὴ τὴν τῶν μελλόντων γνῶσιν ὡς καὶ τὰς λοιπὰς θεοσημίας. Ὥσπερ γὰρ ἡ σὰρξ τῶν ἀνθρώπων κατὰ τὴν οἰκείαν φύσιν οὐκ ἔστι ζωοποιός (ἡ δὲ τοῦ κυρίου σὰρξ ἑνωθεῖσα καθ᾽ ὑπόστασιν αὐτῷ τῷ θεῷ λόγῳ τῆς μὲν κατὰ φύσιν θνητότητος οὐκ ἀπέστη, ζωοποιὸς δὲ γέγονε διὰ τὴν πρὸς τὸν λόγον καθ᾽ ὑπόστασιν ἕνωσιν) καὶ οὐ δυνάμεθα λέγειν, ὅτι οὐκ ἦν καὶ ἔστιν ἀεὶ ζωοποιός, οὕτως ἡ μὲν ἀνθρωπίνη φύσις οὐσιωδῶς οὐ κέκτηται τῶν μελλόντων τὴν γνῶσιν· ἡ δὲ τοῦ κυρίου ψυχὴ διὰ τὴν πρὸς τὸν θεὸν λόγον ἕνωσιν καὶ τὴν ὑποστατικὴν ταυτότητα κατεπλούτησεν, ὡς ἔφην, μετὰ τῶν λοιπῶν θεοσημιῶν καὶ τὴν τῶν μελλόντων γνῶσιν.

Ἰστέον δέ, ὅτι οὔτε δοῦλον αὐτὸν λέγειν δυνάμεθα· τὸ γὰρ τῆς δουλείας καὶ τῆς δεσποτείας ὄνομα οὐ φύσεώς εἰσι γνωρίσματα, ἀλλὰ τῶν πρός τι, ὥσπερ τὸ τῆς πατρότητος καὶ τῆς υἱότητος. Ταῦτα γὰρ οὐκ οὐσίας, ἀλλὰ σχέσεώς εἰσι δηλωτικά. Ὥσπερ οὖν ἐπὶ τῆς ἀγνοίας εἴπομεν, ὅτι, ἐὰν ἰσχναῖς ἐπινοίαις ἤτοι νοῦ λεπταῖς φαντασίαις διέλῃς τὸ κτιστὸν ἐκ τοῦ ἀκτίστου, δούλη ἐστὶν ἡ σάρξ, εἰ μὴ ἥνωτο τῷ θεῷ λόγῳ. Ἅπαξ δὲ ἑνωθεῖσα καθ᾽ ὑπόστασιν πῶς ἔσται δούλη; Εἷς γὰρ ὢν ὁ Χριστὸς οὐ δύναται δοῦλος ἑαυτοῦ εἶναι κύριος ὤν· ταῦτα γὰρ οὐ τῶν ἁπλῶς λεγομένων εἰσίν, ἀλλὰ πρὸς ἕτερον. Τίνος οὖν ἔσται δοῦλος; Τοῦ πατρός; Οὐκοῦν οὐ πάντα, ὅσα ἔχει ὁ πατήρ, καὶ τοῦ υἱοῦ εἰσιν, εἴπερ τοῦ πατρός ἐστι δοῦλος, ἑαυτοῦ δὲ οὐδαμῶς. Πῶς δὲ περὶ ἡμῶν λέγει ὁ ἀπόστολος· «Ὥστε οὐκέτι εἶ δοῦλος, ἀλλ᾽ υἱός», δι᾽

65 On ignorance and servitude

One needs to know that he assumed a nature that is certainly ignorant and a servant. For human nature is a servant of God who made
it and does not possess knowledge of the future. "If, then," according
to Gregory the Theologian, "you separate what is seen from what is
apprehended spiritually,"[1] the flesh is said to be both a servant and
ignorant, but on the other hand through the identity of the hypostasis and its unbreakable union the Lord's soul possessed knowledge
of future events and other miraculous powers in abundance. For just
as the flesh of human beings is not life-giving by virtue of its own
nature (but the Lord's flesh, united hypostatically with God the Word
himself, although not abandoning natural mortality nevertheless
became life-giving through its hypostatic union with the Word), and
we cannot say that it was not but is forever life-giving, so too human
nature does not of itself possess knowledge of future events. But the
Lord's soul, on account of its union with God the Word and its hypostatic identity, also possessed, as I have said, along with the other
miraculous powers, the knowledge of future events in abundance.[2]

One should also note that we cannot call him a servant either.
For the words servitude and lordship are not natural properties but
relative terms, like fatherhood and sonship. These are indicative not
of essence but of relation. It is therefore just as we said in the case of
ignorance, namely, that if you use subtle conceptions or fine mental
constructions you can separate the created from the uncreated; the
flesh is a servant unless it is united to God the Word. But once it is
united hypostatically [with him] how can it be a servant? For since
Christ is one, he cannot be his own servant, being, as he is, Lord.
For these terms do not belong to things that are predicated simply
but refer to a relation with something else. Whose servant would he
then be? The Father's? But then not everything that the Father has
would also belong to the Son if indeed he were the Father's servant

---

[1] Gregory of Nazianzus, *Oration* 30.15 (PG 36:124B; Moreschini, 736).
[2] Cf. Cyril of Alexandria, *Thesaurus* 21–22 (PG 75:368–80).

αὐτοῦ υἱοθετηθέντων, εἴπερ αὐτὸς δοῦλός ἐστι; Προσηγορικῶς
οὖν λέγεται δοῦλος οὐκ αὐτὸς ὢν τοῦτο, δι' ἡμᾶς δὲ δούλου
μορφὴν εἰληφὼς καὶ δοῦλος μεθ' ἡμῶν κεκλημένος. Ἀπαθὴς γὰρ
ὢν δι' ἡμᾶς ἐδούλευσε πάθεσι καὶ διάκονος τῆς ἡμῶν σωτηρίας
γέγονεν. Οἱ δὲ λέγοντες αὐτὸν δοῦλον διιστῶσι τὸν ἕνα Χριστὸν
εἰς δύο καθάπερ Νεστόριος. Ἡμεῖς δὲ δεσπότην αὐτόν φαμεν καὶ
κύριον πάσης τῆς κτίσεως, τὸν ἕνα Χριστόν, τὸν αὐτὸν θεόν τε
ὁμοῦ καὶ ἄνθρωπον, καὶ πάντα εἰδέναι· «ἐν αὐτῷ γάρ εἰσι πάντες
οἱ θησαυροὶ τῆς σοφίας καὶ τῆς γνώσεως ἀπόκρυφοι».

66 Περὶ προκοπῆς

Προκόπτειν δὲ λέγεται «σοφίᾳ καὶ ἡλικίᾳ καὶ χάριτι», τῇ μὲν
ἡλικίᾳ αὔξων, διὰ δὲ τῆς αὐξήσεως τῆς ἡλικίας τὴν ἐνυπάρχουσαν
αὐτῷ σοφίαν εἰς φανέρωσιν ἄγων, ἔτι δὲ τὴν τῶν ἀνθρώπων ἐν
σοφίᾳ καὶ χάριτι προκοπὴν καὶ τὴν τελείωσιν τῆς τοῦ πατρὸς
εὐδοκίας ἤγουν τὴν τῶν ἀνθρώπων θεογνωσίαν τε καὶ σωτηρίαν
οἰκείαν προκοπὴν ποιούμενος καὶ οἰκειούμενος πανταχοῦ τὸ
ἡμέτερον. Οἱ δὲ προκόπτειν αὐτὸν λέγοντες σοφίᾳ καὶ χάριτι ὡς
προσθήκην τούτων δεχόμενον οὐκ ἐξ ἄκρας ὑπάρξεως τῆς σαρκὸς
γεγενῆσθαι τὴν ἕνωσιν λέγουσιν οὐδὲ τὴν καθ' ὑπόστασιν ἕνωσιν
πρεσβεύουσι, Νεστορίῳ δὲ τῷ ματαιόφρονι πειθόμενοι σχετικὴν
ἕνωσιν καὶ ψιλὴν ἐνοίκησιν τερατεύονται, «μὴ γινώσκοντες,
μήτε ἃ λέγουσι μήτε περὶ τίνων διαβεβαιοῦνται». Εἰ γὰρ ἀληθῶς
ἡνώθη τῷ θεῷ λόγῳ ἡ σὰρξ ἐξ ἄκρας ὑπάρξεως, μᾶλλον δὲ ἐν
αὐτῷ ὑπῆρξε καὶ τὴν ὑποστατικὴν πρὸς αὐτὸν ἔσχε ταυτότητα,

but not in any way his own. And how would the Apostle say about us, "So you are no longer a servant but a son," having been adopted by him, if he himself were a servant?[3] He is therefore called a servant by way of mere appellation, not himself being such but because of "having assumed the form of a servant"[4] for our sake and being called a servant along with us. For although he was impassible, he made himself a servant to passions for our sake and became the agent of our salvation. Those who call him a servant divide the one Christ into two, like Nestorius. But we call him Master and Lord of the whole of creation, the one Christ, the same both God and man, who knows all things. "For in him are hidden all the treasures of wisdom and of knowledge."[5]

66   *On progress*

He is also said to have advanced "in wisdom and maturity and grace,"[1] growing in maturity, and through his growth in maturity bringing into view the wisdom inherent within him, and, moreover, making the progress of human beings in wisdom and grace his own, along with the perfection of God's good pleasure, that is to say, knowledge of God by human beings and their salvation, and so making what belongs to us his own in every respect. Those who say that he advanced in wisdom and grace in the sense that he received these as an addition are not saying that the union took place from the first moment of the existence of the flesh, nor are they advocating the hypostatic union, but persuaded by the foolish Nestorius, they maintain the monstrous idea that the union was relative and a mere indwelling, "without understanding either what they are saying or the things about which they make assertions."[2] For if the flesh was really united with God the Word from the first moment of its existence, or rather, existed in him and had the same hypostatic

---

[3]Gal 4.7.   [4]Phil 2.7.   [5]Col 2.3.

[1]Lk 2.52.   [2]1 Tim 1.7.

πῶς οὐ τελείως κατεπλούτησε πᾶσαν σοφίαν καὶ χάριν, οὐκ αὐτὴ
τῆς χάριτος μεταλαμβάνουσα οὐδὲ κατὰ χάριν τῶν τοῦ λόγου
μετέχουσα, ἀλλὰ μᾶλλον διὰ τὴν καθ᾽ ὑπόστασιν ἕνωσιν τῶν τε
ἀνθρωπίνων τῶν τε θείων τοῦ ἑνὸς Χριστοῦ γεγονότων, ἐπειδὴ
ὁ αὐτὸς ἦν θεός τε ὁμοῦ καὶ ἄνθρωπος τὴν χάριν καὶ τὴν σοφίαν
καὶ πάντων τῶν ἀγαθῶν τὴν πληρότητα κόσμῳ πηγάζουσα;

67 Περὶ δειλίας

Τὸ τῆς δειλίας ὄνομα διπλῆν ἔχει τὴν ἔννοιαν. Ἔστι γὰρ δειλία
φυσικὴ μὴ θελούσης τῆς ψυχῆς διαιρεθῆναι τοῦ σώματος διὰ
τὴν ἐξ ἀρχῆς ὑπὸ τοῦ δημιουργοῦ ἐντεθεῖσαν αὐτῇ φυσικὴν
συμπάθειάν τε καὶ οἰκειότητα, δι᾽ ἣν φυσικῶς φοβεῖται καὶ ἀγωνιᾷ
καὶ παραιτεῖται τὸν θάνατον. Ἧς ὅρος· «Κατὰ φύσιν δειλία ἐστὶ
δύναμις κατὰ συστολὴν τοῦ ὄντος ἀνθεκτική». Εἰ γὰρ τοῦ μὴ
ὄντος εἰς τὸ εἶναι παρήχθη ὑπὸ τοῦ δημιουργοῦ τὰ πάντα, τοῦ
εἶναι καὶ οὐ τοῦ μὴ εἶναι τὴν ἔφεσιν ἔχει φυσικῶς. Τούτων δὲ
κατὰ φύσιν ἴδιον ἡ πρὸς τὰ συστατικὰ ὁρμή. Καὶ ὁ θεὸς λόγος
τοίνυν ἄνθρωπος γενόμενος ἔσχε ταύτην τὴν ἔφεσιν ἐν μὲν τοῖς
συστατικοῖς τῆς φύσεως τὴν ὁρμὴν ἐνδειξάμενος βρώσεώς τε
καὶ πόσεως, ὕπνου τε ἐφιέμενος καὶ φυσικῶς ἐν πείρᾳ τούτων
γενόμενος, ἐν δὲ τοῖς φθαρτικοῖς τὴν ὁρμὴν ὡς τῷ καιρῷ τοῦ
πάθους ἑκουσίως τὴν πρὸς τὸν θάνατον συστολὴν ποιήσασθαι.
Εἰ γὰρ καὶ νόμῳ φύσεως ἐγίνετο τὰ γινόμενα, ἀλλ᾽ οὐ καθ᾽
ἡμᾶς ἠναγκασμένως· ἑκουσίως γὰρ τὰ φυσικὰ θέλων κατεδέξατο.
Ὥστε αὕτη ἡ δειλία καὶ ὁ φόβος καὶ ἀγωνία τῶν φυσικῶν ἐστι
καὶ ἀδιαβλήτων παθῶν καὶ μὴ ὑποκειμένων ἁμαρτίᾳ. Ἔστι πάλιν
δειλία ἡ ἐκ προδοσίας λογισμῶν συνισταμένη ἢ καὶ ἀπιστίας καὶ
τοῦ ἀγνοεῖν τὴν τοῦ θανάτου ὥραν, ὡς ὅταν νυκτὸς δειλιῶμεν

identity as he had, how is it that it did not possess in perfection all wisdom and grace, not because it partook of grace or had a share by grace in what belonged to the Word, but rather because through the hypostatic union what is human and what is divine belong to the one Christ, since the same was simultaneously both God and man, and so produced in abundance grace and wisdom and the fullness of every good thing for the world?[3]

67   *On fear*

The word "fear" (δειλεία, *deileia*) has a dual meaning. For there is a natural fear when the soul does not wish to be separated from the body because of the natural attachment and affinity implanted in it from the beginning by the Creator, on account of which it naturally fears death and is anxious about it and seeks to avoid it. Hence the definition: "Fear is by nature a power of clinging to being by shrinking."[1] For if all things were brought out of non-being into being by the Creator, they naturally have a desire for being, not for non-being. The impulse to conserve what constitutes them is a property that belongs to them by nature. And therefore when God the Word became man, he possessed this desire, on the one hand in matters that sustained nature, demonstrating this impulse by desiring food, drink, and sleep and naturally experiencing them, and on the other in matters destructive of nature, demonstrating the same impulse by voluntarily shrinking from death at the time of his passion. For even though what occurred took place by the law of nature, it was not by compulsion as it is with us. For he voluntarily accepted what was natural because he willed to do so. As a result, this fear and terror and anguish belong to the natural and blameless passions and are not subject to sin.

---

[3]Cf. Athanasius of Alexandria, *Orations against the Arians* 3.51–53 (PG 26:429–36); Gregory of Nazianzus, *Letter* 101.24–25 (PG 37:181A).

[1]Maximus the Confessor, *Disputation with Pyrrhus* 35 (PG 91:297D).

ψόφου τινὸς γινομένου· ἥτις παρὰ φύσιν ἐστίν, ἣν καὶ ὁριζόμενοι
λέγομεν· «Παρὰ φύσιν δειλία ἐστὶ παράλογος συστολή». Ταύτην
ὁ κύριος οὐ προσήκατο· διὸ οὐδὲ ἐδειλίασέ ποτε εἰ μὴ ἐν τῷ τοῦ
πάθους καιρῷ, εἰ καὶ οἰκονομικῶς ἑαυτὸν συνέστελλε πολλάκις·
οὐ γὰρ ἠγνόει τὸν καιρόν.

Ὅτι δὲ ἀληθῶς ἐδειλίασε, φησὶν ὁ ἱερὸς Ἀθανάσιος ἐν τῷ
κατὰ Ἀπολιναρίου λόγῳ· «Διὰ τοῦτο ὁ κύριος ἔλεγεν· 'Νῦν ἡ
ψυχή μου τετάρακται.' Τὸ δὲ 'νῦν' τοῦτό ἐστιν, ὅτε ἠθέλησεν,
ὅμως μέντοι τὸ ὂν ἐπιδείκνυται· οὐ γὰρ τὸ μὴ ὂν ὡς παρὸν
ὠνόμαζεν ὡς δοκήσει γινομένων τῶν λεγομένων. Φύσει γὰρ καὶ
ἀληθείᾳ τὰ πάντα ἐγίνετο». Καὶ μεθ' ἕτερα· «Οὐδαμῶς δὲ θεότης
πάθος προσίεται δίχα πάσχοντος σώματος οὐδὲ ταραχὴν καὶ
λύπην ἐπιδείκνυται δίχα ψυχῆς λυπουμένης καὶ ταρασσομένης
οὔτε ἀδημονεῖ καὶ προσεύχεται δίχα νοήσεως ἀδημονούσης καὶ
προσευχομένης, ἀλλὰ γὰρ κἂν μὴ ἡττήματι φύσεως συνέβαινε τὰ
γινόμενα, ἀλλ' ἐπιδείξει ὑπάρξεως ἐγίνετο τὰ γινόμενα». Τὸ δὲ
«ἡττήματι φύσεως μὴ συμβαίνειν τὰ γινόμενα» τὸ μὴ ἀκουσίως
ταῦτα ὑπομένειν δηλοῖ.

68 Περὶ τῆς τοῦ κυρίου προσευχῆς

Προσευχή ἐστιν ἀνάβασις νοῦ πρὸς θεὸν ἢ αἴτησις τῶν
προσηκόντων παρὰ θεοῦ. Πῶς οὖν ὁ κύριος ἐπὶ Λαζάρου καὶ τῷ

[2]Maximus the Confessor, *Disputation with Pyrrhus* 35 (PG 91:297D).
[3]Jn 12.27.
[4](Ps.-)Athanasius of Alexandria, *On the Incarnation against Apollinaris* 1.16 (PG 26:1124A).
[5](Ps.-)Athanasius of Alexandria, *On the Incarnation against Apollinaris* 2.13 (PG 26:1153B).
[6]Cf. Cyril of Alexandria, *Thesaurus* 23 (PG 75:389–401); Maximus the Confessor, *Disputation with Pyrrhus* 35 (PG 91:297AD).

Then again there is the fear that occurs when thought betrays us, or through lack of trust and not knowing the hour of our death, as when we are afraid in the night when some noise occurs. This fear is contrary to nature. It is that which we define thus: "Fear contrary to nature is an unreasonable shrinking."[2] This was not a fear that the Lord possessed. Consequently, he was never afraid except at the time of his passion, even though he frequently withdrew out of prudence. For he was not ignorant of the appointed time.

That he was truly afraid, the holy Athanasius says in his treatise against Apollinarius: "That is why the Lord said, 'Now my soul is troubled.'[3] The word 'now' means this: 'when he willed.' At the same time, however, it reveals the reality. For he did not name what was not real as if it were present, as if what was spoken of only seemed to have happened. For everything happened by nature and in truth."[4] And after a little: "And in no way does divinity accept suffering without a body that suffers, nor does it display distress and sorrow without a soul that is distressed and sorrowful, nor is it troubled nor does it pray without a mind that is troubled and prays. On the contrary, even though it was not through a defect of nature that what happened occurred, nevertheless what happened came about as a proof of existence."[5] The phrase "it was not through a defect of nature that what happened occurred" reveals that he did not experience these things against his will.[6]

68   *On the Lord's praying*

Prayer is the ascent of the mind to God or the petitioning of God for what is fitting.[1] How then did the Lord pray in the case of Lazarus and

---

[1]The first half of John's definition, "the ascent of the mind to God" (ἀνάβασις νοῦ πρὸς θεόν, *anabasis nou pros theon*) is from Evagrius Ponticus, *On Prayer* (preserved under the name of Nilus of Ancyra) 35 (PG 79:1173D). The definition is also included in the *Doctrina Patrum*, Diekamp, 264. The second half, "the petitioning of God for what is fitting" (αἴτησις τῶν προσηκόντων παρὰ θεοῦ, *aitēsis tōn prosēkontōn para theou*) is a commonplace in various forms in the commentators on Plato and Aristotle.

καιρῷ τοῦ πάθους προσηύχετο; Οὔτε γὰρ ἀναβάσεως τῆς πρὸς
τὸν θεὸν ἐδεῖτο ὁ ἅγιος αὐτοῦ νοῦς ἅπαξ καθ' ὑπόστασιν τῷ θεῷ
λόγῳ ἡνωμένος οὔτε τῆς παρὰ θεοῦ αἰτήσεως· εἷς γάρ ἐστιν ὁ
Χριστός· ἀλλὰ τὸ ἡμέτερον οἰκειούμενος πρόσωπον καὶ τυπῶν ἐν
ἑαυτῷ τὸ ἡμέτερον καὶ ὑπογραμμὸς ἡμῖν γινόμενος καὶ διδάσκων
ἡμᾶς παρὰ θεοῦ αἰτεῖν καὶ πρὸς αὐτὸν ἀνατείνεσθαι καὶ διὰ τοῦ
ἁγίου αὐτοῦ νοῦ ὁδοποιῶν ἡμῖν τὴν πρὸς θεὸν ἀνάβασιν. Ὥσπερ
γὰρ τὰ πάθη ὑπέμεινεν ἡμῖν τὴν κατ' αὐτῶν νίκην βραβεύων, οὕτω
καὶ προσεύχεται ἡμῖν ὁδοποιῶν, ὡς ἔφην, τὴν πρὸς θεὸν ἀνάβασιν
καὶ καταλλάττων ἡμῖν τὸν ἑαυτοῦ πατέρα καὶ ὡς ἀρχὴν καὶ
αἰτίαν ἑαυτοῦ τοῦτον τιμῶν καὶ δεικνύς, ὡς οὐκ ἔστιν ἀντίθεος.
Ὅτε μὲν γὰρ ἔλεγεν ἐπὶ Λαζάρου· «Πάτερ, εὐχαριστῶ σοι, ὅτι
ἤκουσάς μου. Ἐγὼ δὲ ᾔδειν, ὅτι πάντοτέ μου ἀκούεις, ἀλλὰ διὰ
τὸν παρεστηκότα ὄχλον εἶπον, ἵνα γνῶσιν, ὅτι σύ με ἀπέστειλας»,
οὐ πᾶσι σαφέστατον πέφυκεν, ὅτι ὡς ἀρχὴν ἑαυτοῦ καὶ αἰτίαν
τιμῶν τὸν ἑαυτοῦ πατέρα καὶ δεικνύς, ὡς οὐκ ἔστιν ἀντίθεος;

Ὅτε δὲ ἔλεγε· «Πάτερ, εἰ δυνατόν, παρελθέτω ἀπ' ἐμοῦ τὸ
ποτήριον τοῦτο· πλὴν οὐχ ὡς ἐγὼ θέλω, ἀλλ' ὡς σύ», οὐ παντί που
δῆλόν ἐστιν, ὡς διδάσκων ἡμᾶς ἐν τοῖς πειρασμοῖς παρὰ μόνου
θεοῦ αἰτεῖν τὴν βοήθειαν καὶ τὸ θεῖον τοῦ ἡμετέρου προκρίνειν
θελήματος καὶ δεικνύς, ὡς ἀληθῶς τὰ τῆς ἡμετέρας ᾠκειώσατο
φύσεως ὅτι τε κατὰ ἀλήθειαν δύο θελήματα φυσικὰ μὲν καὶ
τῶν αὐτοῦ κατάλληλα φύσεων, ἀλλ' οὐχ ὑπεναντία κέκτηται;
«Πάτερ», φησὶν ὡς ὁμοούσιος, «εἰ δυνατόν», οὐκ ἀγνοῶν—τί δὲ
καὶ τῷ θεῷ ἀδύνατον; —, ἀλλὰ παιδαγωγῶν ἡμᾶς τὸ θεῖον τοῦ
ἡμετέρου προκρίνειν θελήματος· τοῦτο γὰρ μόνον ἀδύνατον, ὃ
θεὸς οὐ βούλεται οὐδὲ παραχωρεῖ. «Πλὴν οὐχ ὡς ἐγὼ θέλω, ἀλλ'
ὡς σύ», ὡς μὲν θεὸς ταυτοτελὴς ὢν τῷ πατρί, ὡς δὲ ἄνθρωπος
τὸ τῆς ἀνθρωπότητος πεφυκὸς ἐνδείκνυται θέλημα· τοῦτο γὰρ
φυσικῶς παραιτεῖται τὸν θάνατον.

---

[2] Jn 11.41–42.
[3] Cf. Gregory of Nazianzus, *Oration* 38.15 (PG 36:328D; Moreschini, 894). "A rival
god" translates ἀντίθεος/*antitheos*, a Homeric word which was taken up by Origen
(fragment 558 of the Fragments from his *Commentary on Matthew*), who says that the

at the time of his passion? His holy mind had no need of ascending to God, seeing that it was already united hypostatically to God the Word, nor did he need to petition God, for Christ is one. Yet he made our human character his own, and typified in himself what belonged to us, and became a model for us, teaching us to petition God and raise ourselves up towards him, and though his holy mind preparing a path for us to ascend to God. For just as he endured his sufferings for us, rewarding us by victory over them, that is also how he prays, preparing a path for us, as I have said, to ascend to God, and reconciling his own Father to us, and honoring him as his own source and cause, and showing that he was not a rival god. For when he said in the case of Lazarus, "Father, I thank you for having heard me. I knew that you always hear me, but I have said this for the sake of the crowd standing here, so that they may believe that you sent me,"[2] was it not absolutely clear to all that he was honoring his own Father as his own source and cause and showing that he was not a rival god?[3]

And when he said, "Father, if it is possible, let this cup pass from me; yet not what I want but what you want,"[4] is it not surely clear to all that he was teaching us to seek help only from God in times of trial, and showing us to prefer the divine will to our own, since he had truly appropriated what belongs to our nature and that he really did possess two natural wills corresponding to his two natures, but not in opposition to each other? "Father," he says, as being of one substance (ὁμοούσιος, *homoousios*) with him, "if it is possible," not that he was ignorant—what is impossible for God?—but in order to teach us to prefer the divine will to our own. For the only thing that is impossible is what God does not will or permit. "Yet not what I want but what you want." This he says as God, since he has the same end in view as the Father, and demonstrates that as man he has the will that is natural to humanity. For he naturally sought to avoid death.

Lord's cry from the cross, "*Eli, Eli, lema sabachthani*" (Mt 27.46), shows that he was not a rival God. Thereafter the word was much used by Christian authors, especially John Chrysostom.

[4]Lk 22.42.

Τὸ δὲ «θεέ μου, θεέ μου, ἱνατί με ἐγκατέλιπες;» τὸ ἡμέτερον
οἰκειούμενος ἔφησε πρόσωπον· οὔτε γὰρ θεὸς αὐτοῦ ὁ πατήρ,
εἰ μή γε διαιρεθέντος ἰσχναῖς τοῦ νοῦ φαντασίαις τοῦ ὁρωμένου
ἐκ τοῦ νοουμένου, τάσσοιτο μεθ᾽ ἡμῶν, οὔτε κατελείφθη ὑπὸ
τῆς οἰκείας θεότητος, ἀλλ᾽ ἡμεῖς ἦμεν οἱ ἐγκαταλελειμμένοι καὶ
παρεωραμένοι. Ὥστε τὸ ἡμέτερον οἰκειούμενος πρόσωπον ταῦτα
προσηύξατο.

69 Περὶ οἰκειώσεως

Χρὴ εἰδέναι, ὡς δύο οἰκειώσεις· μία φυσικὴ καὶ οὐσιώδης, καὶ
μία προσωπικὴ καὶ σχετική. Φυσικὴ μὲν οὖν καὶ οὐσιώδης, καθ᾽
ἣν διὰ φιλανθρωπίαν ὁ κύριος τήν τε φύσιν ἡμῶν καὶ τὰ φυσικὰ
πάντα ἀνέλαβε φύσει καὶ ἀληθείᾳ γενόμενος ἄνθρωπος καὶ
τῶν φυσικῶν ἐν πείρᾳ γενόμενος· προσωπικὴ δέ, ὅτε τις τὸ
ἑτέρου ὑποδύεται πρόσωπον διὰ σχέσιν, οἶκτόν φημι ἢ ἀγάπην,
καὶ ἀντ᾽ αὐτοῦ τοὺς ὑπὲρ αὐτοῦ ποιεῖται λόγους μηδὲν αὐτῷ
προσήκοντας, καθ᾽ ἣν τήν τε κατάραν καὶ τὴν ἐγκατάλειψιν ἡμῶν
καὶ τὰ τοιαῦτα οὐκ ὄντα φυσικά, οὐκ αὐτὸς ταῦτα ὢν ἢ γενόμενος
ᾠκειώσατο, ἀλλὰ τὸ ἡμέτερον ἀναδεχόμενος πρόσωπον καὶ μεθ᾽
ἡμῶν τασσόμενος.

70 Περὶ τοῦ πάθους τοῦ σώματος τοῦ κυρίου καὶ τῆς
ἀπαθείας τῆς αὐτοῦ θεότητος

Αὐτὸς οὖν ὁ τοῦ θεοῦ λόγος πάντα ὑπέμεινε σαρκὶ τῆς θείας καὶ
μόνης ἀπαθοῦς αὐτοῦ φύσεως ἀπαθοῦς μενούσης. Τοῦ γὰρ ἑνὸς

---

[5]Mt 27.46.
[6]Cf. Gregory of Nazianzus, *Oration* 30.5 (PG 36:109B; Moreschini, 724).

[1]The BCEGHKMN family of manuscripts adds: "And his becoming a curse for us
(cf. Gal 3.13) belongs to this category." For the whole chapter, cf. Gregory of Nazianzus,

He uttered the phrase, "My God, my God, why have you forsaken me"[5] in virtue of having made our human character his own. For the Father was not his God, unless by separating what is visible from the mental image through the imaginative working of the mind, we set him alongside us. Nor was he forsaken by his own divinity. On the contrary, it was we who were forsaken and abandoned. And so it was through appropriating our own human character that he prayed in this way.[6]

69 *On appropriation*

One should know that there are two appropriations. One is natural and substantial, the other is personal and relational. The natural and substantial appropriation is that by which the Lord out of his love for humanity assumed our nature and all the natural characteristics that belong to it, by nature and in truth becoming a human being and experiencing the natural characteristics that pertain to humanity. The personal appropriation occurs when someone takes on the character of someone else through a relationship, I mean a relationship of pity or love, and in his place says things on his behalf which do not in any way belong to him personally. It is in this sense that Christ appropriated our curse and abandonment and such things that are not part of our nature, not because he himself was these things or became them, but because he took our character upon himself and set himself alongside us.[1]

70 *On the suffering of the Lord's body and the impassibility of his divinity*

The Word of God himself, then, bore everything in the flesh, with his divine nature, which alone is impassible, remaining free from

Orations 30. 5 (PG 36:109AB; Moreschini, 724) and 37.1 (PG 36:284A; Moreschini, 858); Maximus the Confessor, *Opusculum* 19 (PG 91:220BC), on the nature of "appropriation" (οἰκείωσις, *oikeiōsis*).

Χριστοῦ τοῦ ἐκ θεότητός τε καὶ ἀνθρωπότητος συντεθειμένου, ἐν θεότητί τε καὶ ἀνθρωπότητι ὄντος, πάσχοντος τὸ μὲν παθητὸν ὡς πεφυκὸς πάσχειν ἔπασχεν, οὐ συνέπασχε δὲ τὸ ἀπαθές. Ἡ μὲν γὰρ ψυχὴ παθητὴ οὖσα, τοῦ σώματος τεμνομένου αὐτὴ μὴ τεμνομένη συναλγεῖ καὶ συμπάσχει τῷ σώματι· ἡ δὲ θεότης ἀπαθὴς οὖσα, οὐ συνέπασχε τῷ σώματι.

Ἰστέον δέ, ὅτι θεὸν μὲν σαρκὶ παθόντα φαμέν, θεότητα δὲ σαρκὶ παθοῦσαν ἢ θεὸν διὰ σαρκὸς παθόντα οὐδαμῶς. Ὥσπερ γὰρ ἡλίου δένδρῳ ἐπιλάμποντος εἰ ἀξίνη τέμνοι τὸ δένδρον, ἄτμητος καὶ ἀπαθὴς διαμένει ὁ ἥλιος, πολλῷ μᾶλλον ἡ ἀπαθὴς τοῦ λόγου θεότης καθ᾽ ὑπόστασιν ἡνωμένη τῇ σαρκὶ τῆς σαρκὸς πασχούσης διαμένει ἀπαθής. Καὶ ὥσπερ, εἴ τις πεπυρακτωμένῳ σιδήρῳ ἐπιχέοι ὕδωρ, τὸ μὲν πέφυκε πάσχειν ὑπὸ τοῦ ὕδατος (τὸ πῦρ λέγω, σβέννυται γάρ), ἀβλαβὴς δὲ διαμένει ὁ σίδηρος (οὐ πέφυκε γὰρ ὑπὸ τοῦ ὕδατος διαφθείρεσθαι), πολλῷ πλέον τῆς σαρκὸς πασχούσης ἡ μόνη ἀπαθὴς θεότης τὸ πάθος οὐ προσήκατο καὶ ἀχώριστος αὐτῆς διαμένουσα· οὐκ ἀνάγκη γὰρ παντελῶς καὶ ἀνελλιπῶς ἐοικέναι τὰ παραδείγματα. Ἀνάγκη γὰρ ἐν τοῖς παραδείγμασι καὶ τὸ ὅμοιον θεωρεῖσθαι καὶ τὸ παρηλλαγμένον, ἐπεὶ οὐ παράδειγμα· τὸ γὰρ ἐν πᾶσιν ὅμοιον ταὐτὸν ἂν εἴη καὶ οὐ παράδειγμα, καὶ μάλιστα ἐπὶ τῶν θείων. Ἀδύνατον γὰρ ἐν πᾶσιν ὅμοιον εὑρεῖν παράδειγμα, ἐπί τε τῆς θεολογίας, ἐπί τε τῆς οἰκονομίας.

passion. For when the one Christ, who is composed of divinity and humanity, and exists as both human and divine, suffered, the passible element suffered, as was natural to it, but the impassible element did not suffer along with it. For since the soul is passible, when the body is cut, the soul feels pain and suffers along with the body, even though the soul itself is not cut. But since the divinity is impassible, it did not suffer along with the body.

Moreover, one should be aware that although we speak of God suffering in the flesh, we do not by any means say that divinity suffered in the flesh or that God suffered through the flesh. It is like the sun shining on a tree. If an axe cuts the tree, the sun remains uncut and unaffected.[1] How much more does the dispassionate divinity of the Word, which is united hypostatically to the flesh, remain unaffected when the flesh suffers. And it is like someone pouring water on a red-hot piece of iron. The one is naturally affected by the water (I mean the fire, for it is extinguished), but the piece of iron remains unharmed (for it is not naturally harmed by water). How much more did the divinity, which is alone impassible, not become involved with the suffering when the flesh suffered, even though it remained inseparable from it. It is not necessary for examples to be absolutely alike in every respect. For what is needed in examples is that which is alike and what is different should be observable, otherwise it is not an example. For what is alike in every respect would be identical and not an example, especially in the case of divine matters. For it is impossible to find an example that is alike in every respect both in the case of theology and in the case of the divine economy.

---

[1]Kotter, referring to Otto Bardenhewer, "Ungedruckte Excerpte aus einer Schrift des Patriarchen Eulogius v. Alexandrien (580–607) über Trinität und Incarnation," *Theologische Quartalschrift* 78 (1896): 363, attributes the origin of this image to a lost work on the Trinity by Eulogius of Alexandria (Chalcedonian patriarch 580–607/8).

71 Περὶ τοῦ ἀχώριστον διαμεῖναι τὴν τοῦ λόγου θεότητα
τῆς ψυχῆς καὶ τοῦ σώματος καὶ ἐν τῷ θανάτῳ τοῦ
κυρίου καὶ μίαν διαμεῖναι ὑπόστασιν

Ἀναμάρτητος ὢν ὁ κύριος ἡμῶν Ἰησοῦς Χριστός—«ἁμαρτίαν γὰρ
οὐκ ἐποίησεν» «ὁ αἴρων τὴν ἁμαρτίαν τοῦ κόσμου» «οὐδὲ εὑρέθη
δόλος ἐν τῷ στόματι αὐτοῦ»—οὐχ ὑπέκειτο θανάτῳ, εἴπερ διὰ τῆς
ἁμαρτίας εἰς τὸν κόσμον εἰσῆλθεν ὁ θάνατος. Θνήσκει τοίνυν
τὸν ὑπὲρ ἡμῶν θάνατον ἀναδεχόμενος καὶ ἑαυτὸν τῷ πατρὶ
προσφέρει θυσίαν ὑπὲρ ἡμῶν· αὐτῷ γὰρ πεπλημμελήκαμεν, καὶ
αὐτὸν ἔδει τὸ ὑπὲρ ἡμῶν λύτρον δέξασθαι καὶ οὕτως ἡμᾶς λυθῆναι
τῆς κατακρίσεως· μὴ γὰρ γένοιτο τῷ τυράννῳ τὸ τοῦ δεσπότου
προσενεχθῆναι αἷμα. Πρόσεισι τοίνυν ὁ θάνατος καὶ καταπιὼν τὸ
τοῦ σώματος δέλεαρ τῷ τῆς θεότητος ἀγκίστρῳ περιπείρεται, καὶ
ἀναμαρτήτου καὶ ζωοποιοῦ γευσάμενος σώματος διαφθείρεται
καὶ πάντας ἀνάγει, οὓς πάλαι κατέπιεν. Ὥσπερ γὰρ τὸ σκότος
τῇ τοῦ φωτὸς ἐπεισαγωγῇ ἐξαφανίζεται, οὕτως ἡ φθορὰ τῇ τῆς
ζωῆς προσβολῇ ἀπελαύνεται, καὶ γίνεται πᾶσι ζωή, φθορὰ δὲ τῷ
φθείροντι.

Εἰ καὶ τέθνηκε τοιγαροῦν ὡς ἄνθρωπος καὶ ἡ ἁγία αὐτοῦ
ψυχὴ τοῦ ἀχράντου διηρέθη σώματος, ἀλλ᾿ ἡ θεότης ἀχώριστος
ἀμφοτέρων διέμεινε, τῆς τε ψυχῆς φημι καὶ τοῦ σώματος, καὶ
οὐδὲ οὕτως ἡ μία ὑπόστασις εἰς δύο ὑποστάσεις διηρέθη· τό τε
γὰρ σῶμα καὶ ἡ ψυχὴ κατὰ ταὐτὸν ἐξ ἀρχῆς ἐν τῇ τοῦ λόγου

---

[1] 1 Pet 2.22. [2] Jn 1.29. [3] 1 Pet 2.22.
[4] The Pauline mention of ransom or redemption (Rom 3:25–6; 1 Cor 1.30) led to
much speculation among the fathers and early Christian thinkers. Origen wonders
to whom the ransom was paid. In his view it could only have been paid to the devil
(*Com. Rom.* 3.8). Gregory of Nazianzus objects strongly to this (*Orat.* 45.22), in contrast to Gregory of Nyssa, who accepts it together with the image of the fishhook (*Cat.
Disc.* 22–24) that had also been suggested by Origen (*Hom. Ex.* 6.9; *Com. Mt.* 16.8).
Maximus the Confessor, following Gregory of Nyssa, finds the idea of the deception
of the devil useful (*Quest. Thal.* 64.509–37), using it to develop a neat theological
pattern: humanity had sinned originally in the hope of becoming divine; the devil
swallowed the humanity represented in Christ in the hope of becoming human—but
was vanquished by the divinity. John objects to a ransom paid to the devil (with
Gregory of Nazianzus) but accepts the fishhook image (with Gregory of Nyssa and

71   On the continuing inseparability of the Word's divinity from the soul and the body even in the Lord's death and his remaining a single hypostasis

Since our Lord Jesus Christ was without sin—for "he committed no sin,"[1] "he who takes away the sin of the world,"[2] "and no deceit was found in his mouth"[3]—he was not subject to death, as in fact death came into the world through sin. He therefore died because he accepted death for our sake and offered himself as a sacrifice to the Father on our behalf. For we had offended the Father, and so it was he who had to receive the ransom for us and thus release us from condemnation. God forbid that the Master's blood should have been offered to the tyrant! Death therefore approached and by swallowing the bait of the body was caught by the hook of the divinity, and having tasted the sinless and life-giving body, he was destroyed and threw up all whom he had previously swallowed. As darkness vanishes at the coming of light, so is destruction driven away by the approach of life, and life comes about for all, but destruction for the destroyer.[4]

Even though he did therefore die as a human being and his holy soul was separated from his immaculate body, nevertheless the divinity remained inseparable from both, I mean from the soul and the body, and there is no sense in which the one hypostasis was divided into two hypostases. For since both the body and the soul had their existence in the same way from the beginning in the hypostasis of the Word, and although they were separated from

Maximus) and through it (like Maximus) emphasizes victory over the demonic. Although clearly aware of Gregory of Nyssa's discussion of these topics in the *Catechetical Discourse,* John's direct source seems to have been Maximus' *Questions to Thalassius* 61–65 (from which he borrows several turns of phrase). One of the points that would have repelled him in Gregory's text is the (Origenist) implication that the devil will be saved—hence his insistence on the destruction of the destroyer. For a basic orientation on these issues, see Norman Russell, "The Work of Christ in Patristic Theology," in *The Oxford Handbook of Christology,* ed. Francesca Murphy (Oxford: Oxford University Press, 2015), 154–66, and for an excellent article on the deception of the devil, Maximos Constas, "The Last Temptation of Satan: Divine Deception in Greek Patristic Interpretations of the Passion Narrative," *Harvard Theological Review* 97 (2004): 139–63.

ὑποστάσει ἔσχον τὴν ὕπαρξιν καὶ ἐν τῷ θανάτῳ ἀλλήλων διαιρεθέντα ἕκαστον αὐτῶν ἔμεινε τὴν μίαν ὑπόστασιν τοῦ λόγου ἔχοντα. Ὥστε ἡ μία τοῦ λόγου ὑπόστασις τοῦ τε λόγου καὶ τῆς ψυχῆς καὶ τοῦ σώματος ὑπῆρχεν ὑπόστασις· οὐδέποτε γὰρ οὔτε ἡ ψυχή, οὐδὲ τὸ σῶμα ἰδίαν ἔσχον ὑπόστασιν παρὰ τὴν τοῦ λόγου ὑπόστασιν· μία δὲ ἀεὶ ἡ τοῦ λόγου ὑπόστασις καὶ οὐδέποτε δύο. Ὥστε μία ἀεὶ τοῦ Χριστοῦ ἡ ὑπόστασις. Ὥστε, εἰ καὶ τοπικῶς ἡ ψυχὴ τοῦ σώματος κεχώριστο, ἀλλ' ὑποστατικῶς διὰ τοῦ λόγου ἥνωτο.

72   Περὶ φθορᾶς καὶ διαφθορᾶς

Τὸ τῆς φθορᾶς ὄνομα δύο σημαίνει. Σημαίνει γὰρ τὰ ἀνθρώπινα ταῦτα πάθη· πεῖναν, δίψαν, κόπον, τὴν τῶν ἥλων διάτρησιν, θάνατον ἤτοι χωρισμὸν τῆς ψυχῆς ἐκ τοῦ σώματος καὶ τὰ τοιαῦτα. Κατὰ τοῦτο τὸ σημαινόμενον φθαρτὸν τὸ τοῦ κυρίου σῶμά φαμεν· πάντα γὰρ ταῦτα ἑκουσίως ἀνέλαβε. Σημαίνει δὲ ἡ φθορὰ καὶ τὴν τελείαν τοῦ σώματος εἰς τά, ἐξ ὧν συνετέθη, στοιχεῖα διάλυσιν καὶ ἀφανισμόν· ἥτις μᾶλλον ὑπὸ πολλῶν διαφθορὰ λέγεταί τε καὶ ὀνομάζεται. Ταύτης πεῖραν τὸ τοῦ κυρίου σῶμα οὐκ ἔσχεν, ὥς φησιν ὁ προφήτης Δαυίδ· «Ὅτι οὐκ ἐγκαταλείψεις τὴν ψυχήν μου εἰς ᾅδου οὐδὲ δώσεις τὸν ὅσιόν σου ἰδεῖν διαφθοράν».

Ἄφθαρτον μὲν οὖν κατὰ τὸν ἄφρονα Ἰουλιανὸν καὶ Γαϊανὸν τὸ σῶμα τοῦ Χριστοῦ λέγειν κατὰ τὸ πρῶτον τῆς φθορᾶς σημαινόμενον πρὸ τῆς ἀναστάσεως ἀσεβές. Εἰ γὰρ ἄφθαρτον, οὐχ ὁμοούσιον ἡμῖν, ἀλλὰ καὶ δοκήσει καὶ οὐκ ἀληθείᾳ γέγονεν, ἃ γεγονέναι φησὶ τὸ εὐαγγέλιον, τὴν πεῖναν, τὴν δίψαν, τοὺς ἥλους, τὴν τῆς πλευρᾶς νύξιν, τὸν θάνατον. Εἰ δὲ δοκήσει γέγονε, φενακισμὸς καὶ σκηνὴ τὸ τῆς οἰκονομίας μυστήριον,

---

[1]Ps 15.10.

[2]Julian of Halicarnassus was an early sixth-century monophysite bishop who held that Christ's body was incorrupt from the moment of its conception (rather than only after the resurrection). He and his followers were therefore dubbed "aphthartodocetists." Forced by the imperial government to flee to Egypt, he wrote there

each other in death, each of them remained because they had the one hypostasis of the Word. Consequently, the one hypostasis of the Word was the hypostasis of the Word and the soul and the body. For neither the soul nor the body ever had its own hypostasis apart from the hypostasis of the Word. The hypostasis of the Word has always been one and never two. Consequently, the hypostasis of Christ has always been one. It also follows that even if the soul was separated from the body in a local sense, they were united hypostatically through the Word.

72   On perishability and corruption

The word "perishability" (φθορά, *phthora*) has two meanings. For it refers to the following human passions: hunger, thirst, toil, the piercing with nails, death, which is a separation of the soul from the body, and suchlike. In this sense we say that the Lord's body is perishable, for he voluntarily assumed all these things. But perishability also indicates the complete dissolution of the body into the elements from which it has been constituted and its disappearance. Many prefer to render this meaning by the word "corruption" (διαφθορά, *diaphthora*). The Lord's body had no experience of perishability in this sense, as the prophet David said: "For you will not abandon my soul to hades, nor will you allow your holy one to see corruption."[1]

It is therefore sacrilegious to call Christ's body exempt from corruption (ἄφθαρτον, *aphtharton*) before the resurrection, in accordance with the first sense of "perishability," as the foolish Julian and Gaianus do.[2] For if it was not subject to corruption, it was not consubstantial with us and what the gospel says happened—the hunger, the thirst, the nails, the piercing of the side, the death—happened in appearance and not in reality. But if these things happened

a polemical work against his fellow monophysite, Severus of Antioch, whose doctrine on this point was perfectly orthodox. Julian's work has not survived but we know of it through Severus' refutation. Gaianus was a disciple of Julian who became briefly patriarch of Alexandria.

καὶ δοκήσει καὶ οὐκ ἀληθείᾳ γέγονεν ἄνθρωπος, καὶ δοκήσει καὶ οὐκ ἀληθείᾳ σεσώσμεθα. Ἀλλ' ἄπαγε, καὶ οἱ ταῦτα λέγοντες τῆς σωτηρίας ἀμοιρείτωσαν. Ἡμεῖς δὲ τῆς ἀληθοῦς σωτηρίας ἐτύχομεν καὶ τευξόμεθα. Κατὰ δὲ τὸ δεύτερον τῆς φθορᾶς σημαινόμενον ἄφθαρτον ἤτοι ἀδιάφθορον ὁμολογοῦμεν τὸ τοῦ κυρίου σῶμα, καθὼς ἡμῖν οἱ θεοφόροι πατέρες παραδεδώκασι. Μετὰ μέντοι τὴν ἐκ νεκρῶν ἀνάστασιν τοῦ σωτῆρος καὶ κατὰ τὸ πρῶτον σημαινόμενον ἄφθαρτον τὸ τοῦ κυρίου σῶμά φαμεν· καὶ τῷ ἡμετέρῳ γὰρ σώματι τήν τε ἀνάστασιν καὶ τὴν μετὰ ταῦτα ἀφθαρσίαν ὁ κύριος διὰ τοῦ ἰδίου ἐδωρήσατο σώματος, αὐτὸς ἀπαρχὴ τῆς τε ἀναστάσεως καὶ τῆς ἀφθαρσίας καὶ τῆς ἀπαθείας ἡμῖν γενόμενος. «Δεῖ γὰρ τὸ φθαρτὸν τοῦτο ἐνδύσασθαι ἀφθαρσίαν», φησὶν ὁ θεῖος ἀπόστολος.

73 Περὶ τῆς ἐν τῷ ᾅδῃ καθόδου

Κάτεισιν εἰς ᾅδην ψυχὴ τεθεωμένη, ἵνα, ὥσπερ τοῖς ἐν γῇ ὁ τῆς δικαιοσύνης ἀνέτειλεν ἥλιος, οὕτω καὶ τοῖς ὑπὸ γῆν ἐν σκότει καὶ σκιᾷ θανάτου καθημένοις ἐπιλάμψῃ τὸ φῶς· ἵνα, ὥσπερ τοῖς ἐν γῇ εὐηγγελίσατο εἰρήνην, αἰχμαλώτοις ἄφεσιν καὶ τυφλοῖς ἀνάβλεψιν, καὶ τοῖς πιστεύσασι γέγονεν αἴτιος σωτηρίας αἰωνίου, τοῖς δὲ ἀπειθήσασιν ἔλεγχος ἀπιστίας, οὕτω καὶ τοῖς ἐν ᾅδου· «ἵνα αὐτῷ κάμψῃ πᾶν γόνυ ἐπουρανίων καὶ ἐπιγείων καὶ καταχθονίων», καὶ οὕτω τοὺς ἀπ' αἰῶνος λύσας πεπεδημένους αὖθις ἐκ νεκρῶν ἀνεφοίτησεν ὁδοποιήσας ἡμῖν τὴν ἀνάστασιν.

in appearance, the mystery of the economy of salvation was a fraud and a charade, and [Christ] became a human being in appearance and not in reality, and we have been saved in appearance and not in reality. But away with this, and may those who say these things have no share in salvation. But we, for our part, have found true salvation and will find it. We confess that the Lord's body is not subject to corruption or to destruction in the second sense of "perishability," as the God-bearing fathers have handed down to us. And indeed we also say that after the Savior's resurrection from the dead the Lord's body is not subject to corruption in the first sense of perishability. For by his own body the Lord also granted resurrection and the accompanying incorruptibility to our own body, since he himself became for us the first-fruits of resurrection and of incorruption and of dispassion. "For this perishable body must put on imperishability," says the divine Apostle.[3]

73   *On the descent into hades*

[The Lord's] deified soul descended into hades, so that just as the sun of righteousness had risen, so too the light might also shine on those sitting below the earth in the darkness and shadow of death.[1] The reason for this was that just as for those living on earth he had brought the good news of peace, and liberty to captives, and sight to the blind, and to those who believed became the cause of eternal salvation, and to those who did not believe a reproach to their unbelief, he might also do the same for those in hades, "so that at the name of Jesus every knee should bend, in heaven and on earth and under the earth."[2] And having thus released those who had been bound with fetters from the beginning of the age, he rose again from the dead and prepared for us the way to resurrection.

[3]1 Cor 15.53. For the whole chapter cf. Theodore of Raithu (Ps.-Leontius of Byzantium), *On the Sects* (PG 86/1:1261CD); *Doctrina Patrum*, Diekamp, 111–14.

[1]Mal 3.20 (= 4.2 MT); Mt 4.16 (cf. Is 9.2).   [2]Phil 2.10.

74   Περὶ τῶν μετὰ τὴν ἀνάστασιν

Μετὰ δὲ τὴν ἐκ νεκρῶν ἀνάστασιν πάντα μὲν τὰ πάθη ἀπέθετο, φθορὰν λέγω πεῖνάν τε καὶ δίψαν, ὕπνον καὶ κάματον καὶ τὰ τοιαῦτα. Εἰ γὰρ καὶ ἐγεύσατο βρώσεως μετὰ τὴν ἀνάστασιν, ἀλλ᾽ οὐ νόμῳ φύσεως (οὐ γὰρ ἐπείνασεν), οἰκονομίας δὲ τρόπῳ τὸ ἀληθὲς πιστούμενος τῆς ἀναστάσεως, ὡς αὐτή ἐστιν ἡ σὰρξ ἡ παθοῦσα καὶ ἀναστᾶσα· οὐδὲν δὲ τῶν τῆς φύσεως μερῶν ἀπέθετο, οὐ σῶμα, οὐ ψυχήν, ἀλλὰ καὶ τὸ σῶμα καὶ τὴν ψυχὴν λογικήν τε καὶ νοεράν, θελητικήν τε καὶ ἐνεργητικὴν κέκτηται, καὶ οὕτως εἰς οὐρανοὺς ἀνεφοίτησεν καὶ οὕτως ἐν δεξιᾷ τοῦ πατρὸς καθέζεται, θέλων θεϊκῶς τε καὶ ἀνθρωπίνως τὴν ἡμῶν σωτηρίαν καὶ ἐνεργῶν, θεϊκῶς μὲν τὴν τῶν ὅλων πρόνοιάν τε καὶ συντήρησιν καὶ κυβέρνησιν, ἀνθρωπίνως δὲ μεμνημένος τῶν ἐπὶ γῆς διατριβῶν, ὁρῶν τε καὶ γινώσκων, ὡς ὑπὸ πάσης προσκυνεῖται τῆς λογικῆς κτίσεως. Γινώσκει γὰρ ἡ ἁγία αὐτοῦ ψυχή, ὅτι τε καθ᾽ ὑπόστασιν ἥνωται τῷ θεῷ λόγῳ, καὶ συμπροσκυνεῖται ὡς θεοῦ ψυχὴ καὶ οὐχ ὡς ἁπλῶς ψυχή. Καὶ τὸ ἀναβῆναι δὲ ἐκ γῆς εἰς οὐρανοὺς καὶ τὸ καταβῆναι πάλιν ἐνέργειαί εἰσι περιγραφομένου σώματος· «Οὕτως» γὰρ πάλιν «ἐλεύσεται», φησί, πρὸς ὑμᾶς, «ὃν τρόπον ἐθεάσασθε αὐτὸν πορευόμενον εἰς τὸν οὐρανόν».

75   Περὶ τῆς ἐκ δεξιῶν τοῦ πατρὸς καθέδρας

Ἐκ δεξιῶν δὲ τοῦ θεοῦ καὶ πατρὸς κεκαθικέναι φαμὲν τὸν Χριστὸν σωματικῶς, οὐ τοπικὴν δὲ δεξιὰν τοῦ πατρὸς λέγομεν. Πῶς γὰρ ὁ ἀπερίγραπτος τοπικὴν σχοίη δεξιάν; Δεξιὰ γὰρ καὶ ἀριστερὰ τῶν περιγραφομένων εἰσί. Δεξιὰν δὲ τοῦ πατρὸς λέγομεν τὴν δόξαν καὶ τιμὴν τῆς θεότητος, ἐν ᾗ ὁ τοῦ θεοῦ υἱὸς πρὸ αἰώνων ὑπάρχων, ὡς θεὸς καὶ τῷ πατρὶ ὁμοούσιος, ἐπ᾽ ἐσχάτων σαρκωθεὶς

74 *On what happened after the resurrection*

After the resurrection from the dead he put aside the passions, by which I mean corruption, hunger and thirst, sleep, tiredness, and such things. Even though he tasted food after the resurrection, it was not on account of the law of nature (for he did not experience hunger) but by way of accommodation to confirm the truth of the resurrection, that it was the same flesh that had suffered and had risen again. He did not put aside any part of his nature, neither body nor soul, but retained possession of his body and his soul with its reason and intellect, its will and activity, and in this manner he ascended into heaven and in this manner he sits at the right hand of the Father, willing and realizing our salvation in a divine manner and a human manner—in a divine manner with regard to his providential care and conservation and government of all things, and in a human manner with regard to his remembering what he had experienced on earth, and seeing and knowing that he is worshiped by the whole of rational creation. For his holy soul knows that it is hypostatically united to God the Word, and it is worshiped along with him as the soul of God and not simply as a soul. And the ascent from earth to heaven and the descent again are operations of a circumscribed body. For "he will come to you" again, says Scripture, "in the same way as you saw him go into heaven."[1]

75 *On the sitting at the right hand of the Father*

When we say that Christ is seated corporeally at the right hand of the Father, we are not saying that he is seated at the right hand of the Father in a local sense. For how would he who is uncircumscribed have a right hand in respect of place? For left and right belong to circumscribed entities. What we call the right hand of the Father is the glory and honor of the divinity, in which the Son of God existed before the ages, since he is God and consubstantial with the Father,

[1] Acts 1.11.

καὶ σωματικῶς κάθηται συνδοξασθείσης τῆς σαρκὸς αὐτοῦ·
προσκυνεῖται γὰρ μιᾷ προσκυνήσει μετὰ τῆς σαρκὸς αὐτοῦ ὑπὸ
πάσης τῆς κτίσεως.

76 *Πρὸς τοὺς λέγοντας· Εἰ δύο φύσεις ὁ Χριστός,*
ἢ καὶ τῇ κτίσει λατρεύετε φύσιν κτιστὴν
προσκυνοῦντες ἢ μίαν φύσιν προσκυνητὴν
λέγετε καὶ μίαν ἀπροσκύνητον

Τὸν υἱὸν τοῦ θεοῦ σὺν τῷ πατρὶ καὶ τῷ ἁγίῳ πνεύματι
προσκυνοῦμεν, ἀσώματον μὲν πρὸ τῆς ἐνανθρωπήσεως καὶ νῦν
τὸν αὐτὸν σεσαρκωμένον καὶ γενόμενον ἄνθρωπον μετὰ τοῦ
εἶναι θεόν. Ἡ τοίνυν σὰρξ αὐτοῦ κατὰ μὲν τὴν ἑαυτῆς φύσιν,
ἂν διέλῃς ἰσχναῖς ἐπινοίαις τὸ ὁρώμενον ἐκ τοῦ νοουμένου,
ἀπροσκύνητός ἐστιν ὡς κτιστή, ἑνωθεῖσα δὲ τῷ θεῷ λόγῳ δι᾽
αὐτὸν καὶ ἐν αὐτῷ προσκυνεῖται. Ὅνπερ γὰρ τρόπον ὁ βασιλεὺς
καὶ γυμνὸς προσκυνεῖται καὶ ἐνδεδυμένος, καὶ ἡ ἁλουργὶς ὡς μὲν
ψιλὴ ἁλουργὶς πατεῖται καὶ περιρρίπτεται, βασιλικὸν δὲ γενομένη
ἔνδυμα τιμᾶται καὶ δοξάζεται καί, εἴ τις αὐτὴν παροικτρώσειε,
θανάτῳ ὡς τὰ πολλὰ κατακρίνεται, ὡς δὲ καὶ ξύλον ψιλὸν οὐκ ἔστι
τῇ ἁφῇ ἀπρόσιτον, πυρὶ δὲ προσομιλῆσαν καὶ ἄνθραξ γενόμενον
οὐ δι᾽ ἑαυτό, διὰ δὲ τὸ συνημμένον πῦρ ἀπρόσιτον γίνεται καὶ
οὐχ ἡ τοῦ ξύλου φύσις ὑπάρχει ἀπρόσιτος, ἀλλ᾽ ὁ ἄνθραξ ἤτοι τὸ
πεπυρωμένον ξύλον, οὕτως ἡ σὰρξ κατὰ μὲν τὴν ἑαυτῆς φύσιν
οὐκ ἔστι προσκυνητή, προσκυνεῖται δὲ ἐν τῷ σεσαρκωμένῳ θεῷ
λόγῳ οὐ δι᾽ ἑαυτήν, ἀλλὰ διὰ τὸν ἡνωμένον αὐτῇ καθ᾽ ὑπόστασιν
θεὸν λόγον, καὶ οὔ φαμεν, ὅτι σάρκα προσκυνοῦμεν ψιλήν, ἀλλὰ
σάρκα θεοῦ ἤτοι σεσαρκωμένον θεόν.

and having become incarnate in these last days he is also seated corporeally with his flesh glorified together with him. For he is worshiped in a single act of worship together with his flesh by the whole of creation.

76 *To those who say: "If Christ has two natures, either you also adore the creature when you worship the created nature, or you say that one nature is to be worshiped but not the other"*

We worship the Son of God with the Father and the Holy Spirit, incorporeal before the inhomination and now the same enfleshed and become human along with being God. His flesh, then, in its own nature—if by subtle concepts you distinguish the visible from what is apprehended mentally—is not to be worshiped in virtue of its being created, but it is to be worshiped as having been united with God the Word on account of him and in him. Consider the following examples. The emperor is held in reverence whether he is naked or dressed, and the purple robe, simply as a purple robe, is trodden on and thrown aside, but when it becomes an imperial vestment it is honored and glorified, and if anyone treats its with contempt he is generally condemned to death. A mere piece of wood is not inaccessible to the sense of touch, but when it is brought into contact with fire and becomes a coal, it does become inaccessible through the fire that is united with it, not because the nature of the wood is inaccessible but because of the coal or the heated wood. In the same way, the flesh is not susceptible of worship in its own nature, but is worshiped in the incarnate Word of God, not in itself but on account of the divine Word united hypostatically with it, and we do not say that we worship mere flesh but the flesh of God, that is to say, God incarnate.

77 Διὰ τί ὁ υἱὸς ἐνηνθρώπησε καὶ οὐχ ὁ πατὴρ οὐδὲ τὸ πνεῦμα καὶ τί ἐνανθρωπήσας κατώρθωσεν

Πατὴρ ὁ πατὴρ καὶ οὐχ υἱός, υἱὸς ὁ υἱὸς καὶ οὐ πατήρ, πνεῦμα ἅγιον τὸ πνεῦμα καὶ οὐ πατὴρ οὐδὲ υἱός· ἡ γὰρ ἰδιότης ἀκίνητος. Ἢ πῶς ἂν ἰδιότης εἴη κινουμένη καὶ μεταπίπτουσα; Διὰ τοῦτο ὁ υἱὸς τοῦ θεοῦ υἱὸς ἀνθρώπου γίνεται, ἵνα μείνῃ ἡ ἰδιότης ἀκίνητος· υἱὸς γὰρ ὢν τοῦ θεοῦ υἱὸς ἀνθρώπου γέγονεν σαρκωθεὶς ἐκ τῆς ἁγίας παρθένου, καὶ οὐκ ἐξέστη τῆς οἰκείας ἰδιότητος.

Ἐνηνθρώπησε δὲ ὁ υἱὸς τοῦ θεοῦ, ἵνα, ἐφ᾽ ὅπερ ἐποίησε τὸν ἄνθρωπον, πάλιν αὐτῷ χαρίσηται· ἐποίησε γὰρ αὐτὸν κατ᾽ εἰκόνα ἑαυτοῦ νοερὸν καὶ αὐτεξούσιον καὶ καθ᾽ ὁμοιότητα ἤτοι ἐν ἀρεταῖς τέλειον ὡς ἐφικτὸν ἀνθρώπου φύσει· αὗται γὰρ οἱονεὶ χαρακτῆρες τῆς θείας ὑπάρχουσι φύσεως· τὸ ἀμέριμνον καὶ ἀπερίσπαστον καὶ ἀκέραιον, τὸ ἀγαθόν, τὸ σοφόν, τὸ δίκαιον, τὸ πάσης κακίας ἐλεύθερον. Ἐν κοινωνίᾳ μὲν οὖν ἑαυτοῦ καταστήσας τὸν ἄνθρωπον («ἐπ᾽ ἀφθαρσίᾳ γὰρ τοῦτον ἐποίησε»), διὰ δὲ τῆς ἑαυτοῦ κοινωνίας ἀνήγαγεν αὐτὸν πρὸς τὸ ἄφθαρτον. Ἐπειδὴ δὲ διὰ τῆς παραβάσεως τῆς ἐντολῆς τοὺς τῆς θείας εἰκόνος χαρακτῆρας ἐζοφώσαμέν τε καὶ συνεχέαμεν καὶ ἐν κακίᾳ γενόμενοι τῆς θείας κοινωνίας ἐγυμνώθημεν («τίς γὰρ μετουσία πρὸς σκότος φωτί;») καὶ ἔξω τῆς ζωῆς γενόμενοι τῇ τοῦ θανάτου φθορᾷ ὑπεπέσαμεν, ἐπειδὴ μετέδωκε τοῦ κρείττονος καὶ οὐκ ἐφυλάξαμεν, μεταλαμβάνει τοῦ χείρονος, τῆς ἡμετέρας λέγω φύσεως, ἵνα δι᾽ ἑαυτοῦ ἐν ἑαυτῷ ἀνακαινίσῃ μὲν τὸ κατ᾽ εἰκόνα καὶ καθ᾽ ὁμοίωσιν, διδάξῃ δὲ ἡμᾶς τὴν ἐνάρετον πολιτείαν καὶ ταύτην δι᾽ ἑαυτοῦ ποιήσῃ ἡμῖν εὐεπίβατον καὶ τῇ τῆς ζωῆς κοινωνίᾳ ἐλευθερώσῃ τῆς φθορᾶς ἀπαρχὴ γενόμενος τῆς ἡμῶν ἀναστάσεως καὶ τὸ ἀχρειωθὲν καὶ συντριβὲν σκεῦος ἀνακαινίσῃ,

[1]Was the incarnation a response to the fall or was it intrinsic to the divine plan for the cosmos? John is in accord with Maximus the Confessor that "the whole of Creation is for the sake of the mystery of Christ." Torstein T. Tollefsen, "Christocentric Cosmology," in *The Oxford Handbook of Maximus the Confessor*, ed. Pauline Allen and Bronwen Neil (Oxford: Oxford University Press, 2015), 307–21, at 308. But cf.

77   Why it was the Son who became inhominated and not the Father or the Spirit and what he achieved by having become inhominated

The Father is father and not son, the Son is son and not father, the Holy Spirit is spirit and neither father nor son, for the distinctive property is unchangeable. Otherwise how would it be a distinctive property if it were subject to change and modification? It was for this reason that the Son of God became Son of Man, that his distinctive property might remain unchanged. For since he was Son of God, he became Son of Man through being made flesh from the holy Virgin, and did not abandon his own distinctive property.

The Son of God became inhominated so that he might again grant humanity that for which he had created it.[1] For he created it in his image as rational and possessing free will and in his likeness, which means as perfect in the virtues as is possible for human nature. For these are impresses, as it were, of the divine nature: absence of anxiety and distraction, integrity, goodness, wisdom, justice, freedom from all evil. For he set humanity to be in communion with himself ("he created it for incorruption"[2]) and through this communion with himself he raised it up to incorruption. But because through the transgression of the commandment we darkened and smudged the characteristics of the divine image, and having entered into an evil state were stripped of divine communion ("for what partnership is there between darkness and light"[3]) and having put ourselves outside life, we became subject to the corruption of death, because he gave us a share of what was better and we did not maintain it, he partakes of what is worse, I mean, of our own nature, in order that through himself and in himself he might renew what is in the image and likeness and also teach us the life of virtue and make this easily attainable for us through him, and having become

Chapter 86, where John presents the historical incarnation as the divine remedy for the consequences of the fall.
   [2]Wis 2.23.
   [3]2 Cor 6.14.

ἵνα τῆς τυραννίδος τοῦ διαβόλου λυτρώσηται πρὸς θεογνωσίαν ἡμᾶς καλέσας καὶ νευρώσῃ καὶ παιδεύσῃ δι' ὑπομονῆς καὶ ταπεινώσεως καταπαλαίειν τὸν τύραννον.

Πέπαυται γοῦν ἡ τῶν δαιμόνων θρησκεία, ἡ κτίσις τῷ θείῳ ἡγίασται αἵματι, βωμοὶ καὶ ναοὶ εἰδώλων καθῄρηνται, θεογνωσία πεφύτευται, τριὰς ἡ ὁμοούσιος, ἡ ἄκτιστος θεότης λατρεύεται, εἷς θεὸς ἀληθής, δημιουργὸς τῶν ἁπάντων καὶ κύριος· ἀρεταὶ πολιτεύονται, ἀναστάσεως ἐλπὶς διὰ τῆς Χριστοῦ δεδώρηται ἀναστάσεως, φρίττουσι τοὺς πάλαι ὑποχειρίους ἀνθρώπους οἱ δαίμονες, καὶ τό γε θαυμαστόν, ὅτι ταῦτα πάντα διὰ σταυροῦ καὶ παθῶν καὶ θανάτου κατώρθωται· εἰς πᾶσαν τὴν γῆν τὸ εὐαγγέλιον τῆς θεογνωσίας κεκήρυκται οὐ πολέμῳ καὶ ὅπλοις καὶ στρατοπέδοις τοὺς ἐναντίους τροπούμενον, ἀλλ' ὀλίγοι πτωχοί, ἀγράμματοι, διωκόμενοι, αἰκιζόμενοι, θανατούμενοι σταυρωθέντα σαρκὶ καὶ θανόντα κηρύττοντες τῶν σοφῶν καὶ δυνατῶν κατεκράτησαν· εἵπετο γὰρ αὐτοῖς τοῦ σταυρωθέντος ἡ παντοδύναμος δύναμις. Ὁ θάνατος ὁ πάλαι φοβερώτατος ἥττηται, καὶ τῆς ζωῆς νῦν ὁ στυγητὸς καὶ μισητὸς πάλαι προκρίνεται. Ταῦτα τῆς Χριστοῦ παρουσίας τὰ κατορθώματα, ταῦτα τῆς αὐτοῦ δυνάμεως τὰ γνωρίσματα. Οὐ γὰρ ὡς διὰ Μωσέως ἕνα λαὸν ἐξ Αἰγύπτου καὶ τῆς Φαραὼ δουλείας θάλασσαν διαστήσας διέσωσε, πᾶσαν δὲ μᾶλλον τὴν ἀνθρωπότητα ἐκ φθορᾶς θανάτου καὶ τοῦ πικροῦ τυράννου, τῆς ἁμαρτίας, ἐρρύσατο, οὐ βίᾳ ἄγων πρὸς ἀρετήν, οὐ γῇ καταχωννὺς καὶ πυρὶ φλέγων καὶ λιθοβολεῖσθαι προστάττων τοὺς ἁμαρτάνοντας, ἀλλὰ πραότητι καὶ μακροθυμίᾳ τοὺς ἀνθρώπους πείθων αἱρεῖσθαι τὴν ἀρετὴν καὶ τοῖς ὑπὲρ ταύτης ἐναμιλλᾶσθαι πόνοις καὶ ἐνηδύνεσθαι· πάλαι μὲν γὰρ ἁμαρτάνοντες ᾐκίζοντο καὶ ἔτι τῆς ἁμαρτίας ἀντείχοντο, καὶ θεὸς αὐτοῖς ἡ ἁμαρτία λελόγιστο· νῦν δὲ ὑπὲρ εὐσεβείας καὶ ἀρετῆς αἰκισμοὺς αἱροῦνται καὶ στρεβλώσεις καὶ θάνατον.

the first-fruits of our resurrection might free us from corruption through communion with life and renew the vessel that had become useless and broken, that he might free us from the tyranny of the devil, having called us to the knowledge of God, and strengthen and teach us by patience and humility how to overcome the tyrant.

The cult of the demons has been stopped, creation has been sanctified by the divine blood, altars and temples of idols have been destroyed, knowledge of God has been implanted, the consubstantial Trinity, the uncreated Godhead, is worshiped as one true God, Creator of all things and Lord, virtues are put into practice, hope of resurrection is granted through the resurrection of Christ, the demons who previously had human beings in their power shudder, and what is amazing is that all these things were achieved through the cross and suffering and death. The gospel of the knowledge of God is proclaimed throughout the whole world, and has put the adversaries to flight not by war and weapons and military camps, but by a few poor men, uneducated, persecuted, tortured, and put to death, who by preaching him who was crucified in the flesh and put to death prevailed over the wise and the powerful, for the almighty power of him who was crucified accompanied them. Death, which was once most dreaded, has been defeated, and now that which was once abominated and hated is preferred to life. These things are the achievements of Christ's appearance. These things are the marks of his power. For he did not save a single people from Egypt and slavery to Pharaoh by dividing the sea, as he did through Moses. Instead, it was humanity as a whole that he delivered from the corruption of death and from the bitter tyrant, which is sin, leading it to virtue without the use of force, not overwhelming sinners with earth and burning them with fire and ordering them to be stoned, but persuading people gently and patiently to choose virtue and for virtue's sake to contend in struggling and to find pleasure in it. For formerly those who sinned were tortured yet still clung to their sin, and sin was considered their god, but now for the sake of piety and virtue they choose torture and stretching on the rack and death.

Εὖγε, ὦ Χριστέ, θεοῦ λόγε καὶ σοφία καὶ δύναμις καὶ θεὲ παντοκράτορ. Τί σοι τούτων ἁπάντων οἱ ἄποροι ἡμεῖς ἀντιδοίημεν; Σὰ γὰρ ἅπαντα, καὶ αἰτεῖς παρ' ἡμῶν οὐδὲν ἢ τὸ σῴζεσθαι, αὐτὸς καὶ τοῦτο διδοὺς καὶ λαμβάνουσι χάριν εἰδὼς δι' ἄφατον ἀγαθότητα—σοὶ χάρις τῷ τὸ εἶναι δεδωκότι καὶ τὸ εὖ εἶναι χαρισαμένῳ—κἀκ τούτου παραπεσόντας αὖθις ἐπαναγαγὼν πρὸς τοῦτο διὰ τῆς ἀφάτου συγκαταβάσεως.

78 *Πρὸς τοὺς ἐρωτῶντας, εἰ ἡ ὑπόστασις τοῦ Χριστοῦ κτιστή ἐστιν ἢ ἄκτιστος*

Ἡ ὑπόστασις τοῦ θεοῦ λόγου πρὸ τῆς σαρκώσεως ἁπλῆ ἦν καὶ ἀσύνθετος καὶ ἀσώματος καὶ ἄκτιστος, σαρκωθεῖσα δὲ αὕτη γέγονε καὶ τῇ σαρκὶ ὑπόστασις καὶ γέγονε σύνθετος ἐκ θεότητος, ἧς ἀεὶ εἶχε, καὶ ἐξ ἧς προσείληφε σαρκός, καὶ φέρει τῶν δύο φύσεων τὰ ἰδιώματα ἐν δυσὶ γνωριζομένη ταῖς φύσεσιν, ὥστε ἡ αὐτὴ μία ὑπόστασις ἄκτιστός τέ ἐστι τῇ θεότητι καὶ κτιστὴ τῇ ἀνθρωπότητι, ὁρατὴ καὶ ἀόρατος· ἐπεὶ ἀναγκαζόμεθα ἢ διαιρεῖν τὸν ἕνα Χριστὸν δύο τὰς ὑποστάσεις λέγοντες ἢ τὴν τῶν φύσεων ἀρνεῖσθαι διαφορὰν καὶ τροπὴν εἰσάγειν καὶ σύγχυσιν.

79 *Περὶ τοῦ πότε ἐκλήθη Χριστός*

Οὐχ, ὥς τινες ψευδηγοροῦσι, πρὸ τῆς ἐκ παρθένου σαρκώσεως ὁ νοῦς ἡνώθη τῷ θεῷ λόγῳ καὶ ἐκ τότε ἐκλήθη Χριστός· τοῦτο τῶν Ὠριγένους ληρημάτων τὸ ἀπότημα προϋπαρξιν τῶν ψυχῶν δογματίσαντος. Ἡμεῖς δὲ Χριστὸν γεγενῆσθαί τε καὶ κεκλῆσθαί φαμεν τὸν υἱὸν καὶ λόγον τοῦ θεοῦ, ἀφ' οὗ ἐν τῇ γαστρὶ τῆς ἁγίας ἀειπαρθένου ἐσκήνωσε καὶ σὰρξ ἀτρέπτως ἐγένετο καὶ ἐχρίσθη ἡ

Well done, O Christ, Word of God and wisdom and power and all sovereign-God! What shall we, who possess nothing, offer you in return for all these things? Everything is yours, and you ask nothing from us except to be saved. Even this you have given yourself and you thank those who accept it through your ineffable goodness—thanks be to you who have granted us being and well-being—and through your ineffable condescension you lead those who have fallen away from it back again to it.

78   *To those who ask whether Christ's hypostasis is created or uncreated*

Before the incarnation the hypostasis of God the Word was simple and non-composite and incorporeal and uncreated, but once it had been enfleshed it also became a hypostasis with regard to the flesh and became composite from the divinity that it always possessed and from the flesh which it received in addition, and bears the properties of the two natures acknowledged in the two natures, with the result that the same single hypostasis is both uncreated with respect to the divinity and created with respect to the humanity, being both visible and invisible. Otherwise we would be obliged either to divide the one Christ by saying that there are two hypostases, or to deny the difference and introduce change and confusion.

79   *On when Christ was called such*

The mind was not united with God the Word before taking flesh from the Virgin, and was called Christ from that time, as some falsely declare. This is the result of the ravings of Origen, who laid down the dogma of the pre-existence of souls.[1] But we say that Christ became the Son and Word of God and was called such from the time that he came to dwell in the womb of the holy ever-Virgin and became

[1]The second of the anti-Origenist canons of 543 anathematized anyone who held that the Lord's soul pre-existed before the incarnation. See Price, *The Acts of the Council of Constantinople of 553*, 2:281.

234 SAINT JOHN OF DAMASCUS

σὰρξ τῇ θεότητι· «χρίσις γὰρ αὕτη τῆς ἀνθρωπότητος», ὥς φησιν ὁ θεολόγος Γρηγόριος. Καὶ ὁ ἱερώτατος δὲ τῆς Ἀλεξανδρέων Κύριλλος πρὸς τὸν βασιλέα Θεοδόσιον γράφων τάδε φησίν· «Χρῆναι γὰρ ἔγωγέ φημι μήτε τὸν ἐκ θεοῦ λόγον ἀνθρωπότητος δίχα μήτε μὴν τὸν ἐκ γυναικὸς ἀποτεχθέντα ναὸν οὐχ ἑνωθέντα τῷ λόγῳ Χριστὸν Ἰησοῦν ὀνομάζεσθαι· ἀνθρωπότητι γὰρ καθ᾽ ἕνωσιν οἰκονομικὴν ἀπορρήτως συνενηνεγμένος ὁ ἐκ θεοῦ λόγος νοεῖται Χριστός». Καὶ πρὸς τὰς βασιλίδας οὕτως· «Τινές φασιν, ὅτι τὸ Χριστὸς ὄνομα πρέπει καὶ μόνῳ καὶ ἰδίᾳ καθ᾽ αὑτὸν νοουμένῳ καὶ ὑπάρχοντι, τῷ ἐκ θεοῦ πατρὸς γεννηθέντι λόγῳ. Ἡμεῖς δὲ οὐχ οὕτως δεδιδάγμεθα φρονεῖν ἢ λέγειν· ὅτε γὰρ γέγονε σὰρξ ὁ λόγος, τότε καὶ ὠνομάσθαι λέγομεν Χριστὸν Ἰησοῦν. Ἐπειδὴ γὰρ κέχρισται τῷ ἐλαίῳ τῆς ἀγαλλιάσεως ἤτοι τῷ ἁγίῳ πνεύματι παρὰ τοῦ θεοῦ καὶ πατρός, ταύτῃ τοι Χριστὸς ὀνομάζεται. Ὅτι δὲ περὶ τὸ ἀνθρώπινον ἡ χρίσις, οὐκ ἂν ἐνδυάσειέ τις τῶν ὀρθὰ φρονεῖν εἰωθότων». Καὶ Ἀθανάσιος δὲ ὁ παναοίδιμος ἐν τῷ περὶ τῆς σωτηριώδους ἐπιφανείας ὧδέ πη λέγει· «Ὁ προϋπάρχων θεὸς πρὸ τῆς ἐν σαρκὶ ἐπιδημίας οὐκ ἦν ἄνθρωπος, ἀλλὰ θεὸς ἦν πρὸς τὸν θεὸν ἀόρατος καὶ ἀπαθὴς ὤν· οὔτε οὖν τὸ Χριστὸς ὄνομα δίχα τῆς σαρκὸς προσάγεται, ἐπειδὴ ἀκολουθεῖ τῷ ὀνόματι τὸ πάθος καὶ ὁ θάνατος».

Εἰ δὲ ἡ θεία γραφή φησι· «Διὰ τοῦτο ἔχρισέ σε ὁ θεὸς ὁ θεός σου», ἰστέον ὡς πολλάκις ἡ θεία γραφὴ κέχρηται τῷ παρῳχηκότι χρόνῳ ἀντὶ τοῦ μέλλοντος, ὡς τὸ «μετὰ ταῦτα ἐπὶ τῆς γῆς ὤφθη καὶ τοῖς ἀνθρώποις συνανεστράφη» (οὔπω γὰρ ὤφθη οὐδὲ συνανεστράφη θεὸς ἀνθρώποις, ὅτε ταῦτα ἐλέγετο) καὶ τὸ «ἐπὶ τῶν ποταμῶν Βαβυλῶνος, ἐκεῖ ἐκαθίσαμεν καὶ ἐκλαύσαμεν» (οὔπω δὲ ταῦτα ἐγεγόνει).

[2]Gregory of Nazianzus, *Oration* 30.2 (Moreschini, 720) and 30.21 (Moreschini, 744).
[3]Cyril of Alexandria, *On the Correct Faith to Theodosius* (ACO I.1.1) 60.17—20. The "economic union" is the union according to the dispensation of the incarnation.
[4]Cyril of Alexandria, *On the Correct Faith to Arcadia and Marina* (ACO I.1.5)

flesh without undergoing change and that the flesh was anointed by the divinity. "For this was the anointing of the humanity," as Gregory the Theologian says.[2] And the most holy Cyril of the Alexandrians, writing to the emperor Theodosius, says the following: "For I myself hold that one should give the name of Christ Jesus neither to the Word from God without his humanity, nor to the temple born from a woman but not united with the Word. For the Word from God is understood to be Christ once he has been united ineffably to the humanity by the economic union."[3] And to the empresses he wrote as follows: "Some say that the name of Christ is given correctly only to the Word begotten from God the Father, to him alone as conceived of separately by himself and existing in his own right. But we have not been taught to think and speak in this way. For it was when the Word became flesh that we say he was called Christ Jesus. It was because he was anointed with the oil of gladness, namely, with the Holy Spirit from God the Father, that he was called Christ. That the anointing concerned what was human, no one who is accustomed to thinking correctly can doubt."[4] And the renowned Athanasius says somewhere in his discourse on the saving coming of Christ: "He who existed as God before his appearance in the flesh was not a human being, but being invisible and impassible was God in relation to God. Therefore neither is the name 'Christ' applicable to him without the flesh, since the passion and death follow upon the name."[5]

And if divine Scripture says: "Therefore God your God has anointed you,"[6] one should know that divine Scripture frequently uses the past tense instead of the future, as in the phrase: "After these things he was seen upon earth and lived among men"[7] (for God had not yet been seen by human beings nor had he lived with them), and: "By the rivers of Babylon, there we sat down and wept"[8] (for these things had not yet happened).

69.31–7. These two passages from Cyril are reproduced in *Doctrina Patrum*, Diekamp, 26.11–14, from which John has clearly taken them.

   [5](Ps.-)Athanasius of Alexandria, *On the Incarnation against Apollinaris* 2.1 (PG 26:1133B). This passage, too, is from the *Doctrina Patrum*, Diekamp, 25.20–26.

   [6]Ps 44.8.   [7]Bar 3.38.   [8]Ps 136.1.

80 Πρὸς τοὺς ἐρωτῶντας, εἰ δύο φύσεις ἐγέννησεν ἡ ἁγία
θεοτόκος, εἰ δύο φύσεις ἐπὶ σταυροῦ ἐκρέμαντο

Φύσεως μέν ἐστι τὸ ἀγένητον καὶ τὸ γενητὸν δι᾽ ἑνὸς τοῦ ν
γραφόμενον, ὅπερ δηλοῖ τὸ ἄκτιστον καὶ κτιστόν· τὸ δὲ ἀγέννητον
καὶ γεννητὸν οὐ φύσεως, ἀλλ᾽ ὑποστάσεως ἤτοι τὸ γεννηθῆναι καὶ
τὸ μὴ γεννηθῆναι, ὅπερ διὰ τῶν δύο νν ἐκφέρεται. Ἔστι οὖν ἡ μὲν
θεία φύσις ἀγένητος ἤτοι ἄκτιστος, πάντα δὲ τὰ μετὰ τὴν θείαν
φύσιν γενητὰ ἤτοι κτιστά. Θεωρεῖται τοίνυν ἐν μὲν τῇ θείᾳ καὶ
ἀκτίστῳ φύσει τὸ μὲν ἀγέννητον ἐν τῷ πατρί (οὐ γὰρ ἐγεννήθη),
τὸ δὲ γεννητὸν ἐν τῷ υἱῷ (ἐκ πατρὸς γὰρ ἀιδίως γεγέννηται), τὸ
δὲ ἐκπορευτὸν ἐν τῷ ἁγίῳ πνεύματι. Ἑκάστου δὲ εἴδους ζῴων
τὰ μὲν πρῶτα ἀγέννητα, ἀλλ᾽ οὐκ ἀγένητα· γεγόνασι μὲν γὰρ
ὑπὸ τοῦ δημιουργοῦ, οὐκ ἐγεννήθησαν δὲ ἐξ ὁμοίων. Γένεσις μὲν
κτιστή ἐστι, γέννησις δὲ ἐπὶ μὲν θεοῦ ἐκ μόνου πατρὸς ὁμοουσίου
υἱοῦ πρόοδος, ἐπὶ δὲ τῶν κτισμάτων ἡ ἐκ συναφείας ἄρρενός τε
καὶ θηλείας ὁμοουσίου ὑποστάσεως πρόοδος. Ὅθεν γινώσκομεν,
ὡς οὐκ ἔστι φύσεως τὸ γεννᾶσθαι, ἀλλ᾽ ὑποστάσεως. Εἰ γὰρ
φύσεως ἦν, οὐκ ἂν ἐν τῇ αὐτῇ φύσει τὸ γεννητὸν ἐθεωρεῖτο καὶ τὸ
ἀγέννητον. Ὑπόστασιν τοίνυν ἐγέννησεν ἡ ἁγία θεοτόκος ἐν δυσὶ
γνωριζομένην ταῖς φύσεσι, θεότητι μὲν ἐκ πατρὸς γεννηθεῖσαν
ἀχρόνως, ἐπ᾽ ἐσχάτων δὲ ἐν χρόνῳ ἐξ αὐτῆς σαρκωθεῖσαν καὶ
σαρκὶ τικτομένην. Εἰ δὲ οἱ ἐρωτῶντες αἰνίττοιντο, ὅτι ὁ γεννηθεὶς
ἐκ τῆς ἁγίας θεοτόκου δύο φύσεις ἐστί, φαμέν· Ναί, δύο φύσεις
ἐστί· «θεὸς γάρ ἐστιν ὁ αὐτὸς καὶ ἄνθρωπος». Ὁμοίως καὶ περὶ
τῆς σταυρώσεως ἀναστάσεώς τε καὶ ἀναλήψεως· οὐ φύσεως
ταῦτά ἐστιν, ἀλλ᾽ ὑποστάσεως. Ἔπαθεν οὖν ὁ Χριστὸς ὁ ἐν
δύο φύσεσιν ὢν τῇ παθητῇ φύσει ἐσταυρώθη τε· σαρκὶ γὰρ ἐπὶ
σταυροῦ ἐκρέματο καὶ οὐ θεότητι. Ἐπεὶ εἴπωσιν, ἡμῖν ἐρωτῶσιν·
Δύο φύσεις ἀπέθανον; Οὐχί, ἐροῦσιν. Οὐκοῦν οὐδὲ δύο φύσεις
ἐσταυρώθησαν, ἀλλ᾽ ἐγεννήθη ὁ Χριστὸς ἤτοι ὁ θεὸς λόγος
ἐνανθρωπήσας, ἐγεννήθη σαρκί, ἐσταυρώθη σαρκί, ἔπαθε σαρκί,
ἀπέθανε σαρκί, ἀπαθοῦς μεινάσης αὐτοῦ τῆς θεότητος.

80 *To those who ask whether the holy Theotokos gave birth to two natures, or whether two natures hung upon the cross*

The terms ἀγένητον (*agenēton*, "unoriginated") and γενητόν (*genēton*, "originated") written with one "ν" ("*n*") belong to a nature, and mean "uncreated" and "created," whereas the terms ἀγέννητον (*agennēton*, "ungenerated") and γεννητόν (*gennēton*, "generated") belong not to a nature but to a hypostasis, as do γεννηθῆναι (*gennēthēnai*, "to be begotten") and μὴ γεννηθῆναι (*mē gennēthēnai*, "to be unbegotten"), which is expressed by the two "ν"s ("*n*"s). Thus, on the one hand, the divine nature is unoriginated or uncreated, but on the other, everything that comes after the divine nature is originated or created. Now, within the divine and uncreated nature unbegottenness is contemplated in the Father (for he was not begotten) but begottenness in the Son (for he is eternally begotten by the Father) and procession in the Holy Spirit. Of each species of animal the first in the series is ungenerated but not unoriginated, for they have been originated by the Creator, and have not been begotten from their own kind. Origin means created but begetting in the case of God refers only to the issuing forth from the Father alone of the consubstantial Son. In the case of creatures, however, begetting refers to the coming forth from the union of male and female of a hypostasis of the same substance. From this we know that begetting belongs not to a nature but to a hypostasis. For if it belonged to a nature, both begottenness and unbegottenness could not be contemplated in the same nature. Therefore the holy Theotokos gave birth to a hypostasis acknowledged in two natures, on the one hand in the divinity begotten timelessly from the Father, and on the other in the flesh enfleshed temporally from her in these last days and brought to birth by her.

If those who question us should intimate that he who was born of the holy Theotokos has two natures, we say, "Yes indeed, there are two natures, for 'the same is both God and man.'"[1] And likewise with

---

[1] Cyril of Alexandria, *Third Letter to Nestorius* (*Letter* 17), Anathema 2 (Wickham, 28).

81 *Πῶς πρωτότοκος λέγεται ὁ μονογενὴς υἱὸς τοῦ θεοῦ*

Πρωτότοκός ἐστιν ὁ πρῶτος γεννηθεὶς εἴτε μονογενής, εἴτε καὶ πρὸ ἄλλων ἀδελφῶν. Εἰ μὲν οὖν ἐλέγετο ὁ υἱὸς τοῦ θεοῦ πρωτότοκος, μονογενὴς δὲ οὐκ ἐλέγετο, ὑπενοήσαμεν ἂν κτισμάτων αὐτὸν εἶναι πρωτότοκον ὡς κτίσμα ὑπάρχοντα. Ἐπειδὴ δὲ καὶ πρωτότοκος καὶ μονογενὴς λέγεται, δεῖ δὲ καὶ ἀμφότερα τηρῆσαι ἐπ᾽ αὐτοῦ. «Πρωτότοκον» μὲν αὐτόν φαμεν «πάσης κτίσεως», ἐπειδὴ καὶ αὐτὸς ἐκ τοῦ θεοῦ καὶ ἡ κτίσις ἐκ τοῦ θεοῦ, ἀλλ᾽ αὐτὸς μὲν ἐκ τῆς οὐσίας τοῦ θεοῦ καὶ πατρὸς μόνος ἀχρόνως γεγεννημένος εἰκότως υἱὸς μονογενὴς πρωτότοκος καὶ οὐ πρωτόκτιστος λεχθήσεται· ἡ γὰρ κτίσις οὐκ ἐκ τῆς οὐσίας τοῦ πατρός, ἀλλὰ θελήματι αὐτοῦ ἐκ τοῦ μὴ ὄντος εἰς τὸ εἶναι παρήχθη. «Πρωτότοκος δὲ ἐν πολλοῖς ἀδελφοῖς»· μονογενὴς γὰρ ὢν καὶ ἐκ μητρὸς ἐπειδήπερ μετέσχηκεν αἵματος καὶ σαρκὸς παραπλησίως ἡμῖν καὶ ἄνθρωπος γέγονε. Γεγόναμεν δὲ καὶ ἡμεῖς δι᾽ αὐτοῦ υἱοὶ θεοῦ υἱοθετηθέντες διὰ τοῦ βαπτίσματος· αὐτὸς ὁ φύσει υἱὸς τοῦ θεοῦ πρωτότοκος ἐν ἡμῖν τοῖς θέσει καὶ χάριτι υἱοῖς θεοῦ γενομένοις καὶ ἀδελφοῖς αὐτοῦ χρηματίσασι γέγονεν. Ὅθεν ἔλεγεν· «Ἀναβαίνω πρὸς τὸν πατέρα μου καὶ πατέρα ὑμῶν.» Οὐκ εἶπε· πατέρα ἡμῶν, ἀλλὰ «πατέρα μου», φύσει δῆλον, καὶ «πατέρα ὑμῶν» χάριτι, καὶ «θεόν μου καὶ θεὸν ὑμῶν». Καὶ οὐκ εἶπε θεὸν ἡμῶν, ἀλλὰ «θεόν μου», ἂν διέλῃς λεπταῖς ἐπινοίαις τὸ

regard to the crucifixion, resurrection, and ascension: these belong
not to the nature but to the hypostasis. Thus Christ, who exists in two
natures, suffered in his passible nature and was crucified, for he hung
upon the cross in the flesh but not in the divinity. When we put the
question to them, "Did two natures die?" they will say, "Certainly not."
Therefore neither were two natures crucified. On the contrary, Christ
was engendered, that is to say, God the Word was inhominated, was
engendered in the flesh, crucified in the flesh, suffered in the flesh,
died in the flesh, while remaining impassible in his divinity.

81   *How it is that the only-begotten Son of God is called
         "first-born"*

A first-born is the first to be born, whether as the only child or as
preceding other brothers and sisters. Therefore if the Son of God
had been called first-born but had not been called only-begotten, we
would have assumed him to be the first-born of creation as himself
a creature. But because he is called both first-born and only-begotten, both of these must be observed in his case. We say that he is
"the first-born of all creation"[1] because he is from God and creation
is also from God, but since he alone has been begotten timelessly
from the essence of God the Father, he is appropriately said to be
first-born but not first-created. For creation is not from the essence
of the Father but has been brought out of non-being into being by
his will. And he is "first-born among many brothers and sisters,"[2]
in that while being only-begotten, he was also born from a mother
since in fact he came to share in blood and flesh like us and became
a human being. And we ourselves became through him sons of God
as a result of our adoption through baptism. He who is by nature Son
of God became first-born among us who have become sons of God
by adoption and grace and have been called his brothers and sisters.
That is why he said: "I am ascending to my Father and your Father."[3]
He did not say: "our Father" but "my Father," that is to say, by nature,

[1] Col 1.15.   [2] Rom 8.29.   [3] Jn 20.17.

ὁρώμενον ἐκ τοῦ νοουμένου, καὶ «θεὸν ὑμῶν» ὡς δημιουργὸν καὶ κύριον.

81b *Πρὸς τοὺς ἐρωτῶντας, εἰ ὑπὸ τὸ συνεχὲς ποσὸν ἀνάγονται ἢ ὑπὸ τὸ διωρισμένον αἱ δύο φύσεις*

Αἱ τοῦ κυρίου φύσεις οὔτε ἓν σῶμά εἰσιν, οὔτε ἐπιφάνεια οὔτε γραμμή, οὐ τόπος, οὐ χρόνος, ἵνα ὑπὸ τὸ συνεχὲς ποσὸν ἀναχθῶσι· ταῦτα γάρ εἰσι τὰ συνεχῶς ἀριθμούμενα. Ἥνωνται δὲ αἱ τοῦ κυρίου φύσεις ἀσυγχύτως καθ᾽ ὑπόστασιν καὶ διῄρηνται ἀδιαιρέτως λόγῳ καὶ τρόπῳ τῆς διαφορᾶς. Καὶ ᾧ μὲν τρόπῳ ἥνωνται, οὐκ ἀριθμοῦνται (οὐ γὰρ λέγομεν δύο ὑποστάσεις εἶναι τὰς φύσεις τοῦ Χριστοῦ ἢ δύο κατὰ τὴν ὑπόστασιν), ᾧ δὲ τρόπῳ ἀδιαιρέτως διῄρηνται, ἀριθμοῦνται (δύο γάρ εἰσι φύσεις λόγῳ καὶ τρόπῳ τῆς διαφορᾶς)· ἡνωμέναι γὰρ καθ᾽ ὑπόστασιν καὶ ἐν ἀλλήλαις περιχωροῦσαι ἀσυγχύτως ἥνωνται τὴν εἰς ἀλλήλας μεταβολὴν οὐ δεξάμεναι, τὴν οἰκείαν ἑκάστη φυσικὴν διαφορὰν καὶ μετὰ τὴν ἕνωσιν διασῴζουσα· τὸ γὰρ κτιστὸν μεμένηκε κτιστόν, καὶ τὸ ἄκτιστον ἄκτιστον. Τῷ τρόπῳ τοίνυν τῆς διαφορᾶς καὶ μόνῳ ἀριθμούμεναι ὑπὸ τὸ διωρισμένον ποσὸν ἀναχθήσονται. Ἀδύνατον γὰρ τὰ κατὰ μηδὲν διαφέροντα ἀριθμεῖσθαι· καθὸ δὲ διαφέρουσι, κατὰ τοῦτο καὶ ἀριθμοῦνται, οἷον ὁ Πέτρος καὶ ὁ Παῦλος, καθὸ μὲν ἥνωνται, οὐκ ἀριθμοῦνται (τῷ λόγῳ γὰρ τῆς οὐσίας ἐνούμενοι δύο φύσεις οὐδὲ εἰσὶν οὐδὲ λέγονται), καθ᾽ ὑπόστασιν δὲ διαφέροντες δύο ὑποστάσεις λέγονται. Ὥστε ἡ διαφορὰ αἰτία τοῦ ἀριθμοῦ.

and "your Father" by grace, and [he added] "my God and your God." He did not say "our God," but "my God" (if by subtle notions you separate what is visible from what is conceived mentally), and "your God," as Creator and Lord.

81b *To those who ask whether the two natures are to be reckoned as a continuous quantity or as a disjunctive quantity*[1]

The Lord's natures neither form a single body, nor are they a surface or a line, nor a place, nor time, that they may be reckoned as forming a continuous quantity, for these are the things that are enumerated by conjunction. The Lord's natures are united hypostatically without confusion and are divided indivisibly by reason and mode of difference. And they are not enumerated in the mode by which they are united (for we do not say that Christ's natures are two hypostases or two hypostatically), but they are enumerated in the mode by which they are indivisibly divided (for there are two natures by reason and mode of difference). For since they are united hypostatically and mutually interpenetrate each other, they are united without confusion. They are not susceptible of change into each other, but each preserves its own natural difference even after the union. For the created remained created and the uncreated remained uncreated. Therefore only when they are enumerated are they to be referred to a disjunctive quantity and then only by the mode of the difference. For it is impossible for things that differ in no way at all to be enumerated. They are enumerated insofar as they differ, like Peter and Paul, but insofar as they are united they are not enumerated (for two natures are not united by reason of the essence, nor are they said to be so), but two hypostases are said to differ hypostatically. Consequently, it is difference that is the cause of number.

---

[1]This chapter is added in manuscripts BEGHIKL. It closely reproduces much of Chapter 52.

82 *Περὶ πίστεως καὶ βαπτίσματος*

Ὁμολογοῦμεν δὲ ἓν βάπτισμα εἰς ἄφεσιν ἁμαρτιῶν καὶ εἰς ζωὴν αἰώνιον· τὸ γὰρ βάπτισμα τὸν τοῦ κυρίου θάνατον δηλοῖ. Συνθαπτόμεθα γοῦν τῷ κυρίῳ διὰ τοῦ βαπτίσματος, ὥς φησιν ὁ θεῖος ἀπόστολος. Ὥσπερ οὖν ἅπαξ ἐτελέσθη ὁ τοῦ κυρίου θάνατος, οὕτω καὶ ἅπαξ δεῖ βαπτίζεσθαι, βαπτίζεσθαι δὲ κατὰ τὸν τοῦ κυρίου λόγον εἰς τὸ ὄνομα τοῦ πατρὸς καὶ τοῦ υἱοῦ καὶ τοῦ ἁγίου πνεύματος διδασκομένους τὴν εἰς πατέρα καὶ υἱὸν καὶ ἅγιον πνεῦμα ὁμολογίαν. Ὅσοι τοίνυν εἰς πατέρα καὶ υἱὸν καὶ ἅγιον πνεῦμα βαπτισθέντες μίαν φύσιν ἐν τρισὶν ὑποστάσεσι τῆς θεότητος διδαχθέντες αὖθις ἀναβαπτίζονται, οὗτοι ἀνασταυροῦσι τὸν Χριστόν, ὥς φησιν ὁ θεῖος ἀπόστολος· «Ἀδύνατον γὰρ τοὺς ἅπαξ φωτισθέντας» καὶ τὰ ἑξῆς, «αὖθις ἀνακαινίζειν εἰς μετάνοιαν ἀνασταυροῦντας ἑαυτοῖς τὸν Χριστὸν καὶ παραδειγματίζοντας». Ὅσοι δὲ μὴ εἰς τὴν ἁγίαν τριάδα ἐβαπτίσθησαν, τούτους δεῖ ἀναβαπτίζεσθαι. Εἰ γὰρ καί φησιν ὁ ἀπόστολος, ὅτι «εἰς Χριστὸν» καὶ «εἰς τὸν θάνατον αὐτοῦ ἐβαπτίσθημεν», οὐχ οὕτω δεῖν γίνεσθαί φησι τὴν ἐπίκλησιν τοῦ βαπτίσματος, ἀλλ᾽ ὅτι τύπος τοῦ θανάτου τοῦ Χριστοῦ ἐστι τὸ βάπτισμα· διὰ γὰρ τῶν τριῶν καταδύσεων τὰς τρεῖς ἡμέρας τῆς τοῦ κυρίου ταφῆς σημαίνει τὸ βάπτισμα. Τὸ οὖν εἰς Χριστὸν βαπτισθῆναι δηλοῖ τὸ πιστεύοντας εἰς αὐτὸν βαπτίζεσθαι. Ἀδύνατον δὲ εἰς Χριστὸν πιστεῦσαι μὴ διδαχθέντας τὴν εἰς πατέρα καὶ υἱὸν καὶ ἅγιον πνεῦμα ὁμολογίαν. Χριστὸς γάρ ἐστιν ὁ υἱὸς τοῦ θεοῦ τοῦ ζῶντος, ὃν ἔχρισεν ὁ πατὴρ τῷ ἁγίῳ πνεύματι, ὥς φησιν ὁ θεῖος Δαυίδ· «Διὰ τοῦτο ἔχρισέ σε ὁ θεὸς ὁ θεός σου ἔλαιον ἀγαλλιάσεως παρὰ τοὺς μετόχους σου», καὶ Ἠσαΐας ἐκ προσώπου τοῦ κυρίου· «Πνεῦμα ἅγιον ἐπ᾽ ἐμέ, οὗ

---

[1]For a commentary on the concluding nineteen chapters, see Louth, *St John Damascene*, 179–89; cf. Kontouma, "The *Fount of Knowledge* between conservation and creation," 13–14.

[2]Rom 6.4.

[3]Heb 6.4–6.

[4]The rebaptism of those who have received baptism correctly in the name of the Trinity is forbidden by Canons 47 and 49 of the fourth-century "Apostolic Canons."

82   On faith and baptism[1]

We confess one baptism for the remission of sins and for eternal life, for baptism indicates the Lord's death. "We are therefore buried together with" the Lord "through baptism," as the divine Apostle says.[2] Thus just as the Lord's death was accomplished only once, so too we should be baptized only once and baptized according to the Lord's command in the name of the Father, and of the Son, and of the Holy Spirit, having been taught to confess the Father and the Son and the Holy Spirit. Those, then, who after having been baptized in the Father and Son and Holy Spirit, and after having been taught about the one nature of the Godhead in three hypostases, are baptized again crucify Christ again, as the divine Apostle says: "For it is impossible to restore again to repentance those who have once been enlightened," and so forth, "since on their own they are crucifying again the Son of God and are holding him up to contempt."[3] Only those who have not been baptized in the Holy Trinity should be baptized again.[4] For even if the Apostle says that we have been baptized "into Christ" and "into his death,"[5] he does not say that this is how the baptismal invocation should be made, but that baptism is a type of Christ's death, for through the three immersions baptism signifies the three days of the Lord's burial. Therefore, to be baptized into Christ means the baptism of those who believe in him. For it is impossible to believe in Christ without having been taught the confession of Father and Son and Holy Spirit. For Christ is the Son of the living God, whom the Father anointed by the Holy Spirit, as the divine David says: "Therefore God, your God, has anointed you with the oil of gladness beyond your companions,"[6] and Isaiah, speaking in the person of the Lord: "The Holy Spirit is upon me because he has anointed me."[7] Indeed it was to teach the invocation to his own

Although the Quinisext Ecumenical Council (the Council in Trullo, 692) rejected the *Apostolic Constitutions*, to which the eighty-five Apostolic Canons were appended, it approved of the canons themselves. In Chapter 90, John lists the Apostolic Canons as a canonical text of the New Testament.

[5]Rom 6.3.   [6]Ps 44.8.   [7]Is 61.1.

εἵνεκεν ἔχρισέ με». Τὴν μέντοι ἐπίκλησιν τοὺς οἰκείους μαθητὰς ὁ κύριος διδάσκων ἔλεγε· «Βαπτίζοντες αὐτοὺς εἰς τὸ ὄνομα τοῦ πατρὸς καὶ τοῦ υἱοῦ καὶ τοῦ ἁγίου πνεύματος». Ἐπειδὴ γὰρ ἐπ᾽ ἀφθαρσίᾳ πεποίηκεν ἡμᾶς ὁ θεός, παραβάντας δὲ τὴν σωτήριον αὐτοῦ ἐντολὴν φθορᾷ θανάτου κατεδίκασεν, ἵνα μὴ ἀθάνατον ᾖ τὸ κακόν, συγκαταβὰς τοῖς δούλοις ὡς εὔσπλαγχνος καὶ καθ᾽ ἡμᾶς γενόμενος τῆς φθορᾶς διὰ τοῦ ἰδίου πάθους ἐλυτρώσατο, ἐπήγασεν ἡμῖν ἐκ τῆς ἁγίας καὶ ἀχράντου αὐτοῦ πλευρᾶς πηγὴν ἀφέσεως, ὕδωρ μὲν εἰς ἀναγέννησιν καὶ ἔκπλυσιν τῆς τε ἁμαρτίας καὶ τῆς φθορᾶς, αἷμα δὲ ποτὸν ζωῆς ἀιδίου πρόξενον, ἐντολάς τε ἡμῖν δέδωκε δι᾽ ὕδατος ἀναγεννᾶσθαι καὶ πνεύματος δι᾽ ἐντεύξεως καὶ ἐπικλήσεως τῷ ὕδατι ἐπιφοιτῶντος τοῦ πνεύματος. Ἐπειδὴ γὰρ διπλοῦς ὁ ἄνθρωπος, ἐκ ψυχῆς καὶ σώματος, διπλῆν ἡμῖν ἔδωκε καὶ τὴν κάθαρσιν, δι᾽ ὕδατός τε καὶ πνεύματος· τοῦ μὲν πνεύματος τὸ «κατ᾽ εἰκόνα καὶ καθ᾽ ὁμοίωσιν» ἐν ἡμῖν ἀνακαινίζοντος, τοῦ δὲ ὕδατος διὰ τῆς τοῦ πνεύματος χάριτος τὸ σῶμα τῆς ἁμαρτίας καθαίροντος καὶ τῆς φθορᾶς ἀπαλλάττοντος, καὶ τὴν μὲν τοῦ θανάτου εἰκόνα ἐκπληροῦντος τοῦ ὕδατος, τὸν δὲ τῆς ζωῆς ἀρραβῶνα παρεχομένου τοῦ πνεύματος.

Ἀπ᾽ ἀρχῆς γὰρ «πνεῦμα θεοῦ τοῖς ὕδασιν ἐπεφέρετο». Καὶ ἄνωθεν ἡ γραφὴ μαρτυρεῖ τῷ ὕδατι, ὡς ἔστι καθαρτήριον. Ἐπὶ Νῶε δι᾽ ὕδατος ὁ θεὸς τὴν κοσμικὴν ἁμαρτίαν κατέκλυσε. Δι᾽ ὕδατος πᾶς ἀκάθαρτος κατὰ τὸν νόμον καθαίρεται, καὶ αὐτῶν τῶν ἱματίων πλυνομένων τῷ ὕδατι. Ἔδειξεν Ἡλίας τὴν χάριν τοῦ πνεύματος συμμεμιγμένην τῷ ὕδατι, ὕδατι φλέξας τὴν ὁλοκαύτωσιν. Καὶ σχεδὸν ἅπαντα κατὰ τὸν νόμον ὕδατι καθαρίζονται (τὰ γὰρ ὁρατὰ σύμβολα τῶν νοουμένων εἰσίν), ἡ μέντοι ἀναγέννησις κατὰ ψυχὴν γίνεται· πίστις γὰρ υἱοθετεῖν

---

[8] Mt 28.19.

[9] The phrase, "that what is evil should not become immortal" (ἵνα μὴ ἀθάνατον ᾖ τὸ κακόν, *hina mē athanaton ē[i] to kakon*) is from Gregory of Nazianzus, *Oration* 38.12 (Moreschini, 890) (=*Oration* 45.8).

[10] The opening words of this sentence (Ἐπειδὴ γὰρ διπλοῦς ὁ ἄνθρωπος ἐκ ψυχῆς καὶ σώματος, *epeidē diplous ho anthrōpos, ek psychēs kai sōmatos*) reproduce the

disciples that the Lord said: "Baptizing them in the name of the Father and of the Son, and of the Holy Spirit."[8] For it was because God made us for incorruption that he condemned the transgressors of his saving commandment to the corruption of death, that what is evil should not become immortal,[9] but in his compassion he condescended to his servants and having become like us delivered us from corruption by his own passion. He made a fountain of remission gush out from his holy and immaculate side, on the one hand water for rebirth and cleansing from sin and corruption, and on the other blood as a drink productive of eternal life, and gave us commandments to be born again through water and Spirit with the Spirit coming upon the water through entreaty and invocation. For because human beings are twofold, consisting of soul and body,[10] he also gave us a twofold cleansing, through water and Spirit, the Spirit renewing in us what is in "in the image and likeness,"[11] and the water purifying the body of sin through the grace of the Spirit and delivering it from corruption, the water fulfilling the image of death, and the Spirit providing the pledge of life.

For from the beginning "the Spirit of God moved over the waters."[12] And Scripture testifies again to water, saying that it is purifying. In the time of Noah it was through water that God washed away the sin of the whole world.[13] It is through water that according to the Law every unclean person is purified, and even the garments themselves are washed in water.[14] By setting fire to the holocaust with water Elijah demonstrated the grace of the Spirit mixed with water.[15] And according to the Law almost everything is purified by water (for the visible things are symbols of what is apprehended spiritually), but the regeneration takes place in the soul, for faith is able to adopt us, even though we are creatures, and raise us up to our original blessedness.

beginning of the fourth paragraph of Cyril of Jerusalem's *Catechetical Lecture* 3 (On Baptism) (PG 33:429A). John goes on to summarize the rest of Cyril's paragraph but enriches it by introducing the idea of renewal "in the image and likeness."
[11]Gen 1.26.   [12]Gen 1.2.   [13]Cf. Gen 6.17.
[14]Cf. Lev 15.10–11.   [15]Cf. 3 Kg 18.34.

οἶδε καίτοι ὄντας κτίσματα διὰ τοῦ πνεύματος καὶ εἰς τὴν ἀρχαίαν ἀνάγειν μακαριότητα.

Ἡ μὲν οὖν τῶν ἁμαρτιῶν ἄφεσις πᾶσιν ὁμοίως διὰ τοῦ βαπτίσματος δίδοται, ἡ δὲ χάρις τοῦ πνεύματος κατὰ τὴν ἀναλογίαν τῆς πίστεως καὶ τῆς προκαθάρσεως. Νῦν μὲν οὖν διὰ τοῦ βαπτίσματος τὴν ἀπαρχὴν τοῦ ἁγίου πνεύματος λαμβάνομεν, καὶ ἀρχὴ ἑτέρου βίου γίνεται ἡμῖν ἡ παλιγγενεσία καὶ σφραγὶς καὶ φυλακτήριον καὶ φωτισμός.

Χρὴ δὲ πάσῃ δυνάμει ἀσφαλῶς τηρεῖν ἑαυτοὺς καθαροὺς ἀπὸ ῥυπαρῶν ἔργων, ἵνα μὴ πάλιν ὥσπερ κύων ἐπὶ τὸν ἴδιον ἔμετον ἐπιστρέψαντες δούλους πάλιν ἑαυτοὺς τῆς ἁμαρτίας ποιήσωμεν. «Πίστις γὰρ χωρὶς ἔργων νεκρά ἐστιν», ὁμοίως καὶ ἔργα χωρὶς πίστεως· ἡ γὰρ ἀληθὴς πίστις διὰ τῶν ἔργων δοκιμάζεται.

Βαπτιζόμεθα δὲ εἰς τὴν ἁγίαν τριάδα, ὅτι αὐτὰ τὰ βαπτιζόμενα χρῄζει τῆς ἁγίας τριάδος εἰς τὴν αὐτῶν σύστασίν τε καὶ διαμονήν, καὶ ἀδύνατον μὴ συμπαρεῖναι ἀλλήλαις τὰς τρεῖς ὑποστάσεις· ἀχώριστος γὰρ ἡ ἁγία τριάς.

Πρῶτον βάπτισμα τὸ τοῦ κατακλυσμοῦ εἰς ἐκκοπὴν ἁμαρτίας. Δεύτερον τὸ διὰ τῆς θαλάσσης καὶ τῆς νεφέλης· σύμβολον γὰρ ἡ μὲν νεφέλη τοῦ πνεύματος, ἡ θάλασσα δὲ τοῦ ὕδατος. Τρίτον τὸ νομικόν· πᾶς γὰρ ἀκάθαρτος ἀπελούετο ὕδατι ἔπλυνέ τε τὰ ἱμάτια καὶ οὕτως εἰσῄει εἰς τὴν παρεμβολήν. Τέταρτον τὸ Ἰωάννου εἰσαγωγικὸν ὑπάρχον καὶ εἰς μετάνοιαν ἄγον τοὺς βαπτιζομένους, ἵνα εἰς Χριστὸν πιστεύσωσιν· «ἐγὼ γὰρ ὑμᾶς», φησί, «βαπτίζω ἐν ὕδατι· ὁ δὲ ὀπίσω μου ἐρχόμενος, αὐτὸς ὑμᾶς βαπτίσει ἐν πνεύματι ἁγίῳ καὶ πυρί». Προκαθαίρει οὖν ὁ Ἰωάννης ἐπὶ τὸ πνεῦμα διὰ τοῦ ὕδατος. Πέμπτον τὸ τοῦ κυρίου βάπτισμα, ὃ αὐτὸς ἐβαπτίσατο. Βαπτίζεται δὲ οὐχ ὡς αὐτὸς χρῄζων καθάρσεως, ἀλλὰ τὴν ἐμὴν οἰκειούμενος κάθαρσιν, ἵνα συντρίψῃ τὰς κεφαλὰς τῶν δρακόντων ἐπὶ τοῦ ὕδατος, ἵνα κλύσῃ τὴν ἁμαρτίαν καὶ πάντα τὸν παλαιὸν Ἀδὰμ ἐνθάψῃ τῷ ὕδατι, ἵνα ἁγιάσῃ τὸν βαπτιστήν, ἵνα πληρώσῃ τὸν νόμον, ἵνα τὸ τῆς τριάδος ἀποκαλύψῃ μυστήριον, ἵνα τύπος καὶ ὑπογραμμὸς ἡμῖν πρὸς τὸ βαπτίζεσθαι γένηται. Βαπτιζόμεθα δὲ ἡμεῖς τὸ τέλειον

So then, the remission of sins is given to all equally through baptism, but the grace of the Spirit is given in proportion to the degree of faith and previous purification. In fact through baptism we now receive the first-fruits of the Holy Spirit, and this rebirth and seal and safeguarding and illumination become for us the beginning of a new life.

It is necessary for us to be on our guard with all our strength to keep ourselves pure from filthy works that we may not make ourselves slaves again to sin like a dog returning to its vomit. For "faith without works is dead"[16] and likewise works without faith. For true faith is proved by works.

We are baptized into the Holy Trinity because those things that are baptized need the Holy Trinity for their support and perseveration in being, and it is impossible for the three hypostases not to be present with each other, for the Holy Trinity is indivisible.

The first baptism was that of the flood, for the eradication of sin.[17] The second was that through the sea and the cloud, for the cloud was a symbol of the Spirit, and the sea a symbol of water.[18] The third was that of the Law, for every unclean person washed himself in water and also washed his clothes and thus entered into the camp.[19] The fourth baptism, that of John, was introductory and led the baptized to repentance, that they might believe in Christ. "I baptize you with water," it says, "but he who is coming after me will baptize you with the Holy Spirit and with fire."[20] Thus John cleanses in advance through water in preparation for the Spirit. The fifth baptism is that of the Lord, who was himself baptized.[21] He was baptized not because he himself needed cleansing but so that by making our cleansing his own he might "crush the heads of the dragons in the water,"[22] that he might wash away sin and bury the whole of the old Adam in the water, that he might sanctify the baptizer, that he might fulfil the Law, that he might reveal the mystery of the Trinity, that he might become for us a model and example for our own baptism. We

---

[16]Jas 2.20.   [17]Cf. Gen 6.11–13.   [18]Cf. Ex 14.21–22; 24.18.
[19]Cf. Num 19.7.   [20]Mt 3.11.   [21]Cf. Mt 3.13–17.   [22]Ps 73.13.

τοῦ κυρίου βάπτισμα τὸ δι᾽ ὕδατός τε καὶ πνεύματος. Πυρὶ δὲ
λέγεται βαπτίζειν Χριστός· ἐν εἴδει γὰρ πυρίνων γλωσσῶν ἐπὶ
τοὺς ἁγίους ἀποστόλους τὴν τοῦ πνεύματος χάριν ἐξέχεεν, ὥς
φησιν αὐτὸς ὁ κύριος· «Ὅτι Ἰωάννης μὲν ἐβάπτισεν ὕδατι, ὑμεῖς
δὲ βαπτισθήσεσθε ἐν πνεύματι ἁγίῳ καὶ πυρὶ οὐ μετὰ πολλὰς
ταύτας ἡμέρας», ἢ διὰ τὸ τοῦ μέλλοντος πυρὸς κολαστικὸν
βάπτισμα. Ἕκτον τὸ διὰ μετανοίας καὶ δακρύων ὄντως ἐπίπονον.
Ἕβδομον τὸ δι᾽ αἵματος καὶ μαρτυρίου, ὃ καὶ αὐτὸς Χριστὸς ὑπὲρ
ἡμῶν ἐβαπτίσατο ὡς λίαν αἰδέσιμον καὶ μακάριον, ὅσῳ δευτέροις
οὐ μολύνεται ῥύποις. Ὄγδοον τὸ τελευταῖον οὐ σωτήριον, ἀλλὰ
τῆς μὲν κακίας ἀναιρετικόν (οὐκ ἔτι γὰρ κακία καὶ ἁμαρτία
πολιτεύεται), κολάζον δὲ ἀτελεύτητα.

Σωματικῷ εἴδει ὡσεὶ περιστερὰ κατεφοίτησε τὸ πνεῦμα τὸ
ἅγιον ἐπὶ τὸν κύριον τὴν ἀπαρχὴν τοῦ ἡμετέρου ὑποδεικνύον
βαπτίσματος καὶ τιμῶν τὸ σῶμα, ἐπεὶ καὶ τοῦτο ἤγουν τὸ σῶμα
τῇ θεώσει θεὸς καὶ ἅμα που ἄνωθεν εἴθισται περιστερὰ λύσιν
κατακλυσμοῦ εὐαγγελίζεσθαι. Ἐπὶ δὲ τοὺς ἁγίους ἀποστόλους
πυροειδῶς κάτεισι· θεὸς γάρ ἐστιν, «ὁ δὲ θεὸς πῦρ καταναλίσκον
ἐστί».

Τὸ ἔλαιον ἐν τῷ βαπτίσματι παραλαμβάνεται τὴν χρίσιν
μηνύον καὶ χριστοὺς ἡμᾶς ἐργαζόμενον καὶ τὸν τοῦ θεοῦ ἡμῖν
ἐπαγγελλόμενον διὰ τοῦ ἁγίου πνεύματος ἔλεον, ἐπεὶ καὶ κάρφος
ἐλαίας τοῖς ἐκ τοῦ κατακλυσμοῦ περισωθεῖσιν ἡ περιστερὰ
κεκόμικεν.

Ἐβαπτίσθη Ἰωάννης τὴν χεῖρα ἐπιθεὶς ἐπὶ τὴν θείαν τοῦ
δεσπότου κορυφὴν καὶ τῷ ἰδίῳ αἵματι. Οὐ χρὴ ὑπερτίθεσθαι τὸ
βάπτισμα, ὅτε δι᾽ ἔργων ἡ πίστις τῶν προσιόντων μαρτυρηθῇ.
Ὁ ἐν δόλῳ προσιὼν τῷ βαπτίσματι κατακριθήσεται μᾶλλον ἢ
ὠφεληθήσεται.

ourselves are baptized in the perfect baptism of the Lord, the baptism that is with water and the Spirit. Christ is said to baptize with fire, for he poured out the grace of the Spirit on the holy apostles in the form of tongues of fire, as the Lord himself says: "John baptized with water, but you will be baptized with the Holy Spirit and with fire not many days from now,"[23] or else it is by the punitive baptism of the fire that is to come. The sixth baptism is by repentance and tears and is truly laborious. The seventh is by blood and martyrdom. Christ himself was baptized by this for our sake, since it is exceedingly venerable and blessed in that it is not polluted by subsequent impurities. The last is the eighth, which is not salvific but on the one hand destroys evil (for evil and sin are no longer prevalent) and on the other punishes endlessly.[24]

The Holy Spirit rested upon the Lord in bodily form like a dove symbolizing the first-fruits of our own baptism and honoring the body, since even this, that is to say, the body was divine by deification. At the same time, rather, the dove was accustomed earlier to bringing the good news of the resolution of the flood.[25] But it descended on the holy apostles in the form of fire, for it is God, and "God is a consuming fire."[26]

The oil in baptism is taken as indicating chrismation, and as making us christs, and as announcing God's mercy to us through the Holy Spirit, since the dove also brought an olive twig to those who had been saved from the flood.

John was baptized when he put his hand on the Master's divine head and also by his own blood.

Baptism should not be deferred when the faith of those who ask for it is supported by works. But anyone who seeks baptism dishonestly will be condemned rather than benefited.

[23] Acts 1.5.
[24] For this paragraph, cf. (Ps.-)Athanasius, *Questions on the Scriptures* 101 (PG 28:760ABC).
[25] Cf. Gen 7.10–11.
[26] Deut 4.24.

83   *Περὶ πίστεως*

Ἡ μέντοι πίστις διπλῆ ἐστιν. «Ἔστι γὰρ πίστις ἐξ ἀκοῆς». Ἀκούοντες γὰρ τῶν θείων γραφῶν πιστεύομεν τῇ διδασκαλίᾳ τοῦ πνεύματος. Αὕτη δὲ τελειοῦται πᾶσι τοῖς νομοθετηθεῖσιν ὑπὸ Χριστοῦ, ἔργῳ πιστεύουσα, εὐσεβοῦσα καὶ τὰς ἐντολὰς πράττουσα τοῦ ἀνακαινίσαντος ἡμᾶς. Ὁ γὰρ μὴ κατὰ τὴν παράδοσιν τῆς καθολικῆς ἐκκλησίας πιστεύων ἢ κοινωνῶν διὰ τῶν ἀτόπων ἔργων τῷ διαβόλῳ ἄπιστός ἐστιν.

«Ἔστι δὲ» πάλιν «πίστις ἐλπιζομένων ὑπόστασις, πραγμάτων ἔλεγχος οὐ βλεπομένων» ἢ ἀδίστακτος καὶ ἀδιάκριτος ἐλπὶς τῶν τε ὑπὸ θεοῦ ἡμῖν ἐπηγγελμένων καὶ τῆς τῶν αἰτήσεων ἡμῶν ἐπιτυχίας. Ἡ μὲν οὖν πρώτη τῆς ἡμετέρας γνώμης ἐστίν, ἡ δὲ δευτέρα τῶν χαρισμάτων τοῦ πνεύματος.

Ἰστέον, ὅτι διὰ τοῦ βαπτίσματος περιτεμνόμεθα ἅπαν τὸ ἀπὸ γενέσεως κάλυμμα ἤτοι τὴν ἁμαρτίαν καὶ Ἰσραηλῖται πνευματικοὶ καὶ θεοῦ λαὸς χρηματίζομεν.

84   *Περὶ σταυροῦ, ἐν ᾧ ἔτι καὶ περὶ πίστεως*

«Ὁ λόγος ὁ τοῦ σταυροῦ τοῖς μὲν ἀπολλυμένοις μωρία ἐστί, τοῖς δὲ σῳζομένοις ἡμῖν δύναμις θεοῦ ἐστιν». «Ὁ μὲν γὰρ πνευματικὸς πάντα ἀνακρίνει, ψυχικὸς δὲ ἄνθρωπος οὐ δέχεται τὰ τοῦ πνεύματος». Μωρία γάρ ἐστι τοῖς μὴ πίστει δεχομένοις καὶ τὸ ἀγαθὸν καὶ παντοδύναμον τοῦ θεοῦ λογιζομένοις, ἀλλ᾽ ἀνθρωπίνοις καὶ φυσικοῖς λογισμοῖς ἐρευνῶσι τὰ θεῖα· πάντα γὰρ τὰ τοῦ θεοῦ ὑπὲρ φύσιν εἰσὶ καὶ λόγον καὶ ἔννοιαν. Εἰ γάρ τις λογίσηται, ὅπως ἐκ τοῦ μὴ ὄντος εἰς τὸ εἶναι τίνος τε ἕνεκεν παρήγαγεν ὁ θεὸς τὰ πάντα, καὶ φυσικοῖς λογισμοῖς φθάσαι βουληθῇ, οὐ καταλαμβάνει· ψυχικὴ γάρ ἐστιν ἡ γνῶσις

---

[1] Rom 10.17.
[2] Cf. 1 Thess 1.3.
[3] Heb 11.1.

83   *On faith*

Now faith is twofold. "For there is faith that comes from what is heard."[1] For by hearing the divine Scriptures we believe in the teaching of the Spirit. This faith is perfected by everything that has been prescribed by Christ, trusting in the work of faith, holding orthodox opinions, and keeping the commandments of him who renewed us.[2] For anyone who does not believe in accordance with the tradition of the Catholic Church or is in communion with the devil through wicked works is without faith.

There is also faith that is "the assurance of things hoped for, the conviction of things not seen,"[3] or an unhesitating and unwavering hope in the things promised to us by God and in the success of our petitions. The first of these depends on our own will, the second on the graces of the Spirit.

One should know that through baptism we are circumcised, cutting away everything that has covered us since birth, namely, sin, and are reckoned as spiritual Israelites and the people of God.

84   *On the cross and in which there is more on faith*

"The teaching concerning the cross is foolishness to those who are perishing, but to us who are being saved it is the power of God."[1] "Those who are spiritual discern all things, but those who are materially minded do not receive the gifts of the Spirit."[2] For the teaching concerning the cross is foolishness to those who do not receive it in faith and do not take account of the goodness and omnipotence of God, but investigate divine matters by the use of natural human reasoning, for everything concerning God transcends nature and reason and concept. For if one were to consider how God brought everything into being from non-being and for what purpose, and wished to achieve this by natural reasoning, one would not succeed.

[1] 1 Cor 1.18.
[2] 1 Cor 2.15.

αὕτη καὶ δαιμονιώδης. Εἰ δέ τις πίστει χειραγωγούμενος ἀγαθὸν καὶ παντοδύναμον καὶ ἀληθὲς καὶ σοφὸν καὶ δίκαιον τὸ θεῖον λογίσηται, εὑρήσει πάντα λεῖα καὶ ὁμαλὰ καὶ ὁδὸν εὐθεῖαν. Ἐκτὸς γὰρ πίστεως ἀδύνατον σωθῆναι· πίστει γὰρ πάντα, τά τε ἀνθρώπινα τά τε πνευματικά, συνίστανται. Οὔτε γὰρ γεωργὸς ἐκτὸς πίστεως τέμνει γῆς αὔλακα, οὐκ ἔμπορος μικρῷ ξύλῳ τὴν ἑαυτοῦ ψυχὴν τῷ μαινομένῳ τῆς θαλάσσης πελάγει παραδίδωσιν, οὐ γάμοι συνίστανται, οὐκ ἄλλο τι τῶν ἐν τῷ βίῳ. Πίστει νοοῦμεν ἐκ τοῦ μὴ ὄντος εἰς τὸ εἶναι τὰ πάντα τῇ τοῦ θεοῦ δυνάμει παρῆχθαι· πάντα, τά τε θεῖα καὶ τὰ ἀνθρώπινα, πίστει κατορθοῦμεν. Πίστις δέ ἐστιν ἀπολυπραγμόνητος συγκατάθεσις.

Πᾶσα μὲν οὖν πρᾶξις καὶ θαυματουργία Χριστοῦ μεγίστη καὶ θεία καὶ θαυμαστή, ἀλλὰ πάντων ἐστὶ θαυμαστότερον ὁ τίμιος αὐτοῦ σταυρός. Δι' οὐδενὸς γὰρ ἑτέρου ὁ θάνατος κατήργηται, ἡ τοῦ προπάτορος ἁμαρτία λέλυται, ὁ ᾅδης ἐσκύλευται, ἡ ἀνάστασις δεδώρηται, δύναμις ἡμῖν τοῦ καταφρονεῖν τῶν παρόντων καὶ αὐτοῦ τοῦ θανάτου δέδοται, ἡ πρὸς τὴν ἀρχαίαν μακαριότητα ἐπάνοδος κατώρθωται, πύλαι παραδείσου ἠνοίγησαν, ἡ φύσις ἡμῶν ἐκ δεξιῶν τοῦ θεοῦ κεκάθικε, τέκνα θεοῦ καὶ κληρονόμοι γεγόναμεν εἰ μὴ διὰ τοῦ σταυροῦ τοῦ κυρίου ἡμῶν Ἰησοῦ Χριστοῦ. Διὰ σταυροῦ γὰρ ταῦτα πάντα κατώρθωται.» Ὅσοι γὰρ ἐβαπτίσθημεν εἰς Χριστόν», φησὶν ὁ ἀπόστολος, «εἰς τὸν θάνατον αὐτοῦ ἐβαπτίσθημεν». Ὅσοι δὲ εἰς Χριστὸν ἐβαπτίσθημεν, Χριστὸν ἐνεδυσάμεθα. Χριστὸς δέ ἐστι θεοῦ δύναμις καὶ σοφία. Ἰδοὺ ὁ θάνατος τοῦ Χριστοῦ ἤτοι ὁ σταυρὸς τὴν ἐνυπόστατον τοῦ θεοῦ σοφίαν καὶ δύναμιν ἡμᾶς περιέβαλε. Δύναμις δὲ θεοῦ ἐστιν ὁ λόγος ὁ τοῦ σταυροῦ, ἢ ὅτι τὸ δυνατὸν τοῦ θεοῦ ἤτοι ἡ κατὰ τοῦ θανάτου νίκη δι' αὐτοῦ ἡμῖν πεφανέρωται, ἢ ὅτι, ὥσπερ τὰ τέσσαρα ἄκρα τοῦ σταυροῦ διὰ τοῦ μέσου κέντρου

---

[3] Jas 3.15.
[4] For this paragraph and the first part of the next, cf. Cyril of Jerusalem, *Catechetical Lecture* 13 (PG 33:772–821). "Unquestioning assent" is not blind faith but faith that does not raise questions simply out of intellectual curiosity.
[5] Rom 6.3.   [6] Gal 3.27.   [7] 1 Cor 1.24.

For such knowledge is earthly and demonic.[3] But if one is guided by faith and reckons the divine to be omnipotent and true and wise and just, one will find all things smooth and even and a straight path. For without faith it is impossible to be saved. For all things, both human and spiritual, are sustained by faith. For without faith neither does a farmer cut a furrow in the soil, nor does a merchant entrust his own soul to the raging of the open sea in a small timber craft, nor are marriages contracted, nor is anything else in this life undertaken. It is by faith that we know that everything by God's power has been brought from non-being into being, and it is by faith that we achieve everything both divine and human. Faith is unquestioning assent.[4]

So then, every act and miracle of Christ was very great and divine and wonderful, but the most wonderful of all is his precious cross. For by nothing else was death abolished, was the sin of our first ancestor absolved, was hades despoiled, was the resurrection granted, was the power given to us to despise the things of this world and death itself, was the return to our original blessedness achieved, were the gates of paradise opened, was our nature seated at the right hand of God, did we become children and heirs of God, except by the cross of our Lord Jesus Christ. For it was by the cross that all these things were accomplished. "All of us who have been baptized into Christ Jesus," says the Apostle, "were baptized into his death."[5] All of us who have been baptized into Christ have put on Christ.[6] Christ is the power and wisdom of God.[7] See how the death of Christ, that is to say, the cross, has clothed us in the substantive wisdom and power of God. And the teaching of the cross is the power of God, either because it was through the cross that the power of God or the victory over death was revealed to us, or because just as the four ends of the cross are held and pressed together by the center, so also is the height and depth, length and breadth, that is to say, the whole of the visible and invisible creation, held together by the power of God.[8]

[8]On the cosmic significance of the cross, cf. Gregory of Nyssa, *Catechetical Discourse* 32.5–10 (PG 45:80C–84A; Green, 132–34).

κρατοῦνται καὶ συσφίγγονται, οὕτω διὰ τῆς τοῦ θεοῦ δυνάμεως τό τε ὕψος καὶ τὸ βάθος μῆκός τε καὶ πλάτος ἤτοι πᾶσα ὁρατή τε καὶ ἀόρατος κτίσις συνέχεται.

Οὗτος ἡμῖν σημεῖον δέδοται ἐπὶ τοῦ μετώπου, ὃν τρόπον τῷ Ἰσραὴλ ἡ περιτομή· δι᾽ αὐτοῦ γὰρ οἱ πιστοὶ τῶν ἀπίστων ἀποδιιστάμεθά τε καὶ γνωριζόμεθα. Οὗτος θυρεὸς καὶ ὅπλον καὶ τρόπαιον κατὰ τοῦ διαβόλου. Οὗτος σφραγίς, ἵνα μὴ θίγῃ ἡμῶν ὁ ὀλοθρεύων, ὥς φησιν ἡ γραφή. Οὗτος τῶν κειμένων ἀνάστασις, τῶν ἑστώτων στήριγμα, ἀσθενῶν βακτηρία, ποιμαινομένων ῥάβδος, ἐπιστρεφόντων χειραγωγία, προκοπτόντων τελείωσις, ψυχῆς σωτηρία καὶ σώματος, πάντων κακῶν ἀποτρόπαιον, πάντων ἀγαθῶν πρόξενος, ἁμαρτίας ἀναίρεσις, φυτὸν ἀναστάσεως, ξύλον ζωῆς αἰωνίου.

Αὐτὸ μὲν οὖν τὸ τίμιον ξύλον ὡς ἀληθῶς καὶ σεβάσμιον, ἐν ᾧ ἑαυτὸν εἰς θυσίαν ὑπὲρ ἡμῶν Χριστὸς προσενήνοχεν, ὡς ἁγιασθὲν τῇ ἁφῇ τοῦ ἁγίου σώματος καὶ αἵματος εἰκότως προσκυνητέον, τοὺς ἥλους, τὴν λόγχην, τὰ ἐνδύματα καὶ τὰ ἱερὰ αὐτοῦ σκηνώματα, ἅτινά εἰσιν ἡ φάτνη, τὸ σπήλαιον, ὁ Γολγοθᾶς ὁ σωτήριος, ὁ ζωοποιὸς τάφος, ἡ Σιὼν τῶν ἐκκλησιῶν ἡ ἀκρόπολις, καὶ τὰ ὅμοια· ὥς φησιν ὁ θεοπάτωρ Δαυίδ· «Εἰσελευσόμεθα εἰς τὰ σκηνώματα αὐτοῦ, προσκυνήσομεν εἰς τὸν τόπον, οὗ ἔστησαν οἱ πόδες αὐτοῦ». Ὅτι δὲ τὸν σταυρὸν λέγει, δηλοῖ τὸ ἑπόμενον· «Ἀνάστηθι, κύριε, εἰς τὴν ἀνάπαυσίν σου»· ἕπεται γὰρ τῷ σταυρῷ ἡ ἀνάστασις. Εἰ γὰρ τῶν ἐρωμένων ποθητὸν οἶκος καὶ κλίνη καὶ περιβόλαιον, πόσῳ μᾶλλον τὰ τοῦ θεοῦ καὶ σωτῆρος, δι᾽ ὧν καὶ σεσῴσμεθα.

Προσκυνοῦμεν δὲ καὶ τὸν τύπον τοῦ τιμίου σταυροῦ, εἰ καὶ ἐξ ἑτέρας ὕλης γένηται, οὐ τὴν ὕλην τιμῶντες—μὴ γένοιτο—, ἀλλὰ τὸν τύπον ὡς Χριστοῦ σύμβολον. Ἔφη γὰρ τοῖς ἑαυτοῦ μαθηταῖς διατιθέμενος· «Τότε φανήσεται τὸ σημεῖον τοῦ υἱοῦ τοῦ ἀνθρώπου ἐν τῷ οὐρανῷ», τὸν σταυρὸν λέγων. Διὸ καὶ ταῖς γυναιξὶν ἔλεγεν ὁ τῆς ἀναστάσεως ἄγγελος· «Ἰησοῦν ζητεῖτε τὸν Ναζαρηνὸν τὸν ἐσταυρωμένον», καὶ ὁ ἀπόστολος· «Ἡμεῖς δὲ κηρύσσομεν Χριστὸν ἐσταυρωμένον». Πολλοὶ μὲν γὰρ Χριστοὶ

This has been given to us upon our forehead as a sign, in the same way as circumcision to Israel. For it is by this that we Christians are distinguished from unbelievers and recognized. It is this that is a shield and weapon and trophy against the devil. It is this that is a seal, so that the destroyer might not touch us, as Scripture says.[9] It is this that is the raising up of the fallen, the support of the standing, the staff of the infirm, the rod of the shepherded, the guidance of those converting, the perfection of those making progress, the salvation of soul and body, the averter of all evils, the procurer of all good, the destruction of sin, the plant of resurrection, the tree of eternal life.

So, then, that precious wood on which Christ offered himself as a sacrifice for our sake is rightly to be venerated, as truly worthy of reverence, as sanctified by contact with his holy body and blood, along with the nails, the lance, the garments, and the sacred places of his sojourning, which are the manger, the cave, saving Golgotha, the life-giving tomb, Sion, the acropolis of the churches, and suchlike. As David, the ancestor of God, says: "Let us enter into his tabernacles, let us worship at the place where his feet stood."[10] The fact that he is referring to the cross is revealed by the following verse: "Arise, O Lord, and go to your resting-place."[11] For the resurrection follows the cross. For if the house and bed and garment of those we love is precious to us, how much more so are the things of our God and Savior, through which we have also been saved.

We also venerate the form of the precious cross, even if it is made of a different material, not honoring the material—God forbid!—but the form as a symbol of Christ. For he said to his disciples, setting it out for them: "Then the sign of the Son of Man will appear in the heavens,"[12] meaning the cross. And it was also on this account that the messenger of the resurrection said to the women: "You are looking for Jesus of Nazareth who was crucified,"[13] and the Apostle said: "But we proclaim Christ crucified."[14] For there were many Christs and Jesuses, but only one crucified. He did not say "pierced by a

[9]Cf. Heb 11.28.   [10]Ps 131.7.   [11]Ps 131.8.
[12]Mt 24.30.   [13]Mk 16.6.   [14]1 Cor 1.23.

καὶ Ἰησοῖ, ἀλλ᾽ εἷς ὁ ἐσταυρωμένος. Οὐκ εἶπε λελογχευμένον, ἀλλ᾽ «ἐσταυρωμένον». Προσκυνητέον τοίνυν τὸ σημεῖον τοῦ Χριστοῦ. Ἔνθα γὰρ ἂν ᾖ τὸ σημεῖον, ἐκεῖ καὶ αὐτὸς ἔσται. Τὴν δὲ ὕλην, ἐξ ἧς ὁ τύπος τοῦ σταυροῦ συνίσταται, εἰ καὶ χρυσὸς ἢ λίθοι εἶεν τίμιοι, μετὰ τὴν τοῦ τύπου (εἰ τύχοι) διάλυσιν οὐ προσκυνητέον. Πάντα τοίνυν τὰ θεῷ ἀνακείμενα προσκυνοῦμεν αὐτῷ τὸ σέβας προσάγοντες.

Τοῦτον τὸν τίμιον σταυρὸν προετύπωσε τὸ ξύλον τῆς ζωῆς τὸ ἐν παραδείσῳ ὑπὸ θεοῦ πεφυτευμένον (ἐπεὶ γὰρ διὰ ξύλου ὁ θάνατος, ἔδει διὰ ξύλου δωρηθῆναι τὴν ζωὴν καὶ τὴν ἀνάστασιν), Ἰακὼβ προσκυνήσας τὸ ἄκρον τῆς ῥάβδου ἐνηλλαγμέναις ταῖς χερσὶ τοὺς υἱοὺς Ἰωσὴφ εὐλογήσας καὶ τὸ σημεῖον τοῦ σταυροῦ διαγράψας σαφέστατα, ῥάβδος Μωσαϊκὴ σταυροτύπως τὴν θάλασσαν πλήξασα καὶ σώσασα μὲν τὸν Ἰσραήλ, Φαραὼ δὲ βυθίσασα, χεῖρες σταυροειδῶς ἐκτεινόμεναι καὶ τὸν Ἀμαλὴκ τροπούμεναι, ξύλῳ τὸ πικρὸν ὕδωρ γλυκαινόμενον καὶ πέτρα ῥηγνυμένη καὶ προχέουσα νάματα, ῥάβδος τῷ Ἀαρὼν τὸ τῆς ἱεραρχίας ἀξίωμα χρηματίζουσα, ὄφις ἐπὶ ξύλου θριαμβευόμενος (ὡς νενέκρωται τοῦ ξύλου τοὺς νεκρὸν ὁρῶντας τὸν ἐχθρὸν διασῴζοντος τοὺς πιστεύοντας, ὡς Χριστὸς ἐν σαρκὶ ἁμαρτίας ἁμαρτίαν οὐκ εἰδυίᾳ προσήλωται), Μωσῆς ὁ μέγας· «Ὄψεσθε», βοῶν, «τὴν ζωὴν ὑμῶν ἐπὶ ξύλου κρεμαμένην ἀπέναντι τῶν ὀφθαλμῶν ὑμῶν», Ἡσαΐας· «Ὅλην τὴν ἡμέραν διεπέτασα τὰς χεῖράς μου πρὸς λαὸν ἀπειθοῦντα καὶ ἀντιλέγοντα». Οἱ τοῦτο προσκυνοῦντες τῆς μερίδος τύχοιμεν Χριστοῦ τοῦ ἐσταυρωμένου. Ἀμήν.

85 Περὶ τοῦ προσκυνεῖν κατὰ ἀνατολάς

Οὐχ ἁπλῶς οὐδ᾽ ὡς ἔτυχε κατὰ ἀνατολὰς προσκυνοῦμεν, ἀλλ᾽ ἐπειδὴ ἐξ ὁρατῆς τε καὶ ἀοράτου ἤτοι νοητῆς καὶ αἰσθητῆς συντεθείμεθα φύσεως, διπλῆν καὶ τὴν προσκύνησιν τῷ

lance" but "crucified." The sign of Christ is therefore to be venerated. For where the sign is, there he is too. The material of which the form of the cross is composed, even if consisting of gold or precious stones, is not to be venerated after the form of the cross should happen to be broken up. We therefore venerate everything that refers to God, directing the adoration to him.

This precious cross was prefigured by the tree of life planted by God in paradise (for since death came through a tree, it was necessary that life and resurrection should be bestowed through a tree).[15] It was also prefigured by Jacob when he venerated the end of his staff, blessing the sons of Joseph with crossed hands and very clearly making the sign of the cross,[16] and by Moses' rod used in the form of a cross to divide the sea, saving Israel and drowning Pharaoh.[17] It was prefigured by Moses stretching out his hands in the form of a cross and routing Amalek;[18] by the tree by which the bitter water was sweetened and the rock split with streams of water gushing forth;[19] by the rod by which the dignity of priesthood was conferred on Aaron;[20] by the serpent raised in triumph upon a tree (as if it had been put to death, the tree preserving the believers who saw the enemy dead, as Christ who knew no sin was nailed to a tree in the flesh of sin),[21] the great Moses crying out: "You shall see your life hanging on a tree before your eyes,"[22] and Isaiah: "I stretched out my hands all day to a disobedient and rebellious people."[23] May we who venerate this attain to the portion of Christ crucified. Amen.

85   *On facing towards the east in worship*

It is not without reason or by chance that we worship facing towards the east, but seeing that we are composed of a nature that is both visible and invisible, that is to say, both intelligible and sensible, we also offer a twofold worship to the Creator. It is like the way in which

---

[15]Cf. Gen 2.9.   [16]Cf. Gen 48.14.   [17]Cf. Ex 14.16–17.
[18]Cf. Ex 17.9–13.   [19]Cf. Ex 17.6; Num 20.11.   [20]Cf. Num 17.16–23.
[21]Cf. Num 21.9; Jn 3.14.   [22]Deut 28.66.   [23]Is 65.2; Rom 10.21.

δημιουργῷ προσάγομεν, ὥσπερ καὶ τῷ νῷ ψάλλομεν καὶ τοῖς σωματικοῖς χείλεσι καὶ βαπτιζόμεθα ὕδατί τε καὶ πνεύματι καὶ διπλῶς τῷ κυρίῳ ἑνούμεθα τῶν μυστηρίων μετέχοντες καὶ τῆς τοῦ πνεύματος χάριτος.

Ἐπεὶ τοίνυν «ὁ θεὸς φῶς ἐστι» νοητόν, καὶ «ἥλιος δικαιοσύνης» καὶ «ἀνατολὴ» ἐν ταῖς γραφαῖς ὠνόμασται ὁ Χριστός, ἀναθετέον αὐτῷ τὴν ἀνατολὴν εἰς προσκύνησιν· πᾶν γὰρ καλὸν τῷ θεῷ ἀναθετέον, ἐξ οὗ πᾶν ἀγαθὸν ἀγαθύνεται. Φησὶ δὲ καὶ ὁ θεῖος Δαυίδ· «Αἱ βασιλεῖαι τῆς γῆς, ᾄσατε τῷ θεῷ, ψάλατε τῷ κυρίῳ τῷ ἐπιβεβηκότι ἐπὶ τὸν οὐρανὸν τοῦ οὐρανοῦ κατὰ ἀνατολάς». Ἔτι δέ φησιν ἡ γραφή· «Ἐφύτευσεν ὁ θεὸς παράδεισον ἐν Ἐδὲμ κατὰ ἀνατολάς· ἔνθα τὸν ἄνθρωπον, ὃν ἔπλασεν, ἔθετο», ὃν παραβάντα τοῦ παραδείσου τῆς τρυφῆς ἐξώρισεν ἀπέναντι τε τοῦ παραδείσου κατῴκισεν, ἐκ δυσμῶν δηλαδή. Τὴν οὖν ἀρχαίαν πατρίδα ἐπιζητοῦντες καὶ πρὸς αὐτὴν ἀτενίζοντες τῷ θεῷ προσκυνοῦμεν. Καὶ ἡ σκηνὴ δὲ ἡ Μωσαϊκὴ κατὰ ἀνατολὰς εἶχε τὸ καταπέτασμα καὶ τὸ ἱλαστήριον. Καὶ ἡ φυλὴ τοῦ Ἰούδα ὡς τιμιωτέρα ἐξ ἀνατολῶν παρενέβαλε. Καὶ ἐν τῷ περιωνύμῳ δὲ τοῦ Σολομῶντος ναῷ ἡ τοῦ κυρίου πύλη κατὰ ἀνατολὰς διέκειτο. Ἀλλὰ μὴν καὶ ὁ κύριος σταυρούμενος ἐπὶ δυσμὰς ἑώρα, καὶ οὕτω προσκυνοῦμεν πρὸς αὐτὸν ἀτενίζοντες. Καὶ ἀναλαμβανόμενος πρὸς ἀνατολὰς ἀνεφέρετο, καὶ οὕτως αὐτῷ οἱ ἀπόστολοι προσεκύνησαν, καὶ οὕτως ἐλεύσεται, ὃν τρόπον ἐθεάσαντο αὐτὸν πορευόμενον εἰς τὸν οὐρανόν, ὡς αὐτὸς ὁ κύριος ἔφησεν· «Ὥσπερ ἡ ἀστραπὴ ἐξέρχεται ἀπὸ ἀνατολῶν καὶ φθάνει ἕως δυσμῶν, οὕτως ἔσται ἡ παρουσία τοῦ υἱοῦ τοῦ ἀνθρώπου». Αὐτὸν οὖν ἐκδεχόμενοι ἐπὶ ἀνατολὰς προσκυνοῦμεν. Ἄγραφος δέ ἐστιν ἡ παράδοσις αὕτη τῶν ἀποστόλων· πολλὰ γὰρ ἀγράφως ἡμῖν παρέδωκαν.

---

[1] Jn 1.5.   [2] Mal 3.20 (= 4.2 MT).   [3] Lk 1.78; cf. Zech 6.12 (LXX).
[4] Ps 67.33–34.   [5] Gen 2.8.   [6] Cf. Gen 3.24.
[7] Ex 37.5; Lev 16.14.   [8] Num 2.3.   [9] Ez 8.16.

we sing psalms with the mind and also without physical lips, and are baptized by water and the Spirit and are united with the Lord in a twofold manner by participating in the rite and in the grace of the Spirit.

Therefore since God is spiritual light,[1] and Christ is called "sun of righteousness"[2] and "sunrise,"[3] the east is assigned to him for worship, for everything beautiful should be assigned to God from whom every good thing derives its goodness. The divine David also says: "Sing to God, O kingdoms of the earth, sing psalms to the Lord who has mounted on the heaven of heaven towards the east."[4] And furthermore Scripture says: "God planted a garden in Eden towards the east and he set there the man whom he had created,"[5] and when this man had transgressed he exiled him from the Paradise of delight and made him dwell over against Paradise, clearly in the west.[6] Therefore yearning for our original homeland, we gaze in its direction when we worship God. Moreover, Moses' tent had the veil and the place of propitiation towards the east.[7] And the tribe of Juda, as the most highly esteemed, had their camp to the east.[8] And in the celebrated temple of Solomon the Lord's gate was on the eastern side.[9] And indeed when the Lord was crucified he faced west, and so we worship gazing towards him.[10] And when he ascended, he was borne up towards the east, and it is thus that the apostles worshiped him and thus that he will come again, in the same way as he was seen going into heaven,[11] as the Lord himself said: "For as the lightning comes from the east and flashes as far as the west, so will be the coming of the Son of Man."[12] Therefore we who await him worship facing east. This tradition of the apostles is unwritten, for they have handed down many things to us orally.[13]

[10]Cf. Ps 67.34.　　　[11]Acts 1.11.　　　[12]Mt 24.27.

[13]On praying eastwards as an unwritten tradition, cf. Basil of Caesarea, *On the Holy Spirit* 27 (PPS 42:104–6; PG 32:188AB). John is no doubt right in saying that this tradition (which Christianity shared with some of the Jewish sects) goes back to the apostles.

86 *Περὶ τῶν ἁγίων καὶ ἀχράντων τοῦ κυρίου μυστηρίων*

Ὁ ἀγαθὸς καὶ πανάγαθος καὶ ὑπεράγαθος θεός, ὁ ὅλος ὢν ἀγαθότης, διὰ τὸν ὑπερβάλλοντα πλοῦτον τῆς αὐτοῦ ἀγαθότητος οὐκ ἠνέσχετο μόνον εἶναι τὸ ἀγαθὸν ἤτοι τὴν ἑαυτοῦ φύσιν ὑπὸ μηδενὸς μετεχόμενον. Τούτου χάριν ἐποίησε πρῶτον μὲν τὰς νοερὰς καὶ οὐρανίους δυνάμεις, εἶτα τὸν ὁρατὸν καὶ αἰσθητὸν κόσμον, εἶτα ἐκ νοεροῦ καὶ αἰσθητοῦ τὸν ἄνθρωπον. Πάντα μὲν οὖν τὰ ὑπ᾽ αὐτοῦ γενόμενα κοινωνοῦσι τῆς αὐτοῦ ἀγαθότητος κατὰ τὸ εἶναι (αὐτὸς γάρ ἐστι τοῖς πᾶσι τὸ εἶναι, ἐπειδὴ ἐν αὐτῷ εἰσι τὰ ὄντα, οὐ μόνον ὅτι αὐτὸς ἐκ τοῦ μὴ ὄντος εἰς τὸ εἶναι αὐτὰ παρήγαγεν, ἀλλ᾽ ὅτι ἡ αὐτοῦ ἐνέργεια τὰ ὑπ᾽ αὐτοῦ γενόμενα συντηρεῖ καὶ συνέχει), ἐκ περισσοῦ δὲ τὰ ζῷα (κατά τε γὰρ τὸ εἶναι καὶ κατὰ τὸ ζωῆς μετέχειν κοινωνοῦσι τοῦ ἀγαθοῦ), τὰ δὲ λογικὰ καὶ κατὰ τὰ προειρημένα μέν, οὐ μὴν ἀλλὰ καὶ κατὰ τὸ λογικόν, καὶ ταῦτα μᾶλλον· οἰκειότερα γάρ πώς εἰσι πρὸς αὐτόν, εἰ καὶ πάντων ὑπέρκειται ἀσυγκρίτως.

Ὁ μέντοι ἄνθρωπος λογικὸς καὶ αὐτεξούσιος γενόμενος ἐξουσίαν εἴληφεν ἀδιαλείπτως διὰ τῆς οἰκείας προαιρέσεως ἑνοῦσθαι τῷ θεῷ, εἴ γε διαμένει ἐν τῷ ἀγαθῷ, τουτέστι τῇ τοῦ κτίσαντος ὑπακοῇ. Ἐπειδὴ τοίνυν ἐν παραβάσει τῆς τοῦ πεποιηκότος αὐτὸν ἐντολῆς γέγονε καὶ θανάτῳ καὶ φθορᾷ ὑποπέπτωκεν, ὁ ποιητὴς καὶ δημιουργὸς τοῦ γένους ἡμῶν διὰ σπλάγχνα ἐλέους αὐτοῦ ὡμοιώθη ἡμῖν κατὰ πάντα γενόμενος ἄνθρωπος χωρὶς ἁμαρτίας καὶ ἡνώθη τῇ ἡμετέρᾳ φύσει· ἐπειδὴ γὰρ μετέδωκεν ἡμῖν τῆς ἰδίας εἰκόνος καὶ τοῦ ἰδίου πνεύματος καὶ

---

[1]For this paragraph, cf. Dionysius the Areopagite, *Divine Names*, 4.1 (PG 3:693B–696A; Suchla, 143–4). The reason for creation is the goodness of God. He does not *need* to create or to share his being but he does so through his overflowing goodness. Everything that exists participates to some degree in God, at the most fundamental level simply because it "is" rather than "is not," at the higher levels because it shares in life and intelligence, which in absolute terms are God. This is linked to the Platonic concept of participation, which in Platonism accounts for why the Many exist besides the One—see, e.g., the first thirteen propositions of Proclus' *Elements of Theology*, ed.

86 *On the Lord's holy and immaculate mysteries*

God, who is good and supremely good and beyond the good, who is utter goodness, was not content through the overwhelming wealth of his goodness to be the only good, that is to say, that his own nature should not be participated in by anything. On account of this he made first the intelligible and heavenly powers, then the visible and sensible world, and then out of both the intelligible and the sensible he made humanity. Therefore everything made by him shares in his goodness by virtue of being, for he is being with regard to all things, since it is in him that beings *are*, not only because he brought them out of non-being into being, but also because it is his activity (ἐνέργεια, *energeia*) that preserves what has been made by him and keeps them in being. Living things share in his goodness more abundantly, by virtue of participating both in being and in life. Rational beings share in his goodness in both the ways already mentioned, and indeed not only in those ways but by virtue of reason too, and more so because of that. For they are somehow closer to him, even though he transcends them all incomparably.[1]

Now because humans were created as rational beings endowed with free will, they received the right to be united with God uninterruptedly by their own choice, provided of course they persevered in the good, that is to say, in obedience to the Creator. Well, when they came to transgress the commandment of him who had made them and became subject to death and corruption, the maker and creator of humankind out of his deep compassion made himself like us and became a human being in every respect except sin and united himself to our nature. For since he imparted to us a share of his own image

E. R. Dodds (Oxford: Clarendon Press, 1963)—but goes beyond Platonism principally because Platonism relies on the notion of emanation for the production of the Many, whereas the Christian doctrine of creation requires a profound gulf to exist between the Creator and all existents. The Platonic concept of participation is very useful to Christian thinkers but only when combined with a doctrine of God who is "beyond the good" and "beyond being." It is significant that although before John we also find "beyond the good" (ὑπεράγαθος, *hyperagathos*) in Dionysius and Maximus, we do not find it in any non-Christian philosopher or commentator.

οὐκ ἐφυλάξαμεν, μεταλαμβάνει αὐτὸς τῆς πτωχῆς καὶ ἀσθενοῦς ἡμῶν φύσεως, ἵνα ἡμᾶς καθάρῃ καὶ ἀφθαρτίσῃ καὶ μετόχους πάλιν τῆς αὐτοῦ καταστήσῃ θεότητος.

Ἔδει δὲ μὴ μόνον τὴν ἀπαρχὴν τῆς ἡμετέρας φύσεως ἐν μετοχῇ γενέσθαι τοῦ κρείττονος, ἀλλὰ καὶ πάντα τὸν βουλόμενον ἄνθρωπον καὶ δευτέραν γέννησιν γεννηθῆναι καὶ τραφῆναι τροφὴν ξένην καὶ τῇ γεννήσει πρόσφορον καὶ οὕτω φθάσαι τὸ μέτρον τῆς τελειότητος. Διὰ μὲν τῆς αὐτοῦ γεννήσεως ἤτοι σαρκώσεως καὶ τοῦ βαπτίσματος καὶ τοῦ πάθους καὶ τῆς ἀναστάσεως ἠλευθέρωσε τὴν φύσιν τῆς ἁμαρτίας τοῦ προπάτορος, τοῦ θανάτου, τῆς φθορᾶς, καὶ τῆς ἀναστάσεως ἀπαρχὴ γέγονε καὶ ὁδὸν καὶ τύπον ἑαυτὸν καὶ ὑπογραμμὸν τέθεικεν, ἵνα καὶ ἡμεῖς τοῖς αὐτοῦ ἀκολουθήσαντες ἴχνεσι γενώμεθα θέσει, ὅπερ αὐτός ἐστι φύσει, υἱοὶ καὶ κληρονόμοι θεοῦ καὶ αὐτοῦ συγκληρονόμοι. Ἔδωκεν οὖν ἡμῖν, ὡς ἔφην, γέννησιν δευτέραν, ἵνα ὥσπερ γεννηθέντες ἐκ τοῦ Ἀδὰμ ὡμοιώθημεν αὐτῷ κληρονομήσαντες τὴν κατάραν καὶ τὴν φθοράν, οὕτω καὶ ἐξ αὐτοῦ γεννηθέντες ὁμοιωθῶμεν αὐτῷ καὶ κληρονομήσωμεν τήν τε ἀφθαρσίαν καὶ τὴν εὐλογίαν καὶ τὴν δόξαν αὐτοῦ.

Ἐπειδὴ δὲ πνευματικός ἐστιν Ἀδάμ, ἔδει καὶ τὴν γέννησιν πνευματικὴν εἶναι, ὁμοίως καὶ τὴν βρῶσιν· ἀλλ' ἐπειδὴ διπλοῖ τινές ἐσμεν καὶ σύνθετοι, δεῖ καὶ τὴν γέννησιν διπλῆν εἶναι, ὁμοίως καὶ τὴν βρῶσιν σύνθετον. Ἡ μὲν οὖν γέννησις δι' ὕδατος ἡμῖν καὶ πνεύματος δέδοται, φημὶ δὴ τοῦ ἁγίου βαπτίσματος, ἡ δὲ βρῶσις αὐτὸς ὁ ἄρτος τῆς ζωῆς, ὁ κύριος ἡμῶν Ἰησοῦς Χριστὸς ὁ ἐκ τοῦ οὐρανοῦ καταβάς. Μέλλων γὰρ τὸν ἑκούσιον ὑπὲρ ἡμῶν καταδέχεσθαι θάνατον ἐν τῇ νυκτί, ἐν ᾗ ἑαυτὸν παρεδίδου, διαθήκην καινὴν διέθετο τοῖς ἁγίοις αὐτοῦ μαθηταῖς καὶ ἀποστόλοις καὶ δι' αὐτῶν πᾶσι τοῖς εἰς αὐτὸν πιστεύουσιν. Ἐν τῷ ὑπερῴῳ τοίνυν τῆς ἁγίας καὶ ἐνδόξου Σιὼν τὸ παλαιὸν πάσχα μετὰ τῶν μαθητῶν αὐτοῦ φαγὼν καὶ πληρώσας τὴν παλαιὰν

---

[2] Cf. 2 Pet 1.4, "partakers of the divine nature" (κοινωνοὶ τῆς θείας φύσεως, koinōnoi tēs theias physeōs). For "partakers," however, John uses the more Platonic word μέτοχοι (metochoi).

and his own Spirit and we did not preserve it, he himself participates in our poor and weak nature that he might cleanse us and make us incorrupt and render us once again partakers of his own divinity.[2]

Moreover, it was necessary that not only the first-fruits of our nature should come to partake of the Almighty[3] but also that every human being who wishes it should be born by a second birth, and be nourished by a food that is novel and appropriate to the birth, and thus arrive at the measure of perfection. Through his own birth, that is to say, incarnation and baptism and passion and resurrection, he freed the nature of our first ancestor from sin, death, and corruption, and became the first-fruits of the resurrection and made himself the way, the model, and the example, so that we too, following in his footsteps, might become by adoption what he is by nature, sons and heirs of God, and fellow-heirs with him. He therefore gave us, as I have said, a second birth, so that just as having been born from Adam we have become like him and have inherited the curse and corruption, so also having been born also from him we might become like him and inherit his incorruption and blessing and glory.

And since Adam is spiritual, it was also necessary that his birth should be spiritual, and likewise his food. But since we are twofold and composite, it was required that our birth should also be twofold, and likewise our food twofold. On the one hand, birth was given to us through water and spirit—I refer to holy baptism—on the other, our food is the bread of life himself, our Lord Jesus Christ, who descended from heaven. For when he was to accept a willing death for our sake on the night in which he surrendered himself, he made a new covenant with his holy disciples and apostles, and through them with all who believe in him. So when he had eaten the old Passover with his disciples in the upper room of holy and glorious Sion and had fulfilled the old covenant, he washed his disciples' feet, providing them with a symbol of holy baptism. Then he broke the

---

[3]"should come to partake of the Almighty" renders ἐν μετοχῇ γένεσθαι τοῦ κρείττονος (*en metochē genesthai tou kreittonos*). On ὁ κρείττων (*ho kreittōn*) as "the Almighty," see Lampe, s.v. κρείσσων (*kreissōn*), 2.a.

διαθήκην νίπτει τῶν μαθητῶν τοὺς πόδας, σύμβολον τοῦ ἁγίου βαπτίσματος παρεχόμενος. Εἶτα κλάσας ἄρτον ἐπεδίδου αὐτοῖς λέγων· «Λάβετε, φάγετε, τοῦτό μού ἐστι τὸ σῶμα» τὸ ὑπὲρ ὑμῶν κλώμενον εἰς ἄφεσιν ἁμαρτιῶν. Ὁμοίως δὲ λαβὼν τὸ ποτήριον ἐξ οἴνου καὶ ὕδατος μετέδωκεν αὐτοῖς λέγων· «Πίετε ἐξ αὐτοῦ πάντες· τοῦτό μού ἐστι τὸ αἷμα τῆς καινῆς διαθήκης τὸ ὑπὲρ ὑμῶν ἐκχυνόμενον εἰς ἄφεσιν ἁμαρτιῶν· τοῦτο ποιεῖτε εἰς τὴν ἐμὴν ἀνάμνησιν. Ὁσάκις γὰρ ἂν ἐσθίητε τὸν ἄρτον τοῦτον καὶ τὸ ποτήριον τοῦτο πίνητε, τὸν θάνατον τοῦ υἱοῦ τοῦ ἀνθρώπου καταγγέλλετε καὶ τὴν ἀνάστασιν αὐτοῦ ὁμολογεῖτε, ἕως ἂν ἔλθῃ».

Εἰ τοίνυν «ὁ λόγος τοῦ θεοῦ ζῶν ἐστι καὶ ἐνεργὴς» καὶ «πάντα, ὅσα ἠθέλησεν ὁ κύριος, ἐποίησεν»· εἰ εἶπε· «Γενηθήτω φῶς, καὶ ἐγένετο· γενηθήτω στερέωμα, καὶ ἐγένετο»· εἰ «τῷ λόγῳ κυρίου οἱ οὐρανοὶ ἐστερεώθησαν, καὶ τῷ πνεύματι τοῦ στόματος αὐτοῦ πᾶσα ἡ δύναμις αὐτῶν·» εἰ οὐρανὸς καὶ ἡ γῆ ὕδωρ τε καὶ πῦρ καὶ ἀὴρ καὶ πᾶς ὁ κόσμος αὐτῶν τῷ λόγῳ κυρίου συνετελέσθησαν καὶ τοῦτο δὴ τὸ πολυθρύλλητον ζῷον ὁ ἄνθρωπος· εἰ θελήσας αὐτὸς ὁ θεὸς λόγος ἐγένετο ἄνθρωπος καὶ τὰ τῆς ἁγίας παρθένου καθαρὰ καὶ ἀμώμητα αἵματα ἑαυτῷ ἀσπόρως σάρκα ὑπεστήσατο, —οὐ δύναται τὸν ἄρτον ἑαυτοῦ σῶμα ποιῆσαι καὶ τὸν οἶνον καὶ τὸ ὕδωρ αἷμα; Εἶπεν ἐν ἀρχῇ· «Ἐξαγαγέτω ἡ γῆ βοτάνην χόρτου», καὶ μέχρι τοῦ νῦν τοῦ ὑετοῦ γινομένου ἐξάγει τὰ ἴδια βλαστήματα τῷ θείῳ συνελαυνομένη καὶ δυναμουμένη προστάγματι. Εἶπεν ὁ θεός· «Τοῦτό μού ἐστι τὸ σῶμα», καί· «Τοῦτό μου τὸ αἷμα», καί· «Τοῦτο ποιεῖτε» καὶ τῷ παντοδυνάμῳ αὐτοῦ προστάγματι, ἕως ἂν ἔλθῃ, γίνεται· οὕτως γὰρ εἶπεν· «Ἕως ἂν ἔλθῃ». Καὶ γίνεται ὑετὸς τῇ καινῇ ταύτῃ γεωργίᾳ διὰ τῆς ἐπικλήσεως ἡ τοῦ ἁγίου πνεύματος ἐπισκιάζουσα δύναμις· ὥσπερ γὰρ πάντα, ὅσα

---

[4]John closely follows the wording of *The Liturgy of St James*, 202.9–24 (ed. B.-Ch. Mercier, *Patrologia Orientalis* 26 [1950], 19–256). This was the Liturgy used in Jerusalem until the thirteenth century.

| [5]Heb 4.12. | [6]Ps 134.6. | [7]Gen 1.3. |
| [8]Gen 1.6. | [9]Ps 32.6. | [10]Gen 1.11. |

bread and gave it to them, saying: "Take, eat, this is my body" which is broken for you for the remission of sins. Likewise taking the cup of wine and water he gave it to them, saying: "Drink of this all of you; this is my blood of the new covenant which is shed for you for the remission of sins. Do this in memory of me. For as often as you eat this bread and drink this cup, you proclaim the death of the Son of Man and you confess his resurrection, until he comes."[4]

Now if "the Word of God is living and active"[5] and "whatever the Lord wanted to do he did;"[6] if he said: "Let there be light and there was light,"[7] "let there be a firmament and there was a firmament;"[8] if "by the Word of the Lord the heavens were established, and all their power by the breath of his mouth;"[9] if heaven and earth, water and fire and air, and the whole order of these were established by the Word of the Lord and indeed that celebrated animal, the human being; if by his will God the Word became a human being and caused the pure and undefiled blood of the holy Virgin to subsist for himself without seed as his flesh—can he not make bread his own body, and wine and water his blood? He said in the beginning: "Let the earth put forth vegetation"[10] and until now when it rains it puts forth its own shoots, drawn on and strengthened by the divine command. God said: "This is my body"[11] and "This is my blood,"[12] and "Do this"[13] and by his almighty command, until he comes again, it happens. For that is what he said: "Until he comes again."[14] And through the epiclesis the overshadowing power of the Holy Spirit becomes the rain for this novel cultivation.[15] For as with everything that he made, God made it by the operation of the Holy Spirit, so in this case, too, the operation of the Spirit brings about things that transcend nature, which cannot be comprehended except by faith

[11]Mt 26.26; Mk 14.22; Lk 22.19; 1 Cor 11.24. This and the following Eucharistic phrases are quoted from *The Liturgy of St James.*
[12]Mt 26.28; Mk 14.24.   [13]1 Cor 11.24.   [14]1 Cor 11.26.
[15]The epiclesis is the liturgical invocation of the Holy Spirit to sanctify the holy gifts and transform the bread and wine into the body and blood of Christ. Its long tradition in the Jerusalem Liturgy is witnessed by Cyril of Jerusalem (*c*. 315–87). See his *Catechetical Lecture* 19.7 (PG 33:1072AB).

ἐποίησεν, ὁ θεὸς τῇ τοῦ ἁγίου πνεύματος ἐνεργείᾳ ἐποίησεν, οὕτω καὶ νῦν ἡ τοῦ πνεύματος ἐνέργεια τὰ ὑπὲρ φύσιν ἐργάζεται, ἃ οὐ δύναται χωρῆσαι, εἰ μὴ μόνη πίστις. «Πῶς ἔσται μοι τοῦτο», φησὶν ἡ ἁγία παρθένος, «ἐπεὶ ἄνδρα οὐ γινώσκω;» Ἀποκρίνεται Γαβριὴλ ὁ ἀρχάγγελος· «Πνεῦμα ἅγιον ἐπελεύσεται ἐπὶ σέ, καὶ δύναμις ὑψίστου ἐπισκιάσει σοι». Καὶ νῦν ἐρωτᾷς· Πῶς ὁ ἄρτος γίνεται σῶμα Χριστοῦ καὶ ὁ οἶνος καὶ τὸ ὕδωρ αἷμα Χριστοῦ; Λέγω σοι κἀγώ· Πνεῦμα ἅγιον ἐπιφοιτᾷ καὶ ταῦτα ποιεῖ τὰ ὑπὲρ λόγον καὶ ἔννοιαν.

Ἄρτος δὲ καὶ οἶνος παραλαμβάνεται· οἶδε γὰρ ὁ θεὸς τὴν ἀνθρωπίνην ἀσθένειαν, ὡς τὰ πολλὰ γὰρ τὰ μὴ κατὰ τὴν συνήθειαν τετριμμένα ἀποστρέφεται δυσχεραίνουσα· τῇ οὖν συνήθει συγκαταβάσει κεχρημένος διὰ τῶν συνήθων τῆς φύσεως ποιεῖ τὰ ὑπὲρ φύσιν· καὶ ὥσπερ ἐπὶ τοῦ βαπτίσματος, ἐπειδὴ ἔθος τοῖς ἀνθρώποις ὕδατι λούεσθαι καὶ ἐλαίῳ χρίεσθαι, συνέζευξε τῷ ἐλαίῳ καὶ ὕδατι τὴν χάριν τοῦ πνεύματος καὶ ἐποίησεν αὐτὸ λουτρὸν ἀναγεννήσεως, οὕτως, ἐπειδὴ ἔθος τοῖς ἀνθρώποις ἄρτον ἐσθίειν ὕδωρ τε καὶ οἶνον πίνειν, συνέζευξεν αὐτοῖς τὴν αὐτοῦ θεότητα καὶ πεποίηκεν αὐτὰ σῶμα καὶ αἷμα αὐτοῦ, ἵνα διὰ τῶν συνήθων καὶ κατὰ φύσιν ἐν τοῖς ὑπὲρ φύσιν γενώμεθα.

Σῶμά ἐστιν ἀληθῶς ἡνωμένον θεότητι, τὸ ἐκ τῆς ἁγίας παρθένου σῶμα, οὐχ ὅτι αὐτὸ τὸ σῶμα τὸ ἀναληφθὲν ἐξ οὐρανῶν κατέρχεται, ἀλλ᾿ ὅτι αὐτὸς ὁ ἄρτος καὶ ὁ οἶνος μεταποιεῖται εἰς σῶμα καὶ αἷμα θεοῦ. Εἰ δὲ τὸν τρόπον ἐπιζητεῖς, πῶς γίνεται, ἀρκεῖ σοι ἀκοῦσαι, ὅτι διὰ πνεύματος ἁγίου, ὥσπερ καὶ ἐκ τῆς ἁγίας θεοτόκου διὰ πνεύματος ἁγίου ἑαυτῷ καὶ ἐν ἑαυτῷ ὁ κύριος σάρκα ὑπεστήσατο· καὶ πλέον οὐδὲν γινώσκομεν, ἀλλ᾿ ὅτι ὁ λόγος τοῦ θεοῦ ἀληθὴς καὶ ἐνεργής ἐστι καὶ παντοδύναμος, ὁ δὲ τρόπος ἀνεξερεύνητος. Οὐ χεῖρον δὲ καὶ τοῦτο εἰπεῖν, ὅτι, ὥσπερ φυσικῶς διὰ τῆς βρώσεως ὁ ἄρτος καὶ ὁ οἶνος καὶ τὸ ὕδωρ διὰ τῆς πόσεως εἰς σῶμα καὶ αἷμα τοῦ ἐσθίοντος καὶ πίνοντος μεταβάλλεται καὶ οὐ γίνεται ἕτερον σῶμα παρὰ τὸ πρότερον αὐτοῦ σῶμα, οὕτως ὁ τῆς προθέσεως ἄρτος οἶνός τε καὶ ὕδωρ διὰ τῆς ἐπικλήσεως καὶ ἐπιφοιτήσεως τοῦ ἁγίου πνεύματος ὑπερφυῶς

alone. "How can this be," said the holy Virgin, "since I do not know a man?"[16] Gabriel the archangel replied: "The Holy Spirit will come upon you, and the power of the Most High will overshadow you."[17] And now you ask: "How does the bread become Christ's body and the wine and water Christ's blood?" And I say to you: "The Holy Spirit descends over it and does these things that transcend reason and understanding."

Bread and wine are used, for God knows our human weakness, how for the most part we turn away with repugnance from what we are not used to by long habit. Therefore by condescending to use what we are used to, he performs that which transcends nature through the familiar things of nature, and as in the case of baptism, since it is customary for people to wash themselves with water and anoint themselves with oil, he united the grace of the Spirit with oil and water and made this the bath of regeneration, so too, since it is customary for people to eat bread and drink water and wine, he united his own divinity to these and made them his body and blood, so that through things that are familiar and natural we should engage with that which transcends nature.

The body that came from the holy Virgin is a body truly united with divinity, not because the same body that ascended descends from heaven, but because the bread and the wine are changed into God's body and blood. If you ask about the manner, how this happens, it is sufficient for you to hear that it is through the Holy Spirit, just as it was also through the Holy Spirit that the Lord caused flesh to subsist for himself and in himself from the holy Theotokos. And beyond that we know nothing except that the Word of God is true and operative and all-powerful, but the manner is not subject to investigation. We may, not inappropriately, add the following, that just as bread through eating and wine and the water through drinking are transformed into the body and blood of the one who eats and drinks, and a different body from the one that previously existed does not come into being, so the bread, wine, and water of

16 Lk 1.34.   17 Lk 1.35.

μεταποιεῖται εἰς τὸ σῶμα τοῦ Χριστοῦ καὶ αἷμα, καὶ οὔκ εἰσι δύο, ἀλλ᾿ ἓν καὶ τὸ αὐτό.

Γίνεται τοίνυν τοῖς πίστει ἀξίως μεταλαμβάνουσιν εἰς ἄφεσιν ἁμαρτιῶν καὶ εἰς ζωὴν αἰώνιον καὶ εἰς φυλακτήριον ψυχῆς τε καὶ σώματος, τοῖς δὲ ἐν ἀπιστίᾳ ἀναξίως μετέχουσιν εἰς κόλασιν καὶ τιμωρίαν, καθάπερ καὶ ὁ τοῦ κυρίου θάνατος τοῖς μὲν πιστεύουσι γέγονε ζωὴ καὶ ἀφθαρσία εἰς ἀπόλαυσιν τῆς αἰωνίου μακαριότητος, τοῖς δὲ ἀπειθοῦσι καὶ τοῖς κυριοκτόνοις εἰς κόλασιν καὶ τιμωρίαν αἰώνιον.

Οὔκ ἔστι τύπος ὁ ἄρτος καὶ ὁ οἶνος τοῦ σώματος καὶ αἵματος τοῦ Χριστοῦ—μὴ γένοιτο—, ἀλλ᾿ αὐτὸ τὸ σῶμα τοῦ κυρίου τεθεωμένον, αὐτοῦ τοῦ κυρίου εἰπόντος· «Τοῦτό μού ἐστι» οὐ τύπος τοῦ σώματος ἀλλὰ «τὸ σῶμα», καὶ οὐ τύπος τοῦ αἵματος ἀλλὰ «τὸ αἷμα», καὶ πρὸ τούτου τοῖς Ἰουδαίοις, ὅτι, «εἰ μὴ φάγητε τὴν σάρκα τοῦ υἱοῦ τοῦ ἀνθρώπου, οὐκ ἔχετε ζωὴν αἰώνιον. Ἡ γὰρ σάρξ μου ἀληθής ἐστι βρῶσις, καὶ τὸ αἷμά μου ἀληθής ἐστι πόσις», καὶ πάλιν· «Ὁ τρώγων με ζήσεται».

Διὸ μετὰ παντὸς φόβου καὶ συνειδήσεως καθαρᾶς καὶ ἀδιστάκτου πίστεως προσέλθωμεν, καὶ πάντως ἔσται ἡμῖν, καθὼς πιστεύομεν μὴ διστάζοντες. Τιμήσωμεν δὲ αὐτὸ πάσῃ καθαρότητι, ψυχικῇ τε καὶ σωματικῇ· διπλοῦν γάρ ἐστι. Προσέλθωμεν αὐτῷ πόθῳ διακαεῖ καὶ σταυροειδῶς τὰς παλάμας τυπώσαντες τοῦ ἐσταυρωμένου τὸ σῶμα ὑποδεξώμεθα καὶ ἐπιθέντες ὀφθαλμοὺς καὶ χείλη καὶ μέτωπα τοῦ θείου ἄνθρακος μεταλάβωμεν, ἵνα τὸ πῦρ τοῦ ἐν ἡμῖν πόθου προσλαβὸν τὴν ἐκ τοῦ ἄνθρακος πύρωσιν καταφλέξῃ ἡμῶν τὰς ἁμαρτίας καὶ φωτίσῃ ἡμῶν τὰς καρδίας

---

[18]Cf. Gregory of Nyssa, *Catechetical Discourse* 37.9 (PG 45:96CD; Green, 147–48), an analogy that goes back to Justin Martyr, *First Apology* 66. John (like Cyril of Jerusalem, *Mystagogical Catechesis* 3.7 and 19) adds the explanation that the transformation is brought about liturgically by the epiclesis and the descent of the Holy Spirit.

[19]Jn 6.53–55.   [20]Jn 6.57.

[21]The exhortation to approach communion with hands folded and also to sanctify the eyes by the sight of the transformed bread and wine echoes Cyril of Jerusalem, *Mystagogical Catechesis* 5.21 (PG 33:1125A; PPS 57:135). The interpretation of Isaiah's burning coal (cf. Is 6.6) as a Eucharistic image symbolizing the sanctified bread on

the offering are transformed supernaturally into the body and blood of Christ through the epiclesis and the descent of the Holy Spirit, and there are not two bodies but one and the same body.[18]

Thus to those who receive communion worthily in faith it brings the remission of sins and life everlasting and the protection of soul and body, but to those who communicate unworthily in unbelief it brings punishment and retribution, just as the Lord's death brought life and incorruption to those who believe that they might enjoy eternal blessedness, but to those without faith and the killers of the Lord it brought eternal punishment and retribution.

The bread and the wine are not a symbol of the body and blood of Christ—God forbid!—but the actual deified body of the Lord, since the Lord himself said: "This is my body," not a symbol of my body, and "This is my blood," not a symbol of my blood, and before this to the Jews: "Unless you eat the flesh of the Son of Man you do not have eternal life. For my flesh is true food and my blood is true drink,"[19] and again: "Whoever eats me will live."[20]

Therefore let us approach with all fear and with a clear conscience and unhesitating faith, and it will certainly be for us as we believe and do not doubt. Let us honor it in all purity, both of soul and of body, for it is twofold. Let us approach it with burning desire and with our hands folded in the form of a cross let us receive the body of the Crucified, and applying our eyes and lips and foreheads let us partake of the divine coal, so that the fire of the desire within us might receive the heat of the coal and burn up our sins and illuminate our hearts and so that by partaking of the divine fire we might be set on fire and deified. Isaiah saw a coal, and a coal is not plain wood but wood united with fire.[21] In the same way the bread of

the altar is prefigured by Cyril of Alexandria (*Commentary on Isaiah*, PG 70:181B) and is also implied by the *Liturgy of St James* (B.-Ch. Mercier, *Patrologia Orientalis* [1946], 162.7 and 232.7) but is developed with particular clarity by John in this passage, which builds on the last paragraph of Chapter 52. Cf. John Damascene's *Homily on Holy Saturday* 29, where Joseph of Arimathea, as he takes down Christ's holy body from the cross, is described as touching the divine coal, not in a symbolic way like the Seraphim, but in reality on account of the hypostatic unity of Christ's humanity with his divinity (PG 96:629C).

καὶ τῇ μετουσίᾳ τοῦ θείου πυρὸς πυρωθῶμεν καὶ θεωθῶμεν. Ἄνθρακα εἶδεν Ἡσαΐας· ἄνθραξ δὲ ξύλον λιτὸν οὐκ ἔστιν, ἀλλ᾽ ἡνωμένον πυρί· οὕτως καὶ ὁ ἄρτος τῆς κοινωνίας οὐκ ἄρτος λιτός ἐστιν, ἀλλ᾽ ἡνωμένος θεότητι· σῶμα δὲ ἡνωμένον θεότητι οὐ μία φύσις ἐστίν, ἀλλὰ μία μὲν τοῦ σώματος, τῆς δὲ ἡνωμένης αὐτῷ θεότητος ἑτέρα· ὥστε τὸ συναμφότερον οὐ μία φύσις, ἀλλὰ δύο.

Ἄρτῳ καὶ οἴνῳ ἐδεξιοῦτο Μελχισεδὲκ τὸν Ἀβραὰμ ἐκ τῆς τῶν ἀλλοφύλων κοπῆς ὑποστρέφοντα, ὁ ἱερεὺς τοῦ θεοῦ τοῦ ὑψίστου· ἐκείνη ἡ τράπεζα ταύτην τὴν μυστικὴν προεικόνιζε τράπεζαν, ὃν τρόπον ἐκεῖνος ὁ ἱερεὺς τοῦ ἀληθινοῦ ἀρχιερέως Χριστοῦ τύπος ἦν καὶ εἰκόνισμα· «Σὺ» γάρ, φησίν, «ἱερεὺς εἰς τὸν αἰῶνα κατὰ τὴν τάξιν Μελχισεδέκ». Τοῦτον τὸν ἄρτον οἱ ἄρτοι εἰκόνιζον τῆς προθέσεως. Αὕτη γάρ ἐστιν ἡ καθαρὰ θυσία, δηλαδὴ καὶ ἀναίμακτος, ἣν ἀπὸ ἀνατολῶν ἡλίου μέχρι δυσμῶν αὐτῷ προσφέρεσθαι διὰ τοῦ προφήτου ὁ κύριος ἔφησε.

Σῶμά ἐστι καὶ αἷμα Χριστοῦ εἰς σύστασιν τῆς ἡμετέρας ψυχῆς τε καὶ σώματος χωροῦν, οὐ δαπανώμενον, οὐ φθειρόμενον, οὐκ εἰς ἀφεδρῶνα χωροῦν—μὴ γένοιτο—, ἀλλ᾽ εἰς τὴν ἡμῶν οὐσίαν τε καὶ συντήρησιν, βλάβης παντοδαποῦς ἀμυντήριον, ῥύπου παντὸς καθαρτήριον—ἂν μὲν χρυσὸν λάβῃ κίβδηλον, διὰ τῆς κριτικῆς πυρώσεως καθαίρει—, ἵνα μὴ ἐν τῷ μέλλοντι σὺν τῷ κόσμῳ κατακριθῶμεν. Καθαίρει γὰρ νόσους καὶ παντοίας ἐπιφοράς, καθὼς φησιν ὁ θεῖος ἀπόστολος· «Εἰ γὰρ ἑαυτοὺς ἐκρίνομεν, οὐκ ἂν ἐκρινόμεθα. Κρινόμενοι δὲ ὑπὸ κυρίου παιδευόμεθα, ἵνα μὴ σὺν τῷ κόσμῳ κατακριθῶμεν». Καὶ τοῦτό ἐστιν, ὃ λέγει· «Ὥστε ὁ μετέχων τοῦ σώματος καὶ τοῦ αἵματος τοῦ κυρίου ἀναξίως κρῖμα ἑαυτῷ ἐσθίει καὶ πίνει». Δι᾽ αὐτοῦ καθαιρόμενοι ἑνούμεθα τῷ σώματι τοῦ κυρίου καὶ τῷ πνεύματι αὐτοῦ καὶ γινόμεθα σῶμα Χριστοῦ.

Οὗτος ὁ ἄρτος ἐστὶν ἡ ἀπαρχὴ τοῦ μέλλοντος ἄρτου, ὅς ἐστιν ὁ ἐπιούσιος· τὸ γὰρ «ἐπιούσιον» δηλοῖ ἢ τὸν μέλλοντα, τουτέστιν

[22]Cf. Gen 14.17–20. [23]Ps 109.4; Heb 7.17.
[24]The shewbread (ἄρτοι τῆς προθέσεως, artoi tēs protheseōs—"bread of the

communion is not plain bread but bread united with divinity. For the body united with divinity is not a single nature, but that of the body is one nature and that of the divinity united with it is another nature. Consequently, both together are not one nature but two.

Melchizedek, the priest of the most high God, received Abraham with bread and wine on his return from the slaughter of the foreign tribes.[22] That table prefigured this mystical table, in the same way that that priest was a type and image of Christ, the true high priest. For Scripture says: "You are a priest forever, according to the order of Melchizedek."[23] This bread was typified by the loaves of the shew-bread.[24] For this is the "pure sacrifice," that is to say, the bloodless sacrifice, which the Lord said through the prophet is offered "from the rising of the sun to its setting."[25]

It is the body and blood of Christ that enters into us for the nourishment of our soul and body. It is not consumed or corrupted, it does not pass out into the sewer—God forbid!—but into our substance for our preservation, a defence against all kinds of harm, a purification from all filth—if gold is adulterated, it is purified by fire that separates—that in the age to come we may not be condemned along with the world. For it clears us from disease and every kind of attack, as the divine Apostle says: "But if we judged ourselves, we would not be judged. But when we are judged by the Lord, we are disciplined so that we may not be condemned along with the world."[26] And this is the meaning of the text: "Therefore all who partake of the Lord's body and blood unworthily eat and drink judgement to themselves."[27] Cleansed by it, we are united to the body of the Lord and to his Spirit and become Christ's body.

This bread is the first-fruits of the bread of the age to come, which is the superessential bread. For the word "superessential" (ἐπιούσιος, *epiousios*) indicates either what belong to the future, that is to say, the future of the age to come, or what is received by us for

Presence" in the NRSV translation) was the twelve loaves set out in two rows each week by the altar of incense in the Jerusalem Temple; cf. Lev 24.5–9; Mk 2.26.
    [25]Mal 1.11.   [26]1 Cor 11.31–32.   [27]1 Cor 11.29.

τὸν τοῦ μέλλοντος αἰῶνος, ἢ τὸν πρὸς συντήρησιν τῆς οὐσίας ἡμῶν λαμβανόμενον. Εἴτε οὖν οὕτως, εἴτε οὕτως, τὸ τοῦ κυρίου σῶμα προσφυῶς λεχθήσεται· πνεῦμα γὰρ ζωοποιοῦν ἐστιν ἡ σὰρξ τοῦ κυρίου, διότι ἐκ τοῦ ζωοποιοῦ πνεύματος συνελήφθη· «τὸ γὰρ γεγεννημένον ἐκ τοῦ πνεύματος πνεῦμά ἐστι». Τοῦτο δὲ λέγω οὐκ ἀναιρῶν τὴν τοῦ σώματος φύσιν, ἀλλὰ τὸ ζωοποιὸν καὶ θεῖον τούτου δηλῶσαι βουλόμενος.

Εἰ δὲ καί τινες ἀντίτυπα τοῦ σώματος καὶ τοῦ αἵματος τοῦ κυρίου τὸν ἄρτον καὶ τὸν οἶνον ἐκάλεσαν, ὡς ὁ θεοφόρος ἔφη Βασίλειος, οὐ μετὰ τὸ ἁγιασθῆναι εἶπον, ἀλλὰ πρὶν ἁγιασθῆναι αὐτὴν τὴν προσφορὰν οὕτω καλέσαντες.

Μετάληψις λέγεται· δι᾽ αὐτῆς γὰρ τῆς Ἰησοῦ θεότητος μεταλαμβάνομεν. Κοινωνία λέγεταί τε καὶ ἔστιν ἀληθῶς διὰ τὸ κοινωνεῖν ἡμᾶς δι᾽ αὐτῆς τῷ Χριστῷ καὶ μετέχειν αὐτοῦ τῆς σαρκός τε καὶ τῆς θεότητος, κοινωνεῖν δὲ καὶ ἐνοῦσθαι καὶ ἀλλήλοις δι᾽ αὐτῆς· ἐπεὶ γὰρ ἐξ ἑνὸς ἄρτου μεταλαμβάνομεν, οἱ πάντες ἓν σῶμα Χριστοῦ καὶ ἓν αἷμα καὶ ἀλλήλων μέλη γινόμεθα σύσσωμοι Χριστοῦ χρηματίζοντες.

Πάσῃ δυνάμει τοίνυν φυλαξώμεθα, μὴ λαμβάνειν μετάληψιν αἱρετικῶν μήτε διδόναι. «Μὴ δῶτε γὰρ τὰ ἅγια τοῖς κυσίν», φησὶν ὁ κύριος, «μηδὲ ῥίπτετε τοὺς μαργαρίτας ὑμῶν ἔμπροσθεν τῶν χοίρων», ἵνα μὴ μέτοχοι τῆς κακοδοξίας καὶ τῆς αὐτῶν γενώμεθα κατακρίσεως. Εἰ γὰρ πάντως ἕνωσίς ἐστι πρὸς Χριστὸν καὶ πρὸς ἀλλήλους, πάντως καὶ πᾶσι τοῖς συμμεταλαμβάνουσιν ἡμῖν κατὰ προαίρεσιν ἑνούμεθα· ἐκ προαιρέσεως γὰρ ἡ ἕνωσις αὕτη γίνεται, οὐ χωρὶς τῆς ἡμῶν γνώμης.

---

[28]The word ἐπιούσιος, here translated as "superessential," is a New Testament coinage that appears in the Lord's Prayer in slightly different settings in Mt 6.11 (τὸν ἄρτον ἡμῶν τὸν ἐπιούσιον δὸς ἡμῖν σήμερον, *ton arton hēmōn ton epiousion dos hēmin sēmeron*) and Lk 11.3 (τὸν ἄρτον ἡμῶν τὸν ἐπιούσιον δίδου ἡμῖν τὸ καθ᾽ ἡμέραν, *ton arton hēmōn ton epiousion didou hēmin to kath' hēmeran*). The meaning is not as clear as the familiar English translation, "daily," would imply. Jerome translated the Matthaean instance as *supersubstantialem* ("superessential") but the Lucan as *quotidianum* ("daily"). John Chrysostom took the ἐπιούσιον bread to be ordinary daily bread

the maintenance of our substance.[28] Therefore, whether it indicates the one or the other, it is said appropriately of the Lord's body, for the Lord's flesh is "life-giving spirit," because it was conceived of the life-giving Spirit:[29] "For what is born of the Spirit is spirit."[30] In saying this I do not deny the nature of the body but wish to emphasize its life-giving and divine character.

If some have called the bread and the wine symbols of the Lord's body and blood, as the God-bearing Basil did,[31] they were not referring to them after the consecration but called them such before the offering itself was consecrated.

It is called "partaking" (μετάληψις, *metalēpsis*), for it is through this that we partake of Jesus' divinity. It is also called "communion" (κοινωνία, *koinōnia*) and is truly so because through it we are in communion with Christ and share in his flesh and divinity, and to be in communion is also to be united with each other through this. For since we partake of one bread, we all become one body of Christ and one blood and members of one another, being reckoned to be one body with Christ.

We should therefore with all our strength guard against receiving communion from heretics or giving it to them. "Do not give what is holy to dogs," says the Lord, "nor cast your pearls before swine,"[32] that we may not become sharers in their heresy and in their condemnation. For if union is assuredly with Christ and with each other, it is evident that we are united by our own deliberate choice with all with whom we receive communion. For this union takes place by deliberate choice, not without our voluntary intention.

(*Homilies on Matthew* 19.5) but many fathers since Origen (cf. Origen, *On the Lord's Prayer* 27.7–11; PPS 29:178–82.) have understood it to be the supernatural bread of Christ. Maximus the Confessor, on the basis of the σήμερον (*sēmeron*) in Matthew's text, understood the superessential bread to belong to the present age (αἰών, *aiōn*) (*On the Lord's Prayer* 562). John Damascene interprets it as the bread of the age to come.
[29]Cf. 1 Cor 15.45; Jn 6.63.   [30]Jn 3.6.
[31]Cf. *Liturgy of St Basil*, 329.24.
[32]Mt 7.6.

Ἀντίτυπα δὲ τῶν μελλόντων λέγονται οὐχ ὡς μὴ ὄντα ἀληθῶς σῶμα καὶ αἷμα Χριστοῦ, ἀλλ᾽ ὅτι νῦν μὲν δι᾽ αὐτῶν μετέχομεν τῆς Χριστοῦ θεότητος, τότε δὲ νοητῶς διὰ μόνης τῆς θέας.

87 Περὶ τῆς γενεαλογίας τοῦ κυρίου καὶ περὶ τῆς ἁγίας θεοτόκου

Περὶ τῆς ἁγίας ὑπερυμνήτου ἀειπαρθένου καὶ θεοτόκου Μαρίας ἐν τοῖς προλαβοῦσι μετρίως διαλαβόντες καὶ τὸ καιριώτατον παραστήσαντες, ὡς κυρίως καὶ ἀληθῶς θεοτόκος ἔστι τε καὶ ὀνομάζεται, νῦν τὰ λείποντα προσαναπληρώσωμεν. Αὕτη γὰρ τῇ προαιωνίῳ προγνωστικῇ βουλῇ τοῦ θεοῦ προορισθεῖσα καὶ διαφόροις εἰκόσι καὶ λόγοις προφητῶν διὰ πνεύματος ἁγίου εἰκονισθεῖσά τε καὶ προκηρυχθεῖσα ἐν τῷ προωρισμένῳ καιρῷ ἐκ Δαυιδικῆς ῥίζης ἐβλάστησε διὰ τὰς πρὸς αὐτὸν γενομένας ἐπαγγελίας. «Ὤμοσε γὰρ κύριος», φησί, «τῷ Δαυὶδ ἀλήθειαν, καὶ οὐ μὴ ἀθετήσει αὐτόν· ἐκ καρποῦ τῆς κοιλίας σου θήσομαι ἐπὶ τοῦ θρόνου σου», καὶ πάλιν· «Ἅπαξ ὤμοσα ἐν τῷ ἁγίῳ μου, εἰ τῷ Δαυὶδ ψεύσομαι. Τὸ σπέρμα αὐτοῦ εἰς τὸν αἰῶνα μένει· καὶ ὁ θρόνος αὐτοῦ ὡς ὁ ἥλιος ἐναντίον μου καὶ ὡς ἡ σελήνη κατηρτισμένη εἰς τὸν αἰῶνα, καὶ ὁ μάρτυς ἐν οὐρανῷ πιστός,» καὶ Ἡσαΐας· «Ἐξανατελεῖ ῥάβδος ἐξ Ἰεσσαί, καὶ ἄνθος ἐκ τῆς ῥίζης ἀναβήσεται».

Ὅτι μὲν οὖν ὁ Ἰωσὴφ ἐκ Δαυιδικοῦ φύλου κατάγεται, ὁ Ματθαῖος καὶ Λουκᾶς, οἱ ἱερώτατοι εὐαγγελισταί, διαρρήδην ὑπέδειξαν, ἀλλ᾽ ὁ μὲν Ματθαῖος ἐκ Δαυὶδ διὰ Σολομῶντος κατάγει τὸν Ἰωσήφ, ὁ δὲ Λουκᾶς διὰ Νάθαν. Τῆς δὲ ἁγίας παρθένου τὴν γέννησιν καὶ ἀμφότεροι παρεσιώπησαν.

---

[33]By means of vision, the highest of the physical senses, but in this case spiritual vision, we shall go beyond the symbols to attain to the reality itself. It may be noted that after the communion of the laity, the priest prays at every Liturgy, in words drawn from John Damascene's Paschal Canon, "O Christ, great and most holy Pascha, O Wisdom, Word, and Power of God, grant that we may more perfectly partake of Thee in the never-ending day of Thy kingdom." (IG)

They are called symbols of the things to come not in the sense that they are not truly the body and blood of Christ, but because now it is through them that we partake of Christ's divinity, whereas then we shall partake of it spiritually through vision alone.[33]

87   *On the Lord's genealogy and on the holy Theotokos*

In the preceding discussions we have, to a limited extent, discussed the holy, supremely praiseworthy, ever-virgin Mary, the Theotokos, setting out the most important point, namely, that she is literally and truly Theotokos and is called such.[1] Now let us complete what still remains to be said. For she was predetermined by the eternal foreknowing will of God, and was symbolized and proclaimed in advance through the Spirit by the various images and words of the prophets, and so at the predetermined time sprouted from the root of David in accordance with the promises made to him. "For the Lord," it says, "swore to David in truth and will not set it aside. From the fruit of your belly I shall set one upon your throne."[2] And again: "Once and for all have I sworn by my holiness. I will not lie to David. His line shall continue forever, and his throne shall be before me like the sun and the like the moon that is established forever, and the witness in the sky is trustworthy."[3] And Isaiah: "A shoot shall come forth out of Jesse, and a flower shall rise up from the root."[4]

That Joseph descended from the tribe of David is stated explicitly by both Matthew and Luke, the most holy evangelists.[5] But Matthew traces his descent from David through Solomon, whereas Luke has him descended from Nathan. Both of them are silent about the birth of the holy Virgin.

One needs to know that it was not a custom among the Hebrews or in holy Scripture for the genealogy of the female line to be given.

[1]See especially Chapters 56 and 80, above.
[2]Ps 131.11.   [3]Ps 88.36–38.   [4]Is 11.1.
[5]Mt 1.1–16; Lk 3.23–38. John's task here is to reconcile the two different genealogies given in Matthew and Luke.

Χρὴ οὖν εἰδέναι, ὡς οὐκ ἦν ἔθος Ἑβραίοις οὐδὲ τῇ θείᾳ γραφῇ
γενεαλογεῖσθαι γυναῖκας. Νόμος δὲ ἦν μὴ μνηστεύεσθαι φυλὴν
ἐξ ἑτέρας φυλῆς. Ὁ δὲ Ἰωσὴφ ἐκ Δαυιδικοῦ καταγόμενος φύλου,
δίκαιος ὑπάρχων (τοῦτο γὰρ αὐτῷ μαρτυρεῖ τὸ θεῖον εὐαγγέλιον),
οὐκ ἂν παρανόμως τὴν ἁγίαν παρθένον πρὸς μνηστείαν ἠγάγετο,
εἰ μὴ ἐκ τοῦ αὐτοῦ σκήπτρου κατήγετο. Δείξας τοίνυν τὸ τοῦ
Ἰωσὴφ καταγώγιον ἠρκέσθη.

Χρὴ δὲ καὶ τοῦτο εἰδέναι, ὡς νόμος ἦν ἀγόνου ἀνδρὸς
τελευτῶντος τὸν τούτου ἀδελφὸν τὴν τοῦ τετελευτηκότος
γαμετὴν πρὸς γάμον ἄγεσθαι καὶ ἐγείρειν σπέρμα τῷ ἀδελφῷ.
Τὸ οὖν τικτόμενον κατὰ φύσιν μὲν τοῦ δευτέρου ἤτοι τοῦ
γεγεννηκότος ἦν, κατὰ δὲ νόμον τοῦ τελευτήσαντος.

Ἐκ τῆς σειρᾶς τοίνυν τοῦ Νάθαν τοῦ υἱοῦ Δαυὶδ Λευὶ
ἐγέννησε τὸν Μελχὶ καὶ τὸν Πάνθηρα· ὁ Πάνθηρ ἐγέννησε τὸν
Βαρπάνθηρα οὕτως ἐπικληθέντα. Οὗτος ὁ Βαρπάνθηρ ἐγέννησε
τὸν Ἰωακείμ, Ἰωακεὶμ ἐγέννησε τὴν ἁγίαν θεοτόκον. Ἐκ δὲ τῆς
σειρᾶς Σολομῶντος τοῦ υἱοῦ Δαυὶδ Ματθὰν ἔσχε γυναῖκα, ἐξ ἧς
ἐγέννησε τὸν Ἰακώβ. Τελευτήσαντος δὲ τοῦ Ματθὰν Μελχὶ ἐκ
τῆς φυλῆς τοῦ Νάθαν, ὁ υἱὸς Λευί, ἀδελφὸς δὲ τοῦ Πάνθηρος,
ἔγημε τὴν γυναῖκα τοῦ Ματθάν, μητέρα δὲ τοῦ Ἰακώβ, καὶ ἐξ
αὐτῆς ἔσχε τὸν Ἠλί. Ἐγένοντο οὖν ἀδελφοὶ ὁμομήτριοι Ἰακὼβ καὶ
Ἠλί, ὁ μὲν Ἰακὼβ ἐκ τῆς φυλῆς Σολομῶντος, ὁ δὲ Ἠλὶ ἐκ φυλῆς
Νάθαν. Ἐτελεύτησε δὲ ὁ Ἠλί, ὁ ἐκ τῆς φυλῆς τοῦ Νάθαν ἄπαις·
καὶ ἔλαβεν Ἰακώβ, ὁ ἀδελφὸς αὐτοῦ ὁ ἐκ τῆς φυλῆς Σολομῶντος,
τὴν γυναῖκα αὐτοῦ καὶ ἐγέννησε τὸν Ἰωσήφ. Ὁ οὖν Ἰωσὴφ φύσει
μέν ἐστιν υἱὸς Ἰακὼβ ἐκ τοῦ καταγωγίου τοῦ Σολομῶντος, κατὰ
δὲ νόμον Ἠλὶ τοῦ ἐκ Νάθαν.

---

[6]Num 36.6–9.   [7]Mt 1.19.   [8]Deut 25.5–6.

[9]Neither Panther nor Barpanther is mentioned in the Matthean and Lukan
genealogies. So where did John find this tradition? Kotter cites Epiphanius, *Against
Heresies* (*Panarion*) III (GCS 37), 457.12–14, but this is not relevant since Epiphanius
(followed by Anastasius of Sinai) posits Panther as an ancestor of Joseph, not of the
Theotokos. A more helpful reference is given by Henry Chadwick in *Origen Contra
Celsum* (Cambridge: Cambridge University Press, 1965), 31 n. 3. In *Against Celsus* 1.32
Origen refutes Celsus' charge (supported by the Talmud) that the Lord's biological

But there was a law that one tribe should not marry into another.[6] And since Joseph, who was a descendant of the tribe of David, was a righteous man (for this is testified about him by the divine gospel),[7] he would not have taken the holy Virgin in marriage, unless she were descended from the same tribe. It was therefore sufficient to have shown the descent of Joseph.

One also needs to know the following. It was the law that when a man died without issue, his brother was to marry the wife of the deceased and raise up offspring for his brother. The child thus born belonged by nature to the second, that is to say, to the one that had begotten it, but by law to the deceased.[8]

So from the line of Nathan the son of David, Levi was the father of Melchi and Panther.[9] Panther was the father of Barpanther, so called. This Barpanther was the father of Joachim, and Joachim was the father of the holy Theotokos. From the line of Solomon the son of David, Matthan took a wife by whom he begot Jacob. When Matthan died, Melchi of the tribe of Nathan, son of Levi and brother of Panther, married Matthan's wife, the mother of Jacob, and by her had Heli. There were therefore two brothers from the same mother, Jacob and Heli, but Jacob was the tribe of Solomon, whereas Heli was of the tribe of Nathan. Now Heli, the one who was of the tribe of Nathan, died childless. And Jacob, his brother of the tribe of Solomon, took his wife and begot Joseph. Therefore Joseph, although by nature son of Jacob and descended from Solomon, was by law son of Heli descended from Nathan.

Then Joachim married the modest and praiseworthy Anna. But just as the earlier Anna was barren but through prayer and a promise gave birth to Samuel,[10] so this Anna, too, as a result of intercession and

father was a Roman soldier called Panther. Chadwick draws attention to a passage in Andrew of Crete's *Homily on the Lord's Circumcision* (PG 97:916B) in which Panther is also mentioned as the brother of Melchi and the great-grandfather of the Theotokos, which Chadwick, very plausibly, thinks was taken up by John Damascene. If the "Karpanther" of Migne's text was already a scribal error in the copy of Andrew's homilies consulted by John, John correctly changed it to Barpanther. (IG)

[10] 1 Kg 1.9–20.

Ἰωακεὶμ τοίνυν τὴν σεμνήν τε καὶ ἀξιέπαινον Ἄνναν πρὸς
γάμον ἠγάγετο. Ἀλλ᾽ ὥσπερ ἡ πάλαι Ἄννα στειρεύσασα δι᾽ εὐχῆς
καὶ ἐπαγγελίας τὸν Σαμουὴλ ἐγέννησεν, οὕτω καὶ αὕτη διὰ λιτῆς
καὶ ἐπαγγελίας πρὸς θεοῦ τὴν θεοτόκον κομίζεται, ἵνα κἂν τούτῳ
μηδενὸς τῶν περιφανῶν καθυστερίζοιτο· τίκτει τοιγαροῦν ἡ
χάρις (τοῦτο γὰρ ἡ Ἄννα ἑρμηνεύεται) τὴν κυρίαν (τοῦτο γὰρ τῆς
Μαρίας σημαίνει τὸ ὄνομα· κυρία γὰρ ὄντως γέγονε πάντων τῶν
ποιημάτων τοῦ δημιουργοῦ χρηματίσασα μήτηρ). Τίκτεται δὲ ἐν
τῷ τῆς προβατικῆς τοῦ Ἰωακεὶμ οἴκῳ καὶ τῷ ἱερῷ προσάγεται. Εἶτα
ἐν τῷ οἴκῳ τοῦ θεοῦ φυτευθεῖσά τε καὶ πιανθεῖσα τῷ πνεύματι
ὡσεὶ ἐλαία κατάκαρπος πάσης ἀρετῆς καταγώγιον γέγονε πάσης
βιωτικῆς καὶ σαρκικῆς ἐπιθυμίας τὸν νοῦν ἀποστήσασα καὶ οὕτω
παρθένον τὴν ψυχὴν τηρήσασα σὺν τῷ σώματι, ὡς ἔπρεπε τὴν
θεὸν ἐγκόλπιον ὑποδέχεσθαι μέλλουσαν· ἅγιος γὰρ ὢν ἐν ἁγίοις
ἀναπαύεται. Οὕτω τοίνυν ἁγιωσύνην μετέρχεται καὶ ναὸς ἅγιος
καὶ θαυμαστὸς τοῦ ὑψίστου θεοῦ ἀναδείκνυται ἀξίως.

Ἐπειδὴ δὲ ἐπετήρει τὰς παρθένους ὁ τῆς ἡμῶν σωτηρίας
ἐχθρὸς διὰ τὴν Ἡσαΐου πρόρρησιν· «Ἰδοὺ ἡ παρθένος ἐν γαστρὶ
ἕξει», φήσαντος, «καὶ τέξεται υἱόν, καὶ καλέσουσι τὸ ὄνομα αὐτοῦ
Ἐμμανουήλ, ὅ ἐστι μεθερμηνευόμενον Μεθ᾽ ἡμῶν ὁ θεός», ὡς ἂν
δελεάσῃ τὸν ἐν σοφίᾳ ἀεὶ ἁβρυνόμενον «ὁ δρασσόμενος τοὺς
σοφοὺς ἐν τῇ πανουργίᾳ αὐτῶν», πρὸς μνηστείαν ἡ νεᾶνις τῷ
Ἰωσὴφ ὑπὸ τῶν ἱερέων δίδοται, ὁ καινὸς τόμος τῷ γράμματα
εἰδότι· ἡ δὲ μνηστεία φυλακή τε τῆς παρθένου ὑπῆρχε καὶ τοῦ
τὰς παρθένους ἐπιτηροῦντος ἀποβουκόλημα. Ὅτε δὲ ἦλθε τὸ
πλήρωμα τοῦ χρόνου», ἀπεστάλη ἄγγελος κυρίου πρὸς αὐτὴν
τὴν τοῦ κυρίου εὐαγγελιζόμενος σύλληψιν· οὕτως τε συνείληφε
τὸν υἱὸν τοῦ θεοῦ, τὴν τοῦ πατρὸς ἐνυπόστατον δύναμιν, «οὐκ ἐκ

---

[11]John is correct about the etymological meaning of Anna (Hannah in Hebrew).
The etymological meaning of Mary (Maria in Greek, Maryam in Aramaic, and
Miriam in Hebrew) is not certain, but John's derivation is a plausible one.
[12]Ps 51.10.
[13]The details of the early life of the Virgin, the names of her parents, her dedica-
tion by them to the Temple, where she grew up, and her betrothal at the age of twelve

a promise, received the Theotokos from God, that even in this matter she might not fall short of any of her eminent predecessors. Grace, then (for this is the translation of Anna) gave birth to the Lady (for this is what the name Mary means, for she truly became Lady of all creatures, since she was called mother of the Creator).[11] She was born in Joachim's house at the Sheepgate and was brought to the Temple. Then planted in the House of God and tended by the Holy Spirit, she became, "like a fruitful olive tree,"[12] the abode of every virtue, having put out of her mind every worldly and carnal desire, and thus keeping her soul virginal as well as her body, as was fitting for one who was to receive God in her womb. For since God is holy, he reposes in holy people. She thus shared in holiness and proved worthily to be a holy and wonderful temple of the God Most High.[13]

The enemy of our salvation kept virgins under observation on account of Isaiah's prophecy. "Behold, the virgin shall conceive in her womb," he says, "and bear a son, and they shall call his name Emmanuel, which means 'God is with us.'"[14] Because of this, so that "he who catches the wise in their craftiness"[15] might deceive him who prides himself on his wisdom, the young woman was given by the priests to Joseph in betrothal, as the new book to one who is learned.[16] The betrothal was a protection for the Virgin, and a ruse to lead astray him who kept virgins under observation. "But when the fullness of time had come,"[17] an angel of the Lord was sent to her to announce the conception of the Lord. And it was thus that she conceived the Son of God, the enhypostatic power of the Father, "not by the will of the flesh, or by the will of a man,"[18] that is to say, by sexual union and procreation, but by the good will of the Father and the cooperation of the Holy Spirit. She furnished the Creator

to the widower Joseph, are traditional. They are encountered for the first time in the apocryphal *Protevangelium of James*, which goes back at least to the third century.
[14]Mt 1.23; cf. Is 7.14.   [15]1 Cor 3.19; cf. Job 5.12–13.
[16]The scholarly image of "the new book" (ὁ καινὸς τόμος, *ho kainos tomos*) is a biblical allusion. Isaiah, the prophet of the coming of Christ, was commanded to take a "new book" and write in it (Is 8.1, LXX).
[17]Gal 4.4.   [18]Jn 1.13.

θελήματος σαρκὸς οὐδὲ ἐκ θελήματος ἀνδρὸς» ἤτοι συναφείας καὶ σπορᾶς, ἀλλ᾽ ἐκ τῆς τοῦ πατρὸς εὐδοκίας καὶ συνεργίας τοῦ ἁγίου πνεύματος· ἐχορήγησέ τε τῷ κτίστῃ τὸ κτισθῆναι καὶ τῷ πλάστῃ τὸ πλασθῆναι καὶ τῷ υἱῷ τοῦ θεοῦ καὶ θεῷ τὸ σαρκωθῆναι καὶ ἀνθρωπισθῆναι ἐκ τῶν ἁγνῶν καὶ ἀμολύντων αὐτῆς σαρκῶν καὶ αἱμάτων, τὸ τῆς προμήτορος ἀποπληροῦσα χρέος· ὥσπερ γὰρ ἐκείνη συναφείας ἐκτὸς ἐξ Ἀδὰμ πεπλαστούργηται, οὕτω καὶ αὕτη τὸν νέον Ἀδὰμ ἀπεκύησε νόμῳ κυήσεως τικτόμενον καὶ ὑπὲρ φύσιν γεννήσεως. Τίκτεται γὰρ ἀπάτωρ ἐκ γυναικὸς ὁ ἐκ πατρὸς ἀμήτωρ· καὶ ὅτι μὲν ἐκ γυναικὸς νόμῳ κυήσεως, ὅτι δὲ ἄνευ πατρός, ὑπὲρ φύσιν γεννήσεως· καὶ ὅτι μὲν τῷ εἰθισμένῳ χρόνῳ (τὸν γὰρ ἐννεαμηνιαῖον τελέσας καὶ τῷ δεκάτῳ ἐπιβὰς γεννᾶται), νόμῳ κυήσεως· ὅτι δὲ ἀνωδίνως, ὑπὲρ θεσμὸν γεννήσεως· ἧς γὰρ ἡδονὴ οὐ προηγήσατο, οὐδὲ ὠδὶν ἐπηκολούθησε, κατὰ τὸν προφήτην τὸν λέγοντα· «Πρὶν ὠδίνησεν, ἔτεκε», καὶ πάλιν· «Πρὶν ἐλθεῖν τὸν καιρὸν τῶν ὠδίνων, ἐξέφυγε καὶ ἔτεκεν ἄρσεν».

Γεγέννηται τοίνυν ἐξ αὐτῆς ὁ υἱὸς τοῦ θεοῦ καὶ θεὸς σεσαρκωμένος, οὐ θεοφόρος ἄνθρωπος, ἀλλὰ θεὸς σεσαρκωμένος, οὐχ ὡς προφήτης ἐνεργείᾳ χριόμενος, παρουσίᾳ δὲ ὅλου τοῦ χρίοντος, ὥστε ἄνθρωπον μὲν γενέσθαι τὸ χρῖσαν καὶ θεὸν τὸ χριόμενον, οὐ μεταβολῇ φύσεως, ἀλλ᾽ ἑνώσει τῇ καθ᾽ ὑπόστασιν. Ὁ αὐτὸς γὰρ ἦν, ὅ τε χρίων καὶ ὁ χριόμενος, χρίων ὡς θεὸς ἑαυτὸν ὡς ἄνθρωπον. Πῶς οὖν οὐ θεοτόκος ἡ θεὸν σεσαρκωμένον ἐξ αὐτῆς γεννήσασα; Ὄντως κυρίως καὶ ἀληθῶς θεοτόκος καὶ κυρία, καὶ πάντων κτισμάτων δεσπόζουσα, δούλη καὶ μήτηρ τοῦ δημιουργοῦ χρηματίσασα. Ὥσπερ δὲ συλληφθεὶς παρθένον τὴν συλλαβοῦσαν ἐτήρησεν, οὕτω καὶ τεχθεὶς τὴν αὐτῆς παρθενίαν ἐφύλαξεν ἄτρωτον μόνος διελθὼν δι᾽ αὐτῆς καὶ κεκλεισμένην τηρήσας αὐτήν· δι᾽ ἀκοῆς μὲν ἡ σύλληψις, ἡ δὲ γέννησις διὰ τῆς συνήθους τῶν τικτομένων ἐξόδου, εἰ καί τινες μυθολογοῦσι διὰ τῆς πλευρᾶς αὐτὸν τεχθῆναι τῆς θεομήτορος. Οὐ γὰρ ἀδύνατος ἦν καὶ διὰ τῆς πύλης διελθεῖν καὶ ταύτης μὴ παραβλάψαι τὰ σήμαντρα.

with the means of being created, and the Fashioner with the means of being fashioned, and the Son of God and God with the means of being enfleshed and becoming human from her pure and undefiled flesh and blood, thus paying the debt of the first mother. For just as the latter was fashioned from the side of Adam without sexual union, so too did the former bring forth the new Adam by the law of conception and of a birth that transcended nature. For he who was from a father without a mother was brought forth from a woman without a father. And because he was brought forth from a woman, it was by the law of conception, but because this occurred without a father, it was by a birth that transcended nature. And because this occurred at the normal time (for he was born at the end of the nine-month period and had entered on the tenth month) it was by the law of conception. But because it was without pain, it was a birth beyond the law of birth. For as it had not been preceded by pleasure, it was not followed by pain, in accordance with the prophet who said: "Before she was in labor she gave birth,"[19] and again: "Before the time of labor came upon her, she escaped and delivered a male."[20]

And so the Son of God was born from her and became God made flesh, not a God-bearing man, but God enfleshed, not as a prophet anointed by [external] operation but by the presence of the whole of the anointer, so that the anointer became man and the anointed became God, not by a change of nature but by hypostatic union. For the same was both the anointer and the anointed, as God anointing himself as man. How, then, was she who gave birth to God incarnate from her own person not Theotokos? In reality she is literally and truly Theotokos and Lady and Mistress of all created beings, since she has been called handmaid and mother of the Creator. When he was conceived, he kept her who had conceived him a virgin. In the same way, when he was born he left her virginity intact, since he alone entered through her and kept her shut. The conception took place through the sense of hearing but the birth took place through the usual passage through which children are born, even if

[19] Is 66.7.   [20] Ibid.

Μένει τοίνυν καὶ μετὰ τόκον παρθένος ἡ ἀειπάρθενος οὐδαμῶς ἀνδρὶ μέχρι θανάτου προσομιλήσασα. Εἰ γὰρ καὶ γέγραπται· «Καὶ οὐκ ἔγνω αὐτήν, ἕως οὗ ἔτεκε τὸν υἱὸν αὐτῆς τὸν πρωτότοκον», ἰστέον ὅτι πρωτότοκός ἐστιν ὁ πρῶτος γεννηθείς, εἰ καὶ μονογενὴς εἴη· τὸ μὲν γὰρ πρῶτον γεννηθῆναι δηλοῖ, οὐ πάντως δὲ καὶ ἑτέρων συνεμφαίνει γέννησιν. Τὸ δὲ «ἕως» τὴν μὲν τοῦ ὡρισμένου χρόνου προθεσμίαν σημαίνει, οὐκ ἀποφάσκει δὲ τὸ μετὰ ταῦτα· φησὶ γὰρ ὁ κύριος· «Καὶ ἰδοὺ ἐγὼ μεθ᾽ ὑμῶν εἰμι πάσας τὰς ἡμέρας ἕως τῆς συντελείας τοῦ αἰῶνος», οὐχ ὡς μετὰ τὴν τοῦ αἰῶνος συντέλειαν χωρισθησόμενος. Φησὶ γοῦν ὁ θεῖος ἀπόστολος· «Καὶ οὕτως πάντοτε σὺν κυρίῳ ἐσόμεθα», μετὰ τὴν κοινὴν ἀνάστασιν λέγων.

Πῶς γὰρ ἂν θεὸν γεννήσασα καὶ ἐκ τῆς τῶν παρηκολουθηκότων πείρας τὸ θαῦμα γνωρίσασα ἀνδρὸς συνάφειαν κατεδέξατο; Ἄπαγε. Οὐ σωφρονοῦντος λογισμοῦ τὰ τοιαῦτα νοεῖν, μὴ ὅτι καὶ πράττειν.

Ἀλλ᾽ αὕτη ἡ μακαρία καὶ τῶν ὑπὲρ φύσιν δωρεῶν ἀξιωθεῖσα τὰς ὠδῖνας, ἃς διέφυγε τίκτουσα, ταύτας ἐν τῷ τοῦ πάθους καιρῷ ὑπέμεινε ὑπὸ τῆς μητρικῆς συμπαθείας τῶν σπλάγχνων τὸν σπαραγμὸν ἀνατλᾶσα καί, ὃν θεὸν ἔγνω διὰ γεννήσεως, τοῦτον ὡς κακοῦργον ἀναιρούμενον βλέπουσα ὡς ῥομφαίᾳ τοῖς λογισμοῖς ἐσπαράττετο· καὶ τοῦτό ἐστι· «Καὶ σοῦ δὲ αὐτῆς τὴν ψυχὴν διελεύσεται ῥομφαία». Ἀλλὰ μεταβάλλει τὴν λύπην ἡ χαρὰ τῆς ἀναστάσεως θεὸν τὸν σαρκὶ θανόντα κηρύττουσα.

88　Περὶ τῶν ἁγίων καὶ τῆς τῶν λειψάνων αὐτῶν τιμῆς

Τιμητέον τοὺς ἁγίους ὡς φίλους Χριστοῦ, ὡς τέκνα καὶ κληρονόμους θεοῦ, ὥς φησιν ὁ θεολόγος εὐαγγελιστής· «Ὅσοι

some invent tales of his being born from the side of the Mother of God. For it was not impossible that he should pass through the gate without breaking its seals.

Thus the Ever-Virgin remained a virgin even after giving birth and in no way had any association with a man until her death. Even if it is written: "he did not know her until she had given birth to her first-born son,"[21] one should know that "first-born" is the first to be born even if it is the only child. To be born first does not necessarily imply the birth of others. The word "until" indicates the interval up to the appointed time; it does not exclude the time after it. For the Lord says: "Behold, I am with you all the days until the end of the age,"[22] not implying that he will be separated from us after the end of the age. It is thus that the Apostle says: "And so we will be with the Lord forever,"[23] meaning after the general resurrection.

For how could she who had given birth to God and been aware of the miracle from subsequent experience have accepted sexual union with a man? Perish the thought! The thinking of such things does not belong to chaste thought, let alone putting them into practice.

Nevertheless, at the time of the Passion this blessed woman, who was considered worthy of gifts that transcended nature, suffered the pains that she had escaped while giving birth. Out of maternal love she endured heart-rending pain, and seeing the one whom she knew by the manner of his birth to be God put to death as a criminal, she was torn apart in her thoughts as if by a sword. This is the meaning of "and a sword will pierce your own soul too."[24] But her grief was transformed by the joy of the resurrection that proclaimed the one who had died in the flesh to be God.

88 *On the honor due to the saints and their relics*

The saints should be honored as friends of Christ, as children and heirs of God, as the Theologian evangelist says: "But to all who

---

[21]Mt 1.25; Lk 2.7.   [22]Mt 28.30.
[23]1 Thess 4.17.   [24]Lk 2.35.

δὲ ἔλαβον αὐτόν, ἔδωκεν αὐτοῖς ἐξουσίαν τέκνα θεοῦ γενέσθαι».
«Ὥστε οὐκέτι εἰσὶν δοῦλοι, ἀλλ᾽ υἱοί· εἰ δὲ υἱοί, καὶ κληρονόμοι, κληρονόμοι μὲν θεοῦ, συγκληρονόμοι δὲ Χριστοῦ». Καὶ ὁ κύριος ἐν τοῖς ἱεροῖς εὐαγγελίοις τοῖς ἀποστόλοις φησίν· «Ὑμεῖς φίλοι μού ἐστε. Οὐκέτι ὑμᾶς καλῶ δούλους· ὁ γὰρ δοῦλος οὐκ οἶδε, τί ποιεῖ αὐτοῦ ὁ κύριος». Εἰ δὲ καὶ «βασιλεὺς βασιλέων καὶ κύριος κυριευόντων» καὶ «θεὸς θεῶν» ὁ δημιουργὸς τῶν ἁπάντων καὶ κύριος λέγεται, πάντως οἱ ἅγιοι θεοί τε καὶ κύριοι καὶ βασιλεῖς. Τούτων θεὸς ὁ θεὸς καὶ κύριος καὶ βασιλεύς ἐστι καὶ λέγεται. «Ἐγὼ γάρ εἰμι», φησὶ τῷ Μωσεῖ, «θεὸς Ἀβραὰμ καὶ θεὸς Ἰσαὰκ καὶ θεὸς Ἰακώβ». Καὶ θεὸν Φαραὼ τὸν Μωσῆν ὁ θεὸς ἐποίησεν. Θεοὺς δὲ λέγω καὶ βασιλεῖς καὶ κυρίους οὐ φύσει, ἀλλ᾽ ὡς τῶν παθῶν βασιλεύσαντας καὶ κυριεύσαντας καὶ τὴν τῆς θείας εἰκόνος ὁμοίωσιν, καθ᾽ ἣν καὶ γεγένηνται, ἀπαραχάρακτον φυλάξαντας (βασιλεὺς γὰρ λέγεται καὶ ἡ τοῦ βασιλέως εἰκών) καὶ ἑνωθέντας θεῷ κατὰ προαίρεσιν καὶ τοῦτον δεξαμένους ἔνοικον καὶ τῇ τούτου μεθέξει γεγονότας χάριτι, ὅπερ αὐτός ἐστι φύσει. Πῶς οὖν οὐ τιμητέον τοὺς θεράποντας καὶ φίλους καὶ υἱοὺς τοῦ θεοῦ χρηματίσαντας; Ἡ γὰρ πρὸς τοὺς εὐγνώμονας τῶν ὁμοδούλων τιμὴ ἀπόδειξιν ἔχει τῆς πρὸς τὸν κοινὸν δεσπότην εὐνοίας.

Οὗτοι ταμιεῖα θεοῦ καὶ καθαρὰ γεγόνασι καταγώγια· «Ἐνοικήσω γὰρ ἐν αὐτοῖς», ὁ θεός φησι, «καὶ ἐμπεριπατήσω καὶ ἔσομαι αὐτῶν θεός». Ὅτι μὲν οὖν «ψυχαὶ δικαίων ἐν χειρὶ θεοῦ, καὶ οὐ μὴ ἅψηται αὐτῶν βάσανος», φησὶν ἡ θεία γραφή· ὁ θάνατος γὰρ τῶν ἁγίων ὕπνος μᾶλλόν ἐστι ἢ θάνατος. «Ἐκοπίασαν γὰρ εἰς τὸν αἰῶνα καὶ ζήσονται εἰς τέλος», καί· «Τίμιος ἐναντίον κυρίου ὁ θάνατος τῶν ὁσίων αὐτοῦ». Τί οὖν τιμιώτερον τοῦ ἐν χειρὶ εἶναι θεοῦ; Ζωὴ γάρ ἐστιν ὁ θεὸς καὶ φῶς καὶ οἱ ἐν χειρὶ θεοῦ ὄντες ἐν ζωῇ καὶ φωτὶ ὑπάρχουσιν.

Ὅτι δὲ διὰ τοῦ νοῦ τοῖς σώμασιν αὐτῶν ἐνῴκησεν ὁ θεός, φησὶν ὁ ἀπόστολος· «Οὐκ οἴδατε, ὅτι τὰ σώματα ὑμῶν ναὸς

[1] Jn 1.12.   [2] Gal 4.7; Rom 8.17.   [3] Jn 15.14–15,
[4] Tim 6.15.   [5] Deut 10.17.   [6] Ex 3.6; Mt 22.32.   [7] Ex 7.1.
[8] Basil of Caesarea, Homily 19, *On the Holy Forty Martyrs* (PG 31:501B) (with the

received him he gave the power to become children of God."[1] "So you are no longer slaves but sons, and if sons then also heirs, fellow heirs with Christ."[2] And in the holy Gospels the Lord says to the apostles: "You are my friends. I do not call you servants any longer, for the servant does not know what the master is doing."[3] And if the Creator and Lord of all is called "King of kings and Lord of lords"[4] and "God of gods,"[5] the saints are necessarily gods and lords and kings. Of these God is and is said to be God and Lord and King. "For I," as he says to Moses, "am the God of Abraham and the God of Isaac and the God of Jacob."[6] And God made Moses a god to Pharaoh.[7] I mean gods and kings and lords not by nature, but because they have ruled over and mastered the passions and have kept inviolate the likeness of the divine image, in which they were created (for the king's image is also called king), and have been united with God by their free will, and have received him as dwelling within them, and by participation in him have become by grace what he is by nature. How then should we not honor those who have been called the servants and friends and sons of God? "For the honor shown to the most faithful of our fellow servants is proof of affection for our common master."[8]

These have become inner chambers and pure dwelling-places of God. "For I will live in them," says God, "and walk among them, and I will be their God."[9] Indeed, "the souls of the righteous are in the hands of God and no torment will touch them,"[10] divine Scripture says, for the death of the saints is sleep rather than death. "For they labored until the aeon and will live until the end,"[11] and: "Honorable in the sight of the Lord is the death of his saints."[12] What then is more honorable than to be in God's hand? For God is life and light and those who are in God's hand exist in life and light.

Seeing that God has dwelt in their bodies by means of the mind, the Apostle says: "Do you not know that your bodies are a temple of

substitution of εὐγνώμονας/*eugnōmonas*, "faithful," or "loyal" for Basil's ἀγαθούς/*agathous*, "good").

[9]2 Cor 6.16.   [10]Wis 3.1.   [11]Ps 48.10.   [12]Ps 115.6.

τοῦ ἐνοικοῦντος ἐν ὑμῖν πνεύματος ἁγίου ἐστίν;» «Ὁ δὲ κύριος τὸ πνεῦμά ἐστι», καί· «Εἴ τις τὸν ναὸν τοῦ θεοῦ φθείρει, φθερεῖ τοῦτον ὁ θεός». Πῶς οὖν οὐ τιμητέον τοὺς ἐμψύχους ναοὺς τοῦ θεοῦ, τὰ ἔμψυχα τοῦ θεοῦ σκηνώματα; Οὗτοι ζῶντες ἐν παρρησίᾳ τῷ θεῷ παρεστήκασι.

Πηγὰς ἡμῖν σωτηρίους ὁ δεσπότης Χριστὸς τὰ τῶν ἁγίων παρέσχετο λείψανα πολυτρόπως τὰς εὐεργεσίας πηγάζοντα, μύρον εὐωδίας βρύοντα. Καὶ μηδεὶς ἀπιστείτω. Εἰ γὰρ ἐξ ἀκροτόμου πέτρας ὕδωρ ἐν ἐρήμῳ, ἐπήγασε βουλομένου θεοῦ καὶ ἐκ σιαγόνος ὄνου τῷ Σαμψὼν διψῶντι, ἐκ μαρτυρικῶν λειψάνων μύρον εὐῶδες ἀναβλύζειν ἄπιστον; Οὐδαμῶς, τοῖς γε εἰδόσι τὴν τοῦ θεοῦ δύναμιν καὶ τὴν τῶν ἁγίων παρ’ αὐτοῦ τιμήν.

Ἐν τῷ νόμῳ πᾶς ὁ νεκροῦ ἁπτόμενος ἀκάθαρτος ἐχρημάτιζεν, ἀλλ’ οὐχ οὗτοι νεκροί. Ἀφ’ οὗ γὰρ ἡ αὐτοζωή, ὁ τῆς ζωῆς αἴτιος, ἐν νεκροῖς ἐλογίσθη, τοὺς ἐπ’ ἐλπίδι ἀναστάσεως καὶ τῇ εἰς αὐτὸν πίστει κοιμηθέντας οὐ νεκροὺς προσαγορεύομεν. Νεκρὸν γὰρ σῶμα πῶς θαυματουργεῖν δύναται; Πῶς οὖν δι’ αὐτῶν δαίμονες ἀπελαύνονται, ἀσθενεῖς θεραπεύονται, τυφλοὶ ἀναβλέπουσι, λεπροὶ καθαίρονται, πειρασμοὶ καὶ ἀνίαι λύονται, πᾶσα δόσις ἀγαθὴ ἐκ τοῦ πατρὸς τῶν φώτων δι’ αὐτῶν τοῖς ἀδιστάκτῳ πίστει αἰτοῦσι κάτεισι; Πόσα ἂν ἔκαμες, ἵνα προστάτην εὕρῃς θνητῷ σε βασιλεῖ προσάγοντα καὶ ὑπὲρ σοῦ πρὸς αὐτὸν τοὺς λόγους ποιούμενον; Τοὺς οὖν προστάτας τοῦ γένους παντὸς τοὺς τῷ θεῷ ὑπὲρ ἡμῶν τὰς ἐντεύξεις ποιουμένους οὐ τιμητέον; Ναὶ μὴν τιμητέον, ναοὺς ἐγείροντας τῷ θεῷ ἐπὶ τῷ τούτων ὀνόματι, καρποφορίας προσάγοντας, τὰς τούτων μνήμας γεραίροντας καὶ ἐν αὐταῖς εὐφραινομένους πνευματικῶς, ἵνα οἰκεία τῶν συγκαλούντων ἡ εὐφροσύνη γένηται, ἵνα μὴ θεραπεύειν πειρώμενοι τοὔμπαλιν αὐτοὺς παροργίσωμεν. Οἷς μὲν γὰρ θεὸς θεραπεύεται, καὶ οἱ τούτου θεράποντες εὐφρανθήσονται· οἷς δὲ προσοχθίζει θεός, καὶ οἱ τούτου προσοχθιοῦσιν ὑπασπισταί.

---

[13]1 Cor 6.19.   [14]2 Cor 3.17.
[15]1 Cor 3.17.   [16]Ex 17.6; Judg 15.19.

the Holy Spirit dwelling within you?";[13] "The Lord is the Spirit";[14] and "If anyone destroys God's temple, God will destroy that person."[15] How, then, should we not honor the living temples of God, the living tabernacles of God? These while still alive have stood confidently in the presence of God.

Christ the Master has provided the relics of the saints for us as saving springs, making benefits well up for us in a variety of ways, causing them to flow with myrrh. And let no one disbelieve this. For if by God's will water flowed from the precipitous rock in the desert and from the ass's jawbone when Sampson was thirsty,[16] is it incredible that fragrant myrrh should flow from the relics of the saints? Not at all, for those who know the power of God and the honor that the saints have received from him.[17]

In the Law anyone who touches a corpse was deemed to be unclean,[18] but these are not corpses. Seeing that Life itself, the cause of life, was reckoned among the dead, we do not regard as dead those who have fallen asleep in the hope of the resurrection and with faith in him. For how can a dead body perform miracles? How, then, are demons expelled through them? How are the sick healed? How do the blind see again? How are lepers healed? How are temptations and vexations dispelled? How does every good gift come down through them from the Father of lights to those who ask with unhesitating faith?[19] How much would you do to find a patron to present you to a mortal king and to speak to him on your behalf? Should we not honor the patrons of the entire race who intercede for us with God? Yes indeed, we should honor them, building churches to God in their name, bringing them offerings, celebrating their anniversaries and finding spiritual joy in these, that the joy may become that of those who have invited us to come together, that in trying to offer them veneration we may not provoke them instead. For the servants of God find joy in the things by which God is worshiped, and what

---

[17]The most famous of the myrrh-flowing (μυρόβλυτα, *myroblyta*) relics of saints in John's time were those of St Demetrius of Thessalonica.

[18]Num 19.11.   [19]Cf. Jas 1.17.

«Ἐν ψαλμοῖς καὶ ὕμνοις καὶ ᾠδαῖς πνευματικαῖς» καὶ κατανύξει καὶ τῶν δεομένων ἐλέῳ τοὺς ἁγίους πιστοὶ θεραπεύσωμεν, οἷς μάλιστα καὶ θεὸς θεραπεύεται. Στήλας αὐτοῖς ἐγείρωμεν ὁρωμένας τε εἰκόνας καὶ αὐτοὶ ἔμψυχοι στῆλαι καὶ εἰκόνες αὐτῶν τῇ τῶν ἀρετῶν μιμήσει γενώμεθα.

Τὴν θεοτόκον ὡς κυρίως καὶ ἀληθῶς θεοῦ μητέρα τιμήσωμεν· τὸν προφήτην Ἰωάννην ὡς πρόδρομον καὶ βαπτιστὴν ἀπόστολόν τε καὶ μάρτυρα («οὔτε γὰρ ἐν γεννητοῖς γυναικῶν μείζων Ἰωάννου ἐγήγερται», ὡς ὁ κύριος ἔφησε, καὶ τῆς βασιλείας αὐτὸς πρῶτος κῆρυξ γεγένηται)· τοὺς ἀποστόλους ὡς ἀδελφοὺς τοῦ κυρίου καὶ αὐτόπτας καὶ ὑπηρέτας τῶν αὐτοῦ παθημάτων, οὓς «προγνοὺς καὶ προώρισε συμμόρφους τῆς εἰκόνος τοῦ υἱοῦ αὐτοῦ» ὁ θεὸς καὶ πατήρ· «πρῶτον ἀποστόλους, δεύτερον προφήτας, τρίτον ποιμένας καὶ διδασκάλους»· τούς τε τοῦ κυρίου μάρτυρας ἐκ παντὸς τάγματος ἐκλελεγμένους ὡς στρατιώτας Χριστοῦ καὶ τὸ αὐτοῦ πεπωκότας ποτήριον τό τε τοῦ ζωοποιοῦ αὐτοῦ θανάτου βαπτισθέντας βάπτισμα ὡς κοινωνοὺς τῶν παθημάτων αὐτοῦ καὶ τῆς δόξης, ὧν ταξίαρχος ὁ πρωτοδιάκονος Χριστοῦ καὶ ἀπόστολος καὶ πρωτομάρτυς Στέφανος· καὶ τοὺς ὁσίους πατέρας ἡμῶν τοὺς θεοφόρους ἀσκητὰς τοὺς τὸ χρονιώτερον καὶ ἐπιπονώτερον μαρτύριον τῆς συνειδήσεως διαθλήσαντας, οἱ «περιῆλθον ἐν μηλωταῖς, ἐν αἰγείοις δέρμασιν, ὑστερούμενοι, θλιβόμενοι, κακοχούμενοι, ἐν ἐρημίαις πλανώμενοι καὶ ὄρεσι καὶ σπηλαίοις καὶ ταῖς ὀπαῖς τῆς γῆς, ὧν οὐκ ἦν ἄξιος ὁ κόσμος»· τοὺς πρὸ τῆς χάριτος προφήτας, πατριάρχας, δικαίους τοὺς προκατηγγελκότας τὴν τοῦ κυρίου παρουσίαν. Τούτων πάντων ἀναθεωροῦντες τὴν πολιτείαν ζηλώσωμεν τὴν πίστιν, τὴν ἀγάπην, τὴν ἐλπίδα, τὸν ζῆλον, τὸν βίον, τὴν καρτερίαν τῶν παθημάτων, τὴν ὑπομονὴν μέχρις αἵματος, ἵνα καὶ τῶν τῆς δόξης στεφάνων αὐτοῖς κοινωνήσωμεν.

offends God also offends his guards. As faithful Christians let us venerate the saints with "psalms and hymns and spiritual songs,"[20] and with compunction and compassion towards the needy, with which God, too, above all is worshiped. Let us put up memorials to them and visible images and become ourselves their living memorials and images by imitating their virtues.

Let us honor the Theotokos as properly and truly Mother of God. Let us honor the prophet John as forerunner and baptist, apostle and martyr ("for no one has arisen among those born of women greater than John,"[21] as the Lord said, and he was the first herald of the kingdom). Let us honor the apostles as brothers of the Lord and eyewitness and servants of his passion, who were those whom God the Father "foreknew and predestined to be conformed to the image of his Son,"[22] "first apostles, second prophets, third shepherds and teachers."[23] Let us honor the Lord's martyrs, chosen from every rank as soldiers of Christ who have drunk from his cup and been baptized by the baptism of his life-giving death, as sharers of his passion and glory, whose commanding officer is Christ's protodeacon and apostle and protomartyr, Stephen. Let us honor our holy fathers the God-bearing ascetics, who have struggled in the longer drawn-out and more laborious martyrdom of the conscience, who "went about in skins of sheep and goats, destitute, persecuted, tormented, wandering in deserts and mountains, and caves and holes in the ground, of whom the world was not worthy."[24] Let us honor the prophets who came before the time of grace, the patriarchs, the righteous who announced in advance the Lord's coming. Reviewing the manner of life of all these, let us emulate their faith, their love, their hope, their zeal, their life, their endurance of suffering, their patience even to the shedding of their blood, that we may also share with them their crowns of glory.

[20]Eph 5.19.   [21]Mt 11.11.   [22]Rom 8.29.
[23]1 Cor 12.28.   [24]Heb 11.37–38.

89 Περὶ εἰκόνων

Ἐπειδὴ δέ τινες ἡμῖν καταμέμφονται προσκυνοῦσί τε καὶ τιμῶσι τήν τε τοῦ σωτῆρος καὶ τῆς δεσποίνης ἡμῶν εἰκόνα, ἔτι δὲ καὶ τῶν λοιπῶν ἁγίων καὶ θεραπόντων Χριστοῦ, ἀκουέτωσαν, ὡς ἐξ ἀρχῆς ὁ θεὸς τὸν ἄνθρωπον κατ᾽ οἰκείαν εἰκόνα ἐποίησε. Τίνος οὖν ἕνεκεν ἀλλήλους προσκυνοῦμεν, εἰ μὴ ὡς κατ᾽ εἰκόνα θεοῦ πεποιημένους; Ὡς γάρ φησιν ὁ θεοφόρος καὶ πολὺς τὰ θεῖα Βασίλειος, «ἡ τῆς εἰκόνος τιμὴ ἐπὶ τὸ πρωτότυπον διαβαίνει»· πρωτότυπον δέ ἐστι τὸ εἰκονιζόμενον, ἐξ οὗ τὸ παράγωγον γίνεται. Τίνος ἕνεκεν ὁ Μωσαϊκὸς λαὸς τῇ σκηνῇ κυκλόθεν προσεκύνει εἰκόνα καὶ τύπον φερούσῃ τῶν ἐπουρανίων, μᾶλλον δὲ τῆς ὅλης κτίσεως; Φησὶ γοῦν ὁ θεὸς τῷ Μωσεῖ· «Ὅρα, ποιήσεις πάντα κατὰ τὸν τύπον τὸν δειχθέντα σοι ἐν τῷ ὄρει». Καὶ τὰ Χερουβὶμ δὲ τὰ σκιάζοντα τὸ ἱλαστήριον οὐχὶ ἔργα χειρῶν ἀνθρώπων; Τί δὲ ὁ ἐν Ἱεροσολύμοις περιώνυμος ναός; Οὐχὶ χειροποίητος καὶ ἀνθρώπων τέχνῃ κατεσκευασμένος;

Ἡ δὲ θεία γραφὴ κατηγορεῖ τῶν προσκυνούντων τοῖς γλυπτοῖς, ἀλλὰ καὶ τῶν θυόντων τοῖς δαιμονίοις. Ἔθυον μὲν καὶ Ἕλληνες, ἔθυον δὲ καὶ Ἰουδαῖοι· ἀλλ᾽ Ἕλληνες μὲν δαίμοσιν, Ἰουδαῖοι δὲ τῷ θεῷ. Καὶ ἀπόβλητος μὲν ἡ τῶν Ἑλλήνων θυσία ἦν καὶ κατάκριτος, ἡ δὲ τῶν δικαίων τῷ θεῷ εὐαπόδεκτος. Ἔθυσε γὰρ Νῶε, καὶ «ὠσφράνθη ὁ θεὸς ὀσμὴν εὐωδίας», τῆς ἀγαθῆς προαιρέσεως καὶ τῆς πρὸς αὐτὸν εὐνοίας τὸ εὐῶδες ἀποδεχόμενος. Οὕτω τὰ μὲν τῶν Ἑλλήνων γλυπτά, ἐπεὶ δαιμόνων ἦσαν ἐξεικονίσματα ἀπόβλητά τε καὶ ἀπηγορευμένα τυγχάνουσι.

Πρὸς δὲ τούτοις τοῦ ἀοράτου καὶ ἀσωμάτου καὶ ἀπεριγράπτου καὶ ἀσχηματίστου θεοῦ τίς δύναται ποιήσασθαι μίμημα; Παραφροσύνης τοίνυν ἄκρας καὶ ἀσεβείας τὸ σχηματίζειν τὸ θεῖον. Ἐντεῦθεν ἐν τῇ παλαιᾷ οὐκ ἦν τετριμμένη ἡ τῶν εἰκόνων

---

[1]Throughout this chapter John draws closely on his three treatises *Against the Iconoclasts* (PPS 24), or rather on the third edition of his treatise *Against the Iconoclasts*, since the three treatises (generally known in English as *On the Divine Images*) are all reworkings of the same text.

89   *On Images*[1]

Since there are some who reproach us for venerating and honoring the image of the Savior and our Lady, and also the images of the rest of the saints and servants of Christ, let them hear that from the beginning God made humankind in his own image. For what reason, then, do we bow in salutation to each other, other than that we were made in the image of God? As the God-bearing Basil, deeply versed in divine matters, says, "the honor offered to the image passes to the archetype."[2] The archetype is that which is represented in the image, from which the copy is made. For what reason did the people of Moses from all around venerate the tabernacle that bore the image and type of the heavenly things, or rather, of the whole of creation? God therefore said to Moses: "See, you shall make everything according to the pattern that was shown you on the mountain."[3] And are the cherubim that overshadow the mercy seat not works of human hands? And what was the famous temple in Jerusalem? Was it not made by the work and skill of human hands?

The divine Scripture condemns those who worship graven images but also those who sacrifice to demons. The Greeks sacrificed and the Jews also sacrificed, but the Greeks sacrificed to demons and the Jews to God. And the sacrifice of the Greeks was rejected and condemned, whereas that of the righteous offered to God was well received. For Noah sacrificed, and "God smelt the pleasing odor,"[4] and accepted the fragrance of the good disposition and love for him. Thus the carved images of the Greeks come to be rejected and forbidden because they were representations of demons.

But beyond these considerations, who can make an image of God, incorporeal and uncircumscribed and without form as he is? It is utterly deranged and impious to give form to the divine. Hence in the Old Testament it was not the practice to use images. But when God in the depths of his compassion became in truth a human

---

[2]Basil of Caesarea, *On the Holy Spirit* 18.45 (PPS 42:81; PG 32:149C).
[3]Heb 8.5; Ex 25.40.   [4]Gen 8.21.

χρῆσις. Ἐπεὶ δὲ ὁ θεὸς διὰ σπλάγχνα ἐλέους αὐτοῦ κατὰ
ἀλήθειαν γέγονεν ἄνθρωπος διὰ τὴν ἡμετέραν σωτηρίαν, οὐχ
ὡς τῷ Ἀβραὰμ ὤφθη ἐν εἴδει ἀνθρώπου, οὐχ ὡς τοῖς προφήταις,
ἀλλὰ κατ' οὐσίαν ἀληθῶς γέγονεν ἄνθρωπος διέτριψέ τε ἐπὶ
τῆς γῆς «καὶ τοῖς ἀνθρώποις συνανεστράφη», ἐθαυματούργησεν,
ἔπαθεν, ἐσταυρώθη, ἀνέστη, ἀνελήφθη, καὶ πάντα ταῦτα κατὰ
ἀλήθειαν γέγονε, καὶ ὡράθη ὑπὸ τῶν ἀνθρώπων, ἐγράφη μὲν εἰς
ὑπόμνησιν ἡμῶν καὶ διδαχὴν τῶν τηνικαῦτα μὴ παρόντων, ἵνα
μὴ ἑωρακότες, ἀκούσαντες δὲ καὶ πιστεύσαντες τύχωμεν τοῦ
μακαρισμοῦ τοῦ κυρίου. Ἐπεὶ δὲ οὐ πάντες ἴσασι γράμματα οὐδὲ
τῇ ἀναγνώσει σχολάζουσιν, οἱ πατέρες συνεῖδον ὥσπερ τινὰς
ἀριστείας ἐν εἰκόσι ταῦτα γράφεσθαι εἰς ὑπόμνησιν σύντομον.
Ἀμέλει πολλάκις μὴ κατὰ νοῦν ἔχοντες τὸ τοῦ κυρίου πάθος,
τὴν εἰκόνα τῆς Χριστοῦ σταυρώσεως ἰδόντες, τοῦ σωτηρίου
πάθους εἰς ἀνάμνησιν ἐλθόντες, πεσόντες προσκυνοῦμεν οὐ τῇ
ὕλῃ, ἀλλὰ τῷ εἰκονιζομένῳ, ὥσπερ οὐ τῇ ὕλῃ τοῦ εὐαγγελίου
οὐδὲ τῇ τοῦ σταυροῦ ὕλῃ προσκυνοῦμεν, ἀλλὰ τῷ ἐκτυπώματι.
Τί γὰρ διαφέρει σταυρὸς μὴ ἔχων τὸ τοῦ κυρίου ἐκτύπωμα τοῦ
ἔχοντος; Ὡσαύτως καὶ τῆς θεομήτορος· ἡ γὰρ εἰς αὐτὴν τιμὴ εἰς
τὸν ἐξ αὐτῆς σαρκωθέντα ἀνάγεται. Ὁμοίως καὶ τὰ τῶν ἁγίων
ἀνδραγαθήματα ἐπαλείφοντα ἡμᾶς πρὸς ἀνδρείαν καὶ ζῆλον
καὶ μίμησιν τῆς αὐτῶν ἀρετῆς καὶ δόξαν θεοῦ. Ὡς γὰρ ἔφημεν, ἡ
πρὸς τοὺς εὐγνώμονας τῶν ὁμοδούλων τιμὴ ἀπόδειξιν ἔχει τῆς
πρὸς τὸν κοινὸν δεσπότην εὐνοίας καὶ ἡ τῆς εἰκόνος τιμὴ πρὸς
τὸ πρωτότυπον διαβαίνει. Ἔστι δὲ ἄγραφος ἡ παράδοσις ὥσπερ
τὸ κατὰ ἀνατολὰς προσκυνεῖν, τὸ προσκυνεῖν σταυρὸν καὶ ἕτερα
πλεῖστα τούτοις ὅμοια.

Φέρεται δὲ καί τις ἱστορία, ὡς ὁ κύριος τῷ Αὐγάρῳ τῆς
Ἐδεσσηνῶν πόλεως βασιλεύοντι ζωγράφον ἀποστείλαντι τὴν τοῦ
κυρίου ὁμοιογραφῆσαι εἰκόνα μὴ δυνηθέντος τοῦ ζωγράφου διὰ
τὴν ἀποστίλβουσαν τοῦ προσώπου λαμπρότητα αὐτὸς ἱμάτιον
τῷ οἰκείῳ καὶ ζωοποιῷ προσώπῳ ἐπιθεὶς ἐναπομάξασθαι τῷ

being for our salvation, he was not seen as he was by Abraham, in a human form, or as he was by the prophets, but truly became a human being in his substance and dwelt on earth, and "lived among men,"[5] performed miracles, suffered, was crucified, rose again, ascended, and all these things happened in reality and were seen by human beings, and written down as a reminder for us and as teaching about things no longer present, so that without having seen we might through hearing and believing attain to the Lord's promise of blessedness. Since not everybody is literate or has the leisure for reading, the fathers acknowledged that these should be depicted in images as memorials to serve as a concise reminder. In point of fact, often when we do not have the Lord's passion in mind, we see the image of Christ's crucifixion, recall the saving passion, and falling down venerate not the matter but the one represented in the image, just as we do not venerate the material of which the gospel is made or the material of the cross, but the representation. For what is special about a cross that does not have the representation of the Lord compared with one that does? It is the same with the Mother of God, for the honor paid to her ascends to the one who became incarnate from her. Similarly, the brave deeds of the saints prepare us like athletes to show bravery and zeal and emulate their virtues and glorification of God. For as we have said,[6] the honor rendered to the most faithful of our fellow servants is proof of our love for our common master and the honor rendered to the image passes over to the original. This is an unwritten tradition, as is praying towards the east, venerating the cross, and many other things similar to these.

There is also a story told about the Lord that, when Abgar, king of Edessa, sent an artist to paint a portrait of him, and as the artist was unable to do so because of the brightness radiating from his face, the Lord himself laid a cloth on his own life-giving face so as

[5]Bar 3.38.
[6]At the end of the first paragraph of Chapter 88 (p. 259), and in the first paragraph of the present chapter (p. 262).

ἱματίῳ τὸ ἑαυτοῦ ἀπεικόνισμα καὶ οὕτως ἀποστεῖλαι ποθοῦντι τῷ Αὐγάρῳ.

Ὅτι δὲ καὶ πλεῖστα οἱ ἀπόστολοι ἀγράφως παραδεδώκασι, γράφει Παῦλος ὁ τῶν ἐθνῶν ἀπόστολος· «Ἄρα οὖν, ἀδελφοί, στήκετε καὶ κρατεῖτε τὰς παραδόσεις ἡμῶν, ἃς ἐδιδάχθητε εἴτε διὰ λόγου εἴτε δι᾽ ἐπιστολῆς ἡμῶν», καὶ πρὸς Κορινθίους· «Ἐπαινῶ δὲ ὑμᾶς, ἀδελφοί, ὅτι πάντα μου μέμνησθε καί, καθὼς παρέδωκα ὑμῖν, τὰς παραδόσεις κατέχετε».

90 Περὶ γραφῆς

Εἷς ἐστιν ὁ θεὸς ὑπό τε παλαιᾶς διαθήκης καὶ καινῆς κηρυττόμενος, ὁ ἐν τριάδι ὑμνούμενός τε καὶ δοξαζόμενος, τοῦ κυρίου φήσαντος· «Οὐκ ἦλθον καταλῦσαι τὸν νόμον, ἀλλὰ πληρῶσαι» (αὐτὸς γὰρ τὴν ἡμῶν σωτηρίαν εἰργάσατο, ὑπὲρ ἧς πᾶσα γραφὴ καὶ ἅπαν μυστήριον), καὶ πάλιν· «Ἐρευνᾶτε τὰς γραφάς· αὗται γὰρ μαρτυροῦσι περὶ ἐμοῦ», καὶ τοῦ ἀποστόλου εἰπόντος· «Πολυμερῶς καὶ πολυτρόπως πάλαι ὁ θεὸς λαλήσας τοῖς πατράσιν ἡμῶν ἐν τοῖς προφήταις, ἐπ᾽ ἐσχάτων τῶν ἡμερῶν τούτων ἐλάλησεν ἡμῖν ἐν υἱῷ». Διὰ πνεύματος τοίνυν ἁγίου ὅ τε νόμος καὶ οἱ προφῆται, εὐαγγελισταὶ καὶ ἀπόστολοι καὶ ποιμένες ἐλάλησαν καὶ διδάσκαλοι.

«Πᾶσα τοίνυν γραφὴ θεόπνευστος πάντως ὠφέλιμος». Ὥστε κάλλιστον καὶ ψυχωφελέστατον ἐρευνᾶν τὰς θείας γραφάς. Ὥσπερ γὰρ δένδρον παρὰ τὰς διεξόδους τῶν ὑδάτων

---

[7]The story is given by Eusebius in his *History of the Church* 1.13. In a footnote Kotter adds a passage that is found in some late manuscripts (the earliest of them is Athous Batop. 280, of the twelfth century) and was also in the manuscript translated by Burgundio of Pisa: "We might also mention that Luke the apostle and evangelist painted the Lord and his mother, copies of which are possessed by the famous city of the Romans. And they are carefully stored in Jerusalem, since also Josephus the Jew, as some say, in accordance with the likeness that they have in Jerusalem, and which they call Roman, records the exact way the Lord looked, with meeting eyebrows, beautiful eyes, long face, inclining forwards, and of good stature, obviously when he lived among us and was seen as a man." Flavius Josephus (37–c. 100), scion of an elite first-century Jewish family, went over to the Roman side during the First Jewish War

to impress his own image upon the cloth and thus send it to Abgar who desired it.[7]

The fact that the apostles transmitted a great many things without writing them down is recorded by Paul, the Apostle to the Gentiles: "So then, brothers and sisters, stand firm and hold fast to the traditions that you were taught by us, either by word of mouth or by our letter";[8] and to the Corinthians: "I commend you because you remember me in everything and maintain the traditions just as I handed them on to you."[9]

90   *On Scripture*

It is the same God, hymned and glorified as a Trinity, who is proclaimed by the Old Testament and the New, as the Lord has said: "I have not come to abolish the Law, but to fulfil it"[1] (for he himself worked our salvation, for the sake of which all Scripture and every sacrament exists); and again: "Search the Scriptures, for these testify on my behalf."[2] The Apostle also says: "Long ago God spoke to our ancestors in many and various ways by the prophets, but in these last days he has spoken to us by a Son."[3] Thus it was through the Holy Spirit that the Law and the prophets spoke, as also did evangelists and apostles and shepherds and teachers.

"All Scripture is inspired by God and is exceedingly useful."[4] It is therefore excellent and most beneficial to the soul to search the divine Scriptures.[5] For the soul is like a tree planted by streams of water.[6] It is irrigated by Scripture and grows luxuriantly and yields ripe fruit—

of 66–73, and afterwards wrote *The Jewish Wars* and *The Antiquities of the Jews*. There are two references to Jesus Christ in *The Antiquities* 18.3 (the so-called Testimonium Flavianum) and 20.9. Even if the Testimonium has been interpolated by the Christian copyists of the manuscript tradition, it is widely agreed by scholars that Josephus was aware of Jesus Christ and his context. The description of the appearance of Christ, however, is not known from any of his works.

[8] 2 Thess 2.15.   [9] 1 Cor 11.2.

[1] Mt 5.17.   [2] Jn 5.39.   [3] Heb 1.1–2.
[4] 2 Tim 3.16.   [5] Cf. Jn 5.39.   [6] Cf. Ps 1.3.

πεφυτευμένον, οὕτω καὶ ψυχὴ τῇ θείᾳ ἀρδευομένη γραφῇ
πιαίνεται καὶ καρπὸν ὥριμον δίδωσι, πίστιν ὀρθόδοξον, καὶ
ἀειθαλέσι τοῖς φύλλοις, ταῖς θεαρέστοις φημὶ ὡραΐζεται πράξεσι·
πρός τε γὰρ πρᾶξιν ἐνάρετον καὶ θεωρίαν ἀθόλωτον ἐκ τῶν
ἁγίων γραφῶν ῥυθμιζόμεθα. Πάσης γὰρ ἀρετῆς παράκλησιν
καὶ κακίας ἁπάσης ἀποτροπὴν ἐν ταύταις εὑρίσκομεν. Ἐὰν οὖν
ἐσόμεθα φιλομαθεῖς, ἐσόμεθα καὶ πολυμαθεῖς· ἐπιμελείᾳ γὰρ
καὶ πόνῳ καὶ τῇ τοῦ διδόντος χάριτι κατορθοῦνται ἅπαντα.
«Ὁ γὰρ αἰτῶν λαμβάνει καὶ ὁ ζητῶν εὑρίσκει καὶ τῷ κρούοντι
ἀνοιγήσεται». Κρούσωμεν τοίνυν εἰς τὸν κάλλιστον παράδεισον
τῶν γραφῶν, τὸν εὐώδη, τὸν γλυκύτατον, τὸν ὡραιότατον, τὸν
παντοίοις νοερῶν θεοφόρων ὀρνέων κελαδήμασι περιηχοῦντα
ἡμῶν τὰ ὦτα, τὸν ἁπτόμενον ἡμῶν τῆς καρδίας, καὶ λυπουμένην
μὲν παρακαλοῦντα, θυμουμένην δὲ κατευνάζοντα καὶ χαρᾶς
ἀιδίου ἐμπιπλῶντα, τὸν ἐπιβιβάζοντα ἡμῶν τὴν διάνοιαν ἐπὶ
τὰ χρυσαυγῆ μετάφρενα τῆς θείας περιστερᾶς καὶ ὑπέρλαμπρα
καὶ ταῖς φανωτάταις αὐτῆς πτέρυξι πρὸς τὸν μονογενῆ υἱὸν καὶ
κληρονόμον τοῦ φυτουργοῦ τοῦ νοητοῦ ἀμπελῶνος ἀνάγοντα καὶ
δι' αὐτοῦ τῷ πατρὶ τῶν φώτων προσάγοντα. Ἀλλὰ μὴ παρέργως
κρούσωμεν, προθύμως δὲ μᾶλλον καὶ ἐπιμόνως· μὴ ἐκκακήσωμεν
κρούοντες. Οὕτω γὰρ ἡμῖν ἀνοιγήσεται. Ἐὰν ἀναγνῶμεν ἅπαξ καὶ
δὶς καὶ μὴ διαγνῶμεν, ἃ ἀναγινώσκομεν, μὴ ἐκκακήσωμεν, ἀλλ'
ἐπιμείνωμεν, ἀδολεσχήσωμεν, ἐρωτήσωμεν· «ἐπερώτησον» γάρ,
φησίν, «τὸν πατέρα σου, καὶ ἀναγγελεῖ σοι, τοὺς πρεσβυτέρους
σου, καὶ ἐροῦσί σοι». Οὐ γὰρ πάντων ἡ γνῶσις. Ἀρυσώμεθα
ἐκ τῆς τούτου τοῦ παραδείσου πηγῆς ἀέννα καὶ καθαρώτατα
νάματα ἀλλόμενα εἰς ζωὴν αἰώνιον, ἐντρυφήσωμεν, ἀπλήστως
κατατρυφήσωμεν· τὴν γὰρ χάριν ἀδάπανον κέκτηνται.

Εἰ δέ τι καὶ παρὰ τῶν ἔξωθεν χρήσιμον καρπώσασθαι
δυνηθείημεν, οὐ τῶν ἀπηγορευμένων ἐστί. Γενώμεθα δόκιμοι
τραπεζῖται τὸ μὲν γνήσιον καὶ καθαρὸν χρυσίον σωρεύοντες, τὸ
δὲ κίβδηλον παραιτούμενοι. Λάβωμεν λόγους καλλίστους, θεοὺς

[7]Mt 7.8.　　[8]Deut 32.7.　　[9]Cf. 1 Cor 8.7.　　[10]Jn 4.14.
[11]The "exterior wisdom" (contained in the writings of the pagan philosophers)

orthodox faith—and its leaves are evergreen, by which I mean that it is made beautiful by actions pleasing to God. For we are trained by the holy Scriptures in virtuous action and unsullied contemplation. For we find exhortation to every virtue and dissuasion from every vice in them. Thus if we have a passion for learning, we will become exceedingly learned. For by diligence and toil and the grace of the Giver all things may be achieved. "For everyone who asks receives, and everyone who seeks finds, and for everyone who knocks, the door will be opened."[7] Let us therefore knock at the most beautiful paradise of the Scriptures, the fragrant, most sweet, most lovely paradise that fills our ears with the songs of all kinds of spiritual God-bearing birds, that touches our heart, that consoles it when it is sad, that calms it when it is angry and fills it with everlasting joy, that lifts our mind on to the golden back of the divine dove, the supremely radiant back, that with its brilliant wings carries us up towards the only-begotten Son and heir of the planter of the spiritual vineyard and through him to the Father of lights. Only let us not knock in a casual manner but rather eagerly and persistently. Let us not lose heart when knocking. For in this way it will be opened to us. If we read something once or twice and do not understand what we have read, let us not lose heart, but let us persist with it, let us meditate on it, let us question it. "Ask your father," it says, "and he will inform you, your elders and they will tell you."[8] For not everyone has knowledge.[9] Let us draw from the spring of this paradise ever-flowing and crystal-clear streams "gushing up to eternal life."[10] Let us delight in them, let us thoroughly delight in them insatiably, for they contain boundless grace.

And if we are able to acquire useful fruit from external sources, this does not belong to what is forbidden. Let us become experienced bankers, piling up the genuine pure gold and rejecting the counterfeit. Let us take up the best writings and throw to the dogs the ridiculous gods and bizarre myths. For we should be able to acquire from the former a great deal of strength.[11]

is not to be rejected but is to be used judiciously, as John himself demonstrates in the *Exposition*.

δὲ γελοίους καὶ μύθους ἀλλοτρίους τοῖς κυσὶν ἀπορρίψωμεν· πλείστην γὰρ ἐξ αὐτῶν ἰσχὺν κτήσασθαι δυνηθείημεν.

Ἰστέον δέ, ὡς εἴκοσι δύο βίβλοι εἰσὶ τῆς παλαιᾶς διαθήκης κατὰ τὰ στοιχεῖα τῆς Ἑβραΐδος φωνῆς. Εἴκοσι δύο γὰρ στοιχεῖα ἔχουσιν, ἐξ ὧν πέντε διπλοῦνται, ὡς γίνεσθαι αὐτὰ εἴκοσι ἑπτά· διπλοῦν γάρ ἐστι τὸ Χὰφ καὶ τὸ Μὲμ καὶ τὸ Νοῦν καὶ τὸ Φὶ καὶ τὸ Σαδί. Διὸ καὶ αἱ βίβλοι κατὰ τοῦτον τὸν τρόπον εἴκοσι δύο μὲν ἀριθμοῦνται, εἴκοσι ἑπτὰ δὲ εὑρίσκονται διὰ τὸ πέντε ἐξ αὐτῶν διπλοῦσθαι. Συνάπτεται γὰρ ἡ Ῥοὺθ τοῖς Κριταῖς καὶ ἀριθμεῖται παρ' Ἑβραίοις μία βίβλος· ἡ πρώτη καὶ δευτέρα τῶν Βασιλειῶν μία βίβλος· ἡ τρίτη καὶ ἡ τετάρτη τῶν Βασιλειῶν μία βίβλος· ἡ πρώτη καὶ ἡ δευτέρα τῶν Παραλειπομένων μία βίβλος· ἡ πρώτη καὶ ἡ δευτέρα τοῦ Ἔσδρα μία βίβλος. Οὕτως οὖν σύγκεινται αἱ βίβλοι ἐν πεντατεύχοις τέτρασι, καὶ μένουσιν ἄλλαι δύο, ὡς εἶναι τὰς ἐνδιαθέτους βίβλους οὕτως· πέντε νομικάς· Γένεσιν, Ἔξοδον, Λευιτικόν, Ἀριθμούς, Δευτερονόμιον· αὕτη πρώτη πεντάτευχος, ἢ καὶ νομοθεσία. Εἶτα ἄλλη πεντάτευχος, τὰ καλούμενα Γραφεῖα, παρά τισι δὲ Ἁγιόγραφα, ἅτινά ἐστιν οὕτως· Ἰησοῦς ὁ τοῦ Ναυῆ, Κριταὶ μετὰ τῆς Ῥούθ, Βασιλειῶν πρώτη μετὰ τῆς δευτέρας, βίβλος μία, Βασιλειῶν τρίτη μετὰ τῆς τετάρτης, βίβλος μία, καὶ αἱ δύο τῶν Παραλειπομένων, βίβλος μία· αὕτη δευτέρα πεντάτευχος. Τρίτη πεντάτευχος αἱ στιχήρεις βίβλοι· τοῦ Ἰώβ, τὸ Ψαλτήριον, Παροιμίαι Σολομῶντος, Ἐκκλησιαστὴς τοῦ αὐτοῦ, τὰ Ἄισματα τῶν ᾀσμάτων τοῦ αὐτοῦ. Τετάρτη πεντάτευχος, ἡ προφητική· τὸ δωδεκαπρόφητον, βίβλος μία, Ἡσαΐας, Ἱερεμίας Ἰεζεκιήλ, Δανιήλ. Εἶτα τοῦ Ἔσδρα, αἱ δύο εἰς μίαν συναπτόμεναι βίβλον, καὶ ἡ Ἐσθήρ.—Ἡ δὲ Πανάρετος, τουτέστιν ἡ Σοφία τοῦ Σολομῶντος,

---

[12]John's information is correct. The five doubled letters are those with a different form at the end of a word.

[13]In most English translations (based upon the Masoretic Text, not the LXX), First and Second Kingdoms = First and Second Samuel; Third and Fourth King-doms = First and Second Kings; First and Second Paralipomena = First and Second Chronicles. First and Second Esdras, however, are more complicated cases: First Esdras contains material from what the Masoretic Text calls 2 Chron 35.1–36.23 and significantly more material from Ezra and Nehemiah, while Second Esdras contains

One should also know that there are twenty-two books in the Old Testament in accordance with the letters of the Hebrew alphabet. For it has twenty-two letters of which five are doubled, making them twenty-seven.[12] The doubled letters are *khaph, mem, nun, phi,* and *sadi.* Hence the books in this way, although counted as twenty-two, are actually twenty-seven through the doubling of five of them. For Ruth is attached to Judges and counted as one book by the Hebrews. First and Second Kingdoms are one book.[13] Third and Fourth Kingdoms are one book. First and Second Paralipomena are one book. First and Second Esdras are one book. Thus the books are grouped into four pentateuchs, with two others remaining, so that the canonical books are as follows. The five books of the Law: Genesis, Exodus, Leviticus, Numbers, Deuteronomy. This is the first pentateuch, otherwise the Legislation.[14] Then there is another pentateuch, known as the Writings, which some call the Hagiographa. These are as follows: Jesus son of Nave, Judges with Ruth, First and Second Kingdoms (one book), Third and Fourth Kingdoms (one book), and the two Paralipomena (one book). This is the second pentateuch. The third pentateuch consists of the books composed in verse, those of Job, the Psalter, the Proverbs of Solomon, Ecclesiastes of the same, the Song of Songs of the same. The fourth pentateuch is the prophetic, consisting of the Twelve Prophets (one book), Isaiah, Jeremiah, Ezekiel, Daniel. Then comes Esdras, the two books being attached to form a single one, and Esther. The Panaretus, that is to say, the Wisdom of Solomon, and the Wisdom of Jesus, which the father of Sirach wrote in Hebrew but was translated into Greek by his grandson Jesus, the son of Sirach, are admirable and good, but are not counted among those that were deposited in the ark.

most of the Masoretic Ezra (2 Esd 1–10) and Nehemiah (2 Esd 11–23). See *A New English Translation of the Septuagint: A Translation of the Greek into Contemporary English—An Essential Resource for Biblical Studies,* ed. Albert Pietersma and Benjamin G. Wright (Oxford: Oxford University Press, 2007), 392, 405–7; Henry Barclay Swete, *Introduction to the Old Testament in Greek,* rev. Richard Rusden Ottley (Cambridge: Cambridge University Press, 1914), 265–67. (IG)

[14]The νομοθεσία (*nomothesia,* "legislation"), i.e., the Torah.

καὶ ἡ Σοφία τοῦ Ἰησοῦ, ἣν ὁ πατὴρ μὲν τοῦ Σιρὰχ ἐξέθετο
Ἑβραϊστί, Ἑλληνιστὶ δὲ ἡρμήνευσεν ὁ τούτου μὲν ἔγγονος Ἰησοῦς,
τοῦ δὲ Σιρὰχ υἱός, ἐνάρετοι μὲν καὶ καλαί, ἀλλ' οὐκ ἀριθμοῦνται
οὐδὲ ἔκειντο ἐν τῇ κιβωτῷ.

Τῆς δὲ νέας διαθήκης εὐαγγέλια τέσσαρα· τὸ κατὰ Ματθαῖον,
τὸ κατὰ Μάρκον, τὸ κατὰ Λουκᾶν, τὸ κατὰ Ἰωάννην· Πράξεις
τῶν ἁγίων ἀποστόλων διὰ Λουκᾶ τοῦ εὐαγγελιστοῦ· καθολικαὶ
ἐπιστολαὶ ἑπτά· Ἰακώβου μία, Πέτρου δύο, Ἰωάννου τρεῖς, Ἰούδα
μία· Παύλου ἀποστόλου ἐπιστολαὶ δεκατέσσαρες, Ἀποκάλυψις
Ἰωάννου εὐαγγελιστοῦ, κανόνες τῶν ἁγίων ἀποστόλων διὰ
Κλήμεντος.

91 Περὶ τῶν ἐπὶ Χριστοῦ λεγομένων

Τῶν ἐπὶ Χριστοῦ λεγομένων τρόποι γενικοί εἰσι τέσσαρες· Α' τὰ
μὲν γὰρ καὶ πρὸ τῆς ἐνανθρωπήσεως ἁρμόσει αὐτῷ, Β' τὰ δὲ ἐν τῇ
ἑνώσει, Γ' τὰ δὲ μετὰ τὴν ἕνωσιν, Δ' τὰ δὲ μετὰ τὴν ἀνάστασιν.

Α' Καὶ τῶν πρὸ τῆς ἐνανθρωπήσεως μὲν τρόποι εἰσὶν ἕξ.—α'
Τὰ μὲν γὰρ αὐτῶν τὸ συναφὲς τῆς φύσεως καὶ τὸ πρὸς τὸν
πατέρα ὁμοούσιον δηλοῖ ὡς τὸ «ἐγὼ καὶ ὁ πατὴρ ἕν ἐσμεν» καὶ
«ὁ ἑωρακὼς ἐμὲ ἑώρακε τὸν πατέρα» καὶ τὸ «ὃς ἐν μορφῇ θεοῦ
ὑπάρχων» καὶ τὰ τοιαῦτα. —β' Τὰ δὲ τὸ τέλειον τῆς ὑποστάσεως
ὡς τὸ «υἱὸς τοῦ θεοῦ» καὶ «χαρακτὴρ τῆς ὑποστάσεως αὐτοῦ»
καὶ τὸ «μεγάλης βουλῆς ἄγγελος, θαυμαστός, σύμβουλος»

---

[15]In John's time the number of canonical books of the New Testament was still
fluid. In his thirty-ninth *Festal Letter* (of 367) Athanasius of Alexandria lists the second-century texts, the *Didache* and the *Shepherd*, as deuterocanonical in the same
category as the Wisdom of Solomon, the Wisdom of Sirach, Esther, Judith, and Tobit.
The surviving Greek fragment of this letter is edited by P. Ioannou, *Fonti, Fasciolo IX.
Discipline générale antique (iv-ix s.). Les canons des pères grecs*, vol. 2 (Rome: Tipo-
graphia Italo-Orientale "S. Nilo," 1963), 71.10–76.8. Gregory of Nazianzus, however,
in his *Carmina dogmatica* excludes everything apart from the four Gospels, Acts, the
fourteen Pauline Epistles and the seven Catholic Epistles. "You have them all. / If it's
anything else, it's not genuine," he says (PPS 46:39; PG 37:474). The Church of Jerusalem evidently regarded not only the Revelation of John as fully canonical but also the

The books of the New Testament are four Gospels, those of Matthew, Mark, Luke, and John; the Acts of the holy apostles written by Luke the Evangelist; seven Catholic Epistles, one of James, two of Peter, three of John, and one of Jude; the fourteen epistles of the Apostle Paul, the Revelation of John the Evangelist, and the Canons of the Holy Apostles transmitted by Clement.[15]

91   *On the statements made about Christ*

The statements made about Christ are of four general kinds: (1) those that also apply to him before the incarnation; (2) those that apply to him in the union; (3) those that apply to him after the union; (4) those that apply to him after the resurrection.

(1) Of the kind that apply to him before the incarnation there are six modes: (a) some statements indicate the unified character of the nature and the consubstantiality with the Father, such as "I and the Father are one,"[1] and "He who has seen me has seen the Father,"[2] and "who although he was in the form of God,"[3] and the like. (b) Others indicate the perfection of the hypostasis, such as "Son of God,"[4] and "the imprint of his hypostasis,"[5] and "Angel of great counsel, Wonderful, Counsellor,"[6] and the like. (c) Others indicate the mutual interpenetration of the hypostases, such as "I am in the Father and the Father is in me,"[7] and their inseparable abiding in each other, such as "Word,"[8] "Wisdom and Power,"[9] and "Radiance."[10] For the word abides inseparably in the mind (I mean the substantial word),

Apostolic Canons. This body of canon law, appended to an Arianizing work known as the *Apostolic Constitutions*, was composed in the last decades of the fourth century on the basis of Ps.-Clement's *Letter to James*. The Quinisext Ecumenical Council (in Trullo, 692) rejected the *Apostolic Constitutions* (in Canon 2) as interpolated by heretics but retained the attached canons.

[1] Jn 10.30.   [2] Jn 14.9.   [3] Phil 2.6.
[4] E.g., Mt 14.33, 27.54; Jn 1.34, 1.49, 5.25, 10.36, 11.27; Acts 9.20; 2 Cor 1.19; Eph 4.13; Heb 4.14; 1 Jn 4.15, 5.12; Rev 2.18.
[5] Heb 1.3.   [6] Is 9.5.   [7] Jn 14.10.
[8] E.g. Jn 1.1, 1.14.   [9] 1 Cor 1.24.   [10] Heb 1.3.

καὶ τὰ ὅμοια. —γ′ Τὰ δὲ τὴν ἐν ἀλλήλαις τῶν ὑποστάσεων περιχώρησιν ὡς τὸ «ἐγὼ ἐν τῷ πατρί, καὶ ὁ πατὴρ ἐν ἐμοί» καὶ τὴν ἀνεκφοίτητον ἵδρυσιν ὡς «λόγος», «σοφία καὶ δύναμις» καὶ «ἀπαύγασμα». Ὅ τε γὰρ λόγος ἐν τῷ νῷ (λόγον δέ φημι τὸν οὐσιώδη), καὶ ἡ σοφία ὁμοίως, καὶ ἐν τῷ δυναμένῳ ἡ δύναμις, καὶ ἐν τῷ φωτὶ τὸ ἀπαύγασμα ἀνεκφοιτήτως ἵδρυται, ἐξ αὐτῶν πηγαζόμενα. —δ′ Τὰ δὲ ὡς ἐξ αἰτίου τοῦ πατρὸς ὡς τὸ «ὁ πατήρ μου μείζων μού ἐστιν»· ἐξ αὐτοῦ γὰρ ἔχει τό τε εἶναι καὶ πάντα, ὅσα ἔχει, τὸ μὲν εἶναι γεννητῶς καὶ οὐ δημιουργητικῶς ὡς τὸ «ἐγὼ ἐκ τοῦ πατρὸς ἐξῆλθον», «κἀγὼ ζῶ διὰ τὸν πατέρα», πάντα δέ, ὅσα ἔχει, οὐ μεταδοτικῶς οὔτε διδακτικῶς, ἀλλ' ὡς ἐξ αἰτίου ὡς τὸ «οὐ δύναται ὁ υἱὸς ποιεῖν ἀφ' ἑαυτοῦ οὐδέν, ἐὰν μή τι βλέπῃ τὸν πατέρα ποιοῦντα». Εἰ μὴ γὰρ ὁ πατήρ ἐστιν, οὐδὲ ὁ υἱός· ἐκ τοῦ πατρὸς γὰρ ὁ υἱὸς καὶ ἐν τῷ πατρὶ καὶ οὐ μετὰ τὸν πατέρα. Ὁμοίως καί, ἃ ποιεῖ, ἐξ αὐτοῦ καὶ σὺν αὐτῷ· μία γὰρ καὶ ἡ αὐτή, οὐχ ὁμοία, ἀλλ' ἡ αὐτὴ τοῦ πατρὸς καὶ τοῦ υἱοῦ καὶ τοῦ ἁγίου πνεύματος θέλησις ἐνέργειά τε καὶ δύναμις. —ε′ Τὰ δὲ ὡς τῆς πατρικῆς εὐδοκίας διὰ τῆς αὐτοῦ ἐνεργείας πληρουμένης οὐχ ὡς δι' ὀργάνου ἢ δούλου, ἀλλ' ὡς δι' οὐσιώδους καὶ ἐνυποστάτου αὐτοῦ λόγου καὶ σοφίας καὶ δυνάμεως διὰ τὸ μίαν ἐν πατρὶ καὶ υἱῷ θεωρεῖσθαι κίνησιν, ὡς τὸ «πάντα δι' αὐτοῦ ἐγένετο», καὶ τὸ «ἀπέστειλε τὸν λόγον αὐτοῦ καὶ ἰάσατο αὐτούς», καὶ τὸ «ἵνα γνῶσιν, ὅτι σύ με ἀπέστειλας». —ϛ′ Τὰ δὲ προφητικῶς, καὶ τούτων τὰ μὲν ὡς μέλλοντα οἷον «ἐμφανῶς ἥξει», καὶ τὸ τοῦ Ζαχαρίου «ἰδοὺ ὁ βασιλεύς σου ἔρχεταί σοι», καὶ τὸ ὑπὸ Μιχαίου εἰρημένον «ἰδοὺ κύριος ἐκπορεύεται ἐκ τοῦ τόπου αὐτοῦ καὶ καταβήσεται καὶ ἐπιβήσεται ἐπὶ τὰ ὑψηλὰ τῆς γῆς»· τὰ δὲ μέλλοντα ὡς παρῳχηκότα· «Οὗτος ὁ θεὸς ἡμῶν μετὰ ταῦτα ἐπὶ τῆς γῆς ὤφθη καὶ τοῖς ἀνθρώποις συνανεστράφη», καὶ τὸ «κύριος ἔκτισέ με ἀρχὴν ὁδῶν αὐτοῦ εἰς ἔργα αὐτοῦ», καὶ «διὰ τοῦτο ἔχρισέ σε ὁ θεὸς ὁ θεός σου ἔλαιον ἀγαλλιάσεως παρὰ τοὺς μετόχους σου» καὶ τὰ τοιαῦτα.—Τὰ μὲν οὖν πρὸ τῆς ἑνώσεως καὶ

and wisdom likewise, and power in him who has power, and radiance in the light, and spring from them. (d) Others indicate that he is from the Father as from his cause, such as "My Father is greater than I,"[11] for it is from him that he has his being and everything that he has, on the one hand the fact that he exists by generation and not by creation, such as "I came from the Father,"[12] "and I live because of the Father,"[13] and on the other the fact that everything that he has is not because it has been transmitted to him or taught to him but is as from his cause, such as "the Son can do nothing on his own but only what he sees the Father doing."[14] For if there is no Father, neither is there a Son. For the Son is from the Father and in the Father and not after the Father. Likewise, what he does is from him and in him, for the will, operation, and power of the Father and the Son and the Holy Spirit are one and the same, not merely similar. (e) Others indicate that when the Father's good pleasure is fulfilled through his operation, it is not as if by an instrument or servant, but by his essential and enhypostatic Word and Wisdom and Power on account of the movement in the Father and the Son being regarded as one, such as the statements "all things came into being through him,"[15] and "He sent out his Word and healed them,"[16] and "that they may know that you have sent me."[17] (f) Others are uttered prophetically, and of these some refer to the future, such as "He will come manifestly,"[18] and the words of Zechariah, "Lo, your king comes to you,"[19] and the saying of Micah, "For lo, the Lord is coming out of his place, and will come down and tread upon the high places of the earth."[20] Others refer to the future as the past: "After these things this God of ours was seen upon earth and lived with men,"[21] and "the Lord created me the beginning of his ways and for his works,"[22] and "therefore God, your God has anointed you with the oil of gladness beyond your companions,"[23] and the like. Some of these were said of him both before the union and after

[11]Jn 14.28.   [12]Jn 16.27.   [13]Jn 6.57.   [14]Jn 5.19.
[15]Jn 1.3.   [16]Ps 106.20.   [17]Jn 11.42.   [18]Ps 49.2.
[19]Zec 9.9.   [20]Mic 1.3.   [21]Bar 3.38.   [22]Prov 8.22.   [23]Ps 44.8.

μετὰ τὴν ἕνωσιν ἐπ᾽ αὐτῷ λεχθήσεται, τὰ δὲ μετὰ τὴν ἕνωσιν πρὸ τῆς ἑνώσεως οὐδαμῶς, εἰ μήτιγε προφητικῶς, ὡς ἔφημεν.

Βʹ Τῶν δὲ ἐν τῇ ἑνώσει τρόποι εἰσὶ τρεῖς. —αʹ Ὅτε μὲν γὰρ ἐκ τοῦ κρείττονος τὸν λόγον ποιούμεθα, θέωσιν τῆς σαρκὸς καὶ λόγωσιν καὶ ὑπερύψωσιν λέγομεν καὶ τὰ τοιαῦτα, τὸν προσγενόμενον τῇ σαρκὶ πλοῦτον ἐκ τῆς πρὸς τὸν ὕψιστον θεὸν λόγον ἑνώσεώς τε καὶ συμφυΐας ἐμφαίνοντες.—βʹ Ὅτε δὲ ἀπὸ τοῦ ἐλάττονος, σάρκωσιν τοῦ λόγου, ἐνανθρώπησιν, κένωσιν, πτωχείαν, ταπείνωσίν φαμεν· ταῦτα γὰρ καὶ τὰ τοιαῦτα ἐκ τῆς πρὸς τὸ ἀνθρώπινον κράσεως ἐπιλέγεται τῷ λόγῳ τε καὶ θεῷ.—γʹ Ὅταν δὲ ἐξ ἀμφοῖν ἅμα, ἕνωσιν, κοινωνίαν, χρίσιν, συμφυΐαν, συμμόρφωσιν καὶ τὰ τοιαῦτα φάσκομεν. Διὰ τοῦτον οὖν τὸν τρίτον τρόπον οἱ προλελεγμένοι δύο τρόποι λέγονται. Διὰ γὰρ τῆς ἑνώσεως δηλοῦται, τί ἔσχεν ἑκάτερον ἐκ τῆς τοῦ συνυφεστῶτος αὐτῷ ἁρμογῆς καὶ περιχωρήσεως· διὰ γὰρ τὴν καθ᾽ ὑπόστασιν ἕνωσιν ἡ σὰρξ τεθεῶσθαι λέγεται καὶ θεὸς γενέσθαι καὶ ὁμόθεος τῷ λόγῳ καὶ ὁ θεὸς λόγος σαρκωθῆναι καὶ ἄνθρωπος γενέσθαι καὶ κτίσμα λέγεσθαι καὶ ἔσχατος καλεῖσθαι, οὐχ ὡς τῶν δύο φύσεων μεταβληθεισῶν εἰς μίαν φύσιν σύνθετον (ἀδύνατον γὰρ ἐν μιᾷ φύσει ἅμα τὰ ἐναντία φυσικὰ γενέσθαι), ἀλλ᾽ ὡς τῶν δύο φύσεων καθ᾽ ὑπόστασιν ἑνωθεισῶν καὶ τὴν εἰς ἀλλήλας περιχώρησιν ἀσύγχυτον καὶ ἀμετάβλητον ἐχουσῶν. Ἡ δὲ περιχώρησις οὐκ ἐκ τῆς σαρκός, ἀλλ᾽ ἐκ τῆς θεότητος γέγονεν· ἀμήχανον γὰρ τὴν σάρκα περιχωρῆσαι διὰ τῆς θεότητος, ἀλλ᾽ ἡ θεία φύσις ἅπαξ περιχωροῦσα διὰ τῆς σαρκὸς ἔδωκε καὶ τῇ σαρκὶ τὴν πρὸς αὐτὴν ἄρρητον περιχώρησιν, ἣν δὴ ἕνωσιν λέγομεν.—Ἰστέον δέ, ὡς ἐπὶ τοῦ πρώτου καὶ δευτέρου τρόπου τῶν ἐν τῇ ἑνώσει τὸ ἀνάπαλιν θεωρεῖται. Ὅτε γὰρ περὶ τῆς σαρκὸς τὸν λόγον ποιούμεθα, θέωσιν

---

[24]John uses here, and again near the end of the paragraph, a coinage of his own, λόγωσις (*logōsis*, perhaps "endowment with reason," but probably, more strongly, "endowment with Word"—literally "Wording"). He balances the "Wording of the flesh" (τῆς σαρκὸς ... λόγωσιν, *tēs sarkos ... logōsin*) with the "enfleshment of the Word" (σάρκωσιν τοῦ λόγου, *sarkōsin tou logou*) in a manner that recalls Gregory

the union, others after the union but in no sense before the union, unless indeed prophetically, as we have said.

(2) Of the kind that apply to him in the union there are three modes: (a) When we are discussing the matter from the point of view of enhancement, we speak of the flesh's deification, its endowment with Word,[24] its supreme exaltation and the like, emphasizing the richness that has been added to the flesh from its union and coming together into one with the Word, the Most High God. (b) But when we are discussing it from the point of view of impairment, we speak of the Word's enfleshment, his inhomination, self-emptying, poverty, humiliation. For these and similar things are attributed to God the Word on account of his blending with the human element. (c) When we are considering it from both points of view at the same time, we speak of union, communion, anointing, coming together into one, unity of form, and suchlike. Through this third mode the first two are therefore said to be implied. For through the union it is shown what each had through conjunction and interpenetration with what subsisted in a unity with it. For through the hypostatic union the flesh is said to have been deified and become God and equally divine as the Word, and God the Word is said to have been enfleshed and to have become a human being, and be referred to as a creature and be called "last," not because the two natures have been changed into a single composite nature (for it is impossible for opposite natures to exist simultaneously in a single nature), but because the two natures have been united hypostatically and possess a mutual indwelling without confusion and without change. The interpenetration (περιχώρησις, *perichōrēsis*) did not originate from the flesh but from the divinity. For it is impossible that the flesh should pass reciprocally into the divinity. Rather, once the divine nature had passed reciprocally into the flesh, it also endowed the flesh with an ineffable interpenetration, which indeed we call the union. One should note, too, that as in the

of Nazianzus' kenosis–theosis wordplay, but unlike Gregory's θέωσις (*theōsis*), his λόγωσις (*logōsis*) did not catch on. It was not used by any of his successors and remained a *hapax legomenon*.

καὶ λόγωσιν καὶ ὑπερύψωσιν καὶ χρίσιν φαμέν (ἀπὸ μὲν γὰρ τῆς
θεότητος ταῦτα, περὶ δὲ τὴν σάρκα θεωρεῖται)· ὅτε δὲ περὶ τοῦ
λόγου, κένωσιν, σάρκωσιν, ἐνανθρώπησιν, ταπείνωσιν καὶ τὰ
τοιαῦτα, ἅτινα, ὡς ἔφημεν, ἐκ τῆς σαρκὸς ἐπιλέγεται τῷ λόγῳ τε
καὶ θεῷ· αὐτὸς γὰρ ταῦτα ὑπέμεινεν ἑκών.

Γ΄ Τῶν δὲ μετὰ τὴν ἕνωσιν τρόποι εἰσὶ τρεῖς. —Πρῶτος ὁ
τῆς θείας φύσεως δηλωτικὸς ὡς τὸ «ἐγὼ ἐν τῷ πατρὶ καὶ ὁ
πατὴρ ἐν ἐμοί», καὶ «ἐγὼ καὶ ὁ πατὴρ ἕν ἐσμεν», καὶ πάντα,
ὅσα πρὸ τῆς ἐνανθρωπήσεως αὐτῷ ἐπιλέγεται, ταῦτα καὶ μετὰ
τὴν ἐνανθρώπησιν αὐτῷ ἐπιλεχθήσεται πλὴν τοῦ μὴ εἰληφέναι
σάρκα καὶ τὰ ταύτης φυσικά.—Δεύτερος ὁ τῆς ἀνθρωπίνης ὡς
τὸ «τί με ζητεῖτε ἀποκτεῖναι ἄνθρωπον, ὃς τὴν ἀλήθειαν ὑμῖν
λελάληκα;» καὶ τὸ «οὕτω δεῖ ὑψωθῆναι τὸν υἱὸν τοῦ ἀνθρώπου»
καὶ τὰ τοιαῦτα. Τούτων δὲ τῶν ἀνθρωποπρεπῶς ἐπὶ τοῦ σωτῆρος
Χριστοῦ γεγραμμένων εἴτε ἐν ῥήμασιν εἴτε ἐν πράγμασιν τρόποι
εἰσὶ ἕξ.—α΄ Τὰ μὲν γὰρ αὐτῶν κατὰ φύσιν οἰκονομικῶς πέπρακταί
τε καὶ λέλεκται οἷον ὁ ἐκ παρθένου τόκος, ἡ καθ᾽ ἡλικίαν αὔξησίς
τε καὶ προκοπή, ἡ πεῖνα, ἡ δίψα, ὁ κόπος, τὸ δάκρυον, ὁ ὕπνος,
ἡ τῶν ἥλων τρῆσις, ὁ θάνατος καὶ τὰ τοιαῦτα, ὅσα φυσικὰ καὶ
ἀδιάβλητα πάθη ὑπάρχουσιν· ἐν τούτοις γὰρ ἅπασι μίξις μέν ἐστι
τοῦ θείου πρὸς τὸ ἀνθρώπινον, πλὴν τοῦ σώματος ἀληθῶς εἶναι
πιστεύεται, οὐδὲν τούτων τοῦ θείου πάσχοντος, δι᾽ αὐτῶν δὲ τὴν
ἡμῶν οἰκονομοῦντος σωτηρίαν.—β΄ Τὰ δὲ κατὰ προσποίησιν τὸ
ἐρωτᾶν «ποῦ τεθείκατε Λάζαρον;», ὁ ὑπὸ τὴν συκῆν δρόμος, τὸ
ὑποδύεσθαι ἤγουν ὑπαναχωρεῖν, ἡ προσευχή, τὸ «προσεποιήσατο
πορρωτέρω πορεύεσθαι». Τούτων γὰρ καὶ τῶν παραπλησίων
οὔτε ὡς θεὸς οὔτε ὡς ἄνθρωπος ἔχρῃζε, πλὴν ἀνθρωποπρεπῶς
ἐσχηματίζετο, πρὸς ὅπερ ἡ χρεία καὶ τὸ λυσιτελὲς ἀπῄτει, οἷον
τὴν μὲν προσευχὴν διὰ τὸ δεῖξαι, ὡς οὐκ ἔστιν ἀντίθεος καὶ
ὡς αἰτίαν αὐτοῦ τιμῶν τὸν πατέρα, τὸ ἐρωτᾶν οὐκ ἀγνοῶν,

---

[25]Jn 14.10.   [26]Jn 10.30.   [27]Jn 7.19, 8.40.   [28]Jn 3.14.
[29]Jn 11.24.   [30]Cf. Mt 21.18–19.   [31]Cf. Lk 9.10.

case of the first and second modes, the converse is perceived in the union. For when we are discussing the flesh, we speak of deification and endowment with Word and supreme exaltation and anointing (for these matters concerning the flesh are perceived from the point of view of divinity). But when we are discussing the Word, we speak of self-emptying, enfleshment, inhomination, abasement, and the like, which, as we have said, are attributed to God the Word as a result of the flesh, for he endured these things voluntarily.

(3) Of the kind that follow the union there are three modes. The first is the one that is indicative of the divine nature, such as "I am in the Father and the Father is in me,"[25] and "I and the Father are one,"[26] and everything that is attributed to him before the inhomination is also attributed to him after the inhomination, except the fact of his not having received the flesh and its natural characteristics. The second is the one that is indicative of the human nature, such as "Why are you looking for an opportunity to kill me, a man who has told you the truth that I heard from God?"[27] and "so must the Son of Man be lifted up,"[28] and the like.

Those things that have been written about Christ the Savior in a manner befitting a human being, whether in his words or his actions, belong to six modes: (a) Some of them were done and said by nature in accordance with the dispensation of the incarnation, such as birth from a virgin, physical development as he grew up, hunger, thirst, weariness, tears, sleep, piercing with nails, death, and suchlike, which are natural and blameless passions. For in all these, although there is a mingling of the divine with the human, nevertheless they are believed to belong truly to the body, the divine suffering none of them but through them bringing about our salvation. (b) Others are by way of pretence: his asking "Where have you laid Lazarus?";[29] his going up to the fig tree;[30] his slipping away or withdrawing;[31] his prayer;[32] his "pretending to go further."[33] For he had no need of these and similar things either as God or as a human being. He was only making a show

[32]Cf. Mt 14.23, 26.36; Mk 1.35; Lk 3.21, 5.16, 6.12, 9.18.
[33]Lk 24.28.

ἀλλ᾽ ἵνα δείξῃ, ὡς κατὰ ἀλήθειάν ἐστιν ἄνθρωπος μετὰ τοῦ εἶναι θεός· τὸ ὑπαναχωρεῖν, ἵνα διδάξῃ μὴ προπετεύεσθαι μηδ᾽ ἑαυτοὺς προδιδόναι.—γ′ Τὰ δὲ κατ᾽ οἰκείωσιν καὶ ἀναφορὰν ὡς τὸ «θεέ μου, θεέ μου, ἵνα τί με ἐγκατέλιπες»; καὶ τὸ «μὴ γνόντα ἁμαρτίαν ὑπὲρ ἡμῶν ἁμαρτίαν ἐποίησε», καὶ τὸ «γενόμενος ὑπὲρ ἡμῶν κατάρα», καὶ τὸ «αὐτὸς ὁ υἱὸς ὑποταγήσεται τῷ ὑποτάξαντι αὐτῷ τὰ πάντα». Οὔτε γὰρ ὡς θεὸς οὔτε ὡς ἄνθρωπος ἐγκατελείφθη ποτὲ ὑπὸ τοῦ πατρὸς οὔτε ἁμαρτία οὔτε κατάρα γέγονεν οὔτε ὑποταγῆναι χρῄζει τῷ πατρί· καθὸ μὲν γὰρ θεὸς ἴσος ἐστὶ τῷ πατρὶ καὶ οὐδὲ ἐναντίος οὐδὲ ὑποτεταγμένος, καθὸ δὲ ἄνθρωπος οὐδέπω ἀνήκοος γέγονε τοῦ γεννήτορος, ἵνα ὑποταγῆς δεηθῇ. Τὸ ἡμέτερον τοίνυν οἰκειούμενος πρόσωπον καὶ μεθ᾽ ἡμῶν τάσσων ἑαυτὸν ταῦτα ἔλεγεν· ἡμεῖς γὰρ ἦμεν οἱ ἁμαρτίας καὶ κατάρας ἔνοχοι ὡς ἀπειθεῖς καὶ παρήκοοι καὶ διὰ τοῦτο ἐγκαταλελειμμένοι. —δ′ Τὰ δὲ διὰ τὴν κατ᾽ ἐπίνοιαν διαίρεσιν. Ἐὰν γὰρ τῇ ἐπινοίᾳ διέλῃς τὰ τῇ ἀληθείᾳ ἀχώριστα ἤτοι τὴν σάρκα ἐκ τοῦ λόγου, λέγεται καὶ δοῦλος καὶ ἀγνοῶν· καὶ γὰρ τῆς δούλης καὶ ἀγνοούσης φύσεως ἦν καί, εἰ μὴ ἥνωτο τῷ θεῷ λόγῳ ἡ σάρξ, δούλη ἦν καὶ ἀγνοοῦσα, ἀλλὰ διὰ τὴν πρὸς θεὸν λόγον καθ᾽ ὑπόστασιν ἕνωσιν οὔτε δούλη ἦν οὔτε ἠγνόει. Οὕτω καὶ θεὸν ἑαυτοῦ τὸν πατέρα ἐκάλεσεν.—ε′ Τὰ δὲ διὰ τὴν πρὸς ἡμᾶς φανέρωσίν τε καὶ πίστωσιν ὡς τὸ «πάτερ, δόξασόν με τῇ δόξῃ, ᾗ εἶχον πρὸ τοῦ τὸν κόσμον εἶναι παρὰ σοί» (αὐτὸς μὲν γὰρ δεδοξασμένος ἦν τε καὶ ἔστιν, ἀλλ᾽ ἡμῖν οὐκ ἦν φανερωθεῖσα καὶ πιστωθεῖσα ἡ δόξα αὐτοῦ), καὶ τὸ ὑπὸ τοῦ ἀποστόλου εἰρημένον «τοῦ ὁρισθέντος υἱοῦ θεοῦ ἐν δυνάμει κατὰ πνεῦμα ἁγιωσύνης, ἐξ ἀναστάσεως νεκρῶν» (διὰ γὰρ τῶν θαυμάτων καὶ τῆς ἀναστάσεως καὶ τῆς ἐπιφοιτήσεως τοῦ ἁγίου πνεύματος ἐφανερώθη καὶ ἐπιστώθη τῷ κόσμῳ, ὅτι υἱός ἐστι τοῦ θεοῦ), καὶ τὸ «προέκοπτε σοφίᾳ καὶ χάριτι».—ς′ Τὰ δὲ κατὰ τὴν τοῦ Ἰουδαίων προσώπου οἰκείωσιν μετὰ τῶν Ἰουδαίων ἀριθμῶν

---

[34]Mt 27.46.   [35]2 Cor 5.21.   [36]Gal 3.13.

of behaving in a human way, in accordance with what was demanded by necessity or profit, such as when he prayed in order to show that he was not a rival god but honored the Father as his cause. He asked not because he was ignorant but in order to show that he was truly a human being as well as being God. He withdrew in order to teach us not to act rashly and not to be false to ourselves. (c) Others are by appropriation and reference, such as "My God, my God, why have you forsaken me?"[34] and "For our sake he made him to be sin who knew no sin,"[35] and "becoming a curse for us,"[36] and "the Son himself will be subjected to the one who put all things in subjection under him."[37] For he was never forsaken by the Father either as God or as man, nor did he ever become sin or a curse, nor did he need to be subjected to the Father. For in that he is God, he is equal to the Father and not opposed to him or subjected to him, and in that he is a human being he was never disobedient to his Father that he should need to be made subject to him. It was therefore by appropriating our own character and putting himself alongside us that he said these things. For we were the ones who were guilty of sin and liable to a curse, since we were disobedient and heedless, and for that reason were forsaken. (d) Others are by conceptual distinction. For if you divide things conceptually that are in reality inseparable, that is to say, divide the flesh from the Word, he is said to be both a servant and ignorant. For since the flesh was of a servile and ignorant nature, if it had not been united to God the Word it would have remained a servant and ignorant. But because of its hypostatic union with God the Word it was neither a servant nor ignorant. It was also thus that he called God his father. (e) Others are for the sake of manifesting and confirming to us, such as "Father, glorify me with the glory that I had in your presence before the world existed"[38] (for he himself was glorified and is glorified, but his glory had not been manifested and confirmed to us), and the Apostle's text, "and was declared to be Son of God with power according to the Spirit of holiness by resurrection from the dead"[39] (for it was by the miracles and the resurrection and the overshadowing of

[37]1 Cor 15.28.   [38]Jn 17.5.   [39]Rom 1.4.

ἑαυτόν, ὡς πρὸς τὴν Σαμαρεῖτίν φησιν· «Ὑμεῖς προσκυνεῖτε, ὃ
οὐκ οἴδατε, ἡμεῖς προσκυνοῦμεν, ὃ οἴδαμεν, ὅτι ἡ σωτηρία ἐκ
τῶν Ἰουδαίων ἐστίν».—Τρίτος τρόπος ὁ τῆς μιᾶς ὑποστάσεως
δηλωτικὸς καὶ τοῦ συναμφοτέρου παραστατικός, οἷον τὸ «ἐγὼ ζῶ
διὰ τὸν πατέρα, καὶ ὁ τρώγων με, κἀκεῖνος ζήσεται δι᾽ ἐμέ», καὶ τὸ
«ὑπάγω πρὸς τὸν πατέρα, καὶ οὐκέτι θεωρεῖτέ με», καὶ τὸ «οὐκ ἂν
τὸν κύριον τῆς δόξης ἐσταύρωσαν», καὶ τὸ «οὐδεὶς ἀναβέβηκεν
εἰς τὸν οὐρανόν, εἰ μὴ ὁ ἐκ τοῦ οὐρανοῦ καταβάς, ὁ υἱὸς τοῦ
ἀνθρώπου ὁ ὢν ἐν τῷ οὐρανῷ» καὶ τὰ τοιαῦτα.

Δ´ Καὶ τῶν μετὰ τὴν ἀνάστασιν τὰ μέν εἰσι θεοπρεπῆ ὡς τὸ
«βαπτίζοντες αὐτοὺς εἰς τὸ ὄνομα τοῦ πατρὸς καὶ τοῦ υἱοῦ (ὡς
θεοῦ δηλονότι) καὶ τοῦ ἁγίου πνεύματος», καὶ τὸ «ἰδοὺ ἐγὼ μεθ᾽
ὑμῶν εἰμι πάσας τὰς ἡμέρας ἕως τῆς συντελείας τοῦ αἰῶνος» καὶ
τὰ τοιαῦτα (ὡς γὰρ θεός ἐστι μεθ᾽ ἡμῶν), τὰ δὲ ἀνθρωποπρεπῆ
ὡς τὸ «ἐκράτησαν αὐτοῦ τοὺς πόδας», καὶ τὸ «κἀκεῖ με ὄψονται»
καὶ τὰ τοιαῦτα.

Ε´ Τῶν δὲ μετὰ τὴν ἀνάστασιν ἀνθρωποπρεπῶν τρόποι εἰσὶ
διάφοροι. Τὰ μὲν γὰρ ἀληθῶς, ἀλλ᾽ οὐ κατὰ φύσιν, ἀλλὰ κατ᾽
οἰκονομίαν πρὸς τὸ πιστώσασθαι, ὅτι αὐτὸ τὸ παθὸν σῶμα
ἀνέστη, ὡς οἱ μώλωπες, ἡ βρῶσις καὶ ἡ πόσις ἡ μετὰ τὴν
ἀνάστασιν, τὰ δὲ ἀληθῶς κατὰ φύσιν ὡς τὸ μεταβαίνειν τόπους
ἐκ τόπων ἀμόχθως καὶ τὸ διὰ τῶν θυρῶν κεκλεισμένων εἰσελθεῖν,
τὰ δὲ κατὰ προσποίησιν ὡς τὸ «προσεποιήσατο πορρωτέρω
πορεύεσθαι», τὰ δὲ τοῦ συναμφοτέρου ὡς τὸ «ἀναβαίνω πρὸς
τὸν πατέρα μου καὶ πατέρα ὑμῶν καὶ θεόν μου καὶ θεὸν ὑμῶν»,
καὶ τὸ «εἰσελεύσεται ὁ βασιλεὺς τῆς δόξης», καὶ τὸ «ἐκάθισεν
ἐν δεξιᾷ τῆς μεγαλωσύνης ἐν τοῖς ὑψηλοῖς», τὰ δὲ ὡς μεθ᾽ ἡμῶν

---

[40]Lk 2.52.   [41]Jn 4.22.

[42]I.e. the third of the modes announced in the first paragraph of section (3).

[43]"The both together" (τὸ συναμφότερον, to synamphoteron) is a compendious
expression for the hypostatic union in Christ of the divinity and the humanity.

the Holy Spirit that it was manifested and confirmed to the world that he is the Son of God), and "he increased in wisdom and grace."[40] (f) Others are by his appropriation of the character of the Jews and his counting himself among them, as when he says to the Samaritan woman, "You worship what you do not know; we worship what we know, for salvation is from the Jews."[41]

The third mode[42] is the one that is indicative of the one hypostasis and proves "the both together,"[43] such as, "I live because of the Father, so whoever eats me will live because of me,"[44] and, "I am going to the Father and you will see me no longer,"[45] and "they would not have crucified the Lord of glory,"[46] and "no one has ascended into heaven except the one who descended from heaven, the Son of Man who is in heaven,"[47] and suchlike.

(4) Of the kind that apply to him after the resurrection, some befit the divinity, such as "baptizing them in the name of the Father and of the Son (clearly as God) and of the Holy Spirit,"[48] and "behold, I am with you always, to the end of the age,"[49] and suchlike (for he is with us as God), whereas others befit the humanity, such as "they took hold of his feet,"[50] and "there they will see me,"[51] and suchlike.

(5) Of the kind that apply to him after the resurrection there are various modes. Some are uttered truly, although not in accordance with nature but in accordance with the economy, in order to give assurance that the body that suffered was the same body that rose again, such as the marks of the wounds, the eating and drinking after the resurrection. Others are uttered truly in accordance with nature, such as the effortless moving from place to place and the passing through closed doors. Others, again, are by pretence, such as "he pretended to be going further."[52] Others are in accordance with "the both together," such as "I am ascending to my Father and your Father, to my God and your God,"[53] and "the King of Glory will come

[44]Jn 6.57.	[45]Jn 16.10.	[46]1 Cor 2.8.	
[47]Jn 3.13.	[48]Mt 28.19.	[49]Mt 28.20.	
[50]Mt 28.9.	[51]Mt 28.10.	[52]Lk 24.28.	[53]Jn 20.17.

ἑαυτὸν τάττοντος τῷ τρόπῳ τῆς κατὰ ψιλὴν ἐπίνοιαν διαιρέσεως
ὡς τὸ «θεόν μου καὶ θεὸν ὑμῶν».

Δεῖ οὖν τὰ μὲν ὑψηλὰ προσνέμειν τῇ θείᾳ καὶ κρείττονι
φύσει παθῶν καὶ σώματος, τὰ δὲ ταπεινὰ τῇ ἀνθρωπίνῃ, τὰ
δὲ κοινὰ τῷ συνθέτῳ ἤγουν τῷ ἑνὶ Χριστῷ, ὅς ἐστι θεὸς καὶ
ἄνθρωπος, καὶ εἰδέναι ἀμφότερα ἑνὸς καὶ τοῦ αὐτοῦ κυρίου
ἡμῶν Ἰησοῦ Χριστοῦ· ἑκάστου γὰρ τὸ ἴδιον γινώσκοντες καὶ
ἀμφότερα ἐξ ἑνὸς πραττόμενα βλέποντες ὀρθῶς πιστεύομεν καὶ
οὐ πλανηθησόμεθα. Ἐξ ὧν ἁπάντων τῶν μὲν ἑνωθεισῶν φύσεων
ἡ διαφορὰ γινώσκεται καὶ «ὅτι μὴ ταὐτόν», ὥς φησιν ὁ θειότατος
Κύριλλος, «ἐν ποιότητι φυσικῇ θεότης τε καὶ ἀνθρωπότης». Εἷς γε
μὴν υἱὸς καὶ Χριστὸς καὶ κύριος, καὶ ὡς ἑνὸς ὄντος ἓν αὐτοῦ καὶ
τὸ πρόσωπον κατ' οὐδένα τρόπον διὰ τὴν ἐπίγνωσιν τῆς φυσικῆς
διαφορᾶς μεριζομένης τῆς καθ' ὑπόστασιν ἑνώσεως.

92 Ὅτι οὐκ ἔστι τῶν κακῶν αἴτιος ὁ θεός

Χρὴ εἰδέναι, ὅτι ἔθος τῇ θείᾳ γραφῇ τὴν παραχώρησιν τοῦ θεοῦ
ἐνέργειαν αὐτοῦ καλεῖν, ὡς ὅταν λέγῃ ὁ ἀπόστολος ἐν τῇ πρὸς
Ῥωμαίους ἐπιστολῇ· «Ἢ οὐκ ἔχει ἐξουσίαν ὁ κεραμεὺς τοῦ πηλοῦ
ἐκ τοῦ αὐτοῦ φυράματος ποιῆσαι, ὃ μὲν εἰς τιμὴν σκεῦος, ὃ δὲ
εἰς ἀτιμίαν;» Ὅτι μὲν γὰρ αὐτὸς ποιεῖ καὶ ταῦτα κἀκεῖνα· μόνος
γὰρ αὐτός ἐστι τῶν ἁπάντων δημιουργός, ἀλλ' οὐκ αὐτὸς τίμια
κατασκευάζει ἢ ἄτιμα, ἀλλ' ἡ οἰκεία ἑκάστου προαίρεσις. Καὶ
τοῦτο δῆλον, ἐξ ὧν ὁ αὐτὸς ἀπόστολος ἐν τῇ πρὸς Τιμόθεον
δευτέρᾳ ἐπιστολῇ φησιν· «Ἐν μεγάλῃ οἰκίᾳ οὐκ ἔστι μόνον σκεύη
χρυσᾶ καὶ ἀργυρᾶ, ἀλλὰ καὶ ξύλινα καὶ ὀστράκινα, καὶ ἃ μὲν εἰς
τιμήν, ἃ δὲ εἰς ἀτιμίαν. Ἐὰν οὖν τις ἐκκαθάρῃ ἑαυτὸν ἀπὸ τούτων,

---

[54]Ps 23.7.   [55]Heb 1.3.   [56]Jn 20.17.
[57]"The composite nature" (τὸ σύνθετον, *to syntheton*), like "the both together"
(τὸ συναμφότερον, *to synamphoteron*), is another compendious expression for the
hypostatic union, this time emphasizing the oneness rather than the twoness.

in,"[54] and "he sat down at the right hand of the Majesty on high."[55] Others are as if he were setting himself alongside us by a merely conceptual distinction, such as "my God and your God."[56]

One should therefore attribute the sublime things to the divine nature that is superior to passions and the body, the humble things to the human nature, and those that are common to both to the composite nature,[57] that is to say, to the one Christ, who is God and man, and one should know that both belong to one and the same, our Lord Jesus Christ. For if we know what is proper to each and see both as performed by the same subject, we believe correctly and will not be in error. From all these we recognize the difference between the united natures and, as the most divine Cyril says, "that divinity and humanity are not the same in their natural quality."[58] There is a single entity who is Son and Christ and Lord, and since he is one, his person is also one, the hypostatic union being in no way divided by our acknowledgement of the natural difference.

92   *That God is not the cause of evils*

One needs to know that it is customary in the divine Scripture to call the permission of God his activity, as, for example, when the Apostle says in his Epistle to the Romans: "Has the potter no right over the clay, to make out of the same lump one object for noble use and another for ignoble use?"[1] This is so because the same makes both sorts, for it is he alone who is the creator of all things. Yet it is not he himself who produces noble or ignoble things, but the personal free choice of each of us. And this is clear from what the Apostle himself says in the Second Epistle to Timothy: "In a large house there are vessels not only of gold and silver but also of wood and clay, some for noble use, some for ignoble use. If one were to cleanse oneself of the things I have mentioned one would become a noble vessel, dedicated

[58]Cyril of Alexandria, *Letter* 40 (ACO I, 1, 4, p. 27.12—16 = *Doctrina Patrum*, Diekamp, 149.19.

[1]Rom 9.21.

ἔσται σκεῦος εἰς τιμήν, ἡγιασμένον καὶ εὔχρηστον τῷ δεσπότῃ, εἰς πᾶν ἔργον ἀγαθὸν ἡτοιμασμένον». Δῆλον δέ, ὡς ἑκουσίως ἡ κάθαρσις γίνεται· «Ἐὰν γάρ τις», φησίν, «ἐκκαθάρῃ ἑαυτόν», ἡ δὲ ἀκόλουθος ἀντιστροφὴ ἀντιφωνεῖ· Ἐὰν δὲ μὴ ἐκκαθάρῃ, ἔσται σκεῦος εἰς ἀτιμίαν, ἄχρηστον τῷ δεσπότῃ, συντριβῆς ἄξιον. Τὸ οὖν προκείμενον ῥητὸν καὶ τὸ «συνέκλεισεν ὁ θεὸς πάντας εἰς ἀπείθειαν», καὶ τὸ «ἔδωκεν αὐτοῖς ὁ θεὸς πνεῦμα κατανύξεως, ὀφθαλμοὺς τοῦ μὴ βλέπειν καὶ ὦτα τοῦ μὴ ἀκούειν», ταῦτα πάντα οὐχ ὡς τοῦ θεοῦ ἐνεργήσαντος ἐκληπτέον, ἀλλ' ὡς τοῦ θεοῦ παραχωρήσαντος διὰ τὸ αὐτεξούσιον καὶ τὸ ἀβίαστον εἶναι τὸ καλόν.

Τὴν οὖν παραχώρησιν αὐτοῦ ὡς ἐνέργειαν καὶ ποίησιν αὐτοῦ λέγειν σύνηθες τῇ θείᾳ γραφῇ. Ἀλλὰ μὴν καὶ ὅτε φησὶ τὸν θεὸν κτίζειν κακὰ καὶ μὴ εἶναι «ἐν πόλει κακίαν, ἣν ὁ κύριος οὐκ ἐποίησεν», οὐ κακῶν αἴτιον τὸν θεὸν δείκνυσιν, ἀλλ', ἐπειδὴ δισέμφατον τὸ τῆς κακίας ὄνομα, δύο σημαῖνον· ποτὲ μὲν γὰρ τὸ τῇ φύσει κακὸν δηλοῖ, ὅπερ ἐναντίον ἐστὶ τῇ ἀρετῇ καὶ τῇ τοῦ θεοῦ θελήσει, ποτὲ δὲ τὸ πρὸς τὴν ἡμετέραν αἴσθησιν κακὸν καὶ ἐπίπονον ἤγουν τὰς θλίψεις καὶ ἐπαγωγάς. Αὗται δὲ τῷ μὲν δοκεῖν κακαί εἰσιν ἀλγειναὶ τυγχάνουσαι, τῇ δὲ ἀληθείᾳ ἀγαθαί· ἐπιστροφῆς γὰρ καὶ σωτηρίας γίνονται τοῖς συνιοῦσι πρόξενοι· ταύτας διὰ θεοῦ γίνεσθαί φησιν ἡ γραφή.

Ἰστέον δέ, ὡς καὶ τούτων ἡμεῖς ἐσμεν αἴτιοι. Τῶν γὰρ ἑκουσίων κακῶν τὰ ἀκούσιά εἰσιν ἔκγονα.—Καὶ τοῦτο δὲ ἰστέον, ὅτι ἔθος τῇ γραφῇ τινα ἐκβατικῶς ὀφείλοντα λέγεσθαι αἰτιολογικῶς λέγειν ὡς τὸ «σοὶ μόνῳ ἥμαρτον καὶ τὸ πονηρὸν ἐνώπιόν σου ἐποίησα, ὅπως ἂν δικαιωθῇς ἐν τοῖς λόγοις σου καὶ νικήσῃς ἐν τῷ κρίνεσθαί σε». Οὐ γὰρ ὁ ἁμαρτήσας, ἵνα νικήσῃ ὁ θεός, ἥμαρτεν, οὔτε δὲ ὁ θεὸς ἐδεῖτο τῆς ἡμῶν ἁμαρτίας, ἵνα ἐκ ταύτης

---

[2]2 Tim 2.20–21. [3]Rom 11.32. [4]Rom 11.8. [5]Am 3.6.

[6]The word John uses for "ambiguous" (δισέμφατον, *disemphaton*) is not otherwise attested. In his lexicon of rare words the fifth-century lexicographer Hesychius of Alexandria does, however, list ἔμφατον (*emphaton*), which he defines as "something

and useful to the owner of the house, ready for every good work."[2] It is clear that the cleansing takes place voluntarily. "If one were to cleanse oneself," it says, and the following clause is implied: "If one were not to cleanse oneself, one will be a vessel for ignoble use, useless to the master and fit to be smashed." Therefore the passage just quoted and the texts "God has imprisoned all in disobedience,"[3] and "God gave them a sluggish spirit, eyes that would not see and ears that would not hear"[4]—all these are to be taken not as actions of God but as concessions of God, because the good depends on free will and is not forced.

It is therefore usual for the divine Scripture to speak of God's conceding things as his acting and effecting. Indeed, even when it says that God creates evil and that "there is no evil in a city that the Lord has not effected,"[5] it does not show God to be the cause of evil. On the contrary, because the word "evil" is ambiguous,[6] it has two meanings. Sometimes it signifies what is naturally evil, that which is contrary to virtue and the will of God, and sometimes it signifies what is distressing and burdensome from our own point of view, that is to say, afflictions and calamities. These are evil in appearance because they are painful, but in reality they are good. For to the perceptive they become the agents of conversion and salvation. It is these that Scripture says come about through God.

One should also know that we are the cause of these too. For involuntary evils are the product of voluntary ones. And there is a further thing that one should know, that it is usual in Scripture for some things that ought to be spoken of as effects to be spoken of as causes, as in "Against you alone have I sinned and done what is evil in your sight, that you might be justified in your pronouncements and prevail in your judgements."[7] The sinner did not sin in order that God might prevail, nor was God in need of our sin in order that as a result of it he might be shown to prevail (for he prevails

said ambiguously." John has clearly added διο- ("twice") to indicate that the ambiguity is specifically twofold.

[7] Ps 50.6.

275 SAINT JOHN OF DAMASCUS

νικητὴς ἀναφανῇ (φέρει γὰρ ἀσυγκρίτως κατὰ πάντων καὶ μὴ
ἁμαρτανόντων τὰ νικητήρια δημιουργὸς ὢν καὶ ἀκατάληπτος
καὶ ἄκτιστος καὶ φυσικὴν ἔχων τὴν δόξαν καὶ οὐκ ἐπίκτητον),
ἀλλ᾽ ὅτι ἡμῶν ἁμαρτανόντων οὐκ ἄδικός ἐστιν ἐπιφέρων τὴν
ὀργὴν καὶ μετανοοῦσι συγχωρῶν νικητὴς τῆς ἡμετέρας κακίας
ἀναδείκνυται. Οὐκ ἐπὶ τούτῳ δὲ ἡμεῖς ἁμαρτάνομεν, ἀλλ᾽ ὅτι
οὕτως ἀποβαίνει τὸ πρᾶγμα, ὥσπερ, ἐὰν κάθηταί τις ἐργαζόμενος,
φίλος δέ τις ἐπιστῇ, φησίν, ὅτι, ἵνα μηδὲ σήμερον ἐργάσωμαι,
παρεγένετο ὁ φίλος. Ὁ μὲν οὖν φίλος οὐχ, ἵνα μὴ ἐργάσηται,
παρεγένετο, οὕτω δὲ ἀπέβη· ἀσχολούμενος γὰρ περὶ τὴν τοῦ
φίλου ὑποδοχὴν οὐκ ἐργάζεται. Λέγεται δὲ ταῦτα ἐκβατικά, ὅτι
οὕτως ἀποβαίνουσι τὰ πράγματα. Οὐ θέλει δὲ ὁ θεὸς μόνος εἶναι
δίκαιος, ἀλλὰ πάντας ὁμοιοῦσθαι αὐτῷ κατὰ δύναμιν.

93 Ὅτι οὐ δύο ἀρχαί

Ὅτι οὐ δύο ἀρχαί, μία ἀγαθὴ καὶ μία πονηρά, ἐντεῦθεν εἰσόμεθα·
ἐναντία γὰρ ἀλλήλοις τὸ ἀγαθὸν καὶ τὸ πονηρὸν καὶ ἀλλήλων
φθαρτικὰ καὶ ἐν ἀλλήλοις ἢ σὺν ἀλλήλοις οὐχ ὑφιστάμενα. Ἐν
μέρει τοίνυν τούτων ἕκαστον ἔσται τοῦ παντός. Καὶ πρῶτον
μὲν περιγραφήσονται οὐχ ὑπὸ τοῦ παντὸς μόνον, ἀλλὰ καὶ ὑπὸ
μέρους τοῦ παντὸς τούτων ἕκαστον.

Ἔπειτα τίς ὁ τὴν χώραν ἑκάστῳ ἀποτεμόμενος; Οὐ γὰρ
ἀλλήλοις συνενεχθῆναι καὶ συμβιβασθῆναι φήσουσιν, ἐπεὶ οὐ
κακὸν τὸ κακὸν εἰρήνην ἄγον πρὸς τὸ ἀγαθόν τε συμβιβαζόμενον,
οὐδ᾽ ἀγαθὸν τὸ ἀγαθὸν πρὸς τὸ κακὸν φιλικῶς διακείμενον. Εἰ δὲ
ἕτερος τούτων ἑκάστῳ τὴν οἰκείαν ἀφώρισε διατριβήν, ἐκεῖνος
μᾶλλον ἔσται θεός.

Ἀνάγκη δὲ καὶ δυοῖν θάτερον ἢ ἅπτεσθαι καὶ φθείρειν
ἀλλήλους ἢ εἶναί τι μέσον, ἐν ᾧ οὐδὲ τὸ ἀγαθὸν οὐδὲ τὸ κακὸν
ἔσται, ὥσπερ τι διάφραγμα διεῖργον ἐξ ἀλλήλων ἀμφότερα. Καὶ
οὐκέτι δύο, ἀλλὰ τρεῖς ἀρχαὶ ἔσονται.

incomparably over all, including those who have not sinned, since he is creator and beyond comprehension and uncreated, and possesses glory by nature, not by acquisition). No, it is because when we sin, God is not unjust in bringing his anger to bear upon us, and by forgiving the repentant he is shown to prevail over our wickedness. It is not for this purpose that we sin, but that is how things turn out. It is like when someone is sitting working and a friend drops by, and he says "My friend has turned up so that I shall not work today." The friend did not turn up in order that he should not work, but that is how it turned out, for occupied as he was with entertaining his friend, he did not work. These events are called chance effects because that is how things turn out. Moreover, God does not wish to be just on his own. On the contrary, he wishes all to become like him according to their capacity.

93   *That there are not two fundamental principles*

Following on from the last point, we shall argue that there are not two fundamental principles, one good and the other evil. For good and evil are opposites; they are mutually destructive, and do not subsist in or with each other.[1] If that were the case, each of the two would be a part of the whole. And first they would be delimited not by the whole itself, but each of them by a part of the whole.

Next, who is it that assigns its space to each? For they would not say that they have come to an agreement with each other and been reconciled, since evil that has made peace with good and been reconciled with it would not be evil, nor would good that has a friendly relationship with evil be good. If it is another who has delimited for each its zone of activity, that other would surely be God.

Also, one of two things would necessarily follow. Either they would be in contact with each other and destroy each other or there would be something in between them, in which case this would be neither good nor evil, but like some barrier separating each from the

---

[1]Cf. Aristotle, *Categories* 10, 11b35–6.

Ἀνάγκη δὲ καὶ τούτων τὸ ἕτερον ἢ εἰρηνεύειν, ὅπερ τὸ κακὸν οὐ δύναται (τὸ γὰρ εἰρηνεῦον οὐ κακόν), ἢ μάχεσθαι, ὅπερ τὸ ἀγαθὸν οὐ δύναται (τὸ γὰρ μαχόμενον οὐ τελέως ἀγαθόν), ἢ τὸ μὲν κακὸν μάχεσθαι, τὸ δὲ ἀγαθὸν μὴ ἀντιμάχεσθαι, ἀλλ᾿ ὑπὸ τοῦ κακοῦ φθείρεσθαι, ἢ λυπεῖσθαι καὶ κακοῦσθαι, ὅπερ οὐ τοῦ ἀγαθοῦ γνώρισμα. Μία τοίνυν ἀρχὴ ἀγαθὴ πάσης κακίας ἀπηλλαγμένη.

Ἀλλ᾿ εἰ τοῦτο, φασί, πόθεν τὸ κακόν; Ἀμήχανον γὰρ ἐκ τοῦ ἀγαθοῦ τὸ κακὸν ἔχειν τὴν γένεσιν. Φαμὲν οὖν, ὅτι τὸ κακὸν οὐδὲν ἕτερόν ἐστιν εἰ μὴ τοῦ ἀγαθοῦ στέρησις καὶ ἐκ τοῦ κατὰ φύσιν εἰς τὸ παρὰ φύσιν παρατροπή· οὐδὲν γὰρ κακὸν κατὰ φύσιν. Πάντα γάρ, ὅσα ἐποίησεν ὁ θεός, καλὰ λίαν, καθὸ γέγονεν. Οὕτω τοίνυν μένοντα, καθὼς ἔκτισται, καλὰ λίαν εἰσίν, ἑκουσίως δὲ ἀποφοιτῶντα ἐκ τοῦ κατὰ φύσιν καὶ εἰς τὸ παρὰ φύσιν ἐρχόμενα, ἐν τῷ κακῷ γίνονται.

Κατὰ φύσιν μὲν οὖν πάντα δοῦλα καὶ ὑπήκοα τοῦ δημιουργοῦ. Ὅταν οὖν ἑκουσίως τι τῶν κτισμάτων ἀφηνιάσῃ καὶ παρήκοον τοῦ ποιήσαντος αὐτὸ γένηται, ἐν ἑαυτῷ συνεστήσατο τὴν κακίαν· κακία γὰρ οὐκ οὐσία τίς ἐστιν οὐδὲ οὐσίας ἰδίωμα, ἀλλὰ συμβεβηκὸς ἤτοι ἐκ τοῦ κατὰ φύσιν εἰς τὸ παρὰ φύσιν ἑκούσιος παρατροπή, ὅπερ ἐστὶν ἡ ἁμαρτία.

Πόθεν οὖν ἡ ἁμαρτία;—Τῆς αὐτεξουσίου γνώμης τοῦ διαβόλου εὕρημα.—Κακὸς οὖν ὁ διάβολος;—Καθὸ μὲν γέγονεν, οὐ κακός, ἀλλ᾿ ἀγαθός· ἄγγελος γὰρ λαμπρὸς καὶ φωτεινὸς ὑπὸ τοῦ δημιουργοῦ ἔκτισται, αὐτεξούσιος ὡς λογικός, ἑκουσίως τε τῆς κατὰ φύσιν ἀρετῆς ἀπεφοίτησε καὶ ἐν τῷ ζόφῳ τῆς κακίας γέγονε, θεοῦ μακρυνθεὶς τοῦ μόνου ἀγαθοῦ καὶ φωτοποιοῦ· ἐξ αὐτοῦ γὰρ πᾶν ἀγαθὸν ἀγαθύνεται, καὶ καθόσον ἐξ αὐτοῦ μακρύνεται γνώμῃ (οὐ γὰρ τόπῳ), ἐν τῷ κακῷ γέγονεν.

other. And then there would be no longer two but three fundamental principles.

One or other of these would also necessarily follow: either they would be at peace, which evil cannot do (for what is at peace is not evil), or they would fight, which good cannot do (for what fights is not perfectly good), or evil would fight and good not fight back, but be destroyed by evil, or be in a state of grief and distress, which is not a mark of the good. Therefore there is a single fundamental principle that is good and free from all evil.

But if this is so, they say, where does evil come from? For it is impossible for evil to have its origin in the good. We therefore say that evil is nothing other than the privation of good and a decline from being in accordance with nature to being contrary to nature.[2] For there is nothing that is evil by nature. For everything that God made was "very good,"[3] in that it was given being. Thus, in so far as they remained as they were created, they are very good. But if they voluntarily fell away from being in accordance with nature and came into a state of being contrary to nature, they entered into a state of evil.

So all that serves the Creator and is obedient to him is in accordance with nature. When anything created therefore voluntarily rebels against its maker and becomes disobedient to him, it brings evil into being within itself. For evil is not some substance or the property of some substance, but an accident, that is to say, a voluntary decline from being in accordance with nature to being contrary to nature, which is sin.

Where, then, does sin come from? It is an invention deriving from the devil's free will. Is the devil therefore evil? In so far as he was given being, he is not evil, but good. For he was created by the Creator as a bright and radiant angel endowed with free will as a rational creature, but he voluntarily departed from virtue in accordance with nature and entered into the darkness of evil, having distanced himself from God, the only good and source of light. For every good

[2]On evil as the privation of good, see p. 102, note 2.
[3]Gen 1.31.

94   Τίνος ἕνεκεν προγινώσκων ὁ θεὸς τοὺς ἁμαρτάνειν καὶ
      μὴ μετανοεῖν μέλλοντας ἔκτισεν

Ὁ θεὸς δι᾽ ἀγαθότητα ἐκ τοῦ μὴ ὄντος εἰς τὸ εἶναι παράγει
τὰ γινόμενα καὶ τῶν ἐσομένων προγνώστης ἐστίν. Εἰ μὲν οὖν
μὴ ἔμελλον ἔσεσθαι, οὐδ᾽ ἂν κακοὶ ἔμελλον ἔσεσθαι οὐδ᾽ ἂν
προεγινώσκοντο. Τῶν γὰρ ὄντων αἱ γνώσεις, καὶ τῶν πάντως
ἐσομένων αἱ προγνώσεις· πρῶτον γὰρ τὸ εἶναι, καὶ τότε τὸ
καλὸν ἢ κακὸν εἶναι. Εἰ δὲ μέλλοντας ἔσεσθαι διὰ τὴν τοῦ θεοῦ
ἀγαθότητα τὸ κακοὺς ἐξ οἰκείας προαιρέσεως μέλλειν ἔσεσθαι
ἐκώλυσεν αὐτοὺς γενέσθαι, τὸ κακὸν ἐνίκα ἂν τὴν τοῦ θεοῦ
ἀγαθότητα. Ποιεῖ τοιγαροῦν ὁ θεὸς ἀγαθὰ ἅπαντα, ἃ ποιεῖ·
ἕκαστος δὲ ἐξ οἰκείας προαιρέσεως καλός τε καὶ κακὸς γίνεται.
Εἰ καὶ τοίνυν ἔφη ὁ κύριος· «Συνέφερε τῷ ἀνθρώπῳ ἐκείνῳ, εἰ
οὐκ ἐγεννήθη», οὐ τὴν οἰκείαν κτίσιν κακίζων ἔλεγεν, ἀλλὰ τὴν
ἐξ οἰκείας προαιρέσεως καὶ ῥαθυμίας ἐπιγενομένην τῷ κτίσματι
αὐτοῦ κακίαν. Ἡ γὰρ τῆς οἰκείας γνώμης ῥαθυμία ἄχρηστον
αὐτῷ τὴν τοῦ δημιουργοῦ εὐεργεσίαν ἐποίησεν, ὥσπερ ἄν, εἴ τις
πλοῦτον καὶ ἀρχὴν παρὰ βασιλέως ἐγχειρισθεὶς τυραννήσει τὸν
εὐεργέτην, ὃν ἀξίως χειρωσάμενος τιμωρήσεται, εἰ μέχρι τέλους
τῇ τυραννίδι κατίδοι τοῦτον ἐναπομένοντα.

95   Περὶ νόμου θεοῦ καὶ νόμου ἁμαρτίας

Ἀγαθὸν τὸ θεῖον καὶ ὑπεράγαθον, καὶ τὸ τούτου θέλημα· τοῦτο
γὰρ ἀγαθόν, ὅπερ ὁ θεὸς βούλεται. Νόμος δέ ἐστιν ἡ τοῦτο

derives its goodness from God, and in so far as it distances itself from him—in its will, not in a spatial sense—it becomes evil.

94   Why God created those whom he foreknew would sin and not repent

God in his goodness brings what exists out of non-being into being and has foreknowledge of what will happen. If, then, they were not going to exist, they were neither going to be evil, nor would they be foreknown to be evil. For knowledge is of what exists, and foreknowledge is necessarily of what is going to exist. For existence comes first and then being either good or evil. But if those who were going to exist through God's goodness were prevented from coming into existence because they were going to be evil through their own deliberate choice, then evil would have prevailed over God's goodness. Everything that God makes he most certainly makes as good. Each of us becomes good or evil by our own deliberate choice. Even if the Lord said: "It would have been better for that one not to have been born,"[1] he did not say it in disparagement of his own creation but because evil had happened to his creature through that creature's own deliberate choice and indolence. For the creature made the Creator's benefaction useless to itself through the indolence of its own will. It is as if someone who had been entrusted with wealth and authority by a king were to rebel against his benefactor. He would rightly be overpowered and punished if the king saw that he was persisting in his rebellion to the end.[2]

95   On the law of God and the law of sin

The divine is good and supremely good, as is also its will. For what is good is what God wills. A law (νόμος, *nomos*) is the commandment

[1] Mt 26.24.
[2] For the contemporary Islamic discussions of the same topic, see Fakhry, *History of Islamic Philosophy*, 44–48.

διδάσκουσα ἐντολή, ἵν' ἐν αὐτῷ μένοντες ἐν φωτὶ ὦμεν. Ἧς ἐντολῆς ἡ παράβασις ἁμαρτία ἐστίν. Αὕτη δὲ διὰ τῆς τοῦ διαβόλου προσβολῆς καὶ τῆς ἡμετέρας ἀβιάστου καὶ ἑκουσίου παραδοχῆς συνίσταται· λέγεται δὲ καὶ αὕτη νόμος.

Ἐπιβαίνων οὖν ὁ τοῦ θεοῦ νόμος τῷ νῷ ἡμῶν ἐφέλκεται πρὸς ἑαυτὸν καὶ νύττει τὴν ἡμετέραν συνείδησιν. Λέγεται δὲ καὶ ἡ ἡμετέρα συνείδησις νόμος τοῦ νοὸς ἡμῶν. Καὶ ἡ προσβολὴ δὲ τοῦ πονηροῦ, τουτέστιν ὁ νόμος τῆς ἁμαρτίας, ἐπιβαίνων τοῖς μέλεσι τῆς σαρκὸς ἡμῶν δι' αὐτῆς ἡμῖν προσβάλλει. Ἅπαξ γὰρ παραβάντες ἑκουσίως τὸν νόμον τοῦ θεοῦ καὶ τὴν προσβολὴν τοῦ πονηροῦ παραδεξάμενοι ἐδώκαμεν αὐτῇ εἴσοδον, πραθέντες ὑφ' ἑαυτῶν τῇ ἁμαρτίᾳ. Ὅθεν ἑτοίμως ἄγεται τὸ σῶμα ἡμῶν πρὸς αὐτήν. Λέγεται οὖν καὶ ἡ ἐναποκειμένη τῷ σώματι ἡμῶν ὀσμὴ καὶ αἴσθησις τῆς ἁμαρτίας ἤτοι ἐπιθυμία καὶ ἡδονὴ τοῦ σώματος νόμος ἐν τοῖς μέλεσι τῆς σαρκὸς ἡμῶν.

Ὁ μὲν οὖν νόμος τοῦ νοός μου ἤτοι ἡ συνείδησις συνήδεται τῷ νόμῳ τοῦ θεοῦ ἤτοι τῇ ἐντολῇ καὶ ταύτην θέλει. Ὁ δὲ νόμος τῆς ἁμαρτίας ἤτοι ἡ προσβολὴ διὰ τοῦ νόμου τοῦ ἐν τοῖς μέλεσιν ἤτοι τῆς τοῦ σώματος ἐπιθυμίας καὶ ῥοπῆς καὶ κινήσεως καὶ τοῦ ἀλόγου μέρους τῆς ψυχῆς ἀντιστρατεύεται τῷ νόμῳ τοῦ νοός μου, τουτέστι τῇ συνειδήσει, καὶ αἰχμαλωτίζει με καὶ θέλοντα τὸν τοῦ θεοῦ νόμον καὶ ἀγαπῶντα καὶ μὴ θέλοντα τὴν ἁμαρτίαν κατὰ ἀνάκρασιν διὰ τοῦ λείου τῆς ἡδονῆς καὶ τῆς τοῦ σώματος ἐπιθυμίας καὶ τοῦ ἀλόγου μέρους τῆς ψυχῆς, ὡς ἔφην, πλανᾷ καὶ πείθει δουλεῦσαι τῇ ἁμαρτίᾳ· ἀλλ' «ὁ θεὸς τὸ ἀδύνατον τοῦ νόμου, ἐν ᾧ ἠσθένει ὁ νόμος διὰ τῆς σαρκός, πέμψας τὸν υἱὸν αὐτοῦ ἐν ὁμοιώματι σαρκὸς ἁμαρτίας» (σάρκα μὲν γὰρ ἀνέλαβεν, ἁμαρτίαν δὲ οὐδαμῶς) «κατέκρινε τὴν ἁμαρτίαν ἐν τῇ σαρκί, ἵνα τὸ δικαίωμα τοῦ νόμου πληρωθῇ ἐν τοῖς μὴ κατὰ σάρκα περιπατοῦσιν, ἀλλὰ κατὰ πνεῦμα». «Τὸ γὰρ πνεῦμα συναντιλαμβάνεται τῇ ἀσθενείᾳ ἡμῶν» καὶ παρέχει δύναμιν τῷ νόμῳ τοῦ νοὸς ἡμῶν κατὰ τοῦ νόμου τοῦ ἐν τοῖς μέλεσιν ἡμῶν. Τὸ γὰρ «τί προσευξώμεθα, καθὸ δεῖ, οὐκ οἴδαμεν, ἀλλ' αὐτὸ τὸ πνεῦμα ἐντυγχάνει ὑπὲρ ἡμῶν στεναγμοῖς ἀλαλήτοις», τουτέστι

that teaches this, that by abiding in it we may be in light. The transgression of this commandment is sin. The latter is brought about through the assault of the devil and our own unforced and voluntary consent. This too is called a law.

Therefore when the law of God enters our mind it draws it towards itself and pricks our conscience. Our own conscience is also called a law of our mind. Moreover, the assault of the evil one, that is to say, the law of sin, enters the members of our flesh and attacks us through it. For once we have voluntarily transgressed the law of God and have consented to the assault of the evil one, we have allowed it entry, having sold ourselves to sin. Hence our body is easily induced to sin. And so the scent and sensation of sin stored up in our body, that is to say, the body's desire and pleasure, is also called a law in the members of our flesh.

Thus on the one hand the law of my mind, that is to say, my conscience, is in harmony with the law of God, that is to say, the commandment, and desires it. But on the other hand, the law of sin, which is to say, the assault that comes about through the law that is in my members, which is to say, the desire and inclination and movement of the irrational part of the soul, fights against the law of my mind, that is to say, my conscience, and takes me prisoner, even though I desire the law of God and love it and do not desire sin, and by a blending, through the softness of pleasure and the desire of the body and the irrational part of the soul, as I have said, leads me astray and persuades me to become a slave to sin. But "God has done what the law, weakened by the flesh, could not do: by sending his own Son in the likeness of sinful flesh" (for he assumed flesh but in no way did he assume sin) "he condemned sin in the flesh, so that the just requirement of the law might be fulfilled in those who walk not according to the flesh but according to the Spirit."[1] For "the Spirit helps us in our weakness"[2] and gives strength to the law of our mind against the law that is in our members. For the text, "we do not know how to pray as we ought, but the Spirit itself intercedes for us with

[1] Rom 8.3–4.   [2] Rom 8.26.

διδάσκει ἡμᾶς, τί προσευξόμεθα. Ὥστε ἀδύνατον, εἰ μὴ δι᾽ ὑπομονῆς καὶ προσευχῆς τὰς ἐντολὰς τοῦ θεοῦ κατεργάσασθαι.

96 Κατὰ Ἰουδαίων περὶ τοῦ σαββάτου

Σάββατον ἡ ἑβδόμη ἡμέρα κέκληται, δηλοῖ δὲ τὴν κατάπαυσιν· ἐν αὐτῇ γὰρ κατέπαυσεν ὁ θεὸς ἀπὸ τῶν ἔργων αὐτοῦ, ὥς φησιν ἡ γραφή. Διὸ καὶ μέχρις ἑπτὰ ὁ τῶν ἡμερῶν ἀριθμὸς προβαίνων πάλιν ἀνακυκλοῦται καὶ ἀπὸ τῆς πρώτης ἄρχεται. Οὗτος ὁ ἀριθμὸς τίμιος παρὰ Ἰουδαίοις τοῦ θεοῦ προστάξαντος τιμᾶσθαι αὐτὸν οὐχ ὡς ἔτυχεν, ἀλλὰ καὶ μετὰ βαρυτάτων τῶν ἐπὶ τῇ παραβάσει ἐπιτιμίων. Οὐχ ἁπλῶς δὲ τοῦτο προσέταξεν, ἀλλὰ διά τινας μυστικῶς τοῖς πνευματικοῖς τε καὶ διορατικοῖς κατανοουμένας αἰτίας.

Ὡς ἐμὲ γοῦν γνῶναι τὸν ἀμαθῆ, ἵν᾽ ἐκ τῶν κατωτέρων καὶ παχυτέρων ἄρξωμαι· Εἰδὼς ὁ θεὸς τὸ παχύ τε καὶ φιλόσαρκον καὶ πρὸς τὴν ὕλην ὅλως ἐπιρρεπὲς τοῦ Ἰσραηλίτου λαοῦ, ἅμα δὲ καὶ τὸ ἀδιάκριτον· πρῶτον μέν, ἵνα ὁ δοῦλος καὶ τὸ ὑποζύγιον ἀναπαύσηται, ὡς γέγραπται· ἐπειδὴ ἀνὴρ «δίκαιος οἰκτείρει ψυχὰς κτηνῶν αὐτοῦ», ἅμα δὲ ἵνα καὶ σχολὴν ἄγοντες ἐκ τοῦ περὶ τὴν ὕλην περισπασμοῦ πρὸς θεὸν συνάγωνται «ἐν ψαλμοῖς καὶ ὕμνοις καὶ ᾠδαῖς πνευματικαῖς» καὶ μελέτῃ τῶν θείων γραφῶν ἅπασαν τὴν ἑβδόμην ἀναλίσκοντες καὶ ἐν τῷ θεῷ καταπαύοντες. Ὅτε μὲν γὰρ οὐκ ἦν νόμος, οὐ γραφὴ θεόπνευστος, οὐδὲ τὸ σάββατον θεῷ ἀφιέρωτο. Ὅτε δὲ ἡ θεόπνευστος γραφὴ διὰ Μωσέως ἐδόθη, ἀφιερώθη τῷ θεῷ τὸ σάββατον, ὡς ἂν περὶ τὴν ταύτης μελέτην ἐν αὐτῷ ἀδολεσχήσωσιν οἱ μὴ πάντα τὸν βίον τῷ θεῷ ἀφιεροῦντες, οἱ μὴ πόθῳ τῷ δεσπότῃ ὡς πατρὶ δουλεύοντες, ἀλλ᾽ ὡς δοῦλοι ἀγνώμονες κἂν μικρὸν καὶ ἐλάχιστον μέρος τῆς ἑαυτῶν ζωῆς τῷ θεῷ ἀποτέμωνται, καὶ τοῦτο φόβῳ τῶν ἐπὶ τῇ παραβάσει εὐθυνῶν

sighs too deep for words,"[3] teaches us what we should pray for. In consequence, it is impossible to fulfill God's commandments except through patience and prayer.

96 *Against the Jews concerning the Sabbath*

The seventh day is called the Sabbath and signifies rest, for it was on this day that God rested from his works, as Scripture says.[1] That is why the number of days advances up to seven, and then the cycle begins again and starts from the first day. This number is held in honor by the Jews since God ordained that it should be honored not in any casual way but with the heaviest penalties for its transgression. He did not command this simply for its own sake, but for certain mystical reasons that are understood by the spiritual and discerning.

I shall begin, to the best of my untutored knowledge, with the lower and less spiritual aspects. Knowing the grossness and sensuality of the Israelite people, and their complete orientation towards the material, as well as their lack of discernment, God ordained first that the slave and the beast of burden should rest, as it is written, since the "righteous man has compassion for the souls of his beasts,"[2] and at the same time that they should break off from their preoccupation with material things and gather together before God to spend the whole of the seventh day "in psalms and hymns and spiritual songs"[3] and in the study of the divine Scriptures, taking their rest in God. For when there was no Law, no inspired written legislation, neither was the Sabbath dedicated to God. But when the inspired legislation was given through Moses, the Sabbath was dedicated to God, so that by studying the legislation those who do not dedicate their whole life to God might meditate on him, that those who do not serve the master with loving desire as a father, but like ungrateful servants might set aside just a small and insignificant portion of their lives for God, and out of fear of punishments and penalties for transgression at that. For

[3]Rom 8.26.

[1]Gen 2.2.   [2]Prov 12.10.   [3]Eph 5.19.

καὶ ἐπιτιμήσεων· «δικαίῳ γὰρ νόμος οὐ κεῖται», ἀλλ᾽ ἀδίκοις. Ἐπεὶ πρῶτος Μωσῆς τεσσαράκοντα ἡμερῶν καὶ αὖθις ἑτέρων τεσσαράκοντα νηστείᾳ προσεδρεύσας τῷ θεῷ, πάντως καὶ τοῖς σάββασι διὰ τῆς νηστείας ἐκάκου ἑαυτὸν τοῦ νόμου μὴ κακοῦν ἑαυτοὺς ἐν τῇ τοῦ σαββάτου ἡμέρᾳ προστάσσοντος. Εἰ δὲ φαῖεν, ὅτι πρὸ τοῦ νόμου τοῦτο, τί φήσουσι περὶ τοῦ Θεσβίτου Ἠλιοῦ τεσσαράκοντα ἡμερῶν ὁδὸν ἀνύσαντος ἐν βρώσει μιᾷ; Οὗτος γὰρ οὐ μόνον διὰ τῆς νηστείας, ἀλλὰ καὶ διὰ τῆς ὁδοιπορίας ἐν τοῖς σάββασι τῶν τεσσαράκοντα ἡμερῶν ἑαυτὸν κακώσας ἔλυσε τὸ σάββατον, καὶ οὐκ ὠργίσθη τούτῳ ὁ τὸν νόμον δεδωκώς, ἀλλὰ καὶ ὡς ἀρετῆς ἔπαθλον ἐν Χωρὴβ ἑαυτὸν ἐνεφάνισε. Τί δὲ περὶ Δανιὴλ φήσουσιν; Οὐχὶ τρεῖς ἑβδομάδας διετέλεσεν ἄσιτος; Τί δὲ πᾶς Ἰσραήλ; Οὐ περιτέμνει τὸ παιδίον ἐν σαββάτῳ, εἰ τύχοι, ὀκταήμερον; Οὐχὶ δὲ καὶ τὴν μεγάλην νηστείαν, ἣν νενομοθέτηνται, εἰ ἐν σαββάτῳ καταντήσοι, νηστεύουσι; Οὐχὶ δὲ καὶ οἱ ἱερεῖς καὶ οἱ Λευῖται ἐν τοῖς τῆς σκηνῆς ἔργοις βεβηλοῦσι τὸ σάββατον καὶ ἀναίτιοί εἰσιν; Ἀλλὰ καὶ κτῆνος, ἂν εἰς βόθρον ἐμπέσοι ἐν σαββάτῳ, ὁ μὲν ἀνασπάσας ἀναίτιος, ὁ δὲ παριδὼν κατάκριτος. Τί δὲ πᾶς Ἰσραήλ; οὐχὶ ἑπτὰ ἡμέρας τὴν τοῦ θεοῦ κιβωτὸν περιφέροντες τὰ Ἱεριχούντια τείχη περιῄεσαν, ἐν αἷς πάντως ἦν καὶ τὸ σάββατον; Ὡς οὖν ἔφην, σχολῆς ἕνεκα τῆς πρὸς θεόν, ἵνα κἂν σμικροτάτην ἀπόμοιραν αὐτῷ ἀπονέμωσι καὶ ἀναπαύσωνται ὅ τε δοῦλος καὶ τὸ ὑποζύγιον, ἡ τοῦ σαββάτου τήρησις ἐπινενόητο τοῖς νηπίοις ἔτι καὶ ὑπὸ τὰ στοιχεῖα τοῦ κόσμου δεδουλωμένοις, τοῖς σαρκικοῖς καὶ μηδὲν ὑπὲρ τὸ σῶμα καὶ τὸ γράμμα ἐννοῆσαι δυναμένοις. «Ὅτε δὲ ἦλθε τὸ πλήρωμα τοῦ χρόνου, ἐξαπέστειλεν ὁ θεὸς τὸν υἱὸν αὐτοῦ τὸν μονογενῆ, γενόμενον ἐκ γυναικὸς ἄνθρωπον, γενόμενον ὑπὸ νόμον, ἵνα τοὺς ὑπὸ νόμον ἐξαγοράσῃ, ἵνα τὴν υἱοθεσίαν ἀπολάβωμεν». Ὅσοι γὰρ ἐλάβομεν αὐτόν, ἔδωκεν ἡμῖν ἐξουσίαν τέκνα θεοῦ

"the law is laid down not for the innocent" but for the guilty.[4] When Moses waited upon God with fasting first for forty days and then again for another forty, he inevitably mortified himself by the fast even on the Sabbaths, despite the law proscribing self-mortification on the Sabbath day.[5] If it should be said that this happened prior to the law, what will they say about Elijah the Tishbite, who made a journey of forty days on a single meal?[6] The latter, by mortifying himself not only through fasting but also through traveling on the Sabbaths of the fast, broke the Sabbath, yet he who gave the Law was not angry with him but manifested himself to him on Horeb as a prize for virtue. And what will they say about Daniel? Did he not go for three weeks without food?[7] And what about Israel as a whole? Do they not circumcise a child on the eighth day, even if it happens to be a Sabbath?[8] Do they not keep the great fast, which is laid down in the Law, even if it falls on a Sabbath?[9] And do not even the priests and Levites profane the Sabbath by their functions in the tabernacle yet remain free of guilt?[10] Moreover, if a beast falls into a pit on a Sabbath the one who pulls it out is guiltless, but the one who ignores it is condemned.[11] And what about Israel as a whole? Did they not carry the ark of God round the walls of Jericho for seven days, one of which must have been the Sabbath?[12]

Therefore as I have said, for the sake of leisure to devote to God, in order that they might assign the smallest portion to him and that the slave and beast of burden might rest, the observance of the Sabbath was imposed even on "minors and those enslaved to the rudiments of the world,"[13] those living according to the flesh and unable to understand anything beyond the body and the letter. "But when the fullness of time had come, God sent his only-begotten Son, a human being born of a woman, born under the law, in order to redeem those who were under the law, so that we might receive adoption."[14] "But to those of us who received him, he gave us power

[4]1 Tim 1.19.   [5]Ex 24.18, 34.28.   [6]3 Kg 19.8.
[7]Dan 10.2–3.   [8]Lev 12.3.   [9]Lev 23. 28–29.   [10]Mt 12.5.
[11]Mt 12.11.   [12]Jos 6.12–15.   [13]Gal 4.3.   [14]Gal 4.4–5.

γενέσθαι, τοῖς πιστεύουσιν εἰς αὐτόν. Ὥστε οὐκέτι ἐσμὲν δοῦλοι ἀλλ' υἱοί, οὐκέτι ὑπὸ νόμον ἀλλ' ὑπὸ χάριν· οὐκέτι μερικῶς τῷ κυρίῳ δουλεύοντες ἐκ φόβου, ἀλλὰ πάντα τὸν τῆς ζωῆς χρόνον αὐτῷ ἀνατιθέναι ὀφείλοντες καὶ ἀεὶ τὸν δοῦλον, τὸν θυμὸν λέγω καὶ τὴν ἐπιθυμίαν, ἀπὸ τῆς ἁμαρτίας καταπαύοντες καὶ τῷ θεῷ σχολάζειν ἐπιτρέποντες· τὴν μὲν ἐπιθυμίαν ἅπασαν ἀεὶ πρὸς θεὸν ἀνατείνοντες, τὸν δὲ θυμὸν κατὰ τῶν τοῦ θεοῦ δυσμενῶν καθοπλίζοντες· καὶ τὸ ὑποζύγιον ἤτοι τὸ σῶμα ὁμοίως τῆς μὲν δουλείας τῆς ἁμαρτίας ἀναπαύοντες, ταῖς δὲ θείαις ἐντολαῖς ἐξυπηρετεῖσθαι προτρέποντες.

Ταῦτα ὁ πνευματικὸς ἡμῖν ἐντέλλεται τοῦ κυρίου νόμος, καὶ οἱ τοῦτον φυλάσσοντες ὑπέρτεροι τοῦ Μωσαϊκοῦ νόμου γεγόνασιν· ἐλθόντος γὰρ τοῦ τελείου τὸ ἐκ μέρους κατήργηται, καὶ τοῦ καλύμματος τοῦ νόμου ἤτοι τοῦ καταπετάσματος διὰ τῆς τοῦ σωτῆρος διαρραγέντος σταυρώσεως καὶ τοῦ πνεύματος πυρίναις γλώσσαις ἐκλάμψαντος τὸ γράμμα κατήργηται, τὰ σωματικὰ πέπαυται καὶ ὁ τῆς δουλείας νόμος πεπλήρωται καὶ νόμος ἐλευθερίας ἡμῖν δεδώρηται. Καὶ ἑορτάζομεν τὴν τελείαν τῆς ἀνθρωπίνης φύσεως κατάπαυσιν, φημὶ δὴ τὴν τῆς ἀναστάσεως ἡμέραν, ἐν ᾗ ἡμᾶς ὁ κύριος Ἰησοῦς, ὁ τῆς ζωῆς ἀρχηγὸς καὶ σωτήρ, εἰς τὴν ἐπηγγελμένην τοῖς πνευματικῶς τῷ θεῷ λατρεύουσι κληρουχίαν εἰσήγαγεν, εἰς ἣν αὐτὸς πρόδρομος ἡμῶν εἰσῆλθεν, ἀναστὰς ἐκ νεκρῶν καὶ ἀνοιγέντων αὐτῷ τῶν οὐρανίων πυλῶν ἐν δεξιᾷ τοῦ πατρὸς κεκάθικε σωματικῶς, ἔνθα καὶ οἱ τὸν πνευματικὸν τηροῦντες νόμον εἰσελεύσονται.

Ἡμῖν τοίνυν τοῖς τῷ πνεύματι στοιχοῦσι καὶ οὐ τῷ γράμματι πᾶσα ἡ τῶν σαρκικῶν ἐστιν ἀπόθεσις καὶ ἡ πνευματικὴ λατρεία καὶ πρὸς θεὸν συνάφεια. Περιτομὴ μὲν γάρ ἐστιν ἡ τῆς σωματικῆς ἡδονῆς καὶ τῶν περιττῶν καὶ οὐκ ἀναγκαίων ἀπόθεσις· ἀκροβυστία γὰρ οὐδὲν ἕτερόν ἐστιν εἰ μὴ δέρμα, ἡδονικοῦ μορίου περίττωμα. Πᾶσα δὲ= ἡδονὴ μὴ ἐκ θεοῦ καὶ ἐν θεῷ γινομένη περίττωμα ἡδονῆς ἐστιν· ἧς τύπος ἡ ἀκροβυστία. Σάββατον δὲ ἡ

to become children of God, who believe in him."[15] So we are "no longer slaves but sons,"[16] no longer "under the law but under grace,"[17] no longer serving the Lord in a partial manner out of fear, but under the obligation to devote all the days of our life to him. And we should always make the slave, by which I mean anger and desire, cease from sin and redirect it towards resting in God, raising up the whole of our desire towards God, and arming our anger against the things that are displeasing to God. We should likewise make the beast of burden, that is to say, the body, cease from slavery to sin and redirect it towards serving the divine commandments.

These are the obligations which the Lord's spiritual law lays upon us, and those who keep it have come to be above the Mosaic Law. For when the perfect has come, the partial is abolished, and when the veil of the law, that is to say, the curtain, was rent in two at the Lord's crucifixion and was illuminated by the fiery tongues of the Spirit, the letter was abolished, the bodily aspects ceased, and the law of slavery came to its fulfilment and the law of freedom was granted to us. And we celebrate the perfect rest of human nature, by which I mean the day of resurrection, through which the Lord Jesus, the author of life and savior, will lead us into the inheritance promised to those who worship God in spirit. He "entered into it" himself as "our forerunner,"[18] when he rose from the dead, and, with the gates of heaven opened to him, took his seat corporeally at the right hand of the Father. Those who keep the spiritual law will enter there, too.

Therefore what is incumbent on us, who conform to the spirit and not the letter,[19] is to set aside completely what belongs to the flesh, and fix our sights on spiritual worship and union with God. For circumcision is the setting aside of bodily pleasure and of what is superfluous and not necessary. For the foreskin is nothing more than skin, a superfluous part of the pleasurable member. Any pleasure that does not come from God and is in God is a superfluous pleasure. The foreskin is a symbol of this. And the Sabbath signifies the

[15]Jn 1.12.   [16]Gal 4.7.   [17]Rom 6.14.   [18]Heb 6.20.
[19]Cf. 2 Cor 3.6

ἐκ τῆς ἁμαρτίας κατάπαυσις. Ὥστε ἀμφότερα ἕν τυγχάνουσι καὶ οὕτως ἀμφότερα ἅμα ὑπὸ τῶν πνευματικῶν τελούμενα, οὐδὲ τὴν τυχοῦσαν παρανομίαν ἐργάζονται.

Ἔτι δὲ ἰστέον, ὅτι ὁ ἑπτὰ ἀριθμὸς πάντα τὸν παρόντα χρόνον δηλοῖ, ὥς φησιν ὁ σοφώτατος Σολομῶν· «Δοῦναι μερίδα τοῖς ἑπτὰ καί γε τοῖς ὀκτώ». Καὶ ὁ θεηγόρος Δαυὶδ περὶ τῆς ὀγδόης ψάλλων περὶ τῆς μελλούσης μετὰ τὴν ἐκ νεκρῶν ἀνάστασιν καταστάσεως ἔψαλλε. Τὴν ἑβδόμην οὖν ἡμέραν ἀργίαν ἄγειν ἐκ τῶν σωματικῶν, τοῖς δὲ πνευματικοῖς ἐνασχολεῖσθαι προστάσσων ὁ νόμος μυστικῶς πάντα τὸν χρόνον τῷ ἀληθινῷ Ἰσραὴλ καὶ νοῦν ὁρῶντα θεὸν ἔχοντι ὑπέφηνε τῷ θεῷ ἑαυτὸν προσάγειν καὶ ὑπεράνω τῶν σωματικῶν γίνεσθαι.

97   Περὶ παρθενίας

Κακίζουσιν οἱ σαρκικοὶ τὴν παρθενίαν, καὶ εἰς μαρτυρίαν προβάλλονται οἱ φιλήδονοι τὸ «ἐπικατάρατος πᾶς, ὃς οὐκ ἐγείρει σπέρμα ἐν τῷ Ἰσραήλ». Ἡμεῖς δέ φαμεν τῷ ἐκ παρθένου σαρκωθέντι θεῷ λόγῳ θαρρήσαντες, ὡς ἡ παρθενία ἄνωθεν καὶ ἐξ ἀρχῆς ἐφυτεύθη τῇ φύσει τῶν ἀνθρώπων· ἐκ παρθένου γὰρ γῆς ὁ ἄνθρωπος πεπλαστούργηται, ἐκ μόνου Ἀδὰμ ἡ Εὔα ἔκτισται, ἐν παραδείσῳ παρθενία ἐπολιτεύετο. Φησὶ γοῦν ἡ θεία γραφή, ὅτι «γυμνοὶ ἦσαν, ὅ τε Ἀδὰμ καὶ ἡ Εὔα, καὶ οὐκ ᾐσχύνοντο». Ἡνίκα

---

[20]Eccl 11.2.

[21]From the earliest days of the Church, as the late first-century *Epistle of Barnabas* testifies, the eighth day, the day of the Lord's resurrection, has been seen as the beginning of a new world (*Ep. Barn.* 15.8). Biblical commentators saw the Christian significance of "eighth" as already implicit in the Septuagint, in the eight persons who emerged from the ark after the flood (Gen 8.18; cf. 2 Pet 2.5) and in the cryptic inscription of Psalm 11, a psalm of "the eighth." In his work *On the Inscriptions of the Psalms*, Gregory of Nyssa says that the title of "the eighth" indicates that the whole of our effort in this world to lead a virtuous life is directed towards the age to come (*In inscriptiones psalm.* 2.5, PG 44:504C–505A). In the following century, Hesychius of Jerusalem (died after 451) interprets the word "eighth" as referring to the consummation of the age. On the eighth day, he says, following the judgement that will

cessation from sin. Consequently, both amount to the same thing, and thus, since both are fulfilled at the same time by the spiritual, the latter are not guilty of any possible wrongdoing.

One should know, moreover, that the number seven signifies the whole of the present time, as the most wise Solomon says: "Give a portion to seven and also to eight."[20] And when David, who speaks of God, was singing a psalm of "the eighth," he sang about the future state after the resurrection of the dead.[21] Therefore when the law commanded that on the seventh day there should be a rest from bodily labors and an application to spiritual matters, it was signifying mystically to the true Israel that has its mind oriented towards seeing God that it should apply itself all the time to God and transcend corporeal things.

97 *On virginity*

Sensual people denigrate virginity, and pleasure-seekers cite the verse, "Accursed is anyone who does not raise up seed in Israel"[1] as testimony. But we say, emboldened by the fact that God the Word took flesh from a virgin, that virginity is from on high and was implanted in human nature from the beginning. For humanity was fashioned from virgin earth; Eve was created from Adam alone; in paradise virginity was the way of life. Therefore the divine Scripture says: "They were naked, both Adam and Eve, and they were not ashamed."[2] But when they transgressed "they knew that they

take place after the resurrection on the seventh day, the condemned will be handed over to punishment but the worthy to everlasting life (*De titulis psalm.*, Psalm. XI, PG27:685D). Maximus the Confessor (7th cent) regards the eighth day as denoting "that state which is beyond nature and time," "the transposition and transmutation of those found worthy into a state of deification," and "the inexpressible mystery of the eternal well-being of created things" (*Chapters on Theology and the Economy* 1.51, 55, 56, PG 90:1101C, 1104B, 1104C; trans. G. Palmer, P. Sherrard and K. Ware, *The Philokalia, The Complete Text*, vol. 2 [London: Faber, 1981], 124, 125). Hesychius, however, who like John had been *hierokēryx* (preacher) of the Anastasis Church in Jerusalem, seems to have been John's main source.

[1]Deut 25.9.   [2]Gen 2.25.

δὲ παρέβησαν, «ἔγνωσαν, ὅτι γυμνοὶ ἦσαν», καὶ αἰσχυνθέντες ἔρραψαν ἑαυτοῖς περιζώματα. Καὶ μετὰ τὴν παράβασιν, «ὅτι γῆ εἶ καὶ εἰς γῆν ἀπελεύσῃ», ὅτε διὰ τῆς παραβάσεως θάνατος εἰς τὸν κόσμον εἰσῆλθε, τότε «ἔγνω Ἀδὰμ Εὔαν τὴν γυναῖκα αὐτοῦ, καὶ συνέλαβε καὶ ἐγέννησεν». Ὥστε διὰ τὸ μὴ ἐκτριβῆναι καὶ ἀναλωθῆναι τὸ γένος ὑπὸ τοῦ θανάτου ὁ γάμος ἐπινενόηται, ὡς ἂν διὰ τῆς παιδοποιίας τὸ γένος τῶν ἀνθρώπων διασῴζηται.

Ἀλλ᾽ ἐροῦσι τυχόν· Τί οὖν τὸ «ἄρρεν καὶ θῆλυ» βούλεται καὶ τὸ «αὐξάνεσθε καὶ πληθύνεσθε»; Πρὸς ὃ λέξομεν, ὅτι τὸ μὲν «αὐξάνεσθε καὶ πληθύνεσθε» οὐ πάντως τὸν διὰ γαμικῆς συναφείας πληθυσμὸν δηλοῖ. Ἐδύνατο γὰρ ὁ θεὸς καὶ ἑτέρῳ τρόπῳ τὸ γένος πληθῦναι, εἰ τὴν ἐντολὴν μέχρι τέλους ἐτήρησαν ἀπαραχάρακτον. Ἀλλ᾽ εἰδὼς ὁ θεὸς τῇ προγνώσει αὐτοῦ, «ὁ πάντα εἰδὼς πρὶν γενέσεως αὐτῶν», ὡς μέλλουσιν ἐν παραβάσει γίνεσθαι καὶ θανάτῳ κατακρίνεσθαι, προλαβὼν ἐποίησε τὸ ἄρρεν καὶ θῆλυ καὶ αὐξάνεσθαι καὶ πληθύνεσθαι προσέταξεν. Ὁδῷ τοίνυν κατέλθωμεν καὶ ἴδωμεν τὰ τῆς παρθενίας αὐχήματα· ταὐτὸν δὲ καὶ ἁγνείας εἰπεῖν.

Νῶε εἰς τὴν κιβωτὸν εἰσελθεῖν προστασσόμενος καὶ κόσμου σπέρμα φυλάττειν ἐγχειριζόμενος οὕτω προστάττεται· «Εἴσελθε σύ», φησί, «καὶ οἱ υἱοί σου καὶ ἡ γυνή σου καὶ αἱ γυναῖκες τῶν υἱῶν σου». Διεῖλεν αὐτοὺς ἐκ τῶν γυναικῶν, ὡς ἂν μετὰ τῆς ἁγνείας τὸ πέλαγος καὶ τὸ παγκόσμιον ἐκεῖνο ναυάγιον διαδράσαιεν. Μετὰ μέντοι τὴν τοῦ κατακλυσμοῦ κατάπαυσιν· «Ἔξελθε σύ», φησί, «καὶ ἡ γυνή σου καὶ οἱ υἱοί σου καὶ αἱ γυναῖκες τῶν υἱῶν σου». Ἰδοὺ πάλιν διὰ τὸν πληθυσμὸν ὁ γάμος συγκεχώρηται. Εἶτα Ἠλίας, ὁ πυρίπνους ἁμαρτηλάτης καὶ οὐρανοφοίτης, οὐκ ἀγαμίαν ἠσπάζετο καὶ τῷ ὑπὲρ ἀνθρώπους ἐμαρτυρήθη μετεωρίσματι; Τίς οὐρανοὺς ἔκλεισε; Τίς νεκροὺς ἤγειρε; Τίς Ἰορδάνην ἔτεμεν; Οὐχ ὁ παρθένος Ἠλίας; Ἐλισσαῖος δέ, ὁ τούτου φοιτητής, οὐ τὴν ἴσην ἀρετὴν ἐπιδειξάμενος ἐν διπλασίῳ τὴν χάριν τοῦ πνεύματος

were naked" and feeling shame, sewed aprons for themselves.[3] And after the transgression, "because you are earth and to earth you will return,"[4] when death entered into the world through the transgression, it was then that "Adam knew Eve his wife, and she conceived and gave birth."[5] Consequently, so that the human race should not waste away and be wiped out by death, marriage was devised, that by having children the human race might be preserved.

But perhaps they will say: "What is meant by 'male and female,' and by the phrase 'increase and multiply'?" To that we would say that the phrase "increase and multiply" does not necessarily mean increase through sexual relations. For God could have multiplied the race by other means if it had kept the commandment inviolate until the end. But since God, "who is aware of all things before they come to be,"[6] knew by his foreknowledge that they would transgress and incur the condemnation of death, he made the male and the female in anticipation of this and commanded them to increase and multiply. Let us, then, go down this path and look at the moral splendors of virginity, which is the same as to say the moral splendors of chastity.

When Noah was commanded to enter the ark and was entrusted with the preservation of the world's seed, he was instructed as follows: "Enter," it says, "you and your sons and your wife and the wives of your sons."[7] The men were separated from the women, that through chastity they might escape the flood and that worldwide disaster. But after the flood had subsided, "Come out," it says, "you and your wife and your sons and the wives of your sons."[8] Notice again that marriage is permitted again for the sake of increase. And then did not Elijah, the fiery charioteer who entered heaven, embrace celibacy, and was his superhuman quality not proved by his assumption?[9] Who closed the heavens? Who raised the dead? Who parted the waters of the Jordan? Was it not the virgin Elijah? And did not his disciple Elisha show the same virtue when he asked for a double share of the grace of the Spirit and inherited it?[10] And

[3]Gen 3.7.   [4]Gen 3.19.   [5]Gen 4.1.   [6]Dan 13 (Sus).42.
[7]Gen 6.18; 7.1.   [8]Gen 8.16.   [9]Cf. 4 Kg 2.11.   [10]Cf. 4 Kg 2.13–14.

αἰτήσας ἐκληρονόμησε; Τί δὲ οἱ τρεῖς παῖδες; Οὐ παρθενίαν ἀσκήσαντες πυρὸς κρείττους γεγόνασι διὰ τῆς παρθενίας τῶν σωμάτων ἀναλώτων τῷ πυρὶ γεγονότων; Οὐ Δανιήλ, οὐ τῷ σώματι παρθενίᾳ στομωθέντι θηρῶν ὀδόντες ἐμπαρεῖναι οὐκ ἴσχυσαν; Οὐ μέλλων τοῖς Ἰσραηλίταις ὁ θεὸς ὀπτάνεσθαι ἁγνίζειν τὸ σῶμα προσέταττεν; Οὐχὶ οἱ ἱερεῖς ἑαυτοὺς ἁγνίζοντες οὕτω τῶν ἀδύτων ἐπέβαινον καὶ τὰς θυσίας προσῆγον; Οὐχ ὁ νόμος μεγάλην εὐχὴν τὴν ἁγνείαν ἀνηγόρευσε;

Χρὴ τοιγαροῦν ἐπὶ τὸ πνευματικώτερον λαμβάνειν τὸ νομικὸν πρόσταγμα. Ἔστι γὰρ σπέρμα πνευματικὸν δι᾽ ἀγάπης καὶ φόβου θεοῦ συλλαμβανόμενον ἐν τῇ ψυχικῇ γαστρὶ ὠδινούσῃ καὶ τικτούσῃ πνεῦμα σωτηρίας. Οὕτω δὲ ἐκληπτέον καὶ τὸ «μακάριος, ὃς ἔχει σπέρμα ἐν Σιὼν καὶ οἰκείους ἐν Ἰερουσαλήμ». Τί γάρ, κἂν πόρνος ᾖ, κἂν μέθυσος καὶ εἰδωλολάτρης, μακάριός ἐστιν, εἰ μόνον ἔχει σπέρμα ἐν Σιὼν καὶ οἰκείους ἐν Ἰερουσαλήμ; Οὐδεὶς εὖ φρονῶν τοῦτο ἐρεῖ.

Παρθενία τὸ τῶν ἀγγέλων πολίτευμα, τὸ πάσης ἀσωμάτου φύσεως ἰδίωμα. Ταῦτα λέγομεν οὐ τὸν γάμον κακίζοντες—μὴ γένοιτο—(οἴδαμεν γὰρ τὸν κύριον ἐν τῇ παρουσίᾳ αὐτοῦ τὸν γάμον εὐλογήσαντα καὶ τὸν εἰπόντα· «Τίμιος ὁ γάμος καὶ ἡ κοίτη ἀμίαντος»), ἀλλὰ καλοῦ κρείττονα τὴν παρθενίαν γινώσκοντες. Ἔν τε γὰρ ταῖς ἀρεταῖς εἰσιν ἐπιτάσεις καὶ ὑφέσεις, ὁμοίως καὶ ἐν ταῖς κακίαις. Γινώσκομεν, ὅτι γάμου ἔκγονοι πάντες βροτοὶ μετὰ τοὺς τοῦ γένους ἀρχηγέτας. Ἐκεῖνοι γὰρ παρθενίας εἰσὶ καὶ οὐ γάμου πλαστούργημα. Ὅσῳ τοιγαροῦν ἄγγελος ἀνθρώπου ὑπέρτερος, τοσούτῳ παρθενία γάμου τιμιωτέρα. Τί δὲ λέγω ἄγγελος; Αὐτὸς ὁ Χριστὸς τῆς παρθενίας τὸ κλέος, οὐ μόνον ἐκ πατρὸς ἀνάρχως καὶ ἀσυνδυάστως γεγεννημένος, ἀλλ᾽ ὅτι καὶ ἄνθρωπος καθ᾽ ἡμᾶς γενόμενος ὑπὲρ ἡμᾶς ἐκ παρθένου συναφείας ἄνευ σεσαρκωμένος καὶ αὐτὸς παρθενίαν τὴν ἀληθῆ καὶ παντελῆ δεικνὺς ἐν ἑαυτῷ. Ὅθεν καὶ ταύτην ἡμῖν οὐκ ἐνομοθέτησε μέν

what of the Three Children? Was it not by practicing virginity that they became superior to fire, since their bodies through virginity had become inconsumable by fire?[11] Was not Daniel's body so hardened by virginity that the teeth of the wild beasts were powerless against it?[12] When God was about to appear to the Israelites, did he not command them to purify their bodies?[13] Did not the priests purify themselves before entering the sanctuary and offering the sacrifices?[14] Did not the law designate chastity a great vow?[15]

It is therefore necessary to take the legal prescription in a more spiritual sense. For there is a spiritual seed that through the fear and love of God is conceived in the soul's womb that suffers labor and gives birth to the spirit of salvation. This is the sense in which we should take the verse: "Blessed is he who has seed in Sion and family members in Jerusalem."[16] What do you think? Even if someone is a fornicator, even if he is a drunkard and an idolater, is he blessed just because he has seed in Sion and family members in Jerusalem? Nobody in their right mind would say this.

Virginity is the angels' mode of life, the characteristic property of all incorporeal nature. We say this not in disparagement of marriage—God forbid!—(for we know that the Lord blessed marriage by attending a wedding and him who said: "Let marriage be held in honor by all, and let the marriage bed be kept undefiled"[17]) but in the knowledge that virginity exceeds the good. For there are higher and lower degrees among the virtues, just as there are among the vices. We know that after the first parents of the race all mortals are the offspring of marriage. For the former were fashioned in virginity, not through marriage. Therefore just as an angel is superior to a human being, so too is virginity more honorable than marriage. But why should I say "an angel"? Christ himself demonstrates the preeminence of virginity, for not only was he begotten of the Father eternally and without pairing, but when he became a human being like us, he assumed flesh in a manner beyond us from a virgin without

[11]Cf. Dan 3.24–26.   [12]Cf. Dan 6.19–22.   [13]Cf. Ex 19.10–15.
[14]Cf. Num 8.21–22.   [15]Cf. Num 6.2.   [16]Is 31.9 (LXX).   [17]Heb 13.4.

(«οὐ γὰρ πάντες χωροῦσι τὸν λόγον», ὡς αὐτὸς ἔφησεν), ἔργῳ δὲ ἡμᾶς ἐξεπαίδευσεν καὶ πρὸς ταύτην ἡμᾶς ἐνεδυνάμωσε. Τίνι γὰρ οὐκ ἔστι σαφές, ὅτι παρθενία ἐν ἀνθρώποις νῦν πολιτεύεται;

Καλὴ μὲν ἡ τεκνογονία, ἥν ὁ γάμος συνέστησε, καὶ καλὸς ὁ γάμος διὰ τὰς πορνείας, ταύτας περικόπτων καὶ τὸ λυσσῶδες τῆς ἐπιθυμίας διὰ τῆς ἐννόμου μίξεως οὐκ ἐῶν πρὸς ἀνόμους ἐκμαίνεσθαι πράξεις. Καλὸς ὁ γάμος, οἷς οὐ πάρεστιν ἐγκράτεια· κρείττων δὲ ἡ παρθενία ψυχῆς τεκνογονίαν αὔξουσα καὶ θεῷ καρπὸν ὥριμον, τὴν προσευχήν, προσάγουσα. «Τίμιος ὁ γάμος καὶ ἡ κοίτη ἀμίαντος· πόρνους δὲ καὶ μοιχοὺς κρινεῖ ὁ θεός».

98 Περὶ τῆς περιτομῆς

Ἡ περιτομὴ πρὸ νόμου ἐδόθη τῷ Ἀβραὰμ μετὰ τὰς εὐλογίας, μετὰ τὴν ἐπαγγελίαν, σημεῖον ἀποδιαστέλλον αὐτὸν καὶ τοὺς αὐτοῦ οἰκογενεῖς ἐκ τῶν ἐθνῶν, μεθ' ὧν συνανεστρέφετο. Καὶ δῆλον· Ὅτε γὰρ ἐν τῇ ἐρήμῳ τεσσαράκοντα ἔτη ὁ Ἰσραὴλ μόνος καθ' ἑαυτὸν διέτριψεν οὐ συναναμεμιγμένος ἑτέρῳ ἔθνει, ὅσοι ἐν τῇ ἐρήμῳ ἐγεννήθησαν, οὐ περιετμήθησαν· ἡνίκα δὲ Ἰησοῦς διεβίβαζεν αὐτοὺς τὸν Ἰορδάνην, περιετμήθησαν, καὶ γέγονε δεύτερος νόμος περιτομῆς. Ἐπὶ Ἀβραὰμ γὰρ ἐδόθη νόμος περιτομῆς, εἶτα ἐπαύσατο ἐν τῇ ἐρήμῳ τεσσαράκοντα ἔτη. Καὶ πάλιν ἐκ δευτέρου ἔδωκεν ὁ θεὸς τῷ Ἰησοῦ νόμον περιτομῆς μετὰ τὸ διαβῆναι τὸν Ἰορδάνην, καθὼς ἐν τῇ βίβλῳ Ἰησοῦ τοῦ Ναυῆ γέγραπται· «Ὑπὸ δὲ τοῦτον τὸν καιρὸν εἶπεν κύριος τῷ Ἰησοῦ· Ποίησον σεαυτῷ μαχαίρας πετρίνας ἐκ πέτρας ἀκροτόμου καὶ καθίσας περίτεμε τοὺς υἱοὺς Ἰσραὴλ ἐκ δευτέρου», καὶ μετ' ὀλίγα·

sexual union, and himself demonstrated in his own person what true and complete virginity is. Therefore he did not lay this down too as a law for us ("for not everyone can accept this teaching,"[18] as he himself said) but he taught us by example and gave us strength to do it. For to whom is it not obvious that virginity is now a way of life among us?

Having children is good, which is why marriage was established, and marriage is good on account of the sexual urge because it curtails it and through licit union does not allow the frenzy of desire to be driven madly to lawless acts. Marriage is good for those who cannot practice continence, but virginity is better because it increases the soul's fecundity and offers ripe fruit, which is prayer, to God. "Let marriage be held in honor and let the marriage bed be kept undefiled, for God will judge fornicators and adulterers."[19]

98   *On circumcision*

Circumcision was given to Abraham before the Law, after the blessings, after the promise, as a sign setting him and his household apart from the Gentiles amongst whom he lived.[1] And this is evident. For when Israel spent forty years in the desert alone by themselves and did not mingle with any other nation, those who were born in the desert were not circumcised. But when Joshua took them across the Jordan, they were circumcised and a second law of circumcision came into being. For a law of circumcision was given in the time of Abraham, then it ceased for forty years in the desert. And God gave the law of circumcision again a second time to Joshua after the crossing of the Jordan, as is written in the Book of Joshua the son of Nun: "At this time the Lord said to Joshua: 'Make yourself knives of sharp stone and sit down and circumcise the sons of Israel a second time,'"[2] and after a little: "For Israel wandered in the desert of Battaris for forty-two years, and for this reason most of the fighting men who

[18]Mt 19.11.   [19]Heb 13.4.

[1]Cf. Gen 17.10–12.   [2]Jos 5.2.

«Ἐπὶ τεσσαράκοντα γὰρ καὶ δύο ἔτη ἀνέστραπται Ἰσραὴλ ἐν τῇ ἐρήμῳ τῇ Βατταρίτιδι, καὶ διὰ τοῦτο ἀπερίτμητοι αὐτῶν ἦσαν οἱ πλεῖστοι τῶν μαχίμων τῶν ἐξεληλυθότων ἐκ γῆς Αἰγύπτου, οἱ ἀπειθήσαντες ταῖς ἐντολαῖς τοῦ θεοῦ, οἷς καὶ διώρισε μὴ ἰδεῖν αὐτοὺς τὴν γῆν τὴν ἀγαθήν, ἣν ὤμοσε κύριος τοῖς πατράσιν ἡμῶν δοῦναι αὐτοῖς, γῆν ῥέουσαν γάλα καὶ μέλι. Ἀντὶ δὲ τούτων ἀντεκατέστησε τοὺς υἱοὺς αὐτῶν, οὓς Ἰησοῦς περιέτεμε, διὰ τὸ γεγενῆσθαι αὐτοὺς ἀπεριτμήτους κατὰ τὴν ὁδόν». Ὥστε σημεῖον ἦν ἡ περιτομὴ ἀφορίζον τὸν Ἰσραὴλ ἐκ τῶν ἐθνῶν, οἷς συνανεστρέφετο.

Τύπος δὲ ἦν τοῦ βαπτίσματος. Καθάπερ γὰρ ἡ περιτομὴ οὐ χρειῶδες μέλος ἀποτέμνει τοῦ σώματος, ἀλλὰ περίττωμα ἄχρηστον, οὕτω διὰ τοῦ ἁγίου βαπτίσματος τὴν ἁμαρτίαν περιτεμνόμεθα· ἡ δὲ ἁμαρτία δῆλον ὡς περίττωμα ἐπιθυμίας ἐστὶ καὶ οὐ χρειώδης ἐπιθυμία (ἀδύνατον γάρ τινα μηδ᾽ ὅλως ἐπιθυμεῖν ἢ τέλεον ἄγευστον ἡδονῆς εἶναι), ἀλλὰ τὸ ἄχρηστον τῆς ἡδονῆς ἤτοι ἡ ἄχρηστος ἐπιθυμία τε καὶ ἡδονή, τουτέστιν ἡ ἁμαρτία, ἣν περιτέμνει τὸ ἅγιον βάπτισμα παρέχον ἡμῖν σημεῖον τὸν τίμιον σταυρὸν ἐπὶ τοῦ μετώπου, οὐκ ἐξ ἐθνῶν ἀφορίζον ἡμᾶς (πάντα γὰρ τὰ ἔθνη τοῦ βαπτίσματος ἔτυχον καὶ τῷ σημείῳ τοῦ σταυροῦ ἐσφραγίσθησαν), ἀλλ᾽ ἐν ἑκάστῳ ἔθνει τὸν πιστὸν ἀποδιαστέλλον τοῦ ἀπίστου. Τῆς τοίνυν ἀληθείας ἐμφανισθείσης ἀνόνητος ὁ τύπος καὶ ἡ σκιά. Ὥστε περιττὸν νῦν τὸ περιτέμνεσθαι καὶ ἐναντίον τοῦ ἁγίου βαπτίσματος. Ὁ γὰρ περιτεμνόμενος χρεωστεῖ ὅλον τὸν νόμον τηρῆσαι· ὁ δὲ κύριος, ἵνα πληρώσῃ τὸν νόμον, περιετμήθη, καὶ πάντα δὲ τὸν νόμον καὶ τὸ σάββατον ἐτήρησεν, ἵνα πληρώσῃ καὶ στήσῃ τὸν νόμον. Ἀφ᾽ οὗ δὲ ἐβαπτίσθη καὶ τὸ ἅγιον πνεῦμα τοῖς ἀνθρώποις ἐνεφανίσθη ἐν εἴδει περιστερᾶς καταβαῖνον ἐπ᾽ αὐτόν, ἔκτοτε ἡ πνευματικὴ λατρεία καὶ πολιτεία καὶ ἡ τῶν οὐρανῶν βασιλεία κεκήρυκται.

had come out of the land of Egypt were uncircumcised, who had disobeyed God's commandments, and whom God had determined should not see the good land which the Lord had sworn to give to these our fathers, a land flowing with milk and honey. And in their place he set their sons, whom Joshua circumcised, because they had not been circumcised on the way."[3] So circumcision was a sign separating Israel from the Gentiles amongst whom they lived.

It was also a figure of baptism. For just as circumcision does not cut off a member of the body that is useful, but a useless and superfluous item, so too through holy baptism we are circumcised with regard to sin. And sin clearly is like a superfluous part of desire and not a useful desire (for it is impossible for anyone not to have any desire at all, or to be entirely without experience of pleasure). No, the useless part of pleasure, that is to say, useless desire and pleasure, which is sin, it is this that holy baptism circumcises, giving us the precious cross as a sign on our foreheads, not setting us apart from the Gentiles (for all the nations have had the opportunity to be baptized and to be sealed by the sign of the cross), but in each nation to distinguish the believer from the unbeliever. Now that the truth has been made manifest, the type and the shadow are unprofitable. It is therefore superfluous now to be circumcised and contrary to holy baptism. For someone who is circumcised is obliged to keep the whole of the Law. The Lord was circumcised in order to fulfill the Law, and he kept the whole of the Law and the Sabbath, so as to fulfill it and bring it to a stop. Once he was baptized and the Holy Spirit was manifested to people in the form of a dove descending upon him, from that time the spiritual worship and manner of life and the kingdom of heaven have been proclaimed.

[3] Jos 5.6–7.

99 Περὶ τοῦ ἀντιχρίστου

Χρὴ γινώσκειν, ὅτι δεῖ τὸν ἀντίχριστον ἐλθεῖν. Πᾶς μὲν οὖν ὁ μὴ ὁμολογῶν τὸν υἱὸν τοῦ θεοῦ καὶ θεὸν ἐν σαρκὶ ἐληλυθέναι καὶ εἶναι θεὸν τέλειον καὶ γενέσθαι ἄνθρωπον τέλειον μετὰ τοῦ μεῖναι θεὸν ἀντίχριστός ἐστιν.

Ὅμως ἰδιοτρόπως καὶ ἐξαιρέτως ἀντίχριστος λέγεται ὁ ἐπὶ τῇ συντελείᾳ τοῦ αἰῶνος ἐρχόμενος. Χρὴ τοιγαροῦν πρῶτον κηρυχθῆναι τὸ εὐαγγέλιον ἐν πᾶσι τοῖς ἔθνεσι, καθὼς ἔφη ὁ κύριος, καὶ τότε ἐλεύσεται εἰς ἔλεγχον τῶν ἀντιθέων Ἰουδαίων. Ἔφη γὰρ αὐτοῖς ὁ κύριος· «Ἐγὼ ἦλθον ἐν τῷ ὀνόματι τοῦ πατρός μου, καὶ οὐ λαμβάνετέ με· ἔρχεται ἄλλος ἐν τῷ ὀνόματι τῷ ἰδίῳ, κἀκεῖνον λήψεσθε». Καὶ ὁ ἀπόστολος· «Ἀνθ᾽ ὧν τὴν ἀγάπην τῆς ἀληθείας οὐκ ἐδέξαντο εἰς τὸ σωθῆναι αὐτούς, καὶ διὰ τοῦτο πέμψει αὐτοῖς ὁ θεὸς ἐνέργειαν πλάνης εἰς τὸ πιστεῦσαι αὐτοὺς τῷ ψεύδει, ἵνα κριθῶσι πάντες οἱ μὴ πιστεύσαντες τῇ ἀληθείᾳ, ἀλλ᾽ εὐδοκήσαντες ἐν τῇ ἀδικίᾳ». Οἱ οὖν Ἰουδαῖοι υἱὸν θεοῦ ὄντα τὸν κύριον Ἰησοῦν Χριστὸν καὶ θεὸν οὐκ ἐδέξαντο, τὸν δὲ πλάνον θεὸν ἑαυτὸν λέγοντα δέξονται. Ὅτι γὰρ θεὸν ἑαυτὸν ἀποκαλέσει, ὁ ἄγγελος τῷ Δανιὴλ διδάσκων οὕτω φησίν· «Ἐπὶ θεοὺς τῶν πατέρων αὐτοῦ οὐ συνήσει», καὶ ὁ ἀπόστολος· «Μή τις ὑμᾶς ἐξαπατήσῃ κατὰ μηδένα τρόπον, ὅτι, ἐὰν μὴ ἔλθῃ ἡ ἀποστασία πρῶτον καὶ ἀποκαλυφθῇ ὁ ἄνθρωπος τῆς ἀνομίας, ὁ υἱὸς τῆς ἀπωλείας ὁ ἀντικείμενος καὶ ὑπεραιρόμενος ἐπὶ πάντα λεγόμενον θεὸν ἢ σέβασμα, ὥστε αὐτὸν εἰς τὸν ναὸν τοῦ θεοῦ ὡς θεὸν καθίσαι ἀποδεικνύντα ἑαυτόν, ὅτι ἔστι θεός». Εἰς τὸν ναὸν δὲ τοῦ θεοῦ οὐ τὸν ἡμέτερον, ἀλλὰ τὸν παλαιόν, τὸν Ἰουδαϊκόν. Οὐ γὰρ ἡμῖν, ἀλλὰ τοῖς Ἰουδαίοις εἰσελεύσεται· οὐχ ὑπὲρ Χριστοῦ ἀλλὰ κατὰ Χριστοῦ καὶ τῶν τοῦ Χριστοῦ, διὸ καὶ ἀντίχριστος λέγεται.

---

[1]The tradition of the coming of Antichrist before the final consummation of the age is found in the Johannine epistles (1 Jn 2.18–22, 4.3; 2 Jn 7—the only places in the New Testament where the word "antichrist" appears), and also in 2 Thessalonians 2.1–12, and Revelation 13 and 17. The teaching is commonly discussed in early Christian literature (e.g., *Didache* 13.3–4, Irenaeus, *Against Heresies* 5. 25–30), at a time when the Church was suffering intermittent persecution from the Roman authorities, but

99   *On the Antichrist*

One needs to know that the Antichrist has to come.[1] It is true that
anyone who does not confess that the Son of God also came as
God in the flesh, and is perfect God and became perfect man while
remaining God, is an antichrist.[2] The one, however, who is to come
at the consummation of the age is called antichrist in a special and
distinctive sense. It is therefore necessary that the gospel should
first be preached among all the nations, just as the Lord said,[3] and
then he will come to condemn the Jews, the enemies of God. For the
Lord himself said: "I have come in my Father's name, and you do not
accept me; if another comes in his own name, him you will accept."[4]
And the Apostle: "Because they refused to love the truth and so be
saved, and for this reason God sends them a powerful delusion, leading them to believe what is false, so that all who have not believed
the truth but took pleasure in unrighteousness will be condemned."[5]
Therefore the Jews, who did not accept that the Lord Jesus Christ is
Son of God and God, will accept the deceiver who calls himself God.
That he will call himself God, is declared by the angel that instructed
Daniel, who says: "He shall pay no respect to the gods of his fathers."[6]
And the Apostle says: "Let no one deceive you in any way; for that
day will not come unless the rebellion comes first and the lawless one
is revealed, the one destined for destruction. He opposes and exalts
himself above every so-called god or object of worship, so that he
takes his seat in the temple of God, declaring himself to be God."[7] In
the temple of God, not ours but the old temple, the Jewish one. For
he will come not to us but to the Jews, not on behalf of Christ but
against Christ and the people of Christ, and that is why he is called
Antichrist.

less commonly after Constantine, the first Christian emperor, became sole ruler in
324. For John Damascene, the figure of Antichrist had become relevant again with the
advent of the new religion of Muhammed. Among patristic sources known to have
been consulted by John, Cyril of Jerusalem's *Catechetical Lectures* (4.15, 15.11–12, and
15.16–17) would have provided him with much of the material he needed.

[2]Cf. 1 Jn 4.2–3.	[3]Mt 24.14.	[4]Jn 5.43.
[5]2 Thess 2.10–12.	[6]Dan 11.37.	[7]2 Thess 2.3–4.

Δεῖ τοίνυν πρῶτον κηρυχθῆναι τὸ εὐαγγέλιον ἐν πᾶσι τοῖς ἔθνεσι. «Καὶ τότε ἀποκαλυφθήσεται ὁ ἄνομος, οὗ ἐστιν ἡ παρουσία κατ᾽ ἐνέργειαν τοῦ σατανᾶ ἐν πάσῃ δυνάμει καὶ σημείοις καὶ τέρασι ψεύδους καὶ ἐν πάσῃ ἀπάτῃ τῆς ἀδικίας ἐν τοῖς ἀπολλυμένοις, ὃν ὁ κύριος ἀνελεῖ τῷ ῥήματι τοῦ στόματος αὐτοῦ καὶ καταργήσει τῇ παρουσίᾳ τῆς ἐπιφανείας αὐτοῦ». Οὐκ αὐτὸς τοίνυν ὁ διάβολος γίνεται ἄνθρωπος κατὰ τὴν τοῦ κυρίου ἐνανθρώπησιν—μὴ γένοιτο—, ἀλλ᾽ ἄνθρωπος ἐκ πορνείας τίκτεται καὶ ὑποδέχεται πᾶσαν τὴν ἐνέργειαν τοῦ σατανᾶ. Προειδὼς γὰρ ὁ θεὸς τὸ ἄτοπον τῆς μελλούσης αὐτοῦ προαιρέσεως παραχωρεῖ ἐνοικῆσαι ἐν αὐτῷ τὸν διάβολον.

Τίκτεται τοίνυν ἐκ πορνείας, ὡς ἔφημεν, καὶ ἀνατρέφεται λεληθότως καὶ αἰφνίδιον ἐπανίσταται καὶ ἀνταίρει καὶ βασιλεύει. Καὶ ἐν τοῖς προοιμίοις μὲν τῆς βασιλείας αὐτοῦ, μᾶλλον δὲ τυραννίδος, ὑποκρίνεται δικαιοσύνην· ἡνίκα δὲ ἐπικρατὴς γένηται, διώκει τὴν ἐκκλησίαν τοῦ θεοῦ καὶ ἐκφαίνει πᾶσαν τὴν πονηρίαν αὐτοῦ. Ἐλεύσεται δὲ «ἐν σημείοις καὶ τέρασι ψεύδους» πεπλασμένοις καὶ οὐκ ἀληθέσι καὶ τοὺς σαθρὰν καὶ ἀστήρικτον τὴν βάσιν τῆς διανοίας ἔχοντας ἀπατήσει καὶ ἀποστήσει ἀπὸ θεοῦ, ὥστε σκανδαλισθῆναι, «εἰ δυνατόν, καὶ τοὺς ἐκλεκτούς».

Ἀποσταλήσεται δὲ Ἐνὼχ καὶ Ἠλίας ὁ Θεσβίτης καὶ ἐπιστρέψουσι καρδίας πατέρων ἐπὶ τέκνα, τουτέστι τὴν συναγωγὴν ἐπὶ τὸν κύριον ἡμῶν Ἰησοῦν Χριστὸν καὶ τὸ τῶν ἀποστόλων κήρυγμα, καὶ ὑπ᾽ αὐτοῦ ἀναιρεθήσονται. Καὶ ἐλεύσεται ὁ κύριος ἐξ οὐρανοῦ, ὃν τρόπον οἱ ἅγιοι ἀπόστολοι ἐθεάσαντο αὐτὸν πορευόμενον εἰς τὸν οὐρανόν, θεὸς τέλειος καὶ ἄνθρωπος τέλειος, μετὰ δόξης καὶ δυνάμεως καὶ ἀνελεῖ τὸν ἄνθρωπον τῆς ἀνομίας, τὸν υἱὸν τῆς ἀπωλείας, τῷ πνεύματι τοῦ στόματος αὐτοῦ. Μηδεὶς τοίνυν ἀπὸ γῆς ἐκδεχέσθω τὸν κύριον, ἀλλ᾽ ἐξ οὐρανοῦ, ὡς αὐτὸς ἡμᾶς ἠσφαλίσατο.

---

[8] 2 Thess 2.8–10.   [9] 2 Thess 2.9.   [10] Mt 24.24.
[11] Cf. Mal 3.21 (4.6 MT); Lk 1.17.
[12] Rev 11.3–12. Although Enoch and Elijah are not named in this passage from Revelation, the "two witnesses" wearing sackcloth who destroy their enemies by fire and are taken up to heaven in a cloud were traditionally identified with the only two

It is therefore necessary that the gospel should first be preached among all the nations. "And then the lawless one will be revealed, whose coming is apparent in the working of Satan, who uses all power, signs, lying wonders, and every kind of wicked deception for those who are perishing, whom the Lord Jesus will destroy with the breath of his mouth, annihilating him by the manifestation of his coming."[8] Therefore the devil himself does not become a human being in the manner of the Lord's incarnation—God forbid!—but a human being is born from fornication and receives the whole of Satan's activity. For since God foresees the outrageousness of his future free choice, he permits the devil to reside in him.

He is therefore born of fornication, as we have said, and is brought up secretly and suddenly rises up and rebels and comes to rule. And in the early days of his reign, or rather his tyranny, he makes a pretence of righteousness, but when he gains complete control, he persecutes the Church of God and makes the whole of his wickedness manifest. He will come "with signs and lying wonders"[9] that are false and not true, and will deceive those whose understanding rests on a rotten and unstable foundation and cause them to revolt from God, so that even "the elect, if possible"[10] are made to stumble.

Enoch and Elijah the Tishbite will be sent, and they will "turn the hearts of fathers to their children,"[11] that is to say, the synagogue to our Lord Jesus Christ and the preaching of the apostles, and they will be destroyed by him.[12] And the Lord will come from heaven in the same way that the holy apostles saw him going into heaven,[13] perfect God and perfect man, with glory and power, and he will destroy the man of lawlessness, the son of perdition, with the breath of his mouth.[14] Let no one, then, expect the Lord from this earth, but from heaven, as he himself assured us.

biblical figures to have been thus translated into heaven. "Many of the teachers," says Andrew of Caesarea (late 6th cent.), "understood these [to be] Enoch and Elias," Andrew of Caesarea, *Commentary on the Apocalypse* 30.11.3–4 (FOC 123:131–32). The identification goes back at least to Irenaeus (*Against Heresies* 5.5.1), who claimed to have a close connection to the author of Revelation through Polycarp. (IG)

[13] Acts 1.11.   [14] 2 Thess 2.3.

100 *Περὶ ἀναστάσεως*

Πιστεύομεν δὲ καὶ εἰς ἀνάστασιν νεκρῶν. Ἔσται γάρ, ὄντως ἔσται νεκρῶν ἀνάστασις. Ἀνάστασιν δὲ λέγοντες σωμάτων φαμὲν ἀνάστασιν. Ἀνάστασις γάρ ἐστι δευτέρα τοῦ πεπτωκότος στάσις· αἱ γὰρ ψυχαὶ ἀθάνατοι οὖσαι πῶς ἀναστήσονται; Εἰ γὰρ θάνατον ὁρίζονται χωρισμὸν ψυχῆς ἀπὸ σώματος, ἀνάστασίς ἐστι πάντως συνάφεια πάλιν ψυχῆς καὶ σώματος καὶ δευτέρα τοῦ διαλυθέντος καὶ πεσόντος ζῴου στάσις. Αὐτὸ οὖν τὸ σῶμα τὸ φθειρόμενον καὶ διαλυόμενον, αὐτὸ ἀναστήσεται ἄφθαρτον· οὐκ ἀδυνατεῖ γὰρ ὁ ἐν ἀρχῇ ἐκ τοῦ χοὸς τῆς γῆς αὐτὸ συστησάμενος πάλιν ἀναλυθὲν καὶ ἀποστραφὲν εἰς τὴν γῆν, ἐξ ἧς ἐλήφθη κατὰ τὴν τοῦ δημιουργοῦ ἀπόφασιν, πάλιν ἀναστῆσαι αὐτό.

Εἰ γὰρ μὴ ἔστιν ἀνάστασις, «φάγωμεν καὶ πίωμεν», τὸν ἐνήδονον καὶ ἀπολαυστικὸν βίον μετέλθωμεν. Εἰ οὐκ ἔστιν ἀνάστασις, ἐν τίνι τῶν ἀλόγων διαφέρομεν; Εἰ οὐκ ἔστιν ἀνάστασις, μακαρίσωμεν τὰ θηρία τοῦ ἀγροῦ τὸν ἄλυπον ἔχοντα βίον. Εἰ οὐκ ἔστιν ἀνάστασις, οὐδὲ θεός ἐστιν οὐδὲ πρόνοια, αὐτομάτως δὲ πάντα ἄγονταί τε καὶ φέρονται. Ἰδοὺ γὰρ ὁρῶμεν πλείστους δικαίους μὲν πενομένους καὶ ἀδικουμένους καὶ μηδεμιᾶς ἐν τῷ παρόντι βίῳ τυγχάνοντας ἀντιλήψεως, ἁμαρτωλοὺς δὲ καὶ ἀδίκους ἐν πλούτῳ καὶ πάσῃ τρυφῇ εὐθηνοῦντας. Καὶ τίς ἂν τοῦτο δικαιοκρισίας ἢ σοφῆς προνοίας ἔργον εὖ φρονῶν ὑπολάβοι; Ἔσται οὖν, ἔσται ἀνάστασις. Δίκαιος γὰρ ὁ θεὸς καὶ τοῖς ὑπομένουσιν αὐτὸν μισθαποδότης γίνεται. Εἰ μὲν οὖν ἡ ψυχὴ μόνη τοῖς τῆς ἀρετῆς ἀγῶσιν ἐνήθλησε, μόνη καὶ στεφανωθήσεται. Καὶ εἰ μόνη ταῖς ἡδοναῖς ἐνεκυλίσθη, μόνη δικαίως ἂν ἐκολάζετο· ἀλλ᾽ ἐπεὶ μήτε τὴν ὕπαρξιν κεχωρισμένην ἔσχον μήτε τὴν ἀρετὴν μήτε τὴν κακίαν ἡ ψυχὴ μετῆλθε δίχα τοῦ σώματος, δικαίως ἄμφω ἅμα καὶ τῶν ἀμοιβῶν τεύξονται.

100 *On resurrection*

We also believe in the resurrection of the dead. For there will be, there really will be, a resurrection of the dead. And when we say resurrection, we mean the resurrection of bodies. For resurrection is a setting up a second time of what has fallen. For since souls are immortal, how will they be set up again? For if death is defined as the separation of the soul from the body, resurrection must be the coming together again of soul and body and the setting up a second time of the animal part that has fallen and dissolved. This body, then, which has corrupted and dissolved, it is this body that will be raised up incorruptible. For he who in the beginning formed it from the dust of the earth is not unable, when it has dissolved and returned again to the earth from which it was taken by the decision of the Creator, to raise it up again.

For if there is no resurrection, "Let us eat and drink,"[1] let us go for a pleasurable and enjoyable life. If there is no resurrection, how do we differ from dumb animals? If there is no resurrection, let us pronounce the wild beasts of the countryside blessed for they have a life without sorrow. If there is no resurrection, there is no God either, or providence, but everything comes and goes of its own accord. For look, we see a great many righteous people suffering penury and injustice, and receiving not the slightest help in this life, whereas sinners and unrighteous people luxuriate in wealth and every kind of self-indulgence. And who in their right mind would take this to be a work of righteous judgement or wise providence? There will, therefore, most certainly be a resurrection. For God is just and recompenses those who wait on him patiently. Now if the soul engaged in the struggle for virtue on its own, it alone would be crowned. And if it wallowed in pleasures on its own, it alone would be justly punished. But since the soul has neither an independent existence, nor engages in virtue or vice without the body, both of them will rightly attain their rewards at the same time.

[1] 1 Cor 15.32.

Μαρτυρεῖ δὲ καὶ ἡ θεία γραφή, ὅτι ἔσται σωμάτων ἀνάστασις. Φησὶ γοῦν ὁ θεὸς πρὸς Νῶε μετὰ τὸν κατακλυσμόν· «Ὡς λάχανα χόρτου δέδωκα ὑμῖν τὰ πάντα. Πλὴν κρέας ἐν αἵματι ψυχῆς οὐ φάγεσθε· καὶ γὰρ τὸ ὑμέτερον αἷμα τῶν ψυχῶν ὑμῶν ἐκζητήσω, ἐκ χειρὸς πάντων τῶν θηρίων ἐκζητήσω αὐτὸ καὶ ἐκ χειρὸς παντὸς ἀνθρώπου ἀδελφοῦ αὐτοῦ ἐκζητήσω τὴν ψυχὴν αὐτοῦ. Ὁ ἐκχέων αἷμα ἀνθρώπου, ἀντὶ τοῦ αἵματος αὐτοῦ ἐκχυθήσεται, ὅτι ἐν εἰκόνι θεοῦ ἐποίησα τὸν ἄνθρωπον». Πῶς ἐκζητήσει τὸ αἷμα τοῦ ἀνθρώπου ἐκ χειρὸς πάντων τῶν θηρίων, ἢ ὅτι ἀναστήσει τὰ σώματα τῶν ἀνθρώπων τῶν ἀποθνησκόντων; Οὐ γὰρ ἀντὶ τοῦ ἀνθρώπου ἀποθανεῖται τὰ θηρία.—καὶ πάλιν τῷ Μωσεῖ· Ἐγώ εἰμι ὁ θεὸς Ἀβραὰμ καὶ θεὸς Ἰσαὰκ καὶ θεὸς Ἰακώβ. Οὐκ ἔστιν ὁ θεὸς νεκρῶν θεὸς» τῶν ἀποθανόντων καὶ οὐκέτι ἐσομένων, ἀλλὰ ζώντων, ὧν αἱ ψυχαὶ μὲν ἐν χειρὶ αὐτοῦ ζῶσι, τὰ δὲ σώματα πάλιν διὰ τῆς ἀναστάσεως ζήσεται. Καὶ ὁ θεοπάτωρ Δαυίδ φησι πρὸς τὸν θεόν· «Ἀντανελεῖς τὸ πνεῦμα αὐτῶν, καὶ ἐκλείψουσι καὶ εἰς τὸν χοῦν αὐτῶν ἐπιστρέψουσιν». Ἰδοὺ περὶ τῶν σωμάτων ὁ λόγος. Εἶτα ἐπάγει· «Ἐξαποστελεῖς τὸ πνεῦμά σου, καὶ κτισθήσονται, καὶ ἀνακαινιεῖς τὸ πρόσωπον τῆς γῆς».—καὶ Ἡσαΐας δέ· «Ἀναστήσονται οἱ νεκροί, καὶ ἐγερθήσονται οἱ ἐν τοῖς μνημείοις». Δῆλον δέ, ὡς οὐχ αἱ ψυχαὶ ἐν τοῖς μνημείοις τίθενται, ἀλλὰ τὰ σώματα. Καὶ ὁ μακάριος δὲ Ἰεζεκιήλ· «Καὶ ἐγένετο», φησίν, «ἐν τῷ με προφητεῦσαι, καὶ ἰδοὺ σεισμός, καὶ προσήγαγε τὰ ὀστᾶ, ὀστέον πρὸς ὀστέον, ἕκαστον πρὸς τὴν ἁρμονίαν αὐτοῦ. Καὶ εἶδον, καὶ ἰδοὺ ἐπεγένετο αὐτοῖς νεῦρα, καὶ σάρκες ἀνεφύοντο, καὶ ἀνέβαινεν ἐπ᾽ αὐτὰ καὶ περιετάθη αὐτοῖς δέρματα ἐπάνωθεν». Εἶτα διδάσκει, πῶς κελευσθέντα ἐπανῆλθε τὰ πνεύματα. Καὶ ὁ θεῖος Δανιήλ· «Καὶ ἐν τῷ καιρῷ ἐκείνῳ ἀναστήσεται Μιχαὴλ ὁ ἄρχων ὁ μέγας ὁ ἑστηκὼς ἐπὶ τοὺς υἱοὺς τοῦ λαοῦ σου· καὶ ἔσται καιρὸς θλίψεως, θλῖψις, οἵα οὐ γέγονεν, ἀφ᾽ οὗ γεγένηται ἔθνος ἐπὶ τῆς γῆς, ἕως τοῦ καιροῦ ἐκείνου. Καὶ ἐν τῷ καιρῷ ἐκείνῳ σωθήσεται ὁ λαός σου, πᾶς ὁ εὑρεθεὶς γεγραμμένος ἐν τῷ βιβλίῳ.

Divine Scripture also testifies that there will be a bodily resurrection. God accordingly says to Noah after the flood: "I have given everything to you as the green plants. Only you shall not eat flesh with the blood of life. For your own lifeblood I will require a reckoning: from the hand of every wild animal I will require it and from the hand of every human being I will require the soul of their brother. Whoever sheds the blood of a human being, instead of that blood their own shall be shed, because I made humankind in the image of God."[2] How will he require the blood of a human being from the hand of all the wild beasts, unless he raises up the bodies of human beings who have died? For the wild animals will not die instead of human beings. And again to Moses: "I am the God of Abraham, the God of Isaac, and the God of Jacob. He is God not of the dead," of those who have died and will be no more, "but of the living," whose souls live in his hand and whose bodies will live again through the resurrection.[3] And David, the ancestor of God, says to God: "You will take away their breath and they will die and return to their dust."[4] See how it refers to bodies. And then he adds: "You shall send forth your Spirit and they shall be created, and you shall renew the face of the earth."[5] And Isaiah: "The dead shall rise and those in the tombs shall awake."[6] It is obvious that it is not souls that are placed in the tombs but bodies. And the blessed Ezekiel: "And it came to pass," he says, "while I was prophesying, that behold, there was a shaking, and the bones came together, bone to bone, each one with its right companion. And I saw, and behold, sinews came upon them, and flesh grew on them, and skin developed upon them and covered their surface."[7] Then he teaches that the spirits came back when they were commanded to do so. And the divine Daniel: "And at that time Michael the great prince, who stands over the sons of your people, will arise. And there shall be a time of anguish, anguish such as has never occurred from the time that there was a nation on the earth until that time. And at that time your people shall be delivered, everyone who is found written in the book. And

[2]Gen 9.3–6.   [3]Cf. Wis 3.1; Mt 22.32–33.   [4]Ps 103.29.
[5]Ps 103.30.   [6]Is 26.19.   [7]Ez 37.7–8.

Καὶ πολλοὶ τῶν καθευδόντων ἐν γῆς χώματι ἐγερθήσονται, οὗτοι εἰς ζωὴν αἰώνιον, καὶ οὗτοι εἰς ὀνειδισμὸν καὶ αἰσχύνην αἰώνιον. Καὶ οἱ συνιόντες ἐκλάμψουσιν ὡς ἡ λαμπρότης τοῦ στερεώματος, καὶ ἀπὸ τῶν δικαίων τῶν πολλῶν ὡς οἱ ἀστέρες εἰς τοὺς αἰῶνας καὶ ἔτι ἐκλάμψουσι».—«Πολλοὶ τῶν καθευδόντων ἐν γῆς χώματι», λέγων, «ἐξεγερθήσονται», δῆλον, ὡς ἀνάστασιν ἐμφαίνει σωμάτων· οὐ γὰρ δήπου τις φήσειε τὰς ψυχὰς ἐν γῆς χώματι καθεύδειν. Ἀλλὰ μὴν καὶ ὁ κύριος ἐν τοῖς ἱεροῖς εὐαγγελίοις τὴν τῶν σωμάτων ἀριδήλως ἀνάστασιν παραδέδωκεν. «Ἀκούσονται» γάρ, φησίν, «οἱ ἐν τοῖς μνημείοις τῆς φωνῆς τοῦ υἱοῦ τοῦ θεοῦ, καὶ ἐξελεύσονται οἱ τὰ ἀγαθὰ ποιήσαντες εἰς ἀνάστασιν ζωῆς, οἱ δὲ τὰ φαῦλα πράξαντες εἰς ἀνάστασιν κρίσεως». Ἐν τοῖς μνημείοις δὲ τὰς ψυχάς ποτε τῶν εὖ φρονούντων εἴποι τις ἄν;

Οὐ λόγῳ δὲ μόνον, ἀλλὰ καὶ ἔργῳ τὴν τῶν σωμάτων ὁ κύριος ἀνάστασιν ἐφανέρωσε. Πρῶτον μὲν τεταρταῖον καὶ ἤδη φθαρέντα καὶ ὀδωδότα ἐγείρας τὸν Λάζαρον· οὐ ψυχὴν γὰρ ἐστερημένην σώματος, ἀλλὰ καὶ σῶμα σὺν τῇ ψυχῇ, καὶ οὐχ ἕτερον, ἀλλ᾽ αὐτὸ τὸ φθαρὲν ἤγειρε. Πῶς γὰρ ἂν ἐγινώσκετο ἢ ἐπιστεύετο ἡ τοῦ τεθνεῶτος ἀνάστασις μὴ τῶν χαρακτηριστικῶν τῆς ὑποστάσεως ἰδιωμάτων ταύτην συνιστώντων; Ἀλλὰ Λάζαρον μὲν πρὸς ἔνδειξιν τῆς οἰκείας θεότητος καὶ πίστωσιν τῆς αὐτοῦ τε καὶ ἡμῶν ἀναστάσεως ἤγειρε, πάλιν ὑποστρέφειν μέλλοντα εἰς θάνατον. Αὐτὸς δὲ ὁ κύριος ἀπαρχὴ τῆς τελείας καὶ μηκέτι θανάτῳ ὑποπιπτούσης ἀναστάσεως γέγονε. Διὸ δὴ καὶ ὁ θεῖος ἀπόστολος Παῦλος ἔλεγεν· «Εἰ νεκροὶ οὐκ ἐγείρονται, οὐδὲ Χριστὸς ἐγήγερται. Ἄρα οὖν ματαία ἡ πίστις ἡμῶν· ἄρα ἔτι ἐσμὲν ἐν ταῖς ἁμαρτίαις ἡμῶν», καὶ ὅτι «Χριστὸς ἐγήγερται, ἀπαρχὴ τῶν κεκοιμημένων», καί· «Πρωτότοκος ἐκ νεκρῶν», καὶ πάλιν· «Εἰ γὰρ πιστεύομεν, ὅτι Ἰησοῦς ἀπέθανε καὶ ἀνέστη, οὕτως ὁ θεὸς τοὺς κοιμηθέντας διὰ τοῦ Ἰησοῦ ἄξει σὺν αὐτῷ». «Οὕτως» ἔφη, ὡς ὁ κύριος ἀνέστη.

many of those who sleep in the dust of the earth shall awake, some to everlasting life and some to reproach and everlasting shame. And the wise shall shine like the brightness of the firmament and out of the multitude of the righteous shall shine like the stars unto the ages and beyond."[8] When he says "many of those who sleep in the dust of the earth shall awake," it is clear that he means the resurrection of bodies. No one, presumably, would speak of souls sleeping in the dust of the earth. Moreover, indeed, the Lord, too, clearly taught the resurrection of bodies in the sacred Gospels. "For those who are in their graves," it says, "will hear the voice of the Son of God and will come out—those who have done good, to the resurrection of life, and those who have done evil, to the resurrection of condemnation."[9] Who in their right mind would ever say that souls were in their graves?

It was not only in speech but also in actions that the Lord made manifest the resurrection of bodies. First he raised Lazarus, who was four days dead and already decaying and stinking.[10] For it was not a soul bereft of a body but the body with the soul, and not another body, but that which had decayed that he raised. For how would the resurrection of the dead man be known or believed other than by the characteristic properties of his hypostasis that attested it? Yet he raised Lazarus as proof of his own divinity and as an assurance of his own resurrection and ours, although Lazarus was to return to a state of death. But the Lord himself became the first-fruit of the perfect resurrection no longer subject to death. That is also why the Apostle Paul said: "For if the dead are not raised, then Christ has not been raised. Therefore our faith is futile, and so we are still in our sins,"[11] and: "Christ has been raised from the dead, the first-fruits of those who have fallen asleep,"[12] and: "the first-born from the dead,"[13] and again: "For if we believe that Jesus died and rose again, that is how, through Jesus, God will bring with him those who have fallen asleep."[14] "That is how," he said, in the same way as the Lord rose again.

[8]Dan 12.1–3.   [9]Jn 5.28–29.   [10]Cf. Jn 11.38–40.
[11]1 Cor 15.16–17.   [12]1 Cor 15.20.   [13]Col 1.18.   [14]1 Thess 4.14.

Ὅτι δὲ ἡ τοῦ κυρίου ἀνάστασις σώματος ἀφθαρτισθέντος καὶ ψυχῆς ἕνωσις ἦν (ταῦτα γὰρ τὰ διαιρεθέντα), δῆλον· ἔφη γάρ· «Λύσατε τὸν ναόν, καὶ ἐν τρισὶν ἡμέραις οἰκοδομήσω αὐτόν». Μάρτυς δὲ ἀξιόπιστος τὸ ἱερὸν εὐαγγέλιον, ὡς περὶ τοῦ ἰδίου ἔλεγε σώματος. «Ψηλαφήσατέ με καὶ ἴδετε», φησὶ τοῖς οἰκείοις μαθηταῖς ὁ κύριος πνεῦμα δοκοῦσιν ὁρᾶν, «ὅτι ἐγώ εἰμι καὶ οὐκ ἠλλοίωμαι· ὅτι πνεῦμα σάρκα καὶ ὀστέα οὐκ ἔχει, καθὼς ἐμὲ θεωρεῖτε ἔχοντα». «Καὶ τοῦτο εἰπὼν ἔδειξεν αὐτοῖς τὰς χεῖρας καὶ τὴν πλευρὰν» καὶ τῷ Θωμᾷ προτείνει πρὸς ψηλάφησιν. Ἆρα οὐχ ἱκανὰ ταῦτα τὴν τῶν σωμάτων πιστώσασθαι ἀνάστασιν;

Πάλιν φησὶν ὁ θεῖος ἀπόστολος· «Δεῖ γὰρ τὸ φθαρτὸν τοῦτο ἐνδύσασθαι ἀφθαρσίαν, καὶ τὸ θνητὸν τοῦτο ἐνδύσασθαι ἀθανασίαν», καὶ πάλιν· «Σπείρεται ἐν φθορᾷ, ἐγείρεται ἐν ἀφθαρσίᾳ· σπείρεται ἐν ἀσθενείᾳ, ἐγείρεται ἐν δυνάμει· σπείρεται ἐν ἀτιμίᾳ, ἐγείρεται ἐν δόξῃ· σπείρεται σῶμα ψυχικὸν» ἤτοι παχύ τε καὶ θνητόν, «ἐγείρεται σῶμα πνευματικόν», ἄτρεπτον, ἀπαθές, λεπτόν· τοῦτο γὰρ σημαίνει τὸ «πνευματικόν», οἷον τὸ τοῦ κυρίου σῶμα μετὰ τὴν ἀνάστασιν κεκλεισμένων τῶν θυρῶν διερχόμενον, ἀκοπίατον, τροφῆς, ὕπνου καὶ πόσεως ἀνενδεές. Ἔσονται γάρ, φησὶν ὁ κύριος, «ὡς οἱ ἄγγελοι τοῦ θεοῦ», οὐ γάμος ἔτι, οὐ τεκνογονία. Φησὶ γοῦν ὁ θεῖος ἀπόστολος· «Ἡμῶν γὰρ τὸ πολίτευμα ἐν οὐρανοῖς ὑπάρχει, ἐξ οὗ καὶ σωτῆρα ἀπεκδεχόμεθα κύριον Ἰησοῦν, ὃς καὶ μετασχηματίσει τὸ σῶμα τῆς ταπεινώσεως ἡμῶν εἰς τὸ γενέσθαι αὐτὸ σύμμορφον τῷ σώματι τῆς δόξης αὐτοῦ», οὐ τὴν εἰς ἑτέραν μορφὴν μεταποίησιν λέγων—ἄπαγε—, τὴν ἐκ φθορᾶς δὲ μᾶλλον εἰς ἀφθαρσίαν ἐναλλαγήν.

«Ἀλλ᾽ ἐρεῖ τις· Πῶς ἐγείρονται οἱ νεκροί;» Ὦ τῆς ἀπιστίας. Ὦ τῆς ἀφροσύνης. Ὁ χοῦν εἰς σῶμα βουλήσει μόνῃ μεταβαλών, ὁ μικρὰν ὕλης ῥανίδα τοῦ σπέρματος ἐν μήτρᾳ αὔξειν προστάξας καὶ τὸ πολυειδὲς τοῦτο καὶ πολύμορφον ἀποτελεῖν τοῦ σώματος ὄργανον, οὐχὶ μᾶλλον τὸ γεγονὸς καὶ διαρρυὲν ἀναστήσει πάλιν

It is clear that the Lord's resurrection was the union of a body rendered incorrupt with a soul (for these had been separated), for he said: "Destroy this temple and in three days I will raise it up."[15] The sacred gospel is a reliable witness that he was speaking about his own body. "Touch me and see," the Lord says to his disciples who think they are seeing a spirit, "see that it is I myself and I have not changed, for a spirit does not have flesh and bones as you see that I have."[16] "And after he said this, he showed them his hands and his side"[17] and invited Thomas to feel him. Are these things not sufficient to convince us of the resurrection of bodies?

The divine Apostle says again: "For this perishable body must put on imperishability, and this mortal body must put on immortality,"[18] and again: "It is sown in perishability, it is raised in imperishability; it is sown in weakness, it is raised in power; it is sown in dishonor, it is raised in glory; it is sown a psychical body," that is to say, a body that is dense and mortal, "it is raised a spiritual body,"[19] immutable, dispassionate, and light, for that is what "spiritual" means, like the Lord's body after the resurrection that passed through closed doors, that did not become weary or need food, sleep, and drink. For they shall be, the Lord says, "like the angels of God,"[20] and there will no longer be any marriage or child-bearing. The divine Apostle therefore says: "For our citizenship is in heaven, and it is from there that we are expecting a Savior, the Lord Jesus, who will transform the body of our humiliation so that it may be conformed to the body of his glory,"[21] not saying a transformation into another form—God forbid!—but rather a change from perishability to imperishability.

"But someone will ask, 'How will the dead rise?'"[22] What lack of faith! What foolishness! He who transformed dust into body by his will alone, he who appointed that a small drop of seed should grow in the womb and result in this complex and multiform organ of the body—is it not all the more likely that he can raise again that which has come into being and has been dissolved simply by willing

[15]Jn 2.19.   [16]Lk 24.39.   [17]Lk 24.40; Jn 20.20.   [18]1 Cor 15.53.
[19]1 Cor 15.42–44.   [20]Mt 22.30.   [21]Phil 3.20–21.   [22]1 Cor 15.35.

βουληθείς; «Ποίῳ δὲ σώματι ἔρχονται; Ἄφρον»· εἰ τοῖς τοῦ θεοῦ λόγοις οὐ πιστεύειν ἡ πώρωσις συγχωρεῖ, κἂν τοῖς ἔργοις πίστευε. «Σὺ γάρ, ὃ σπείρεις, οὐ ζωοποιεῖται, ἐὰν μὴ ἀποθάνῃ· καὶ ὃ σπείρεις, οὐ τὸ σῶμα τὸ γενησόμενον σπείρεις, ἀλλὰ γυμνὸν κόκκον, εἰ τύχοι, σίτου ἤ τινος τῶν λοιπῶν. Ὁ δὲ θεὸς αὐτῷ δίδωσι σῶμα, καθὼς ἠθέλησε, καὶ ἑκάστῳ τῶν σπερμάτων τὸ ἴδιον σῶμα». Θέασαι τοίνυν ὡς ἐν τάφοις ταῖς αὔλαξι τὰ σπέρματα καταχωννύμενα. Τίς ὁ τούτοις ῥίζας ἐντιθείς, καλάμην καὶ φύλλα, καὶ ἀστάχυας καὶ τοὺς λεπτοτάτους ἀνθέρικας; Οὐχ ὁ τῶν ὅλων δημιουργός; Οὐ τοῦ τὰ πάντα τεκτηναμένου τὸ πρόσταγμα; Οὕτω τοίνυν πίστευε καὶ τῶν νεκρῶν τὴν ἀνάστασιν ἔσεσθαι θείᾳ βουλήσει καὶ νεύματι· σύνδρομον γὰρ ἔχει τῇ βουλήσει τὴν δύναμιν.

Ἀναστησόμεθα τοιγαροῦν τῶν ψυχῶν πάλιν ἑνουμένων τοῖς σώμασιν ἀφθαρτιζομένοις καὶ ἀποδυομένοις τὴν φθορὰν καὶ παραστησόμεθα τῷ φοβερῷ τοῦ Χριστοῦ βήματι, καὶ παραδοθήσεται ὁ διάβολος καὶ οἱ δαίμονες αὐτοῦ καὶ ὁ ἄνθρωπος αὐτοῦ ἤγουν ὁ ἀντίχριστος καὶ οἱ ἀσεβεῖς καὶ οἱ ἁμαρτωλοὶ εἰς τὸ πῦρ τὸ αἰώνιον, οὐχ ὑλικὸν οἷον τὸ παρ' ἡμῖν, ἀλλ' οἷον εἰδείη θεός. Οἱ δὲ τὰ ἀγαθὰ πράξαντες ἐκλάμψουσιν ὡς ὁ ἥλιος σὺν ἀγγέλοις εἰς ζωὴν αἰώνιον σὺν τῷ κυρίῳ ἡμῶν Ἰησοῦ Χριστῷ, ὁρῶντες αὐτὸν καὶ ὁρώμενοι καὶ ἄληκτον τὴν ἀπ' αὐτοῦ εὐφροσύνην καρπούμενοι.

it? "With what kind of body do they come? Fool!"[23] If a hardening does not allow you to believe the words of God, at least "believe the works":[24] "For what you sow does not come to life until it dies. And as for what you sow, you do not sow the body that is to be, but a bare seed, perhaps of wheat or of some other grain. But God gives it a body as he has chosen, and to each kind of seed its own body."[25] Therefore look at the seeds covered up in the furrows as if in graves. Who put roots into them, and stem, and leaves, and ears and beards? Was it not the Creator of all? Was it not at the command of him who has fashioned everything? Therefore believe from this that the resurrection of the dead too will take place by the divine will and command. For God's power is concurrent with his will.[26]

We shall consequently rise again with souls united once more with bodies that have become incorrupt and have been freed from decay, and we shall stand at Christ's dread tribunal, and the devil and his demons and his own man, that is to say, the Antichrist, and the impious and sinners will be handed over to eternal fire, not a material fire such as we know, but such as God knows. Those who have done good will shine like the sun together with the angels in life eternal with our Lord Jesus Christ, seeing him and being seen and bearing as fruit the endless joy that comes from him.[27]

[23] 1 Cor 15.35–36.
[24] Jn 10.38.
[25] 1 Cor 15.36–38.
[26] Gregory of Nyssa, *Catechetical Discourse* 2.3 (PG 45:17C; Green, 69).
[27] Some manuscripts add "Amen" (DG). Others conclude with the addition of a scribal comment, e.g., "Conclusion of John's one hundred and fifty chapters" (H); "Lord, grant the copyist of this book a place [in your kingdom]"(I).

Concordance of chapters in the Latin and Greek versions

Latin	Greek	Latin	Greek	Latin	Greek
1.1	1	2.18	32	3.23	67
1.2	2	2.19	33	3.24	68
1.3	3	2.20	34	3.25	69
1.4	4	2.21	35	3.26	70
1.5	5	2.22	36	3.27	71
1.6	6	2.23	37	3.28	72
1.7	7	2.24	38	3.29	73
1.8	8	2.25	39	4.1	74
1.9	9	2.26	40	4.2	75
1.10	10	2.27	41	4.3	76
1.11	11	2.28	42	4.4	77
1.12	12	2.29	43	4.5	78
1.12b	12b	2.30	44	4.6	79
1.13	13	3.1	45	4.7	80
1.14	14	3.2	46	4.8	81
2.1	15	3.3	47		81b

Latin	Greek	Latin	Greek	Latin	Greek
2.2	16	3.4	48	4.9	82
2.3	17	3.5	49	4.10	83
2.4	18	3.6	50	4.11	84
2.5	19	3.7	51	4.12	85
2.6	20	3.8	52	4.13	86
2.7	21	3.9	53	4.14	87
2.8	22	3.10	54	4.15	88
	22b	3.11	55	4.16	89
2.9	23	3.12	56	4.17	90
	23b	3.13	57	4.18	91
2.10	24	3.14	58	4.19	92
	24b	3.15	59	4.20	93
2.11	25	3.16	60	4.21	94
2.12	26	3.17	61	4.22	95
2.13	27	3.18	62	4.23	96
2.14	28	3.19	63	4.24	97
2.15	29	3.20	64	4.25	98
2.16	30	3.21	65	4.26	99
2.17	31	3.22	66	4.27	100

Select Bibliography

Editions and translations of *On the Orthodox Faith*

Ἔκδοσις ἀκριβὴς τῆς ὀρθοδόξου πίστεως. *Expositio fidei.* Edited by P. Boni-
fatius Kotter, OSB. Die Schriften des Johannes von Damaskos, Band
II. Berlin and New York: Walter de Gruyter, 1973. (The modern critical
edition.)

Ἰωάννου τοῦ Δαμασκηνοῦ ἔκδοσις τῆς ὀρθοδόξου πίστεως. *Joannis Dama-
sceni editio orthodoxae fidei. Eiusdem de iis qui in fide dormierunt.*
Edited by Bernardinus Donatus. Verona: Apud Stephanum et Fratres
Sabios, 1531. (The *editio princeps.*)

John of Damascus, *Exposition of the Orthodox Faith*. Translated (on the
basis of Lequien's text reprinted by Migne) by S. D. F. Salmond. NPNF,
Second Series, volume 9, part 2. (Reprinted by T&T Clark and W. B.
Eerdmans, 1997.)

La foi orthodoxe/Jean Damascène. Kotter's critical Greek text with French
translation and notes by P. Ledrux, with the collaboration of G.-M. de
Durand. Introduction and notes by P. Ledrux, with the collaboration of
V. Kontouma-Conticello and G.-M. de Durand. SC 535 and 540. Paris:
Éditions du Cerf, 2010.

*Saint John Damascene, De Fide Orthodoxa: Versions of Burgundio and Cer-
banus*. Edited by Eligius M. Buytaert. St Bonaventure, NY: Franciscan
Institute, 1955.

*Saint John of Damascus, Writings. The Fount of Knowledge: The Philosophi-
cal Chapters, On Heresies, and On the Orthodox Faith*. Translated (on
the basis of Lequien's text reprinted by Migne) by Frederic H. Chase, Jr.
FOC 37. Washington: The Catholic University of America Press, 1958.
(Reprinted by Ex Fontibus Co., 2012.)

Τοῦ πατρὸς ἡμῶν Ἰωάννου τοῦ Δαμασκηνοῦ τὰ εὐρισκόμενα. *S. Johannis
Damasceni opera omnia quae extant*. Greek text with Latin translation by Michel Lequien, OP. Paris, 1712. (Reprinted in Venice in 1748,

and in Paris by J.-P. Migne in 1864. The *Expositio fidei* occupies PG
94:789–1228.)

Other works by John Damascene in translation

Dialectica. Translated (on the basis of Lequien's text, reprinted in PG
94:525–676) by Frederic H. Chase, Jr. FOC 37. Washington: The Catholic
University of America Press, 1958. Pp. 3–110.

Homily for the Feast of the Transfiguration. In *Light on the Mountain: Greek
Patristic Homilies on the Transfiguration of the Lord*. Translated (on the
basis of Kotter's critical Greek text) by Brian E. Daley, SJ. PPS 48. Yonkers, NY: St Vladimir's Seminary Press, 2013. Pp. 205–31.

On Heresies. Translated (on the basis of Lequien's text, reprinted in PG
94:677–780) by Frederic H. Chase, Jr. FOC 37. Washington: The Catholic University of America Press, 1958. Pp. 111–63.

Three Homilies on the Dormition of the Mother of God, and a Canon for the
Dormition of the Mother of God. In *On the Dormition of Mary: Early
Patristic Homilies*. Translation (on the basis of Kotter's critical Greek
text) and introduction by Brian E. Daley, SJ. PPS 18. Crestwood, NY: St
Vladimir's Seminary Press, 1998. Pp. 183–246.

Three Treatises on the Divine Images. In *St John of Damascus, Three Treatises
on the Divine Images*. Translation (on the basis of Kotter's critical Greek
text) and introduction by Andrew Louth. PPS 24. Crestwood, NY: St
Vladimir's Seminary Press, 2003.

Primary Sources

The Acts of the Council of Chalcedon. Translated with an introduction and
notes by Richard Price and Michael Gaddis. 3 volumes. TTH 45. Liverpool: Liverpool University Press, 2005.

The Acts of the Second Council of Nicaea (787). Translated with notes and an
introduction by Richard Price. TTH 68. Liverpool: Liverpool University Press, 2020.

Andrew of Caesarea. *Commentary on the Apocalypse*. Translated by Eugenia
Scarvelis Constantinou. FOC 123. Washington: The Catholic University
of America Press, 2011.

Aristotle. *The Complete Works of Aristotle: The Revised Oxford Translation.* Edited by Jonathan Barnes, 2 vols. Bollingen Series 71. Princeton, NJ: Princeton University Press, 1984.

Basil of Caesarea. *Basilio di Caesarea, Sulla Genesi (Omelie sull'Esamerone).* Edited with an Italian translation by Mario Naldini. Milan: Fondazione Lorenzo Valla and Arnaldo Mondadori, 1990. English translation by Sister Agnes Clare Way, C.D.P., *Saint Basil: Exegetic Homilies.* Fathers of the Church 46. Washington, DC: The Catholic University of America Press, 1963. Pp. 3–150.

Cyril of Alexandria. *Cyril of Alexandria: Select Letters.* Edited and translated by Lionel R. Wickham. Oxford Early Christian Texts. Oxford: Clarendon Press, 1983.

Doctrina Patrum de Incarnatione Verbi: Ein griechische Florilegium aus der Wende des 7. und 8. Jahrhunderts. Edited by F. Diekamp. Revised edition by B. Phanourgakis and E. Chrysos. Münster: Aschendorff Verlag, 1981.

Dionysius the Areopagite. *Corpus Dionysiacum I. Pseudo-Dionysius Areopagita. De divinis nominibus.* Edited by Beata Regina Suchla. Berlin and New York: Walter de Gruyter, 1990. *Corpus Dionysiacum II. Pseudo-Dionysius Areopagita. De coelesti hierarchia, De ecclesiastica hierarchia, De mystica theologia, Epistulae.* Edited by Günter Heil and Adolf Martin Ritter. Berlin and New York: Walter de Gruyter, 1991. English translation (to be used with caution because often a loose paraphrase) by Colm Luibheid with Paul Rorem, *Pseudo-Dionysius, The Complete Works.* CWS. Mahwah, NJ: Paulist Press, and London: SPCK, 1987.

Gregory of Nazianzus. *Gregorio di Nazianzo, Tutte le Orazioni.* Edited by Claudio Moreschini (critical Greek text of the SC edition conveniently printed in a single volume) with an Italian translation by Chiara Sani and Maria Vincelli. Milan: Fondazione Lorenzo Valla and Arnaldo Mondadori, 1990. Partial English translations by Frederick Williams and Lionel Wickham, *On God and Christ: The Five Theological Orations and Two Letters to Cledonius of St Gregory of Nazianzus,* PPS 23. Crestwood, NY: St Vladimir's Seminary Press, 2002; Martha Vinson, *St Gregory of Nazianzus, Select Orations,* FOC 107, Washington: Catholic University of America Press, 2003; Nonna Verna Harrison, *Festal Orations of St Gregory of Nazianzus,* PPS 36. Yonkers, NY: St Vladimir's Seminary Press, 2008. The translation (often reprinted) of *St Gregory*

Nazianzen, Select Orations by Charles Gordon Browne and James Edward Swallow in NPNF, Second Series, volume 7, is unreliable.

Gregory of Nyssa. *Catechetical Discourse.* Srawley's critical Greek text with Introduction, Translation, Notes, Glossary, and Bibliography by Ignatius Green. PPS 60. Yonkers, NY: St Vladimir's Seminary Press, 2019.

Leontius of Byzantium. *Leontius of Byzantium: The Complete Works.* Critical text with English translation by Brian E. Daley, SJ. Oxford Early Christian Texts. Oxford: Oxford University Press, 2017.

Maximus the Confessor. *Disputation with Pyrrhus.* Edited with a Latin translation by François Combéfis, O.P., and reprinted by J.-P. Migne in PG 91:288–353. English translation by Joseph P. Farrell, *The Disputation with Pyrrhus of our Father among the Saints Maximus the Confessor.* Waymart, PA: St Tikhon's Seminary Press, 1990.

———. *Massimo Confessore: Capitoli sulla carità.* Edited by A. Ceresa-Gastaldo (Rome: Editrice Studium, 1969), 48–238. English translation by George C. Berthold, *Maximus Confessor: Selected Writings.* CWS. Mahwah, NJ: Paulist Press, 1985. Pp. 35–98.

———. *Maximi Confessoris Quaestiones as Thalassium.* Edited by Carl Laga and Carlos Steel. 2 vols. Corpus Christianorum, Series Graeca 7 (Quaestiones 1–55) and 22 (Quaestiones 56–65). Turnhout: Brepols, 1980–90.

———. *Maximos the Confessor: On Difficulties in the Church Fathers, The Ambigua.* Edited and translated by Nicholas Constas. 2 vols. Dumbarton Oaks Medieval Library 28 and 29. Cambridge, MA: Harvard University Press, 2014.

———. *Opuscula theologica et polemica.* Edited with a Latin translation by François Combéfis, O.P., and reprinted by J.-P. Migne in PG 91:9–286.

Nemesius of Emesa. *On Human Nature.* Edited by C. F. Matthaei with a Latin translation, and reprinted by J.-P. Migne in PG 40:504–817. Critical edition by M. Morani, *Nemesii Emeseni de natura hominis.* Bibliotheca scriptorum Graecorum et Romanorum Teubneriana. Leipzig: Teubner, 1987. English Translation by R. W. Sharples and P. J. van der Eijk, *Nemesius, On the Nature of Man.* TTH 49. Liverpool: Liverpool University Press, 2008.

Origen of Alexandria. *Origen: Contra Celsum.* Translated with an introduction and notes by Henry Chadwick. Cambridge: Cambridge University Press, 1965.

_____. *Origen: On First Principles*. Edited and translated by John Behr. 2 vols. Oxford Early Christian Texts. Oxford: Oxford University Press, 2017.

Philoponus. *Against Aristotle on the Eternity of the World*. Translated by Christian Wildberg. Ancient Commentators on Aristotle. London: Duckworth, 1987.

Plotinus. *Plotinus*. With an English translation by A. H. Armstrong. 7 vols. Loeb Classical Library. Cambridge, MA: Harvard University Press, 1978–88.

Theophanes. *The Chronicle of Theophanes Confessor: Byzantine and Near Eastern History AD 284–813*. Translated by Cyril Mango and Roger Scott with Geoffrey Greatrex. Oxford: Clarendon Press, 1997.

Secondary Sources

Ables, Scott. "Development in Theological Method and Argument in John of Damascus." *Journal of Early Christian Studies* (forthcoming). http://oregonstate.academia.edu/ScottAbles.

_____. "Was the Reestablishment of the Jerusalem Patriarchate a 'Proto-Melkite' Gambit Orchestrated by John of Damascus—*Quid pro Quo*: Cathedral for Patriarchate?" *ARAM Periodical* (forthcoming). http://oregonstate.academia.edu/ScottAbles.

Auzépy, Marie-France. "From Palestine to Constantinople (Eighth–Ninth Centuries): Stephen the Sabaite and John of Damasus." In *Languages and Cultures of Eastern Christianity*. Edited by Scott Fitzgerald Johnson. The Worlds of Eastern Christianity, 300–1500, volume 6. Farnham, UK and Burlington, VT: Ashgate Variorum, 2015. Pp. 399–442. Translated by Elodie Turquois from "De la Palestine à Constantinople (VIIIe–IXe siècles): Étienne le sabaite et Jean Damascène." *Travaux et Mémoires* 12 (1994): 183–218.

Backus, Irena. "John of Damascus, *De Fide Orthodoxa*: Translations by Burgundio (1153/54), Grosseteste (1235/40) and Lefèvre d'Etaples (1507)." *Journal of the Warburg and Courtauld Institutes* 49 (1986): 211–17.

Bathrellos, Demetrios. *The Byzantine Christ: Person, Nature, and Will in the Christology of Maximus the Confessor*. Oxford: Oxford University Press, 2004.

Bradshaw, David. "Sexual Difference and the Difference It Makes: The Greek Fathers and Their Sources." In *The Reception of Greek Ethics in Late Antiquity and Byzantium*. Edited by Sophia Xenophontos and Anna Marmodoro. Cambridge: Cambridge University Press, forthcoming.

Constas, Maximos. "The Last Temptation of Satan: Divine Deception in Greek Patristic Interpretations of the Passion Narrative." *Harvard Theological Review* 97 (2004): 139–63.

Cross, Richard. "Perichoresis, Deification, and Christological Predication in John of Damascus." *Medieval Studies* 62 (2000): 69–124.

_____. "The Reception of John of Damascus in the *Summa Halensis*." In *The Summa Halensis: Sources and Content*. Edited by Lydia Schumacher. Veröffentlichungen des Grabmann-Institutes zur Erforschung der mittelalterlichen Theologie und Philosophie 66. Berlin and Boston: Walter de Gruyter, 2020. Pp. 71–90.

Daley, Brian E., SJ. *God Visible: Patristic Christology Reconsidered*. Oxford: Oxford University Press, 2018.

_____. "Maximus the Confessor and John of Damascus on the Trinity." In *The Holy Trinity in the Life of the Church*. Edited by Khaled Anatolios. Holy Cross Studies in Patristic Theology and History. Grand Rapids, Michigan: Baker Academic, 2014. Pp. 79–99.

Demetracopoulos, John A. "In Search of the Pagan and Christian Sources of John of Damascus' Theodicy." In *Byzantine Theology and its Philosophical Background*. Edited by Antonio Rigo, in collaboration with Pavel Ermilov and Michele Trizio. Byzantios: Studies in Byzantine History and Civilization 4. Turnhout: Brepols, 2011. Pp. 50–86.

Farrington, Benjamin. *Greek Science*, vol. 2, *Theophrastus to Galen*. Harmondsworth, UK: Penguin Books, 1949.

Flusin, Bernard. "From Arabic to Greek, then to Georgian: A Life of Saint John of Damascus." In *Languages and Cultures of Eastern Christianity*. Edited by Scott Fitzgerald Johnson. The Worlds of Eastern Christianity, 300–1500, volume 6. Farnham, UK and Burlington, VT: Ashgate Variorum, 2015. Pp. 483–93. Translated by Emily Corran from "De l'arabe au grec, puis au géorgien: Une Vie de saint Jean Damascène." In *Traduction et traducteurs au Moyen Âge*. Edited by G. Contamine. Paris: CNRS, 1989. Pp. 51–61.

Frede, Michael. "John of Damascus on Human Action, the Will, and Human Freedom." In *Byzantine Philosophy and its Ancient Sources*. Edited by Katerina Ierodiakonou. Oxford: Clarendon Press, 2002. Pp. 63–95.

Georgi, Deacon Porphyrios (Fadi), editor. *Saint John the Damascene: Theology, Image and Melody*. Balamand Theological Conferences 3. Tripoli, Lebanon: St John of Damascus Institute of Theology, University of Balamand, 2012.

Griffith, Sidney H. "John of Damascus and the Church in Syria in the Umayyad Era: The Intellectual and Cultural Milieu of Orthodox Christians in the World of Islam." *Hugoye: Journal of Syriac Studies* 11/2 (2011): 207–37.

———. "The Manṣūr Family and Saint John of Damascus: Christians and Muslims in Umayyad Times." In *Christians and Others in the Umayyad State*. Edited by Antoine Borrut and Fred M. Donner. Chicago: The Oriental Institute of the University of Chicago, 2016. Pp. 29–51.

Haldon, John. "The Works of Anastasius of Sinai: A Key Source for the History of Seventh-Century East Mediterranean Society and Belief." In *Languages and Cultures of Eastern Christianity*. Edited by Scott Fitzgerald Johnson. The Worlds of Eastern Christianity, 300–1500, volume 6. Farnham, UK and Burlington, VT: Ashgate Variorum, 2015. Pp. 323–63. First published in *Byzantine and Early Islamic Near East: Problems with the Literary Source Material*. Edited by Averil M. Cameron and Lawrence I. Conrad. Studies in Late Antiquity and Early Islam 1. Princeton, NJ: Darwin Press, 1992. Pp. 107–47.

Hoyland, Robert G. *Seeing Islam as Others Saw It: A Survey and Evaluation of Christian, Jewish and Zoroastrian Writings on Early Islam*. Studies in Late Antiquity and Early Islam 13. Princeton, NJ: The Darwin Press, 1997.

Jugie, Martin. "Jean Damascène (Saint)." In *Dictionnaire de théologie catholique*, volume 8, part 2. Edited by A. Vacant, E. Mangenot, and É. Amann. Paris: Librairie Letouzey et Ané, 1925. Cols 693–751.

Kaegi, Walter E. *Byzantium and the Early Islamic Conquests*. Cambridge: Cambridge University Press, 1992.

Kalvesmaki, Joel. "Evagrius in the Byzantine Genre of Chapters." In *Evagrius and His Legacy*. Edited by Joel Kalvesmaki and Robin Darling Young. Notre Dame, IN: University of Notre Dame Press, 2016. Pp. 257–87.

Karamanolis, George. *The Philosophy of Early Christianity*, second edition. Ancient Philosophies. New York and London: Routledge, 2021.

Kontouma, Vassa. "At the Origins of Byzantine Systematic Dogmatics: the *Exposition of the Orthodox Faith* of St John of Damascus." In Vassa Kontouma. *John of Damascus: New Studies on his Life and Works*. Variorum Collected Studies Series CS1053. Farnham, UK: Ashgate Publishing, 2015. Study VI. English translation by Augustine Casiday of "À l'origine de la dogmatique systématique byzantine: l'*Édition precise de la foi orthodoxe* de saint Jean Damascène." In *Byzantine Theologians. The Systematization of Their Own Doctrine and Their Perception of Foreign Doctrines*. Edited by A. Rigo and P. Ermilov. Quaderni di Νέα Ῥώμη 3. Rome: Università degli Studi di Roma "Tor Vergata," 2009. Pp. 3–17.

———. "John III of Antioch (996–1021) and the *Life of John of Damascus* (BHG 884)." In Vassa Kontouma. *John of Damascus: New Studies on his Life and Works*. Variorum Collected Studies Series CS1053. Farnham, UK: Ashgate Publishing, 2015. Study II. English translation by Augustine Casiday of "Jean III d'Antioche (996–1021) et la *Vie de Jean Damascène* (BHG 884)." *Revue des études byzantines* 68 (2010): 127–47.

———. "John of Damascus (*c*. 655–*c*. 745)." In Vassa Kontouma. *John of Damascus: New Studies on his Life and Works*. Variorum Collected Studies Series CS1053. Farnham, UK: Ashgate Publishing, 2015. Study I. English translation by Augustine Casiday of "Jean Damascène." In *Dictionnaire des philosophes antiques*, vol 3. Edited by R. Goulet. Paris: CNRS Éditions, 2000. Pp. 989–1012.

———. *John of Damascus: New Studies on His Life and Works*. Variorum Collected Studies Series CS1053. Farnham, UK: Ashgate Publishing, 2015.

———. "Pseudo-Cyril's *De SS. Trinitate*: A Compilation of Joseph the Philosopher." In Vassa Kontouma. *John of Damascus: New Studies on his Life and Works*. Variorum Collected Studies Series CS1053. Farnham, UK: Ashgate Publishing, 2015. Study IV. Reprinted from *Orientalia Christiana Periodica* 61 (1995): 117–29.

———. "Remarques sur la situation de la philosophie byzantine du concile de Chalcédoine à Jean Damascène." La "Source de connaissance" de Jean Damascène (*ca* 650—*ca* 750). Traduction française et commentaire des livres I (*Dialectica*) et III (*Expositio fidei*). Ph.D., University of Paris-IV Sorbonne, Paris, 1996. Pp. cxviii–clxx. First publication, updated and

augmented, in Vassa Kontouma. *John of Damascus: New Studies on his Life and Works.* Variorum Collected Studies Series CS1053. Farnham, UK: Ashgate Publishing, 2015. Study III.

―――――. "The *Fount of Knowledge* between Conservation and Creation." In Vassa Kontouma. *John of Damascus: New Studies on his Life and Works.* Variorum Collected Studies Series CS1053. Farnham, UK: Ashgate Publishing, 2015. Study V. English translation by Augustine Casiday of "La Fonte della Conoscenza tra conservazione e creazione." In *Giovanni di Damasco. Un Padre al sorgere dell' Islam. Atti del XIII Convegno ecumenico internazionale di spiritualità ortodossa, sezione bizantina, Bose, 11—13 sett. 2005.* Edited by S. Chialà and L. Cremaschi. Bose, 2006. Pp. 177–203.

Krausmüller, Dirk. "A Conceptualist Turn: The Ontological Status of Created Species in Late Greek Patristic Theology." *Scrinium* 16 (2020): 233–52.

―――――. "Responding to John Philoponus: Hypostasis, Particular Substances, and *Perichoresis* in the Trinity." *Journal for Late Antique Religion and Culture* 9 (2015): 13–28.

―――――. "Under the Spell of John Philoponus: How Chalcedonian Theologians of the Late Patristic Period Attempted to Safeguard the Oneness of God." *Journal of Theological Studies* 68 (2015): 625–49.

Lang, U. Michael. "Anhypostatos–enhypostatos: Church Fathers, Protestant Orthodoxy and Karl Barth." *Journal of Theological Studies* ns 49/2 (1998): 630–57.

Louth, Andrew. "Christology in the East from the Council of Chalcedon to John Damascene." In *The Oxford Handbook of Christology.* Edited by Francesca Murphy. Oxford: Oxford University Press, 2015. Pp. 139–53.

―――――. *St John Damascene: Tradition and Originality in Byzantine Theology.* Oxford: Oxford University Press, 2002.

―――――. "The Πηγὴ Γνώσεως of St John Damascene: Its Date and Development." In *Porphyrogenita: Essays on the History and Literature of Byzantium and the Latin East in Honour of Julian Chrysostomides.* Edited by Charalambos Dendrinos, Jonathan Harris, Eirene Harvalia-Crook, and Judith Herrin. London and Burlington, VT: Ashgate, 2003. Pp. 335–40.

Maltezou, Chryssa. "*Nazione greca* καὶ cose sacre: Λείψανα ἁγίων στὸν ναὸ τοῦ Ἁγίου Γεωργίου τῆς Βενετίας." *Thesaurismata: Bolletino dell'Istituto Ellenico di Studi Bizantini e Postbizantini* 29 (1999): 9–31.

Mango, Cyril. "Greek Culture in Palestine after the Arab Conquest." In *Languages and Cultures of Eastern Christianity*. Edited by Scott Fitzgerald Johnson. The Worlds of Eastern Christianity, 300–1500, volume 6. Farnham, UK and Burlington, VT: Ashgate Variorum, 2015. Pp. 375–86. First published in *Scritture, libri e testi nelle aree provinciali di bisanzio (Atti del seminario di Erice, 18–21 settembre 1988)*, volume 1. Spoleto: Centro italiano di studi sull'alto Medioevo, 1991. Pp. 149–60.

Meyendorff, John. "An Effort at Systemization: St. John of Damascus." In John Meyendorff, *Christ in Eastern Christian Thought*. Crestwood, NY: St Vladimir's Seminary Press, 1975. Pp. 153–72.

Nellas, Panayiotis. *Deification in Christ: The Nature of the Human Person*. Crestwood, NY: St Vladimir's Seminary Press, 1987. English translation by Norman Russell of Ζῶον θεούμενον: Προοπτικὲς γιὰ μιὰ ὀρθόδοξη κατανόηση τοῦ ἀνθρώπου. Athens: Epopteia, 1979 (and frequently reprinted).

Piccirillo, Michele, OFM. "The Christians in Palestine during a Time of Transition: 7th–9th Centuries." In *The Christian Heritage in the Holy Land*. Edited by Anthony O'Mahony with Göran Gunner and Kevork Hintlian. London: Scorpion Cavendish, 1995. Pp. 47–56.

Plested, Marcus. "Thomas Aquinas and John of Damascus on the Light of the Transfiguration: Can We Speak of a Greek Patristic Turn in Thomas?" In *Thomas Aquinas and the Greek Fathers*. Edited by Michael Dauphinais, Andrew Hofer, and Roger Nutt. Ave Maria, FL: Sapientia Press, 2019. Pp. 206–20.

Russell, Norman. "The Work of Christ in Patristic Theology." In *The Oxford Handbook of Christology*. Edited by Francesca Murphy. Oxford: Oxford University Press, 2015. Pp. 153–66.

Sambursky, S. *The Physical World of Late Antiquity*. London: Routledge and Kegan Paul, 1962.

Scott, Alan. *Origen and the Life of the Stars: A History of an Idea*. Oxford: Clarendon Press, 1991.

Scott, Mark S. M. *Journey Back to God: Origen on the Problem of Evil*. Oxford: Oxford University Press, 2015.

Stead, Christopher. *Divine Substance*. Oxford: Clarendon Press, 1977.

Thomas, David. *Anti-Christian polemic in early Islam: Abū ʿĪsā al-Warrāq's "Against the Trinity."* Cambridge: Cambridge University Press, 1992.

Thunberg, Lars. *Microcosm and Mediator: The Theological Anthropology of Maximus the Confessor*. Second edition. Chicago and La Salle, Illinois: Open Court, 1995.

Tollefsen, Torstein T. *Activity and Participation in Late Antique and Early Christian Thought*. Oxford: Oxford University Press, 2012.

_____. "Christocentric Cosmology." In *The Oxford Handbook of Maximus the Confessor*. Edited by Pauline Allen and Bronwen Neil. Oxford: Oxford University Press, 2015. Pp. 307–21.

Trombley, F. R. "A Note on the See of Jerusalem and the Synodal List of the Sixth Ecumenical Council (680–681)." *Byzantion* 53/2 (1983): 632–38.

Twombly, Charles C. *Perichoresis and Personhood: God, Christ, and Salvation in John of Damascus*. Princeton Theological Monograph Series 216. Eugene, OR: Pickwick Publications, 2015.

Zachhuber, Johannes. "John of Damascus in the *Summa Halensis*." In *The Summa Halensis: Sources and Content*. Edited by Lydia Schumacher. Veröffentlichungen des Grabmann-Institutes zur Erforschung der mittelalterlichen Theologie und Philosophie 66. Berlin and Boston: Walter de Gruyter, 2020. Pp. 91–116.

Indexes

Index of Scriptural References

Index of Ancient Texts

Index of Modern Authors

General Index

POPULAR PATRISTICS SERIES

ST VLADIMIR'S SEMINARY PRESS
1-800-204-2665 • www.svspress.com

CPSIA information can be obtained
at www.ICGtesting.com
Printed in the USA
LVHW081341231122
733879LV00009B/687

9 780881 416947